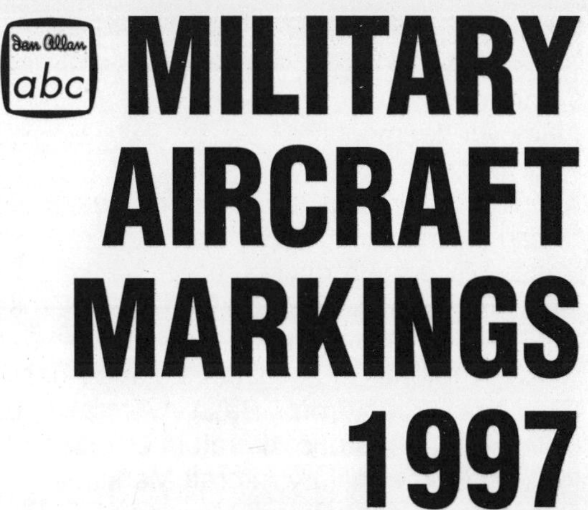

MILITARY AIRCRAFT MARKINGS 1997

Peter R. March

Contents

Photographs by Peter R. March (PRM) unless otherwise credited

This eighteenth edition published 1997

ISBN 0 7110 2499 5

Published by Ian Allan Publishing

an imprint of Ian Allan Ltd,
Terminal House, Station Approach,
Shepperton, Surrey TW17 8AS.
Printed by Ian Allan Printing Ltd,
at its works at Coombelands in Runnymede, England

Code: 9703/G

Front cover: Tornado GR1, RAF. *Denis J. Calvert/Inter Air Press*
Back cover: F-16A, Royal Netherlands Air Force. *PRM*

Introduction

This eighteenth annual edition of *abc Military Aircraft Markings*, a companion to *abc Civil Aircraft Markings*, lists in alphabetical and numerical order all of the aircraft that carry a United Kingdom military serial, and **which are based, or might be seen, in the UK**. The term *aircraft* used here covers powered, manned aeroplanes, helicopters, airships and gliders. Included are all the current Royal Air Force, Royal Navy, Army Air Corps, Ministry of Defence (Procurement Executive), Defence Research Agency, manufacturers' test aircraft and civilian-owned aircraft with military markings.

Aircraft withdrawn from operational use but which are retained in the UK for ground training purposes or otherwise preserved by the Services and in the numerous museums and collections are listed. The serials of some incomplete aircraft have been included, such as the cockpit sections of machines displayed by the RAF Exhibition Flight, aircraft used by airfield fire sections and for service battle damage repair training (BDRT), together with significant parts of aircraft held by preservation groups and societies. Where only part of the aircraft fuselage remains the abbreviation <ff> for front fuselage/cockpit section or <rf> for rear fuselage is shown after the type. Many of these aircraft are allocated, and sometimes wear, a secondary identity, such as an RAF Support Command 'M' maintenance number. These numbers are listed against those aircraft to which they have been allocated.

A serial 'missing' is either because it was never issued as it formed part of a 'black-out block' (a practice that has now ceased) or because the aircraft is written off, scrapped, sold abroad or allocated an alternative marking. Aircraft used as targets on MoD ranges to which access is restricted, and un-manned target drones, are omitted, as are UK military aircraft that have been permanently grounded and are based overseas and unlikely to return to Britain.

In the main, the serials listed are those markings presently displayed on the aircraft. Aircraft which bear a false serial are quoted in *italic type*. Very often these serials are carried by replicas, that are denoted by <R> after the type. The manufacturer and aircraft type are given, together with recent alternative, previous, secondary or civil identity shown in round brackets. Complete records of multiple previous identities are only included where space permits. The operating unit and its based location, along with any known unit and base code markings in square brackets, are given as accurately as possible. The unit markings are normally carried boldly on the sides of the fuselage or on the aircraft's fin. In the case of RAF and AAC machines currently in service, they are usually one or two letters or numbers, while the RN continues to use a well-established system of three-figure codes between 000 and 999 together with a fin letter code denoting the aircraft s operational base. RN squadrons, units and bases are allocated blocks of numbers from which individual aircraft codes are issued. To help identification of RN bases and landing platforms on ships, a list of tail-letter codes with their appropriate name, helicopter code number, ship pennant number and type of vessel, is included; as is a helicopter code number/ships' tail-letter code grid cross-reference.

Codes change, for example when aircraft move between units, and therefore the markings currently painted on a particular aircraft might not be those shown in this edition because of subsequent events. The implementation of the Government's continuing civilian contractorisation and the RAF's Front Line First reductions and re-organisation, again accounts for the large number of changes in this new edition. In particular the transfer of helicopter aircrew training for all three services, and RAF initial pilot training have, and will continue to play a key part. Those airframes which may not appear in the next edition because of sale, accident, etc, have their fates, where known, given in italic type in the *locations* column.

The Irish Army Air Corps fleet is listed, together with the serials of other overseas air arms whose aircraft might be seen visiting the UK from time to time. The serial numbers are as usually presented on the individual machine or as they are normally identified. Where possible, the aircraft's base and operating unit have been shown.

USAF, US Army and US Navy aircraft based in the UK and in Western Europe, and of types which regularly visit the UK from the USA, are each listed in separate sections by aircraft type. The serial number actually displayed on the aircraft is shown in full, with additional Fiscal Year (FY) or full serial information also provided. Where appropriate, details of the operating wing, squadron allocation and base are added. The USAF is, like the RAF, continuing a major reorganisation which is producing new unit titles, many squadron changes and the closure of bases worldwide. Only details that concern changes effected by December 1996 are shown.

Veteran and Vintage aircraft which carry overseas military markings but which are based in the UK have been separately listed showing their principal means of identification. There is an additional section in this edition, listing the growing number of aircraft in government or military service, often under contract to private operating companies, that carry civil registrations. In the UK this category is steadily increasing as more military training passes to civilian contractors.

Information shown is believed to be correct at 31 January 1997, and significant changes can be monitored through the monthly 'Military Markings' column in *Aircraft Illustrated*.

Acknowledgements

The compiler again wishes to thank the many people who have taken trouble to send comments, criticism and other useful information following the publication of the previous editions of *abc Military Aircraft Markings*. In particular the following correspondents: D. Braithwaite, P. F. Burton, B. Dunnell, G. Fraser, H. W. Gandy, A. Helden, I. Logan, A. P. March, D. J. March, M. K. Thompson and P. Wiggins.

This compilation has relied heavily on the publications of the following aviation groups and societies: *Airfield Review* (Airfield Research Group), *Air Link* (Lincolnshire Aviation Society), *BAC News* (Bristol Aero Collection), *Review* (British Aviation Research Group), *International Auster Club News*, *Irish Air Letter*, *North-West Air News* (Air Britain, Merseyside Branch), *Osprey* (Solent Aviation Society), *Prestwick Airport Letter* (Prestwick Airport Aviation Group), *RAF News*, *Stansted Aviation News* (Stansted Aviation Society), *Strobe/Military Aviation Review* (MAP), *Ulster Air Mail* (Ulster Aviation Society) and *Update* (British Aviation Preservation Council).

This fully revised edition of *abc Military Aircraft Markings* would not have been possible without considerable research, collation and checking by Howard Curtis, to whom I am indebted.

PRM   **January 1997**

Fairey Swordfish II W5856 operated by the RN Historic Flight at RNAS Yeovilton. *Andrew March*

Tiger Moth T7230 is privately owned G-AFVE. *PRM*

AAC	Army Air Corps
AACS	Airborne Air Control Squadron
AACTS	Airborne Air Control Training Squadron
AAS	Aeromedical Airlift Squadron
ABS	Air Base Squadron
ACC	Air Combat Command
ACCGS	Air Cadets Central Gliding School
ACCS	Airborne Command and Control Squadron
ACW	Airborne Control Wing
AD&StA	Aberdeen, Dundee & St Andrews
AEF	Air Experience Flight
AES	Air Engineering School
AEW	Airborne Early Warning
AF	Arméflyget (Army Air Battalion)
AFB	Air Force Base
AFRES	Air Force Reserve
AFSC	Air Force System Command
AFSK	Armeflygskolan (Army Flying School)
AFWF	Advanced Fixed Wing Flight
AG	Airlift Group
AGA	Academia General del Aire (General Air Academy)
AkG	Aufklärüngsgeschwader (Reconnaissance Wing)
AMC	Air Mobility Command
AMD-BA	Avions Marcel Dassault-Breguet Aviation
AMF	Aircraft Maintenance Flight
AMG	Aircraft Maintenance Group
AMIF	Aircraft Maintenance Instruction Flight
AMS	Air Movements School
AMW	Air Mobility Wing
ANG	Air National Guard
APS	Aircraft Preservation Society
ARS	Air Refuelling Squadron
ARW	Air Refuelling Wing
ARWS	Advanced Rotary Wing Squadron
AS	Airlift Squadron/Air Squadron
ASCW	Airborne Surveillance Control Wing
ASF	Aircraft Servicing Flight
AS&RU	Aircraft Salvage and Repair Unit
ATC	Air Training Corps
ATCC	Air Traffic Control Centre
Avn	Aviation
Avn Co	Aviation Company
AW	Airlift Wing/Armstrong Whitworth Aircraft
AWC	Air Warfare Centre
BAC	British Aircraft Corporation
BAe	British Aerospace PLC
BAOR	British Army of the Rhine
BAPC	British Aviation Preservation Council
BATUS	British Army Training Unit Support
BBMF	Battle of Britain Memorial Flight
BDRF	Battle Damage Repair Flight
BDRT	Battle Damage Repair Training
Be	Beech
Bf	Bayerische Flugzeugwerke
BFWF	Basic Fixed Wing Flight
BG	Bomber Group
BGA	British Gliding & Soaring Association
bk	black (squadron colours and markings)
bl	blue (squadron colours and markings)
BNFL	British Nuclear Fuels Ltd
BnHATk	Helicopter Attack Battalion
BnHLn	Liaison Battalion
BP	Boulton & Paul
BS	Bomber Squadron
B-V	Boeing-Vertol
BW	Bomber Wing
CAC	Commonwealth Aircraft Corporation
CARG	Cotswold Aircraft Restoration Group
CASA	Construcciones Aeronautics SA
Cav	Cavalry
CC	County Council
CCF	Combined Cadet Force/Canadian Car & Foundry Company
CDE	Chemical Defence Establishment
CEAM	Centre d'Expérimentation Aériennes Militaires (Military Air Experimental Centre)
CEV	Centre d'Essais en Vol (Flight Test Centre)
CFS	Central Flying School
CGMF	Central Glider Maintenance Flight
CIEH	Centre d'Instruction des Equipages D'Hélicoptäre (Helicopter Crew Training Centre)
CIFAS	Centre d'Instruction des Forces Aériennes Stratégiques (Air Strategic Training Centre)
CinC	Commander in Chief
CINCAFSE	Commander in Chief, Allied Forces Southern Europe
CINCLANT	Commander in Chief Atlantic
CITac	Centre d'Instruction Tactique (Tactical Training Centre)
Co	Company
Comp	Composite with
CT	College of Technology
CTE	Central Training Establishment
CTTS	Civilian Technical Training School
CV	Chance-Vought
D-BA	Daimler-Benz Aerospace
D-BD	Dassault-Breguet Dornier
DEODS	Defence Explosives Ordnance Disposal School
Det	Detachment
DH	de Havilland
DHC	de Havilland Canada
DHFS	Defence Helicopter Flying School
DRA	Defence Research Agency
DTEO	Defence Test and Evaluation Organisation
DTI	Department of Trade and Industry
EA	Escadron Aérien (Air Squadron)
EAC	Ecole de l'Aviation de Chasse (Fighter Aviation School)
EAP	European Aircraft Project
EAT	Ecole de l'Aviation de Transport (Transport Aviation School)
EC	Escadre de Chasse (Fighter Wing)
ECS	Electronic Countermeasures Squadron
EDA	Escadre de Detection Aéroportée (Air Detection Wing)
EdC	Escadron de Convoyage
EDCA	Escadre de Détection et de Control Aéroportée (Airborne Detection & Control Sqn)
EE	English Electric
EET	Escadron Electronique Tactique (Tactical Electronics Flight)
EHI	European Helicopter Industries
EL	Escadre de Liaison (Liaison Wing)
EMA	East Midlands Airport
EMVO	Elementaire Militaire Vlieg Opleiding (Elementary Flying Training)
ENOSA	Ecole des Navigateurs Operationales Systemes d'Armees (Navigation School)
EoN	Elliot's of Newbury

EP&TU	Exhibition, Production & Transportation Unit
EPAA	Ecole de Pilotage Elementaire de l'Armée de l'Air (Air Force Elementary Flying School)
EPE	Ecole de Pilotage Elementaire (Elementary Flying School)
ER	Escadre de Reconnaissance (Reconnaissance Wing)
ERS	Escadron de Reconnaissance Stratégique (Strategic Reconnaissance Squadron)
ERV	Escadre de Ravitaillement en Vol (Air Refuelling Wing)
ES	Escadrille de Servitude
Esc	Escuadron (Squadron)
Esk	Eskadrille (Squadron)
Eslla	Escuadrilla (Squadron)
Esq	Esquadra (Squadron)
ET	Escadre de Transport (Transport Squadron)
ETE	Escadron de Transport et Entrainment (Transport Training Squadron)
ETEC	Escadron de Transport d'Entrainement et de Calibration (Transport Training & Calibration Sqn)
ETL	Escadron de Transport Légäre (Light Transport Squadron)
ETO	Escadron de Transition Operationnelle
ETOM	Escadron de Transport Outre Mer (Overseas Transport Squadron)
ETPS	Empire Test Pilots' School
ETS	Engineering Training School
FAA	Fleet Air Arm/Federal Aviation Administration
FACF	Forward Air Control Flight
FBS	Flugbereitschaftstaffel
FBW	Fly by wire
FC	Forskokcentralen (Flight Centre)
FE	Further Education
FETC	Fire and Emergency Training Centre
ff	Front fuselage
FG	Fighter Group
FH	Fairchild-Hiller
FI	Falkland Islands
FLG FFB	Fluglehrgruppe Furstenfeldbruck (Flight Training Group Furstenfeldbruck)
FISt	Flieger Staffel (Flight Squadron)
Flt	Flight
FMA	Fabrica Militar de Aviones
FMV	Forsvarets Materielwerk
FONA	Flag Officer Naval Aviation
FRADU	Fleet Requirements and Air Direction Unit
FRA	FR Aviation
FS	Fighter Squadron
FSAIU	Flight Safety & Accident Investigation Unit
FSCTE	Fire School Central Training Establishment
FTS	Flying Training School
FTW	Flying Training Wing
Fw	Focke Wulf
FW	Fighter Wing/Foster Wickner
FWTS	Fixed Wing Test Squadron
FY	Fiscal Year
F3 OCU	Tornado F3 Operational Conversion Unit
GAL	General Aircraft Ltd
GAM	Groupe Aerien Mixte (Composite Air Group)
gd	gold (squadron colours and markings)
GD	General Dynamics
GHL	Groupe d'Helicopteres Legeres (Light Helicopter Group)

GI	Ground Instruction/Groupement d'Instruction (Instructional Group)
gn	green (squadron colours and markings)
GRD	Gruppe fur Rustunggdienste (Group for Service Preparation)
GT	Grupo de Transporte (Transport Wing)
GTT	Grupo de Transporte de Tropos (Troop Carrier Wing)
gy	grey (squadron colours and markings)
HAF	Historic Aircraft Flight
HC	Helicopter Combat Support Squadron
HF	Historic Flying Ltd
HFR	Heeresfliegerregiment (Army Air Regiment)
HFWS	Heeresflieger Waffenschule (Army Air Weapons School)
Hkp Div	Helikopterdivisionen (Helicopter Division)
HMA	Helicopter Maritime Attack
HMF	Harrier Maintenance Flight/Helicopter Maintenance Flight
HMS	Her Majesty's Ship
HOCU	Harrier OCU
HP	Handley-Page
HQ	Headquarters
HS	Hawker Siddeley
HSF	Harrier Servicing Flight
IAF	Israeli Air Force
IHM	International Helicopter Museum
IWM	Imperial War Museum
JATE	Joint Air Transport Establishment
JbG	Jagdbombergeschwader (Fighter Bomber Wing)
JFACSTU	Joint Forward Air Control Students Training Unit
JG	Jagdgeschwader (Fighter Wing)
Kridlo	Wing
Letka	Squadron
LTG	Lufttransportgeschwader (Air Transport Wing)
LTV	Ling-Temco-Vought
LVG	Luftwaffen Versorgungs Geschwader (Air Force Maintenance Wing)/ Luft Verkehrs Gesellschaft
LZS	Letecké Zkušcbní Středisko (Air Test Centre)
m	multi-coloured (squadron colours and markings)
MARPAT	Maritime Patrouillegroep (Maritime Patrol Group)
MBB	Messerschmitt Bolkow-Blohm
MCAS	Marine Corps Air Station
McD	McDonnell Douglas
Med	Medical
MFG	Marine Flieger Geschwader (Naval Air Wing)
MH	Max Holste
MIB	Military Intelligence Battalion
MiG	Mikoyan Gurevich
MoD(PE)	Ministry of Defence (Procurement Executive)
Mod	Modified
MR	Maritime Reconnaissance
MRF	Meteorological Research Flight
MS	Morane-Saulnier
MTM	Mira Taktikis Metaforon
MU	Maintenance Unit
Mus'm	Museum
NA	North American
NACDS	Naval Air Command Driving School
NAEWF	NATO Airborne Early Warning Force
NAF	Naval Air Facility
NARO	Naval Aircraft Repair Organisation
NAS	Naval Air Station
NASU	Naval Air Support Unit

NATO	North Atlantic Treaty Organisation
NE	North-East
NI	Northern Ireland
NMSU	Nimrod Major Servicing Unit
NYARC	North Yorks Aircraft Restoration Centre
OCU	Operational Conversion Unit
OEU	Operation Evaluation Unit
OFMC	Old Flying Machine Company
or	orange (squadron colours and markings)
PBN	Pilatus Britten-Norman
pr	purple (squadron colours and markings)
PRU	Photographic Reconnaissance Unit
r	red (squadron colours and markings)
R	Replica
RAeS	Royal Aeronautical Society
RAF	Royal Aircraft Factory/Royal Air Force
RAFC	Royal Air Force College
RAFM	Royal Air Force Museum
RAFGSA	Royal Air Force Gliding and Soaring Association
RAOC	Royal Army Ordnance Corps
RCAF	Royal Canadian Air Force
RE	Royal Engineers
Regt	Regiment
REME	Royal Electrical & Mechanical Engineers
rf	Rear fuselage
RJAF	Royal Jordanian Air Force
RM	Royal Marines
RMC of S	Royal Military College of Science
RN	Royal Navy
RNAS	Royal Naval Air Station
RNAW	Royal Naval Aircraft Workshop
RNEC	Royal Naval Engineering College
RNGSA	Royal Navy Gliding and Soaring Association
ROF	Royal Ordnance Factory
RQS	Rescue Squadron
R-R	Rolls-Royce
RS	Reid & Sigrist/Reconnaissance Squadron
RSV	Reparto Sperimentale Volo (Experimental Flight School)
RW	Reconnaissance Wing
RWTS	Rotary Wing Test Squadron
SA	Scottish Aviation
Saab	Svenska Aeroplan Aktieboleg
SAH	School of Air Handling
SAL	Scottish Aviation Limited
SAM	School of Aviation Medicine
SAOEU	Strike/Attack Operational Evaluation Unit
SAR	Search and Rescue
Saro	Saunders-Roe
SARTU	Search and Rescue Training Unit
SBoLK	Stíhacie Bombardovacie Letecké Kridlo (Fighter Bomber Air Wing)
SCW	Sea Control Wing
SEAE	School of Electrical & Aeronautical Engineering
SEPECAT	Société Européenne de Production de l'avion Ecole de Combat et d'Appui Tactique
SFDO	School of Flight Deck Operations
SHAPE	Supreme Headquarters Allied Forces Europe
si	silver (squadron colours and markings)
SKTU	Sea King Training Unit
Skv	Skvadron (Squadron)
SLK	Stíhacie Letecké Kridlo (Fighter Air Wing)
SLV	School Licht Vliegwezen (Flying School)
Sm	Smaldeel (Squadron)
SNCAN	Société Nationale de Constructions Aéronautiques du Nord
SOES	Station Operations & Engineering Squadron
SOG	Special Operations Group
SOS	Special Operations Squadron
SoTT	School of Technical Training
SOW	Special Operations Wing
SPAD	Société Pour les Appareils Deperdussin
Sqn	Squadron
SSF	Station Servicing Flight
SWWAPS	Second World War Aircraft Preservation Society
TA	Territorial Army
T&EE	Test & Evaluation Establishment
TFC	The Fighter Collection
TGp	Test Groep
TMF	Tornado Maintenance Flight
TMTS	Trade Management Training School
TS	Test Squadron
TsAGI	Tsentral'ny Aerogidrodinamicheski Instut (Central Aero & Hydrodynamics Institute)
TsLw	Technische Schule der Luftwaffe (Luftwaffe Technical School)
TSW	Tactical Supply Wing
TTTE	Tri-national Tornado Training Establishment
TW	Test Wing
UAS	University Air Squadron
Uberwg	Uberwachunggeschwader (Surveillance Wing)
UK	United Kingdom
UKAEA	United Kingdom Atomic Energy Authority
UNFICYP	United Nations' Forces in Cyprus
US	United States
USAF	United States Air Force
USAFE	United States Air Forces in Europe
USAREUR	US Army Europe
USEUCOM	United States European Command
USMC	United States Marine Corps
USN	United States Navy
VFW	Vereinigte Flugtechnische Werke
VGS	Volunteer Gliding School
VMGR	Marine Aerial Refuelling/Transport Squadron
VMGRT	Marine Aerial Refuelling/Transport Training Squadron
VQ	Fleet Air Reconnaissance Squadron
VR	Fleet Logistic Support Squadron
VS	Vickers-Supermarine
VSL	Vycvikové Stredisko Letectva (Flying Training Centre)
w	white (squadron colours and markings)
Wg	Wing
WLT	Weapons Loading Training
WRS	Weather Reconnaissance Squadron
WS	Westland
WTD	Wehrtechnische Dienstelle (Technical Support Unit)
WW2	World War II
y	yellow (squadron colours and markings)
zDL	základna Dopravního Letectva
ZmDK	Zmiesany Dopravny Kridlo (Mixed Transport Wing)
zSL	základna Skolního Letectva
zTL	základna Taktického Letectva

This section is to assist the reader to locate the places in the United Kingdom where operational military aircraft are based. The term *aircraft* also includes helicopters and gliders.

The alphabetical order listing gives each location in relation to its county and to its nearest classified road(s) (*by* means adjoining; *of* means proximate to), together with its approximate direction and mileage from the centre of a nearby major town or city.

Some civil airports are included where active military units are also based, but **excluded** are MoD sites with non-operational aircraft (eg *gate guardians*), the bases of privately-owned civil aircraft that wear military markings and museums.

User	Base name	County/Region	Location	Distance/direction from (town)
DTEO	Aberporth	Dyfed	N of A487	6m ENE of Cardigan
RAF	Abingdon	Oxfordshire	W by B4017, W of A34	5m SSW of Oxford
RAF	Aldergrove/Belfast Airport	Co Antrim	W by A26	13m W of Belfast
RAF/ Hunting	Barkston Heath	Lincolnshire	W by B6404, S of A153	5m NNE of Grantham
RAF	Benson	Oxfordshire	E by A423	1m NE of Wallingford
DTEO/ RAF	Boscombe Down	Wiltshire	S by A303, W of A338	6m N of Salisbury
RAF	Boulmer	Northumberland	E of B1339	4m E of Alnwick
RAF	Brize Norton	Oxfordshire	W of A4095	5m SW of Witney
RAF/ Marshall	Cambridge Airport/ Teversham	Cambridgeshire	S by A1303	2m E of Cambridge
RM/RAF	Chivenor	Devon	S of A361	4m WNW of Barnstaple
RAF	Church Fenton	Yorkshire North	S of B1223	7m WNW of Selby
RAF	Colerne	Wiltshire	S of A420, E of Fosse Way	5m NE of Bath
RAF	Coltishall	Norfolk	W of B1150	9m NNE of Norwich
RAF	Coningsby	Lincolnshire	S of A153, W by B1192	10m NW of Boston
RAF	Cosford	Shropshire	W of A41, N of A464	9m WNW of Wolverhampton
RAF	Cottesmore	Leicestershire	W of A1, N of B668	9m NW of Stamford
RAF	Cranwell	Lincolnshire	N by A17, S by B1429	5m WNW of Sleaford
RNAS	Culdrose	Cornwall	E by A3083	1m SE of Helston
AAC	Dishforth	Yorkshire North	E by A1	4m E of Ripon
BAe	Dunsfold	Surrey	W of A281, S of B2130	9m S of Guildford
USAF	Fairford	Gloucestershire	S of A417	9m ESE of Cirencester
BAe	Filton	Avon	E by M5 jn 17, W by A38	4m N of Bristol
RNAY	Fleetlands	Hampshire	E by A32	2m SE of Fareham
RAF	Glasgow Airport	Strathclyde	N by M8 jn 28	7m W of city
RAF	Halton	Buckinghamshire	N of A4011, S of B4544	4m ESE of Aylesbury
RAF	Henlow	Bedfordshire	E of A600, W of A6001	1m SW of Henlow
RAF	Honington	Suffolk	E of A134, W of A1088	6m S of Thetford
RAF	Hullavington	Wiltshire	W of A429	1m N of M4 jn 17
RAF	Kenley	Greater London	W of A22	1m W of Warlingham
RAF	Kinloss	Grampian	E of B9011, N of B9089	3m NE of Forres
RAF	Kirknewton	Lothian	E by B7031, N by A70	8m SW of Edinburgh
USAF	Lakenheath	Suffolk	W by A1065	8m W of Thetford
RAF	Leeming	Yorkshire North	E by A1	5m SW of Northallerton
RAF	Leuchars	Fife	E of A919	7m SE of Dundee
RAF	Linton-on-Ouse	Yorkshire North	E of B6265	10m NW of York
DTEO	Llanbedr	Gwynedd	W of A496	7m NNW of Barmouth
RAF	Lossiemouth	Grampian	W of B9135, S of B9040	4m N of Elgin
RAF	Lyneham	Wiltshire	W of A3102, S of A420	10m WSW of Swindon
RAF	Manston	Kent	N by A253	3m W of Ramsgate
RAF	Marham	Norfolk	N by A1122	6m W of Swaffham
AAC	Middle Wallop	Hampshire	S by A343	6m SW of Andover
USAF	Mildenhall	Suffolk	S by A1101	9m NNE of Newmarket
RAF	Newton	Nottinghamshire	N of A52, W of A46	7m E of Nottingham
RAF	Northolt	Greater London	N by A40	3m E of M40 jn 1
RAF	Odiham	Hampshire	E of A32	2m S of M3 jn 5
RNAS	Portland	Dorset	E by A354	3m S of Weymouth
RN	Predannack	Cornwall	W by A3083	7m S of Helston
RN	Prestwick Airport	Strathclyde	E by A79	3m N of Ayr
RAF	St Athan	South Glamorgan	N of B4265	13m WSW of Cardiff
RAF	St Mawgan/Newquay Airport	Cornwall	N of A3059	4m ENE of Newquay
RAF	Sealand	Flint	W by A550	6m WNW of Chester
RAF	Shawbury	Shropshire	W of B5063	7m NNE of Shrewsbury

User	Base name	County/Region	Location	Distance/direction from (town)
RAF	Swansea Airport/ Fairwood Common	West Glamorgan	W by A4118	6m W of Swansea
RAF/ Shorts	Sydenham/ Belfast City Airport	Co Down	W by A2	2m E of city
RAF	Syerston	Nottinghamshire	W by A46	5m SW of Newark
RAF DTEO	Ternhill	Shropshire	SW by A41	3m SW of Market
RAF/ ACC	Topcliffe	Yorkshire North	E of A167, W of A168	3m SW of Thirsk
RAF	Upavon	Wiltshire	S by A342	14m WNW of Andover
RAF	Valley	Gwynedd	S of A5 on Anglesey	5m SE of Holyhead
RAF	Waddington	Lincolnshire	E by A607, W by A15	5m S of Lincoln
BAe	Warton	Lancashire	S by A584	8m SE of Blackpool
AAC/ RAF	Wattisham	Suffolk	N of B1078	5m SSW of Stowmarket
DTEO	West Freugh	Dumfries & Galloway	S by A757, W by A715	5m SE of Stranraer
RAF	Weston-on-the-Green	Oxfordshire	E by A43	9m N of Oxford
RAF	Wethersfield	Essex	E of B1053	7m NNW of Braintree
RAF	Wittering	Cambridgeshire	W by A1, N of A47	3m S of Stamford
RAF	Woodvale	Merseyside	W by A565	5m SSW of Southport
RAF	Wyton	Cambridgeshire	E of A141, N of B1090	3m NE of Huntingdon
WS	Yeovil	Somerset	N of A30, S of A3088	1m W of Yeovil
RNAS	Yeovilton	Somerset	S by B3151, S of A303	5m N of Yeovil

British Military Aircraft Serials

The Committee of Imperial Defence through its Air Committee introduced a standardised system of numbering aircraft in November 1912. The Air Department of the Admiralty was allocated the first batch 1-200 and used these to cover aircraft already in use and those on order. The Army was issued with the next block from 201-800, which included the number 304 which was given to the Cody Biplane now preserved in the Science Museum. By the outbreak of World War 1 the Royal Navy was on its second batch of serials 801-1600 and this system continued with alternating allocations between the Army and Navy until 1916 when number 10000, a Royal Flying Corps BE2C, was reached.

It was decided not to continue with five digit numbers but instead to start again from 1, prefixing RFC aircraft with the letter A and RNAS aircraft with the prefix N. The RFC allocations commenced with A1 an FE2D and before the end of the year had reached A9999 an Armstrong Whitworth FK8. The next group commenced with B1 and continued in logical sequence through the C, D, E and F prefixes. G was used on a limited basis to identify captured German aircraft, while H was the last block of wartime-ordered aircraft. To avoid confusion I was not used, so the new postwar machines were allocated serials in the J range. A further minor change was made in the serial numbering system in August 1929 when it was decided to maintain four numerals after the prefix letter, thus omitting numbers 1 to 999. The new K series therefore commenced at K1000, which was allocated to an AW Atlas.

The Naval N prefix was not used in such a logical way. Blocks of numbers were allocated for specific types of aircraft such as seaplanes or flying-boats. By the late 1920s the sequence had largely been used up and a new series using the prefix S was commenced. In 1930 separate naval allocations were stopped and subsequent serials were issued in the military range which had by this time reached the K series. A further change in the pattern of allocations came in the L range. Commencing with L7272 numbers were issued in blocks with smaller blocks of serials between not used. These were known as blackout blocks. As M had already been used as a suffix for Maintenance Command instructional airframes it was not used as a prefix. Although N had previously been used for naval aircraft it was used again for serials allocated from 1937.

With the build-up to World War 2 the rate of allocations quickly accelerated and the prefix R was being used when war was declared. The letters O and Q were not allotted, and nor was S which had been used up to S1865 for naval aircraft before integration into the RAF series. By 1940 the serial Z9999 had been reached, as part of a blackout block, with the letters U and Y not used to avoid confusion. The option to recommence serial allocation at A1000 was not taken up; instead it was decided to use an alphabetical two-letter prefix with three numerals running from 100 to 999. Thus AA100 was allocated to a Blenheim IV.

This two-letter, three-numeral serial system which started in 1940 continues today. The letters C, I, O, Q, U and Y were, with the exception of NC, not used. For various reasons the following letter combinations were not issued: DA, DB, DH, EA, GA to GZ, HA, HT, JE, JH, JJ, KR to KT, MR, NW, NZ, SA to SK, SV, TN, TR and VE. The first postwar serials issued were in the VP range while the end of the WZs had been reached by the Korean War. The current new issues are in the ZJ range and there are now no blackout blocks of unallocated serials. This being so, and at the current rate of issue the Z range will last well into the 21st century.

Note: Whilst every effort has been made to ensure the accuracy of this publication, no part of the contents has been obtained from official sources. The compiler will be pleased to continue to receive comments, corrections and further information for inclusion in subsequent editions of *Military Aircraft Markings* and the monthly up-date of additions and amendments that is published in *Aircraft Illustrated*. Please send your information to Military Aircraft Markings, PO Box 46, Westbury-on-Trym, Bristol BS9 1TF; or fax to 0117 968 3928.

British Military Aircraft Markings

A serial in *italics* denotes that it is not the genuine marking for that airframe.

Serial	Type (other identity) [code]	Owner/operator, location or fate	Notes
164	Bleriot Type XI (BAPC 106/9209M)	RAF Museum Rest'n Centre, Cardington	
168	Sopwith Tabloid Scout <R> (G-BFDE)	RAF Museum, Hendon	
304	Cody Biplane (BAPC 62)	Science Museum, South Kensington	
433	Bleriot Type XXVII (BAPC 107/9202M)	RAF Museum, Hendon	
687	RAF BE2b <R> (BAPC 181)	RAF Museum, Hendon	
1701	RAF BE2c <R> (BAPC 117)	Privately owned, Sevenoaks	
2345	Vickers FB5 Gunbus <R> (G-ATVP)	RAF Museum, Hendon	
2699	RAF BE2c	Imperial War Museum, Lambeth	
2882	Vickers FB5 Gunbus <R> (BAPC 234)	Macclesfield Historical Av Soc, Barton	
3066	Caudron GIII (G-AETA/9203M)	RAF Museum, Hendon	
5492	Sopwith LC-1T Triplane <R> (G-PENY)	*Re-registered as G-BWRA, April 1996*	
5894	DH2 <R> (G-BFVH) [FB2]	Wessex Aviation & Transport, Chalmington	
5964	DH2 <R> (BAPC 112)	Museum of Army Flying, stored Middle Wallop	
6232	RAF BE2c <R> (BAPC 41)	Yorkshire Air Museum, stored Elvington	
8359	Short 184 <ff>	FAA Museum, RNAS Yeovilton	
A301	Morane BB (frame)	RAF Museum Rest'n Centre, Cardington	
A1325	RAF BE2e (G-BVGR)	Aero Vintage, Hatch	
A1742	Bristol Scout D <R> (BAPC 38)	The Aircraft Restoration Co, Duxford	
A4850	RAF SE5a <R> (BAPC 176)	Macclesfield Historical Av Soc, Barton	
A7317	Sopwith Pup <R> (BAPC 179)	Midland Air Museum, Coventry	
A8226	Sopwith 1½ Strutter <R> (G-BIDW)	RAF Museum, Hendon	
B415	AFEE 10/42 Rotabuggy <R> (BAPC 163)	Museum of Army Flying, Middle Wallop	
B1807	Sopwith Pup (G-EAVX) [A7]	Privately owned, Keynsham, Avon	
B2458	Sopwith 1F.1 Camel <R> (G-BPOB/*F542*) [R]	Privately owned, Booker	
B6401	Sopwith 1F.1 Camel <R> (G-AWYY/C1701)	FAA Museum, RNAS Yeovilton	
B7270	Sopwith 1F.1 Camel <R> (G-BFCZ)	Brooklands Museum, Weybridge	
B9708	Sopwith 1½ Strutter <R>	*Repainted as N3177*	
C1904	RAF SE5a <R> (G-PFAP) [Z]	Privately owned, Syerston	
C3011	Phoenix Currie Super Wot (G-SWOT) [S]	The Real Aeroplane Company, Breighton	
C4451	Avro 504J <R> (BAPC 210)	Southampton Hall of Aviation	
C4912	Bristol M1C <R> (BAPC 135)	Northern Aeroplane Workshops	
C4940	Bristol M1C <R>	Bygone Times Warehouse, Euxton, Lancs	
C4994	Bristol M1C <R> (G-BLWM)	RAF Museum, Hendon	
C9533	RAF SE5a <R> (G-BUWE) [M]	Privately owned, Boscombe Down	
D276	RAF SE5a <R> (BAPC 208)	Prince's Mead Shopping Centre, Farnborough	
D2700	RAF SE5a <R> (BAPC 208)	*Repainted as D276*	
D3419	Sopwith 1F.1 Camel <R> (BAPC 59)	RAF Cosford Aerospace Museum	
D7560	Avro 504K	Museum of Army Flying, Middle Wallop	
D7889	Bristol F2b Fighter (G-AANM/BAPC 166)	Aero Vintage, St Leonards-on-Sea	
D8084	Bristol F2b Fighter (G-ACAA/F4516) [S]	The Fighter Collection, Old Warden	
D8096	Bristol F2b Fighter (G-AEPH) [D]	The Shuttleworth Collection, Old Warden	
D8781	Avro 504K <R> (G-ECKE)	Privately owned, Rougham	
E373	Avro 504K <R> (BAPC 178)	Privately owned,	
E449	Avro 504K (G-EBJE/9205M)	RAF Museum, Hendon	
E2466	Bristol F2b Fighter (BAPC 165) [I]	RAF Museum, Hendon	
E2581	Bristol F2b Fighter	Imperial War Museum, Duxford	

Notes	Serial	Type (other identity) [code]	Owner/operator, location or fate
	F141	RAF SE5a <R> (G-SEVA) [G]	Privately owned, Boscombe Down
	F344	Avro 504K <R>	*Repainted as G-AACA*
	F542	Sopwith 1F.1 Camel <R> (G-BPOB)	*Painted as B2458*
	F760	SE5a Microlight <R> [A]	Privately owned, Redhill
	F904	RAF SE5a (G-EBIA)	The Shuttleworth Collection, Old Warden
	F938	RAF SE5a (G-EBIC/9208M)	RAF Museum, Hendon
	F943	RAF SE5a <R> (G-BIHF) [S]	Privately owned, White Waltham
	F943	RAF SE5a <R> (G-BKDT)	Yorkshire Air Museum, Elvington
	F1010	Airco DH9A [C]	RAF Museum, Hendon
	F3556	RAF RE8	Imperial War Museum, Duxford
	F4013	Sopwith 1F.1 Camel <R>	Privately owned, Coventry
	F5447	RAF SE5a <R> (G-BKER) [N]	Privately owned, Cumbernauld
	F5459	RAF SE5a <R> (G-INNY) [Y]	Privately owned, Old Sarum
	F5475	RAF SE5a <R> (BAPC 250)	Brooklands Museum, Weybridge
	F6314	Sopwith 1F.1 Camel (9206M) [B]	RAF Museum, Hendon
	F8010	RAF SE5a <R> (G-BDWJ) [Z]	Privately owned, Graveley
	F8614	Vickers FB27A Vimy IV <R> (G-AWAU)	RAF Museum, Hendon
	H1968	Avro 504K <R> (BAPC 42)	Yorkshire Air Museum, stored Elvington
	H2311	Avro 504K (G-ABAA)	Gr Manchester Mus of Science & Industry
	H3426	Hawker Hurricane <R> (BAPC 68)	Privately owned,
	H5199	Avro 504K (BK892/3118M/ G-ACNB/G-ADEV)	The Shuttleworth Collection, Old Warden
	J7326	DH53 Humming Bird (G-EBQP)	Privately owned, Audley End
	J8067	Westland Pterodactyl 1a	Science Museum, South Kensington
	J9941	Hawker Hart 2 (G-ABMR)	RAF Museum, Hendon
	K1786	Hawker Tomtit (G-AFTA)	The Shuttleworth Collection, Old Warden
	K2050	Isaacs Fury II (G-ASCM)	Privately owned, Brize Norton
	K2059	Isaacs Fury II (G-PFAR)	Privately owned, Dunkeswell
	K2060	Isaacs Fury II (G-BKZM)	Privately owned, Haverfordwest
	K2075	Isaacs Fury II (G-BEER)	Privately owned, Temple Bruer
	K2227	Bristol 105 Bulldog IIA (G-ABBB) (wreck)	RAF Museum/Skysport Engineering, Hatch
	K2567	DH82A Tiger Moth (DE306/ 7035M/G-MOTH)	Privately owned, Bishop's Stortford
	K2572	DH82A Tiger Moth (NM129/ G-AOZH)	Privately owned, Shoreham
	K2572	DH82A Tiger Moth <R>	The Aeroplane Collection, Hooton Park
	K2587	DH82A Tiger Moth <R> (G-BJAP)	Privately owned, Shoreham
	K3215	Avro 621 Tutor (G-AHSA)	The Shuttleworth Collection, Old Warden
	K3661	Hawker Nimrod II (G-BURZ)	Aero Vintage, St Leonards-on-Sea
	K3731	Isaacs Fury <R> (G-RODI)	Privately owned, Hailsham
	K4232	Avro 671 Rota I (SE-AZB)	RAF Museum, Hendon
	K4235	Avro 671 Rota I (G-AHMJ) [KX-H]	The Shuttleworth Collection, Old Warden
	K4972	Hawker Hart Trainer IIA (1764M)	RAF Cosford Aerospace Museum
	K5054	Supermarine Spitfire <R> (BAPC 190/*EN398*)	Macclesfield Historical Av Soc, Barton
	K5054	Supermarine Spitfire <R> (BAPC 214)	The Spitfire Society, Lee-on-Solent
	K5054	Supermarine Spitfire <R> (G-BRDV)	Privately owned, Hullavington
	K5414	Hawker Hind (G-AENP/BAPC 78) [XV]	The Shuttleworth Collection, Old Warden
	K5600	Hawker Audax I (2015M/G-BVVI)	Aero Vintage, St Leonards-on-Sea
	K5673	Hawker Fury I <R> (BAPC 249)	Brooklands Museum, Weybridge
	K6035	Westland Wallace II (2365M)	RAF Museum, Hendon
	K7271	Hawker Fury II <R> (BAPC 148)	RAF Cosford Aerospace Museum, stored
	K8042	Gloster Gladiator II (8372M)	RAF Museum, Hendon
	K8203	Hawker Demon I (G-BTVE/2292M)	Demon Displays, Hatch
	K9853	VS300 Spitfire IA (AR213/G-AIST) [QV-H]	Privately owned, Booker
	K9926	VS300 Spitfire I <R> (BAPC 217) [JH-C]	RAF Bentley Priory, on display
	K9942	VS300 Spitfire IA (8383M) [SD-V]	RAF Museum, Hendon
	L1070	VS300 Spitfire I <R> (BAPC 227) [XT-A]	RAF Turnhouse, on display
	L1592	Hawker Hurricane I [KW-Z]	Science Museum, South Kensington
	L1592	Hawker Hurricane I <R> (BAPC 63) [KW-Z]	*Painted as P3208 by February 1996*

Serial	Type (other identity) [code]	Owner/operator, location or fate	Notes
L1679	Hawker Hurricane I <R> (BAPC 241) [JX-G]	Tangmere Military Aviation Museum	
L1710	Hawker Hurricane I <R> (BAPC 219) [AL-D]	RAF Biggin Hill, on display	
L2301	VS Walrus I (G-AIZG)	FAA Museum, RNAS Yeovilton	
L2940	Blackburn Skua I	FAA Museum, RNAS Yeovilton	
L5343	Fairey Battle I [VO-S]	RAF Museum, Hendon	
L6906	Miles M14A Magister I (G-AKKY/ T9841/BAPC 44)	Museum of Berkshire Aviation, Woodley	
L8756	Bristol 149 Bolingbroke IVT (RCAF 10001) [XD-E]	RAF Museum, Hendon	
L8841	Bristol 149 Bolingbroke IVT (G-BPIV/Z5722) [QY-C]	The Aircraft Restoration Company, Duxford	
N248	Supermarine S6A	Southampton Hall of Aviation	
N546	Wright Quadruplane 1 <R> (BAPC 164)	Southampton Hall of Aviation	
N1671	Boulton Paul P82 Defiant I (8370M) [EW-D]	RAF Museum, Hendon	
N1854	Fairey Fulmar II (G-AIBE)	FAA Museum, RNAS Yeovilton	
N2078	Sopwith Baby (8214/8215)	FAA Museum, RNAS Yeovilton	
N2276	Gloster Sea Gladiator II (N5903/ G-GLAD) [H]	The Fighter Collection, Duxford	
N2308	Gloster Gladiator I (L8032/ G-AMRK)[HP-B]	The Shuttleworth Collection, Old Warden	
N2980	Vickers Wellington IA [R]	Brooklands Museum, Weybridge	
N3177	Sopwith 1½ Strutter <R>	Macclesfield Historical Av Soc, Barton	
N3194	VS300 Spitfire I <R> (BAPC 220) [GR-Z]	RAF Biggin Hill, on display	
N3289	VS300 Spitfire I <R> (BAPC 65) [DW-K]	Kent Battle of Britain Museum, Hawkinge	
N3313	VS300 Spitfire I <R> (BAPC 69) [KL-B]	Kent Battle of Britain Museum, Hawkinge	
N3378	Boulton Paul P82 Defiant I (wreck)	Boulton Paul Association, Wolverhampton	
N4389	Fairey Albacore (N4172) [4M]	FAA Museum, RNAS Yeovilton	
N4877	Avro 652A Anson I (G-AMDA) [VX-F]	Imperial War Museum, Duxford	
N5182	Sopwith Pup <R> (G-APUP/9213M)	RAF Museum, Hendon	
N5195	Sopwith Pup (G-ABOX)	Museum of Army Flying, Middle Wallop	
N5419	Bristol Scout D <R> (N5419)	Bristol Aircraft Collection, stored Kemble	
N5492	Sopwith Triplane <R> (BAPC 111)	FAA Museum, RNAS Yeovilton	
N5628	Gloster Gladiator II	RAF Museum, Hendon	
N5912	Sopwith Triplane (8385M)	RAF Museum, Hendon	
N6181	Sopwith Pup (G-EBKY)	The Shuttleworth Collection, Old Warden	
N6290	Sopwith Triplane <R> (G-BOCK)	The Shuttleworth Collection, Old Warden	
N6452	Sopwith Pup <R> (G-BIAU)	FAA Museum, RNAS Yeovilton	
N6466	DH82A Tiger Moth (G-ANKZ)	Privately owned, Barton	
N6720	DH82A Tiger Moth (7014M) [RUO-B]	Privately owned, Hatch	
N6740	DH82A Tiger Moth (G-AISY)	Privately owned, Sandtoft, S Yorks	
N6797	DH82A Tiger Moth (G-ANEH)	Privately owned, Goodwood	
N6812	Sopwith 2F.1 Camel	Imperial War Museum, Lambeth	
N6847	DH82A Tiger Moth (G-APAL)	Privately owned, Little Gransden	
N6848	DH82A Tiger Moth (G-BALX)	Privately owned, Headcorn	
N6965	DH82A Tiger Moth (G-AJTW) [FL-J]	Privately owned, Tibenham	
N6985	DH82A Tiger Moth (G-AHMN)	AAC Historic Aircraft Flt, Middle Wallop	
N9191	DH82A Tiger Moth (G-ALND)	Privately owned, Abergavenny	
N9192	DH82A Tiger Moth (G-BSTJ) [RCO-N]	Privately owned, Sywell	
N9389	DH82A Tiger Moth (G-ANJA)	Privately owned, Shipmeadow, Suffolk	
N9899	Supermarine Southampton I (fuselage)	RAF Museum, Hendon	
P1344	HP52 Hampden I (9175M) [PL-K]	RAF Museum Rest'n Centre, Cardington	
P1344	HP52 Hampden I <rf> (parts Hereford L6012)	RAF Museum, Hendon	
P2617	Hawker Hurricane I (8373M) [AF-A]	RAF Museum, Hendon	
P2793	Hawker Hurricane I <R> (BAPC 236) [SD-M]	Eden Camp Theme Park, Malton, North Yorkshire	•
P2902	Hawker Hurricane I (G-ROBT)	Privately owned, Sudbury	
P3059	Hawker Hurricane I <R> (BAPC 64) [SD-N]	Kent Battle of Britain Museum, Hawkinge	

Notes	Serial	Type (other identity) [code]	Owner/operator, location or fate
	P3175	Hawker Hurricane I (wreck)	RAF Museum, Hendon
	P3208	Hawker Hurricane I <R> (BAPC 63/ *L1592*) [SD-T]	Kent Battle of Britain Museum, Hawkinge
	P3386	Hawker Hurricane I <R> (BAPC 218) [FT-A]	RAF Bentley Priory, on display
	P3395	Hawker Hurricane IV (KX829)[JX-B]	Birmingham Mus of Science & Technology
	P3554	Hawker Hurricane I (composite)	The Air Defence Collection, Salisbury
	P4139	Fairey Swordfish II (HS618) [5H]	FAA Museum, RNAS Yeovilton
	P5865	CCF T-6J Harvard IV (G-BKCK) [LE-W]	Privately owned, North Weald
	P6382	Miles M14A Hawk Trainer 3 (G-AJRS) [C]	The Shuttleworth Collection, Old Warden
	P7350	VS329 Spitfire IIA (G-AWIJ) [RN-S]	RAF BBMF, Coningsby
	P7540	VS329 Spitfire IIA [DU-W]	Dumfries & Galloway Avn Mus, Dumfries
	P8140	VS329 Spitfire II <R> (BAPC 71) [ZF-K]	Norfolk & Suffolk Avn Museum, Flixton
	P8448	VS329 Spitfire II <R> (BAPC 225) [UM-D]	RAF Cranwell
	P9444	VS300 Spitfire IA [RN-D]	Science Museum, South Kensington
	R1914	Miles M14A Magister (G-AHUJ)	The Real Aeroplane Company, Breighton
	R4897	DH82A Tiger Moth II (G-ERTY)	*Sold to Germany*
	R4907	DH82A Tiger Moth II (G-ANCS)	Privately owned, Wreningham, Norfolk
	R5250	DH82A Tiger Moth II (G-AODT)	Privately owned, Tibenham
	R5868	Avro 683 Lancaster I (7325M) [PO-S]	RAF Museum, Hendon
	R6915	VS300 Spitfire I	Imperial War Museum, Lambeth
	R9125	Westland Lysander III (8377M)	RAF Museum, Hendon
	R9371	HP59 Halifax II <ff> [LX-L]	Cotswold Aircraft Rest'n Group, Innsworth
	S1287	Fairey Flycatcher <R> (G-BEYB) [5]	FAA Museum, RNAS Yeovilton
	S1579	Hawker Nimrod I <R> (G-BBVO) [571]	Privately owned, Dunkeswell
	S1581	Hawker Nimrod I (G-BWWK) (fuselage)	Aero Vintage, St Leonards-on-Sea
	S1595	Supermarine S6B	Science Museum, South Kensington
	T5298	Bristol 156 Beaufighter I (4552M) <ff>	Midland Air Museum, Coventry
	T5424	DH82A Tiger Moth II (G-AJOA)	Privately owned, Chiseldon
	T5672	DH82A Tiger Moth II (G-ALRI)	Privately owned, Chalmington
	T5854	DH82A Tiger Moth II (G-ANKK)	Privately owned, Halfpenny Green *(rebuild)*
	T5879	DH82A Tiger Moth II (G-AXBW)	Privately owned, Tongham
	T5968	DH82A Tiger Moth II (G-ANNN)	Privately owned, Hollybush
	T6099	DH82A Tiger Moth II (G-AOGR)	*Painted as XL714 by May 1996*
	T6256	DH82A Tiger Moth II (G-APLR/ I-JENA)	*Sold as I-JENA, 1996*
	T6296	DH82A Tiger Moth II (8387M)	RAF Museum, Hendon
	T6313	DH82A Tiger Moth II (G-AHVU)	Privately owned, Liphook
	T6390	DH82A Tiger Moth II (G-ANIX)	Island Aeroplane Company, Sandown
	T6818	DH82A Tiger Moth II (G-ANKT) [91]	The Shuttleworth Collection, Old Warden
	T6991	DH82A Tiger Moth II (G-ANOR/ DE694)	Privately owned, Paddock Wood
	T7109	DH82A Tiger Moth II (G-AOIM)	Privately owned, Shobdon
	T7230	DH82A Tiger Moth II (G-AFVE)	Privately owned, Biggin Hill
	T7281	DH82A Tiger Moth II (G-ARTL)	Privately owned, Egton, nr Whitby
	T7404	DH82A Tiger Moth II (G-ANMV)	Privately owned, Booker
	T7471	DH82A Tiger Moth II (G-AJHU)	*Sold to Italy*
	T7793	DH82A Tiger Moth II (G-ANKV)	Privately owned, Croydon, on display
	T7842	DH82A Tiger Moth II (G-AMTF)	Privately owned, Boughton, Suffolk
	T7909	DH82A Tiger Moth II (G-ANON)	Privately owned, Sherburn-in-Elmet
	T7997	DH82A Tiger Moth II (NL750/ G-AHUF)	Privately owned, Shoreham
	T8191	DH82A Tiger Moth II (G-BWMK)	Privately owned, Welshpool
	T9707	Miles M14A Magister I (G-AKKR/ 8378M/T9708)	Gr Manchester Mus of Science & Industry
	T9738	Miles M14A Magister I (G-AKAT)	Privately owned, Breighton
	V1075	Miles M14A Magister I (G-AKPF)	Privately owned, Sandown
	V3388	Airspeed AS10 Oxford I (G-AHTW)	Imperial War Museum, Duxford
	V6028	Bristol 149 Bolingbroke IVT (G-MKIV) [GB-D] <rf>	The Aircraft Restoration Co, *stored* Duxford

Serial	Type (other identity) [code]	Owner/operator, location or fate	Notes
V7350	Hawker Hurricane I (fuselage)	Brenzett Aeronautical Museum	
V7467	Hawker Hurricane I <R> (BAPC 223) [LE-D]	RAF Coltishall, on display	
V7767	Hawker Hurricane I <R> (BAPC 72)	Privately owned, Sopley, Hants	
V9281	WS Lysander IIIA (G-BCWL) [RU-M]	Repainted as V9545, 1996	
V9441	WS Lysander IIIA (G-AZWT) [AR-A]	Privately owned, stored Strathallan	
V9545	WS Lysander IIIA (G-BCWL/V9281) [BA-C]	Privately owned, Duxford	
V9673	WS Lysander IIIA (V9300/G-LIZY) [MA-J]	Imperial War Museum, Duxford	
W1048	HP59 Halifax II (8465M) [TL-S]	RAF Museum, Hendon	
W2068	Avro 652A Anson I [68]	RAF Museum, Duxford (restoration by TFC)	
W2718	VS Walrus I (G-RNLI)	Dick Melton Aviation, Great Yarmouth	
W4041	Gloster E28/39 [G]	Science Museum, South Kensington	
W4050	DH98 Mosquito	Mosquito Aircraft Museum, London Colney	
W5856	Fairey Swordfish II (G-BMGC) [A2A]	RN Historic Flight, Yeovilton	
W9385	DH87B Hornet Moth (G-ADND) [YG-L,3]	The Shuttleworth Collection, Old Warden	
X4474	VS361 Spitfire LF XVIE (TE311/ 7241M) [QV-I]	Repainted as MK178, 1996	
X4590	VS300 Spitfire I (8384M) [PR-F]	RAF Museum, Hendon	
X7688	Bristol 156 Beaufighter I (3858M/ G-DINT)	Privately owned, Hatch	
Z2033	Fairey Firefly I (G-ASTL) [275]	Imperial War Museum, Duxford	
Z5027	Hawker Hurricane IIb	Privately owned, Audley End	
Z5053	Hawker Hurricane IIb (G-BWHA)	Historic Flying, Audley End	
Z5252	Hawker Hurricane IIb	Privately owned, Cheltenham	
Z5722	Bristol 149 Bolingbroke IVT (G-BPIV) [WM-Z]	Repainted as L8841	
Z7015	Hawker Sea Hurricane Ib (G-BKTH) [7-L]	The Shuttleworth Collection, Duxford	
Z7197	Percival P30 Proctor III (G-AKZN/ 8380M)	RAF Museum, Hendon	
Z7258	DH89A Dragon Rapide (NR786/ G-AHGD)	Privately owned, Membury (wreck)	
Z7381	Hawker Hurricane XIIb (G-HURI) [XR-T]	The Fighter Collection, Duxford	
AA908	VS349 Spitfire VB <R> (BAPC 230) [UM-W]	Eden Camp Theme Park, Malton, North Yorkshire	
AB130	VS349 Spitfire VA (parts)	Privately owned,	
AB910	VS349 Spitfire VB [ZD-C]	RAF BBMF, Audley End	
AD540	VS349 Spitfire VB (wreck)	Dumfries & Galloway Avn Mus, Dumfries	
AE436	HP52 Hampden I (parts)	Lincolnshire Avn Heritage Centre, E Kirkby	
AE977	Hawker Sea Hurricane X (G-TWTD)	Hawker Restorations Ltd, Milden	
AL246	Grumman Martlet I	FAA Museum, RNAS Yeovilton	
AM561	Lockheed Hudson V (parts)	Cornwall Aero Park, Helston	
AP506	Cierva C30A (G-ACWM)	IHM, Weston-super-Mare	
AP507	Cierva C30A (G-ACWP) [KX-P]	Science Museum, South Kensington	
AR213	VS300 Spitfire IA (G-AIST) [PR-D]	Repainted as K9853, 1996	
AR501	VS349 Spitfire LF VC (G-AWII) [NN-A]	The Shuttleworth Collection, Old Warden	
AR614	VS349 Spitfire VC (5378M/7555M/ G-BUWA) [DU-Z]	To New Zealand, 1997	
BB807	DH82A Tiger Moth (G-ADWO)	Southampton Hall of Aviation	
BE417	Hawker Hurricane XIIb (G-HURR) [AE-K]	Privately owned, Brooklands	
BE421	Hawker Hurricane IIc <R> (BAPC 205) [XP-G]	RAF Museum, Hendon	
BL370	VS349 Spitfire VB	Sold to the USA, November 1996	
BL614	VS349 Spitfire VB (4354M) [ZD-F]	Medway Aircraft Preservation Society, Rochester	
BL655	VS349 Spitfire VB (wreck)	Lincolnshire Avn Heritage Centre, East Kirkby	
BL924	VS349 Spitfire VB <R> (BAPC 242) [AZ-G]	Tangmere Military Aviation Museum	

Notes	Serial	Type (other identity) [code]	Owner/operator, location or fate
	BM597	VS349 Spitfire LF VB (5718M/ G-MKVB) [JH-B]	Historic Aircraft Collection, Audley End
	BN230	Hawker Hurricane IIc (LF751/ 5466M) [FT-A]	RAF Manston, Memorial Pavilion
	BR600	VS361 Spitfire IX <R> (BAPC 222) [SH-V]	RAF Uxbridge, on display
	BR600	VS361 Spitfire IX <R> (BAPC 224) [JP-A]	Ambassador Hotel, Norwich
	BR600	VS361 Spitfire IX <R> (fuselage)	Privately owned, Dunkeswell, derelict
	BW853	Hawker Sea Hurricane XII (G-BRKE)	*Used in the rebuild of BW881*
	BW881	Hawker Sea Hurricane XIIA (G-KAMM)	Privately owned, Eye, Suffolk
	DD931	Bristol 152 Beaufort VIII (9131M) [L]	RAF Museum, Hendon
	DE208	DH82A Tiger Moth II (G-AGYU)	Privately owned, Ronaldsway
	DE363	DH82A Tiger Moth II (G-ANFC)	Privately owned, Rochester
	DE470	DH82A Tiger Moth II (G-ANMY)	Privately owned, Durley, Hants
	DE623	DH82A Tiger Moth II (G-ANFI)	Privately owned, Shobdon
	DE673	DH82A Tiger Moth II (6948M/ G-ADNZ)	Privately owned, Hampton
	DE970	DH82A Tiger Moth II (G-AOBJ)	Privately owned, Cardiff
	DE992	DH82A Tiger Moth II (G-AXXV)	Privately owned, Swanton Morley
	DF128	DH82A Tiger Moth II (G-AOJJ) [RCO-U]	Privately owned, White Waltham
	DF155	DH82A Tiger Moth II (G-ANFV)	Privately owned, Shempston Fm, Lossiemouth
	DF198	DH82A Tiger Moth II (G-BBRB)	Privately owned, Biggin Hill
	DG202	Gloster F9/40 (5758M) [G]	RAF Cosford Aerospace Museum
	DG590	Miles M2H Hawk Major (8379M/ G-ADMW)	RAF Museum Restoration Centre, Cardington
	DP872	Fairey Barracuda II (fuselage)	FAA Museum, stored Yeovilton
	DR613	Foster-Wikner GM1 Wicko (G-AFJB)	Privately owned, stored Berkswell, W Midlands
	DV372	Avro 683 Lancaster I <ff>	Imperial War Museum, Lambeth
	EE416	Gloster Meteor F3 <ff>	Science Museum, Wroughton
	EE425	Gloster Meteor F3 <ff>	Rebel Air Museum, Earls Colne
	EE531	Gloster Meteor F4 (7090M)	Midland Air Museum, Coventry
	EE549	Gloster Meteor F4 (7008M)	Tangmere Military Aviation Museum
	EF545	VS349 Spitfire VC <ff>	Privately owned, High Wycombe
	EM720	DH82A Tiger Moth II (G-AXAN)	Privately owned, Little Gransden
	EM727	DH82A Tiger Moth II (G-AOXN)	Privately owned, Yeovil
	EM903	DH82A Tiger Moth II (G-APBI)	Privately owned, Halstead
	EN224	VS366 Spitfire F XII (G-FXII)	Privately owned, Newport Pagnell
	EN343	VS365 Spitfire PR XI <R> (BAPC 226)	RAF Benson, on display
	EN398	VS361 Spitfire F IX <R> (BAPC 184) [WO-A]	Privately owned, North Weald
	EN398	VS361 Spitfire F IX <R> (BAPC 190) [JE-J]	*Repainted as K5054*
	EP120	VS349 Spitfire LF VB (5377M/ 8070M/G-LFVB) [AE-A]	The Fighter Collection, Duxford
	EX976	NA AT-6D Harvard III (FAP.1657)	FAA Museum, RNAS Yeovilton
	EZ259	NA AT-6D Harvard III (G-BMJW)	Privately owned, Wakefield, West Yorkshire
	EZ407	NA AT-6D Harvard III	*Sold to the USA as N407EZ, March 1996*
	FB226	Bonsall Mustang <R> (G-BDWM) [MT-A]	Privately owned, Gamston
	FE695	Noorduyn AT-16 Harvard IIB (G-BTXI)	The Fighter Collection, Duxford
	FE905	Noorduyn AT-16 Harvard IIB (LN-BNM)	RAF Museum, Hendon
	FE992	Noorduyn AT-16 Harvard IIB (G-BDAM) [KT]	Privately owned, Duxford
	FH153	Noorduyn AT-16 Harvard IIB (G-BBHK) [GW-A]	Privately owned, stored Cardiff
	FJ992	Boeing-Stearman PT-17 Kaydet (442/G-BPTB)	Privately owned, Audley End
	FM118	Avro 683 Lancaster B X <ff>	Privately owned, Gosport, Hants
	FR886	Piper L-4J Cub (G-BDMS)	Privately owned, Old Sarum
	FS728	Noorduyn AT-16 Harvard IIB (G-BAFM) [F]	Privately owned, Goodwood

Serial	Type (other identity) [code]	Owner/operator, location or fate	Notes
FS890	Noorduyn AT-16 Harvard IIB (7554M)	MoD(PE), stored DTEO Boscombe Down	
FT239	CCF T-6J Texan (G-BIWX)	Privately owned, North Weald	
FT323	NA AT-6D Harvard III (FAP 1513)	Air Engineering Services, Swansea	
FT375	Noorduyn AT-16 Harvard IIB [5]	Sold to Italy, July 1996	
FT391	Noorduyn AT-16 Harvard IIB (G-AZBN)	Privately owned, Shoreham	
FX301	NA AT-6D Harvard III (EX915/ G-JUDI)	Privately owned, Bryngwyn Bach, Clwyd	
FX360	Noorduyn AT-16 Harvard IIB (KF435)	Booker Aircraft Museum	
FX442	Noorduyn AT-16 Harvard IIB [TO-M]	Privately owned, South Gorley, Hants	
FX760	Curtiss P-40N Kittyhawk IV (9150M) [GA-?]	RAF Museum, Hendon	
HB275	Beech C-45 Expeditor II (G-BKGM)	Privately owned, North Weald	
HB751	Fairchild Argus III (G-BCBL)	Privately owned, Little Gransden	
HH379	GAL48 Hotspur II <rf>	Museum of Army Flying, Middle Wallop	
HH982	Taylorcraft Plus D (LB312/G-AHXE)	Privately owned, Shoreham	
HJ711	DH98 Mosquito NF II [VI-C]	Night Fighter Preservation Tm, Elvington	
HM354	Percival P34 Proctor III (G-ANPP)	Privately owned, Stansted	
HM580	Cierva C-30A (G-ACUU)	Imperial War Museum, Duxford	
HS503	Fairey Swordfish IV (BAPC 108)	RAF Cosford Aerospace Museum, stored	
JM135	Bristol 156 Beaufighter XIC (A19-144)	The Fighter Collection, Duxford	
JR505	Hawker Typhoon IB <ff>	Midland Air Museum, Coventry	
JV482	Grumman Wildcat V	Ulster Aviation Society, Langford Lodge	
KB889	Avro 683 Lancaster B X (G-LANC) [NA-I]	Imperial War Museum, Duxford	
KB976	Avro 683 Lancaster B X (G-BCOH)	Aces High, North Weald	
KB994	Avro 683 Lancaster B X (G-BVBP)	Aces High, North Weald	
KD431	CV Corsair IV [E2-M]	FAA Museum, RNAS Yeovilton	
KD572	Goodyear FG-1D Corsair (88297/ G-FGID)	The Fighter Collection, Duxford	
KE209	Grumman Hellcat II	FAA Museum, RNAS Yeovilton	
KE418	Hawker Tempest <rf>	RAF Museum Store, Cardington	
KF183	Noorduyn AT-16 Harvard IIB [3]	MoD(PE)/HATS, DTEO Boscombe Down	
KF388	Noorduyn AT-16 Harvard IIB <ff>	Privately owned, Bournemouth	
KF435	Noorduyn AT-16 Harvard IIB <ff>	Privately owned, Swindon	
KF487	Noorduyn AT-16 Harvard IIB (KLu B-168)	British Aerial Museum, Duxford, spares use	
KF532	Noorduyn AT-16 Harvard IIB <ff>	Newark Air Museum, Winthorpe	
KG374	Douglas Dakota IV (KN645/8355M) [YS]	RAF Cosford Aerospace Museum	
KG391	Douglas C-47A Dakota III (G-BVOL) [AG]	Sold to the Netherlands, February 1996	
KJ351	Airspeed AS58 Horsa II (TL659/ BAPC 80) [23]	Museum of Army Flying, Middle Wallop	
KK995	Sikorsky Hoverfly I [E]	RAF Museum, Hendon	
KL161	NA B-25D Mitchell II (N88972) [VO-B]	The Fighter Collection, Duxford	
KL216	Republic P-47D Thunderbolt (45-49295/9212M) [RS-L]	RAF Cosford Aerospace Museum	
KN448	Douglas Dakota C4 <ff>	Science Museum, South Kensington	
KN751	Consolidated Liberator C VI [F]	RAF Cosford Aerospace Museum	
KP208	Douglas Dakota IV [YS]	Airborne Forces Museum, Aldershot	
KZ191	Hawker Hurricane IV (frame only)	Privately owned, North Weald	
KZ321	Hawker Hurricane IV (G-HURY) (frame only)	The Fighter Collection, Duxford	
LA198	VS356 Spitfire F21 (7118M) [RAI-G]	City of Glasgow Museum	
LA226	VS356 Spitfire F21 (7119M)	RAF Museum Rest'n Centre, Cardington	
LA255	VS356 Spitfire F21 (6490M) [JX-U]	RAF No 1 Sqn, Wittering (preserved)	
LA546	VS Seafire F46	Charleston Aviation Services, Colchester	
LB294	Taylorcraft Plus D (G-AHWJ)	Museum of Army Flying, Whitchurch	
LB375	Taylorcraft Plus D (G-AHGW)	Privately owned, Edge Hill	
LF363	Hawker Hurricane IIc	RAF, Audley End (on rebuild)	
LF738	Hawker Hurricane IIc (5405M) [UH-A]	RAF Cosford Aerospace Museum	

Notes	Serial	Type (other identity) [code]	Owner/operator, location or fate
	LF789	DH82 Queen Bee (BAPC 186)	Mosquito Aircraft Museum, London Colney
	LF858	DH82 Queen Bee (G-BLUZ)	Privately owned, Rush Green
	LH208	Airspeed AS51 Horsa I (8596M) (parts only)	Used in the rebuild of KJ351
	LS326	Fairey Swordfish II (G-AJVH) [L2]	RN Historic Flight, RNAS Yeovilton
	LV907	HP59 Halifax III (HR792) [NP-F]	Yorkshire Air Museum, Elvington
	LZ551	DH100 Vampire [P]	FAA Museum, RNAS Yeovilton
	LZ551	DH100 Vampire FB6 (J-1173/ G-DHXX) [P]	Source Classic Jet Flight, Bournemouth
	LZ766	Percival P34 Proctor III (G-ALCK)	Imperial War Museum, Duxford
	LZ842	VS361 Spitfire IX (remains)	Sold to Australia
	MF628	Vickers Wellington T10 (9210M)	RAF Museum, Hendon
	MH434	VS361 Spitfire LF IXB (G-ASJV) [ZD-B]	The Old Flying Machine Company, Duxford
	MH486	VS361 Spitfire LF IX <R> (BAPC 206) [FF-A]	RAF Museum, Hendon
	MH777	VS361 Spitfire IX <R> (BAPC 221) [RF-N]	RAF Northolt, on display
	MJ147	VS361 Spitfire LF IX	Privately owned, Kent
	MJ627	VS509 Spitfire T9 (G-BMSB) [9G-P]	Privately owned, Bruntingthorpe
	MJ730	VS361 Spitfire HF IXE (G-HFIX) [GZ-?]	Privately owned, Staverton
	MJ751	VS361 Spitfire IX <R> (BAPC 209) [DU-V]	D-Day Museum, Shoreham Airport
	MJ832	VS361 Spitfire IX <R> (BAPC 229) [DN-Y]	RAF Digby, on display
	MK178	VS361 Spitfire LF XVIE (TE311/ X4474/7241M) [QV-I]	RAF EP&TU, St Athan
	MK356	VS361 Spitfire LF IXC (5690M)	RAF BBMF, St Athan
	MK673	VS361 Spitfire LF XVIE (TB382/ X4277/7244M) [SK-E]	RAF EP&TU, St Athan
	MK805	VS361 Spitfire LF IX <R> [SH-B]	Privately owned, Lowestoft
	MK912	VS361 Spitfire LF IXE (G-BRRA) [MN-P]	Privately owned, Paddock Wood, Kent
	ML407	VS509 Spitfire T9 (G-LFIX) [OU-V]	Privately owned, Duxford
	ML411	VS361 Spitfire LF IXE	Privately owned, Kent
	ML417	VS361 Spitfire LF IXE (G-BJSG) [21-T]	The Fighter Collection, Duxford
	ML427	VS361 Spitfire IX (6457M) [ST-I]	Birmingham Mus of Science & Industry
	ML796	Short S25 Sunderland V	Imperial War Museum, Duxford
	ML824	Short S25 Sunderland V [NS-Z]	RAF Museum, Hendon
	MN235	Hawker Typhoon IB	RAF Museum, Hendon
	MP425	Airspeed AS10 Oxford I (G-AITB) [G]	RAF Museum, Hendon
	MT438	Auster III (G-AREI)	Privately owned, Old Sarum
	MT847	VS379 Spitfire FR XIVE (6960M) [AX-H]	Gr Manchester Mus of Science & Industry
	MT928	VS359 Spitfire HF VIIIC (G-BKMI/ MV154) [ZX-M]	Privately owned, Filton
	MV262	VS379 Spitfire FR XIV (G-CCVV)	Privately owned, Booker
	MV293	VS379 Spitfire FR XIV (G-SPIT) [01-C]	The Fighter Collection, Duxford
	MW376	Hawker Tempest II (G-BSHW)	Sold to France, June 1996
	MW401	Hawker Tempest II (G-PEST)	Privately owned, Sandtoft, S Yorks
	MW404	Hawker Tempest II (IAF HA557)	Privately owned
	MW467	VS349 Spitfire V <R> (BAPC 202)	Repainted as MAV467
	MW758	Hawker Tempest II (IAF HA580)	Privately owned
	MW763	Hawker Tempest II (G-TEMT)	Privately owned, Sandtoft, S Yorks
	NF370	Fairey Swordfish III	Imperial War Museum, Duxford
	NF389	Fairey Swordfish III [D]	RN Historic Flight, Yeovilton
	NF875	DH89A Dragon Rapide 6 (G-AGTM)	Repainted as G-AGTM by September 1996
	NJ673	Auster 5D (G-AOCR)	Privately owned, Wellesbourne Mountford
	NJ695	Auster 4 (G-AJXV)	Privately owned, Tollerton
	NJ703	Auster 5 (G-AKPI)	Privately owned, Croft, Lincs
	NJ719	Auster 5 (TW385/G-ANFU)	Privately owned, Newcastle
	NL750	DH82A Tiger Moth II (T7997/ G-AOBH)	Privately owned, Thruxton
	NL846	DH82A Tiger Moth II (F-BGEQ)	Brooklands Museum, Chessington (rebuild)
	NL985	DH82A Tiger Moth I (7015M/ G-BWIK)	Privately owned, Sywell
	NM181	DH82A Tiger Moth I (G-AZGZ)	Privately owned, Rush Green

Serial	Type (other identity) [code]	Owner/operator, location or fate	Notes
NP181	Percival P31 Proctor IV (G-AOAR)	*Scrapped*	
NP184	Percival P31 Proctor IV (G-ANYP) [K]	*Sold to Australia*	
NP294	Percival P31 Proctor IV [TB-M]	Lincolnshire Avn Heritage Centre, E Kirkby	
NP303	Percival P31 Proctor IV (G-ANZJ)	Privately owned, Byfleet, Surrey	
NV778	Hawker Tempest TT5 (8386M)	RAF Museum Rest'n Centre, Cardington	
NX534	Auster III (G-BUDL)	Privately owned, Middle Wallop	
NX611	Avro 683 Lancaster B VII (8375M/ G-ASXX) [LE-C, DX-C]	Lincolnshire Avn Heritage Centre, E Kirkby	
PA474	Avro 683 Lancaster B I [WS-J]	RAF BBMF, Coningsby	
PF179	HS Gnat T1 (XR541/8602M)	Privately owned, Ipswich	
PK624	VS356 Spitfire F22 (8072M) [RAU-T]	The Fighter Collection, Duxford	
PK664	VS356 Spitfire F22 (7759M) [V6-B]	RAF Museum Rest'n Centre, Cardington	
PK683	VS356 Spitfire F24 (7150M)	Southampton Hall of Aviation	
PK724	VS356 Spitfire F24 (7288M)	RAF Museum, Hendon	
PL344	VS361 Spitfire LF IXE (G-IXCC) [Y2-B]	Privately owned, Booker	
PL965	VS365 Spitfire PR XI (G-MKXI) [R]	Privately owned, Duxford	
PM631	VS390 Spitfire PR XIX [S]	RAF BBMF, Coningsby	
PM651	VS390 Spitfire PR XIX (7758M) [X]	RAF Museum Rest'n Centre, Cardington	
PN323	HP Halifax VII <ff>	Imperial War Museum, Lambeth	
PP566	Fairey Firefly I (fuselage)	South Yorkshire Avn Museum, Firbeck	
PP972	VS358 Seafire LF IIIC (G-BUAR) [6M-D]	Flying A Services, Earls Colne	
PR536	Hawker Tempest II (IAF HA457) [OQ-H]	RAF Museum, Hendon	
PS853	VS390 Spitfire PR XIX (G-MXIX) [C]	Rolls-Royce, Filton/East Midlands	
PS915	VS390 Spitfire PR XIX (7548M/ 7711M) [P]	RAF BBMF, Coningsby	
PV202	VS509 Spitfire T9 (G-TRIX) [VZ-M]	Privately owned, Goodwood	
PZ865	Hawker Hurricane IIc (G-AMAU) [J]	RAF BBMF, Coningsby	
RA848	Slingsby Cadet TX1	The Aeroplane Collection, stored Wigan	
RA854	Slingsby Cadet TX1	Privately owned, Breighton	
RA897	Slingsby Cadet TX1	Newark Air Museum store, Hucknall	
RD253	Bristol 156 Beaufighter TF X (7931M)	RAF Museum, Hendon	
RF342	Avro 694 Lincoln B II (G-29-1/ G-APRJ)	Aces High, North Weald	
RF398	Avro 694 Lincoln B II (8376M)	RAF Cosford Aerospace Museum	
RG333	Miles M38 Messenger IIA (G-AIEK)	Privately owned, Felton, Bristol	
RG333	Miles M38 Messenger IIA (G-AKEZ)	Privately owned, Chelmsford	
RH377	Miles M38 Messenger 4A (G-ALAH)	Privately owned, Stretton, Cheshire	
RH746	Bristol 164 Brigand TF1 (fuselage)	North-East Aircraft Museum, stored Usworth	
RL962	DH89A Dominie II (G-AHED)	RAF Museum Store, Cardington	
RM221	Percival P31 Proctor IV (G-ANXR)	Privately owned, Biggin Hill	
RM689	VS379 Spitfire F XIV (G-ALGT) (remains)	Rolls-Royce, East Midlands	
RN218	Isaacs Spitfire <R> (G-BBJI) [N]	Privately owned, Langham	
RR232	VS361 Spitfire HF IXC (G-BRSF)	Sussex Spraying Services, Lancing, W Sussex	
RR299	DH98 Mosquito T III (G-ASKH) [HT-E]	*Crashed, 21 July 1996, Barton*	
RT486	Auster 5 (G-AJGJ) [PF-A]	Privately owned, Henstridge, Somerset	
RT520	Auster 5 (G-ALYB)	*Repainted as G-ALYB*	
RT610	Auster 5A-160 (G-AKWS)	Privately owned, Exeter	
RW388	VS361 Spitfire LF XVIE (6946M) [U4-U]	Stoke-on-Trent City Museum, Hanley	
RW393	VS361 Spitfire LF XVIE (7293M) [XT-A]	RAF Cosford Aerospace Museum	
RX168	VS358 Seafire L IIIC (IAC 157/ G-BWEM)	Privately owned, Battle	
SL674	VS361 Spitfire LF IX (8392M)	RAF Museum Rest'n Centre, Cardington	
SM520	VS361 Spitfire LF IX	Privately owned, Oxford	
SM832	VS379 Spitfire F XIVE (G-WWII) [YB-A]	The Fighter Collection, Duxford	
SM845	VS394 Spitfire FR XVIII (G-BUOS)	Privately owned, Audley End	
SX137	VS384 Seafire F XVII	FAA Museum, RNAS Yeovilton	

Notes	Serial	Type (other identity) [code]	Owner/operator, location or fate
	SX300	VS384 Seafire F XVII	Privately owned, Twyford, Bucks
	SX336	VS384 Seafire F XVII (G-BRMG)	Privately owned, Twyford, Bucks
	TA122	DH98 Mosquito FB VI [UP-G]	Mosquito Aircraft Museum, London Colney
	TA634	DH98 Mosquito TT35 (G-AWJV) [8K-K]	Mosquito Aircraft Museum, London Colney
	TA639	DH98 Mosquito TT35 (7806M) [AZ-E]	RAF Cosford Aerospace Museum
	TA719	DH98 Mosquito TT35 (G-ASKC)	Imperial War Museum, Duxford
	TA805	VS361 Spitfire IX (G-PMNF)	Privately owned, Sandown, IOW
	TB252	VS361 Spitfire LF XVIE (G-XVIE) [GW-H]	Privately owned, Audley End
	TB752	VS361 Spitfire LF XVIE (8086M) [KH-Z]	RAF Manston, Memorial Pavilion
	TB885	VS361 Spitfire LF XVIE	Shoreham Aircraft Preservation Society
	TD248	VS361 Spitfire LF XVIE (7246M/ G-OXVI) [D]	*Sold to Belgium, May 1996*
	TD314	VS361 Spitfire LF IX (*N601DA*)	Privately owned, Norwich
	TE184	VS361 Spitfire LF XVIE (6850M/ G-MXVI)	Privately owned, North Weald
	TE462	VS361 Spitfire LF XVIE (7243M)	Royal Scottish Mus'm of Flight, E Fortune
	TE566	VS361 Spitfire LF IXE (G-BLCK) [DU-A]	Historic Aircraft Collection, Duxford
	TG263	Saro SR A1 (G-12-1) [P]	Southampton Hall of Aviation
	TG511	HP67 Hastings C1 (8554M)	RAF Cosford Aerospace Museum
	TG517	HP67 Hastings T5	Newark Air Museum, Winthorpe
	TG528	HP67 Hastings C1A	Imperial War Museum, Duxford
	TJ118	DH98 Mosquito TT35 <ff>	Mosquito Aircraft Museum, stored
	TJ138	DH98 Mosquito B35 (7607M) [VO-L]	RAF Museum, Hendon
	TJ324	Auster 5 (G-APAH)	Privately owned, Cumbernauld
	TJ343	Auster 5 (G-AJXC)	Privately owned, stored Hook
	TJ398	Auster AOP6 (BAPC 70)	Aircraft Pres'n Soc of Scotland, E Fortune
	TJ569	Auster 5 (G-AKOW)	Museum of Army Flying, Middle Wallop
	TJ672	Auster 5D (G-ANIJ)	Privately owned, Whitchurch, Hants
	TJ704	Beagle A61 Terrier 2 (G-ASCD) [JA]	Yorkshire Air Museum, Elvington
	TJ707	Auster 5 (frame)	Air Service Training, Perth
	TK718	GAL59 Hamilcar I	Royal Tank Museum, Bovington
	TK777	GAL59 Hamilcar I (fuselage)	Museum of Army Flying, Middle Wallop
	TL615	Airspeed AS58 Horsa II	Robertsbridge Aviation Society, Mayfield
	TP367	VS394 Spitfire XVIII	*Sold to the USA*
	TS291	Slingsby Cadet TX1 (BGA852)	Royal Scottish Mus'm of Flight, E Fortune
	TS423	Douglas C-47A Dakota C3 (G-DAKS)	Aces High Ltd, North Weald
	TS798	Avro 685 York C1 (G-AGNV)	RAF Cosford Aerospace Museum
	TV959	DH98 Mosquito T III [AF-V]	The Fighter Collection, stored Duxford
	TV959	DH98 Mosquito T III <R>	Privately owned, Heald Green, Cheshire
	TW384	Auster 5 (G-ANHZ)	Privately owned, Headcorn
	TW439	Auster 5 (G-ANRP)	The Real Aeroplane Company, Breighton
	TW448	Auster 5 (G-ANLU)	Privately owned, Hedge End
	TW462	Beagle A61 Terrier 1 (G-ARLO)	Privately owned, Chandlers Ford, Hants
	TW467	Auster 5 (G-ANIE)	Privately owned, Middle Wallop
	TW511	Auster 5 (G-APAF)	Privately owned, North Coates
	TW533	Beagle A61 Terrier 2 (G-ASAX)	Privately owned, Netherly, Grampian
	TW536	Auster AOP6 (7704M/G-BNGE) [TS-V]	Privately owned, Middle Wallop
	TW591	Auster 6A (G-ARIH) [N]	Privately owned, Abbots Bromley
	TW641	Beagle A61 Terrier 2 (G-ATDN)	Privately owned, Biggin Hill
	TX183	Avro 652A Anson C19 (G-BSMF)	Privately owned, Arbroath
	TX213	Avro 652A Anson C19 (G-AWRS)	North-East Aircraft Museum, Usworth
	TX214	Avro 652A Anson C19 (7817M)	RAF Cosford Aerospace Museum
	TX226	Avro 652A Anson C19 (7865M)	Imperial War Museum, stored Duxford
	TX235	Avro 652A Anson C19	Caernarfon Air World
	VD165	Slingsby T7 Kite (BGA 400)	Privately owned, Dunstable
	VF301	DH100 Vampire F1 (7060M) [RAL-G]	Midland Air Museum, Coventry
	VF512	Auster 6A (G-ARRX) [PF-M]	Privately owned, White Waltham
	VF516	Beagle A61 Terrier 2 (G-ASMZ) [T]	Privately owned, Bagby
	VF526	Auster 6A (G-ARXU) [T]	Privately owned, Middle Wallop
	VF548	Beagle A61 Terrier 1 (G-ASEG)	Privately owned, Dunkeswell
	VF611	Beagle A61 Terrier 2 (G-ATBU)	Privately owned, Hucknall

Serial	Type (other identity) [code]	Owner/operator, location or fate	Notes
VH127	Fairey Firefly TT4 [200/R]	FAA Museum, RNAS Yeovilton	
VL348	Avro 652A Anson C19 (G-AVVO)	Newark Air Museum, Winthorpe	
VL349	Avro 652A Anson C19 (G-AWSA)	Norfolk & Suffolk Aviation Mus'm, Flixton	
VM325	Avro 652A Anson C19	Midland Air Museum, Coventry	
VM360	Avro 652A Anson C19 (G-APHV)	Royal Scottish Mus'm of Flight, E Fortune	
VM791	Slingsby Cadet TX3 (XA312/ 8876M)	No 450 Sqn ATC, RAF Kenley	
VN148	Grunau Baby IIb (BAPC 33/ BGA2400)	Privately owned, Dunstable	
VN485	VS356 Spitfire F24 (7326M)	Imperial War Museum, Duxford	
VP293	Avro 696 Shackleton T4 <ff>	Lincolnshire Avn Heritage Centre, E Kirkby	
VP519	Avro 652A Anson C19 (G-AVVR) <ff>	The Aeroplane Collection, Manchester	
VP952	DH104 Devon C2 (8820M)	RAF Cosford Aerospace Museum	
VP955	DH104 Devon C2 (G-DVON)	Privately owned, Little Staughton	
VP957	DH104 Devon C2 (8822M) <ff>	No 1137 Sqn ATC, Belfast	
VP959	DH104 Devon C2 (G-BWFB) [L]	Privately owned, Little Staughton	
VP967	DH104 Devon C2 (G-KOOL)	East Surrey Technical College, Redhill	
VP968	DH104 Devon C2	*Scrapped at Boscombe Down, October 1994*	
VP971	DH104 Devon C2 (8824M)	FSCTE, RAF Manston	
VP975	DH104 Devon C2 [M]	Science Museum, Wroughton	
VP978	DH104 Devon C2 (8553M)	RAF Brize Norton, instructional use	
VP981	DH104 Devon C2	RAF, stored Coningsby	
VR137	Westland Wyvern TF1	FAA Museum, stored RNAS Yeovilton	
VR192	Pervical P40 Prentice T1 (G-APIT)	SWWAPS, Lasham	
VR249	Percival P40 Prentice T1 (G-APIY) [FA-EL]	Newark Air Museum, Winthorpe	
VR259	Percival P40 Prentice T1 (G-APJB) [M]	Air Atlantique Historic Flight, Coventry	
VR930	Hawker Sea Fury FB11 (8382M)	RN Historic Flight, Brough	
VS356	Percival P40 Prentice T1 (G-AOLU)	Privately owned, Montrose	
VS562	Avro 652A Anson T21 (8012M)	Maes Artro Craft Village, Llanbedr	
VS610	Percival P40 Prentice T1 (G-AOKL) [K-L]	Privately owned, Bassingbourn	
VS623	Percival P40 Prentice T1 (G-AOKZ) [KQ-F]	Midland Air Museum, Coventry	
VT260	Gloster Meteor F4 (8813M) [67]	*To the USA, 1997*	
VT409	Fairey Firefly AS5 <rf>	North-East Aircraft Museum, stored Usworth	
VT812	DH100 Vampire F3 (7200M) [N]	RAF Museum, Hendon	
VT935	Boulton Paul P111A (VT769)	Midland Air Museum, Coventry	
VT987	Auster AOP6 (G-BKXP)	Aerobuild Ltd, Little Gransden, Cambs	
VV106	Supermarine 510 (7175M)	FAA Museum, stored Wroughton	
VV217	DH100 Vampire FB5 (7323M)	North-East Aircraft Museum, stored Usworth	
VV901	Avro 652A Anson T21	Yorkshire Air Museum, Elvington	
VW453	Gloster Meteor T7 (8703M) [Z]	RAF Innsworth, on display	
VW985	Auster AOP6 (G-ASEF)	Privately owned, Upper Arncott, Oxon	
VX118	Auster AOP6 (G-ASNB)	Privately owned, Kingston Deverill	
VX147	Alon A2 Aircoupe (G-AVIL)	Privately owned, Headcorn	
VX185	EE Canberra B(I)8 (7631M) <ff>	Science Museum, Wroughton	
VX250	DH103 Sea Hornet 21 [48] <rf>	Mosquito Aircraft Museum, London Colney	
VX272	Hawker P.1052 (7174M)	FAA Museum, stored Wroughton	
VX275	Slingsby T21B Sedbergh TX1 (8884M/BGA 572)	RAF Museum Rest'n Centre, Cardington	
VX461	DH100 Vampire FB5 (7646M)	RAF Cosford Aerospace Museum, stored	
VX573	Vickers Valetta C2 (8389M)	RAF Cosford Aerospace Museum, stored	
VX577	Vickers Valetta C2	North-East Aircraft Museum, Usworth	
VX580	Vickers Valetta C2	Norfolk & Suffolk Avn Museum, Flixton	
VX595	WS51 Dragonfly HR1 [29]	Gosport Aviation Society, HMS *Sultan*	
VX653	Hawker Sea Fury FB11 (G-BUCM)	*Repainted as WE724*	
VX665	Hawker Sea Fury FB11 <rf>	RN Historic Flight, at BAe Brough	
VX926	Auster T7 (G-ASKJ)	Privately owned, Little Gransden	
VZ304	DH100 Vampire FB6 (J-1167/ G-MKVI) [A-T]	De Havilland Aviation, Swansea	
VZ345	Hawker Sea Fury T20S	RN Historic Flight, Brough (on rebuild)	
VZ462	Gloster Meteor F8	*Used in the rebuild of WM366*	
VZ467	Gloster Meteor F8 (G-METE) [01]	Classic Jets Flying Museum, Biggin Hill	
VZ477	Gloster Meteor F8 (7741M) <ff>	Midland Air Museum, Coventry	
VZ608	Gloster Meteor FR9	Newark Air Museum, Winthorpe	
VZ634	Gloster Meteor T7 (8657M)	Newark Air Museum, Winthorpe	
VZ638	Gloster Meteor T7 (G-JETM) [HF]	Vallance By-Ways, Charlwood, Surrey	

Notes	Serial	Type (other identity) [code]	Owner/operator, location or fate
	VZ728	RS4 Desford Trainer (G-AGOS)	Snibston Discovery Park, stored Coalville
	VZ962	WS51 Dragonfly HR1 [904]	IHM, Weston-super-Mare
	VZ965	WS51 Dragonfly HR5	FAA Museum, at RNAS Culdrose
	WA473	VS Attacker F1 [102/J]	FAA Museum, RNAS Yeovilton
	WA576	Bristol 171 Sycamore 3 (7900M/ G-ALSS)	Dumfries & Galloway Avn Mus, Dumfries
	WA577	Bristol 171 Sycamore 3 (7718M/ G-ALST)	North-East Aircraft Museum, Usworth
	WA591	Gloster Meteor T7 (7917M/ G-BWMF) [W]	Meteor Flight, Yatesbury
	WA630	Gloster Meteor T7 [69] <ff>	Robertsbridge Aviation Society, Mayfield
	WA634	Gloster Meteor T7/8	RAF Cosford Aerospace Museum
	WA638	Gloster Meteor T7(mod)	Martin Baker Aircraft, Chalgrove, spares use
	WA662	Gloster Meteor T7	South Yorkshire Avn Museum, Firbeck
	WA984	Gloster Meteor F8 [A]	Tangmere Military Aviation Museum
	WB188	Hawker Hunter F3 (7154M)	Tangmere Military Aviation Museum
	WB271	Fairey Firefly AS5 [204/R]	RN Historic Flight, RNAS Yeovilton
	WB440	Fairey Firefly AS6 <ff>	South Yorkshire Aviation Museum, Firbeck
	WB491	Avro 706 Ashton 2 (TS897/	Avro Aircraft Heritage Society, BAe Woodford
	WB550	DHC1 Chipmunk T10 [D]	*To Canada, September 1996*
	WB556	DHC1 Chipmunk T10	RAFGSA, Bicester
	WB560	DHC1 Chipmunk T10	Privately owned, Fownhope, H&W
	WB565	DHC1 Chipmunk T10 [X]	AAC BFWF/2 Regiment, Middle Wallop
	WB567	DHC1 Chipmunk T10	*Sold, February 1997*
	WB569	DHC1 Chipmunk T10 [R]	*Sold as SE-BON, 1996*
	WB571	DHC1 Chipmunk T10 (G-AOSF) [34]	*Sold to Germany*
	WB584	DHC1 Chipmunk T10 (7706M) <ff>	No 327 Sqn ATC, Kilmarnock
	WB585	DHC1 Chipmunk T10 (G-AOSY) [RCU-X]	Privately owned, Blackbushe
	WB586	DHC1 Chipmunk T10 [A]	*Sold as LN-DHC, 1996*
	WB588	DHC1 Chipmunk T10 (G-AOTD) [D]	Privately owned, Biggin Hill
	WB615	DHC1 Chipmunk T10 [E]	AAC BFWF/2 Regiment, Middle Wallop
	WB624	DHC1 Chipmunk T10 <ff>	Newark Air Museum, Winthorpe
	WB626	DHC1 Chipmunk T10 <ff>	Privately owned, Fownhope, H&W
	WB627	DHC1 Chipmunk T10 (9248M) [N]	Dulwich College CCF
	WB645	DHC1 Chipmunk T10 (8218M)	RAFGSA, Bicester, spares use
	WB647	DHC1 Chipmunk T10 [R]	AAC BFWF/2 Regiment, Middle Wallop
	WB652	DHC1 Chipmunk T10 [V]	*Sold, February 1997*
	WB654	DHC1 Chipmunk T10 [U]	AAC BFWF/2 Regiment, Middle Wallop
	WB657	DHC1 Chipmunk T10 [908]	RN Historic Flight, Yeovilton
	WB660	DHC1 Chipmunk T10 (G-ARMB)	Privately owned, Shipdham
	WB670	DHC1 Chipmunk T10 (8361M) <ff>	No 1312 Sqn ATC, Southend Airport
	WB671	DHC1 Chipmunk T10 [910]	*Sold as G-BWTG, June 1996*
	WB685	DHC1 Chipmunk T10 (comp WP969/G-ATHC)	North-East Aircraft Museum, Usworth
	WB693	DHC1 Chipmunk T10 [S]	AAC BFWF/2 Regiment, Middle Wallop
	WB697	DHC1 Chipmunk T10 [95]	*Sold, February 1997*
	WB702	DHC1 Chipmunk T10 (G-AOFE)	Privately owned, Goodwood
	WB703	DHC1 Chipmunk T10 (G-ARMC)	Privately owned, White Waltham
	WB711	DHC1 Chipmunk T10 (G-APPM)	The Aircraft Restoration Co, Duxford
	WB733	DHC1 Chipmunk T10 (comp WG422)	South Yorkshire Avn Museum, Firbeck
	WB739	DHC1 Chipmunk T10 [8]	*Sold as F-AZVA, February 1996*
	WB754	DHC1 Chipmunk T10 [H]	AAC BFWF/2 Regiment, Middle Wallop
	WB758	DHC1 Chipmunk T10 (7729M) [P]	Privately owned, Torbay
	WB763	DHC1 Chipmunk T10 (G-BBMR) [14]	Privately owned, Ottershaw
	WB922	Slingsby T21B Sedburgh TX1	Privately owned, stored Rufforth
	WB943	Slingsby T21B Sedburgh TX1 (BGA 2941)	Privately owned, Rufforth
	WB981	Slingsby T21B Sedburgh TX1 (BGA 3238)	Privately owned, Aston Down
	WD286	DHC1 Chipmunk T10 (G-BBND) [J]	Privately owned, Bourn
	WD288	DHC1 Chipmunk T10 (G-AOSO) [38]	Privately owned, Charlton Park, Wilts
	WD289	DHC1 Chipmunk T10 [E]	*Sold, February 1997*

Serial	Type (other identity) [code]	Owner/operator, location or fate	Notes
WD292	DHC1 Chipmunk T10 (G-BCRX)	Privately owned, White Waltham	
WD293	DHC1 Chipmunk T10 (7645M) <ff>	No 1367 Sqn ATC, Caerleon, Gwent	
WD305	DHC1 Chipmunk T10 (G-ARGG)	Privately owned, Coventry	
WD310	DHC1 Chipmunk T10 (G-BWUN) [B]	Privately owned,	
WD318	DHC1 Chipmunk T10 (8207M) <ff>	No 145 Sqn ATC, Timperley, Gr Manchester	
WD325	DHC1 Chipmunk T10 [N]	AAC BFWF/2 Regiment, Middle Wallop	
WD331	DHC1 Chipmunk T10 [J]	*Sold, February 1997*	
WD355	DHC1 Chipmunk T10 (WD335) <ff>	No 1955 Sqn ATC, Wells, Somerset	
WD356	DHC1 Chipmunk T10 (7625M)	Privately owned, St Ives, Cambridgeshire	
WD363	DHC1 Chipmunk T10 (G-BCIH) [5]	Privately owned, Andrewsfield	
WD370	DHC1 Chipmunk T10 <ff>	No 176 Sqn ATC, Hove	
WD373	DHC1 Chipmunk T10 [12]	*Sold, February 1997*	
WD377	DHC1 Chipmunk T10	Dumfries & Galloway Avn Mus, stored Dumfries	
WD379	DHC1 Chipmunk T10 (WB696/ G-APLO) [K]	Privately owned, Jersey	
WD386	DHC1 Chipmunk T10	South Yorkshire Avn Museum, stored Firbeck	
WD388	DHC1 Chipmunk T10 (G-BDIC)	*Sold as D-EPAK, September 1996*	
WD390	DHC1 Chipmunk T10 (G-BWNK) [68]	Privately owned, Bristol	
WD413	Avro 652A Anson T21 (7881M/ G-BFIR)	Privately owned, Lee-on-Solent	
WD646	Gloster Meteor TT20 (8189M) [R]	39 Restoration Group, North Weald	
WD686	Gloster Meteor NF11	Muckleburgh Collection, Weybourne	
WD790	Gloster Meteor NF11 (8743M)<ff>	North-East Aircraft Museum, Usworth	
WD889	Fairey Firefly AS5 <ff>	North-East Aircraft Museum, Usworth	
WD931	EE Canberra B2 <ff>	RAF Cosford Aerospace Museum	
WD935	EE Canberra B2 (8440M) <ff>	Privately owned, Bridgnorth	
WD954	EE Canberra B2 <ff>	Privately owned, Romford, Essex	
WE113	EE Canberra T4 <ff>	Privately owned, Woodhurst, Cambridgeshire	
WE122	EE Canberra TT18 [845] <ff>	Blyth Valley Aviation Collection, Walpole, Suffolk	
WE139	EE Canberra PR3 (8369M)	RAF Museum, Hendon	
WE168	EE Canberra PR3 (8049M) <ff>	Privately owned, Colchester	
WE173	EE Canberra PR3 (8740M) <ff>	Privately owned, Stock, Essex	
WE188	EE Canberra T4	Solway Aviation Society, Carlisle	
WE192	EE Canberra T4 <ff>	Blyth Valley Aviation Collection, Walpole, Suffolk	
WE275	DH112 Venom FB50 (J-1601/ G-VIDI)	BAe Hawarden Fire Section	
WE402	DH112 Venom FB50 (J-1523/ G-VENI)	Source Classic Jet Flight, Bournemouth	
WE410	DH112 Venom FB50 (J-1539/ G-DHUU)	*Repainted as WR410, early 1996*	
WE569	Auster T7 (G-ASAJ)	Privately owned, Bassingbourn	
WE600	Auster T7 Antarctic (7602M)	RAF Cosford Aerospace Museum	
WE724	Hawker Sea Fury FB11 (VX653/ G-BUCM)	The Fighter Collection, Duxford	
WE925	Gloster Meteor F8	Classic Jet Aircraft Group, Loughborough	
WE982	Slingsby T30B Prefect TX1 (8781M)	RAF Cosford Aerospace Museum	
WE990	Slingsby T30B Prefect TX1 (BGA 2583)	Privately owned, RAF Swanton Morley	
WF118	Percival P57 Sea Prince T1 (G-DACA)	Vallance By-Ways, Charlwood, Surrey	
WF122	Percival P57 Sea Prince T1 [575/CU]	Flambards Village Theme Park, Helston	
WF125	Percival P57 Sea Prince T1 [576]	*Burnt at Predannack, 1995*	
WF128	Percival P57 Sea Prince T1 (8611M)	Norfolk & Suffolk Avn Museum, Flixton	
WF137	Percival P57 Sea Prince C1	SWWAPS, Lasham	
WF145	Hawker Sea Hawk F1 <ff>	Privately owned, South Molton, Devon	
WF225	Hawker Sea Hawk F1 [CU]	RNAS Culdrose, at main gate	
WF259	Hawker Sea Hawk F2 [171/A]	Royal Scottish Mus'm of Flight, E Fortune	
WF369	Vickers Varsity T1 [F]	Newark Air Museum, Winthorpe	
WF372	Vickers Varsity T1 [A]	Brooklands Museum, Weybridge	
WF376	Vickers Varsity T1	Bristol Airport Fire Section	
WF408	Vickers Varsity T1 (8395M)	RAF Northolt, for ground instruction	

Notes	Serial	Type (other identity) [code]	Owner/operator, location or fate
	WF410	Vickers Varsity T1 [F]	Brunel Technical College, Lulsgate
	WF643	Gloster Meteor F8 [X]	Norfolk & Suffolk Avn Museum, Flixton
	WF714	Gloster Meteor F8 (WK914)	The Old Flying Machine Co, stored Duxford
	WF784	Gloster Meteor T7 (7895M)	Gloucestershire Avn Coll, RAF Quedgeley
	WF825	Gloster Meteor T7 (8359M) [A]	Avon Air Museum, stored Malmesbury
	WF877	Gloster Meteor T7 (G-BPOA)	Privately owned, Kemble
	WF911	EE Canberra B2 <ff>	Pennine Avn Museum, stored Charnock Richard, Lancs
	WF922	EE Canberra PR3	Midland Air Museum, Coventry
	WG300	DHC1 Chipmunk T10 <ff>	RAFGSA, Bicester
	WG303	DHC1 Chipmunk T10 (8208M) <ff>	RAFGSA, Bicester
	WG307	DHC1 Chipmunk T10 (G-BCYJ)	Privately owned, Shempston Fm, Lossiemouth
	WG308	DHC1 Chipmunk T10 [8]	*Sold, February 1997*
	WG316	DHC1 Chipmunk T10 (G-BCAH)	Privately owned, Shoreham
	WG321	DHC1 Chipmunk T10 [G]	AAC BFWF/2 Regiment, Middle Wallop
	WG323	DHC1 Chipmunk T10 [F]	AAC BFWF/2 Regiment, Middle Wallop
	WG348	DHC1 Chipmunk T10 (G-BBMV)	Privately owned, Moulton St Mary
	WG350	DHC1 Chipmunk T10 (G-BPAL)	Privately owned, Thruxton
	WG362	DHC1 Chipmunk T10 (8437M/ T10 (G-BPAL)	Privately owned, Thruxton
	WG362	DHC1 Chipmunk T10 (8437M/ 8630M) <ff>	*Painted as WX643*
	WG403	DHC1 Chipmunk T10 [O] <ff>	Privately owned, Doncaster
	WG407	DHC1 Chipmunk T10 (G-BWMX)	Privately owned, Spanhoe Lodge
	WG418	DHC1 Chipmunk T10 (8209M/ G-ATDY) <ff>	No 1940 Sqn ATC, Levenshulme
	WG419	DHC1 Chipmunk T10 (8206M) <ff>	No 1053 Sqn ATC, Armthorpe
	WG422	DHC1 Chipmunk T10 (8394M/ G-BFAX) [116]	The Aircraft Restoration Co, Duxford
	WG430	DHC1 Chipmunk T10 [3]	*Sold, February 1997*
	WG432	DHC1 Chipmunk T10 [L]	AAC BFWF/2 Regiment, Middle Wallop
	WG458	DHC1 Chipmunk T10 [B]	*Sold, February 1997*
	WG463	DHC1 Chipmunk T10 (8363M/ G-ATDX) <ff>	*Scrapped*
	WG465	DHC1 Chipmunk T10 (G-BCEY)	Privately owned, White Waltham
	WG469	DHC1 Chipmunk T10 (G-BWJY) [72]	Privately owned,
	WG471	DHC1 Chipmunk T10 (8210M) <ff>	No 301 Sqn ATC, Bury St Edmunds
	WG472	DHC1 Chipmunk T10 (G-AOTY)	Privately owned, Netherthorpe
	WG477	DHC1 Chipmunk T10 (8362M/ G-ATDP) <ff>	No 281 Sqn ATC, Birkdale, Merseyside
	WG478	DHC1 Chipmunk T10	*Sold to South Africa, July 1995*
	WG479	DHC1 Chipmunk T10 [F]	*Sold as F-AZLO, 1996*
	WG480	DHC1 Chipmunk T10 [D]	*Sold to Australia, October 1996*
	WG486	DHC1 Chipmunk T10	RAF BBMF, Coningsby
	WG511	Avro 696 Shackleton T4 (fuselage)	Flambards Village Theme Park, Helston
	WG718	WS51 Dragonfly HR3 [934]	Privately owned, Elvington
	WG719	WS51 Dragonfly HR5 (G-BRMA) [902]	IHM, Weston-super-Mare
	WG724	WS51 Dragonfly HR5 [932]	North-East Aircraft Museum, Usworth
	WG751	WS51 Dragonfly HR5	Privately owned, Condover, Shropshire
	WG754	WS51 Dragonfly HR3 (WG725/ 7703M) [912/CU]	Flambards Village Theme Park, Helston
	WG760	EE P1A (7755M)	RAF Cosford Aerospace Museum
	WG763	EE P1A (7816M)	Gr Manchester Mus of Science & Industry
	WG768	Short SB5 (8005M)	RAF Cosford Aerospace Museum
	WG774	BAC 221	Science Museum, RNAS Yeovilton
	WG777	Fairey FD2 (7986M)	RAF Cosford Aerospace Museum
	WG789	EE Canberra B2/6 <ff>	Privately owned, Mendlesham, Suffolk
	WH132	Gloster Meteor T7 (7906M) [J]	No 276 Sqn ATC, Chelmsford
	WH166	Gloster Meteor T7 (8052M)	Privately owned, Birlingham, Worcs
	WH291	Gloster Meteor F8	SWWAPS, Lasham
	WH301	Gloster Meteor F8 (7930M) [T]	RAF Museum, Hendon
	WH364	Gloster Meteor F8 (8169M)	Privately owned, Kemble
	WH453	Gloster Meteor D16 [L]	MoD(PE), stored DTEO Llanbedr
	WH646	EE Canberra T17A <ff>	Midland Air Museum, Coventry
	WH657	EE Canberra B2	Brenzett Aeronautical Museum
	WH665	EE Canberra T17 (8763M) [J]	BAe Filton, Fire Section
	WH699	EE Canberra B2T (WJ637/8755M)	*Scrapped at Stock, 1996*

Serial	Type (other identity) [code]	Owner/operator, location or fate	Notes
WH725	EE Canberra B2	Imperial War Museum, Duxford	
WH734	EE Canberra B2(mod)	MoD(PE), DTEO Llanbedr	
WH739	EE Canberra B2 <ff>	No 2475 Sqn ATC, Ammanford, Dyfed	
WH740	EE Canberra T17 (8762M) [K]	East Midlands Airport Aero Park	
WH773	EE Canberra PR7 (8696M)	Vallance By-Ways, Charlwood, Surrey	
WH775	EE Canberra PR7 (8128M/ 8868M) <ff>	Privately owned, Welshpool	
WH779	EE Canberra PR7 [BP]	RAF No 39(1 PRU) Sqn, Marham	
WH780	EE Canberra T22 <ff>	*Scrapped at Stock, 1995*	
WH780	EE Canberra T22 <rf>	RAF St Athan, Fire Section	
WH791	EE Canberra PR7 (8165M/8176M/ 8187M)	RAF Cottesmore, at main gate	
WH796	EE Canberra PR7 <ff>	Privately owned, Stock, Essex	
WH797	EE Canberra T22 <ff>	*Scrapped at Stock, 1995*	
WH797	EE Canberra T22 <rf>	RAF St Athan, Fire Section	
WH801	EE Canberra T22 <ff>	*Scrapped at Stock, 1995*	
WH803	EE Canberra T22 <ff>	Privately owned, Stock, Essex	
WH840	EE Canberra T4 (8350M) <ff>	Privately owned, Flixton	
WH846	EE Canberra T4	Yorkshire Air Museum, Elvington	
WH849	EE Canberra T4 [BE]	FR Aviation, Bournemouth	
WH850	EE Canberra T4 <ff>	Macclesfield Historical Avn Soc, Barton	
WH854	EE Canberra T4 <ff>	Martin Baker Aircraft, Chalgrove	
WH863	EE Canberra T17 (8693M) <ff>	Newark Air Museum, Winthorpe	
WH876	EE Canberra B2(mod)	DTEO Aberporth, instructional use	
WH887	EE Canberra TT18 [847]	MoD(PE), stored DTEO Llanbedr	
WH902	EE Canberra T17A [EK]	*Scrapped at Wyton, 1995*	
WH903	EE Canberra B2 <ff>	Yorkshire Air Museum, Elvington	
WH903	EE Canberra B2 (8584M) <ff>	Vallance By-Ways, Charlwood, Surrey	
WH904	EE Canberra T19	Newark Air Museum, Winthorpe	
WH946	EE Canberra B6(mod) (8185M) <ff>	Privately owned, Tetney, Grimsby	
WH952	EE Canberra B6	*Scrapped at Stock, 1994*	
WH953	EE Canberra B6(mod) <ff>	Blyth Valley Aviation Collection, Walpole, Suffolk	
WH957	EE Canberra E15 (8869M) <ff>	Lincolnshire Avn Heritage Centre, East Kirkby	
WH960	EE Canberra B15 (8344M) <ff>	Privately owned, Hucknall	
WH964	EE Canberra E15 (8870M) <ff>	Phoenix Aviation, Bruntingthorpe	
WH984	EE Canberra B15 (8101M) <ff>	No 198 Sqn ATC, Hinckley, Leics	
WH991	WS51 Dragonfly HR3	Privately owned, Elvington	
WJ231	Hawker Sea Fury FB11 (WE726) [115/O]	FAA Museum, Yeovilton	
WJ237	WAR Sea Fury <R> (G-BLTG) [113/O]	*Crashed, 1 September 1996, Crosland Moor*	
WJ358	Auster AOP6 (G-ARYD)	Museum of Army Flying, stored Middle Wallop	
WJ565	EE Canberra T17 (8871M) <ff>	Phoenix Aviation, Bruntingthorpe	
WJ567	EE Canberra B2 <ff>	Privately owned, Houghton, Cambs	
WJ576	EE Canberra T17 <ff>	Phoenix Aviation, Bruntingthorpe	
WJ581	EE Canberra PR7 <ff>	Privately owned, Canterbury	
WJ603	EE Canberra B2 (8664M) <ff>	Privately owned, Stock, Essex	
WJ614	EE Canberra TT18 (N76765) [846]	*Sold to the USA, September 1995*	
WJ630	EE Canberra T17 [ED]		
WJ633	EE Canberra T17A [EF]	*Scrapped at Wyton, 1995*	
WJ636	EE Canberra TT18 [CX]	*Scrapped at Wyton, August 1995*	
WJ639	EE Canberra TT18 [39]	North-East Aircraft Museum, Usworth	
WJ640	EE Canberra B2 (8722M) <ff>	Privately owned, Guildford	
WJ676	EE Canberra B2 (7796M) <ff>	Privately owned, Liverpool	
WJ677	EE Canberra B2 <ff>	RNAS Culdrose, Fire Section	
WJ680	EE Canberra TT18 (G-BURM) [CT]	Canberra Flight, Kemble	
WJ717	EE Canberra TT18 (9052M)	RAF CTTS, St Athan	
WJ721	EE Canberra TT18 [21]	Dundonald Aviation Centre, Strathclyde	
WJ731	EE Canberra B2T [BK] <ff>	Derby World War 2 Avionics Museum	
WJ775	EE Canberra B6 (8581M) [J] (fuselage)	Stanford Training Area, Bodney Camp, Norfolk	
WJ821	EE Canberra PR7 (8668M)	Army, Bassingbourn, on display	
WJ863	EE Canberra T4 <ff>	Cambridge Airport Fire Section	
WJ865	EE Canberra T4	Privately owned, Stock, Essex	
WJ866	EE Canberra T4 [AV]	RAF No 39(1 PRU) Sqn, Marham	
WJ872	EE Canberra T4 (8492M) <ff>	No 327 Sqn ATC, Kilmarnock	
WJ874	EE Canberra T4 [AS]	RAF No 39(1 PRU) Sqn, Marham	
WJ876	EE Canberra T4 <ff>		
WJ880	EE Canberra T4 (8491M) <ff>	Dumfries & Galloway Avn Mus, Dumfries	

Notes	Serial	Type (other identity) [code]	Owner/operator, location or fate
	WJ893	Vickers Varsity T1	T&EE Aberporth Fire Section
	WJ903	Vickers Varsity T1 [C] <ff>	Dumfries & Galloway Avn Mus, Dumfries
	WJ945	Vickers Varsity T1 (G-BEDV) [21]	Imperial War Museum, Duxford
	WJ975	EE Canberra T19 [S]	Bomber County Aviation Museum, Hemswell
	WJ981	EE Canberra T17A [EN]	*Scrapped at Wyton, August 1995*
	WJ992	EE Canberra T4	Bournemouth Int'l Airport, Fire Section
	WK102	EE Canberra T17 (8780M) <ff>	Privately owned, Welshpool
	WK118	EE Canberra TT18 <ff>	Privately owned, Worcester
	WK119	EE Canberra B2 <ff>	*Scrapped at Wyton by 1994*
	WK122	EE Canberra TT18 [22]	Flambards Village Theme Park, Helston
	WK124	EE Canberra TT18 (9093M) [CR]	FSCTE, RAF Manston
	WK126	EE Canberra TT18 (N2138J) [843]	Gloucestershire Avn Coll, Staverton
	WK127	EE Canberra TT18 (8985M) <ff>	No 2424 Sqn ATC, Bassingbourn
	WK128	EE Canberra B2	MoD(PE), DTEO Llanbedr
	WK142	EE Canberra TT18 (N76764) [848]	*Sold to the USA, September 1995*
	WK143	EE Canberra B2	DTEO Llanbedr Fire Section
	WK144	EE Canberra B2 (8689M) <ff>	*Scrapped at Stock, 1995*
	WK163	EE Canberra B6(mod) (G-BVWC)	Classic Aviation Projects, Bruntingthorpe
	WK198	VS Swift F4 (7428M) (fuselage)	North-East Aircraft Museum, Usworth
	WK275	VS Swift F4	Privately owned, Upper Hill, nr Leominster
	WK277	VS Swift FR5 (7719M) [N]	Newark Air Museum, Winthorpe
	WK281	VS Swift FR5 (7712M) [S]	Tangmere Military Aviation Museum
	WK511	DHC1 Chipmunk T10 (G-BVBT) [905]	Kennet Aviation, Cranfield
	WK512	DHC1 Chipmunk T10 [A]	AAC BFWF/2 Regiment, Middle Wallop
	WK517	DHC1 Chipmunk T10 (G-ULAS) [84]	Privately owned, Spanhoe Lodge
	WK518	DHC1 Chipmunk T10	RAF BBMF, Coningsby
	WK522	DHC1 Chipmunk T10 (G-BCOU)	Privately owned, High Easter
	WK549	DHC1 Chipmunk T10 (G-BTWF) [Y]	Privately owned, Rufforth
	WK550	DHC1 Chipmunk T10 [G]	*Sold, February 1997*
	WK554	DHC1 Chipmunk T10 [4]	*Sold, February 1997*
	WK558	DHC1 Chipmunk T10 (G-ARMG)	Privately owned, Wellesbourne Mountford
	WK559	DHC1 Chipmunk T10 [M]	AAC BFWF/2 Regiment, Middle Wallop
	WK562	DHC1 Chipmunk T10 [91]	Privately owned, Booker
	WK570	DHC1 Chipmunk T10 (8211M) <ff>	No 424 Sqn ATC, Southampton
	WK572	DHC1 Chipmunk T10 [92]	*Sold, February 1997*
	WK576	DHC1 Chipmunk T10 (8357M) <ff>	No 1206 Sqn ATC, Lichfield
	WK584	DHC1 Chipmunk T10 (7556M) <ff>	No 216 Sqn ATC, Bawtry
	WK585	DHC1 Chipmunk T10	RAF, stored Newton
	WK586	DHC1 Chipmunk T10 [V]	AAC BFWF/2 Regiment, Middle Wallop
	WK589	DHC1 Chipmunk T10 [C]	The Aircraft Restoration Co, Duxford
	WK590	DHC1 Chipmunk T10 [69]	*Sold to Belgium, May 1996*
	WK608	DHC1 Chipmunk T10 [906]	RN Historic Flt, Yeovilton
	WK609	DHC1 Chipmunk T10 [93]	*Sold, February 1997*
	WK611	DHC1 Chipmunk T10 (G-ARWB)	Privately owned, White Waltham
	WK613	DHC1 Chipmunk T10 [P]	Pennine Aviation Museum, Bacup
	WK620	DHC1 Chipmunk T10 [T] (fuselage)	Privately owned, Tattershall Thorpe
	WK622	DHC1 Chipmunk T10 (G-BCZH)	Privately owned, Horsford
	WK624	DHC1 Chipmunk T10 (G-BWHI) [M]	The Aircraft Restoration Co, Duxford
	WK626	DHC1 Chipmunk T10 (8213M) <ff>	Wiltshire Historic Aviation Grp, Salisbury
	WK628	DHC1 Chipmunk T10 (G-BBMW)	Privately owned, Shoreham
	WK630	DHC1 Chipmunk T10 [11]	*Sold, February 1997*
	WK633	DHC1 Chipmunk T10 [B]	Privately owned, Shoreham
	WK635	DHC1 Chipmunk T10	*Sold to Canada*
	WK638	DHC1 Chipmunk T10 (G-BWJZ) [83]	Privately owned, Spanhoe Lodge
	WK639	DHC1 Chipmunk T10 (G-BWJU) [L]	Privately owned, Blackpool
	WK640	DHC1 Chipmunk T10 (G-BWUV) [C]	Privately owned,
	WK642	DHC1 Chipmunk T10 [94]	*Sold, February 1997*
	WK643	DHC1 Chipmunk T10 [G]	*Sold, February 1997*
	WK654	Gloster Meteor F8 (8092M) [X]	City of Norwich Aviation Museum
	WK800	Gloster Meteor D16 [Z]	MoD(PE), DTEO Llanbedr
	WK864	Gloster Meteor F8 (WL168/7750M) [C]	Yorkshire Air Museum, Elvington
	WK935	Gloster Meteor Prone Pilot (7869M)	RAF Cosford Aerospace Museum
	WK991	Gloster Meteor F8 (7825M)	Imperial War Museum, Duxford
	WL131	Gloster Meteor F8 (7751M) <ff>	South Yorkshire Avn Museum, Firbeck
	WL181	Gloster Meteor F8 [X]	North-East Aircraft Museum, Usworth

Serial	Type (other identity) [code]	Owner/operator, location or fate	Notes
WL332	Gloster Meteor T7 [888]	Privately owned, Long Marston	
WL345	Gloster Meteor T7	St Leonard's Motors, Hollington, E Sussex	
WL349	Gloster Meteor T7 [Z]	Gloucestershire Avn Coll, Staverton	
WL360	Gloster Meteor T7 (7920M) [G]	Gloucestershire Avn Coll, Staverton	
WL375	Gloster Meteor T7(mod)	Dumfries & Galloway Avn Mus, Dumfries	
WL405	Gloster Meteor T7	Martin Baker Aircraft, Chalgrove, spares use	
WL419	Gloster Meteor T7	Martin Baker Aircraft, Chalgrove	
WL505	DH100 Vampire FB9 (7705M/ G-FBIX)	De Havilland Aviation, Swansea	
WL626	Vickers Varsity T1 (G-BHDD) [P]	East Midlands Airport Aero Park	
WL627	Vickers Varsity T1 (8488M) [D] <ff>	Privately owned, Preston, E Yorkshire	
WL635	Vickers Varsity T1	*Scrapped at Machrihanish*	
WL679	Vickers Varsity T1 (9155M)	RAF Cosford Aerospace Museum	
WL732	BP P108 Sea Balliol T21	RAF Cosford Aerospace Museum	
WL756	Avro 696 Shackleton AEW2 (9101M)	RAF St Mawgan, Fire Section	
WL795	Avro 696 Shackleton MR2C (8753M) [T]	RAF St Mawgan, on display	
WL798	Avro 696 Shackleton MR2C (8114M) <ff>	Privately owned, Elgin	
WL925	Slingsby T31B Cadet TX3 (WV925) <ff>	RAF No 633 VGS, Cosford	
WM145	AW Meteor NF11 <ff>	N Yorks Aircraft Recovery Centre, Chop Gate	
WM167	AW Meteor NF11 (G-LOSM)	Jet Heritage Ltd, Bournemouth	
WM223	AW Meteor TT20	SWWAPS, Lasham	
WM267	Gloster Meteor NF11 <ff>	South Yorkshire Avn Museum, Firbeck	
WM292	AW Meteor TT20 [841]	Phoenix Aviation, Bruntingthorpe	
WM311	AW Meteor TT20 (WM224/8177M)	39 Restoration Group, North Weald	
WM366	AW Meteor NF13 (4X-FNA) (comp VZ462)	SWWAPS, Lasham	
WM367	AW Meteor NF13 <ff>	39 Restoration Group, North Weald	
WM571	DH112 Sea Venom FAW21 [VL]	Southampton Hall of Aviation	
WM729	DH113 Vampire NF10 [A] <ff>	Mosquito Aircraft Museum, London Colney	
WM913	Hawker Sea Hawk FB5 (8162M) [456/J]	Newark Air Museum, Winthorpe	
WM961	Hawker Sea Hawk FB5 [J]	Caernarfon Air World	
WM969	Hawker Sea Hawk FB5 [10/Z]	Imperial War Museum, Duxford	
WM993	Hawker Sea Hawk FB5 [034]	Privately owned, Peasedown St John, Avon	
WN105	Hawker Sea Hawk FB3 (WF299/ 8164M)	Privately owned, Birlingham, Worcs	
WN108	Hawker Sea Hawk FB5 [033]	Ulster Aviation Society, Langford Lodge	
WN149	BP P108 Balliol T2 <ff>	Boulton Paul Association, Wolverhampton	
WN411	Fairey Gannet AS1 (fuselage)	Privately owned, Southampton	
WN493	WS51 Dragonfly HR5	FAA Museum, RNAS Yeovilton	
WN499	WS51 Dragonfly HR5 [Y]	Caernarfon Air World	
WN516	BP P108 Balliol T2 <ff>	North-East Aircraft Museum, Usworth	
WN534	BP P108 Balliol T2 <ff>	Boulton Paul Association, Wolverhampton	
WN890	Hawker Hunter F2 <ff>	Robertsbridge Aviation Society, Mayfield	
WN904	Hawker Hunter F2 (7544M) [3]	RE 39 Regt, Waterbeach, on display	
WN907	Hawker Hunter F2 (7416M) <ff>	Blyth Valley Aviation Collection, Walpole, Suffolk	
WP180	Hawker Hunter F5 (WP190/ 7582M/8473M) [K]	*Repainted as WP190*	
WP185	Hawker Hunter F5 (7583M)	Privately owned, Great Dunmow, Essex	
WP190	Hawker Hunter F5 (7582M/8473M/ *WP180*) [K]	RAF Quedgeley, Glos.	
WP250	DH113 Vampire NF10 <ff>	Privately owned, Baxterley, Warwickshire	
WP255	DH113 Vampire NF10 <ff>	South Yorkshire Avn Museum, Firbeck	
WP270	EoN Eton TX1 (8598M)	Gr Manchester Mus of Science & Industry	
WP271	EoN Eton TX1	Privately owned, stored Keevil	
WP309	Percival P57 Sea Prince T1 [570/CU]	*Scrapped at Carlisle, 1995*	
WP313	Percival P57 Sea Prince T1 [568/CU]	FAA Museum, stored Wroughton	
WP314	Percival P57 Sea Prince T1 (8634M) [573/CU]	Privately owned, Carlisle Airport	
WP321	Percival P57 Sea Prince T1 (G-BRFC) [750/CU]	Aces High, North Weald	
WP503	WS51 Dragonfly HR3 [901]	Privately owned, Carnforth, Lancs	

Notes	Serial	Type (other identity) [code]	Owner/operator, location or fate
	WP515	EE Canberra B2 <ff>	No 1002 Sqn ATC, Bridgend
	WP772	DHC1 Chipmunk T10 [Q] (wreck)	Privately owned, St Athan
	WP776	DHC1 Chipmunk T10 [817/CU]	*Sold to Canada*
	WP784	DHC1 Chipmunk T10 <ff>	The Vampire Collection, Hemel Hempstead
	WP786	DHC1 Chipmunk T10 [G]	*Sold to Australia, October 1996*
	WP788	DHC1 Chipmunk T10 (G-BCHL)	Privately owned, Sleap
	WP790	DHC1 Chipmunk T10 (G-BBNC) [T]	Mosquito Aircraft Museum, London Colney
	WP795	DHC1 Chipmunk T10 (G-BVZZ) [901]	Privately owned, Lee-on-Solent
	WP800	DHC1 Chipmunk T10 (G-BCXN) [2]	Privately owned, Halton
	WP803	DHC1 Chipmunk T10 (G-HAPY) [G]	Privately owned, Booker
	WP805	DHC1 Chipmunk T10 (G-MAJR) [D]	Privately owned,
	WP808	DHC1 Chipmunk T10 (G-BDEU)	Privately owned, Binham
	WP809	DHC1 Chipmunk T10 (G-BVTX) [778]	Privately owned, Husbands Bosworth
	WP831	DHC1 Chipmunk T10 (G-BBMT)	Privately owned, Little Gransden
	WP833	DHC1 Chipmunk T10 [H]	RAF Newton
	WP835	DHC1 Chipmunk T10 (G-BDCB)	*Sold to Germany as D-ERTY, August 1995*
	WP837	DHC1 Chipmunk T10 [L]	*Sold, February 1997*
	WP839	DHC1 Chipmunk T10 [A]	Privately owned,
	WP840	DHC1 Chipmunk T10 [9]	*Sold, February 1997*
	WP843	DHC1 Chipmunk T10 (G-BDBP)	Privately owned, Booker
	WP844	DHC1 Chipmunk T10 (G-BWOX) [85]	Privately owned, Spanhoe Lodge
	WP845	DHC1 Chipmunk T10 <ff>	Vintage Aircraft Team, Bruntingthorpe
	WP855	DHC1 Chipmunk T10 [5]	*Sold, February 1997*
	WP856	DHC1 Chipmunk T10 (G-BVWP) [904]	Privately owned, Cuckfield
	WP857	DHC1 Chipmunk T10 (G-BDRJ) [24]	Privately owned, Elstree
	WP859	DHC1 Chipmunk T10 [E]	*Sold, February 1997*
	WP860	DHC1 Chipmunk T10 [6]	*Sold, February 1997*
	WP863	DHC1 Chipmunk T10 (8360M/ G-ATJI) <ff>	FR Aviation, Bournemouth
	WP864	DHC1 Chipmunk T10 (8214M) <ff>	RAF, stored Newton
	WP869	DHC1 Chipmunk T10 (8215M) <ff>	Privately owned, Wittering
	WP871	DHC1 Chipmunk T10 [W]	AAC BFWF/2 Regiment, Middle Wallop
	WP872	DHC1 Chipmunk T10	*Sold, February 1997*
	WP896	DHC1 Chipmunk T10 (G-BWVY) [M]	Privately owned, London
	WP900	DHC1 Chipmunk T10 (G-BWRX) [V]	*Sold to France, October 1996*
	WP901	DHC1 Chipmunk T10 (G-BWNT) [B]	Privately owned, East Midlands Airport
	WP903	DHC1 Chipmunk T10 (G-BCGC)	Privately owned, Shoreham
	WP906	DHC1 Chipmunk T10 [816/CU]	*Sold to Canada*
	WP907	DHC1 Chipmunk T10 <ff> (7970M)	Privately owned, Reading
	WP912	DHC1 Chipmunk T10 (8467M)	RAF Cosford Aerospace Museum
	WP914	DHC1 Chipmunk T10 [E]	*Sold as F-AZSM, February 1996*
	WP920	DHC1 Chipmunk T10 [10]	*Sold, February 1997*
	WP921	DHC1 Chipmunk T10 (G-ATJJ) <ff>	Privately owned, Brooklands
	WP925	DHC1 Chipmunk T10 [C]	AAC BFWF/2 Regiment, Middle Wallop
	WP927	DHC1 Chipmunk T10 (8216M/ G-ATJK) <ff>	No 247 Sqn ATC, Ashton-under-Lyne
	WP928	DHC1 Chipmunk T10 [D]	AAC BFWF/2 Regiment, Middle Wallop
	WP929	DHC1 Chipmunk T10 [F]	*Sold, February 1997*
	WP930	DHC1 Chipmunk T10 [J]	AAC BFWF/2 Regiment, Middle Wallop
	WP962	DHC1 Chipmunk T10 [C]	RAF, stored Cambridge
	WP964	DHC1 Chipmunk T10 [Y]	AAC BFWF/2 Regiment, Middle Wallop
	WP967	DHC1 Chipmunk T10	*Sold, February 1997*
	WP970	DHC1 Chipmunk T10 [T]	*Sold, February 1997*
	WP971	DHC1 Chipmunk T10 (G-ATHD)	Privately owned, Denham
	WP972	DHC1 Chipmunk T10 (8667M) <ff>	
	WP974	DHC1 Chipmunk T10 [96]	*Sold, February 1997*
	WP976	DHC1 Chipmunk T10 (WP791/ G-APTS)	Privately owned, Booker
	WP977	DHC1 Chipmunk T10 (G-BHRD) [N]	Privately owned, Kidlington

Serial	Type (other identity) [code]	Owner/operator, location or fate	Notes
WP978	DHC1 Chipmunk T10 (7467M) <ff>	RAF	
WP981	DHC1 Chipmunk T10 [D]	*Sold, February 1997*	
WP983	DHC1 Chipmunk T10 [B]	AAC BFWF/2 Regiment, Middle Wallop	
WP984	DHC1 Chipmunk T10 (G-BWTO) [H]	Privately owned, Duxford	
WR410	DH112 Venom FB50 (J-1539/ G-DHUU/*WE410*)	Source Classic Jet Flight, Bournemouth	
WR410	DH112 Venom FB54 (J-1790/ G-BLKA) [N]	Vintage Aircraft Team, Bruntingthorpe	
WR539	DH112 Venom FB4 (8399M) [F]	Mosquito Aircraft Museum, London Colney	
WR960	Avro 696 Shackleton AEW2 (8772M)	Gr Manchester Mus of Science & Industry	
WR963	Avro 696 Shackleton AEW2	Air Atlantique Historic Flight, Coventry	
WR971	Avro 696 Shackleton MR3 (8119M) [Q]	Privately owned, Narborough, Norfolk	
WR974	Avro 696 Shackleton MR3 (8117M) [K]	Vallance By-Ways, Charlwood, Surrey	
WR977	Avro 696 Shackleton MR3 (8186M) [B]	Newark Air Museum, Winthorpe	
WR982	Avro 696 Shackleton MR3 (8106M) [J]	Vallance By-Ways, Charlwood, Surrey	
WR985	Avro 696 Shackleton MR3 (8103M) [H]	Privately owned, Long Marston	
WS103	Gloster Meteor T7 [709/VL]	FAA Museum, Crawley Technical College	
WS692	Gloster Meteor NF12 (7605M) [C]	Newark Air Museum, Winthorpe	
WS726	Gloster Meteor NF14 (7960M) [G]	No 1855 Sqn ATC, Royton, Gr Manchester	
WS739	Gloster Meteor NF14 (7961M)	Newark Air Museum, Winthorpe	
WS760	Gloster Meteor NF14 (7964M)	Meteor Flight, stored Yatesbury	
WS774	Gloster Meteor NF14 (7959M)	Privately owned, RAF Quedgeley, Glos	
WS776	Gloster Meteor NF14 (7716M) [K]	RAF North Luffenham, at main gate	
WS788	Gloster Meteor NF14 (7967M) [Z]	Yorkshire Air Museum, Elvington	
WS792	Gloster Meteor NF14 (7965M) [K]	Brighouse Bay Caravan Park, Borgue, D&G	
WS807	Gloster Meteor NF14 (7973M) [N]	Gloucestershire Avn Coll, stored Yatesbury	
WS832	Gloster Meteor NF14 [W]	Solway Aviation Society, Carlisle Airport	
WS838	Gloster Meteor NF14	Midland Air Museum, Coventry	
WS843	Gloster Meteor NF14 (7937M) [Y]	RAF Cosford Aerospace Museum, stored	
WT121	Douglas Skyraider AEW1 (WT983) [415/CU]	FAA Museum, stored RNAS Yeovilton	
WT205	EE Canberra B(I)6	No 2341 Sqn ATC, Eastwood, Essex	
WT308	EE Canberra B(I)6	RN, Predannack Fire School	
WT309	EE Canberra B(I)6	Privately owned, stored Farnborough	
WT327	EE Canberra B(I)8	MoD(PE), stored DTEO Boscombe Down	
WT333	EE Canberra B6(mod) (G-BVXC)	Classic Aviation Projects, Bruntingthorpe	
WT339	EE Canberra B(I)8 (8198M)	RAF Barkston Heath Fire Section	
WT480	EE Canberra T4 [AT]	RAF, stored Shawbury	
WT482	EE Canberra T4 <ff>	Privately owned,	
WT483	EE Canberra T4 [83]	Privately owned, Long Marston	
WT486	EE Canberra T4 (8102M) <ff>	Flight Experience Workshop, Belfast	
WT488	EE Canberra T4	BAe Dunsfold Fire Section	
WT507	EE Canberra PR7 (8131M/8548M) [44] <ff>	No 384 Sqn ATC, Mansfield	
WT509	EE Canberra PR7 [BR]	RAF No 39(1 PRU) Sqn, Marham	
WT510	EE Canberra T22 <ff>	Privately owned, Stock, Essex	
WT519	EE Canberra PR7 [CH]	RAF Wyton, Fire Section	
WT520	EE Canberra PR7 (8094M/ 8184M) <ff>	South West Aviation Heritage, Eaglescott	
WT525	EE Canberra T22 <ff>	Privately owned, South Woodham Ferrers	
WT532	EE Canberra PR7 (8728M/8890M) [Z]	Bournemouth Int'l Airport, Fire Section	
WT534	EE Canberra PR7 (8549M) [43] <ff>	No 492 Sqn ATC, Shirley, W. Midlands	
WT536	EE Canberra PR7 (8063M) <ff>	Phoenix Aviation, Bruntingthorpe	
WT537	EE Canberra PR7	BAe Samlesbury, on display	
WT555	Hawker Hunter F1 (7499M)	Vanguard Haulage, Greenford, London	
WT569	Hawker Hunter F1 (7491M)	No 2117 Sqn ATC, Kenfig Hill, Mid-Glamorgan	
WT612	Hawker Hunter F1 (7496M)	RAF Henlow on display	
WT619	Hawker Hunter F1 (7525M)	Gr Manchester Mus of Science & Industry	
WT648	Hawker Hunter F1 (7530M) <ff>	The Air Defence Collection, Salisbury	
WT651	Hawker Hunter F1 [C]	Newark Air Museum, Winthorpe	
WT660	Hawker Hunter F1 (7421M) [C]	Privately owned, Cullen, Grampian	

Notes	Serial	Type (other identity) [code]	Owner/operator, location or fate
	WT680	Hawker Hunter F1 (7533M) [J]	No 1429 Sqn ATC, at DTEO Aberporth
	WT684	Hawker Hunter F1 (7422M)	Jet Avn Preservation Grp, Long Marston
	WT694	Hawker Hunter F1 (7510M)	Caernarfon Air World
	WT711	Hawker Hunter GA11 [833/DD]	Air Atlantique, Coventry
	WT720	Hawker Hunter F51 (RDAF E-408/ 8565M) [B]	RAF Sealand, on display
	WT722	Hawker Hunter T8C (G-BWGN) [878/VL]	Classic Jet Aircraft Co, Exeter
	WT723	Hawker Hunter PR11 [866/VL,3]	SFDO, RNAS Culdrose
	WT744	Hawker Hunter GA11 [868/VL]	South West Aviation Heritage, Eaglescott
	WT746	Hawker Hunter F4 (7770M) [A]	Army, Saighton, Chester
	WT799	Hawker Hunter T8C [879/VL]	Privately owned, stored Ipswich
	WT804	Hawker Hunter GA11 [831/DD]	FETC, Moreton-in-Marsh
	WT806	Hawker Hunter GA11	Privately owned, Ipswich
	WT859	Supermarine 544 <ff>	Brooklands Museum, Weybridge
	WT867	Slingsby T31B Cadet TX3	Privately owned, Eaglescott
	WT898	Slingsby T31B Cadet TX3 (BGA 3284)	Privately owned, Rufforth
	WT899	Slingsby T31B Cadet TX3	Privately owned, Swindon
	WT902	Slingsby T31B Cadet TX3 (BGA 3147)	Privately owned, Lleweni Parc, Clwyd
	WT905	Slingsby T31B Cadet TX3	Privately owned,
	WT910	Slingsby T31B Cadet TX3 (BGA 3953)	Privately owned, Challock
	WT933	Bristol 171 Sycamore 3 (G-ALSW/ 7709M)	Newark Air Museum, Winthorpe
	WV106	Douglas Skyraider AEW1 [427/C]	FAA Museum, at Flambards Village Theme Park, Helston
	WV198	Sikorsky S55 Whirlwind HAR21 (G-BJWY) [K]	Solway Aviation Society, Carlisle
	WV256	Hawker Hunter GA11 [862/VL]	RN, stored Shawbury
	WV276	Hawker Hunter F4 (7847M) [D]	DRA Avionics & Sensors Dept, Farnborough
	WV318	Hawker Hunter T7B (G-FFOX)	Delta Engineering Aviation, Kemble
	WV322	Hawker Hunter T8C (9096M) [Y]	AMIF, RAFC Cranwell
	WV332	Hawker Hunter F4 (7673M) <ff>	No 1254 Sqn ATC, Godalming
	WV372	Hawker Hunter T7 [877/VL]	RNAS Culdrose, on display
	WV381	Hawker Hunter GA11 [732/VL]	UKAEA, Culham, Oxon
	WV382	Hawker Hunter GA11 [830/VL]	Jet Avn Preservation Grp, Long Marston
	WV383	Hawker Hunter T7	MoD(PE)/DRA, DTEO Boscombe Down
	WV395	Hawker Hunter F4 (8001M)	BAe Dunsfold, Fire Section
	WV396	Hawker Hunter T8C [91]	RAF Valley, at main gate
	WV483	Percival P56 Provost T1 (7693M) [N-E]	Privately owned
	WV486	Percival P56 Provost T1 (7694M) [N-D]	Privately owned, Grazeley, Berks
	WV493	Percival P56 Provost T1 (G-BDYG/ 7696M) [29]	Royal Scottish Mus'm of Flight, stored E Fortune
	WV499	Percival P56 Provost T1 (7698M) [P-G]	39 Restoration Group, North Weald
	WV562	Percival P56 Provost T1 (7606M) [P-C]	RAF Cosford Aerospace Museum, stored
	WV605	Percival P56 Provost T1 [T-B]	Norfolk & Suffolk Avn Museum, Flixton
	WV606	Percival P56 Provost T1 (7622M) [P-B]	Newark Air Museum, Winthorpe
	WV666	Percival P56 Provost T1 (7925M/ G-BTDH) [O-D]	Privately owned, Shoreham
	WV679	Percival P56 Provost T1 (7615M) [O-J]	Wellesbourne Wartime Museum
	WV703	Percival P66 Pembroke C1 (8108M/*G-IIIM*)	Privately owned, Tattershall Thorpe
	WV705	Percival P66 Pembroke C1 <ff>	Southampton Hall of Aviation, stored
	WV740	Percival P66 Pembroke C1 (G-BNPH)	Privately owned, Jersey
	WV746	Percival P66 Pembroke C1 (8938M)	RAF Cosford Aerospace Museum
	WV753	Percival P66 Pembroke C1 (8113M)	*Scrapped at Coventry, 1995*
	WV781	Bristol 171 Sycamore HR12 (G-ALTD/7839M)	Caernarfon Air World
	WV783	Bristol 171 Sycamore HR12 (G-ALSP/7841M)	RAF Museum Restoration Centre, Cardington
	WV787	EE Canberra B2/8 (8799M)	Newark Air Museum, Winthorpe

Serial	Type (other identity) [code]	Owner/operator, location or fate	Notes
WV795	Hawker Sea Hawk FGA6 (8151M)	Phoenix Aviation, Bruntingthorpe	
WV797	Hawker Sea Hawk FGA6 (8155M) [491/J]	Midland Air Museum, Coventry	
WV798	Hawker Sea Hawk FGA6 [026/CU]	SWWAPS, Lasham	
WV826	Hawker Sea Hawk FGA6 [147/Z]	*Repainted as WV906*	
WV838	Hawker Sea Hawk FGA4	Privately owned, Chippenham, Wilts	
WV856	Hawker Sea Hawk FGA6 [163]	FAA Museum, RNAS Yeovilton	
WV903	Hawker Sea Hawk FGA4 (8153M) [128/C]	RN Historic Flight, at BAe Dunsfold	
WV906	Hawker Sea Hawk FGA6 (WV826)	Phoenix Aviation, Bruntingthorpe	
WV908	Hawker Sea Hawk FGA6 (8154M) [188/A]	RN Historic Flight, Yeovilton	
WW138	DH112 Sea Venom FAW22 [227/Z]	FAA Museum, RNAS Yeovilton	
WW145	DH112 Sea Venom FAW22 [680/LM]	Royal Scottish Mus'm of Flight, E Fortune	
WW217	DH112 Sea Venom FAW22 [736]	Newark Air Museum, Winthorpe	
WW388	Percival P56 Provost T1 (7616M) [O-F]	Bomber County Air Museum, Hemswell	
WW421	Percival P56 Provost T1 (7688M) [P-B]	TDL Replicas Ltd, Lowestoft	
WW442	Percival P56 Provost T1 (7618M) [N]	Privately owned, Kings Langley, Herts	
WW444	Percival P56 Provost T1 [D]	Privately owned, Rugeley, Staffs	
WW447	Percival P56 Provost T1	Privately owned, Grazeley, Berks	
WW453	Percival P56 Provost T1 (G-TMKI) [W-S]	Kennet Aviation, Cranfield	
WW654	Hawker Hunter GA11 [834/DD]	Privately owned, Portsmouth	
WX643	DHC1 Chipmunk T10 (8437M/8630M/WG362) <ff>	RAF Newton	
WX660	Hover-Air HA-5 Hoverhawk III (XW660)	Privately owned, Cheltenham	
WX788	DH112 Venom NF3	Night Fighter Preservation Team, Elvington	
WX853	DH112 Venom NF3 (7443M)	Mosquito Aircraft Museum, London Colney	
WX905	DH112 Venom NF3 (7458M)	Newark Air Museum, Winthorpe	
WZ415	DH115 Vampire T11 [72]	*Scrapped, 1993*	
WZ425	DH115 Vampire T11	Privately owned, Birlingham, Worcs	
WZ450	DH115 Vampire T11 <ff>	Lashenden Air Warfare Museum, Headcorn	
WZ458	DH115 Vampire T11 (7728M) [31] <ff>	*Scrapped*	
WZ464	DH115 Vampire T11 (N62430) [40]	Vintage Aircraft Team, Bruntingthorpe	
WZ507	DH115 Vampire T11 (G-VTII)	De Havilland Aviation, Swansea	
WZ515	DH115 Vampire T11 [60]	Solway Aviation Society, Carlisle	
WZ518	DH115 Vampire T11	North-East Aircraft Museum, Usworth	
WZ549	DH115 Vampire T11 (8118M) [F]	Ulster Aviation Society, Langford Lodge	
WZ553	DH115 Vampire T11 (G-DHYY) [40]	Source Classic Jet Flight, Bruntingthorpe	
WZ557	DH115 Vampire T11	N Yorks Aircraft Recovery Centre, Chop Gate	
WZ559	DH115 Vampire T11 (7736M) [45] <ff>	*Scrapped at Halton, 1994*	
WZ581	DH115 Vampire T11 <ff>	The Vampire Collection, Hemel Hempstead	
WZ584	DH115 Vampire T11 [K]	St Albans College of FE	
WZ589	DH115 Vampire T11 [19]	Lashenden Air Warfare Museum, Headcorn	
WZ589	DH115 Vampire T55 (U-1230/G-DHZZ)	Source Classic Jet Flight, Bournemouth	
WZ590	DH115 Vampire T11 [19]	Imperial War Museum, Duxford	
WZ608	DH115 Vampire T11 [56] <ff>	Privately owned, Romford, Essex	
WZ620	DH115 Vampire T11 [68]	Avon Aviation Museum, Yatesbury	
WZ662	Auster AOP9 (G-BKVK)	Privately owned, Middle Wallop	
WZ706	Auster AOP9 (7851M/G-BURR)	Privately owned, Middle Wallop	
WZ711	Auster AOP9/Beagle E3 (G-AVHT)	Privately owned, Middle Wallop	
WZ721	Auster AOP9	Museum of Army Flying, Middle Wallop	
WZ724	Auster AOP9 (7432M)	AAC Middle Wallop, at main gate	
WZ729	Auster AOP9	Privately owned, Newark-on-Trent	
WZ736	Avro 707A (7868M)	Gr Manchester Mus of Science & Industry	
WZ744	Avro 707C (7932M)	RAF Cosford Aerospace Museum	
WZ753	Slingsby T38 Grasshopper TX1	Southampton Hall of Aviation	
WZ765	Slingsby T38 Grasshopper TX1	RAFGSA, Bicester	
WZ767	Slingsby T38 Grasshopper TX1	North-East Aircraft Museum, stored Usworth	
WZ768	Slingsby T38 Grasshopper TX1 (comp XK820)	Privately owned, Kirton-in-Lindsey, Lincs	

Notes	Serial	Type (other identity) [code]	Owner/operator, location or fate
	WZ769	Slingsby T38 Grasshopper TX1	Privately owned, stored Rufforth
	WZ772	Slingsby T38 Grasshopper TX1	Museum of Army Flying, Middle Wallop
	WZ779	Slingsby T38 Grasshopper TX1	Privately owned, Old Sarum
	WZ784	Slingsby T38 Grasshopper TX1	Privately owned, Thurrock College
	WZ791	Slingsby T38 Grasshopper TX1 (8944M)	RAF Museum, Hendon
	WZ792	Slingsby T38 Grasshopper TX1	Privately owned, stored Falgunzeon, D&G
	WZ793	Slingsby T38 Grasshopper TX1	Whitgift School, Croydon
	WZ796	Slingsby T38 Grasshopper TX1	Privately owned, stored Nympsfield, Glos
	WZ816	Slingsby T38 Grasshopper TX1 (BGA 3979)	Privately owned, stored Ashford, Kent
	WZ822	Slingsby T38 Grasshopper TX1 (BGA 3875)	Robertsbridge Aviation Society, Mayfield
	WZ824	Slingsby T38 Grasshopper TX1	Privately owned, stored Strathaven, Strathclyde
	WZ826	Vickers Valiant B(K)1 (XD826/ 7872M) <ff>	Privately owned, Rayleigh, Essex
	WZ829	Slingsby T38 Grasshopper TX1 (BGA 3662)	RAFGSA, Bicester
	WZ831	Slingsby T38 Grasshopper TX1	Privately owned, stored Nympsfield, Glos
	WZ845	DHC1 Chipmunk T10 [6]	*Sold, February 1997*
	WZ846	DHC1 Chipmunk T10 (G-BCSC/ 8439M) <ff>	No 1404 Sqn ATC, Chatham
	WZ847	DHC1 Chipmunk T10 (G-CPMK) [F]	Privately owned, Ashbourne
	WZ856	DHC1 Chipmunk T10	*Sold, February 1997*
	WZ862	DHC1 Chipmunk T10 [A]	*Sold, February 1997*
	WZ866	DHC1 Chipmunk T10 (8217M/ G-ATEB) <ff>	Dumfries & Galloway Avn Mus, Dumfries
	WZ868	DHC1 Chipmunk T10 (G-BCIW) [H]	Privately owned, Fownhope, H&W
	WZ868	DHC1 Chipmunk T10 (WG322/ G-ARMF) [H]	Ragwing Aviation, Tadlow, Cambs
	WZ869	DHC1 Chipmunk T10 (8019M) [R] <ff>	No 395 Sqn ATC, Handforth, Cheshire
	WZ872	DHC1 Chipmunk T10 [E]	*Sold, February 1997*
	WZ876	DHC1 Chipmunk T10 (G-BBWN)	Privately owned, Netherthorpe
	WZ877	DHC1 Chipmunk T10 [75]	Privately owned,
	WZ878	DHC1 Chipmunk T10 [86]	*Sold, February 1997*
	WZ879	DHC1 Chipmunk T10 (G-BWUT) [73]	Aero Vintage, Rye
	WZ882	DHC1 Chipmunk T10 [K]	AAC BFWF/2 Regiment, Middle Wallop
	WZ884	DHC1 Chipmunk T10 [P]	AAC BFWF/2 Regiment, Middle Wallop
	XA109	DH115 Sea Vampire T22	Royal Scottish Mus'm of Flight, E Fortune
	XA127	DH115 Sea Vampire T22 <ff>	FAA Museum, stored RNAS Yeovilton
	XA129	DH115 Sea Vampire T22	FAA Museum, stored Wroughton
	XA225	Slingsby T38 Grasshopper TX1	Churchers College, Petersfield, Hants
	XA230	Slingsby T38 Grasshopper TX1 (BGA 4098)	Privately owned, Henlow
	XA231	Slingsby T38 Grasshopper TX1 (8888M)	E Cheshire & S Manchester Wg ATC, Sealand
	XA241	Slingsby T38 Grasshopper TX1	Shuttleworth Collection, Old Warden
	XA243	Slingsby T38 Grasshopper TX1 (8886M)	Privately owned, Gransden Lodge, Cambs
	XA244	Slingsby T38 Grasshopper TX1	RAF, stored Cosford
	XA282	Slingsby T31B Cadet TX3	Caernarfon Air World
	XA286	Slingsby T31B Cadet TX3	Privately owned, stored Rufforth
	XA289	Slingsby T31B Cadet TX3	Privately owned, Eaglescott
	XA290	Slingsby T31B Cadet TX3	Privately owned, stored Rufforth
	XA293	Slingsby T31B Cadet TX3	Privately owned, Breighton
	XA302	Slingsby T31B Cadet TX3 (BGA3786)	Privately owned, Syerston
	XA454	Fairey Gannet COD4	RNAS Yeovilton Fire Section
	XA459	Fairey Gannet ECM6 [E]	Privately owned, Cirencester
	XA460	Fairey Gannet ECM6 [768/BY]	NE Wales Institute, Connah's Quay, Clwyd
	XA466	Fairey Gannet COD4 [777/LM]	FAA Museum, stored Wroughton
	XA508	Fairey Gannet T2 [627/GN]	FAA Museum, at Midland Air Museum, Coventry
	XA553	Gloster Javelin FAW1 (7470M)	RAF Stanmore Park, on display
	XA564	Gloster Javelin FAW1 (7464M)	RAF Cosford Aerospace Museum
	XA571	Gloster Javelin FAW1 (7663M/ 7722M) <ff>	*Really XH783*
	XA634	Gloster Javelin FAW4 (7641M) [L]	RAF Leeming, on display
	XA699	Gloster Javelin FAW5 (7809M)	Midland Air Museum, Coventry

Serial	Type (other identity) [code]	Owner/operator, location or fate	Notes
XA801	Gloster Javelin FAW2 (7739M) <ff>	*Scrapped at Stock, September 1994*	
XA847	EE P1B (8371M)	Privately owned, Southampton Docks	
XA862	WS55 Whirlwind HAR1 (G-AMJT) [9]	IHM, Weston-super-Mare	
XA864	WS55 Whirlwind HAR1	FAA Museum, stored Wroughton	
XA868	WS55 Whirlwind HAR1	IHM, Weston-super-Mare	
XA870	WS55 Whirlwind HAR1	Flambards Village Theme Park, Helston	
XA880	DH104 Devon C2 (G-BVXR)	Privately owned, Staverton	
XA893	Avro 698 Vulcan B1 (8591M) <ff>	RAF Cosford Aerospace Museum	
XA896	Avro 698 Vulcan B1 <ff>	Privately owned, Reigate	
XA903	Avro 698 Vulcan B1 <ff>	Privately owned, Sidcup, Kent	
XA909	Avro 698 Vulcan B1 <ff>	*Really XA896*	
XA917	HP80 Victor B1 (7827M) <ff>	Privately owned, Guardbridge, Fife	
XB259	Blackburn B101 Beverley C1 (G-AOAI)	Museum of Army Transport, Beverley	
XB261	Blackburn B101 Beverley C1 <ff>	Duxford Aviation Society, Duxford	
XB446	Grumman TBM-3 Avenger ECM6B	FAA Museum, Yeovilton	
XB480	Hiller HT1 [537]	FAA Museum, stored Wroughton	
XB812	Canadair CL-13 Sabre F4 (9227M) [U]	RAF Museum, Hendon	
XD145	Saro SR53	RAF Cosford Aerospace Museum	
XD163	WS55 Whirlwind HAR10 (8645M) [X]	IHM, Weston-super-Mare	
XD165	WS55 Whirlwind HAR10 (8673M) [B]	AAC Middle Wallop, instructional use	
XD186	WS55 Whirlwind HAR10 (8730M)		
XD215	VS Scimitar F1 <ff>	Privately owned, Cheltenham	
XD234	VS Scimitar F1 [834]	DRA, derelict Farnborough	
XD235	VS Scimitar F1 <ff>	No 424 Sqn ATC, Southampton	
XD244	VS Scimitar F1 <ff>	*Scrapped, May 1994*	
XD317	VS Scimitar F1 [112/R]	FAA Museum, RNAS Yeovilton	
XD332	VS Scimitar F1 [194/C]	Flambards Village Theme Park, Helston	
XD375	DH115 Vampire T11 (7887M) [72]	City of Norwich Aviation Museum	
XD377	DH115 Vampire T11 (8203M) [A] <ff>	Privately owned, Barton	
XD382	DH115 Vampire T11 (8033M)	Anchor Surplus, Ripley, Derbys	
XD425	DH115 Vampire T11 <ff>	RAF Millom Museum, Haverigg	
XD434	DH115 Vampire T11 [25]	Fenland & W Norfolk Aviation Museum, Wisbech	
XD435	DH115 Vampire T11 [26] <ff>	Privately owned, Lapworth, Warwicks	
XD445	DH115 Vampire T11 [51]	Bomber County Aviation Museum, Hemswell	
XD447	DH115 Vampire T11 [50]	Jet Avn Preservation Grp, Long Marston	
XD452	DH115 Vampire T11 (7990M) [47] <ff>	Vampire Support Team, RAF Sealand	
XD453	DH115 Vampire T11 (7890M) [64] <ff>	Privately owned, Crosland Moor	
XD459	DH115 Vampire T11 [63] <ff>	Privately owned, Bruntingthorpe	
XD463	DH115 Vampire T11 (8023M)	Privately owned, Ripley	
XD506	DH115 Vampire T11 (7983M)	Aircraft Maintenance Support Svs, Pyle, Mid Glam	
XD515	DH115 Vampire T11 (7998M/ XM515)	Newark Air Museum, Winthorpe	
XD525	DH115 Vampire T11 (7882M) <ff>	Campbell College CCF, Belfast	
XD528	DH115 Vampire T11 (8159M) <ff>	Gamston Aerodrome Fire Section	
XD534	DH115 Vampire T11 [41]	Military Aircraft Pres'n Grp, Barton	
XD535	DH115 Vampire T11 <ff>	Macclesfield Historical Avn Soc, Barton	
XD536	DH115 Vampire T11 (7734M) [H]	Alleyn's School CCF, Northolt	
XD542	DH115 Vampire T11 (7604M) [28]	RAF Edzell, Tayside, on display	
XD547	DH115 Vampire T11 [Z] (composite)	Dumfries & Galloway Avn Mus, Dumfries	
XD593	DH115 Vampire T11 [50]	Newark Air Museum, Winthorpe	
XD595	DH115 Vampire T11 <ff>	Privately owned, Glentham, Lincs	
XD596	DH115 Vampire T11 (7939M)	Southampton Hall of Aviation	
XD599	DH115 Vampire T11	Caernarfon Air World, stored	
XD602	DH115 Vampire T11 (7737M) <ff>	Privately owned, Brands Hatch	
XD614	DH115 Vampire T11 (8124M) <ff>	Privately owned, Southampton	
XD616	DH115 Vampire T11 [56]	Mosquito Aircraft Museum, London Colney	
XD622	DH115 Vampire T11 (8160M)	No 2214 Sqn ATC, Usworth	
XD624	DH115 Vampire T11 [O]	Macclesfield Technical College	
XD626	DH115 Vampire T11 [Q]	Midland Air Museum, Coventry	
XD674	Hunting Jet Provost T1 (7570M) [T]	RAF Cosford Aerospace Museum	

Notes	Serial	Type (other identity) [code]	Owner/operator, location or fate
	XD693	Hunting Jet Provost T1 (XM129/ G-AOBU) [Q-Z]	Kennet Aviation, Cranfield
	XD816	Vickers Valiant B(K)1 <ff>	Brooklands Museum, Weybridge
	XD818	Vickers Valiant B(K)1 (7894M)	RAF Museum, Hendon
	XD857	Vickers Valiant B(K)1 <ff>	Privately owned, Rayleigh, Essex
	XD875	Vickers Valiant B(K)1 <ff>	British Aviation Heritage, Bruntingthorpe
	XE317	Bristol 171 Sycamore HR14 (G-AMWO) [S-N]	Newark Air Museum, Winthorpe
	XE327	Hawker Sea Hawk FGA6 [644/LH]	Privately owned, Kings Langley, Herts
	XE339	Hawker Sea Hawk FGA6 (8156M) [149/E]	BAe Dunsfold (under restoration)
	XE340	Hawker Sea Hawk FGA6 [131/Z]	FAA Museum, at Montrose Air Station Museum, Montrose
	XE368	Hawker Sea Hawk FGA6 [200/J]	Flambards Village Theme Park, Helston
	XE489	Hawker Sea Hawk FGA6 (G-JETH)	Vallance By-Ways, Charlwood, Surrey
	XE521	Fairey Rotodyne Y (parts)	IHM, Weston-super-Mare
	XE584	Hawker Hunter FGA9 <ff>	Macclesfield Historical Avn Soc, Barton
	XE597	Hawker Hunter FGA9 (8874M) <ff>	
	XE601	Hawker Hunter FGA9	MoD(PE)/FJTS, DTEO Boscombe Down
	XE624	Hawker Hunter FGA9 (8875M) [G]	Army, Cawdor Barracks, Brawdy, on display
	XE627	Hawker Hunter F6A [T]	Imperial War Museum, Duxford
	XE643	Hawker Hunter FGA9 (8586M) <ff>	RAF EP&TU, Aldergrove
	XE650	Hawker Hunter FGA9 (G-9-449) <ff>	Privately owned, Welshpool
	XE656	Hawker Hunter F6 (8678M)	Privately owned, Ipswich
	XE665	Hawker Hunter T8C (G-BWGM)	Classic Jet Aircraft Co, Exeter [876/VL]
	XE668	Hawker Hunter GA11 [832/DD]	RN, Predannack Fire School
	XE670	Hawker Hunter F4 (7762M/8585M) <ff>	RAF Cosford Aerospace Museum
	XE677	Hawker Hunter F4 (G-HHUN)	Jet Heritage Ltd, Bournemouth
	XE685	Hawker Hunter GA11 (G-GAII) [861/VL]	Classic Jet Aircraft Co, Exeter
	XE689	Hawker Hunter GA11 (G-BWGK) [864/VL]	Classic Jet Aircraft Co, Exeter
	XE712	Hawker Hunter GA11 [708]	RN, Predannack Fire School
	XE793	Slingsby T31B Cadet TX3 (8666M)	RAF
	XE796	Slingsby T31B Cadet TX3	Privately owned, stored North Weald
	XE799	Slingsby T31B Cadet TX3 (8943M) [R]	RAFGSA, Syerston
	XE802	Slingsby T31B Cadet TX3	Privately owned, stored Cupar, Fife
	XE807	Slingsby T31B Cadet TX3 (BGA3545)	Privately owned, Bath
	XE849	DH115 Vampire T11 (7928M) [V3]	Privately owned, Mildenhall
	XE852	DH115 Vampire T11 [H]	No 2247 Sqn ATC, Hawarden
	XE855	DH115 Vampire T11 <ff>	Midland Air Museum, Coventry
	XE856	DH115 Vampire T11	Privately owned, Catfoss, E Yorkshire
	XE864	DH115 Vampire T11 (composite with XD435)	Privately owned, Stretton, Cheshire
	XE872	DH115 Vampire T11 [62]	Midland Air Museum, Coventry
	XE874	DH115 Vampire T11 (8582M) [61]	Montrose Air Station Museum
	XE897	DH115 Vampire T11 (XD403)	Privately owned, Errol, Tayside
	XE897	DH115 Vampire T55 (U-1214/ G-DHVV)	Source Classic Jet Flight, Bournemouth
	XE920	DH115 Vampire T11 (8196M/ G-VMPR) [D]	Vampire Support Team, Swansea
	XE921	DH115 Vampire T11 [64] <ff>	South Yorkshire Avn Museum, stored Firbeck
	XE935	DH115 Vampire T11 [30]	South Yorkshire Avn Museum, Firbeck
	XE946	DH115 Vampire T11 (7473M) <ff>	RAF Museum Restoration Centre, Cardington
	XE956	DH115 Vampire T11 (G-OBLN)	De Havilland Aviation, Swansea
	XE979	DH115 Vampire T11 [54]	Privately owned, Birlingham, Worcs
	XE982	DH115 Vampire T11 (7564M) [01]	Privately owned, Dunkeswell
	XE985	DH115 Vampire T11 (*WZ476*)	De Havilland Aviation, Swansea
	XE993	DH115 Vampire T11 (8161M)	Privately owned, Cosford
	XE995	DH115 Vampire T11 [53]	Privately owned, High Halden, Kent
	XE998	DH115 Vampire T11 (*U-1215*)	Brooklands Museum, Weybridge
	XF113	VS Swift F7 [19] <ff>	The Air Defence Collection, Salisbury
	XF114	VS Swift F7 (G-SWIF)	Jet Heritage Ltd, Bournemouth

Serial	Type (other identity) [code]	Owner/operator, location or fate	Notes
XF300	Hawker Hunter GA11 [860/VL]	RN, stored Shawbury	
XF301	Hawker Hunter GA11 [834/VL]	*Sold to the USA as N2111H, February 1996*	
XF310	Hawker Hunter T8C [869/VL,2]	SFDO, RNAS Culdrose	
XF314	Hawker Hunter F51 (RDAF E-412) [N]	Tangmere Military Aviation Museum	
XF321	Hawker Hunter T7	Privately owned, stored Yeovilton	
XF324	Hawker Hunter F51 (RDAF E-427) [D]	British Aviation Heritage, Bruntingthorpe	
XF357	Hawker Hunter T8C (G-BWGL) [871/VL]	Classic Jet Aircraft Co, Exeter	
XF358	Hawker Hunter T8C [870/VL]	RN, stored Shawbury	
XF368	Hawker Hunter GA11 [863/VL]	RN, stored Shawbury	
XF375	Hawker Hunter F6A (8736M/ G-BUEZ) [05]	The Old Flying Machine Co, Duxford	
XF382	Hawker Hunter F6A [15]	Midland Air Museum, Coventry	
XF383	Hawker Hunter F6 (8706M) <ff>	Privately owned, Kidlington	
XF509	Hawker Hunter F6 (8708M)	Humbrol Paints, Marfleet, E Yorkshire	
XF515	Hawker Hunter F6A (8830M/ G-KAXF) [C]	Kennet Aviation, Cranfield	
XF519	Hawker Hunter FGA9 (8677M/ 8738M/9183M)	FSCTE, RAF Manston (comp XJ695) [J]	
XF522	Hawker Hunter F6 <ff>	No 1365 Sqn ATC, Aylesbury	
XF526	Hawker Hunter F6 (8679M) [78/E]	Privately owned, Birlingham, Worcs	
XF527	Hawker Hunter F6 (8680M)	RAF Halton, on display	
XF545	Percival P56 Provost T1 (7957M) [O-K]	Privately owned, Cranfield	
XF597	Percival P56 Provost T1 (G-BKFW) [AH]	Privately owned, Aldermaston	
XF603	Percival P56 Provost T1 [H]	Kennet Aviation, Cranfield	
XF690	Percival P56 Provost T1 (8041M/ G-MOOS)	Kennet Aviation, Cranfield	
XF708	Avro 716 Shackleton MR3 [203/C]	Imperial War Museum, Duxford	
XF785	Bristol 173 (7648M/G-ALBN)	RAF Museum Rest'n Centre, Cardington	
XF836	Percival P56 Provost T1 (8043M/ G-AWRY) [JG]	Privately owned, Thatcham	
XF844	Percival P56 Provost T1 [70]	British Aviation Heritage, Bruntingthorpe	
XF877	Percival P56 Provost T1 (G-AWVF) [JX]	Privately owned, Goodwood	
XF926	Bristol 188 (8368M)	RAF Cosford Aerospace Museum	
XF967	Hawker Hunter T8C (9186M) [T]	AMIF, RAFC Cranwell	
XF994	Hawker Hunter T8C [873/VL]	RN, stored Shawbury	
XF995	Hawker Hunter T8B (9237M) [K]	AMIF, RAFC Cranwell	
XG154	Hawker Hunter FGA9 (8863M) [54]	RAF Museum, Hendon	
XG160	Hawker Hunter F6A (8831M/ G-BWAF) [U]	Royal Jordanian AF Historic Flt, stored Bournemouth	
XG164	Hawker Hunter F6 (8681M)	RAF Halton	
XG172	Hawker Hunter F6A (8832M) [A]	Privately owned, Ipswich	
XG194	Hawker Hunter FGA9 (8839M) [55] <rf>	RAF North Luffenham Training Area	
XG193	Hawker Hunter FGA9 (comp with XG297)	Bomber County Aviation Museum, Hemswell	
XG195	Hawker Hunter FGA9 (comp with XG297)	*Repainted as XG193 by April 1996*	
XG196	Hawker Hunter F6A (8702M) [31]	RAF Bracknell, on display	
XG209	Hawker Hunter F6 (8709M) <ff>	Privately owned, Chelmsford	
XG210	Hawker Hunter F6	Privately owned, Beck Row, Suffolk	
XG225	Hawker Hunter F6A (8713M) [S]	RAF Cosford on display	
XG226	Hawker Hunter F6A (8800M) [28] <ff>	No 1242 Sqn ATC, Faversham, Kent	
XG252	Hawker Hunter FGA9 (8840M) [U]	Privately owned, Hereford	
XG254	Hawker Hunter FGA9 (8881M)	RAF Coltishall Fire Section	
XG274	Hawker Hunter F6 (8710M) [71]	Privately owned, Ipswich	
XG290	Hawker Hunter F6 (8711M) [74] (fuselage)	Jet Heritage Ltd, Bournemouth	
XG297	Hawker Hunter FGA9 <ff>	South Yorkshire Avn Museum, stored Firbeck	
XG325	EE Lightning F1 <ff>	No 1476 Sqn ATC, Southend	
XG329	EE Lightning F1 (8050M)	Privately owned, Flixton	
XG331	EE Lightning F1 <ff>	Gloucestershire Avn Coll, Staverton	
XG337	EE Lightning F1 (8056M) [M]	RAF Cosford Aerospace Museum	

Notes	Serial	Type (other identity) [code]	Owner/operator, location or fate
	XG452	Bristol 192 Belvedere HC1 (7997M/G-BRMB)	IHM, Weston-super-Mare
	XG454	Bristol 192 Belvedere HC1 (8366M)	Gr Manchester Mus of Science & Industry
	XG462	Bristol 192 Belvedere HC1 <ff>	IHM, stored Weston-super-Mare
	XG474	Bristol 192 Belvedere HC1 (8367M) [O]	RAF Museum, Hendon
	XG496	DH104 Devon C2 (G-ANDX) [K]	Privately owned, Newcastle
	XG502	Bristol 171 Sycamore HR14	Museum of Army Flying, Middle Wallop
	XG506	Bristol 171 Sycamore HR14 (7852M)	Bomber County Aviation Museum, Hemswell
	XG518	Bristol 171 Sycamore HR14 (8009M) [S-E]	North-East Aircraft Museum, Usworth
	XG523	Bristol 171 Sycamore HR14 <ff>	North-East Aircraft Museum, Usworth
	XG540	Bristol 171 Sycamore HR14 (7899M/8345M) [Y-S]	Bygone Times Warehouse, Euxton, Lancs
	XG544	Bristol 171 Sycamore HR14	Privately owned, Lower Tremar, Cornwall
	XG547	Bristol 171 Sycamore HR14 (G-HAPR) [S-T]	IHM, Weston-super-Mare
	XG574	WS55 Whirlwind HAR3	FAA Museum, stored Wroughton
	XG577	WS55 Whirlwind HAR3 (9050M)	RAF Leconfield Crash Rescue Training
	XG594	WS55 Whirlwind HAS7 [517/PO]	FAA Museum, at R. Scottish Mus'm of Flt, E Fortune
	XG596	WS55 Whirlwind HAS7 [66]	IHM/Westland, Yeovil (under restoration)
	XG597	WS55 Whirlwind HAS7	Privately owned, Siddal, West Yorkshire
	XG613	DH112 Sea Venom FAW21	Imperial War Museum, Duxford
	XG629	DH112 Sea Venom FAW22 <ff>	Privately owned, Stone, Staffs
	XG680	DH112 Sea Venom FAW22 [438]	North-East Aircraft Museum, Usworth
	XG691	DH112 Sea Venom FAW22 [93/J]	Gloucestershire Avn Coll, Staverton
	XG692	DH112 Sea Venom FAW22 [668/LM]	Privately owned, Baxterley, Warwickshire
	XG730	DH112 Sea Venom FAW22 [499/A]	Mosquito Aircraft Museum, London Colney
	XG736	DH112 Sea Venom FAW22	Ulster Aviation Society, Newtownards
	XG737	DH112 Sea Venom FAW22 [220/Z]	Jet Avn Preservation Grp, stored Long Marston
	XG743	DH115 Sea Vampire T22 [597/LM]	Wymondham College, Norfolk
	XG775	DH115 Vampire T55 (U-1219/ G-DHWW) [VL]	Source Classic Jet Flight, Bournemouth
	XG797	Fairey Gannet ECM6 [277]	Imperial War Museum, Duxford
	XG831	Fairey Gannet ECM6 [396]	Flambards Village Theme Park, Helston
	XG882	Fairey Gannet T5 (8754M) [771/LM]	Privately owned, Errol, Tayside
	XG883	Fairey Gannet T5 [773/BY]	FAA Museum, at Museum of Berkshire Aviation, Woodley
	XG900	Short SC1	Science Museum, at FAA Museum, RNAS Yeovilton
	XG905	Short SC1	Ulster Folk & Transpt Mus, Holywood, Co Down
	XH131	EE Canberra PR9 [AA]	RAF No 39 (1 PRU) Sqn, Marham
	XH132	Short SC9 Canberra (8915M) <ff>	Privately owned, St Austell
	XH133	EE Canberra PR9 <ff>	*Scrapped at Stock, 1996*
	XH134	EE Canberra PR9 [AB]	RAF No 39(1 PRU) Sqn, Marham
	XH135	EE Canberra PR9 [AC]	RAF No 39(1 PRU) Sqn, Marham
	XH136	EE Canberra PR9 (8782M) <ff>	Phoenix Aviation, Bruntingthorpe
	XH165	EE Canberra PR9 <ff>	Blyth Valley Aviation Collection, Walpole
	XH168	EE Canberra PR9 [AD]	RAF No 39(1 PRU) Sqn, Marham
	XH169	EE Canberra PR9	RAF No 39(1 PRU) Sqn, Marham
	XH170	EE Canberra PR9 (8739M)	RAF Wyton, on display
	XH171	EE Canberra PR9 (8746M) [U]	RAF Cosford Aerospace Museum
	XH174	EE Canberra PR9 <ff>	RAF, stored St Athan
	XH175	EE Canberra PR9 <ff>	Privately owned, Stock, Essex
	XH177	EE Canberra PR9 <ff>	Privately owned, Stock, Essex
	XH278	DH115 Vampire T11 (8595M/ 7866M)	Privately owned, Felton, Northumberland
	XH312	DH115 Vampire T11 [18]	Privately owned, Dodleston, Cheshire
	XH313	DH115 Vampire T11 [E]	St Albans College of FE
	XH328	DH115 Vampire T11	Jet Heritage Ltd, Bournemouth (dismantled)
	XH330	DH115 Vampire T11 [73]	Privately owned, Bridgnorth
	XH537	Avro 698 Vulcan B2MRR (8749M) <ff>	Privately owned, Sidcup, Kent
	XH558	Avro 698 Vulcan B2 (G-VLCN)	British Aviation Heritage, Bruntingthorpe
	XH560	Avro 698 Vulcan K2 <ff>	Privately owned, Romford, Essex

Serial	Type (other identity) [code]	Owner/operator, location or fate	Notes
XH563	Avro 698 Vulcan B2MRR <ff>	Privately owned, Banchory, Fife	
XH567	EE Canberra B6(mod)	MoD(PE), stored DTEO Boscombe Down	
XH568	EE Canberra B6(mod) (G-BVIC)	Classic Aviation Projects, Bruntingthorpe	
XH584	EE Canberra T4 (G-27-374) <ff>	South Yorkshire Avn Museum, Firbeck	
XH592	HP80 Victor K1A (8429M) <ff>	Phoenix Aviation, Bruntingthorpe	
XH648	HP80 Victor K1A	Imperial War Museum, Duxford	
XH669	HP80 Victor K2 (9092M) <ff>	Privately owned, Southend Airport	
XH670	HP80 Victor SR2 <ff>	Privately owned, Romford, Essex	
XH672	HP80 Victor K2	RAF Cosford Aerospace Museum	
XH673	HP80 Victor K2 (8911M)	RAF Marham, on display	
XH767	Gloster Javelin FAW9 (7955M) [A]	City of Norwich Aviation Museum	
XH783	Gloster Javelin FAW7 (7798M) <ff>	Privately owned, Catford	
XH837	Gloster Javelin FAW7 (8032M) <ff>	Caernarfon Air World	
XH892	Gloster Javelin FAW9 (7982M) [J]	Norfolk & Suffolk Avn Museum, Flixton	
XH897	Gloster Javelin FAW9	Imperial War Museum, Duxford	
XH903	Gloster Javelin FAW9 (7938M)	Gloucestershire Avn Coll, Staverton	
XH980	Gloster Javelin FAW8 (7867M) <ff>	*Scrapped at Stock, 1995*	
XH992	Gloster Javelin FAW8 (7829M) [P]	Newark Air Museum, Winthorpe	
XJ314	RR Thrust Measuring Rig	Science Museum, at FAA Museum, RNAS Yeovilton	
XJ380	Bristol 171 Sycamore HR14 (8628M)	Montrose Air Station Museum	
XJ389	Fairey Jet Gyrodyne (XD759/ G-AJJP)	Museum of Berkshire Aviation, Woodley	
XJ393	WS55 Whirlwind HAR3 (XD763)	Privately owned, Codmore Hill, Sussex	
XJ409	WS55 Whirlwind HAR10 (XD779)	Maes Artro Craft Village, Llanbedr	
XJ435	WS55 Whirlwind HAR10 (8671M) [V]	AAC Dishforth, instructional use	
XJ476	DH110 Sea Vixen FAW1 <ff>	No 424 Sqn ATC, Southampton Hall of Avn	
XJ481	DH110 Sea Vixen FAW1 [VL]	FAA Museum, at NARO, RNAY Fleetlands Museum	
XJ482	DH110 Sea Vixen FAW1 [713/VL]	Norfolk & Suffolk Avn Museum, Flixton	
XJ488	DH110 Sea Vixen FAW1 <ff>	Privately owned, Hucknall, Notts	
XJ494	DH110 Sea Vixen FAW2	Privately owned, Kings Langley, Herts	
XJ560	DH110 Sea Vixen FAW2 (8142M) [242]	Newark Air Museum, Winthorpe	
XJ565	DH110 Sea Vixen FAW2 [127/E]	Mosquito Aircraft Museum, London Colney	
XJ571	DH110 Sea Vixen FAW2 (8140M) [242/R]	Brooklands Museum, Weybridge	
XJ575	DH110 Sea Vixen FAW2 <ff>	Wellesbourne Wartime Museum	
XJ579	DH110 Sea Vixen FAW2 <ff>	Midland Air Museum, Coventry	
XJ580	DH110 Sea Vixen FAW2 [131/E]	Sea Vixen Society, Christchurch	
XJ607	DH110 Sea Vixen FAW2 (8171M) <ff>	Privately owned, Enstone	
XJ634	Hawker Hunter F6A (8684M) [29]	Aces High Ltd, North Weald	
XJ639	Hawker Hunter F6A (8687M) [H]	Aces High Ltd, North Weald	
XJ676	Hawker Hunter F6A (8844M) <ff>	Privately owned, Leavesden	
XJ690	Hawker Hunter FGA9 <ff>	*Inc into Hunter R–BHAC at Bournemouth*	
XJ714	Hawker Hunter FR10	Jet Avn Preservation Grp, Long Marston	
XJ723	WS55 Whirlwind HAR10	Montrose Air Station Museum, Montrose	
XJ726	WS55 Whirlwind HAR10	Caernarfon Air World	
XJ727	WS55 Whirlwind HAR10 (8661M) [L]	AAC Dishforth, BDRT	
XJ729	WS55 Whirlwind HAR10 (8732M/ G-BVGE)	Privately owned, Cricklade	
XJ758	WS55 Whirlwind HAR10 (8464M) <ff>	Privately owned, Oswestry	
XJ763	WS55 Whirlwind HAR10 (G-BKHA) [P]	Privately owned, stored Thornicombe, Dorset	
XJ772	DH115 Vampire T11 [H]	Mosquito Aircraft Museum, London Colney	
XJ823	Avro 698 Vulcan B2A	Solway Aviation Society, Carlisle Airport	
XJ824	Avro 698 Vulcan B2A	Imperial War Museum, Duxford	
XJ917	Bristol 171 Sycamore HR14 [H-S]	Bristol Aero Collection, stored Kemble	
XJ918	Bristol 171 Sycamore HR14 (8190M)	RAF Cosford Aerospace Museum	
XK149	Hawker Hunter F6A (8714M) [L]	Privately owned, Bruntingthorpe	
XK378	Auster AOP9 (TAD200)	Privately owned, Dale, Dyfed	
XK416	Auster AOP9 (7855M/G-AYUA)	De Havilland Aviation, Swansea	
XK417	Auster AOP9 (G-AVXY)	Privately owned, Newton, Notts	
XK418	Auster AOP9 (7976M)	SWWAPS, Lasham	
XK421	Auster AOP9 (8365M) (frame)	Privately owned, Thurcroft, South Yorkshire	

Notes	Serial	Type (other identity) [code]	Owner/operator, location or fate
	XK482	Saro Skeeter AOP12 (7840M/ G-BJWC) [C]	Privately owned, Sywell
	XK488	Blackburn NA39 Buccaneer S1	FAA Museum, RNAS Yeovilton
	XK526	Blackburn NA39 Buccaneer S2 (8648M)	RAF Honington, at main gate
	XK527	Blackburn NA39 Buccaneer S2D	Privately owned, New Milton, Hants
	XK530	Blackburn NA39 Buccaneer S1	Scrapped at Bedford by 1995
	XK532	Blackburn NA39 Buccaneer S1 (8867M) [632/LM]	The Fresson Trust, Inverness Airport
	XK533	Blackburn NA39 Buccaneer S1 <ff>	Royal Scottish Mus'm of Flight, E Fortune
	XK590	DH115 Vampire T11 [V]	Wellesbourne Wartime Museum
	XK623	DH115 Vampire T11 (G-VAMP) [56]	Caernarfon Air World
	XK624	DH115 Vampire T11 [32]	Norfolk & Suffolk Avn Museum, Flixton
	XK625	DH115 Vampire T11 [12]	Brenzett Aeronautical Museum
	XK627	DH115 Vampire T11	Privately owned, Barton
	XK632	DH115 Vampire T11 [67]	No 2370 Sqn ATC, Denham
	XK637	DH115 Vampire T11 [56]	No 1855 Sqn ATC, Royton, Gr Manchester
	XK655	DH106 Comet C2(RC) <ff>	Gatwick Airport, on display (BOAC colours)
	XK659	DH106 Comet C2(RC) <ff>	Privately owned, Elland, West Yorkshire
	XK695	DH106 Comet C2(RC) (9164M) <ff>	Mosquito Aircraft Museum, London Colney
	XK699	DH106 Comet C2 (7971M)	RAF Lyneham on display
	XK724	Folland Gnat F1 (7715M)	RAF Cosford Aerospace Museum
	XK740	Folland Gnat F1 (8396M)	Southampton Hall of Aviation
	XK741	Folland Gnat F1 (fuselage)	Midland Air Museum, Coventry
	XK776	ML Utility 1	Museum of Army Flying, Middle Wallop
	XK789	Slingsby T38 Grasshopper TX1	Warwick School, Warwick
	XK790	Slingsby T38 Grasshopper TX1	Privately owned, stored Husbands Bosworth
	XK819	Slingsby T38 Grasshopper TX1	The Real Aeroplane Company, Breighton
	XK820	Slingsby T38 Grasshopper TX1	Used in the rebuild of WZ768
	XK822	Slingsby T38 Grasshopper TX1	Privately owned, West Malling
	XK895	DH104 Sea Devon C20 (G-SDEV) [19/CU]	De Havilland Aviation, Swansea
	XK896	DH104 Sea Devon C20 (G-RNAS)	Privately owned, North Coates, Lincs
	XK907	WS55 Whirlwind HAS7 [U]	Midland Air Museum, Coventry
	XK911	WS55 Whirlwind HAS7 [519/PO]	Privately owned, Ipswich
	XK936	WS55 Whirlwind HAS7 [62]	Imperial War Museum, Duxford
	XK940	WS55 Whirlwind HAS7 (G-AYXT)	Privately owned, Diss, Norfolk
	XK944	WS55 Whirlwind HAS7	No 617 Sqn ATC, Malpas School, Cheshire
	XK968	WS55 Whirlwind HAR10 (8445M) [E]	FSCTE, RAF Manston
	XK987	WS55 Whirlwind HAR10 (8393M)	MoD Swynnerton, Staffs
	XK988	WS55 Whirlwind HAR10 [D]	AAC Middle Wallop Fire Section
	XL149	Blackburn B101 Beverley C1 (7988M) <ff>	Newark Air Museum, Winthorpe
	XL160	HP80 Victor K2 (8910M) <ff>	HP Victor Association, Walpole
	XL161	HP80 Victor K2 (9214M)	Scrapped at Lyneham, August 1995
	XL163	HP80 Victor K2 (8916M)	Scrapped at Stock
	XL164	HP80 Victor K2 (9215M) <ff>	Vallance By-Ways, Charlwood, Surrey
	XL188	HP80 Victor K2 (9100M) (fuselage)	RAF Kinloss Fire Section
	XL190	HP80 Victor K2 (9216M)	RAF St Mawgan Fire Section
	XL192	HP80 Victor K2 (9024M)	Scrapped at Stock, 1996
	XL231	HP80 Victor K2	Yorkshire Air Museum, Elvington
	XL318	Avro 698 Vulcan B2 (8733M)	RAF Museum, Hendon
	XL319	Avro 698 Vulcan B2	North-East Aircraft Museum, Usworth
	XL360	Avro 698 Vulcan B2A	Midland Air Museum, Coventry
	XL388	Avro 698 Vulcan B2 <ff>	Blyth Valley Aviation Collection, Walpole
	XL391	Avro 698 Vulcan B2	Privately owned, Blackpool
	XL426	Avro 698 Vulcan B2 (G-VJET)	Vulcan Restoration Trust, Southend
	XL445	Avro 698 Vulcan K2 (8811M) <ff>	Blyth Valley Aviation Collection, Walpole
	XL449	Fairey Gannet AEW3 <ff>	Privately owned, Camberley, Surrey
	XL472	Fairey Gannet AEW3 [044/R]	Vallance By-Ways, Charlwood, Surrey
	XL497	Fairey Gannet AEW3 [041/R]	RN, Prestwick, on display
	XL500	Fairey Gannet AEW3 [CU]	RNAS Culdrose, on display
	XL502	Fairey Gannet AEW3 (8610M/ G-BMYP)	Privately owned, Sandtoft, S Yorks
	XL503	Fairey Gannet AEW3 [070/E]	FAA Museum, RNAS Yeovilton
	XL563	Hawker Hunter T7 (9218M)	Privately owned, on display Farnborough
	XL564	Hawker Hunter T7 [4]	MoD(PE)/ETPS, DTEO Boscombe Down
	XL565	Hawker Hunter T7 (parts of WT745)	Privately owned, Colsterworth, Lincs
	XL567	Hawker Hunter T7 (8723M) [84]	Privately owned, Exeter
	XL568	Hawker Hunter T7A (9224M) [C]	AMIF, RAFC Cranwell

Serial	Type (other identity) [code]	Owner/operator, location or fate	Notes
XL569	Hawker Hunter T7 (8833M) [80]	East Midlands Airport Aero Park	
XL572	Hawker Hunter T7 (G-HNTR) [83]	Yorkshire Air Museum, Elvington	
XL573	Hawker Hunter T7 (G-BVGH)	Classic Jet Aircraft Co, Exeter Airport	
XL577	Hawker Hunter T7 (8676M) [W]	Delta Engineering Aviation, Kemble	
XL578	Hawker Hunter T7 (fuselage)	Vintage Aircraft Team, Bruntingthorpe	
XL580	Hawker Hunter T8M [723]	FAAM, stored RNAS Yeovilton	
XL586	Hawker Hunter T7 <rf>	Privately owned, Colsterworth, Lincs	
XL587	Hawker Hunter T7 (8807M) [Z]	Privately owned, Duxford	
XL591	Hawker Hunter T7	Privately owned, Colsterworth, Lincs	
XL592	Hawker Hunter T7 (8836M) [Y]	Privately owned, Bruntingthorpe	
XL600	Hawker Hunter T7 (G-BVWN/ G-VETA) [Y/FL]	Jet Heritage Ltd, Bournemouth	
XL601	Hawker Hunter T7 [874/VL]	RNAS Culdrose, on display	
XL602	Hawker Hunter T8M (G-BWFT)	South West Aviation Heritage, Exeter	
XL603	Hawker Hunter T8M [724]	Privately owned, Bruntingthorpe	
XL612	Hawker Hunter T7 [2]	MoD(PE)/ETPS, DTEO Boscombe Down	
XL613	Hawker Hunter T7 (G-BVMB)	Classic Jet Aircraft Co, Exeter	
XL614	Hawker Hunter T7 (9235M)	*Sold to the USA as N614XL, May 1996*	
XL616	Hawker Hunter T7 (9223M/ G-BWIE)	Privately owned, Cranfield	
XL618	Hawker Hunter T7 (8892M) [05]	Caernarfon Air World	
XL621	Hawker Hunter T7 (G-BNCX)	Privately owned, Brooklands Museum	
XL623	Hawker Hunter T7 (8770M)	The Planets Leisure Centre, Woking	
XL629	EE Lightning T4	DTEO Boscombe Down, at main gate	
XL703	SAL Pioneer CC1 (8034M)	RAF Cosford Aerospace Museum, stored	
XL714	DH82A Tiger Moth II (T6099/ G-AOGR)	Privately owned, Swanton Morley	
XL728	WS58 Wessex HAS1	*Scrapped at Brawdy*	
XL735	Saro Skeeter AOP12	Privately owned	
XL738	Saro Skeeter AOP12 (7860M)	Museum of Army Flying, Middle Wallop	
XL739	Saro Skeeter AOP12	AAC Wattisham, instructional use	
XL762	Saro Skeeter AOP12 (8017M)	Royal Scottish Mus'm of Flight, E Fortune	
XL763	Saro Skeeter AOP12	Privately owned, Ottershaw	
XL764	Saro Skeeter AOP12 (7940M)	Newark Air Museum, Winthorpe	
XL765	Saro Skeeter AOP12	Privately owned, Clapham, Beds	
XL770	Saro Skeeter AOP12 (8046M)	Southampton Hall of Aviation	
XL809	Saro Skeeter AOP12 (G-BLIX)	Privately owned, Wilden, Beds	
XL811	Saro Skeeter AOP12	IHM, Weston-super-Mare	
XL812	Saro Skeeter AOP12 (G-SARO)	Privately owned, Old Buckenham	
XL813	Saro Skeeter AOP12	Museum of Army Flying, Middle Wallop	
XL814	Saro Skeeter AOP12	AAC Historic Aircraft Flight, Middle Wallop	
XL824	Bristol 171 Sycamore HR14 (8021M)	Gr Manchester Mus of Science & Industry	
XL829	Bristol 171 Sycamore HR14	Bristol Industrial Museum	
XL836	WS55 Whirlwind HAS7 [65]	RN, Predannack Fire School	
XL840	WS55 Whirlwind HAS7	Privately owned, Long Marston	
XL847	WS55 Whirlwind HAS7 [83]	AAC Middle Wallop Fire Section	
XL853	WS55 Whirlwind HAS7 [LS]	NARO, RNAY Fleetlands Museum	
XL875	WS55 Whirlwind HAR9	Air Service Training, Perth	
XL880	WS55 Whirlwind HAR9 [35]	*Burnt at Predannack by June 1996*	
XL929	Percival P66 Pembroke C1 (G-BNPU)	D-Day Museum, Shoreham Airport	
XL954	Percival P66 Pembroke C1 (9042M/N4234C)	Air Atlantique Historic Flight, Coventry	
XL993	SAL Twin Pioneer CC1 (8388M)	RAF Cosford Aerospace Museum	
XM135	BAC Lightning F1	Imperial War Museum, Duxford	
XM144	BAC Lightning F1 (8417M) <ff>	South West Aviation Heritage, Eaglescott	
XM169	BAC Lightning F1A (8422M) <ff>	N Yorks Aircraft Recovery Centre, Chop Gate	
XM172	BAC Lightning F1A (8427M) [B]	RAF Coltishall, gate guard	
XM173	BAC Lightning F1A (8414M) [A]	RAF Bentley Priory, at main gate	
XM191	BAC Lightning F1A (7854M/ 8590M) <ff>	RAF EP&TU, St Athan	
XM192	BAC Lightning F1A (8413M) [K]	Bomber County Air Museum, Hemswell	
XM223	DH104 Devon C2 (G-BWWC) [J]	Privately owned, Glasgow	
XM279	EE Canberra B(I)8 <ff>	Privately owned, Flixton	
XM300	WS58 Wessex HAS1	Welsh Industrial & Maritime Mus'm, Cardiff	
XM327	WS58 Wessex HAS3 [401/KE]	College of Nautical Studies, Warsash	
XM328	WS58 Wessex HAS3	SFDO, RNAS Culdrose	
XM330	WS58 Wessex HAS1	IHM, Weston-super-Mare	
XM349	Hunting Jet Provost T3A (9046M) [T]	Global Aviation	

Notes	Serial	Type (other identity) [code]	Owner/operator, location or fate
	XM350	Hunting Jet Provost T3A (9036M) [89]	South Yorkshire Avn Museum, Firbeck
	XM351	Hunting Jet Provost T3 (8078M) [Y]	RAF, stored Cosford
	XM355	Hunting Jet Provost T3 (8229M) [D]	Arbury College, Cambridge
	XM358	Hunting Jet Provost T3A (8987M) [53]	Privately owned, Colsterworth, Lincs
	XM362	Hunting Jet Provost T3 (8230M)	RAF No 1 SoTT, Cosford
	XM363	Hunting Jet Provost T3 <ff>	RAF Cranwell
	XM365	Hunting Jet Provost T3A [37]	Global Aviation, Binbrook
	XM367	Hunting Jet Provost T3 (8083M) [Z]	*Scrapped at Bruntingthorpe, April 1995*
	XM369	Hunting Jet Provost T3 (8084M) [C]	Privately owned, Portsmouth
	XM370	Hunting Jet Provost T3A (G-BVSP) [10]	Privately owned, Bruntingthorpe
	XM372	Hunting Jet Provost T3A (8917M) [55]	RAF Linton-on-Ouse Fire Section
	XM375	Hunting Jet Provost T3 (8231M) [B]	RAF Linton-on-Ouse Fire Section
	XM376	Hunting Jet Provost T3A (G-BWDR) [27]	Global Aviation, Binbrook
	XM378	Hunting Jet Provost T3A (G-BWZE) [34]	Global Aviation, Binbrook
	XM379	Hunting Jet Provost T3	AAC SEAE, Arborfield
	XM381	Hunting Jet Provost T3 (8232M) [A]	*Scrapped at Marham, February 1996*
	XM383	Hunting Jet Provost T3A [90]	Newark Air Museum, Winthorpe
	XM401	Hunting Jet Provost T3A [17]	
	XM402	Hunting Jet Provost T3 (8055AM) [J]	Fenland & W Norfolk Aviation Museum, Wisbech
	XM403	Hunting Jet Provost T3A (9048M)	RAF No 1 SoTT, Cosford
	XM404	Hunting Jet Provost T3 (8055BM)	FETC, Moreton-in-Marsh, Glos
	XM405	Hunting Jet Provost T3A (G-TORE) [42]	Kennet Aviation, Cranfield
	XM408	Hunting Jet Provost T3 (8333M) [D]	*Sold to the USA, 1995*
	XM409	Hunting Jet Provost T3 (8082M) <rf>	Air Scouts, Guernsey Airport
	XM410	Hunting Jet Provost T3 (8054AM) [B]	RAF North Luffenham Training Area
	XM412	Hunting Jet Provost T3A (9011M) [41]	Privately owned, Ipswich
	XM413	Hunting Jet Provost T3	AAC SEAE, Arborfield
	XM414	Hunting Jet Provost T3A (8996M)	Flight Experience Workshop, Belfast
	XM417	Hunting Jet Provost T3 (8054BM) [D] <ff>	Privately owned, Hednesford, Staffs
	XM419	Hunting Jet Provost T3A (8990M) [102]	RAF CTTS, St Athan
	XM424	Hunting Jet Provost T3A (G-BWDS)	Global Aviation, Binbrook
	XM425	Hunting Jet Provost T3A (8995M) [88]	ATC, King's Lynn, Norfolk
	XM426	Hunting Jet Provost T3 (XN511) [64] <ff>	Repainted as XN511
	XM455	Hunting Jet Provost T3A (8960M) [K]	Global Aviation, Binbrook
	XM459	Hunting Jet Provost T3A [F]	Global Aviation,
	XM463	Hunting Jet Provost T3A [38] (fuselage)	RAF Museum, Hendon
	XM464	Hunting Jet Provost T3A [23]	*Sold to the USA*
	XM465	Hunting Jet Provost T3A [55]	
	XM467	Hunting Jet Provost T3 (8085M)	*Sunk at Gildenburgh Lakes Diving Club, Cambs 1994*
	XM468	Hunting Jet Provost T3 (8081M)	Privately owned, King's Lynn
	XM470	Hunting Jet Provost T3A (G-BWZZ) [12]	Global Aviation, Binbrook
	XM471	Hunting Jet Provost T3A (8968M) [L,93]	RAF No 1 SoTT, Cosford
	XM473	Hunting Jet Provost T3A (8974M/ G-TINY)	Air UK, Norwich, instructional use
	XM474	Hunting Jet Provost T3 (8121M)	No 1330 Sqn ATC, Warrington
	XM475	Hunting Jet Provost T3A (9112M) [44]	FSCTE, RAF Manston
	XM478	Hunting Jet Provost T3A (8983M) [33]	Global Aviation, Binbrook
	XM479	Hunting Jet Provost T3A (G-BVEZ)	Privately owned, Newcastle
	XM480	Hunting Jet Provost T3 (8080M)	4x4 Car Centre, Chesterfield

Serial	Type (other identity) [code]	Owner/operator, location or fate	Notes
XM529	Saro Skeeter AOP12 (7979M/ G-BDNS)	Privately owned, Handforth	
XM553	Saro Skeeter AOP12 (G-AWSV)	Privately owned, Middle Wallop	
XM555	Saro Skeeter AOP12 (8027M)	RAF Cosford Aerospace Museum, stored	
XM561	Saro Skeeter AOP12 (7980M)	South Yorkshire Avn Museum, Firbeck	
XM564	Saro Skeeter AOP12	Royal Armoured Corps Museum, Bovington	
XM569	Avro 698 Vulcan B2 <ff>	Privately owned, Enstone	
XM575	Avro 698 Vulcan B2A (G-BLMC)	East Midlands Airport Aero Park	
XM594	Avro 698 Vulcan B2	Newark Air Museum, Winthorpe	
XM597	Avro 698 Vulcan B2	Royal Scottish Mus'm of Flight, E Fortune	
XM598	Avro 698 Vulcan B2 (8778M)	RAF Cosford Aerospace Museum	
XM602	Avro 698 Vulcan B2 (8771M) <ff>	Avro Aircraft Heritage Society, Woodford	
XM603	Avro 698 Vulcan B2	Avro Aircraft Heritage Society, Woodford	
XM607	Avro 698 Vulcan B2 (8779M)	RAF Waddington, on display	
XM612	Avro 698 Vulcan B2	City of Norwich Aviation Museum	
XM652	Avro 698 Vulcan B2 <ff>	Privately owned, Burntwood, Staffs	
XM655	Avro 698 Vulcan B2 (G-VULC)	Delta Engineering, Wellesbourne Mountford	
XM656	Avro 698 Vulcan B2 (8757M) <ff>	*Scrapped at Stock*	
XM660	WS55 Whirlwind HAS7 [78]	North-East Aircraft Museum, Usworth	
XM685	WS55 Whirlwind HAS7 (G-AYZJ) [513/PO]	Newark Air Museum, Winthorpe	
XM692	HS Gnat T1 <ff>	Robertsbridge Aviation Society, Mayfield	
XM693	HS Gnat T1 (7891M)	BAe Hamble on display	
XM693	HS Gnat T1 (8618M/XP504/ G-TIMM)	Kennet Aviation, Cranfield	
XM694	HS Gnat T1	Privately owned, Ipswich	
XM697	HS Gnat T1 (G-NAAT)	Jet Heritage Ltd, Bournemouth	
XM708	HS Gnat T1 (8573M)	Privately owned, Kings Langley, Herts	
XM709	HS Gnat T1 (8617M) [67]	Privately owned	
XM715	HP80 Victor K2	British Aviation Heritage, Bruntingthorpe	
XM717	HP80 Victor K2 <ff>	RAF Museum Rest'n Centre, Cardington	
XM819	Lancashire EP9 Prospector (G-APXW)	Museum of Army Flying, Middle Wallop	
XM833	WS58 Wessex HAS3	SWWAPS, Lasham	
XM843	WS58 Wessex HAS1 [527]	RN	
XM868	WS58 Wessex HAS1 [517]	RN, Predannack Fire School	
XM870	WS58 Wessex HAS3 [PO]	RN, Predannack Fire School	
XM874	WS58 Wessex HAS1 [521/CU]	RN, Predannack Fire School	
XM927	WS58 Wessex HAS3 (8814M) [660/PO]	RAF Shawbury Fire Section	
XN126	WS55 Whirlwind HAR10 (8655M) [S]	RAF Benson BDRT	
XN137	Hunting Jet Provost T3 <ff>	*Repainted as XN493*	
XN185	Slingsby T21B Sedburgh TX1 (BGA 4077)	RAFGSA, Syerston	
XN198	Slingsby T31B Cadet TX3	Privately owned, Challock Lees	
XN238	Slingsby T31B Cadet TX3 <ff>	Robertsbridge Aviation Society, Mayfield	
XN239	Slingsby T31B Cadet TX3 (8889M) [G]	Imperial War Museum, Duxford	
XN243	Slingsby T31B Cadet TX3 (BGA 3145)	RAFGSA, Bicester	
XN246	Slingsby T31B Cadet TX3	Southampton Hall of Aviation	
XN258	WS55 Whirlwind HAR9 [589/CU]	North-East Aircraft Museum, Usworth	
XN259	WS55 Whirlwind HAS7	London City Airport Fire Section	
XN263	WS55 Whirlwind HAS7	Privately owned,	
XN297	WS55 Whirlwind HAR9 (XN311) [12]	Privately owned, Hull	
XN298	WS55 Whirlwind HAR9 [810/LS]	International Fire Training Centre, Chorley	
XN299	WS55 Whirlwind HAS7 [ZZ]	Royal Marines' Museum, stored Portsmouth	
XN302	WS55 Whirlwind HAS7 (9037M)	Privately owned, Stock, Essex	
XN304	WS55 Whirlwind HAS7 [64]	Norfolk & Suffolk Avn Museum, Flixton	
XN332	Saro P531 (G-APNV) [759]	FAA Museum, stored Wroughton	
XN334	Saro P531	FAA Museum, stored Wroughton	
XN341	Saro Skeeter AOP12 (8022M)	Stondon Transport Museum & Garden Centre, Herts	
XN344	Saro Skeeter AOP12 (8018M)	Science Museum, South Kensington	
XN351	Saro Skeeter AOP12 (G-BKSC)	Privately owned, Shempston Fm, Lossiemouth	
XN359	WS55 Whirlwind HAR9 [34/ED]	RN	
XN380	WS55 Whirlwind HAS7	Lashenden Air Warfare Museum, Headcorn	
XN385	WS55 Whirlwind HAS7	Phoenix Aviation, Bruntingthorpe	

Notes	Serial	Type (other identity) [code]	Owner/operator, location or fate
	XN386	WS55 Whirlwind HAR9 [435/ED]	
	XN412	Auster AOP9	Cotswold Aircraft Rest'n Grp, Innsworth
	XN435	Auster AOP9 (G-BGBU)	Privately owned, Egham
	XN437	Auster AOP9 (G-AXWA)	Privately owned,
	XN441	Auster AOP9 (G-BGKT)	Auster 9 Group, Melton Mowbray
	XN458	Hunting Jet Provost T3 (8234M)	*Repainted as XN594*
	XN459	Hunting Jet Provost T3A (G-BWOT) [N]	Transair(UK) Ltd, North Weald
	XN461	Hunting Jet Provost T3A (G-BVBE) [28]	*Sold to France, August 1996*
	XN462	Hunting Jet Provost T3A [17]	Privately owned,
	XN466	Hunting Jet Provost T3A [29] <ff>	No 1005 Sqn ATC, Radcliffe, Gtr Manchester
	XN470	Hunting Jet Provost T3A [41]	Global Aviation, Binbrook
	XN472	Hunting Jet Provost T3A (8959M) [J,86]	*Sold as N3497, July 1996*
	XN473	Hunting Jet Provost T3A (8862M) [98] <ff>	
	XN492	Hunting Jet Provost T3 (8079M) <ff>	RAF Odiham Fire Section
	XN493	Hunting Jet Provost T3 (XN137) <ff>	Privately owned, Ottershaw
	XN494	Hunting Jet Provost T3A (9012M) [43]	AAC Middle Wallop Fire Section
	XN495	Hunting Jet Provost T3A (8786M) [102]	RAF
	XN497	Hunting Jet Provost T3A [52]	RAF St Athan
	XN498	Hunting Jet Provost T3A (G-BWSH) [16]	Global Aviation, Binbrook
	XN500	Hunting Jet Provost T3A [48]	CSE Ltd, Oxford, ground instruction
	XN501	Hunting Jet Provost T3A (8958M) [G]	Privately owned, Billockby, Norfolk
	XN503	Hunting Jet Provost T3 <ff>	No 1284 Sqn ATC, Milford Haven
	XN505	Hunting Jet Provost T3A [25]	
	XN508	Hunting Jet Provost T3A [47]	RAF St Athan
	XN509	Hunting Jet Provost T3A [50]	*Sold to the USA*
	XN510	Hunting Jet Provost T3A [40]	Global Aviation, Binbrook
	XN511	Hunting Jet Provost T3 (*XM426*) [64] <ff>	Robertsbridge Aviation Society, Mayfield
	XN512	Hunting Jet Provost T3 (8435M)	Phoenix Aviation, Bruntingthorpe
	XN549	Hunting Jet Provost T3 (8235M) [32,P]	RAF Shawbury Fire Section
	XN551	Hunting Jet Provost T3A (8984M)	RAF CTTS, St Athan
	XN554	Hunting Jet Provost T3 (8436M) [K]	RAF North Luffenham Training Area
	XN573	Hunting Jet Provost T3 [E] <ff>	Newark Air Museum, Winthorpe
	XN577	Hunting Jet Provost T3A (8956M) [89,F]	Privately owned, Billockby, Norfolk
	XN579	Hunting Jet Provost T3A (9137M) [14]	RAF North Luffenham Training Area
	XN582	Hunting Jet Provost T3A (8957M) [95,H]	Privately owned, Cambridge
	XN584	Hunting Jet Provost T3A (9014M) [E]	Phoenix Aviation, Bruntingthorpe
	XN586	Hunting Jet Provost T3A (9039M) [91,S]	Brooklands Technical College
	XN589	Hunting Jet Provost T3A (9143M) [46]	RAF Linton-on-Ouse, on display
	XN592	Hunting Jet Provost T3 <ff>	No 1105 Sqn ATC, Winchester
	XN593	Hunting Jet Provost T3A (8988M) [97,Q]	Privately owned, Billockby, Norfolk
	XN594	Hunting Jet Provost T3 (8077M) [W]	Privately owned,
	XN594	Hunting Jet Provost T3 (8234M/ XN458)	Privately owned, Storrington, West Sussex
	XN595	Hunting Jet Provost T3A [43]	*Sold to the USA, 1994*
	XN597	Hunting Jet Provost T3 (7984M) <ff>	No 1940 Sqn ATC, Levenshulme, Cheshire
	XN602	Hunting Jet Provost T3 (8088M)	FSCTE, RAF Manston
	XN607	Hunting Jet Provost T3 <ff>	N Yorks Aircraft Recovery Centre, Chop Gate
	XN629	Hunting Jet Provost T3A (G-BVEG) [49]	Transair (UK) Ltd, North Weald
	XN632	Hunting Jet Provost T3 (8352M)	Privately owned, Pershore, Worcs

Serial	Type (other identity) [code]	Owner/operator, location or fate	Notes
XN634	Hunting Jet Provost T3A <ff>	Privately owned, Ipswich	
XN634	Hunting Jet Provost T3A [53] <rf>	BAe Warton Fire Section	
XN636	Hunting Jet Provost T3A (9045M) [15]	Privately owned	
XN637	Hunting Jet Provost T3 (G-BKOU) [3]	Privately owned, North Weald	
XN641	Hunting Jet Provost T3A (8865M) [47]	*Burnt at Newton by November 1995*	
XN643	Hunting Jet Provost T3A (8704M) <ff>	*Burnt at Barkston Heath*	
XN647	DH110 Sea Vixen FAW2 [707/VL]	Flambards Village Theme Park, Helston	
XN649	DH110 Sea Vixen FAW2 [126]	MoD(PE), stored DRA Farnborough	
XN650	DH110 Sea Vixen FAW2 <ff>	Phoenix Aviation, stored Bruntingthorpe	
XN651	DH110 Sea Vixen FAW2 <ff>	Communications & Electronics Museum, Bletchley Park	
XN657	DH110 Sea Vixen D3 [TR-1]	Privately owned, Stock, Essex	
XN685	DH110 Sea Vixen FAW2 (8173M) [03/VL]	Midland Air Museum, Coventry	
XN688	DH110 Sea Vixen FAW2 (8141M) [511]	DRA Farnborough Fire Section	
XN691	DH110 Sea Vixen FAW2 (8143M) [247/H]	39 Restoration Group, North Weald	
XN692	DH110 Sea Vixen FAW2 [125/E]	*Scrapped at Stock, 1996*	
XN696	DH110 Sea Vixen FAW2 <ff>	Blyth Valley Aviation Collection, Walpole	
XN714	Hunting H126	RAF Cosford Aerospace Museum	
XN724	EE Lightning F2A (8513M) [F]	Privately owned, Newcastle-upon-Tyne	
XN726	EE Lightning F2A (8545M) <ff>	Privately owned, Rayleigh, Essex	
XN728	EE Lightning F2A (8546M) [V]	Privately owned, Balderton, Notts	
XN734	EE Lightning F3A (8346M/ G-BNCA) <ff>	Privately owned, Cranfield	
XN769	EE Lightning F2 (8402M) <ff>	Privately owned, Sidcup, Kent	
XN774	EE Lightning F2A (8551M) [F]	*Burnt at Coningsby by September 1995*	
XN776	EE Lightning F2A (8535M) [C]	Royal Scottish Mus'm of Flight, E Fortune	
XN795	EE Lightning F2A <ff>	Privately owned, Rayleigh, Essex	
XN817	AW660 Argosy C1	DTEO West Freugh Fire Section	
XN819	AW660 Argosy C1 (8205M) <ff>	Newark Air Museum, Winthorpe	
XN923	HS Buccaneer S1 [13]	Vallance By-Ways, Charlwood, Surrey	
XN928	HS Buccaneer S1 (8179M) <ff>	Phoenix Aviation, Bruntingthorpe	
XN929	HS Buccaneer S1 (8051M) <ff>	AMIF, RAFC Cranwell	
XN930	HS Buccaneer S1 (8180M) [632/LM] <ff>	*Scrapped at Stock*	
XN934	HS Buccaneer S1 [631] (fuselage)	RN, Predannack Fire School	
XN953	HS Buccaneer S1 (8182M)	RN, Predannack Fire School	
XN957	HS Buccaneer S1 [630/LM]	FAA Museum, stored RNAS Yeovilton	
XN964	HS Buccaneer S1 [613/LM]	Newark Air Museum, Winthorpe	
XN967	HS Buccaneer S1 <ff>	Muckleburgh Collection, Weybourne, Norfolk	
XN972	HS Buccaneer S1 (8183M/XN962) <ff>	RAF Cosford Aeropsace Museum	
XN974	HS Buccaneer S2A	Yorkshire Air Museum, Elvington	
XN979	HS Buccaneer S2 <ff>		
XP110	WS58 Wessex HAS3 <rf>	RNAY Fleetlands Apprentice School	
XP137	WS58 Wessex HAS3 [CU]	RN, Predannack Fire School	
XP140	WS58 Wessex HAS3 (8806M) [653/PO]	*Scrapped at Chilmark*	
XP142	WS58 Wessex HAS3	FAA Museum, stored Wroughton	
XP150	WS58 Wessex HAS3	FETC, Moreton-in-Marsh, Glos	
XP151	WS58 Wessex HAS1 [047/R]	RN, Predannack Fire School	
XP157	WS58 Wessex HAS1 [AN]	RNAS Yeovilton Fire Section	
XP158	WS58 Wessex HAS1 [522]	RN, Predannack Fire School	
XP159	WS58 Wessex HAS1 (8877M) [047/R]	Privately owned, Brands Hatch	
XP160	WS58 Wessex HAS1 [521/CU]	RN, Predannack Fire School	
XP165	WS Scout AH1	IHM, Weston-super-Mare	
XP166	WS Scout AH1 (G-APVL)	Privately owned, Old Buckenham	
XP190	WS Scout AH1	South Yorkshire Avn Museum, Firbeck	
XP191	WS Scout AH1	AAC Middle Wallop, BDRT	
XP226	Fairey Gannet AEW3 [073/E]	Newark Air Museum, Winthorpe	
XP241	Auster AOP9	Rebel Air Museum, Andrewsfield	
XP242	Auster AOP9 (G-BUCI)	AAC Historic Aircraft Flight, Middle Wallop	
XP244	Auster AOP9 (7864M/*M7922*)	AAC SEAE, Arborfield	
XP248	Auster AOP9 (7863M/*WZ679*)	Privately owned, Sandy, Beds	
XP254	Auster AOP11 (G-ASCC)	Privately owned, Turweston	

Notes	Serial	Type (other identity) [code]	Owner/operator, location or fate
	XP279	Auster AOP9 (G-BWKK)	Privately owned, Popham
	XP280	Auster AOP9	Snibston Discovery Park, Coalville
	XP281	Auster AOP9	Imperial War Museum, Duxford
	XP282	Auster AOP9 (G-BGTC)	*Badly damaged, Widmerpoll 7 October 1996*
	XP283	Auster AOP9 (7859M) (frame)	Privately owned, Baxterley, Warwickshire
	XP299	WS55 Whirlwind HAR10 (8726M)	RAF Cosford Aerospace Museum
	XP329	WS55 Whirlwind HAR10 (8791M) [V]	Privately owned, Tattershall Thorpe
	XP330	WS55 Whirlwind HAR10	CAA Fire School, Teesside Airport
	XP344	WS55 Whirlwind HAR10 (8764M) [X]	*Scrapped at North Luffenham by July 1996*
	XP345	WS55 Whirlwind HAR10 (8792M)	Melbourne Autos, Storwood, E Yorkshire
	XP346	WS55 Whirlwind HAR10 (8793M)	Privately owned, Long Marston
	XP350	WS55 Whirlwind HAR10	Flambards Village Theme Park, Helston
	XP351	WS55 Whirlwind HAR10 (8672M) [Z]	RAF Shawbury, on display
	XP353	WS55 Whirlwind HAR10 (8720M)	Privately owned, Brands Hatch
	XP354	WS55 Whirlwind HAR10 (8721M)	Privately owned, Cricklade, Wilts
	XP355	WS55 Whirlwind HAR10 (8463M/ G-BEBC)	City of Norwich Aviation Museum
	XP359	WS55 Whirlwind HAR10 (8447M)	*Scrapped at Coventry, April 1995*
	XP360	WS55 Whirlwind HAR10 [V]	Privately owned,
	XP361	WS55 Whirlwind HAR10 (8731M)	Phoenix Aviation, Bruntingthorpe
	XP395	WS55 Whirlwind HAR10 (8674M) [A]	Privately owned, Tattershall Thorpe
	XP398	WS55 Whirlwind HAR10 (8794M)	Vallance By-Ways, Charlwood, Surrey
	XP399	WS55 Whirlwind HAR10	Privately owned, Rettendon, Essex
	XP404	WS55 Whirlwind HAR10 (8682M)	IHM, Weston-super-Mare
	XP405	WS55 Whirlwind HAR10 (8656M) [Y]	
	XP411	AW660 Argosy C1 (8442M) [C]	RAF Cosford Aerospace Museum
	XP454	Slingsby T38 Grasshopper TX1	Wellingborough School, Wellingborough
	XP458	Slingsby T38 Grasshopper TX1	City of Norwich Aviation Museum
	XP463	Slingsby T38 Grasshopper TX1	Privately owned, stored Rufforth
	XP488	Slingsby T38 Grasshopper TX1	Fenland & W Norfolk Aviation Museum, stored Wisbech
	XP490	Slingsby T38 Grasshopper TX1	Ipswich School, Ipswich
	XP493	Slingsby T38 Grasshopper TX1	Privately owned, stored Aston Down
	XP494	Slingsby T38 Grasshopper TX1	The Real Aeroplane Company, Breighton
	XP502	HS Gnat T1 (8576M)	RAF CTTS, stored St Athan
	XP503	HS Gnat T1 (8568M) [73]	Phoenix Aviation, Bruntingthorpe
	XP505	HS Gnat T1	Science Museum, Wroughton
	XP516	HS Gnat T1 (8580M) [16]	DRA Structures Dept, Farnborough
	XP540	HS Gnat T1 (8608M) [62]	Phoenix Aviation, Bruntingthorpe
	XP542	HS Gnat T1 (8575M) [42]	Royal Military College of Science, Shrivenham
	XP547	Hunting Jet Provost T4 (8992M) [N,03]	Global Aviation, Binbrook
	XP556	Hunting Jet Provost T4 (9027M) [B]	Cranwell Aviation Heritage Centre
	XP557	Hunting Jet Provost T4 (8494M)	Bomber County Aviation Museum, Hemswell
	XP558	Hunting Jet Provost T4 (8627M) [20]	RAF St Athan Fire Section
	XP563	Hunting Jet Provost T4 (9028M) [C]	Witney Technical College, Oxon
	XP568	Hunting Jet Provost T4	Jet Avn Preservation Grp, Long Marston
	XP573	Hunting Jet Provost T4 (8236M) [19]	Jersey Airport Fire Section
	XP585	Hunting Jet Provost T4 (8407M) [24]	NE Wales Institute, Wrexham
	XP627	Hunting Jet Provost T4	North-East Aircraft Museum, Usworth
	XP629	Hunting Jet Provost T4 (9026M) [P]	RAF North Luffenham Training Area
	XP638	Hunting Jet Provost T4 (9034M) [A]	RAF Waddington, BDRT
	XP640	Hunting Jet Provost T4 (8501M) [D]	Yorkshire Air Museum, Elvington
	XP642	Hunting Jet Provost T4 (fuselage)	Phoenix Aviation, Bruntingthorpe
	XP672	Hunting Jet Provost T4 (8458M/ G-RAFI) [27]	Privately owned, Jurby, Isle of Man
	XP677	Hunting Jet Provost T4 (8587M) <ff>	No 2530 Sqn ATC, East Grinstead
	XP680	Hunting Jet Provost T4 (8460M)	FETC, Moreton-in-Marsh, Glos
	XP686	Hunting Jet Provost T4 (8401M/ 8502M) [G]	RAF North Luffenham Training Area
	XP688	Hunting Jet Provost T4 (9031M) [E]	Phoenix Aviation, Bruntingthorpe

Serial	Type (other identity) [code]	Owner/operator, location or fate	Notes
XP693	BAC Lightning F6 (G-FSIX)	Lightning Flying Club, Exeter Airport	
XP701	BAC Lightning F3 (8924M) <ff>	Robertsbridge Aviation Society, Mayfield	
XP703	BAC Lightning F3 <ff>	Lightning Preservation Grp, RAF Coltishall	
XP706	BAC Lightning F3 (8925M)	Lincs Lightning Pres'n Soc, Strubby	
XP741	BAC Lightning F3 (8939M) [AR]	*Burnt at Manston by August 1995*	
XP745	BAC Lightning F3 (8453M) <ff>	Greenford Haulage, West London	
XP772	DHC2 Beaver AL1 (G-BUCJ)	The Aircraft Restoration Co, Duxford	
XP775	DHC2 Beaver AL1	Privately owned	
XP806	DHC2 Beaver AL1	Privately owned, Cumbernauld	
XP820	DHC2 Beaver AL1	AAC Historic Aircraft Flight, Middle Wallop	
XP821	DHC2 Beaver AL1 [MCO]	Museum of Army Flying, Middle Wallop	
XP822	DHC2 Beaver AL1	Museum of Army Flying, Middle Wallop	
XP831	Hawker P.1127 (8406M)	Science Museum, South Kensington	
XP841	Handley-Page HP115	FAA Museum, RNAS Yeovilton	
XP846	WS Scout AH1 [B,H] (fuselage)	RE 39 Regiment, Waterbeach, instructional use	
XP847	WS Scout AH1	Museum of Army Flying, Middle Wallop	
XP848	WS Scout AH1	AAC Arborfield, on display	
XP849	WS Scout AH1	MoD(PE)/ETPS, DTEO Boscombe Down	
XP850	WS Scout AH1 (fuselage)	*Burnt at Dishforth*	
XP853	WS Scout AH1	AAC SEAE, Arborfield	
XP854	WS Scout AH1 (7898M/TAD043)	AAC SEAE, Arborfield	
XP855	WS Scout AH1	AAC SEAE, Arborfield	
XP856	WS Scout AH1	AAC Middle Wallop, BDRT	
XP857	WS Scout AH1	AAC Middle Wallop Fire Section	
XP883	WS Scout AH1	MoD(PE)/ETPS, DTEO Boscombe Down	
XP884	WS Scout AH1	AAC SEAE, Arborfield	
XP886	WS Scout AH1	AAC SEAE, Arborfield	
XP888	WS Scout AH1	AAC SEAE, Arborfield	
XP890	WS Scout AH1 [G] (fuselage)	AAC, stored RNAW Almondbank	
XP891	WS Scout AH1 [S]	*Sold to New Zealand as ZK-HZS, October 1995*	
XP893	WS Scout AH1	AAC, stored Middle Wallop	
XP899	WS Scout AH1 [D]	AAC SEAE, Arborfield	
XP902	WS Scout AH1	Army, Redford Barracks, Edinburgh, instructional use	
XP905	WS Scout AH1	AAC SEAE, Arborfield	
XP907	WS Scout AH1 (G-SROE)	Privately owned, Ipswich	
XP908	WS Scout AH1 [Y]	AAC, stored Sek Kong	
XP910	WS Scout AH1	AAC SEAE, Arborfield	
XP919	DH110 Sea Vixen FAW2 (8163M) [706/VL]	Blyth Valley Aviation Collection, Walpole	
XP924	DH110 Sea Vixen D3 (G-CVIX)	De Havilland Aviation, Swansea	
XP925	DH110 Sea Vixen FAW2 [752] <ff>	No 1268 Sqn ATC, Hazlemere	
XP956	DH110 Sea Vixen FAW2	Privately owned, Dunsfold	
XP980	Hawker P.1127	FAA Museum, RNAS Yeovilton	
XP984	Hawker P.1127	BAe Dunsfold (under restoration)	
XR137	AW660 Argosy E1	Caernarfon Air World	
XR220	BAC TSR2 (7933M)	RAF Cosford Aerospace Museum	
XR222	BAC TSR2	Imperial War Museum, Duxford	
XR232	Sud Alouette AH2 (F-WEIP)	Museum of Army Flying, Middle Wallop	
XR240	Auster AOP9 (G-BDFH)	Privately owned, Booker	
XR241	Auster AOP9 (G-AXRR)	The Aircraft Restoration Co, Duxford	
XR244	Auster AOP9	AAC Historic Aircraft Flight, Middle Wallop	
XR246	Auster AOP9 (7862M/G-AZBU)	Auster 9 Group, Melton Mowbray	
XR267	Auster AOP9 (G-BJXR)	Cotswold Aircraft Rest'n Grp, Innsworth	
XR271	Auster AOP9	Museum of Artillery, Woolwich	
XR371	SC5 Belfast C1	RAF Cosford Aerospace Museum	
XR379	Sud Alouette AH2	AAC Historic Aircraft Flight, Middle Wallop	
XR436	Saro Scout AH1	AAC Middle Wallop, BDRT	
XR453	WS55 Whirlwind HAR10 (8873M) [A]	RAF Odiham, on gate	
XR458	WS55 Whirlwind HAR10 (8662M) [H]	Museum of Army Flying, Middle Wallop	
XR485	WS55 Whirlwind HAR10 [Q]	Norfolk & Suffolk Avn Museum, Flixton	
XR486	WS55 Whirlwind HCC12 (8727M/ G-RWWW)	Privately owned, Redhill	
XR497	WS58 Wessex HC2 [F]	RAF No 72 Sqn, Aldergrove	
XR498	WS58 Wessex HC2 [X]	RAF No 72 Sqn, Aldergrove	
XR499	WS58 Wessex HC2 [W]	RAF No 60 Sqn, Benson	
XR501	WS58 Wessex HC2	RAF No 22 Sqn, C Flt, Valley	
XR502	WS58 Wessex HC2 [Z]	RAF No 60 Sqn, Benson	

Notes	Serial	Type (other identity) [code]	Owner/operator, location or fate
	XR503	WS58 Wessex HC2	MoD(PE)/ETPS, DTEO Boscombe Down
	XR504	WS58 Wessex HC2 [*Joker*]	RAF No 84 Sqn, Akrotiri
	XR505	WS58 Wessex HC2 [WA]	RAF No 2 FTS, Shawbury
	XR506	WS58 Wessex HC2 [V]	RAF No 60 Sqn, Benson
	XR507	WS58 Wessex HC2	RAF, stored NARO, RNAY Fleetlands
	XR508	WS58 Wessex HC2 [B]	RAF No 60 Sqn, Benson
	XR511	WS58 Wessex HC2 [L]	RAF No 60 Sqn, Benson
	XR515	WS58 Wessex HC2 [B]	RAF, Kai Tak/*Uruguay AF from June 1997*
	XR516	WS58 Wessex HC2 [WB]	RAF No 2 FTS, Shawbury
	XR517	WS58 Wessex HC2 [N]	RAF No 60 Sqn, Benson
	XR518	WS58 Wessex HC2 [O]	RAF No 60 Sqn, Benson
	XR520	WS58 Wessex HC2	RAF No 22 Sqn, C Flt, Valley
	XR521	WS58 Wessex HC2 [WD]	RAF No 2 FTS, Shawbury
	XR522	WS58 Wessex HC2 [A]	RAF, Kai Tak/*Uruguay AF from June 1997*
	XR523	WS58 Wessex HC2 [M]	RAF No 60 Sqn, Benson
	XR525	WS58 Wessex HC2 [G]	RAF No 72 Sqn, Aldergrove
	XR526	WS58 Wessex HC2 (8147M)	Westlands, Yeovil, instructional use
	XR527	WS58 Wessex HC2 [K]	RAF No 72 Sqn, Aldergrove
	XR528	WS58 Wessex HC2 [T]	RAF HMF, St Mawgan, *instructional use*
	XR529	WS58 Wessex HC2 [E]	RAF No 72 Sqn, Aldergrove
	XR534	HS Gnat T1 (8578M) [65]	RAF Valley
	XR535	HS Gnat T1 (8569M) [05]	RAF Halton
	XR537	HS Gnat T1 (8642M/G-NATY) [T]	Jet Heritage Ltd, Bournemouth
	XR538	HS Gnat T1 (8621M/G-RORI) [69]	Gosh That's Aviation Ltd, North Weald
	XR569	HS Gnat T1 (8560M) [08]	Phoenix Aviation, Bruntingthorpe
	XR571	HS Gnat T1 (8493M)	RAF *Red Arrows*, Cranwell, on display
	XR574	HS Gnat T1 (8631M) [72]	RAF No 1 SoTT, Cosford
	XR588	WS58 Wessex HC2 [*Hearts*]	RAF No 84 Sqn, Akrotiri
	XR595	WS Scout AH1 (G-BWHU) [M]	Privately owned, Plymouth
	XR597	WS Scout AH1	AAC SEAE, Arborfield
	XR600	WS Scout AH1 (fuselage)	AAC Middle Wallop, BDRT
	XR601	WS Scout AH1	AAC SEAE, Arborfield
	XR627	WS Scout AH1 [X]	AAC SEAE, Arborfield
	XR628	WS Scout AH1	AAC, stored RNAW Almondbank
	XR629	WS Scout AH1 (fuselage)	AAC, stored RNAW Almondbank
	XR630	WS Scout AH1 [U]	AAC Middle Wallop, BDRT
	XR632	WS Scout AH1	Privately owned, Hawarden
	XR635	WS Scout AH1	AAC SEAE, Arborfield
	XR639	WS Scout AH1 [X] (fuselage)	AAC
	XR650	Hunting Jet Provost T4 (8459M) [28]	DTEO Boscombe Down, GI use
	XR651	Hunting Jet Provost T4 (8431M) [A]	
	XR654	Hunting Jet Provost T4 [34]	Macclesfield Hist Avn Society, Barton
	XR658	Hunting Jet Provost T4 (8192M)	NE Wales Institute, Connah's Quay, Clwyd
	XR662	Hunting Jet Provost T4 (8410M) [25]	*Sold to the USA, 1996*
	XR670	Hunting Jet Provost T4 (8498M)	*Scrapped at Stock, 1996*
	XR672	Hunting Jet Provost T4 (8495M) [50]	RAF Halton Fire Section
	XR673	Hunting Jet Provost T4 (9032M) [L]	Gosh That's Aviation Ltd, North Weald
	XR679	Hunting Jet Provost T4 (8991M/ G-BWGT) [M,04]	*Repainted as G-BWGT*
	XR681	Hunting Jet Provost T4 (8588M) <ff>	No 1216 Sqn ATC, Newhaven, E Sussex
	XR700	Hunting Jet Provost T4 (8589M) <ff>	RAF EP&TU, Aldergrove
	XR713	BAC Lightning F3 (8935M) [C]	RAF Leuchars, on display
	XR718	BAC Lightning F6 (8932M) [DA]	Blyth Valley Aviation Collection, Walpole
	XR724	BAC Lightning F6 (G-BTSY)	The Lightning Association, Binbrook
	XR725	BAC Lightning F6	Privately owned, Binbrook
	XR726	BAC Lightning F6 <ff>	Privately owned, Harrogate
	XR728	BAC Lightning F6 [JS]	Lightning Preservation Grp, Bruntingthorpe
	XR747	BAC Lightning F6 <ff>	Lightning Flying Club, Plymouth
	XR749	BAC Lightning F3 (8934M) [DA]	Tees-side Airport, on display
	XR751	BAC Lightning F3	Privately owned, Lower Tremar, Cornwall
	XR753	BAC Lightning F6 (8969M) [BP]	RAF Leeming on display
	XR754	BAC Lightning F6 (8972M) <ff>	Blyth Valley Aviation Collection, Walpole
	XR755	BAC Lightning F6	Privately owned, Callington, Cornwall
	XR757	BAC Lightning F6 <ff>	NATO Aircraft Museum, New Waltham, Humberside
	XR759	BAC Lightning F6 <ff>	Privately owned, Haxey, Lincs
	XR770	BAC Lightning F6 [AA]	NATO Aircraft Museum, New Waltham, Humberside

Serial	Type (other identity) [code]	Owner/operator, location or fate	Notes
XR771	BAC Lightning F6 [BM]	Midland Air Museum, Coventry	
XR773	BAC Lightning F6 (G-OPIB)	Lightning Flying Club, Exeter Airport	
XR777	WS Scout AH1 (really XT625)	AAC, stored Middle Wallop	
XR806	BAC VC10 C1K	RAF No 10 Sqn, Brize Norton	
XR807	BAC VC10 C1K	RAF No 10 Sqn, Brize Norton	
XR808	BAC VC10 C1K	RAF No 10 Sqn, Brize Norton	
XR810	BAC VC10 C1K	RAF No 10 Sqn, Brize Norton	
XR944	Wallis WA116 (G-ATTB)	RAF Museum, Hendon	
XR953	HS Gnat T1 (8609M) [63]	*Sold to the USA as N953RH, February 1996*	
XR954	HS Gnat T1 (8570M) [30]	Privately owned, Ipswich	
XR955	HS Gnat T1 [SAH-2]	Privately owned, Leavesden	
XR977	HS Gnat T1 (8640M) [3]	RAF Cosford Aerospace Museum	
XR985	HS Gnat T1 (7886M)	Vintage Aircraft Team, Bruntingthorpe	
XR991	HS Gnat T1 (8624M/XS102/ G-MOUR)	Intrepid Aviation Co, North Weald	
XR993	HS Gnat T1 (8620M/XP534/ G-BVPP)	Kennet Aviation, Cranfield	
XS100	HS Gnat T1 (8561M) [57]	Privately owned, Ipswich	
XS101	HS Gnat T1 (8638M) (G-GNAT)	Privately owned, Cranfield	
XS122	WS58 Wessex HAS3 [655/PO]	RN	
XS128	WS58 Wessex HAS1 [37]	RNAS Yeovilton Fire Section	
XS149	WS58 Wessex HAS3 [661/GL]	IHM, Weston-super-Mare	
XS165	Hiller UH12E (G-ASAZ) [37]	Privately owned, Luton	
XS176	Hunting Jet Provost T4 (8514M) [N]	University of Salford, Manchester	
XS177	Hunting Jet Provost T4 (9044M) [N]	RAF Valley Fire Section	
XS179	Hunting Jet Provost T4 (8237M) [20]	University of Salford, Manchester	
XS180	Hunting Jet Provost T4 (8238M) [21]	RAF Lyneham (dismantled)	
XS181	Hunting Jet Provost T4 (9033M) [F]	Phoenix Aviation, Bruntingthorpe	
XS183	Hunting Jet Provost T4 <ff>	Imperial War Museum, stored Duxford	
XS186	Hunting Jet Provost T4 (8408M) [M]	RAF North Luffenham Training Area	
XS209	Hunting Jet Provost T4 (8409M) [29]	Gloucestershire Avn Coll, Staverton	
XS215	Hunting Jet Provost T4 (8507M) [17]		
XS216	Hunting Jet Provost T4 <ff>	RAF	
XS217	Hunting Jet Provost T4 (9029M) [O]	Privately owned, Bruntingthorpe	
XS218	Hunting Jet Provost T4 (8508M) <ff>	No 447 Sqn ATC, Henley-on-Thames, Berks	
XS230	BAC Jet Provost T5P (G-BVWF)	*Repainted as G-VIVM*	
XS231	BAC Jet Provost T5 (G-ATAJ)	Phoenix Aviation, Bruntingthorpe	
XS235	DH106 Comet 4C	MoD(PE)/HATS, DTEO Boscombe Down	
XS416	BAC Lightning T5 <ff>	NATO Aircraft Museum, New Waltham, Humberside	
XS417	BAC Lightning T5	Newark Air Museum, Winthorpe	
XS420	BAC Lightning T5	Fenland & W Norfolk Aviation Museum, Wisbech	
XS421	BAC Lightning T5 <ff>	Privately owned, Rayleigh, Essex	
XS422	BAC Lightning T5	Privately owned, Southampton Docks	
XS451	BAC Lightning T5 (8503M/G-LTNG)	Lightning Flying Club, Plymouth	
XS452	BAC Lightning T5 (G-BPFE) [BT]	*Sold to South Africa as ZU-BBD, September 1996*	
XS456	BAC Lightning T5	Privately owned, Wainfleet	
XS457	BAC Lightning T5 <ff>	NATO Aircraft Museum, New Waltham, Humberside	
XS458	BAC Lightning T5	T5 Projects, Cranfield	
XS459	BAC Lightning T5 [AW]	Fenland & W Norfolk Aviation Museum, Wisbech	
XS463	WS Wasp HAS1 (XT431)	IHM, Weston-super-Mare	
XS463	WS Wasp HAS1	RN, Predannack Fire School	
XS479	WS58 Wessex HU5 (8819M) [XF]	JATE, RAF Brize Norton	
XS481	WS58 Wessex HU5	AAC Dishforth, BDRT	
XS482	WS58 Wessex HU5 [A/D]	FSCTE, RAF Manston	
XS483	WS58 Wessex HU5 [T/VL]		
XS484	WS58 Wessex HU5 [821/CU]	Privately owned, Stock, Essex	
XS485	WS58 Wessex HC5C [*Hearts*]	*Scrapped at Shawbury by May 1996*	
XS486	WS58 Wessex HU5 [524/CU,F]	RN Recruiting Team, Wroughton	
XS488	WS58 Wessex HU5 (9056M) [XK]	AAC Wattisham, instructional use	
XS489	WS58 Wessex HU5 [R]		

Notes	Serial	Type (other identity) [code]	Owner/operator, location or fate
	XS491	WS58 Wessex HU5 [XM]	RAF No 16 MU Stafford Fire Section
	XS492	WS58 Wessex HU5 [623]	RN, stored
	XS493	WS58 Wessex HU5	RN, stored Fleetlands
	XS496	WS58 Wessex HU5 [625/PO]	RN AES, *HMS Sultan*, Gosport
	XS498	WS58 Wessex HC5C [*Joker*]	*Scrapped at Shawbury by May 1996*
	XS507	WS58 Wessex HU5 [627/PO]	RN AES, *HMS Sultan*, Gosport
	XS508	WS58 Wessex HU5	FAA Museum, RNAS Yeovilton
	XS509	WS58 Wessex HU5	MoD(PE)/ETPS, DTEO Boscombe Down
	XS510	WS58 Wessex HU5 [626/PO]	RN AES, *HMS Sultan*, Gosport
	XS511	WS58 Wessex HU5 [M]	RN AES, *HMS Sultan*, Gosport
	XS513	WS58 Wessex HU5 [419/PO]	RN AES, *HMS Sultan*, Gosport, BDRT
	XS514	WS58 Wessex HU5 [L]	RN AES, *HMS Sultan*, Gosport
	XS515	WS58 Wessex HU5 [N]	RN AES, *HMS Sultan*, Gosport
	XS516	WS58 Wessex HU5 [Q]	RN
	XS517	WS58 Wessex HC5C [*Diamonds*]	*Scrapped at Shawbury by May 1996*
	XS520	WS58 Wessex HU5 [F]	RN AES, *HMS Sultan*, Gosport
	XS521	WS58 Wessex HU5	Army, Saighton, Cheshire
	XS522	WS58 Wessex HU5 [ZL]	RN
	XS523	WS58 Wessex HU5 [824/CU]	
	XS527	WS Wasp HAS1	FAA Museum, RNAS Yeovilton
	XS529	WS Wasp HAS1 [461]	RN, Predannack Fire School
	XS535	WS Wasp HAS1 [432]	*Scrapped*
	XS539	WS Wasp HAS1 [435]	RNAY Fleetlands Apprentice School
	XS545	WS Wasp HAS1 [635]	
	XS567	WS Wasp HAS1 [434/E]	Imperial War Museum, Duxford
	XS568	WS Wasp HAS1 [441]	RNAY Fleetlands Apprentice School
	XS569	WS Wasp HAS1	RNAY Fleetlands Apprentice School
	XS570	WS Wasp HAS1 [445/P]	Warship Preservation Trust, Birkenhead
	XS572	WS Wasp HAS1 (8845M) [414]	RAF No 16 MU Stafford Fire Section
	XS576	DH110 Sea Vixen FAW2 [125/E]	Imperial War Museum, Duxford
	XS577	DH110 Sea Vixen D3 <ff>	Phoenix Aviation, stored Bruntingthorpe
	XS587	DH110 Sea Vixen FAW(TT)2 (8828M/G-VIXN)	Vallance By-Ways, Charlwood, Surrey
	XS590	DH110 Sea Vixen FAW2 [131/E]	FAA Museum, RNAS Yeovilton
	XS596	HS Andover C1(PR)	MoD(PE)/HATS, DTEO Boscombe Down
	XS598	HS Andover C1 (fuselage)	FETC, Moreton-in-Marsh, Glos
	XS603	HS Andover E3	*Sold as P4-PVS, October 1996*
	XS605	HS Andover E3	RAF Northolt Fire Section
	XS606	HS Andover C1	*Sold as 9Q-CPW, October 1996*
	XS607	HS Andover C1 (G-BEBY)	DTEO Boscombe Down, wfu
	XS610	HS Andover E3	*Sold as P4-BLL, October 1996*
	XS639	HS Andover E3A	RAF Cosford Aerospace Museum
	XS640	HS Andover E3	*Sold as P4-TBL, October 1996*
	XS641	HS Andover C1(PR) (9198M) [Z]	RAF No 1 SoTT, Cosford
	XS643	HS Andover E3A	DTEO Boscombe Down Fire Section
	XS646	HS Andover C1(mod)	MoD(PE)/DRA, DTEO Boscombe Down
	XS652	Slingsby T45 Swallow TX1 (BGA 1107)	Privately owned, Rufforth
	XS674	WS58 Wessex HC2 [R]	RAF No 60 Sqn, Benson
	XS675	WS58 Wessex HC2 [*Spades*]	RAF No 84 Sqn, Akrotiri
	XS676	WS58 Wessex HC2 [WJ]	RAF No 2 FTS, Shawbury
	XS677	WS58 Wessex HC2 [WK]	RAF No 2 FTS, Shawbury
	XS679	WS58 Wessex HC2 [WG]	RAF No 2 FTS, Shawbury
	XS695	HS Kestrel FGA1	RAF Museum Rest'n Centre, Cardington
	XS709	HS125 Dominie T2 [M]	RAF No 3 FTS/55(R) Sqn, Cranwell
	XS710	HS125 Dominie T1 [O]	RAF No 1 SoTT, Cosford
	XS711	HS125 Dominie T2 [L]	RAF No 3 FTS/55(R) Sqn, Cranwell
	XS712	HS125 Dominie T2 [A]	RAF No 3 FTS/55(R) Sqn, Cranwell
	XS713	HS125 Dominie T2 [C]	RAF No 3 FTS/55(R) Sqn, Cranwell
	XS714	HS125 Dominie T1 (9246M) [P]	FSCTE, RAF Manston
	XS726	HS125 Dominie T1 [T]	RAF No 1 SoTT, Cosford
	XS727	HS125 Dominie T2 [D]	RAF No 3 FTS/55(R) Sqn, Cranwell
	XS728	HS125 Dominie T2 [E]	MoD(PE)/HATS, DTEO Boscombe Down
	XS729	HS125 Dominie T1 [G]	RAF No 3 FTS/55(R) Sqn, Cranwell
	XS730	HS125 Dominie T2 [H]	RAF No 3 FTS/55(R) Sqn, Cranwell
	XS731	HS125 Dominie T2 [J]	RAF No 3 FTS/55(R) Sqn, Cranwell
	XS732	HS125 Dominie T1 [B] (fuselage)	DERA, Fort Halstead, Kent
	XS733	HS125 Dominie T1 [Q]	RAF No 3 FTS/55(R) Sqn, Cranwell
	XS734	HS125 Dominie T1 [N]	RAF No 1 SoTT, Cosford
	XS735	HS125 Dominie T1 [R]	RAF Cranwell, instructional use
	XS736	HS125 Dominie T2 [S]	RAF No 3 FTS/55(R) Sqn, Cranwell
	XS737	HS125 Dominie T2 [K]	RAF No 3 FTS/55(R) Sqn, Cranwell
	XS738	HS125 Dominie T1 [U]	RAF No 3 FTS/55(R) Sqn, Cranwell

Serial	Type (other identity) [code]	Owner/operator, location or fate	Notes
XS739	HS125 Dominie T2 [F]	RAF No 3 FTS/55(R) Sqn, Cranwell	
XS743	Beagle B206Z Basset CC1	MoD(PE)/ETPS, DTEO Boscombe Down	
XS765	Beagle B206Z Basset CC1 (G-BSET)	Privately owned, Cranfield	
XS770	Beagle B206Z Basset CC1 (G-HRHI)	Privately owned, Cranfield	
XS790	HS748 Andover CC2	MoD(PE)/DRA, DTEO Boscombe Down	
XS791	HS748 Andover CC2	Phoenix Aviation, Bruntingthorpe	
XS793	HS748 Andover CC2 (9178M) [Y]	RAF No 1 SoTT, Cosford	
XS862	WS58 Wessex HAS3	NB&C Defence Centre, Winterbourne Gunner	
XS863	WS58 Wessex HAS1	Imperial War Museum, Duxford	
XS866	WS58 Wessex HAS1 [520/CU]	RN AES, *HMS Sultan*, Gosport, BDRT	
XS868	WS58 Wessex HAS1	RN AES, *HMS Sultan*, Gosport, BDRT	
XS870	WS58 Wessex HAS1 [PO]	RN Portland Fire Section	
XS871	WS58 Wessex HAS1 (8457M) [AI]	RAF Odiham Fire Section	
XS872	WS58 Wessex HAS1 [572/CU]	RNAY Fleetlands Apprentice School	
XS876	WS58 Wessex HAS1 [523]	RN AES, *HMS Sultan*, Gosport	
XS877	WS58 Wessex HAS1 [516/PO]	RN, Predannack Fire School	
XS881	WS58 Wessex HAS1 [046/CU]	RNAS Yeovilton, BDRT	
XS885	WS58 Wessex HAS1 [12/CU]	SFDO, RNAS Culdrose	
XS886	WS58 Wessex HAS1 [527/CU]	Sea Scouts, Evesham, Worcs	
XS887	WS58 Wessex HAS1 [403/FI]	Flambards Village Theme Park, Helston	
XS888	WS58 Wessex HAS1 [521]	Guernsey Airport Fire Section	
XS897	BAC Lightning F6	South Yorkshire Avn Museum, Firbeck	
XS898	BAC Lightning F6 <ff>	Privately owned, Lavendon, Bucks	
XS899	BAC Lightning F6 <ff>	RAF Coltishall	
XS903	BAC Lightning F6 [BA]	Yorkshire Air Museum, Elvington	
XS904	BAC Lightning F6 [BQ]	Lightning Preservation Grp, Bruntingthorpe	
XS919	BAC Lightning F6	Privately owned, Torpoint, Devon	
XS922	BAC Lightning F6 (8973M) <ff>	The Air Defence Collection, Salisbury	
XS923	BAC Lightning F6 <ff>	Privately owned, Welshpool	
XS925	BAC Lightning F6 (8961M) [BA]	RAF Museum, Hendon	
XS928	BAC Lightning F6 [AD]	BAe Warton	
XS932	BAC Lightning F6 <ff>	Privately owned, Shoreham	
XS933	BAC Lightning F6 <ff>	Privately owned, Terrington St Clement	
XS936	BAC Lightning F6	Castle Motors, Liskeard, Cornwall	
XT108	Agusta-Bell 47G-3 Sioux AH1 [U]	Museum of Army Flying, Middle Wallop	
XT123	Agusta-Bell 47G-3 Sioux AH1 (7883M/XT150) [D]	AAC Middle Wallop, at main gate	
XT131	Agusta-Bell 47G-3 Sioux AH1 [B]	AAC Historic Aircraft Flight, Middle Wallop	
XT133	Agusta-Bell 47G-3 Sioux AH1 (7923M)	Royal Engineers' Museum, Chatham, stored	
XT140	Agusta-Bell 47G-3 Sioux AH1	Air Service Training, Perth	
XT148	Agusta-Bell 47G-3 Sioux AH1	IHM, stored Weston-super-Mare	
XT151	WS Sioux AH1 [W]	Museum of Army Flying, stored Middle Wallop	
XT175	WS Sioux AH1 (TAD175)	CSE Oxford for ground instruction	
XT176	WS Sioux AH1 [U]	FAA Museum, stored Wroughton	
XT190	WS Sioux AH1	IHM, Weston-super-Mare	
XT200	WS Sioux AH1 [F]	Newark Air Museum, Winthorpe	
XT236	WS Sioux AH1 (frame only)	North-East Aircraft Museum, stored Usworth	
XT242	WS Sioux AH1 (composite) [12]	The Aeroplane Collection, Firbeck	
XT255	WS58 Wessex HAS3 (8751M)	RAF No 14 MU, Carlisle, BDRT	
XT257	WS58 Wessex HAS3 (8719M)	RAF No 1 SoTT, Cosford	
XT272	HS Buccaneer S2	DRA Farnborough Fire Section	
XT277	HS Buccaneer S2A (8853M) <ff>	Privately owned, Welshpool	
XT280	HS Buccaneer S2A <ff>	Dundonald Aviation Centre, Strathclyde	
XT284	HS Buccaneer S2A (8855M)	RAF St Athan, BDRT	
XT288	HS Buccaneer S2B (9134M)	Royal Scottish Museum of Flight, stored E Fortune	
XT420	WS Wasp HAS1 [606]	Privately owned,	
XT422	WS Wasp HAS1 [324]	Privately owned, Burgess Hill	
XT427	WS Wasp HAS1 [606]	FAA Museum, at Flambards Village Theme Park, Helston	
XT434	WS Wasp HAS1 [455]	RNAY Fleetlands Apprentice School	
XT437	WS Wasp HAS1 [423]		
XT439	WS Wasp HAS1 [605]	Privately owned, King's Lynn	
XT443	WS Wasp HAS1 [422/AU]	IHM, Weston-super-Mare	
XT449	WS58 Wessex HU5 [C]	RN, Predannack Fire School	

Notes	Serial	Type (other identity) [code]	Owner/operator, location or fate
	XT450	WS58 Wessex HU5	RN, Predannack Fire School
	XT453	WS58 Wessex HU5 [A/B]	RN AES, *HMS Sultan*, Gosport
	XT455	WS58 Wessex HU5 [U]	RN AES, *HMS Sultan*, Gosport
	XT456	WS58 Wessex HU5 (8941M) [XZ]	RAF Aldergrove, BDRT
	XT458	WS58 Wessex HU5 [622]	RN AES, *HMS Sultan*, Gosport
	XT460	WS58 Wessex HU5 [K]	*Scrapped at Lee-on-Solent, 1995*
	XT463	WS58 Wessex HC5C [*Clubs*]	*Scrapped at Shawbury by May 1996*
	XT466	WS58 Wessex HU5 (8921M) [XV]	
	XT467	WS58 Wessex HU5 (8922M) [BF]	RAF Odiham Fire Section
	XT468	WS58 Wessex HU5 [628]	RN
	XT469	WS58 Wessex HU5 (8920M)	RAF No 16 MU, Stafford, ground instruction
	XT470	WS58 Wessex HU5 [A]	*Burnt at Netheravon*
	XT471	WS58 Wessex HU5	AAC Dishforth, BDRT
	XT472	WS58 Wessex HU5 [XC]	IHM, Weston-super-Mare
	XT475	WS58 Wessex HU5 (9108M) [624]	FSCTE, RAF Manston
	XT480	WS58 Wessex HU5 [468/RG]	NARO, RNAY Fleetlands, on display
	XT481	WS58 Wessex HU5	RN, Predannack Fire School
	XT482	WS58 Wessex HU5 [ZM/VL]	FAA Museum, RNAS Yeovilton
	XT484	WS58 Wessex HU5 [H]	RN AES, *HMS Sultan*, Gosport
	XT485	WS58 Wessex HU5	RN AES, *HMS Sultan*, Gosport
	XT486	WS58 Wessex HU5 (8919M) [XR]	RAF JATE, preserved Brize Norton
	XT550	WS Sioux AH1 [D]	AAC Wattisham, on display
	XT575	Vickers Viscount 837 <ff>	Brooklands Museum, Weybridge
	XT595	McD F-4K Phantom FG1 (8851M) <ff>	RAF EP&TU, St Athan
	XT596	McD F-4K Phantom FG1	FAA Museum, RNAS Yeovilton
	XT597	McD F-4K Phantom FG1	DTEO Boscombe Down, for lightning tests
	XT601	WS58 Wessex HC2	RAF Shawbury, spares recovery
	XT602	WS58 Wessex HC2	RAF, stored NARO, RNAY Fleetlands
	XT603	WS58 Wessex HC2 [WF]	RAF No 2 FTS, Shawbury
	XT604	WS58 Wessex HC2	RAF, stored NARO, RNAY Fleetlands
	XT605	WS58 Wessex HC2 [E]	RAF, Kai Tak/*Uruguay AF from June 1997*
	XT606	WS58 Wessex HC2 [WL]	RAF No 2 FTS, Shawbury
	XT607	WS58 Wessex HC2 [P]	RAF No 72 Sqn, Aldergrove
	XT616	WS Scout AH1 (fuselage)	AAC
	XT617	WS Scout AH1	AAC Wattisham, instructional use
	XT620	WS Scout AH1	AAC Dishforth Fire Section
	XT621	WS Scout AH1	R. Military College of Science, Shrivenham
	XT623	WS Scout AH1	AAC SEAE, Arborfield
	XT624	WS Scout AH1 [D]	Privately owned, Lincolnshire
	XT626	WS Scout AH1 [Q]	AAC Historic Aircraft Flt, Middle Wallop
	XT630	WS Scout AH1 [X]	Privately owned, Colsterworth, Lincs
	XT631	WS Scout AH1 [D]	DTEO Boscombe Down (spares use)
	XT632	WS Scout AH1	Privately owned, Hawarden
	XT633	WS Scout AH1	AAC SEAE, Arborfield
	XT634	WS Scout AH1 [T]	Privately owned, Hawarden
	XT637	WS Scout AH1 (fuselage)	*Scrapped at Yeovilton, 1994*
	XT638	WS Scout AH1 [N]	AAC Middle Wallop, at gate
	XT639	WS Scout AH1 [Y] (fuselage)	AAC
	XT640	WS Scout AH1	AAC SEAE, Arborfield
	XT642	WS Scout AH1 (fuselage)	AAC
	XT643	WS Scout AH1 [Z]	RE 39 Regiment, Waterbeach, instructional use
	XT644	WS Scout AH1 [Y]	Privately owned, Hawarden
	XT645	WS Scout AH1 (fuselage)	AAC Thorney Island, BDRT
	XT646	WS Scout AH1 [Z]	*Sold to New Zealand as ZK-HYS*
	XT649	WS Scout AH1	Privately owned,
	XT661	Vickers Viscount 838 <ff>	*Scrapped at Stock*
	XT668	WS58 Wessex HC2 [S]	RAF No 72 Sqn, Aldergrove
	XT669	WS58 Wessex HC2 (8894M) [T]	*Burnt at Aldergrove*
	XT670	WS58 Wessex HC2	RAF SARTU, Valley
	XT671	WS58 Wessex HC2 [D]	RAF No 60 Sqn, Benson
	XT672	WS58 Wessex HC2 [WE]	RAF No 2 FTS, Shawbury
	XT673	WS58 Wessex HC2 [G]	RAF, Kai Tak/*Uruguay AF from June 1997*
	XT675	WS58 Wessex HC2 [C]	RAF, Kai Tak/*Uruguay AF from June 1997*
	XT676	WS58 Wessex HC2 [I]	RAF No 72 Sqn, Aldergrove
	XT677	WS58 Wessex HC2 (8016M)	RAF Brize Norton Fire Section
	XT678	WS58 Wessex HC2 [H]	RAF, Kai Tak/*Uruguay AF from June 1997*
	XT680	WS58 Wessex HC2 [*Diamonds*]	RAF No 84 Sqn, Akrotiri
	XT681	WS58 Wessex HC2 [U]	RAF No 72 Sqn, Aldergrove
	XT755	WS58 Wessex HU5 (9053M) [V]	*Scrapped at Bruntingthorpe, January 1996*
	XT756	WS58 Wessex HU5 [ZJ]	

Serial	Type (other identity) [code]	Owner/operator, location or fate	Notes
XT759	WS58 Wessex HU5 [XY]	RNAY Fleetlands, derelict	
XT760	WS58 Wessex HU5 [418]	RN ETS, Culdrose	
XT761	WS58 Wessex HU5	RN AES, *HMS Sultan*, Gosport	
XT762	WS58 Wessex HU5	SFDO, RNAS Culdrose	
XT765	WS58 Wessex HU5 [J]	RN AES, *HMS Sultan*, Gosport	
XT766	WS58 Wessex HU5 (9054M) [822/CU]	Privately owned,	
XT769	WS58 Wessex HU5 [823]	FAA Museum, RNAS Yeovilton	
XT770	WS58 Wessex HU5 (9055M) [P]	Privately owned, Shawell, Leics	
XT771	WS58 Wessex HU5 [620/PO]	RN AES, *HMS Sultan*, Gosport	
XT772	WS58 Wessex HU5 (8805M)	SARTU RAF Valley, ground instruction	
XT773	WS58 Wessex HU5 (9123M)	RAF St Athan, BDRT	
XT778	WS Wasp HAS1 [430]	RAOC, West Moors, Dorset	
XT780	WS Wasp HAS1 [636]	RNAY Fleetlands Apprentice School	
XT788	WS Wasp HAS1 [442] (G-BMIR)	Privately owned, Charlwood, Surrey	
XT793	WS Wasp HAS1 [456]	Privately owned, East Dereham, Norfolk	
XT803	WS Sioux AH1 [Y]	Privately owned, Panshanger	
XT827	WS Sioux AH1 [D] (spares)	AAC Historic Aircraft Flight, Middle Wallop	
XT852	McD YF-4M Phantom FGR2	DTEO West Freugh Fire Section	
XT858	McD F-4K Phantom FG1	MoD(PE), stored Aston Down	
XT863	McD F-4K Phantom FG1 <ff>	Privately owned, Cowes, IOW	
XT864	McD F-4K Phantom FG1 (8998M/ *XT684*) [BJ]	RAF Leuchars on display	
XT867	McD F-4K Phantom FG1 (9064M) [BH]	RAF Leuchars BDRT	
XT891	McD F-4M Phantom FGR2 (9136M)	RAF Coningsby, on display	
XT895	McD F-4M Phantom FGR2 (9171M) [Q]	*Scrapped at Valley, November 1996*	
XT900	McD F-4M Phantom FGR2 (9099M) [CO]	*Scrapped at Stock, 1995*	
XT903	McD F-4M Phantom FGR2 [X]	RAF Leuchars, BDRT	
XT905	McD F-4M Phantom FGR2 [P]	RAF Coningsby, stored	
XT907	McD F-4M Phantom FGR2 (9151M) [W]	DEODS, Chattenden, Kent	
XT911	McD F-4M Phantom FGR2 <ff>	*Scrapped at Stock, 1995*	
XT914	McD F-4M Phantom FGR2 [Z]	RAF Leeming, decoy	
XV101	BAC VC10 C1K	RAF No 10 Sqn, Brize Norton	
XV102	BAC VC10 C1K	RAF No 10 Sqn, Brize Norton	
XV103	BAC VC10 C1K	RAF No 10 Sqn, Brize Norton	
XV104	BAC VC10 C1K	RAF No 10 Sqn, Brize Norton	
XV105	BAC VC10 C1K	RAF No 10 Sqn, Brize Norton	
XV106	BAC VC10 C1K	RAF No 10 Sqn, Brize Norton	
XV107	BAC VC10 C1K	RAF No 10 Sqn, Brize Norton	
XV108	BAC VC10 C1K	RAF No 10 Sqn, Brize Norton	
XV109	BAC VC10 C1K	RAF No 10 Sqn, Brize Norton	
XV118	WS Scout AH1 (9141M)	RAF Air Movements School, Brize Norton	
XV119	WS Scout AH1 [T]	AAC Dishforth, instructional use	
XV121	WS Scout AH1	Privately owned, Hawarden	
XV122	WS Scout AH1 [D]	R. Military College of Science, Shrivenham	
XV123	WS Scout AH1	IHM, Weston-super-Mare	
XV124	WS Scout AH1 [W]	AAC SEAE, Arborfield	
XV126	WS Scout AH1 (G-SCTA) [X]	Privately owned, Hawarden	
XV127	WS Scout AH1	Army, Middle Wallop (children's playground)	
XV128	WS Scout AH1	Privately owned,	
XV129	WS Scout AH1 [V]	Privately owned,	
XV130	WS Scout AH1 (G-BWJW) [R]	Privately owned, Cricklade, Wilts	
XV131	WS Scout AH1 [Y]	AAC Middle Wallop, BDRT	
XV134	WS Scout AH1 (G-BWLX) [P]	Privately owned, East Dereham, Norfolk	
XV135	WS Scout AH1	AAC	
XV136	WS Scout AH1 [X]	AAC Middle Wallop, on display	
XV137	WS Scout AH1	Privately owned,	
XV138	WS Scout AH1	AAC, stored RNAW Almondbank	
XV139	WS Scout AH1	AAC SEAE, Arborfield	
XV140	WS Scout AH1 (G-KAXL) [K]	Kennet Aviation, Cranfield	
XV141	WS Scout AH1	AAC SEAE, Arborfield	
XV147	HS Nimrod MR1(mod)	MoD(PE)/BAe Warton	
XV148	HS Nimrod MR1(mod) (fuselage)	BAe, stored Woodford	
XV161	HS Buccaneer S2B (9117M) <ff>	Privately owned, Birtley, Tyne & Wear	
XV163	HS Buccaneer S2A <ff>	Phoenix Aviation, Bruntingthorpe	
XV165	HS Buccaneer S2B <ff>	Gloucestershire Avn Coll, Staverton	
XV168	HS Buccaneer S2B	BAe Brough, on display	
XV176	Lockheed C-130K Hercules C3	RAF Lyneham Transport Wing	

Notes	Serial	Type (other identity) [code]	Owner/operator, location or fate
	XV177	Lockheed C-130K Hercules C3	RAF Lyneham Transport Wing
	XV178	Lockheed C-130K Hercules C1	RAF Lyneham Transport Wing
	XV179	Lockheed C-130K Hercules C1	RAF Lyneham Transport Wing
	XV181	Lockheed C-130K Hercules C1	RAF Lyneham Transport Wing
	XV182	Lockheed C-130K Hercules C1	RAF Lyneham Transport Wing
	XV183	Lockheed C-130K Hercules C3	RAF Lyneham Transport Wing
	XV184	Lockheed C-130K Hercules C3	RAF Lyneham Transport Wing
	XV185	Lockheed C-130K Hercules C1	MoD(PE)/HATS, DTEO Boscombe Down
	XV186	Lockheed C-130K Hercules C1	RAF Lyneham Transport Wing
	XV187	Lockheed C-130K Hercules C1	RAF No 1312 Flt, Mount Pleasant, FI
	XV188	Lockheed C-130K Hercules C3	RAF Lyneham Transport Wing
	XV189	Lockheed C-130K Hercules C3	RAF Lyneham Transport Wing
	XV190	Lockheed C-130K Hercules C3	RAF Lyneham Transport Wing
	XV191	Lockheed C-130K Hercules C1	RAF Lyneham Transport Wing
	XV192	Lockheed C-130K Hercules C1	RAF Lyneham Transport Wing
	XV195	Lockheed C-130K Hercules C1	RAF Lyneham Transport Wing
	XV196	Lockheed C-130K Hercules C1	RAF Lyneham Transport Wing
	XV197	Lockheed C-130K Hercules C3	RAF Lyneham Transport Wing
	XV199	Lockheed C-130K Hercules C3	RAF Lyneham Transport Wing
	XV200	Lockheed C-130K Hercules C1	RAF Lyneham Transport Wing
	XV201	Lockheed C-130K Hercules C1K	RAF, stored Cambridge
	XV202	Lockheed C-130K Hercules C3	RAF Lyneham Transport Wing
	XV203	Lockheed C-130K Hercules C1K	RAF, stored Cambridge
	XV204	Lockheed C-130K Hercules C1K	RAF, stored Cambridge
	XV205	Lockheed C-130K Hercules C1	RAF Lyneham Transport Wing
	XV206	Lockheed C-130K Hercules C1	RAF Lyneham Transport Wing
	XV207	Lockheed C-130K Hercules C3	RAF Lyneham Transport Wing
	XV208	Lockheed C-130K Hercules W2	MoD(PE)/MRF, DTEO Boscombe Down
	XV209	Lockheed C-130K Hercules C3	RAF Lyneham Transport Wing
	XV210	Lockheed C-130K Hercules C1	RAF Lyneham Transport Wing
	XV211	Lockheed C-130K Hercules C1	RAF Lyneham Transport Wing
	XV212	Lockheed C-130K Hercules C3	RAF Lyneham Transport Wing
	XV213	Lockheed C-130K Hercules C1K	RAF, stored Cambridge
	XV214	Lockheed C-130K Hercules C3	MoD(PE)/HATS, DTEO Boscombe Down
	XV215	Lockheed C-130K Hercules C1	RAF Lyneham Transport Wing
	XV217	Lockheed C-130K Hercules C3	RAF Lyneham Transport Wing
	XV218	Lockheed C-130K Hercules C1	RAF Lyneham Transport Wing
	XV219	Lockheed C-130K Hercules C3	RAF Lyneham Transport Wing
	XV220	Lockheed C-130K Hercules C3	RAF Lyneham Transport Wing
	XV221	Lockheed C-130K Hercules C3	RAF Lyneham Transport Wing
	XV222	Lockheed C-130K Hercules C3	RAF Lyneham Transport Wing
	XV223	Lockheed C-130K Hercules C3	RAF Lyneham Transport Wing
	XV226	HS Nimrod MR2	RAF No 120 Sqn, Kinloss
	XV227	HS Nimrod MR2	RAF No 42(R) Sqn, Kinloss
	XV228	HS Nimrod MR2	RAF No 42(R) Sqn, Kinloss
	XV229	HS Nimrod MR2	RAF No 206 Sqn, Kinloss
	XV230	HS Nimrod MR2	RAF No 201 Sqn, Kinloss
	XV231	HS Nimrod MR2	RAF No 206 Sqn, Kinloss
	XV232	HS Nimrod MR2	RAF No 201 Sqn, Kinloss
	XV233	HS Nimrod MR2	RAF No 42(R) Sqn, Kinloss
	XV234	BAe Nimrod 2000 (fuselage)	MoD(PE)/FR Aviation, Bournemouth (conversion)
	XV235	HS Nimrod MR2	RAF No 120 Sqn, Kinloss
	XV236	HS Nimrod MR2	RAF No 42(R) Sqn, Kinloss
	XV238	HS Nimrod <R> (parts of G-ALYW)	RAF EP&TU, St Athan
	XV240	HS Nimrod MR2	RAF No 120 Sqn, Kinloss
	XV241	HS Nimrod MR2	RAF No 206 Sqn, Kinloss
	XV242	BAe Nimrod 2000 (fuselage)	MoD(PE)/FR Aviation, Bournemouth (conversion)
	XV243	HS Nimrod MR2	RAF No 120 Sqn, Kinloss
	XV244	HS Nimrod MR2	RAF No 201 Sqn, Kinloss
	XV245	HS Nimrod MR2	RAF No 201 Sqn, Kinloss
	XV246	HS Nimrod MR2	RAF No 201 Sqn, Kinloss
	XV247	BAe Nimrod 2000 (fuselage)	MoD(PE)/FR Aviation, Bournemouth (conversion)
	XV248	HS Nimrod MR2	RAF No 206 Sqn, Kinloss
	XV249	HS Nimrod R1	RAF No 51 Sqn, Waddington
	XV250	HS Nimrod MR2	RAF No 120 Sqn, Kinloss
	XV251	HS Nimrod MR2	RAF No 206 Sqn, Kinloss
	XV252	HS Nimrod MR2	RAF No 201 Sqn, Kinloss
	XV253	HS Nimrod MR2 (9118M)	RAF Kinloss (spares use)
	XV254	HS Nimrod MR2	RAF No 201 Sqn, Kinloss
	XV255	HS Nimrod MR2	RAF Kinloss MR Wing

Serial	Type (other identity) [code]	Owner/operator, location or fate	Notes
XV258	HS Nimrod MR2	RAF No 206 Sqn, Kinloss	
XV259	BAe Nimrod AEW3	DEODS, Chattenden, Kent	
XV260	HS Nimrod MR2	RAF No 120 Sqn, Kinloss	
XV263	BAe Nimrod AEW3P (8967M) (fuselage)	FR Aviation, Bournemouth	
XV268	DHC2 Beaver AL1 (G-BVER)	Privately owned	
XV277	HS P.1127(RAF)	Privately owned, Ipswich	
XV279	HS P.1127(RAF) (8566M)	RAF Harrier Maintenance School, Wittering	
XV280	HS P.1127(RAF) <ff>	RNAS Yeovilton Fire Section	
XV281	HS Harrier GR3	BAe Warton, instructional use	
XV290	Lockheed C-130K Hercules C3	RAF Lyneham Transport Wing	
XV291	Lockheed C-130K Hercules C1	RAF Lyneham Transport Wing	
XV292	Lockheed C-130K Hercules C1	RAF Lyneham Transport Wing	
XV293	Lockheed C-130K Hercules C1	RAF Lyneham Transport Wing	
XV294	Lockheed C-130K Hercules C3	RAF Lyneham Transport Wing	
XV295	Lockheed C-130K Hercules C1	RAF Lyneham Transport Wing	
XV296	Lockheed C-130K Hercules C1K	RAF, stored Cambridge	
XV297	Lockheed C-130K Hercules C1	RAF Lyneham Transport Wing	
XV298	Lockheed C-130K Hercules C1	RAF Lyneham Transport Wing	
XV299	Lockheed C-130K Hercules C3	RAF Lyneham Transport Wing	
XV300	Lockheed C-130K Hercules C1	RAF Lyneham Transport Wing	
XV301	Lockheed C-130K Hercules C3	RAF Lyneham Transport Wing	
XV302	Lockheed C-130K Hercules C3	RAF Lyneham Transport Wing	
XV303	Lockheed C-130K Hercules C3	RAF Lyneham Transport Wing	
XV304	Lockheed C-130K Hercules C3	RAF Lyneham Transport Wing	
XV305	Lockheed C-130K Hercules C3	RAF Lyneham Transport Wing	
XV306	Lockheed C-130K Hercules C1	RAF Lyneham Transport Wing	
XV307	Lockheed C-130K Hercules C3	RAF Lyneham Transport Wing	
XV328	BAC Lightning T5 <ff>	Phoenix Aviation, Bruntingthorpe	
XV332	HS Buccaneer S2B (9232M)	RAF Marham Fire Section	
XV333	HS Buccaneer S2B [234/H]	FAA Museum, RNAS Yeovilton	
XV337	HS Buccaneer S2C (8852M)	RAF St Athan, BDRT	
XV338	HS Buccaneer S2A (8774M) <ff>	Scrapped	
XV344	HS Buccaneer S2C	MoD(PE), stored DTEO Boscombe Down	
XV350	HS Buccaneer S2B	East Midlands Aero Park	
XV352	HS Buccaneer S2B <ff>	Privately owned, Stock, Essex	
XV353	HS Buccaneer S2B (9144M) <ff>	Privately owned,	
XV359	HS Buccaneer S2B	RN, Predannack Fire School	
XV361	HS Buccaneer S2B	Ulster Aviation Society, Langford Lodge	
XV370	Sikorsky SH-3D	RN AES, *HMS Sultan*, Gosport	
XV371	WS61 Sea King HAS1(DB)	RNAY Fleetlands	
XV372	WS61 Sea King HAS1	RAF St Mawgan, instructional use	
XV393	McD F-4M Phantom FGR2 [Q]	Scrapped at Marham, 1994	
XV399	McD F-4M Phantom FGR2 <ff>	Privately owned, Stock, Essex	
XV401	McD F-4M Phantom FGR2 [I]	DTEO Boscombe Down, GI use	
XV402	McD F-4M Phantom FGR2 <ff>	Scrapped at Stock, 1995	
XV406	McD F-4M Phantom FGR2 (9098M) [CK]	RAF Carlisle, on display	
XV408	McD F-4M Phantom FGR2 (9165M) [Z]	RAF Cranwell, on display	
XV411	McD F-4M Phantom FGR2 (9103M) [L]	FSCTE, RAF Manston	
XV415	McD F-4M Phantom FGR2 (9163M) [E]	RAF Boulmer, on display	
XV420	McD F-4M Phantom FGR2 (9247M) [O]	RAF Neatishead, at main gate	
XV422	McD F-4M Phantom FGR2 (9157M) [T]	Stornoway Airport, on display	
XV423	McD F-4M Phantom FGR2 [Y]	RAF Leeming, BDRT	
XV424	McD F-4M Phantom FGR2 (9152M) [I]	RAF Museum, Hendon	
XV426	McD F-4M Phantom FGR2 [P]	RAF Coningsby, BDRT	
XV435	McD F-4M Phantom FGR2 [R]	DTEO Llanbedr Fire Section	
XV460	McD F-4M Phantom FGR2 [R]	RAF Coningsby	
XV465	McD F-4M Phantom FGR2 [S]	RAF Leeming, decoy	
XV467	McD F-4M Phantom FGR2 (9158M) [F]	Benbecula Airport, on display	
XV468	McD F-4M Phantom FGR2 (9159M) [H]	RAF Woodvale, on display	
XV474	McD F-4M Phantom FGR2 [T]	The Old Flying Machine Company, Duxford	
XV482	McD F-4M Phantom FGR2 (9107M) [T]	Scrapped at Leuchars, 1995	
XV489	McD F-4M Phantom FGR2 <ff>	Privately owned, Bruntingthorpe	

Notes	Serial	Type (other identity) [code]	Owner/operator, location or fate
	XV490	McD F-4M Phantom FGR2 <ff>	Privately owned, Bruntingthorpe
	XV497	McD F-4M Phantom FGR2	RAF Coningsby
	XV499	McD F-4M Phantom FGR2	RAF Leeming, WLT
	XV500	McD F-4M Phantom FGR2 (9113M)	RAF St Athan, on display
	XV577	McD F-4K Phantom FG1 (9065M) [AM]	RAF Leuchars, BDRT
	XV581	McD F-4K Phantom FG1 (9070M) [AE]	RAF Buchan, on display
	XV582	McD F-4K Phantom FG1 (9066M) [M]	RAF Leuchars on display
	XV585	McD F-4K Phantom FG1 [AP]	*Scrapped at Leuchars, 1995*
	XV586	McD F-4K Phantom FG1 (9067M) [AJ]	RAF Leuchars BDRT
	XV588	McD F-4K Phantom FG1 [007] <ff>	*Burnt at Predannack by June 1996*
	XV591	McD F-4K Phantom FG1 <ff>	RAF Cosford Aerospace Museum
	XV625	WS Wasp HAS1 [471]	RN AES, *HMS Sultan*, Gosport
	XV629	WS Wasp HAS1	AAC Middle Wallop, BDRT
	XV642	WS61 Sea King HAS2A	RN AES, *HMS Sultan*, Gosport
	XV643	WS61 Sea King HAS6 [703/PW]	RN No 819 Sqn, Prestwick
	XV647	WS61 Sea King HU5 [820/CU]	RN No 771 Sqn, Culdrose
	XV648	WS61 Sea King HU5 [827/CU]	MoD(PE)/RWTS, DTEO Boscombe Down
	XV649	WS61 Sea King AEW2A [186/N]	RN No 849 Sqn, A Flt, Culdrose
	XV650	WS61 Sea King AEW2A [184/L]	RN No 849 Sqn, B Flt, Culdrose
	XV651	WS61 Sea King HU5 [599]	RN No 706 Sqn, Culdrose
	XV653	WS61 Sea King HAS6 [500]	RN No 810 Sqn, Culdrose
	XV654	WS61 Sea King HAS6 [705/PW] (wreck)	RN, stored Fleetlands
	XV655	WS61 Sea King HAS6 [267/N]	RN No 814 Sqn, Culdrose
	XV656	WS61 Sea King AEW2A [180/CU]	RN No 849 Sqn, HQ Flt, Culdrose
	XV657	WS61 Sea King HAS5 [132]	RN ETS, Culdrose
	XV659	WS61 Sea King HAS6 [510/CU]	RN No 810 Sqn, Culdrose
	XV660	WS61 Sea King HAS6 [511/CW]	RN No 810 Sqn, Culdrose
	XV661	WS61 Sea King HU5 [824/CU]	NARO, RNAY Fleetlands
	XV663	WS61 Sea King HAS6 [501/CU]	RN AMG, Culdrose
	XV664	WS61 Sea King AEW2A [181]	NARO, RNAY Fleetlands
	XV665	WS61 Sea King HAS6 [505/CU]	RN No 810 Sqn, Culdrose
	XV666	WS61 Sea King HU5 [823/CU]	NARO, RNAY Fleetlands
	XV669	WS61 Sea King HAS1 [10]	RN ETS, Culdrose
	XV670	WS61 Sea King HU5 [188]	RN No 706 Sqn, Culdrose
	XV671	WS61 Sea King AEW2A [181]	RN No 849 Sqn, HQ Flt, Culdrose
	XV672	WS61 Sea King AEW2A [182/L]	RN No 849 Sqn, B Flt, Culdrose
	XV673	WS61 Sea King HU5 [597]	RN No 706 Sqn, Culdrose
	XV674	WS61 Sea King HAS6 [705/PW]	RN AMG, Culdrose
	XV675	WS61 Sea King HAS6 [598/CU]	RN No 706 Sqn, Culdrose
	XV676	WS61 Sea King HAS6 [515/CM]	RN No 810 Sqn, Culdrose
	XV677	WS61 Sea King HAS6 [269/N]	RN No 814 Sqn, Culdrose
	XV696	WS61 Sea King HAS6 [708/PW]	RN No 819 Sqn, Prestwick
	XV697	WS61 Sea King AEW2A [183/L]	RN No 849 Sqn, B Flt, Culdrose
	XV699	WS61 Sea King HU5 [826/PW]	RN No 819 Sqn, Prestwick
	XV700	WS61 Sea King HAS6 [008/CU]	RN No 810 Sqn, Culdrose
	XV701	WS61 Sea King HAS6 [268/N]	RN No 814 Sqn, Culdrose
	XV703	WS61 Sea King HAS6 [011/L]	RN No 820 Sqn, Culdrose
	XV704	WS61 Sea King AEW2A [183/L]	RN No 849 Sqn, B Flt, Culdrose
	XV705	WS61 Sea King HU5 [821/CU]	RN No 771 Sqn, Culdrose
	XV706	WS61 Sea King HAS6 [583/CU]	RN No 706 Sqn, Culdrose
	XV707	WS61 Sea King AEW2A [185/N]	RN No 849 Sqn, A Flt, Culdrose
	XV708	WS61 Sea King HAS6 [510/CU]	RN AMG, Culdrose
	XV709	WS61 Sea King HAS6 [585]	RN No 706 Sqn, Culdrose
	XV710	WS61 Sea King HAS6 [012/L]	RN No 820 Sqn, Culdrose
	XV711	WS61 Sea King HAS6 [709/PW]	RN No 819 Sqn, Prestwick
	XV712	WS61 Sea King HAS6 [266/N]	RN No 814 Sqn, Culdrose
	XV713	WS61 Sea King HAS6 [018/L]	RN No 820 Sqn, Culdrose
	XV714	WS61 Sea King AEW2A [187/N]	RN No 849 Sqn, A Flt, Culdrose
	XV720	WS58 Wessex HC2	RAF SARTU, Valley
	XV721	WS58 Wessex HC2 [H]	RAF No 72 Sqn, Aldergrove
	XV722	WS58 Wessex HC2 [WH]	RAF No 2 FTS, Shawbury
	XV723	WS58 Wessex HC2 [Q]	RAF No 60 Sqn, Benson
	XV724	WS58 Wessex HC2	RAF No 22 Sqn, C Flt, Valley
	XV725	WS58 Wessex HC2 [C]	RAF No 72 Sqn, Aldergrove
	XV726	WS58 Wessex HC2 [J]	RAF No 72 Sqn, Aldergrove
	XV728	WS58 Wessex HC2 [A]	RAF No 72 Sqn, Aldergrove
	XV729	WS58 Wessex HC2	RAF SARTU, Valley

Serial	Type (other identity) [code]	Owner/operator, location or fate	Notes
XV730	WS58 Wessex HC2 [*Clubs*]	RAF No 84 Sqn, Akrotiri	
XV731	WS58 Wessex HC2 [Y]	RAF No 72 Sqn, Aldergrove	
XV732	WS58 Wessex HCC4	RAF No 32(The Royal) Sqn, Northolt	
XV733	WS58 Wessex HCC4	RAF No 32(The Royal) Sqn, Northolt	
XV738	HS Harrier GR3 (9074M) [B]	Phoenix Aviation, Bruntingthorpe	
XV741	HS Harrier GR3 [1,5]	SFDO, RNAS Culdrose	
XV744	HS Harrier GR3 (9167M) [3K]	R. Military College of Science, Shrivenham	
XV747	HS Harrier GR3 (8979M) (fuselage)	No 1803 Sqn ATC, Hucknall	
XV748	HS Harrier GR3 [3D]	Cranfield University	
XV751	HS Harrier GR3	Vallance By-Ways, Charlwood	
XV752	HS Harrier GR3 (9078M) [B,HF]	RAF No 1 SoTT, Cosford	
XV753	HS Harrier GR3 (9075M) [3F,4]	SFDO, RNAS Culdrose	
XV755	HS Harrier GR3 [M]	RNAS Yeovilton Fire Section	
XV760	HS Harrier GR3 [VL]	BAe Dunsfold	
XV779	HS Harrier GR3 (8931M) [01,A]	RAF Wittering on display	
XV783	HS Harrier GR3 [N]	SFDO, RNAS Culdrose	
XV784	HS Harrier GR3 (8909M) <ff>	DTEO Boscombe Down, GI use	
XV786	HS Harrier GR3 <ff>	RNAS Culdrose	
XV786	HS Harrier GR3 [S] <rf>	RN, Predannack Fire School	
XV798	HS Harrier GR1(mod)	Bristol Aero Collection, stored Kemble	
XV804	HS Harrier GR3 [O]	Defence NBC Centre, Winterbourne Gunner	
XV806	HS Harrier GR3 [E]	SFDO, RNAS Culdrose	
XV808	HS Harrier GR3 (9076M) [3J,6]	SFDO, RNAS Culdrose	
XV810	HS Harrier GR3 (9038M) [K]	RAF St Athan, BDRT	
XV814	DH106 Comet 4 (G-APDF)	DTEO Boscombe Down, spares use	
XV863	HS Buccaneer S2B (9115M/ 9139M/9145M) [S]	RAF Lossiemouth, on display	
XV864	HS Buccaneer S2B (9234M)	FSCTE, RAF Manston	
XV865	HS Buccaneer S2B (9226M)	RAF Coningsby Fire Section	
XV867	HS Buccaneer S2B <ff>	N Yorks Aircraft Recovery Centre, Chop Gate	
XW175	HS Harrier T4(VAAC)	MoD(PE)/DRA, DTEO Boscombe Down	
XW198	WS Puma HC1	RAF No 230 Sqn, Aldergrove	
XW199	WS Puma HC1 [NB]	RAF No 27(R) Sqn, Odiham	
XW200	WS Puma HC1	RAF No 230 Sqn, Aldergrove	
XW201	WS Puma HC1	RAF No 33 Sqn, Odiham	
XW202	WS Puma HC1 [NE]	RAF No 27(R) Sqn, Odiham	
XW204	WS Puma HC1 [BY]	RAF No 18 Sqn, Laarbruch	
XW206	WS Puma HC1 [NG]	RAF No 27(R) Sqn, Odiham	
XW207	WS Puma HC1	RAF No 33 Sqn, Odiham	
XW208	WS Puma HC1	RAF No 33 Sqn, Odiham	
XW209	WS Puma HC1 [NH]	RAF No 27(R) Sqn, Odiham	
XW210	WS Puma HC1	Westland, Weston-super-Mare (on rebuild)	
XW211	WS Puma HC1 [NJ]	RAF No 27(R) Sqn, Odiham	
XW212	WS Puma HC1	RAF No 33 Sqn, Odiham	
XW213	WS Puma HC1 [NE]	RAF No 27(R) Sqn, Odiham	
XW214	WS Puma HC1	RAF No 230 Sqn, Aldergrove	
XW215	WS Puma HC1	RAF No 33 Sqn, Odiham	
XW216	WS Puma HC1 [BY]	RAF No 18 Sqn, Laarbruch	
XW217	WS Puma HC1 [NK]	RAF No 230 Sqn, Aldergrove	
XW218	WS Puma HC1 [BX]	RAF No 18 Sqn, Laarbruch	
XW219	WS Puma HC1	RAF No 230 Sqn, Aldergrove	
XW220	WS Puma HC1 [CZ]	RAF No 230 Sqn, Aldergrove	
XW221	WS Puma HC1	RAF No 33 Sqn, Odiham	
XW222	WS Puma HC1	RAF No 230 Sqn, Aldergrove	
XW223	WS Puma HC1	RAF No 33 Sqn, Odiham	
XW224	WS Puma HC1	RAF No 230 Sqn, Aldergrove	
XW225	WS Puma HC1	RAF No 33 Sqn, Odiham	
XW226	WS Puma HC1 [NK]	RAF No 27(R) Sqn, Odiham	
XW227	WS Puma HC1 [NJ]	RAF No 27(R) Sqn, Odiham	
XW229	WS Puma HC1	RAF No 33 Sqn, Odiham	
XW231	WS Puma HC1 [NM]	RAF No 230 Sqn, Aldergrove	
XW232	WS Puma HC1	RAF No 33 Sqn, Odiham	
XW234	WS Puma HC1	RAF No 230 Sqn, Aldergrove	
XW235	WS Puma HC1	RAF No 33 Sqn, Odiham	
XW236	WS Puma HC1 [NO]	RAF No 230 Sqn, Aldergrove	
XW237	WS Puma HC1	RAF No 33 Sqn, Odiham	
XW241	Sud SA330E Puma	DRA Avionics & Sensors Dept, Farnborough	
XW249	Cushioncraft CC7	Flambards Village Theme Park, Helston	
XW264	HS Harrier T2 <ff>	Gloucestershire Avn Coll, Staverton	
XW265	HS Harrier T4A [W]	RAF No 2 SoTT, Cosford	

Notes	Serial	Type (other identity) [code]	Owner/operator, location or fate
	XW266	HS Harrier T4N [719]	RNAS Yeovilton, spares recovery
	XW267	HS Harrier T4 [SA]	RAF, stored DTEO Boscombe Down
	XW268	HS Harrier T4N (fuselage)	RNAS Yeovilton, spares recovery
	XW269	HS Harrier T4 [BD]	RAF, stored DTEO Boscombe Down
	XW270	HS Harrier T4 (fuselage)	Privately owned, Bruntingthorpe
	XW271	HS Harrier T4 [X,1]	SFDO, RNAS Culdrose
	XW272	HS Harrier T4 (8783M) <ff>	BAe Dunsfold Fire Section
	XW276	Aérospatiale SA341 Gazelle (F-ZWRI)	North-East Aircraft Museum, Usworth
	XW281	WS Scout AH1 [U]	Privately owned, Hawarden
	XW282	WS Scout AH1 [W]	Privately owned,
	XW283	WS Scout AH1 [U]	RM, stored Yeovilton
	XW284	WS Scout AH1 [A] (fuselage)	AAC, stored RNAW Almondbank
	XW289	BAC Jet Provost T5A (G-BVXT/ G-JPVA)	Kennet Aviation, Cranfield
	XW290	BAC Jet Provost T5A (9199M) [41,MA]	RAF No 1 SoTT, Cosford
	XW291	BAC Jet Provost T5 (G-BWOF) [N]	Transair(UK) Ltd, North Weald
	XW292	BAC Jet Provost T5A (9128M) [32]	RAF No 1 SoTT, Cosford
	XW293	BAC Jet Provost T5 (G-BWCS) [Z]	Privately owned, Liverpool
	XW294	BAC Jet Provost T5A (9129M) [45]	RAF No 1 SoTT, Cosford
	XW299	BAC Jet Provost T5A (9146M) [60,MB]	RAF No 1 SoTT, Cosford
	XW301	BAC Jet Provost T5A (9147M) [63,MC]	RAF No 1 SoTT, Cosford
	XW302	BAC Jet Provost T5 [T]	*Sold to the USA as N166A, November 1995*
	XW303	BAC Jet Provost T5A (9119M) [127]	RAF No 1 SoTT, Cosford
	XW304	BAC Jet Provost T5 (9172M) [MD]	RAF No 1 SoTT, Cosford
	XW305	BAC Jet Provost T5A [42]	*Sold to the USA as N453MS, March 1996*
	XW306	BAC Jet Provost T5 [O]	*Sold to the USA as N313A, November 1995*
	XW309	BAC Jet Provost T5 (9179M) [V,ME]	RAF No 1 SoTT, Cosford
	XW310	BAC Jet Provost T5A (G-BWGS) [37]	*Repainted as G-BWGS*
	XW311	BAC Jet Provost T5 (9180M) [W,MF]	RAF No 1 SoTT, Cosford
	XW312	BAC Jet Provost T5A (9109M) [64]	RAF No 1 SoTT, Cosford
	XW315	BAC Jet Provost T5A <ff>	Privately owned, Long Marston
	XW317	BAC Jet Provost T5A [79]	*Sold to the USA as N355A, November 1995*
	XW318	BAC Jet Provost T5A (9190M) [78,MG]	RAF No 1 SoTT, Cosford
	XW319	BAC Jet Provost T5A [76]	*Sold to the USA as N8087V, 1994*
	XW320	BAC Jet Provost T5A (9015M) [71]	RAF No 1 SoTT, Cosford
	XW321	BAC Jet Provost T5A (9154M) [62,MH]	RAF No 1 SoTT, Cosford
	XW323	BAC Jet Provost T5A (9166M) [86]	RAF Museum, Hendon
	XW324	BAC Jet Provost T5 (G-BWSG) [U]	Global Aviation, Binbrook
	XW325	BAC Jet Provost T5B (G-BWGF) [E]	Global Aviation, Binbrook
	XW326	BAC Jet Provost T5A [62]	*Sold to the USA as N326GV, December 1995*
	XW327	BAC Jet Provost T5A (9130M) [62]	RAF No 1 SoTT, Cosford
	XW328	BAC Jet Provost T5A (9177M) [75,MI]	RAF No 1 SoTT, Cosford
	XW330	BAC Jet Provost T5A (9195M) [82,MJ]	RAF No 1 SoTT, Cosford
	XW333	BAC Jet Provost T5A (G-BVTC)	Global Aviation, Binbrook
	XW335	BAC Jet Provost T5A (9061M) [74]	RAF No 1 SoTT, Cosford
	XW351	BAC Jet Provost T5A (9062M) [31]	RAF No 1 SoTT, Cosford
	XW352	BAC Jet Provost T5 [R]	Privately owned, Bruntingthorpe
	XW353	BAC Jet Provost T5A (9090M) [3]	RAF Cranwell, on display
	XW355	BAC Jet Provost T5A (G-JPTV) [20]	Privately owned, Bruntingthorpe
	XW358	BAC Jet Provost T5A (9181M) [59,MK]	RAF No 1 SoTT, Cosford
	XW360	BAC Jet Provost T5A (9153M) [61,ML]	RAF No 1 SoTT, Cosford
	XW361	BAC Jet Provost T5A (9192M) [81,MM]	RAF No 1 SoTT, Cosford
	XW363	BAC Jet Provost T5A [36]	BAe Training School, Warton
	XW364	BAC Jet Provost T5A (9188M) [35,MN]	RAF No 1 SoTT, Cosford

Serial	Type (other identity) [code]	Owner/operator, location or fate	Notes
XW365	BAC Jet Provost T5A (9018M) [73]	RAF No 1 SoTT, Cosford	
XW366	BAC Jet Provost T5A (9097M) [75]	RAF No 1 SoTT, Cosford	
XW367	BAC Jet Provost T5A (9193M) [64,MO]	RAF No 1 SoTT, Cosford	
XW370	BAC Jet Provost T5A (9196M) [72,MP]	RAF No 1 SoTT, Cosford	
XW372	BAC Jet Provost T5A [M]	*Sold to the USA as N372JP, March 1996*	
XW375	BAC Jet Provost T5A (9149M) [52]	RAF No 1 SoTT, Cosford	
XW404	BAC Jet Provost T5A (9049M)	RAF CTTS, St Athan	
XW405	BAC Jet Provost T5A (9187M) [J,MQ]	RAF No 1 SoTT, Cosford	
XW409	BAC Jet Provost T5A (9047M)	RAF CTTS, St Athan	
XW410	BAC Jet Provost T5A (9125M) [80,MR]	RAF No 1 SoTT, Cosford	
XW413	BAC Jet Provost T5A (9126M) [69]	RAF No 1 SoTT, Cosford	
XW416	BAC Jet Provost T5A (9191M) [84,MS]	RAF No 1 SoTT, Cosford	
XW418	BAC Jet Provost T5A (9173M) [MT]	RAF No 1 SoTT, Cosford	
XW419	BAC Jet Provost T5A (9120M) [125]	RAF No 1 SoTT, Cosford	
XW420	BAC Jet Provost T5A (9194M) [83,MU]	RAF No 1 SoTT, Cosford	
XW421	BAC Jet Provost T5A (9111M) [60]	RAF No 1 SoTT, Cosford	
XW422	BAC Jet Provost T5A (G-BWEB) [3]	*Repainted as G-BWEB*	
XW423	BAC Jet Provost T5A (G-BWUW) [14]	Privately owned, North Weald	
XW425	BAC Jet Provost T5A (9200M) [H,MV]	RAF No 1 SoTT, Cosford	
XW427	BAC Jet Provost T5A (9124M) [67]	RAF No 1 SoTT, Cosford	
XW428	Hunting Jet Provost T4 (XR674/ G-TOMG/9030M)	Privately owned, North Weald	
XW429	BAC Jet Provost T5B [C]	*Sold to the USA as N556A, November 1995*	
XW430	BAC Jet Provost T5A (9176M) [77,MW]	RAF No 1 SoTT, Cosford	
XW431	BAC Jet Provost T5B (G-BWBS) [A]	Downbird UK Ltd, Tatenhill	
XW432	BAC Jet Provost T5A (9127M) [76,MX]	RAF No 1 SoTT, Cosford	
XW433	BAC Jet Provost T5A (G-JPRO) [63]	Global Aviation, Binbrook	
XW434	BAC Jet Provost T5A (9091M) [78,MY]	RAF No 1 SoTT, Cosford	
XW436	BAC Jet Provost T5A (9148M) [68]	RAF No 1 SoTT, Cosford	
XW438	BAC Jet Provost T5B [B]	*To Oman, 1995*	
XW527	HS Buccaneer S2B <ff>	Privately owned, Wittering	
XW528	HS Buccaneer S2B (8861M) [C]	RAF Coningsby Fire Section	
XW530	HS Buccaneer S2B	Buccaneer Service Station, Elgin	
XW544	HS Buccaneer S2B (8857M) [Y]	Privately owned, Shawbury	
XW547	HS Buccaneer S2B (9095M/ 9169M) [R]	RAF Cosford Aerospace Museum	
XW549	HS Buccaneer S2B (8860M) (fuselage)	RAF Kinloss, BDRT	
XW550	HS Buccaneer S2B <ff>	Privately owned, West Horndon, Essex	
XW566	SEPECAT Jaguar T2	DRA Avionics & Sensors Dept, Farnborough	
XW612	WS Scout AH1 [A]	Privately owned, Colsterworth, Lincs	
XW613	WS Scout AH1 [W]	Privately owned, Colsterworth, Lincs	
XW614	WS Scout AH1	AAC Historic Flight, Middle Wallop	
XW616	WS Scout AH1	AAC Dishforth, instructional use	
XW630	HS Harrier GR3	RN AES, *HMS Sultan*, Gosport	
XW635	Beagle D5/180 (G-AWSW)	Privately owned, Spanhoe Lodge	
XW664	HS Nimrod R1	RAF No 51 Sqn, Waddington	
XW665	HS Nimrod R1	RAF No 51 Sqn, Waddington	
XW666	HS Nimrod R1 (fuselage)	BAe Woodford, spares use	
XW750	HS748 Series 107	MoD(PE)/DRA, DTEO Boscombe Down	
XW763	HS Harrier GR3 (9002M/9041M) <ff>	Privately owned, stored Bruntingthorpe	
XW764	HS Harrier GR3 (8981M)	*Scrapped at Leeming, 1994*	
XW768	HS Harrier GR3 (9072M) [N]	RAF No 1 SoTT, Cosford	
XW784	Mitchell-Procter Kittiwake I (G-BBRN)	Privately owned, Henstridge	
XW795	WS Scout AH1 (fuselage)	AAC, stored Middle Wallop	

Notes	Serial	Type (other identity) [code]	Owner/operator, location or fate
	XW796	WS Scout AH1	AAC Wattisham, BDRT
	XW798	WS Scout AH1	AAC, Middle Wallop
	XW799	WS Scout AH1	Privately owned,
	XW835	WS Lynx	AAC Wattisham, instructional use
	XW836	WS Lynx	AAC Middle Wallop Fire Section
	XW837	WS Lynx (fuselage)	RNAS Yeovilton Fire Section
	XW838	WS Lynx (TAD 009)	AAC SEAE, Arborfield
	XW839	WS Lynx	IHM, Weston-super-Mare
	XW843	WS Gazelle AH1	AAC SEAE, Arborfield
	XW844	WS Gazelle AH1	AAC No 12 Flt, Brüggen
	XW845	WS Gazelle HT2 [47/CU]	RN No 705 Sqn, Culdrose
	XW846	WS Gazelle AH1 [M]	AAC No 670 Sqn/2 Regiment, Middle Wallop
	XW847	WS Gazelle AH1	AAC No 665 Sqn/5 Regiment, Aldergrove
	XW848	WS Gazelle AH1 [D]	AAC No 670 Sqn/2 Regiment, Middle Wallop
	XW849	WS Gazelle AH1 [G]	RM No 847 Sqn, Yeovilton
	XW851	WS Gazelle AH1	RM No 847 Sqn, Yeovilton
	XW852	WS Gazelle HCC4	RAF, stored NARO, RNAY Fleetlands
	XW853	WS Gazelle HT2 [53/CU]	RN No 705 Sqn, Culdrose
	XW854	WS Gazelle HT2 [46/CU]	RN No 705 Sqn, Culdrose
	XW855	WS Gazelle HCC4	RAF, stored NARO, RNAY Fleetlands
	XW856	WS Gazelle HT2 [49/CU]	RN No 705 Sqn, Culdrose
	XW857	WS Gazelle HT2 [55/CU]	RN No 705 Sqn, Culdrose
	XW858	WS Gazelle HT3 [C]	RAF No 2 FTS, Shawbury
	XW860	WS Gazelle HT2	AAC SEAE, Arborfield
	XW861	WS Gazelle HT2 [52/CU]	RN No 705 Sqn, Culdrose
	XW862	WS Gazelle HT3 [D]	RAF No 2 FTS, Shawbury
	XW863	WS Gazelle HT2 [42/CU]	AAC SEAE, Arborfield
	XW864	WS Gazelle HT2 [54/CU]	RN No 705 Sqn, Culdrose
	XW865	WS Gazelle AH1 [C]	AAC No 670 Sqn/2 Regiment, Middle Wallop
	XW866	WS Gazelle HT3 [E]	RAF No 2 FTS, Shawbury
	XW868	WS Gazelle HT2 [50/CU]	RN, stored Culdrose
	XW870	WS Gazelle HT3 [F]	RAF Shawbury, wfu (damaged)
	XW871	WS Gazelle HT2 [44/CU]	RN No 705 Sqn, Culdrose
	XW884	WS Gazelle HT2 [41/CU]	RN, stored Culdrose
	XW885	WS Gazelle AH1	AAC No 667 Sqn/2 Regiment, Middle Wallop
	XW887	WS Gazelle HT2 [FL]	NARO, RNAY Fleetlands Station Flight
	XW888	WS Gazelle AH1	AAC SEAE, Arborfield
	XW889	WS Gazelle AH1	AAC SEAE, Arborfield
	XW890	WS Gazelle HT2	RNAS Yeovilton, on display
	XW891	WS Gazelle HT2 [49] (fuselage)	*Burnt at Culdrose by 1994*
	XW892	WS Gazelle AH1 [C]	AAC No 666(V) Sqn/7 Regiment, Middle Wallop
	XW893	WS Gazelle AH1	AAC No 665 Sqn/5 Regiment, Aldergrove
	XW894	WS Gazelle HT2 [37/CU]	RN No 705 Sqn, Culdrose
	XW895	WS Gazelle HT2 [51/CU]	RN No 705 Sqn, Culdrose
	XW897	WS Gazelle AH1 [Z]	AAC No 670 Sqn/2 Regiment, Middle Wallop
	XW898	WS Gazelle HT3 [G]	RAF No 2 FTS, Shawbury
	XW899	WS Gazelle AH1 [K]	AAC, stored NARO, RNAY Fleetlands
	XW900	WS Gazelle AH1 (TAD-900)	AAC SEAE, Arborfield
	XW902	WS Gazelle HT3 [H]	RAF No 2 FTS, Shawbury
	XW903	WS Gazelle AH1	AAC No 3(V) Flt/7 Regiment, Leuchars
	XW904	WS Gazelle AH1 [H1]	AAC No 670 Sqn/2 Regiment, Middle Wallop
	XW906	WS Gazelle HT3 [J]	RAF No 2 FTS, Shawbury
	XW907	WS Gazelle HT2 [48/CU]	RN No 705 Sqn, Culdrose
	XW908	WS Gazelle AH1 [E]	AAC No 670 Sqn/2 Regiment, Middle Wallop
	XW909	WS Gazelle AH1	AAC No 654 Sqn/4 Regiment, Wattisham
	XW910	WS Gazelle HT3 [K]	RAF No 2 FTS, Shawbury
	XW911	WS Gazelle AH1 [H]	AAC No 666(V) Sqn/7 Regiment, Middle Wallop
	XW912	WS Gazelle AH1	AAC SEAE, Arborfield
	XW913	WS Gazelle AH1 [Y]	AAC No 662 Sqn/3 Regiment, Wattisham
	XW916	HS Harrier GR3 [W]	RAF Wittering Fire Section
	XW919	HS Harrier GR3 [W]	SFDO, RNAS Culdrose
	XW922	HS Harrier GR3 (8855M)	FSCTE, RAF Manston
	XW923	HS Harrier GR3 (8724M) <ff>	RAF Wittering for rescue training
	XW930	HS125-1B	BAe Dunsfold, spares reclamation

Serial	Type (other identity) [code]	Owner/operator, location or fate	Notes
XW934	HS Harrier T4 [Y]	DRA Farnborough	
XW986	HS Buccaneer S2B	Delta Engineering Aviation, Kemble	
XW987	HS Buccaneer S2B	*Sold as ZU-BCR, 1996*	
XW988	HS Buccaneer S2B	*Sold as ZU-AVI, November 1995*	
XX101	Cushioncraft CC7	IHM, Weston-super-Mare	
XX102	Cushioncraft CC7	Museum of Army Transport, Beverley	
XX105	BAC 1-11/201AC (G-ASJD)	MoD(PE)/DRA, DTEO Boscombe Down	
XX108	SEPECAT Jaguar GR1 [A]	MoD(PE)/FJTS, DTEO Boscombe Down	
XX109	SEPECAT Jaguar GR1 (8918M) [US]	RAF Coltishall, ground instruction	
XX110	SEPECAT Jaguar GR1 <R> (BAPC 169)	RAF No 1 SoTT, Cosford	
XX110	SEPECAT Jaguar GR1 (8955M) [EP]	RAF No 1 SoTT, Cosford	
XX112	SEPECAT Jaguar GR1A [EC]	RAF, stored Shawbury	
XX115	SEPECAT Jaguar GR1 (8821M) (fuselage)	RAF No 1 SoTT, Cosford	
XX116	SEPECAT Jaguar GR1A	RAF St Athan	
XX117	SEPECAT Jaguar GR1A [06]	MoD(PE)/DRA, DTEO Boscombe Down	
XX119	SEPECAT Jaguar GR1A (8898M) [E]	RAF No 16(R) Sqn, Lossiemouth	
XX121	SEPECAT Jaguar GR1 (92..M) [EQ]	RAF No 1 SoTT, Cosford	
XX139	SEPECAT Jaguar T2A [T]	RAF No 16(R) Sqn, Lossiemouth	
XX140	SEPECAT Jaguar T2 (9008M) [D,JJ]	RAF No 1 SoTT, Cosford	
XX141	SEPECAT Jaguar T2A [EV]	RAF No 6 Sqn, Coltishall	
XX143	SEPECAT Jaguar T2B [X] (wreck)	RAF Lossiemouth	
XX144	SEPECAT Jaguar T2A [U]	RAF AMF, Coltishall	
XX145	SEPECAT Jaguar T2	MoD(PE)/ETPS, DTEO Boscombe Down	
XX146	SEPECAT Jaguar T2B [GT]	RAF No 54 Sqn, Coltishall	
XX150	SEPECAT Jaguar T2A [W]	RAF No 16(R) Sqn, Lossiemouth	
XX153	WS Lynx AH1	AAC Wattisham, instructional use	
XX154	HS Hawk T1	MoD(PE), DTEO Llanbedr	
XX156	HS Hawk T1 [PP]	RAF No 4 FTS/19(R) Sqn, Valley	
XX157	HS Hawk T1A	RN FRADU, Culdrose	
XX158	HS Hawk T1A [PA]	RAF No 4 FTS/19(R) Sqn, Valley	
XX159	HS Hawk T1A	RAF, stored Shawbury	
XX160	HS Hawk T1	MoD(PE), DTEO Llanbedr	
XX161	HS Hawk T1 [DQ]	RAF No 4 FTS/208(R) Sqn, Valley	
XX162	HS Hawk T1	MoD(PE)/SAM, DTEO Boscombe Down	
XX163	HS Hawk T1 (9243M) [PH] (wreck)	RAF St Athan, BDRT	
XX164	HS Hawk T1 [CN]	*Crashed, 13 February 1996, Valley*	
XX165	HS Hawk T1	RN, stored Shawbury	
XX167	HS Hawk T1 [PU]	RAF No 4 FTS/19(R) Sqn, Valley	
XX168	HS Hawk T1 [CA]	RAF No 100 Sqn/JFACSTU, Leeming	
XX169	HS Hawk T1 [TH]	RAF No 4 FTS/74(R) Sqn, Valley	
XX170	HS Hawk T1 [DS]	MoD(PE), DTEO Llanbedr	
XX171	HS Hawk T1 [DW]	RAF No 4 FTS/208(R) Sqn, Valley	
XX172	HS Hawk T1	RAF St Althan Station Flight	
XX173	HS Hawk T1 [TE]	RAF No 4 FTS/74(R) Sqn, Valley	
XX174	HS Hawk T1	RAF No 4 FTS/74(R) Sqn, Valley	
XX175	HS Hawk T1	RN, stored Shawbury	
XX176	HS Hawk T1 [DS]	RAF No 4 FTS/208(R) Sqn, Valley	
XX177	HS Hawk T1 [CP]	BAe, Warton, test rig	
XX178	HS Hawk T1 [PQ]	RAF No 4 FTS/19(R) Sqn, Valley	
XX179	HS Hawk T1 [TW]	RAF No 4 FTS/74(R) Sqn, Valley	
XX181	HS Hawk T1 [PS]	RAF No 4 FTS/19(R) Sqn, Valley	
XX183	HS Hawk T1	RN FRADU, Culdrose	
XX184	HS Hawk T1	RAF St Athan Station Flight	
XX185	HS Hawk T1 [TM]	RAF, stored Shawbury	
XX186	HS Hawk T1A [PB]	RAF No 4 FTS/19(R) Sqn, Valley	
XX187	HS Hawk T1A [TN]	RAF No 4 FTS/74(R) Sqn, Valley	
XX188	HS Hawk T1A [TI]	RAF No 4 FTS/74(R) Sqn, Valley	
XX189	HS Hawk T1A [TB]	RAF No 4 FTS/74(R) Sqn, Valley	
XX190	HS Hawk T1A	RAF, stored Shawbury	
XX191	HS Hawk T1A [DT]	RAF No 4 FTS/208(R) Sqn, Valley	
XX193	HS Hawk T1A [CB]	RAF No 100 Sqn, Leeming	
XX194	HS Hawk T1A [CO]	RAF No 100 Sqn, Leeming	
XX195	HS Hawk T1A [DD]	RAF No 4 FTS/208(R) Sqn, Valley	
XX196	HS Hawk T1A [DB]	RAF No 4 FTS/208(R) Sqn, Valley	
XX198	HS Hawk T1A [DC]	RAF, stored Shawbury	

Notes	Serial	Type (other identity) [code]	Owner/operator, location or fate
	XX199	HS Hawk T1A [TG]	RAF No 4 FTS/74(R) Sqn, Valley
	XX200	HS Hawk T1A [CF]	RAF No 100 Sqn, Leeming
	XX201	HS Hawk T1A [N]	RAF, stored Shawbury
	XX202	HS Hawk T1A	RAF No 4 FTS/74(R) Sqn, Valley
	XX203	HS Hawk T1A [PC]	RAF, stored Shawbury
	XX204	HS Hawk T1A [PC]	RAF No 4 FTS/19(R) Sqn, Valley
	XX205	HS Hawk T1A	RN FRADU, Culdrose
	XX217	HS Hawk T1A	RAF, stored Shawbury
	XX218	HS Hawk T1A	RAF No 4 FTS/208(R) Sqn, Valley
	XX219	HS Hawk T1A	RAF, stored Shawbury
	XX220	HS Hawk T1A [PD]	RAF, stored Shawbury
	XX221	HS Hawk T1A [DG]	RAF No 4 FTS/208(R) Sqn, Valley
	XX222	HS Hawk T1A [TJ]	RAF No 4 FTS/74(R) Sqn, Valley
	XX223	HS Hawk T1 (fuselage)	Privately owned, Charlwood, Surrey
	XX224	HS Hawk T1 [PW]	RAF No 4 FTS/19(R) Sqn, Valley
	XX225	HS Hawk T1 [PN]	RAF No 4 FTS/19(R) Sqn, Valley
	XX226	HS Hawk T1 [74]	RAF No 4 FTS/74(R) Sqn, Valley
	XX226	HS Hawk T1 <R> (BAPC . . .)	RAF EP&TU, St Athan
	XX227	HS Hawk T1A	RAF *Red Arrows*, Cranwell
	XX228	HS Hawk T1A [CC]	RAF No 100 Sqn, Leeming
	XX230	HS Hawk T1A	RAF, stored Shawbury
	XX231	HS Hawk T1W	RAF No 4 FTS/19(R) Sqn, Valley
	XX232	HS Hawk T1	RAF No 4 FTS/74(R) Sqn, Valley
	XX233	HS Hawk T1	RAF *Red Arrows*, Cranwell
	XX234	HS Hawk T1 [DV]	RN FRADU, Culdrose
	XX235	HS Hawk T1	RAF No 4 FTS/74(R) Sqn, Valley
	XX236	HS Hawk T1 [PK]	RAF No 4 FTS/19(R) Sqn, Valley
	XX237	HS Hawk T1	RAF *Red Arrows*, Cranwell
	XX238	HS Hawk T1 [TP]	RAF No 4 FTS/74(R) Sqn, Valley
	XX239	HS Hawk T1 [DZ]	RAF No 4 FTS/208(R) Sqn, Valley
	XX240	HS Hawk T1 [TX]	RAF No 4 FTS/74(R) Sqn, Valley
	XX242	HS Hawk T1 [Y]	RN FRADU, Culdrose
	XX244	HS Hawk T1	RAF No 4 FTS/74(R) Sqn, Valley
	XX245	HS Hawk T1	RN FRADU, Culdrose
	XX246	HS Hawk T1A	RAF No 4 FTS/208(R) Sqn, Valley
	XX247	HS Hawk T1A [CM]	RAF No 100 Sqn, Leeming
	XX248	HS Hawk T1A [CJ]	RAF No 100 Sqn, Leeming
	XX249	HS Hawk T1W [PM]	RAF No 4 FTS/19(R) Sqn, Valley
	XX250	HS Hawk T1 [CG]	RAF No 100 Sqn, Leeming
	XX252	HS Hawk T1A	RAF *Red Arrows*, Cranwell
	XX253	HS Hawk T1A	RAF *Red Arrows*, Cranwell
	XX253	HS Hawk T1 <R> (BAPC 171)	RAF EP&TU, St Athan
	XX254	HS Hawk T1A	BAe Brough, fatigue test rig
	XX255	HS Hawk T1A [TE]	RAF, stored Shawbury
	XX256	HS Hawk T1A	RAF No 4 FTS/19(R) Sqn, Valley
	XX258	HS Hawk T1A [TS]	RAF No 4 FTS/74(R) Sqn, Valley
	XX260	HS Hawk T1A	RAF *Red Arrows*, Cranwell
	XX261	HS Hawk T1A	RAF, stored Shawbury
	XX263	HS Hawk T1A	RN FRADU, Culdrose
	XX263	HS Hawk T1 <R> (BAPC 152)	RAF EP&TU, St Athan
	XX264	HS Hawk T1A	RAF *Red Arrows*, Cranwell
	XX265	HS Hawk T1A [CN]	RAF No 100 Sqn, Leeming
	XX266	HS Hawk T1A	RAF *Red Arrows*, Cranwell
	XX278	HS Hawk T1A [PD]	RAF No 4 FTS/19(R) Sqn, Valley
	XX280	HS Hawk T1A	RAF No 4 FTS, Valley
	XX281	HS Hawk T1A [PE]	RAF No 4 FTS/19(R) Sqn, Valley
	XX282	HS Hawk T1A	RAF, stored Shawbury
	XX283	HS Hawk T1 [DY]	RAF No 4 FTS/208(R) Sqn, Valley
	XX284	HS Hawk T1A [CL]	RAF No 100 Sqn, Leeming
	XX285	HS Hawk T1A [CH]	RAF Leeming (damaged)
	XX286	HS Hawk T1A [DK]	RN FRADU, Culdrose
	XX287	HS Hawk T1A [PF]	RAF No 4 FTS/19(R) Sqn, Valley
	XX289	HS Hawk T1A [CI]	RAF No 100 Sqn, Leeming
	XX290	HS Hawk T1 [DV]	RAF No 4 FTS/208(R) Sqn, Valley
	XX292	HS Hawk T1W	RAF *Red Arrows*, Cranwell
	XX294	HS Hawk T1	RAF *Red Arrows*, Cranwell
	XX295	HS Hawk T1 [DA]	RAF No 4 FTS/208(R) Sqn, Valley
	XX296	HS Hawk T1 [DR]	RAF, stored Shawbury
	XX297	HS Hawk T1A (8933M)	*Scrapped at Finningley*
	XX299	HS Hawk T1W [DO]	RAF No 4 FTS/208(R) Sqn, Valley
	XX301	HS Hawk T1A	RN FRADU, Culdrose
	XX302	HS Hawk T1A [TI]	*Crashed, 26 May 1996, Beja, Portugal*
	XX303	HS Hawk T1A [TU]	RAF No 4 FTS/74(R) Sqn, Valley

Serial	Type (other identity) [code]	Owner/operator, location or fate	Notes
XX304	HS Hawk T1A (fuselage)	RAF, stored Shawbury	
XX306	HS Hawk T1A [TQ]	RAF No 4 FTS/74(R) Sqn, Valley	
XX307	HS Hawk T1	RAF *Red Arrows*, Cranwell	
XX308	HS Hawk T1	RAF *Red Arrows*, Cranwell	
XX309	HS Hawk T1 [TQ]	RAF No 4 FTS/74(R) Sqn, Valley	
XX310	HS Hawk T1W [PX]	RAF No 4 FTS/19(R) Sqn, Valley	
XX311	HS Hawk T1	RN FRADU, Culdrose	
XX312	HS Hawk T1	RAF No 4 FTS/74(R) Sqn, Valley	
XX313	HS Hawk T1 [DX]	RAF No 4 FTS/208(R) Sqn, Valley	
XX314	HS Hawk T1 [DU]	RAF No 4 FTS/208(R) Sqn, Valley	
XX315	HS Hawk T1A [DA]	RN FRADU, Culdrose	
XX316	HS Hawk T1A [DF]	RAF No 4 FTS/208(R) Sqn, Valley	
XX317	HS Hawk T1A [DL]	RAF No 4 FTS/208(R) Sqn, Valley	
XX318	HS Hawk T1A [PG]	RAF No 4 FTS/19(R) Sqn, Valley	
XX319	HS Hawk T1A	RAF No 4 FTS/74(R) Sqn, Valley	
XX320	HS Hawk T1A	RAF, stored Shawbury	
XX321	HS Hawk T1A [DH]	RAF No 4 FTS/208(R) Sqn, Valley	
XX322	HS Hawk T1A [W]	RN FRADU, Culdrose	
XX323	HS Hawk T1A [TD]	RAF No 4 FTS/74(R) Sqn, Valley	
XX324	HS Hawk T1A [DM]	RAF No 4 FTS/208(R) Sqn, Valley	
XX325	HS Hawk T1A [CE]	RAF No 100 Sqn, Leeming	
XX326	HS Hawk T1A [PH]	RAF No 4 FTS/19(R) Sqn, Valley	
XX327	HS Hawk T1	MoD(PE)/SAM, DTEO Boscombe Down	
XX329	HS Hawk T1A [PJ]	RAF No 4 FTS/19(R) Sqn, Valley	
XX330	HS Hawk T1A [DE]	RAF No 4 FTS/208(R) Sqn, Valley	
XX331	HS Hawk T1A [CK]	RAF Leeming (damaged)	
XX332	HS Hawk T1A [PL]	RAF No 4 FTS/19(R) Sqn, Valley	
XX335	HS Hawk T1A [CD]	RAF No 100 Sqn, Leeming	
XX337	HS Hawk T1A	RN FRADU, Culdrose	
XX338	HS Hawk T1W [PV]	RAF No 4 FTS/19(R) Sqn, Valley	
XX339	HS Hawk T1A [TV]	RAF No 4 FTS/74(R) Sqn, Valley	
XX341	HS Hawk T1 ASTRA [1]	MoD(PE)/ETPS, DTEO Boscombe Down	
XX342	HS Hawk T1 [2]	MoD(PE)/ETPS, DTEO Boscombe Down	
XX343	HS Hawk T1 [3]	MoD(PE)/ETPS, DTEO Boscombe Down	
XX344	HS Hawk T1 (8847M) (fuselage)	DRA Farnborough Fire Section	
XX345	HS Hawk T1A [DJ]	RAF No 4 FTS/208(R) Sqn, Valley	
XX346	HS Hawk T1A	RN FRADU, Culdrose	
XX348	HS Hawk T1A [DN]	RAF No 4 FTS/208(R) Sqn, Valley	
XX349	HS Hawk T1W [PY]	RAF No 4 FTS/19(R) Sqn, Valley	
XX350	HS Hawk T1A [TC]	RAF No 4 FTS/74(R) Sqn, Valley	
XX351	HS Hawk T1A [DP]	RAF No 4 FTS/208(R) Sqn, Valley	
XX352	HS Hawk T1A [CP]	RAF No 100 Sqn, Leeming	
XX370	WS Gazelle AH1	AAC No 665 Sqn/5 Regiment, Aldergrove	
XX371	WS Gazelle AH1	AAC No 12 Flt, Brüggen	
XX372	WS Gazelle AH1	AAC No 657 Sqn/9 Regiment, Dishforth	
XX375	WS Gazelle AH1 [E1]	AAC No 670 Sqn/2 Regiment, Middle Wallop	
XX378	WS Gazelle AH1 [Q]	AAC No 667 Sqn/2 Regiment, Middle Wallop	
XX379	WS Gazelle AH1	AAC No 658 Sqn/7 Regiment, Middle Wallop	
XX380	WS Gazelle AH1	RM No 847 Sqn, Yeovilton	
XX381	WS Gazelle AH1	AAC No 664 Sqn/9 Regiment, Dishforth	
XX382	WS Gazelle HT3 [M]	RAF No 2 FTS, Shawbury	
XX383	WS Gazelle AH1 [D]	AAC No 658 Sqn/7 Regiment, Middle Wallop	
XX384	WS Gazelle AH1	AAC No 669 Sqn/4 Regiment, Wattisham	
XX385	WS Gazelle AH1 [X]	AAC No 670 Sqn/2 Regiment, Middle Wallop	
XX386	WS Gazelle AH1	AAC No 12 Flt, Brüggen	
XX387	WS Gazelle AH1 (TAD 014)	AAC SEAE, Arborfield	
XX388	WS Gazelle AH1	AAC, stored NARO, RNAY Fleetlands	
XX389	WS Gazelle AH1	AAC No 661 Sqn/1 Regiment, Gütersloh	
XX391	WS Gazelle HT2 [56/CU]	RN No 705 Sqn, Culdrose	
XX392	WS Gazelle AH1 [A1]	AAC No 670 Sqn/2 Regiment, Middle Wallop	
XX393	WS Gazelle AH1 [W]	AAC No 654 Sqn/4 Regiment, Wattisham	
XX394	WS Gazelle AH1 [X]	AAC No 669 Sqn/4 Regiment, Wattisham	
XX395	WS Gazelle AH1	AAC No 651 Sqn/1 Regiment, Gütersloh	
XX396	WS Gazelle HT3 (8718M) [N]	RAF EP&TU, Henlow	
XX398	WS Gazelle AH1 [2]	AAC No 656 Sqn/9 Regiment, Dishforth	
XX399	WS Gazelle AH1 [Y]	AAC No 2(V) Flt, Middle Wallop	
XX403	WS Gazelle AH1 [U]	AAC No 670 Sqn/2 Regiment, Middle Wallop	

Notes	Serial	Type (other identity) [code]	Owner/operator, location or fate
	XX405	WS Gazelle AH1 [C1]	AAC No 670 Sqn/2 Regiment, Middle Wallop
	XX406	WS Gazelle HT3 [P]	RAF No 7 Sqn, Odiham
	XX407	WS Gazelle AH1 [D1]	AAC No 670 Sqn/2 Regiment, Middle Wallop
	XX408	WS Gazelle AH1	AAC No 654 Sqn/4 Regiment, Wattisham
	XX409	WS Gazelle AH1	AAC No 669 Sqn/4 Regiment, Wattisham
	XX410	WS Gazelle HT2 [58/CU]	RN
	XX411	WS Gazelle AH1 [X]	Scrapped at Stock, 1996
	XX411	WS Gazelle AH1 <rf>	FAA Museum, RNAS Yeovilton
	XX412	WS Gazelle AH1 [B]	RM No 847 Sqn, Yeovilton
	XX413	WS Gazelle AH1 [C]	RM No 847 Sqn, Yeovilton
	XX414	WS Gazelle AH1	AAC No 661 Sqn/1 Regiment, Gütersloh
	XX416	WS Gazelle AH1 [W]	AAC No 657 Sqn/9 Regiment, Dishforth
	XX417	WS Gazelle AH1	AAC No 667 Sqn/2 Regiment, Middle Wallop
	XX418	WS Gazelle AH1	AAC No 651 Sqn/1 Regiment, Gütersloh
	XX419	WS Gazelle AH1 [X]	AAC No 662 Sqn/3 Regiment, Wattisham
	XX431	WS Gazelle HT2 [43/CU]	RN No 705 Sqn, Culdrose
	XX432	WS Gazelle AH1	AAC No 669 Sqn/4 Regiment, Wattisham
	XX433	WS Gazelle AH1 [F]	AAC, stored NARO, RNAY Fleetlands
	XX435	WS Gazelle AH1 [W]	AAC No 670 Sqn/2 Regiment, Middle Wallop
	XX436	WS Gazelle HT2 [39/CU]	RN No 705 Sqn, Culdrose
	XX437	WS Gazelle AH1	AAC No 652 Sqn/1 Regiment, Gütersloh
	XX438	WS Gazelle AH1	AAC No 661 Sqn/1 Regiment, Gütersloh
	XX439	WS Gazelle AH1	AAC No 662 Sqn/3 Regiment, Wattisham
	XX440	WS Gazelle AH1 (G-BCHN)	AAC, stored NARO, RNAY Fleetlands
	XX441	WS Gazelle HT2 [38/CU]	RN No 705 Sqn, Culdrose
	XX442	WS Gazelle AH1 [E]	AAC No 666(V) Sqn/7 Regiment, Middle Wallop
	XX443	WS Gazelle AH1 [Y]	AAC No 658 Sqn/7 Regiment, Middle Wallop
	XX444	WS Gazelle AH1 [E]	AAC, stored NARO, RNAY Fleetlands
	XX445	WS Gazelle AH1 [T]	AAC No 658 Sqn/7 Regiment, Middle Wallop
	XX446	WS Gazelle HT2 [57/CU]	RN No 705 Sqn, Culdrose
	XX447	WS Gazelle AH1 [D1]	AAC No 670 Sqn/2 Regiment, Middle Wallop
	XX448	WS Gazelle AH1	AAC No 654 Sqn/4 Regiment, Wattisham
	XX449	WS Gazelle AH1	AAC No 662 Sqn/3 Regiment, Wattisham
	XX450	WS Gazelle AH1 [D]	RM No 847 Sqn, Yeovilton
	XX451	WS Gazelle HT2 [58/CU] (wreck)	RN FSAIU, Yeovilton
	XX452	WS Gazelle AH1	AAC Middle Wallop Fire Section
	XX453	WS Gazelle AH1 [2]	AAC No 663 Sqn/3 Regiment, Wattisham
	XX454	WS Gazelle AH1 [W]	AAC No 662 Sqn/3 Regiment, Wattisham
	XX455	WS Gazelle AH1	AAC No 652 Sqn/1 Regiment, Gütersloh
	XX456	WS Gazelle AH1	AAC No 3(V) Flt/7 Regiment, Leuchars
	XX457	WS Gazelle AH1	AAC SEAE, Arborfield
	XX460	WS Gazelle AH1	AAC No 654 Sqn/4 Regiment, Wattisham
	XX462	WS Gazelle AH1 [W]	AAC No 658 Sqn/7 Regiment, Middle Wallop
	XX466	HS Hunter T66B/T7 (XL620) [830/DD]	RN, Predannack Fire School
	XX467	HS Hunter T66B/T7 (XL605) [86]	Air Service Training, Perth
	XX469	WS Lynx HAS2 (G-BNCL)	
	XX475	HP137 Jetstream T2 (N1036S)	MoD(PE), DTEO West Freugh
	XX476	HP137 Jetstream T2 (N1037S) [561/CU]	RN No 750 Sqn, Culdrose
	XX477	HP137 Jetstream T1 (G-AXXS/ 8462M) <ff>	RAF
	XX478	HP137 Jetstream T2 (G-AXXT) [564/CU]	RN No 750 Sqn, Culdrose
	XX479	HP137 Jetstream T2 (G-AXUR) [563/CU]	RN, stored St Athan
	XX480	HP137 Jetstream T2 (G-AXXU) [565/CU]	RN, stored Shawbury
	XX481	HP137 Jetstream T2 (G-AXUP) [560/CU]	RN No 750 Sqn, Culdrose
	XX482	SA Jetstream T1 [J]	RAF No 3 FTS/45(R) Sqn, Cranwell
	XX483	SA Jetstream T2 [562/CU]	RN, stored Shawbury
	XX484	SA Jetstream T2 [566/CU]	RN No 750 Sqn, Culdrose
	XX485	SA Jetstream T2 [567/CU]	RN No 750 Sqn, Culdrose

Serial	Type (other identity) [code]	Owner/operator, location or fate	Notes
XX486	SA Jetstream T2 [569/CU]	RN No 750 Sqn, Culdrose	
XX487	SA Jetstream T2 [568/CU]	RN No 750 Sqn, Culdrose	
XX488	SA Jetstream T2 [562/CU]	RN No 750 Sqn, Culdrose	
XX490	SA Jetstream T2 [570/CU]	RN No 750 Sqn, Culdrose	
XX491	SA Jetstream T1 [K]	RAF No 3 FTS/45(R) Sqn, Cranwell	
XX492	SA Jetstream T1 [A]	RAF No 3 FTS/45(R) Sqn, Cranwell	
XX493	SA Jetstream T1 [L]	RAF No 3 FTS/45(R) Sqn, Cranwell	
XX494	SA Jetstream T1 [B]	RAF No 3 FTS/45(R) Sqn, Cranwell	
XX495	SA Jetstream T1 [C]	RAF No 3 FTS/45(R) Sqn, Cranwell	
XX496	SA Jetstream T1 [D]	RAF No 3 FTS/45(R) Sqn, Cranwell	
XX497	SA Jetstream T1 [E]	RAF No 3 FTS/45(R) Sqn, Cranwell	
XX498	SA Jetstream T1 [F]	RAF No 3 FTS/45(R) Sqn, Cranwell	
XX499	SA Jetstream T1 [G]	RAF No 3 FTS/45(R) Sqn, Cranwell	
XX500	SA Jetstream T1 [H]	RAF No 3 FTS/45(R) Sqn, Cranwell	
XX507	HS125 CC2	RAF No 32(The Royal) Sqn, Northolt	
XX508	HS125 CC2	RAF No 32(The Royal) Sqn, Northolt	
XX510	WS Lynx HAS2 [69/LS]	RN AES, *HMS Sultan*, Gosport	
XX513	SA Bulldog T1 [10]	RAF CFS, Cranwell	
XX515	SA Bulldog T1 [4]	RAF Manchester & Salford Universities AS/ No 10 AEF, Woodvale	
XX516	SA Bulldog T1 [C]	RAF Cambridge UAS/No 5 AEF, Cambridge	
XX518	SA Bulldog T1 [B]	RAF Cambridge UAS/No 5 AEF, Cambridge	
XX519	SA Bulldog T1 [14]	RAF CFS, Cranwell	
XX520	SA Bulldog T1 [A]	RAF East Midlands UAS/No 7 AEF, Newton	
XX521	SA Bulldog T1 [G]	RAF University of Birmingham AS/ No 8 AEF, Cosford	
XX522	SA Bulldog T1 [06]	RAF East Lowlands UAS, Leuchars	
XX523	SA Bulldog T1 [X]	RAF Liverpool UAS, Woodvale	
XX524	SA Bulldog T1 [04]	RAF University of London AS/No 6 AEF, Benson	
XX525	SA Bulldog T1 [03]	RAF East Lowlands UAS, Leuchars	
XX526	SA Bulldog T1 [C]	RAF Oxford UAS, Benson	
XX527	SA Bulldog T1 [05]	RAF East Lowlands UAS, Leuchars	
XX528	SA Bulldog T1 [D]	RAF Oxford UAS, Benson	
XX529	SA Bulldog T1 [F]	RAF Cambridge UAS/No 5 AEF, Cambridge	
XX531	SA Bulldog T1 [06]	RAF University of Wales AS, St Athan	
XX532	SA Bulldog T1 [E]	RAF Cambridge UAS/No 5 AEF, Cambridge	
XX533	SA Bulldog T1 [U]	RAF Northumbrian Universities AS/ No 11 AEF, Leeming	
XX534	SA Bulldog T1 [B]	RAF University of Birmingham AS/ No 8 AEF, Cosford	
XX535	SA Bulldog T1 [S]	RAF East Midlands UAS/No 7 AEF, Newton	
XX536	SA Bulldog T1	RAF University of Birmingham AS/ No 8 AEF, Cosford	
XX537	SA Bulldog T1 [02]	RAF East Lowlands UAS, Leuchars	
XX538	SA Bulldog T1 [18]	RAF CFS, Cranwell	
XX539	SA Bulldog T1 [L]	RAF Liverpool UAS, Woodvale	
XX540	SA Bulldog T1 [15]	RAF CFS, Cranwell	
XX541	SA Bulldog T1 [F]	RAF Bristol UAS/No 3 AEF, Colerne	
XX543	SA Bulldog T1 [F]	RAF Yorkshire Universities AS/No 9 AEF, Church Fenton	
XX544	SA Bulldog T1 [01]	RAF University of London AS/No 6 AEF, Benson	
XX545	SA Bulldog T1 [02]	RAF East Lowlands UAS, Leuchars, GI use	
XX546	SA Bulldog T1 [03]	RAF University of London AS/No 6 AEF, Benson	
XX547	SA Bulldog T1 [05]	RAF University of London AS/No 6 AEF, Benson	
XX548	SA Bulldog T1 [06]	RAF University of London AS/No 6 AEF, Benson	
XX549	SA Bulldog T1 [6]	RAF Southampton UAS/No 2 AEF, DTEO Boscombe Down	
XX550	SA Bulldog T1 [Z]	RAF Northumbrian Universities AS/ No 11 AEF, Leeming	
XX551	SA Bulldog T1 [E]	RAF Oxford UAS, Benson	
XX552	SA Bulldog T1 [08]	RAF University of London AS/No 6 AEF, Benson	
XX553	SA Bulldog T1 [07]	RAF University of London AS/No 6 AEF, Benson	

Notes	Serial	Type (other identity) [code]	Owner/operator, location or fate
	XX554	SA Bulldog T1 [09]	RAF University of London AS/No 6 AEF, Benson
	XX555	SA Bulldog T1 [U]	RAF Liverpool UAS, Woodvale
	XX556	SA Bulldog T1 [M]	RAF East Midlands UAS/No 7 AEF, Newton
	XX557	SA Bulldog T1	RAF Linton-on-Ouse, ground instruction
	XX558	SA Bulldog T1 [A]	RAF University of Birmingham AS/ No 8 AEF, Cosford
	XX559	SA Bulldog T1	RAF Universities of Glasgow & Strathclyde AS, Glasgow
	XX560	SA Bulldog T1	RAF East Lowlands UAS, Leuchars
	XX561	SA Bulldog T1 [7]	RAF CFS, Cranwell
	XX562	SA Bulldog T1	RAF CFS, Cranwell
	XX611	SA Bulldog T1	RAF Universities of Glasgow & Strathclyde AS, Glasgow
	XX612	SA Bulldog T1 [05]	RAF University of Wales AS, St Athan
	XX614	SA Bulldog T1 [B]	RAF Oxford UAS, Benson
	XX615	SA Bulldog T1 [2]	RAF Manchester & Salford Universities AS/ No 10 AEF, Woodvale
	XX616	SA Bulldog T1 [3]	RAF Manchester & Salford Universities AS/ No 10 AEF, Woodvale
	XX617	SA Bulldog T1 [2]	RAF CFS, Cranwell
	XX619	SA Bulldog T1 [T]	RAF Northumbrian Universities AS/ No 11 AEF, Leeming
	XX620	SA Bulldog T1 [C]	RAF Yorkshire Universities AS/No 9 AEF, Church Fenton
	XX621	SA Bulldog T1 [G]	RAF Yorkshire Universities AS/No 9 AEF, Church Fenton
	XX622	SA Bulldog T1 [B]	RAF Yorkshire Universities AS/No 9 AEF, Church Fenton
	XX623	SA Bulldog T1 [M]	RAF, stored Newton
	XX624	SA Bulldog T1 [D]	RAF Cambridge UAS/No 5 AEF, Cambridge
	XX625	SA Bulldog T1 [01]	RAF University of Wales AS, St Athan
	XX626	SA Bulldog T1 [02]	RAF University of Wales AS, St Athan
	XX627	SA Bulldog T1 [O]	RAF
	XX628	SA Bulldog T1 [J]	RAF Bristol UAS/No 3 AEF, Colerne
	XX629	SA Bulldog T1 [V]	RAF Northumbrian Universities AS/ No 11 AEF, Leeming
	XX630	SA Bulldog T1 [5]	RAF CFS, Cranwell
	XX631	SA Bulldog T1	RAF Queen's UAS/No 13 AEF, Belfast City Airport
	XX632	SA Bulldog T1 [A]	RAF Yorkshire Universities AS/No 9 AEF, Church Fenton
	XX633	SA Bulldog T1 [X]	RAF Northumbrian Universities AS/ No 11 AEF, Leeming
	XX634	SA Bulldog T1 [1]	RAF CFS, Cranwell
	XX635	SA Bulldog T1 (8767M)	RAF CTTS, St Athan
	XX636	SA Bulldog T1 [Y]	RAF Northumbrian Universities AS/ No 11 AEF, Leeming
	XX637	SA Bulldog T1 (9197M) [U]	SERCO, RAF St Athan
	XX638	SA Bulldog T1	RAF CFS, Cranwell
	XX639	SA Bulldog T1 [02]	RAF University of London AS/ No 6 AEF, Benson
	XX640	SA Bulldog T1 [K]	RAF Bristol UAS/No 3 AEF, Colerne
	XX653	SA Bulldog T1	RAF Bristol UAS/No 3 AEF, Colerne
	XX654	SA Bulldog T1 [3]	RAF CFS, Cranwell
	XX655	SA Bulldog T1 [B]	RAF Bristol UAS/No 3 AEF, Colerne
	XX656	SA Bulldog T1 [C]	RAF Bristol UAS/No 3 AEF, Colerne
	XX657	SA Bulldog T1 [U]	RAF Cambridge UAS/No 5 AEF, Cambridge
	XX658	SA Bulldog T1 [A]	RAF Cambridge UAS/No 5 AEF, Cambridge
	XX659	SA Bulldog T1 [S]	RAF Cambridge UAS/No 5 AEF, Cambridge
	XX661	SA Bulldog T1	RAF Universities of Glasgow & Strathclyde AS, Glasgow
	XX663	SA Bulldog T1 [01]	RAF East Lowlands UAS, Leuchars
	XX664	SA Bulldog T1 [04]	RAF East Lowlands UAS, Leuchars
	XX665	SA Bulldog T1	RAF East Lowlands UAS, Leuchars
	XX666	SA Bulldog T1	RAF Universities of Glasgow & Strathclyde AS, Glasgow
	XX667	SA Bulldog T1 [16]	RAF CFS, Cranwell

Serial	Type (other identity) [code]	Owner/operator, location or fate	Notes
XX668	SA Bulldog T1 [1]	RAF Manchester & Salford Universities AS/ No 10 AEF, Woodvale	
XX669	SA Bulldog T1 (8997M) [B]	Phoenix Aviation, Bruntingthorpe	
XX670	SA Bulldog T1 [C]	RAF University of Birmingham AS/ No 8 AEF, Cosford	
XX671	SA Bulldog T1 [D]	RAF University of Birmingham AS/ No 8 AEF, Cosford	
XX672	SA Bulldog T1 [E]	RAF University of Birmingham AS/ No 8 AEF, Cosford	
XX685	SA Bulldog T1 [11]	RAF CFS, Cranwell	
XX686	SA Bulldog T1 [4]	RAF CFS, Cranwell	
XX687	SA Bulldog T1 [13]	RAF CFS, Cranwell	
XX688	SA Bulldog T1 [8]	RAF CFS, Cranwell	
XX689	SA Bulldog T1 [D]	RAF Bristol UAS/No 3 AEF, Colerne	
XX690	SA Bulldog T1 [A]	RAF Liverpool UAS, Woodvale	
XX691	SA Bulldog T1 [10]	RAF University of London AS/No 6 AEF, Benson	
XX692	SA Bulldog T1 [A]	RAF Bristol UAS/No 3 AEF, Colerne	
XX693	SA Bulldog T1 [Y]	RAF Universities of Glasgow & Strathclyde AS, Glasgow	
XX694	SA Bulldog T1 [E]	RAF East Midlands UAS/No 7 AEF, Newton	
XX695	SA Bulldog T1 [A]	RAF Oxford UAS, Benson	
XX696	SA Bulldog T1 [S]	RAF Liverpool UAS, Woodvale	
XX697	SA Bulldog T1 [H]	RAF Bristol UAS/No 3 AEF, Colerne	
XX698	SA Bulldog T1 [9]	RAF CFS, Cranwell	
XX699	SA Bulldog T1 [F]	RAF University of Birmingham AS/ No 8 AEF, Cosford	
XX700	SA Bulldog T1 [17]	RAF CFS, Cranwell	
XX701	SA Bulldog T1 [02]	RAF Southampton UAS/No 2 AEF, DTEO Boscombe Down	
XX702	SA Bulldog T1 [Π]	RAF East Midlands UAS/No 7 AEF, Newton	
XX704	SA Bulldog T1 [U]	RAF East Midlands UAS/No 7 AEF, Newton	
XX705	SA Bulldog T1 [05]	RAF Southampton UAS/No 2 AEF, DTEO Boscombe Down	
XX706	SA Bulldog T1 [01]	RAF Southampton UAS/No 2 AEF, DTEO Boscombe Down	
XX707	SA Bulldog T1 [04]	RAF Southampton UAS/No 2 AEF, DTEO Boscombe Down	
XX708	SA Bulldog T1 [03]	RAF Southampton UAS/No 2 AEF, DTEO Boscombe Down	
XX709	SA Bulldog T1 [E]	RAF Yorkshire Universities AS/No 9 AEF, Church Fenton	
XX710	SA Bulldog T1 [5]	RAF Manchester & Salford Universities AS/ No 10 AEF, Woodvale	
XX711	SA Bulldog T1 [S]	RAF University of London AS/No 6 AEF, Benson	
XX713	SA Bulldog T1 [G]	RAF Bristol UAS/No 3 AEF, Colerne	
XX714	SA Bulldog T1 [D]	RAF Yorkshire Universities AS/No 9 AEF, Church Fenton	
XX719	SEPECAT Jaguar GR1A [EE]	BAe Warton (for Oman)	
XX720	SEPECAT Jaguar GR1A [GB]	RAF No 54 Sqn, Coltishall	
XX722	SEPECAT Jaguar GR1 [EF]	RAF St Athan	
XX723	SEPECAT Jaguar GR1A [GQ]	RAF No 54 Sqn, Coltishall	
XX724	SEPECAT Jaguar GR1A [GA]	RAF, stored Shawbury	
XX725	SEPECAT Jaguar GR1B [GU]	RAF No 54 Sqn, Coltishall	
XX725	SEPECAT Jaguar GR1 <R> (BAPC 150) [GU]	RAF EP&TU, St Athan	
XX726	SEPECAT Jaguar GR1 (8947M) [EB]	RAF No 1 SoTT, Cosford	
XX727	SEPECAT Jaguar GR1 (8951M) [ER]	RAF No 1 SoTT, Cosford	
XX729	SEPECAT Jaguar GR1B [EL]	RAF No 6 Sqn, Coltishall	
XX730	SEPECAT Jaguar GR1 (8952M) [EC]	RAF No 1 SoTT, Cosford	
XX733	SEPECAT Jaguar GR1B [ER]	RAF, stored Coltishall (wreck)	
XX736	SEPECAT Jaguar GR1 (9110M)	RAF Coltishall, BDRT	
XX737	SEPECAT Jaguar GR1A [EE]	RAF No 6 Sqn, Coltishall	
XX738	SEPECAT Jaguar GR1B	MoD(PE)/FJTS, DTEO Boscombe Down	
XX739	SEPECAT Jaguar GR1 (8902M) [I]	RAF No 1 SoTT, Cosford	
XX741	SEPECAT Jaguar GR1A [04]	RAF, stored Shawbury	

Notes	Serial	Type (other identity) [code]	Owner/operator, location or fate
	XX743	SEPECAT Jaguar GR1 (8949M) [EG]	RAF No 1 SoTT, Cosford
	XX744	SEPECAT Jaguar GR1 (92.M) [DJ]	RAF No 1 SoTT, Cosford
	XX745	SEPECAT Jaguar GR1A [D]	RAF No 16(R) Sqn, Lossiemouth
	XX746	SEPECAT Jaguar GR1A (8895M) [07]	RAF No 1 SoTT, Cosford
	XX747	SEPECAT Jaguar GR1 (8903M)	AMIF, RAFC Cranwell
	XX748	SEPECAT Jaguar GR1B [GK]	RAF No 54 Sqn, Coltishall
	XX751	SEPECAT Jaguar GR1 (8937M) [10]	RAF No 1 SoTT, Cosford
	XX752	SEPECAT Jaguar GR1A [EQ]	RAF No 6 Sqn, Coltishall
	XX753	SEPECAT Jaguar GR1 (9087M) <ff>	RAF EP&TU, St Athan
	XX756	SEPECAT Jaguar GR1 (8899M) [AM]	RAF No 1 SoTT, Cosford
	XX757	SEPECAT Jaguar GR1 (8948M) [CU]	RAF No 1 SoTT, Cosford
	XX761	SEPECAT Jaguar GR1 (8600M) <ff>	BAe Warton, instructional use
	XX763	SEPECAT Jaguar GR1 (9009M)	RAF CTTS, St Athan
	XX764	SEPECAT Jaguar GR1 (9010M)	RAF CTTS, St Athan
	XX765	SEPECAT Jaguar ACT	RAF Cosford Aerospace Museum
	XX766	SEPECAT Jaguar GR1A [EA]	RAF No 6 Sqn, Coltishall
	XX767	SEPECAT Jaguar GR1B [GE]	RAF No 54 Sqn, Coltishall
	XX818	SEPECAT Jaguar GR1 (8945M) [DE]	RAF No 1 SoTT, Cosford
	XX819	SEPECAT Jaguar GR1 (8923M) [CE]	RAF No 1 SoTT, Cosford
	XX821	SEPECAT Jaguar GR1 (8896M) [P]	AMIF, RAFC Cranwell
	XX824	SEPECAT Jaguar GR1 (9019M) [AD]	RAF No 1 SoTT, Cosford
	XX825	SEPECAT Jaguar GR1 (9020M) [BN]	RAF No 1 SoTT, Cosford
	XX826	SEPECAT Jaguar GR1 (9021M) [34,JH]	RAF No 1 SoTT, Cosford
	XX829	SEPECAT Jaguar T2A [Y]	RAF No 16(R) Sqn, Lossiemouth
	XX830	SEPECAT Jaguar T2	MoD(PE)/ETPS, DTEO Boscombe Down
	XX832	SEPECAT Jaguar T2A [Z]	RAF No 16(R) Sqn, Lossiemouth
	XX833	SEPECAT Jaguar T2B	RAF AWC/SAOEU, DTEO Boscombe Down
	XX835	SEPECAT Jaguar T2B [FY]	RAF No 41 Sqn, Coltishall
	XX836	SEPECAT Jaguar T2A [ER]	RAF, stored Shawbury
	XX837	SEPECAT Jaguar T2 (8978M) [Z]	RAF No 1 SoTT, Cosford
	XX838	SEPECAT Jaguar T2A [X]	RAF, stored Shawbury
	XX839	SEPECAT Jaguar T2A [GW]	RAF, stored St Athan
	XX840	SEPECAT Jaguar T2A [X]	RAF, stored Shawbury
	XX841	SEPECAT Jaguar T2A [ES]	RAF No 6 Sqn, Coltishall
	XX842	SEPECAT Jaguar T2A [FV]	RAF No 41 Sqn, Coltishall
	XX844	SEPECAT Jaguar T2 (9023M) [F,JF]	RAF St Athan
	XX845	SEPECAT Jaguar T2A [ET]	RAF No 6 Sqn, Coltishall
	XX846	SEPECAT Jaguar T2A [GV]	RAF No 54 Sqn, Coltishall
	XX847	SEPECAT Jaguar T2A	RAF, stored St Athan
	XX885	HS Buccaneer S2B (9225M)	RAF Lossiemouth, BDRT
	XX886	HS Buccaneer S2B	*Scrapped at Stock, 1995*
	XX888	HS Buccaneer S2B <ff>	Dundonald Aviation Centre, Strathclyde
	XX889	HS Buccaneer S2B	Privately owned, Enstone
	XX892	HS Buccaneer S2B <ff>	Christies Garden Centre, Forres, Grampian
	XX893	HS Buccaneer S2B <ff>	Privately owned, Birtley, Tyne & Wear
	XX894	HS Buccaneer S2B [020/R]	Buccaneer Preservation Society, Kemble
	XX895	HS Buccaneer S2B	The Planets Leisure Centre, Woking
	XX897	HS Buccaneer S2B	Source Classic Jet Flight, Bournemouth
	XX899	HS Buccaneer S2B <ff>	Midland Air Museum, Coventry
	XX900	HS Buccaneer S2B	British Aviation Heritage, Bruntingthorpe
	XX901	HS Buccaneer S2B	Yorkshire Air Museum, Elvington
	XX907	WS Lynx AH1	DRA Structures Dept, Farnborough
	XX910	WS Lynx HAS2	DRA Structures Dept, Farnborough
	XX914	BAC VC10/1103 (8777M) <rf>	RAF AMS, Brize Norton
	XX919	BAC 1-11/402AP (PI-C1121)	MoD(PE)/DRA, DTEO Boscombe Down
	XX946	Panavia Tornado (P02) (8883M)	RAF Museum, Hendon
	XX947	Panavia Tornado (P03) (8797M)	RAF, stored St Athan
	XX948	Panavia Tornado (P06) (8879M) [P]	RAF No 1 SoTT, Cosford

Serial	Type (other identity) [code]	Owner/operator, location or fate	Notes
XX955	SEPECAT Jaguar GR1A [GK]	RAF, stored Shawbury	
XX956	SEPECAT Jaguar GR1 (8950M) [BE]	RAF No 1 SoTT, Cosford	
XX958	SEPECAT Jaguar GR1 (9022M) [BK,JG]	RAF No 1 SoTT, Cosford	
XX959	SEPECAT Jaguar GR1 (8953M) [CJ]	RAF No 1 SoTT, Cosford	
XX962	SEPECAT Jaguar GR1B [EK]	AMIF, RAFC Cranwell	
XX965	SEPECAT Jaguar GR1A [C]	AMIF, RAFC Cranwell	
XX966	SEPECAT Jaguar GR1A (8904M) [EL]	RAF No 1 SoTT, Cosford	
XX967	SEPECAT Jaguar GR1 (9006M) [AC,JD]	RAF No 1 SoTT, Cosford	
XX968	SEPECAT Jaguar GR1 (9007M) [AJ,JE]	RAF No 1 SoTT, Cosford	
XX969	SEPECAT Jaguar GR1A (8897M) [01]	RAF No 1 SoTT, Cosford	
XX970	SEPECAT Jaguar GR1B [EH]	RAF St Athan (conversion)	
XX974	SEPECAT Jaguar GR1A [GH]	RAF No 54 Sqn, Coltishall	
XX975	SEPECAT Jaguar GR1 (8905M) [07]	RAF No 1 SoTT, Cosford	
XX976	SEPECAT Jaguar GR1 (8906M) [BD]	RAF No 1 SoTT, Cosford	
XX977	SEPECAT Jaguar GR1 (9132M) [DL,05]	RAF St Athan, BDRT	
XX979	SEPECAT Jaguar GR1A	MoD(PE)/FJTS, DTEO Boscombe Down	
XZ101	SEPECAT Jaguar GR1A [D]	RAF, stored Coltishall	
XZ103	SEPECAT Jaguar GR1A [P]	RAF No 41 Sqn, Coltishall	
XZ104	SEPECAT Jaguar GR1A [FM]	RAF No 41 Sqn, Coltishall	
XZ106	SEPECAT Jaguar GR1A [R]	RAF No 41 Sqn, Coltishall	
XZ107	SEPECAT Jaguar GR1A [H]	RAF No 41 Sqn, Coltishall	
XZ108	SEPECAT Jaguar GR1A [GL]	RAF No 54 Sqn, Coltishall	
XZ109	SEPECAT Jaguar GR1A [EN]	RAF No 6 Sqn, Coltishall	
XZ111	SEPECAT Jaguar GR1A	RAF, stored St Athan	
XZ112	SEPECAT Jaguar GR1A [GA]	RAF No 54 Sqn, Coltishall	
XZ113	SEPECAT Jaguar GR1A [FD]	RAF, stored Coltishall	
XZ114	SEPECAT Jaguar GR1A [FB]	RAF, stored Shawbury	
XZ115	SEPECAT Jaguar GR1A [FC]	RAF Coltishall	
XZ117	SEPECAT Jaguar GR1A [GG]	RAF St Athan	
XZ118	SEPECAT Jaguar GR1A [FF]	RAF, stored Coltishall	
XZ119	SEPECAT Jaguar GR1A [FG]	AMIF, RAFC Cranwell	
XZ129	HS Harrier GR3 [ETS]	RN ETS, Yeovilton	
XZ130	HS Harrier GR3 (9079M) [A,HE]	RAF No 1 SoTT, Cosford	
XZ131	HS Harrier GR3 (9174M) <ff>	RAF EP&TU, St Athan	
XZ132	HS Harrier GR3 (9168M) [C]	AMIF, RAFC Cranwell	
XZ133	HS Harrier GR3 [10]	Imperial War Museum, Duxford	
XZ135	HS Harrier GR3 (8848M) <ff>	RAF EP&TU, St Athan	
XZ138	HS Harrier GR3 (9040M) <ff>	RAFC Cranwell, Trenchard Hall	
XZ145	HS Harrier T4 [T]	RAF, stored Shawbury	
XZ146	HS Harrier T4 [S]	RAF, stored Shawbury	
XZ170	WS Lynx AH9	MoD(PE)/Westland, Yeovil	
XZ171	WS Lynx AH7 [UN]	AAC No 664 Sqn/9 Regiment, Dishforth	
XZ172	WS Lynx AH7	AAC No 655 Sqn/5 Regiment, Aldergrove	
XZ173	WS Lynx AH7	AAC No 669 Sqn/4 Regiment, Wattisham	
XZ174	WS Lynx AH7	AAC No 655 Sqn/5 Regiment, Aldergrove	
XZ175	WS Lynx AH7 [Z]	AAC No 671 Sqn/2 Regiment, Middle Wallop	
XZ176	WS Lynx AH7	AAC No 669 Sqn/4 Regiment, Wattisham	
XZ177	WS Lynx AH7	AAC, stored NARO, RNAY Fleetlands	
XZ178	WS Lynx AH7 [1]	AAC No 662 Sqn/3 Regiment, Wattisham	
XZ179	WS Lynx AH7	AAC No 654 Sqn/4 Regiment, Wattisham	
XZ180	WS Lynx AH7 [R]	RM No 847 Sqn, Yeovilton	
XZ181	WS Lynx AH1	AAC SEAE, Arborfield	
XZ182	WS Lynx AH7 [M]	RM No 847 Sqn, Yeovilton	
XZ183	WS Lynx AH7	AAC No 654 Sqn/4 Regiment, Wattisham	
XZ184	WS Lynx AH7 [W]	AAC, stored NARO, RNAY Fleetlands	
XZ185	WS Lynx AH7	AAC No 662 Sqn/3 Regiment, Wattisham	
XZ186	WS Lynx AH7 (wreckage)	AAC, NARO, RNAY Fleetlands	
XZ187	WS Lynx AH7	AAC No 667 Sqn/2 Regiment, Middle Wallop	
XZ188	WS Lynx AH7	AAC No 662 Sqn/3 Regiment, Wattisham	
XZ190	WS Lynx AH7	AAC No 663 Sqn/3 Regiment, Wattisham	

Notes	Serial	Type (other identity) [code]	Owner/operator, location or fate
	XZ191	WS Lynx AH7 [X]	AAC, stored NARO, RNAY Fleetlands
	XZ192	WS Lynx AH7	AAC No 655 Sqn/5 Regiment, Aldergrove
	XZ193	WS Lynx AH7 [I]	AAC No 671 Sqn/2 Regiment, Middle Wallop
	XZ194	WS Lynx AH7	AAC No 654 Sqn/4 Regiment, Wattisham
	XZ195	WS Lynx AH7 [T]	AAC SEAE, Arborfield
	XZ196	WS Lynx AH7	AAC No 652 Sqn/1 Regiment, Gütersloh
	XZ197	WS Lynx AH7	AAC No 669 Sqn/4 Regiment, Wattisham
	XZ198	WS Lynx AH7	AAC No 655 Sqn/5 Regiment, Aldergrove
	XZ199	WS Lynx AH7	AAC No 657 Sqn/9 Regiment, Dishforth
	XZ203	WS Lynx AH7	AAC, stored NARO, RNAY Fleetlands
	XZ205	WS Lynx AH7	AAC No 655 Sqn/5 Regiment, Aldergrove
	XZ206	WS Lynx AH7	AAC No 662 Sqn/3 Regiment, Wattisham
	XZ207	WS Lynx AH7	AAC No 669 Sqn/4 Regiment, Wattisham
	XZ208	WS Lynx AH7 [Z]	AAC No 664 Sqn/9 Regiment, Dishforth
	XZ209	WS Lynx AH1	AAC, stored NARO, RNAY Fleetlands
	XZ210	WS Lynx AH7 [T]	AAC No 663 Sqn/3 Regiment, Wattisham
	XZ211	WS Lynx AH7	AAC No 654 Sqn/4 Regiment, Wattisham
	XZ212	WS Lynx AH7	AAC 9 Regiment, Dishforth
	XZ213	WS Lynx AH1 (TAD 213)	RNAY Fleetlands Apprentice School
	XZ214	WS Lynx AH7	AAC No 657 Sqn/9 Regiment, Dishforth
	XZ215	WS Lynx AH7 [4]	AAC No 655 Sqn/5 Regiment, Aldergrove
	XZ216	WS Lynx AH7 [2]	AAC No 663 Sqn/3 Regiment, Wattisham
	XZ217	WS Lynx AH7 [UN]	AAC 9 Regiment, Dishforth
	XZ218	WS Lynx AH7	AAC No 655 Sqn/5 Regiment, Aldergrove
	XZ219	WS Lynx AH7	AAC No 651 Sqn/1 Regiment, Gütersloh
	XZ220	WS Lynx AH7	AAC No 654 Sqn/4 Regiment, Wattisham
	XZ221	WS Lynx AH7	AAC No 662 Sqn/3 Regiment, Wattisham
	XZ222	WS Lynx AH7 [P]	AAC No 657 Sqn/9 Regiment, Dishforth
	XZ228	WS Lynx HAS3S [407/YK]	RN No 815 Sqn, Portland
	XZ229	WS Lynx HAS3S [334/SN]	RN AMG, Portland
	XZ230	WS Lynx HAS3S [365/AY]	RN No 815 Sqn, Portland
	XZ231	WS Lynx HAS3	RNAY Fleetlands Apprentice School
	XZ232	WS Lynx HAS3S [410/GC]	RN No 815 Sqn, Portland
	XZ233	WS Lynx HAS3ICE [435/ED]	RN, stored Fleetlands
	XZ234	WS Lynx HAS3S	RN AMG, Portland
	XZ235	WS Lynx HAS3S [635]	RN No 702 Sqn, Portland
	XZ236	WS Lynx HMA8	MoD(PE)/RWTS, DTEO Boscombe Down
	XZ237	WS Lynx HAS3S [361/NF]	RN No 815 Sqn, Portland
	XZ238	WS Lynx HAS3SICE [434/ED]	RN No 815 Sqn, Portland
	XZ239	WS Lynx HAS3S [411/EB]	RN No 815 Sqn, Portland
	XZ241	WS Lynx HAS3S	RN, stored Fleetlands
	XZ243	WS Lynx HAS3 (wreck)	RN Portland, GI use
	XZ245	WS Lynx HAS3S [306]	RN No 815 Sqn, Portland
	XZ246	WS Lynx HAS3ICE [435/ED]	RN No 815 Sqn, Portland
	XZ248	WS Lynx HAS3S [634]	RN No 702 Sqn, Portland
	XZ250	WS Lynx HAS3S [405/LO]	RN No 815 Sqn, Portland
	XZ252	WS Lynx HAS3S	RN, stored Fleetlands
	XZ254	WS Lynx HAS3S [308]	RN No 815 Sqn, Portland
	XZ255	WS Lynx HAS3S [631]	NARO, RNAY Fleetlands
	XZ256	WS Lynx HMA8 [671]	RN AMG, Portland
	XZ257	WS Lynx HAS3S [355/SM]	RN No 815 Sqn, Portland
	XZ284	HS Nimrod MR2	RAF No 42(R) Sqn, Kinloss
	XZ286	BAe Nimrod AEW3 (fuselage)	RAF Kinloss Fire Section
	XZ287	BAe Nimrod AEW3 (9140M) (fuselage)	RAF TSW, Stafford
	XZ290	WS Gazelle AH1 [F]	AAC No 670 Sqn/2 Regiment, Middle Wallop
	XZ291	WS Gazelle AH1	AAC No 12 Flt, Brüggen
	XZ292	WS Gazelle AH1 [3]	AAC No 663 Sqn/3 Regiment, Wattisham
	XZ294	WS Gazelle AH1 [X]	AAC No 658 Sqn/7 Regiment, Middle Wallop
	XZ295	WS Gazelle AH1	AAC No 12 Flt, Brüggen
	XZ296	WS Gazelle AH1	AAC No 654 Sqn/4 Regiment, Wattisham
	XZ298	WS Gazelle AH1 [V]	AAC No 662 Sqn/3 Regiment, Wattisham
	XZ299	WS Gazelle AH1	AAC No 665 Sqn/5 Regiment, Aldergrove
	XZ300	WS Gazelle AH1 [L]	AAC No 670 Sqn/2 Regiment, Middle Wallop
	XZ301	WS Gazelle AH1 [U]	AAC No 662 Sqn/3 Regiment, Wattisham
	XZ302	WS Gazelle AH1	AAC, on rebuild NARO, RNAY Fleetlands
	XZ303	WS Gazelle AH1 [4]	AAC No 656 Sqn/9 Regiment, Dishforth
	XZ304	WS Gazelle AH1	AAC No 6(V) Flt/7 Regiment, Shawbury
	XZ305	WS Gazelle AH1	AAC SEAE, Arborfield

Serial	Type (other identity) [code]	Owner/operator, location or fate	Notes
XZ307	WS Gazelle AH1	AAC, stored NARO, RNAY Fleetlands	
XZ308	WS Gazelle AH1 [V]	AAC No 657 Sqn/9 Regiment, Dishforth	
XZ309	WS Gazelle AH1	AAC No 6(V) Flt/7 Regiment, Shawbury	
XZ310	WS Gazelle AH1 [U]	AAC No 670 Sqn/2 Regiment, Middle Wallop	
XZ311	WS Gazelle AH1	AAC No 6(V) Flt/7 Regiment, Shawbury	
XZ312	WS Gazelle AH1	AAC No 664 Sqn/9 Regiment, Dishforth	
XZ313	WS Gazelle AH1 [A]	AAC No 663 Sqn/3 Regiment, Wattisham	
XZ314	WS Gazelle AH1	AAC No 8 Flt, Middle Wallop	
XZ315	WS Gazelle AH1	AAC No 665 Sqn/5 Regiment, Aldergrove	
XZ316	WS Gazelle AH1 [B]	AAC No 666(V) Sqn/7 Regiment, Middle Wallop	
XZ317	WS Gazelle AH1 [R]	AAC No 670 Sqn/2 Regiment, Middle Wallop	
XZ318	WS Gazelle AH1	AAC No 664 Sqn/9 Regiment, Dishforth	
XZ320	WS Gazelle AH1	AAC No 669 Sqn/4 Regiment, Wattisham	
XZ321	WS Gazelle AH1	AAC No 665 Sqn/5 Regiment, Aldergrove	
XZ322	WS Gazelle AH1 [N]	AAC No 670 Sqn/2 Regiment, Middle Wallop	
XZ323	WS Gazelle AH1	AAC No 16 Flt, Dhekelia, Cyprus	
XZ324	WS Gazelle AH1	AAC No 3(V) Flt/7 Regiment, Leuchars	
XZ325	WS Gazelle AH1 [T]	AAC No 670 Sqn/2 Regiment, Middle Wallop	
XZ326	WS Gazelle AH1	RM, stored Fleetlands	
XZ327	WS Gazelle AH1 [B1]	AAC No 670 Sqn/2 Regiment, Middle Wallop	
XZ328	WS Gazelle AH1	AAC No 654 Sqn/4 Regiment, Wattisham	
XZ329	WS Gazelle AH1 [J]	AAC No 670 Sqn/2 Regiment, Middle Wallop	
XZ330	WS Gazelle AH1 [Y]	AAC No 670 Sqn/2 Regiment, Middle Wallop	
XZ331	WS Gazelle AH1 [B]	AAC No 663 Sqn/3 Regiment, Wattisham	
XZ332	WS Gazelle AH1 [O]	AAC No 670 Sqn/2 Regiment, Middle Wallop	
XZ333	WS Gazelle AH1 [A]	AAC No 670 Sqn/2 Regiment, Middle Wallop	
XZ334	WS Gazelle AH1 [S]	AAC No 670 Sqn/2 Regiment, Middle Wallop	
XZ335	WS Gazelle AH1	AAC No 6(V) Flt/7 Regiment, Shawbury	
XZ337	WS Gazelle AH1 [5]	AAC No 656 Sqn/9 Regiment, Dishforth	
XZ338	WS Gazelle AH1	AAC No 661 Sqn/1 Regiment, Gütersloh	
XZ339	WS Gazelle AH1	AAC No 667 Sqn/2 Regiment, Middle Wallop	
XZ340	WS Gazelle AH1	AAC No 29 Flt, BATUS, Suffield, Canada	
XZ341	WS Gazelle AH1	AAC No 3(V) Flt/7 Regiment, Leuchars	
XZ342	WS Gazelle AH1	AAC, stored NARO, RNAY Fleetlands	
XZ343	WS Gazelle AH1	AAC 1 Regiment, Gütersloh	
XZ344	WS Gazelle AH1 [I]	AAC No 670 Sqn/2 Regiment, Middle Wallop	
XZ345	WS Gazelle AH1 [A]	AAC	
XZ346	WS Gazelle AH1	AAC No 665 Sqn/5 Regiment, Aldergrove	
XZ347	WS Gazelle AH1 [6]	AAC No 656 Sqn/9 Regiment, Dishforth	
XZ348	WS Gazelle AH1 (wreck)	AAC, stored NARO, RNAY Fleetlands	
XZ349	WS Gazelle AH1 [G1]	AAC No 670 Sqn/2 Regiment, Middle Wallop	
XZ355	SEPECAT Jaguar GR1A [FJ]	RAF AWC/SAOEU, DTEO Boscombe Down	
XZ356	SEPECAT Jaguar GR1A [EP]	RAF No 6 Sqn, Coltishall	
XZ357	SEPECAT Jaguar GR1A [FK]	RAF No 41 Sqn, Coltishall	
XZ358	SEPECAT Jaguar GR1A [L]	AMIF, RAFC Cranwell	
XZ360	SEPECAT Jaguar GR1A [N]	RAF No 41 Sqn, Coltishall	
XZ361	SEPECAT Jaguar GR1A [T]	RAF No 41 Sqn, Coltishall	
XZ362	SEPECAT Jaguar GR1B [GC]	Crashed 24 July 1996, Alaska	
XZ363	SEPECAT Jaguar GR1A [O]	RAF, St Athan	
XZ363	SEPECAT Jaguar GR1A <R>	RAF EP&TU, St Athan (BAPC 151) [A]	
XZ364	SEPECAT Jaguar GR1A [GJ]	RAF No 54 Sqn, Coltishall	
XZ366	SEPECAT Jaguar GR1A [FS]	RAF No 41 Sqn, Coltishall	
XZ367	SEPECAT Jaguar GR1A [GP]	RAF No 54 Sqn, Coltishall	
XZ368	SEPECAT Jaguar GR1 [8900M] [AG]	RAF No 1 SoTT, Cosford	
XZ369	SEPECAT Jaguar GR1B [EF]	RAF No 6 Sqn, Coltishall	
XZ370	SEPECAT Jaguar GR1 (9004M) [JB]	RAF No 1 SoTT, Cosford	

Notes	Serial	Type (other identity) [code]	Owner/operator, location or fate
	XZ371	SEPECAT Jaguar GR1 (8907M) [AP]	RAF No 1 SoTT, Cosford
	XZ372	SEPECAT Jaguar GR1A	MoD(PE)/FJTS, DTEO Boscombe Down
	XZ374	SEPECAT Jaguar GR1 (9005M) [JC]	RAF No 1 SoTT, Cosford
	XZ375	SEPECAT Jaguar GR1B [GR]	RAF St Athan (conversion)
	XZ377	SEPECAT Jaguar GR1A [EB]	RAF No 6 Sqn, Coltishall
	XZ378	SEPECAT Jaguar GR1A [EP]	RAF, stored Shawbury
	XZ381	SEPECAT Jaguar GR1B [EC]	RAF No 6 Sqn, Coltishall
	XZ382	SEPECAT Jaguar GR1 (8908M) [AE]	RAF Coltishall BDRF
	XZ383	SEPECAT Jaguar GR1 (8901M) [AF]	RAF No 1 SoTT, Cosford
	XZ384	SEPECAT Jaguar GR1 (8954M) [BC]	RAF No 1 SoTT, Cosford
	XZ385	SEPECAT Jaguar GR1A [C]	RAF No 16(R) Sqn, Lossiemouth
	XZ389	SEPECAT Jaguar GR1 (8946M) [BL]	RAF No 1 SoTT, Cosford
	XZ390	SEPECAT Jaguar GR1A (9003M) [35,JA]	RAF No 1 SoTT, Cosford
	XZ391	SEPECAT Jaguar GR1A [A]	RAF No 16(R) Sqn, Lossiemouth
	XZ392	SEPECAT Jaguar GR1A [GQ]	RAF, stored Shawbury
	XZ394	SEPECAT Jaguar GR1A [GN]	RAF No 54 Sqn, Coltishall
	XZ396	SEPECAT Jaguar GR1A [EM]	RAF AMF, Coltishall
	XZ398	SEPECAT Jaguar GR1A [FA]	RAF No 41 Sqn, Coltishall
	XZ399	SEPECAT Jaguar GR1A [EJ]	RAF AMF, Coltishall
	XZ400	SEPECAT Jaguar GR1A [EG]	RAF, stored Shawbury
	XZ431	HS Buccaneer S2B (9233M)	RAF Marham Fire Section
	XZ439	BAe Sea Harrier FA2	MoD(PE)/BAe, Dunsfold
	XZ440	BAe Sea Harrier FA2 [126/N]	MoD(PE)/BAe Dunsfold (conversion)
	XZ445	BAe Harrier T4A [721] (wreck)	RN FSAIU, Yeovilton
	XZ455	BAe Sea Harrier FA2 [001] (wreck)	RN FSAIU, Yeovilton
	XZ457	BAe Sea Harrier FA2 [714] (wreck)	RN FSAIU, Yeovilton
	XZ459	BAe Sea Harrier FA2 [126]	RN AMG, Yeovilton
	XZ492	BAe Sea Harrier FA2 [127]	RN No 800 Sqn, Yeovilton
	XZ493	BAe Sea Harrier FRS1 [126]	FAA Museum, at BAe Brough (restoration)
	XZ494	BAe Sea Harrier FA2	MoD(PE)/BAe Dunsfold (conversion)
	XZ497	BAe Sea Harrier FA2 [712/R]	MoD(PE)/BAe Dunsfold
	XZ499	BAe Sea Harrier FA2	MoD(PE)/BAe Dunsfold (conversion)
	XZ559	Slingsby T61F Venture T2 (G-BUEK)	Privately owned, Tibenham
	XZ570	WS61 Sea King HAS5(mod)	MoD(PE)/Westland, Yeovil
	XZ571	WS61 Sea King HAS6 [014/L]	RN No 820 Sqn, Culdrose
	XZ574	WS61 Sea King HAS6 [015/L]	RN No 820 Sqn, Culdrose
	XZ575	WS61 Sea King HU5 [599]	NARO, RNAY Fleetlands
	XZ576	WS61 Sea King HAS6	MoD(PE)/RWTS, DTEO Boscombe Down
	XZ578	WS61 Sea King HU5 [581]	RN, stored Fleetlands
	XZ579	WS61 Sea King HAS6 [706/PW]	RN No 819 Sqn, Prestwick
	XZ580	WS61 Sea King HAS6 [704/PW]	RN No 819 Sqn, Prestwick
	XZ581	WS61 Sea King HAS6 [514]	RN No 810 Sqn OEU, DTEO Boscombe Down
	XZ585	WS61 Sea King HAR3	RAF No 202 Sqn, E Flt, Leconfield
	XZ586	WS61 Sea King HAR3 [S]	RAF, NARO, RNAY Fleetlands
	XZ587	WS61 Sea King HAR3	RAF No 202 Sqn, A Flt, Boulmer
	XZ588	WS61 Sea King HAR3	RAF No 22 Sqn, B Flt, Wattisham
	XZ589	WS61 Sea King HAR3	RAF No 22 Sqn, A Flt, Chivenor
	XZ590	WS61 Sea King HAR3	RAF No 202 Sqn, D Flt, Lossiemouth
	XZ591	WS61 Sea King HAR3 [S]	RAF No 203(R) Sqn, St Mawgan
	XZ592	WS61 Sea King HAR3 [S]	RAF HMF, St Mawgan
	XZ593	WS61 Sea King HAR3	RAF No 22 Sqn, B Flt, Wattisham
	XZ594	WS61 Sea King HAR3	RAF HMF, St Mawgan
	XZ595	WS61 Sea King HAR3	RAF No 203(R) Sqn, St Mawgan
	XZ596	WS61 Sea King HAR3	RAF No 202 Sqn, E Flt, Leconfield
	XZ597	WS61 Sea King HAR3 [S]	RAF HMF, St Mawgan
	XZ598	WS61 Sea King HAR3	RAF No 203(R) Sqn, St Mawgan
	XZ599	WS61 Sea King HAR3 [S]	RAF No 78 Sqn, Mount Pleasant, FI
	XZ605	WS Lynx AH7 [Y]	RM No 847 Sqn, Yeovilton
	XZ606	WS Lynx AH7	AAC No 667 Sqn/2 Regiment, Middle Wallop
	XZ607	WS Lynx AH7 [J]	AAC No 662 Sqn/3 Regiment, Wattisham
	XZ608	WS Lynx AH7	AAC No 657 Sqn/9 Regiment, Dishforth
	XZ609	WS Lynx AH7 [O]	AAC No 669 Sqn/4 Regiment, Wattisham
	XZ610	WS Lynx AH7 [K]	AAC No 662 Sqn/3 Regiment, Wattisham

Serial	Type (other identity) [code]	Owner/operator, location or fate	Notes
XZ611	WS Lynx AH7 [Y]	AAC 9 Regiment, Dishforth	
XZ612	WS Lynx AH7 [N]	RM No 847 Sqn, Yeovilton	
XZ613	WS Lynx AH7 [F]	AAC SEAE, Arborfield	
XZ614	WS Lynx AH7 [X]	RM No 847 Sqn, Yeovilton	
XZ615	WS Lynx AH7	AAC No 655 Sqn/5 Regiment, Aldergrove	
XZ616	WS Lynx AH7 [2]	AAC No 656 Sqn/9 Regiment, Dishforth	
XZ617	WS Lynx AH7 [UN]	AAC 9 Regiment, Dishforth	
XZ631	Panavia Tornado GR4	MoD(PE)/BAe Warton	
XZ641	WS Lynx AH7 [G]	AAC No 671 Sqn/2 Regiment, Middle Wallop	
XZ642	WS Lynx AH7 [L]	AAC 3 Regiment, Wattisham	
XZ643	WS Lynx AH7 [3]	AAC No 662 Sqn/3 Regiment, Wattisham	
XZ644	WS Lynx AH7 (wreck)	*Scrapped*	
XZ645	WS Lynx AH7 [M]	AAC No 663 Sqn/3 Regiment, Wattisham	
XZ646	WS Lynx AH7 [UN]	AAC No 657 Sqn/9 Regiment, Dishforth	
XZ647	WS Lynx AH7	AAC No 655 Sqn/5 Regiment, Aldergrove	
XZ648	WS Lynx AH7	AAC 1 Regiment, Gütersloh	
XZ649	WS Lynx AH7	AAC No 655 Sqn/5 Regiment, Aldergrove	
XZ650	WS Lynx AH7	*Crashed 22 September 1994, near Koblenz*	
XZ651	WS Lynx AH7	AAC No 657 Sqn/9 Regiment, Dishforth	
XZ652	WS Lynx AH7 [T]	AAC No 671 Sqn/2 Regiment, Middle Wallop	
XZ653	WS Lynx AH7 [UN]	AAC No 664 Sqn/9 Regiment, Dishforth	
XZ654	WS Lynx AH7	AAC, stored NARO, RNAY Fleetlands	
XZ655	WS Lynx AH7	AAC No 655 Sqn/5 Regiment, Aldergrove	
XZ661	WS Lynx AH1	AAC, stored NARO, RNAY Fleetlands	
XZ662	WS Lynx AH7	AAC No 655 Sqn/5 Regiment, Aldergrove	
XZ663	WS Lynx AH7	AAC No 655 Sqn/5 Regiment, Aldergrove	
XZ664	WS Lynx AH7 [N]	AAC No 662 Sqn/3 Regiment, Wattisham	
XZ665	WS Lynx AH7	AAC No 652 Sqn/1 Regiment, Gütersloh	
XZ666	WS Lynx AH7	AAC No 661 Sqn/1 Regiment, Gütersloh	
XZ667	WS Lynx AH7	AAC No 655 Sqn/5 Regiment, Aldergrove	
XZ669	WS Lynx AH7	AAC No 669 Sqn/4 Regiment, Wattisham	
XZ670	WS Lynx AH7 [UN]	AAC No 664 Sqn/9 Regiment, Dishforth	
XZ671	WS Lynx AH7 <ff>	Westland, Yeovil, instructional use	
XZ672	WS Lynx AH7	AAC No 655 Sqn/5 Regiment, Aldergrove	
XZ673	WS Lynx AH7	AAC No 655 Sqn/5 Regiment, Aldergrove	
XZ674	WS Lynx AH7	AAC No 651 Sqn/1 Regiment, Gütersloh	
XZ675	WS Lynx AH7 [E]	AAC No 671 Sqn/2 Regiment, Middle Wallop	
XZ676	WS Lynx AH7 [N]	AAC No 671 Sqn/2 Regiment, Middle Wallop	
XZ677	WS Lynx AH7 [Y]	AAC No 663 Sqn/3 Regiment, Wattisham	
XZ678	WS Lynx AH7	AAC No 662 Sqn/3 Regiment, Wattisham	
XZ679	WS Lynx AH7 [UN]	AAC No 664 Sqn/9 Regiment, Dishforth	
XZ680	WS Lynx AH7	AAC No 652 Sqn/1 Regiment, Gütersloh	
XZ681	WS Lynx AH1	AAC Middle Wallop, BDRT	
XZ689	WS Lynx HAS3S [403/BX]	RN No 815 Sqn, Portland	
XZ690	WS Lynx HAS3S [462/WM]	RN No 815 Sqn, Portland	
XZ691	WS Lynx HMA8 [474/RM]	RN No 815 Sqn, Portland	
XZ692	WS Lynx HMA8	NARO, RNAY Fleetlands (conversion)	
XZ693	WS Lynx HAS3S [301]	RN No 815 Sqn, Portland	
XZ694	WS Lynx HAS3S	RN AMG, Portland	
XZ695	WS Lynx HAS3S [345/NC]	RN No 815 Sqn, Portland	
XZ696	WS Lynx HAS3S [479]	RN No 815 Sqn, Portland	
XZ697	WS Lynx HMA8	RN AMG, Portland	
XZ698	WS Lynx HAS3S [303]	RN No 815 Sqn, Portland	
XZ699	WS Lynx HAS3 [301]	RN AMG, Portland	
XZ719	WS Lynx HAS3S [644]	RN No 702 Sqn, Portland	
XZ720	WS Lynx HAS3S	NARO, RNAY Fleetlands	
XZ721	WS Lynx HAS3S [307]	RN No 815 Sqn, Portland	
XZ722	WS Lynx HMA8	NARO, RNAY Fleetlands (conversion)	
XZ723	WS Lynx HMA8	NARO, RNAY Fleetlands (conversion)	
XZ724	WS Lynx HAS3S	RN AMG, Portland	
XZ725	WS Lynx HAS3S [338/CT]	RN No 815 Sqn, Portland	
XZ726	WS Lynx HAS3S	RN AMG, Portland	
XZ727	WS Lynx HAS3S [332/LP]	RN No 815 Sqn, Portland	
XZ728	WS Lynx HMA8 [415/MM]	RN No 815 Sqn, Portland	
XZ729	WS Lynx HAS3S	RN No 702 Sqn, Portland	
XZ730	WS Lynx HAS3CTS [304]	RN No 815 Sqn, Portland	
XZ731	WS Lynx HMA8	NARO, RNAY Fleetlands (conversion)	
XZ732	WS Lynx HMA8 [670]	RN No 815 Sqn OEU, Portland	

Notes	Serial	Type (other identity) [code]	Owner/operator, location or fate
	XZ733	WS Lynx HAS3S	NARO, RNAY Fleetlands
	XZ735	WS Lynx HAS3S [352]	RN No 815 Sqn, Portland
	XZ736	WS Lynx HAS3S [376/XB]	RN No 815 Sqn, Portland
	XZ918	WS61 Sea King HAS5	*Sold to Royal Australian Navy, July 1996*
	XZ920	WS61 Sea King HU5 [822/CU]	RN No 771 Sqn, Culdrose
	XZ921	WS61 Sea King HAS6 [587]	RN No 706 Sqn, Culdrose
	XZ922	WS61 Sea King HAS6 [503/CU]	RN No 810 Sqn, Culdrose
	XZ930	WS Gazelle HT3 [Q]	RAF No 2 FTS, Shawbury
	XZ931	WS Gazelle HT3 [R]	RAF No 2 FTS, Shawbury
	XZ932	WS Gazelle HT3 [S]	RAF No 2 FTS, Shawbury
	XZ933	WS Gazelle HT3 [T]	RAF No 2 FTS, Shawbury
	XZ934	WS Gazelle HT3 [U]	RAF No 2 FTS, Shawbury
	XZ935	WS Gazelle HCC4	RAF, stored NARO, RNAY Fleetlands
	XZ936	WS Gazelle HT2 [6]	MoD(PE)/ETPS, DTEO Boscombe Down
	XZ937	WS Gazelle HT2 [Y]	RAF No 2 FTS, Shawbury
	XZ938	WS Gazelle HT2 [45/CU]	RN No 705 Sqn, Culdrose
	XZ939	WS Gazelle HT2 [Z]	MoD(PE)/ETPS, DTEO Boscombe Down
	XZ940	WS Gazelle HT2 [O]	RAF No 2 FTS, Shawbury
	XZ941	WS Gazelle HT2 [B]	RAF No 2 FTS, Shawbury
	XZ942	WS Gazelle HT2 [42/CU]	RN No 705 Sqn, Culdrose
	XZ964	BAe Harrier GR3 [D]	Royal Engineers Museum, Chatham
	XZ965	BAe Harrier GR3 (9184M) [L]	*To Beijing Aviation Museum*
	XZ966	BAe Harrier GR3 (9221M) [G]	RAF Cottesmore Fire Section
	XZ967	BAe Harrier GR3 (9077M) [F]	Military Aircraft Spares Ltd, Taunton
	XZ968	BAe Harrier GR3 (9222M) [3G]	Muckleborough Collection, Weybourne
	XZ969	BAe Harrier GR3 [D]	SFDO, RNAS Culdrose
	XZ970	BAe Harrier GR3	*Preserved in Chile*
	XZ971	BAe Harrier GR3 (9219M) [G]	RAF Benson, at main gate
	XZ987	BAe Harrier GR3 (9185M) [C]	RAF Stafford, at main gate
	XZ990	BAe Harrier GR3 <ff>	No ... Sqn ATC, March, Cambs
	XZ990	BAe Harrier GR3 <rf>	RAF Wittering, derelict
	XZ991	BAe Harrier GR3 (9162M) [3A]	RAF St Athan, BDRT
	XZ993	BAe Harrier GR3 (9240M) [M]	*To RAF Laarbruch for BDRT*
	XZ994	BAe Harrier GR3 (9170M) [U]	RAF Air Movements School, Brize Norton
	XZ995	BAe Harrier GR3 (9220M) [3G]	RAF St Mawgan Fire Section
	XZ996	BAe Harrier GR3 [2,3]	SFDO, RNAS Culdrose
	XZ997	BAe Harrier GR3 (9122M) [V]	RAF Museum, Hendon
	ZA101	BAe Hawk 100 (G-HAWK)	MoD(PE)/BAe Warton
	ZA105	WS61 Sea King HAR3 [S]	RAF No 78 Sqn, Mount Pleasant, FI
	ZA110	BAe Jetstream T2 (F-BTMI) [573/CU]	RN No 750 Sqn, Culdrose
	ZA111	BAe Jetstream T2 (9Q-CTC) [565/CU]	RN No 750 Sqn, Culdrose
	ZA126	WS61 Sea King HAS6 [509/CU]	RN No 810 Sqn, Culdrose
	ZA127	WS61 Sea King HAS6 [592]	RN No 706 Sqn, Culdrose
	ZA128	WS61 Sea King HAS6 [013/L]	RN No 820 Sqn, Culdrose
	ZA129	WS61 Sea King HAS6 [502/CU]	RN No 810 Sqn, Culdrose
	ZA130	WS61 Sea King HU5 [587/CU]	NARO, RNAY Fleetlands
	ZA131	WS61 Sea King HAS6 [011/L]	RN AMG, Culdrose
	ZA133	WS61 Sea King HAS6 [703/PW]	RN No 819 Sqn, Prestwick
	ZA134	WS61 Sea King HU5 [824]	RN No 771 Sqn, Culdrose
	ZA135	WS61 Sea King HAS6 [010/L]	RN No 820 Sqn, Culdrose
	ZA136	WS61 Sea King HAS6 [015/L]	RN, stored Fleetlands
	ZA137	WS61 Sea King HU5 [597]	NARO, RNAY Fleetlands
	ZA140	BAe VC10 K2 (G-ARVL) [A]	RAF No 101 Sqn, Brize Norton
	ZA141	BAe VC10 K2 (G-ARVG) [B]	RAF No 101 Sqn, Brize Norton
	ZA142	BAe VC10 K2 (G-ARVI) [C]	RAF, stored St Athan
	ZA143	BAe VC10 K2 (G-ARVK) [D]	RAF No 101 Sqn, Brize Norton
	ZA144	BAe VC10 K2 (G-ARVC) [E]	RAF No 101 Sqn, Brize Norton
	ZA147	BAe VC10 K3 (5H-MMT) [F]	RAF No 101 Sqn, Brize Norton
	ZA148	BAe VC10 K3 (5Y-ADA)	RAF No 101 Sqn, Brize Norton
	ZA149	BAe VC10 K3 (5X-UVJ)	RAF, stored St Athan
	ZA150	BAe VC10 K3 (5H-MOG) [J]	RAF No 101 Sqn, Brize Norton
	ZA166	WS61 Sea King HU5 [581]	RN No 706 Sqn, Culdrose
	ZA167	WS61 Sea King HU5 [825/CU]	RN No 771 Sqn, Culdrose
	ZA168	WS61 Sea King HAS6 [512]	RN No 810 Sqn OEU, DTEO Boscombe Down
	ZA169	WS61 Sea King HAS6 [265]	RN No 814 Sqn, Culdrose
	ZA170	WS61 Sea King HU5 [584]	RN, stored Fleetlands
	ZA175	BAe Sea Harrier FA2	RN AMG, Yeovilton
	ZA176	BAe Sea Harrier FA2	RN AMG, Yeovilton
	ZA195	BAe Sea Harrier FA2	MoD(PE)/BAe Dunsfold

Serial	Type (other identity) [code]	Owner/operator, location or fate	Notes
ZA250	BAe Harrier T52 (G-VTOL)	Brooklands Museum, Weybridge	
ZA254	Panavia Tornado F2 (fuselage)	RAF Coningsby, instructional use	
ZA267	Panavia Tornado F2	MoD(PE)/FJTS, DTEO Boscombe Down	
ZA283	Panavia Tornado F2	MoD(PE)/BAe Warton	
ZA291	WS61 Sea King HC4 [ZX]	NARO, RNAY Fleetlands	
ZA292	WS61 Sea King HC4 [ZR]	MoD(PE)/Westland, Weston-super-Mare	
ZA293	WS61 Sea King HC4 [ZO]	RN No 848 Sqn, Yeovilton	
ZA295	WS61 Sea King HC4 [VM]	RN No 846 Sqn, Yeovilton	
ZA296	WS61 Sea King HC4 [VO]	RN No 846 Sqn, Yeovilton	
ZA297	WS61 Sea King HC4 [C]	RN No 845 Sqn, Yeovilton	
ZA298	WS61 Sea King HC4 [G]	RN No 845 Sqn, Yeovilton	
ZA299	WS61 Sea King HC4 [ZT]	RN No 848 Sqn, Yeovilton	
ZA310	WS61 Sea King HC4 [ZY]	RN No 848 Sqn, Yeovilton	
ZA312	WS61 Sea King HC4 [ZS]	RN No 848 Sqn, Yeovilton	
ZA313	WS61 Sea King HC4 [M]	RN No 845 Sqn, Yeovilton	
ZA314	WS61 Sea King HC4 [F]	RN No 845 Sqn, Yeovilton	
ZA319	Panavia Tornado GR1 [B-11]	RAF TTTE, Cottesmore	
ZA320	Panavia Tornado GR1 [B-01]	RAF TTTE, Cottesmore	
ZA321	Panavia Tornado GR1 [B-58]	RAF TTTE, Cottesmore	
ZA322	Panavia Tornado GR1 [B-50]	RAF TTTE, Cottesmore	
ZA323	Panavia Tornado GR1 [B-14]	RAF TTTE, Cottesmore	
ZA324	Panavia Tornado GR1 [B-02]	RAF TTTE, Cottesmore	
ZA325	Panavia Tornado GR1 [B-03]	RAF TTTE, Cottesmore	
ZA326	Panavia Tornado GR1P	MoD(PE)/DRA, DTEO Boscombe Down	
ZA327	Panavia Tornado GR1	MoD(PE)/BAe, Warton	
ZA328	Panavia Tornado GR1	MoD(PE)/BAe, Warton	
ZA330	Panavia Tornado GR1 [B-08]	RAF TTTE, Cottesmore	
ZA352	Panavia Tornado GR1 [B-04]	RAF TTTE, Cottesmore	
ZA353	Panavia Tornado GR1	MoD(PE)/FJTS, DTEO Boscombe Down	
ZA354	Panavia Tornado GR1	MoD(PE)/BAe, Warton	
ZA355	Panavia Tornado GR1 [B-54]	RAF TTTE, Cottesmore	
ZA356	Panavia Tornado GR1 [B-07]	RAF TTTE, Cottesmore	
ZA357	Panavia Tornado GR1 [B-05]	RAF TTTE, Cottesmore	
ZA358	Panavia Tornado GR1	MoD(PE)/BAe Warton	
ZA359	Panavia Tornado GR1 [B-55]	RAF TTTE, Cottesmore	
ZA360	Panavia Tornado GR1 [B-56]	RAF TTTE, Cottesmore	
ZA361	Panavia Tornado GR1 [B-57]	RAF TTTE, Cottesmore	
ZA362	Panavia Tornado GR1 [B-09]	RAF TTTE, Cottesmore	
ZA365	Panavia Tornado GR1 [JT]	RAF AMF, Lossiemouth	
ZA367	Panavia Tornado GR1 [II]	RAF No 2 Sqn, Marham	
ZA368	Panavia Tornado GR1 <R> (BAPC 155) [AJ-P]	RAF EP&TU, St Athan	
ZA369	Panavia Tornado GR4A	MoD(PE)/BAe Warton (conversion)	
ZA370	Panavia Tornado GR1A [A]	RAF No 2 Sqn, Marham	
ZA371	Panavia Tornado GR4A	MoD(PE)/BAe Warton (conversion)	
ZA372	Panavia Tornado GR1A [E]	RAF No 2 Sqn, Marham	
ZA373	Panavia Tornado GR1A [H]	RAF No 2 Sqn, Marham	
ZA374	Panavia Tornado GR1B [AJ-L]	RAF No 617 Sqn, Lossiemouth	
ZA375	Panavia Tornado GR1B [AJ-W]	RAF No 617 Sqn, Lossiemouth	
ZA393	Panavia Tornado GR1 [BE]	RAF No 14 Sqn, Brüggen	
ZA395	Panavia Tornado GR1A [N]	RAF No 2 Sqn, Marham	
ZA398	Panavia Tornado GR1A [S]	RAF No 2 Sqn, Marham	
ZA399	Panavia Tornado GR1B [AJ-C]	RAF No 617 Sqn, Lossiemouth	
ZA400	Panavia Tornado GR1A [T]	RAF No 2 Sqn, Marham	
ZA401	Panavia Tornado GR4A	MoD(PE)/BAe Warton (conversion)	
ZA402	Panavia Tornado GR1	MoD(PE)/FJTS, DTEO Boscombe Down	
ZA404	Panavia Tornado GR1A [W]	RAF No 2 Sqn, Marham	
ZA405	Panavia Tornado GR1A [Y]	RAF No 2 Sqn, Marham	
ZA406	Panavia Tornado GR1 [CI]	RAF No 17 Sqn, Brüggen	
ZA407	Panavia Tornado GR1B [AJ-G]	RAF No 617 Sqn, Lossiemouth	
ZA409	Panavia Tornado GR1B	RAF No 12 Sqn, Lossiemouth	
ZA410	Panavia Tornado GR1 [FZ]	RAF No 12 Sqn, Lossiemouth	
ZA411	Panavia Tornado GR1B [AJ-S]	RAF No 617 Sqn, Lossiemouth	
ZA412	Panavia Tornado GR1 [FX]	RAF, stored St Athan	
ZA446	Panavia Tornado GR1B [U]	RAF AWC/SAOEU, DTEO Boscombe Down	
ZA447	Panavia Tornado GR1B [FA]	RAF No 12 Sqn, Lossiemouth	
ZA449	Panavia Tornado GR1	MoD(PE), stored St Anthan	
ZA450	Panavia Tornado GR1B [FB]	RAF No 12 Sqn, Lossiemouth	
ZA452	Panavia Tornado GR1B [FC]	RAF No 12 Sqn, Lossiemouth	
ZA453	Panavia Tornado GR1B [FD]	RAF No 12 Sqn, Lossiemouth	
ZA455	Panavia Tornado GR1B [FE]	RAF No 12 Sqn, Lossiemouth	
ZA456	Panavia Tornado GR1B [AJ-Q]	RAF No 617 Sqn, Lossiemouth	

Notes	Serial	Type (other identity) [code]	Owner/operator, location or fate
	ZA457	Panavia Tornado GR1B [AJ-J]	RAF No 617 Sqn, Lossiemouth
	ZA458	Panavia Tornado GR1 [CE]	RAF No 17 Sqn, Brüggen
	ZA459	Panavia Tornado GR1B [AJ-B]	RAF No 617 Sqn, Lossiemouth
	ZA460	Panavia Tornado GR1B [AJ-A]	RAF No 617 Sqn, Lossiemouth
	ZA461	Panavia Tornado GR1B [AJ-M]	RAF No 617 Sqn, Lossiemouth
	ZA462	Panavia Tornado GR1	RAF No 17 Sqn, Brüggen
	ZA463	Panavia Tornado GR1 [CR]	RAF No 17 Sqn, Brüggen
	ZA465	Panavia Tornado GR1B [AJ-F]	RAF No 617 Sqn, Lossiemouth
	ZA466	Panavia Tornado GR1 <ff>	RAF St Athan, BDRT
	ZA468	*Panavia Tornado GR1 <R>* (BAPC 155)	*Painted as ZA368 by July 1996*
	ZA469	Panavia Tornado GR1B [AJ-O]	RAF St Athan
	ZA470	Panavia Tornado GR1	RAF No 14 Sqn, Brüggen
	ZA471	Panavia Tornado GR1B [AJ-K]	RAF No 617 Sqn, Lossiemouth
	ZA472	Panavia Tornado GR1 [CT]	RAF No 17 Sqn, Brüggen
	ZA473	Panavia Tornado GR1B [FG]	RAF No 12 Sqn, Lossiemouth
	ZA474	Panavia Tornado GR1B [FF]	RAF No 12 Sqn, Lossiemouth
	ZA475	Panavia Tornado GR1B [FH]	RAF No 12 Sqn, Lossiemouth
	ZA490	Panavia Tornado GR1B [FJ]	MoD(PE)/FJTS, DTEO Boscombe Down
	ZA491	Panavia Tornado GR1B [FK]	RAF No 12 Sqn, Lossiemouth
	ZA492	Panavia Tornado GR1B [FL]	RAF No 12 Sqn, Lossiemouth
	ZA541	Panavia Tornado GR1 [TO]	RAF No 15(R) Sqn, Lossiemouth
	ZA542	Panavia Tornado GR1 [JA]	RAF, stored St Athan
	ZA543	Panavia Tornado GR1	RAF, stored St Athan
	ZA544	Panavia Tornado GR1 [TP]	RAF No 15(R) Sqn, Lossiemouth
	ZA546	Panavia Tornado GR1 [AJ-C]	RAF Cottesmore, instructional use
	ZA547	Panavia Tornado GR1 [JC]	RAF, stored St Athan
	ZA548	Panavia Tornado GR1 [TQ]	RAF No 15(R) Sqn, Lossiemouth
	ZA549	Panavia Tornado GR1 [TR]	RAF No 15(R) Sqn, Lossiemouth
	ZA550	Panavia Tornado GR1 [JD]	RAF, stored St Athan
	ZA551	Panavia Tornado GR1 [IV]	RAF No 2 Sqn, Marham
	ZA552	Panavia Tornado GR1 [TS]	RAF No 15(R) Sqn, Lossiemouth
	ZA553	Panavia Tornado GR1 [JE]	RAF, stored St Athan
	ZA554	Panavia Tornado GR1 [DM]	RAF, stored St Athan
	ZA556	Panavia Tornado GR1 [TA]	RAF No 15(R) Sqn, Lossiemouth
	ZA557	Panavia Tornado GR4	MoD(PE)/BAe Warton (conversion)
	ZA559	Panavia Tornado GR1 [F]	RAF No 15(R) Sqn, Lossiemouth
	ZA560	Panavia Tornado GR1 [TG]	RAF No 15(R) Sqn, Lossiemouth
	ZA562	Panavia Tornado GR1 [TT]	RAF No 15(R) Sqn, Lossiemouth
	ZA563	Panavia Tornado GR1 [TC]	RAF No 15(R) Sqn, Lossiemouth
	ZA564	Panavia Tornado GR1 [CK]	RAF No 17 Sqn, Brüggen
	ZA585	Panavia Tornado GR1	RAF, stored St Athan
	ZA587	Panavia Tornado GR1 [TD]	RAF No 15(R) Sqn, Lossiemouth
	ZA588	Panavia Tornado GR1 [AJ-N]	RAF No 617 Sqn, Lossiemouth
	ZA589	Panavia Tornado GR1 [TE]	RAF No 15(R) Sqn, Lossiemouth
	ZA590	Panavia Tornado GR1	RAF, stored St Athan
	ZA591	Panavia Tornado GR1	RAF, stored St Athan
	ZA592	Panavia Tornado GR1 [B]	RAF, stored St Athan
	ZA594	Panavia Tornado GR1 [TU]	RAF No 15(R) Sqn, Lossiemouth
	ZA595	Panavia Tornado GR1 [TV]	RAF No 15(R) Sqn, Lossiemouth
	ZA596	Panavia Tornado GR1	RAF, stored St Athan
	ZA597	Panavia Tornado GR1 [FW]	RAF No 12 Sqn, Lossiemouth
	ZA598	Panavia Tornado GR1B [AJ-T]	RAF No 617 Sqn, Lossiemouth
	ZA599	Panavia Tornado GR1 [FX]	RAF No 12 Sqn, Lossiemouth
	ZA600	Panavia Tornado GR1 [TH]	RAF No 15(R) Sqn, Lossiemouth
	ZA601	Panavia Tornado GR1 [TI]	RAF No 15(R) Sqn, Lossiemouth
	ZA602	Panavia Tornado GR1 [TX]	RAF No 15(R) Sqn, Lossiemouth
	ZA604	Panavia Tornado GR1 [TY]	RAF No 15(R) Sqn, Lossiemouth
	ZA606	Panavia Tornado GR1	RAF, stored St Athan
	ZA607	Panavia Tornado GR1 [TJ]	RAF No 15(R) Sqn, Lossiemouth
	ZA608	Panavia Tornado GR1 [TK]	RAF No 15(R) Sqn, Lossiemouth
	ZA609	Panavia Tornado GR1 [J]	RAF, stored St Athan
	ZA611	Panavia Tornado GR1	RAF, stored St Athan
	ZA612	Panavia Tornado GR1 [TZ]	RAF No 15(R) Sqn, Lossiemouth
	ZA613	Panavia Tornado GR1 [TL]	RAF No 15(R) Sqn, Lossiemouth
	ZA614	Panavia Tornado GR1 [TB]	RAF No 15(R) Sqn, Lossiemouth
	ZA634	Slingsby T61F Venture T2 (G-BUHA) [C]	Privately owned, Rufforth
	ZA663	Slingsby T61F Venture T2 (G-BUFP)	Privately owned, Currock Hill
	ZA670	B-V Chinook HC2 (N37010)	RAF No 7 Sqn, Odiham
	ZA671	B-V Chinook HC2 (N37011) [BB]	RAF No 18 Sqn, Laarbruch
	ZA673	B-V Chinook HC2 (N37016) [NX]	RAF No 27(R) Sqn, Odiham

Serial	Type (other identity) [code]	Owner/operator, location or fate	Notes
ZA674	B-V Chinook HC2 (N37019) [NY]	NARO, RNAY Fleetlands	
ZA675	B-V Chinook HC2 (N37020) [EB]	RAF No 7 Sqn, Odiham	
ZA676	B-V Chinook HC1 (N37021/ 9230M) [FG] (wreck)	FSCTE, RAF Manston	
ZA677	B-V Chinook HC2 (N37022) [EG]	RAF No 7 Sqn, Odiham	
ZA678	B-V Chinook HC1 (N37023/9229M) [EZ] (wreck)	RAF Odiham, BDRT	
ZA679	B-V Chinook HC2 (N37025) [D]	RAF No 78 Sqn, Mount Pleasant, FI	
ZA680	B-V Chinook HC2 (N37026) [BD]	RAF No 18 Sqn, Laarbruch	
ZA681	B-V Chinook HC2 (N37027) [ED]	RAF No 7 Sqn, Odiham	
ZA682	B-V Chinook HC2 (N37029)	NARO, RNAY Fleetlands	
ZA683	B-V Chinook HC2 (N37030) [C]	RAF No 78 Sqn, Mount Pleasant, FI	
ZA684	B-V Chinook HC2 (N37031) [EL]	RAF No 7 Sqn, Odiham	
ZA704	B-V Chinook HC2 (N37033) [EJ]	RAF No 7 Sqn, Odiham	
ZA705	B-V Chinook HC2 (N37035) [BE]	RAF No 18 Sqn, Laarbruch	
ZA707	B-V Chinook HC2 (N37040) [EV]	RAF No 7 Sqn, Odiham	
ZA708	B-V Chinook HC2 (N37042) [BC]	RAF No 18 Sqn, Laarbruch	
ZA709	B-V Chinook HC2 (N37043) [EQ]	RAF No 7 Sqn, Odiham	
ZA710	B-V Chinook HC2 (N37044) [EC]	RAF No 7 Sqn, Odiham	
ZA711	B-V Chinook HC2 (N37046) [ET]	RAF No 7 Sqn, Odiham	
ZA712	B-V Chinook HC2 (N37047) [ER]	RAF No 7 Sqn, Odiham	
ZA713	B-V Chinook HC2 (N37048) [EM]	RAF No 7 Sqn, Odiham	
ZA714	B-V Chinook HC2 (N37051) {EN]	RAF No 7 Sqn, Odiham	
ZA717	B-V Chinook HC1 (N37056/9238M) (wreck)	RAF St Athan, BDRT	
ZA718	B-V Chinook HC2 (N37058) [BN]	MoD(PE)/RWTS, DTEO Boscombe Down	
ZA720	B-V Chinook HC2 (N37060) [EP]	RAF No 7 Sqn, Odiham	
ZA726	WS Gazelle AH1 [F1]	AAC No 670 Sqn/2 Regiment, Middle Wallop	
ZA728	WS Gazelle AH1 [E]	RM No 847 Sqn, Yeovilton	
ZA729	WS Gazelle AH1 [V]	AAC No 658 Sqn/7 Regiment, Middle Wallop	
ZA730	WS Gazelle AH1	AAC No 665 Sqn/5 Regiment, Aldergrove	
ZA731	WS Gazelle AH1 [A]	AAC, NARO, RNAY Fleetlands	
ZA733	WS Gazelle AH1	AAC, stored NARO, RNAY Fleetlands	
ZA734	WS Gazelle AH1	AAC, stored NARO, RNAY Fleetlands	
ZA735	WS Gazelle AH1	AAC No 25 Flt, Belize	
ZA736	WS Gazelle AH1 [S]	AAC No 29 Flt, BATUS, Suffield, Canada	
ZA737	WS Gazelle AH1 [V]	AAC No 670 Sqn/2 Regiment, Middle Wallop	
ZA765	WS Gazelle AH1	AAC, NARO, RNAY Fleetlands	
ZA766	WS Gazelle AH1	AAC No 651 Sqn/1 Regiment, Gütersloh	
ZA767	WS Gazelle AH1	AAC, NARO, RNAY Fleetlands	
ZA768	WS Gazelle AH1 [F] (wreck)	AAC, stored Fleetlands	
ZA769	WS Gazelle AH1 [K]	AAC No 670 Sqn/2 Regiment, Middle Wallop	
ZA771	WS Gazelle AH1 [D]	AAC No 663 Sqn/3 Regiment, Wattisham	
ZA772	WS Gazelle AH1	AAC No 665 Sqn/5 Regiment, Aldergrove	
ZA773	WS Gazelle AH1 [F]	AAC No 658 Sqn/7 Regiment, Middle Wallop	
ZA774	WS Gazelle AH1	AAC No 665 Sqn/5 Regiment, Aldergrove	
ZA775	WS Gazelle AH1	AAC No 665 Sqn/5 Regiment, Aldergrove	
ZA776	WS Gazelle AH1 [F]	RM No 847 Sqn, Yeovilton	
ZA777	WS Gazelle AH1 [B]	AAC No 670 Sqn/2 Regiment, Middle Wallop	
ZA802	WS Gazelle HT3 [W]	RAF No 2 FTS, Shawbury	
ZA803	WS Gazelle HT3 [X]	RAF No 2 FTS, Shawbury	
ZA804	WS Gazelle HT3 [I]	RAF No 2 FTS, Shawbury	
ZA934	WS Puma HC1 [BZ]	RAF No 230 Sqn, Aldergrove	
ZA935	WS Puma HC1 [NR]	RAF No 230 Sqn, Aldergrove	
ZA936	WS Puma HC1	RAF No 230 Sqn, Aldergrove	
ZA937	WS Puma HC1	RAF No 230 Sqn, Aldergrove	
ZA938	WS Puma HC1	RAF No 18 Sqn, Laarbruch	
ZA939	WS Puma HC1 [DN]	RAF No 230 Sqn, Aldergrove	
ZA940	AS355F-1 Twin Squirrel (G-MOBI)	Repainted as G-MOBI, 1996	
ZA947	Douglas Dakota C3 [YS-DM]	RAF BBMF, Coningsby	
ZB500	WS Lynx 800 (G-LYNX)	IHM, Weston-super-Mare	
ZB506	WS61 Sea King Mk 4X	MoD(PE)/DRA, DTEO Boscombe Down	
ZB507	WS61 Sea King Mk 4X	MoD(PE)/DRA, DTEO Boscombe Down	
ZB600	BAe Harrier T4 [Z]	BAe Dunsfold	
ZB601	BAe Harrier T4 (fuselage)	BAe Dunsfold, spares use	
ZB602	BAe Harrier T4 [X]	BAe Dunsfold	

Notes	Serial	Type (other identity) [code]	Owner/operator, location or fate
	ZB603	BAe Harrier T4 [721/VL]	RN No 899 Sqn, Yeovilton
	ZB604	BAe Harrier T4N [722]	RN No 899 Sqn, Yeovilton
	ZB605	BAe Harrier T8 [720]	RN No 899 Sqn, Yeovilton
	ZB615	SEPECAT Jaguar T2	MoD(PE)/FJTS, DTEO Boscombe Down
	ZB625	WS Gazelle HT3 [N]	RAF No 2 FTS, Shawbury
	ZB626	WS Gazelle HT3 [L]	RAF No 2 FTS, Shawbury
	ZB627	WS Gazelle HT3 [A]	RAF No 7 Sqn, Odiham
	ZB629	WS Gazelle HCC4	RAF, stored NARO, RNAY Fleetlands
	ZB646	WS Gazelle HT2 [59/CU]	RN No 705 Sqn, Culdrose
	ZB647	WS Gazelle HT2 [40/CU]	RN No 705 Sqn, Culdrose
	ZB648	WS Gazelle HT2 [40/CU] (wreck)	RN, Predannack Fire School
	ZB649	WS Gazelle HT2 [VL]	RN FONA, Yeovilton
	ZB665	WS Gazelle AH1	AAC No 665 Sqn/5 Regiment, Aldergrove
	ZB666	WS Gazelle AH1 [G]	AAC No 670 Sqn/2 Regiment, Middle Wallop
	ZB667	WS Gazelle AH1	AAC, UNFICYP, Nicosia
	ZB668	WS Gazelle AH1 (TAD 015)	AAC SEAE, Arborfield
	ZB669	WS Gazelle AH1	AAC No 669 Sqn/4 Regiment, Wattisham
	ZB670	WS Gazelle AH1	AAC No 665 Sqn/5 Regiment, Aldergrove
	ZB671	WS Gazelle AH1	AAC No 29 Flt, BATUS, Suffield, Canada
	ZB672	WS Gazelle AH1 [C]	AAC No 663 Sqn/3 Regiment, Wattisham
	ZB673	WS Gazelle AH1 [P]	AAC No 670 Sqn/2 Regiment, Middle Wallop
	ZB674	WS Gazelle AH1	AAC No 665 Sqn/5 Regiment, Aldergrove
	ZB676	WS Gazelle AH1	AAC No 9 Regiment, Dishforth
	ZB677	WS Gazelle AH1	AAC No 29 Flt, BATUS, Suffield, Canada
	ZB678	WS Gazelle AH1	AAC SEAE, Arborfield
	ZB679	WS Gazelle AH1	AAC No 16 Flt, Dhekelia, Cyprus
	ZB682	WS Gazelle AH1	AAC No 665 Sqn/5 Regiment, Aldergrove
	ZB683	WS Gazelle AH1	AAC, NARO, RNAY Fleetlands
	ZB684	WS Gazelle AH1	AAC No 665 Sqn/5 Regiment, Aldergrove
	ZB685	WS Gazelle AH1	AAC No 665 Sqn/5 Regiment, Aldergrove
	ZB686	WS Gazelle AH1	AAC No 665 Sqn/5 Regiment, Aldergrove
	ZB688	WS Gazelle AH1 [H]	AAC No 670 Sqn/2 Regiment, Middle Wallop
	ZB689	WS Gazelle AH1 [W]	AAC No 670 Sqn/2 Regiment, Middle Wallop
	ZB690	WS Gazelle AH1	AAC No 16 Flt, Dhekelia, Cyprus
	ZB691	WS Gazelle AH1 [C]	AAC No 664 Sqn/9 Regiment, Dishforth
	ZB692	WS Gazelle AH1 [E]	AAC No 664 Sqn/9 Regiment, Dishforth
	ZB693	WS Gazelle AH1	AAC, NARO, RNAY Fleetlands
	ZD230	BAC Super VC10 K4 (G-ASGA) [K]	RAF No 101 Sqn, Brize Norton
	ZD232	BAC Super VC10 (G-ASGD/ 8699M)	*Burnt at Brize Norton, May 1994*
	ZD234	BAC Super VC10 (G-ASGF/ 8700M)	RAF Brize Norton, tanker simulator
	ZD235	BAC Super VC10 K4 (G-ASGG) [L]	RAF No 101 Sqn, Brize Norton
	ZD239	BAC Super VC10 (G-ASGK)	FSCTE, RAF Manston
	ZD240	BAC Super VC10 K4 (G-ASGL) [M]	RAF No 101 Sqn, Brize Norton
	ZD241	BAC Super VC10 K4 (G-ASGM) [N]	RAF No 101 Sqn, Brize Norton
	ZD242	BAC Super VC10 K4 (G-ASGP) [P]	RAF No 101 Sqn, Brize Norton
	ZD243	BAC Super VC10 (G-ASGR)	BAe, Filton (spares use)
	ZD249	WS Lynx HAS3S [642]	RN No 702 Sqn, Portland
	ZD250	WS Lynx HAS3S [417/NM]	RN No 815 Sqn, Portland
	ZD251	WS Lynx HAS3S [631]	RN No 702 Sqn, Portland
	ZD252	WS Lynx HMA8	NARO, RNAY Fleetlands (conversion)
	ZD253	WS Lynx HAS3S [410/GC]	RN AMG, Portland
	ZD254	WS Lynx HAS3S [645]	RN No 702 Sqn, Portland
	ZD255	WS Lynx HAS3S [374/VB]	RN No 815 Sqn, Portland
	ZD256	WS Lynx HAS3S [328/BA]	RN No 815 Sqn, Portland
	ZD257	WS Lynx HAS3S	RN AMG, Portland
	ZD258	WS Lynx HAS3S (*XZ258*) [633]	RN No 702 Sqn, Portland
	ZD259	WS Lynx HAS3S [333/BM]	RN No 815 Sqn, Portland
	ZD260	WS Lynx HAS3S [305]	RN No 815 Sqn, Portland
	ZD261	WS Lynx HMA8 [672]	RN No 815 Sqn OEU, Portland
	ZD262	WS Lynx HAS3S [641]	RN No 702 Sqn, Portland
	ZD263	WS Lynx HAS3S [636]	RN No 702 Sqn, Portland
	ZD264	WS Lynx HAS3S [420/EX]	RN No 815 Sqn, Portland
	ZD265	WS Lynx HMA8 [372/NL]	RN No 815 Sqn, Portland
	ZD266	WS Lynx HMA8	MoD(PE)/Westland, Yeovil
	ZD267	WS Lynx HMA8	MoD(PE)/Westland, Yeovil

Serial	Type (other identity) [code]	Owner/operator, location or fate	Notes
ZD268	WS Lynx HMA8	NARO, RNAY Fleetlands (conversion)	
ZD272	WS Lynx AH7 [H]	AAC No 671 Sqn/2 Regiment, Middle Wallop	
ZD273	WS Lynx AH7	AAC, stored NARO, RNAY Fleetlands	
ZD274	WS Lynx AH7	AAC No 664 Sqn/9 Regiment, Dishforth	
ZD276	WS Lynx AH7	AAC No 669 Sqn/4 Regiment, Wattisham	
ZD277	WS Lynx AH7 [0]	AAC No 663 Sqn/3 Regiment, Wattisham	
ZD278	WS Lynx AH7 [A]	AAC No 671 Sqn/2 Regiment, Middle Wallop	
ZD279	WS Lynx AH7 [C]	AAC No 671 Sqn/2 Regiment, Middle Wallop	
ZD280	WS Lynx AH7	AAC, stored NARO, RNAY Fleetlands	
ZD281	WS Lynx AH7 [K]	AAC No 671 Sqn/2 Regiment, Middle Wallop	
ZD282	WS Lynx AH7 [L]	RM No 847 Sqn, Yeovilton	
ZD283	WS Lynx AH7 [P]	AAC No 671 Sqn/2 Regiment, Middle Wallop	
ZD284	WS Lynx AH7	AAC No 663 Sqn/3 Regiment, Wattisham	
ZD285	WS Lynx AH7	MoD(PE)/DRA, DTEO Boscombe Down	
ZD318	BAe Harrier GR5	MoD(PE)/BAe Dunsfold	
ZD319	BAe Harrier GR5	MoD(PE)/BAe Dunsfold	
ZD320	BAe Harrier GR5	MoD(PE)/BAe Dunsfold	
ZD321	BAe Harrier GR5	MoD(PE)/BAe Dunsfold	
ZD322	BAe Harrier GR7 [03]	RAF No 4 Sqn, Laarbruch	
ZD323	BAe Harrier GR7 [04]	RAF St Athan	
ZD324	BAe Harrier GR7 [05]	RAF HOCU/No 20(R) Sqn, Wittering	
ZD326	BAe Harrier GR7 [07]	RAF No 3 Sqn, Laarbruch	
ZD327	BAe Harrier GR7 [08]	RAF No 3 Sqn, Laarbruch	
ZD328	BAe Harrier GR7 [09]	RAF No 1 Sqn, Wittering	
ZD329	BAe Harrier GR7 [10]	RAF No 1 Sqn, Wittering	
ZD330	BAe Harrier GR7 [11]	RAF No 3 Sqn, Laarbruch	
ZD345	BAe Harrier GR7 [12]	RAF HOCU/No 20(R) Sqn, Wittering	
ZD346	BAe Harrier GR7	MoD(PE)/BAe Dunsfold	
ZD347	BAe Harrier GR7 [F]	RAF HOCU/No 20(R) Sqn, Wittering	
ZD348	BAe Harrier GR7 [C]	RAF St Athan	
ZD350	BAe Harrier GR5 (9189M) [A]	RAF St Athan, BDRT	
ZD351	BAe Harrier GR7 [18]	RAF No 4 Sqn, Laarbruch	
ZD352	BAe Harrier GR7 [19]	RAF No 1 Sqn, Wittering	
ZD353	BAe Harrier GR5 (fuselage)	BAe Dunsfold	
ZD354	BAe Harrier GR7 [21]	RAF No 1 Sqn, Wittering	
ZD375	BAe Harrier GR7 [23]	RAF No 3 Sqn, Laarbruch	
ZD376	BAe Harrier GR7 [24]	RAF No 3 Sqn, Laarbruch	
ZD377	BAe Harrier GR7 [25]	*Crashed, 9 January 1997, Laarbruch*	
ZD378	BAe Harrier GR7	RAF St Athan	
ZD379	BAe Harrier GR7 [27]	RAF No 3 Sqn/No 4 Sqn, Laarbruch	
ZD380	BAe Harrier GR7 [28]	RAF No 1 Sqn, Wittering	
ZD400	BAe Harrier GR7 [29]	RAF No 1 Sqn, Wittering	
ZD401	BAe Harrier GR7 [30]	RAF No 1 Sqn, Wittering	
ZD402	BAe Harrier GR7 [31]	RAF HOCU/No 20(R) Sqn, Wittering	
ZD403	BAe Harrier GR7 [32]	RAF No 3 Sqn, Laarbruch	
ZD404	BAe Harrier GR7 [33]	RAF HOCU/No 20(R) Sqn, Wittering	
ZD405	BAe Harrier GR7 [34]	RAF HOCU/No 20(R) Sqn, Wittering	
ZD406	BAe Harrier GR7 [35]	RAF No 4 Sqn, Laarbruch	
ZD407	BAe Harrier GR7 [36]	RAF HOCU/No 20(R) Sqn, Wittering	
ZD408	BAe Harrier GR7 [37]	RAF No 4 Sqn, Laarbruch	
ZD409	BAe Harrier GR7 [38]	RAF No 3 Sqn, Laarbruch	
ZD410	BAe Harrier GR7 [39]	RAF HOCU/No 20(R) Sqn, Wittering	
ZD411	BAe Harrier GR7 [40]	RAF No 1 Sqn, Wittering	
ZD412	BAe Harrier GR5 (wreck)	BAe Dunsfold	
ZD431	BAe Harrier GR7 [43]	RAF HOCU/No 20(R) Sqn, Wittering	
ZD433	BAe Harrier GR7	MoD(PE)/BAe Dunsfold	
ZD434	BAe Harrier GR7 [46]	RAF St Athan	
ZD435	BAe Harrier GR7 [47]	RAF No 4 Sqn, Laarbruch	
ZD436	BAe Harrier GR7	MoD(PE)/DRA, DTEO Boscombe Down	
ZD437	BAe Harrier GR7 [49]	RAF HOCU/No 20R) Sqn, Wittering	
ZD438	BAe Harrier GR7 [50]	RAF No 1 Sqn, Wittering	
ZD461	BAe Harrier GR7 [51]	RAF HOCU/No 20(R) Sqn, Wittering	
ZD462	BAe Harrier GR7 [52]	RAF No 1 Sqn, Wittering	
ZD463	BAe Harrier GR7 [53]	RAF HOCU/No 20(R) Sqn, Wittering	
ZD464	BAe Harrier GR7 [54]	RAF HOCU/No 20(R) Sqn, Wittering	
ZD465	BAe Harrier GR7 [55]	RAF St Athan	
ZD466	BAe Harrier GR7 [56]	RAF No 3 Sqn/No 4 Sqn, Laarbruch	
ZD467	BAe Harrier GR7	RAF AWC/SAOEU, DTEO Boscombe Down	

Notes	Serial	Type (other identity) [code]	Owner/operator, location or fate
	ZD468	BAe Harrier GR7 [58]	RAF No 1 Sqn, Wittering
	ZD469	BAe Harrier GR7	RAF AWC/SAOEU, DTEO Boscombe Down
	ZD470	BAe Harrier GR7 [60]	RAF No 1 Sqn, Wittering
	ZD472	BAe Harrier GR5 <R> (BAPC 191) [01]	RAF EP&TU, St Athan
	ZD476	WS61 Sea King HC4 [ZU]	RN No 848 Sqn, Yeovilton
	ZD477	WS61 Sea King HC4 [H]	RN No 845 Sqn, Yeovilton
	ZD478	WS61 Sea King HC4 [VG]	RN No 846 Sqn, Yeovilton
	ZD479	WS61 Sea King HC4 [ZV]	RN AMG, Yeovilton
	ZD480	WS61 Sea King HC4 [E]	RN No 845 Sqn, Yeovilton
	ZD559	WS Lynx AH5X	MoD(PE)/DRA, DTEO Boscombe Down
	ZD560	WS Lynx AH7	MoD(PE)/ETPS, DTEO Boscombe Down
	ZD565	WS Lynx HAS3S [630]	RN No 702 Sqn, Portland
	ZD566	WS Lynx HMA8	NARO, RNAY Fleetlands (conversion)
	ZD574	B-V Chinook HC2 (N37077) [EH]	RAF No 7 Sqn, Odiham
	ZD575	B-V Chinook HC2 (N37078) [NZ]	RAF No 27(R) Sqn, Odiham
	ZD578	BAe Sea Harrier FA2 [000]	RN AMG, Yeovilton
	ZD579	BAe Sea Harrier FA2 [712]	RN AMG, Yeovilton
	ZD580	BAe Sea Harrier FA2 [002]	RN, stored St Athan
	ZD581	BAe Sea Harrier FA2 [124]	MoD(PE)/BAe Dunsfold (conversion)
	ZD582	BAe Sea Harrier FA2 [712]	RN No 899 Sqn, Yeovilton
	ZD607	BAe Sea Harrier FA2 [123]	RN No 800 Sqn, Yeovilton
	ZD608	BAe Sea Harrier FA2 [717]	RN No 899 Sqn, Yeovilton
	ZD610	BAe Sea Harrier FA2	RN, St Athan
	ZD611	BAe Sea Harrier FA2 [714]	RN No 899 Sqn, Yeovilton
	ZD612	BAe Sea Harrier FA2 [719]	RN No 899 Sqn, Yeovilton
	ZD613	BAe Sea Harrier FA2 [005]	RN AMG, Yeovilton
	ZD614	BAe Sea Harrier FA2 [000]	RN No 801 Sqn, Yeovilton
	ZD615	BAe Sea Harrier FA2 [718]	RN No 899 Sqn, Yeovilton
	ZD620	BAe 125 CC3	RAF No 32(The Royal) Sqn, Northolt
	ZD621	BAe 125 CC3	RAF No 32(The Royal) Sqn, Northolt
	ZD625	WS61 Sea King HC4 [VF]	RN No 846 Sqn, Yeovilton
	ZD626	WS61 Sea King HC4 [ZZ]	RN No 848 Sqn, Yeovilton
	ZD627	WS61 Sea King HC4 [VL]	RN No 846 Sqn, Yeovilton
	ZD630	WS61 Sea King HAS6 [271/N]	RN No 814 Sqn, Culdrose
	ZD631	WS61 Sea King HAS6 [66] (fuselage)	RNAS Lee-on-Solent
	ZD633	WS61 Sea King HAS6 [507]	RN No 810 Sqn, Culdrose
	ZD634	WS61 Sea King HAS6 [506/CU]	RN No 810 Sqn, Culdrose
	ZD636	WS61 Sea King AEW7 [702]	Westlands, Weston-super-Mare (conversion)
	ZD637	WS61 Sea King HAS6 [700/PW]	RN No 819 Sqn, Prestwick
	ZD657	Schleicher ASW-19B Valiant TX1 [YW]	RAF/Dunstable Sailplanes, Dunstable
	ZD658	Schleicher ASW-19B Valiant TX1 [YX]	RAF ACCGS, Syerston
	ZD659	Schleicher ASW-19B Valiant TX1	RAF No 631 VGS, Sealand
	ZD660	Schleicher ASW-19B Valiant TX1 [YZ]	RAF ACCGS, Syerston
	ZD667	BAe Harrier GR3 (9201M) [3,2]	SFDO, RNAS Culdrose
	ZD668	BAe Harrier GR3 [3E]	Phoenix Aviation, Bruntingthorpe
	ZD670	BAe Harrier GR3 [3A]	Privately owned, Leicester Square, London
	ZD703	BAe 125 CC3	RAF No 32(The Royal) Sqn, Northolt
	ZD704	BAe 125 CC3	RAF No 32(The Royal) Sqn, Northolt
	ZD707	Panavia Tornado GR1 [BK]	RAF No 14 Sqn, Brüggen
	ZD708	Panavia Tornado GR4	MoD(PE)/BAe Warton
	ZD709	Panavia Tornado GR1 [DG]	RAF No 31 Sqn, Brüggen
	ZD711	Panavia Tornado GR1 [DY]	RAF No 31 Sqn, Brüggen
	ZD712	Panavia Tornado GR1 [BY]	RAF No 14 Sqn, Brüggen
	ZD713	Panavia Tornado GR1 [TW]	RAF No 15(R) Sqn, Lossiemouth
	ZD714	Panavia Tornado GR1	RAF No 9 Sqn, Brüggen
	ZD715	Panavia Tornado GR1 [CC]	RAF No 17 Sqn, Brüggen
	ZD716	Panavia Tornado GR1 [O]	RAF AWC/SAOEU, DTEO Boscombe Down
	ZD719	Panavia Tornado GR1 [DE]	RAF No 31 Sqn, Brüggen
	ZD720	Panavia Tornado GR1 [AG]	RAF No 9 Sqn, Brüggen
	ZD739	Panavia Tornado GR1 [AC]	RAF No 9 Sqn, Brüggen
	ZD740	Panavia Tornado GR1 [DA]	RAF No 31 Sqn, Brüggen
	ZD741	Panavia Tornado GR1 [CY]	RAF No 17 Sqn, Brüggen
	ZD742	Panavia Tornado GR1	RAF No 17 Sqn, Brüggen
	ZD743	Panavia Tornado GR1 [CX]	RAF No 17 Sqn, Brüggen
	ZD744	Panavia Tornado GR1 [BD]	RAF No 14 Sqn, Brüggen
	ZD745	Panavia Tornado GR1 [BM]	RAF No 14 Sqn, Brüggen

Serial	Type (other identity) [code]	Owner/operator, location or fate	Notes
ZD746	Panavia Tornado GR1 [AB]	RAF No 9 Sqn, Brüggen	
ZD747	Panavia Tornado GR1 [AL]	RAF No 9 Sqn, Brüggen	
ZD748	Panavia Tornado GR1 [AK]	RAF No 9 Sqn, Brüggen	
ZD749	Panavia Tornado GR1 [U]	RAF AWC/SAOEU, DTEO Boscombe Down	
ZD788	Panavia Tornado GR1 [CB]	RAF No 17 Sqn, Brüggen	
ZD789	Panavia Tornado GR1 [AM]	RAF No 9 Sqn, Brüggen	
ZD790	Panavia Tornado GR1 [BB]	RAF No 14 Sqn, Brüggen	
ZD792	Panavia Tornado GR1	RAF No 17 Sqn, Brüggen	
ZD793	Panavia Tornado GR1 [CA]	RAF No 17 Sqn, Brüggen	
ZD809	Panavia Tornado GR1 [BA]	RAF No 14 Sqn, Brüggen	
ZD810	Panavia Tornado GR1 [DB]	RAF No 31 Sqn, Brüggen	
ZD811	Panavia Tornado GR1 [BC]	RAF No 14 Sqn, Brüggen	
ZD812	Panavia Tornado GR1 [BW]	RAF No 14 Sqn, Brüggen	
ZD842	Panavia Tornado GR1 [CY]	RAF, stored St Athan	
ZD843	Panavia Tornado GR1 [CJ]	RAF No 17 Sqn, Brüggen	
ZD844	Panavia Tornado GR1 [DE]	RAF TMF, Marham	
ZD845	Panavia Tornado GR1 [AF]	*Crashed 26 February 1996, Laarbruch*	
ZD846	Panavia Tornado GR1 [BL]	*Crashed 11 January 1996, near Munster*	
ZD847	Panavia Tornado GR1 [CH]	RAF No 17 Sqn, Brüggen	
ZD848	Panavia Tornado GR1 [CD]	RAF No 17 Sqn, Brüggen	
ZD849	Panavia Tornado GR1 [BT]	RAF No 14 Sqn, Brüggen	
ZD850	Panavia Tornado GR1 [DR]	RAF No 31 Sqn, Brüggen	
ZD851	Panavia Tornado GR1 [AJ]	RAF No 9 Sqn, Brüggen	
ZD890	Panavia Tornado GR1 [AE]	RAF No 9 Sqn, Brüggen	
ZD892	Panavia Tornado GR1 [BJ]	RAF No 14 Sqn, Brüggen	
ZD895	Panavia Tornado GR1 [BF]	RAF No 14 Sqn, Brüggen	
ZD899	Panavia Tornado F2	MoD(PE)/BAe Warton	
ZD900	Panavia Tornado F2	To be used in the rebuild of ZE343 at BAe Warton	
ZD901	Panavia Tornado F2 (comp ZE154)	RAF, stored St Athan	
ZD902	Panavia Tornado F2TIARA	MoD(PE)/DRA, DTEO Boscombe Down	
ZD903	Panavia Tornado F2 [AB]	To be used in the rebuild of ZE728 at BAe Warton	
ZD904	Panavia Tornado F2 (comp ZE755)	RAF, stored St Athan	
ZD905	Panavia Tornado F2 (comp ZE258)	RAF, stored St Athan	
ZD906	Panavia Tornado F2 (comp ZE294)	RAF, stored St Athan	
ZD932	Panavia Tornado F2 (comp ZE255)	RAF, stored St Athan	
ZD933	Panavia Tornado F2 (comp ZE729)	RAF, stored St Athan	
ZD934	Panavia Tornado F2 (comp ZE786) [AD]	RAF, stored St Athan	
ZD935	Panavia Tornado F2	To be used in the rebuild of ZE793 at BAe Warton	
ZD936	Panavia Tornado F2 (comp ZE251)	RAF, stored St Athan	
ZD937	Panavia Tornado F2 (comp ZE736)	RAF, stored St Athan	
ZD938	Panavia Tornado F2 (comp ZE295)	RAF, stored St Athan	
ZD939	Panavia Tornado F2 (comp ZE292)	RAF, stored St Athan	
ZD940	Panavia Tornado F2 (comp ZE288)	RAF, stored St Athan	
ZD941	Panavia Tornado F2 (comp ZE254)	RAF, stored St Athan	
ZD948	Lockheed TriStar KC1 (G-BFCA)	RAF No 216 Sqn, Brize Norton	
ZD949	Lockheed TriStar K1 (G-BFCB)	RAF No 216 Sqn, Brize Norton	
ZD950	Lockheed TriStar KC1 (G-BFCC)	RAF No 216 Sqn, Brize Norton	
ZD951	Lockheed TriStar K1 (G-BFCD)	RAF No 216 Sqn, Brize Norton	
ZD952	Lockheed TriStar KC1 (G-BFCE)	RAF No 216 Sqn, Brize Norton	
ZD953	Lockheed TriStar KC1 (G-BFCF)	RAF No 216 Sqn, Brize Norton	
ZD974	Schempp-Hirth Kestrel TX1 [SY]	RAF No 615 VGS, Kenley	
ZD975	Schempp-Hirth Kestrel TX1 [SZ]	RAF CGMF, Syerston	
ZD980	B-V Chinook HC2 (N37082) [EA]	RAF No 7 Sqn, Odiham	
ZD981	B-V Chinook HC2 (N37083) [NW]	RAF No 27(R) Sqn, Odiham	
ZD982	B-V Chinook HC2 (N37085) [EK]	RAF No 7 Sqn, Odiham	
ZD983	B-V Chinook HC2 (N37086) [EI]	RAF No 7 Sqn, Odiham	
ZD984	B-V Chinook HC2 (N37088) [EE]	RAF No 7 Sqn, Odiham	
ZD990	BAe Harrier T8	RAF AMG, Yeovilton	
ZD991	BAe Harrier T4 (9228M) [V]	SFDO, RNAS Culdrose	
ZD992	BAe Harrier T8 [724]	RN No 899 Sqn, Yeovilton	
ZD993	BAe Harrier T8 [723]	RN No 899 Sqn, Yeovilton	
ZD996	Panavia Tornado GR1A [I]	RAF No 2 Sqn, Marham	
ZE116	Panavia Tornado GR1A [O]	RAF No 2 Sqn, Marham	
ZE154	Panavia Tornado F3 (comp ZD901) [AN]	RAF F3 OCU/No 56(R) Sqn, Coningsby	
ZE155	Panavia Tornado F3	MoD(PE)/BAe Warton	
ZE156	Panavia Tornado F3 [HE]	RAF No 111 Sqn, Leuchars	
ZE157	Panavia Tornado F3 [AI]	RAF F3 OCU/No 56(R) Sqn, Coningsby	

Notes	Serial	Type (other identity) [code]	Owner/operator, location or fate
	ZE158	Panavia Tornado F3 [DC]	RAF No 11 Sqn, Leeming
	ZE159	Panavia Tornado F3 [DE]	RAF No 11 Sqn, Leeming
	ZE160	Panavia Tornado F3 [DV]	RAF No 11 Sqn, Leeming
	ZE161	Panavia Tornado F3 [FG]	RAF No 25 Sqn, Leeming
	ZE162	Panavia Tornado F3 [FK]	RAF No 25 Sqn, Leeming
	ZE163	Panavia Tornado F3 [AA]	RAF F3 OCU/No 56(R) Sqn, Coningsby
	ZE164	Panavia Tornado F3 [DA]	RAF No 11 Sqn, Leeming
	ZE165	Panavia Tornado F3 [FO]	RAF No 25 Sqn, Leeming
	ZE166	Panavia Tornado F3 [AF]	*Collided with ZE862 near Sleaford, 10 January 1996*
	ZE167	Panavia Tornado F3 [HX]	*For Italian AF as MM7234*
	ZE168	Panavia Tornado F3 [FN]	RAF No 25 Sqn, Leeming
	ZE199	Panavia Tornado F3 [FL]	RAF No 25 Sqn, Leeming
	ZE200	Panavia Tornado F3 [DB]	RAF No 11 Sqn, Leeming
	ZE201	Panavia Tornado F3 [DO]	RAF No 11 Sqn, Leeming
	ZE203	Panavia Tornado F3 [FI]	RAF No 25 Sqn, Leeming
	ZE204	Panavia Tornado F3 [DD]	RAF No 11 Sqn, Leeming
	ZE205	Panavia Tornado F3 [AM]	*For Italian AF as MM55061*
	ZE206	Panavia Tornado F3 [FH]	RAF No 25 Sqn, Leeming
	ZE207	Panavia Tornado F3 [GC]	RAF No 43 Sqn, Leuchars
	ZE208	Panavia Tornado F3 [AN]	*To Italy as MM55060, February 1997*
	ZE209	Panavia Tornado F3 [AP]	RAF F3 OCU/No 56(R) Sqn, Coningsby
	ZE210	Panavia Tornado F3	RAF AMF, Leuchars (spares use)
	ZE250	Panavia Tornado F3 [HZ]	RAF No 111 Sqn, Leuchars
	ZE251	Panavia Tornado F3 (comp ZD936) [GA]	RAF No 43 Sqn, Leuchars
	ZE252	Panavia Tornado F3 [AS]	*For Italiian AF as MM7225*
	ZE253	Panavia Tornado F3 [AC]	RAF F3 OCU/No 56(R) Sqn, Coningsby
	ZE254	Panavia Tornado F3 (comp ZD941) [GE]	RAF No 43 Sqn, Leuchars
	ZE255	Panavia Tornado F3 (comp ZD932) [AY]	RAF F3 OCU/No 56(R) Sqn, Coningsby
	ZE256	Panavia Tornado F3 [BX]	RAF No 29 Sqn, Coningsby
	ZE257	Panavia Tornado F3 [HN]	RAF No 111 Sqn, Leuchars
	ZE258	Panavia Tornado F3 (comp ZD905)	RAF Coningsby
	ZE287	Panavia Tornado F3 [AH]	RAF F3 OCU/No 56(R) Sqn, Coningsby
	ZE288	Panavia Tornado F3 (comp ZD932) [BH]	RAF No 29 Sqn, Coningsby
	ZE289	Panavia Tornado F3 [HF]	RAF No 111 Sqn, Leuchars
	ZE290	Panavia Tornado F3 [AD]	RAF F3 OCU/No 56(R) Sqn, Coningsby
	ZE291	Panavia Tornado F3 [GQ]	RAF No 43 Sqn, Leuchars
	ZE292	Panavia Tornado F3 (comp ZD939) [AZ]	RAF F3 OCU/No 56(R) Sqn, Coningsby
	ZE293	Panavia Tornado F3 [HT]	RAF No 111 Sqn, Leuchars
	ZE294	Panavia Tornado F3 (comp ZD906)	RAF No 43 Sqn, Leuchars
	ZE295	Panavia Tornado F3 (comp ZD938) [AV]	RAF F3 OCU/No 56(R) Sqn, Coningsby
	ZE296	Panavia Tornado F3 [GR]	RAF No 43 Sqn, Leuchars
	ZE338	Panavia Tornado F3 [HG]	RAF No 111 Sqn, Leuchars
	ZE339	Panavia Tornado F3 [BK]	RAF No 29 Sqn, Coningsby
	ZE340	Panavia Tornado F3 [36-12]	RAF F3 OCU/No 56(R) Sqn, Coningsby
	ZE341	Panavia Tornado F3	RAF ASF, Coningsby
	ZE342	Panavia Tornado F3 [HW]	RAF No 111 Sqn, Leuchars
	ZE343	Panavia Tornado F3 (comp ZD900) [AI]	RAF, stored St Athan (for rebuild at BAe Warton)
	ZE353	McD F-4J(UK) Phantom (9083M) [E]	FSCTE, RAF Manston
	ZE354	McD F-4J(UK) Phantom (9084M) [R]	RAF Coningsby Fire Section
	ZE356	McD F-4J(UK) Phantom (9060M) [Q]	RAF Waddington Fire Section
	ZE360	McD F-4J(UK) Phantom (9059M) [O]	FSCTE, RAF Manston
	ZE361	McD F-4J(UK) Phantom (9057M) [P]	RAF Honington Fire Section
	ZE364	McD F-4J(UK) Phantom (9085M) [Z]	*Scrapped at Coventry, 1996*
	ZE368	WS61 Sea King HAR3	RAF No 203(R) Sqn, St Mawgan
	ZE369	WS61 Sea King HAR3	RAF No 22 Sqn, A Flt, Chivenor
	ZE370	WS61 Sea King HAR3	RAF HMF, St Mawgan
	ZE375	WS Lynx AH9 [2]	AAC No 659 Sqn/4 Regiment, Wattisham
	ZE376	WS Lynx AH9 [4]	AAC No 659 Sqn/4 Regiment, Wattisham
	ZE376	WS Lynx AH9 [4]	AAC No 659 Sqn/4 Regiment, Wattisham

Serial	Type (other identity) [code]	Owner/operator, location or fate	Notes
ZE378	WS Lynx AH7	AAC, stored NARO, RNAY Fleetlands	
ZE379	WS Lynx AH7	AAC No 655 Sqn/5 Regiment, Aldergrove	
ZE380	WS Lynx AH9 [1]	AAC No 659 Sqn/4 Regiment, Wattisham	
ZE381	WS Lynx AH7	AAC No 655 Sqn/5 Regiment, Aldergrove	
ZE382	WS Lynx AH9 [3]	AAC No 659 Sqn/4 Regiment, Wattisham	
ZE395	BAe 125 CC3	RAF No 32(The Royal) Sqn, Northolt	
ZE396	BAe 125 CC3	RAF No 32(The Royal) Sqn, Northolt	
ZE410	Agusta A109A (AE-334)	AAC No 8 Flt, Middle Wallop, Hereford	
ZE411	Agusta A109A (AE-331)	AAC No 8 Flt, Middle Wallop, Hereford	
ZE412	Agusta A109A	AAC No 8 Flt, Middle Wallop, Hereford	
ZE413	Agusta A109A	AAC No 8 Flt, Middle Wallop, Hereford	
ZE418	WS61 Sea King AEW7 [826]	RN AMG, Culdrose (conversion)	
ZE419	WS61 Sea King HAS6 (fuselage)	RN, Predannack Fire School	
ZE420	WS61 Sea King AEW7	Westlands, Weston-super-Mare (conversion)	
ZE422	WS61 Sea King HAS6 [588]	RN No 706 Sqn, Culdrose	
ZE425	WS61 Sea King HC4 [J]	RN No 845 Sqn, Yeovilton	
ZE426	WS61 Sea King HC4 [VI]		
ZE427	WS61 Sea King HC4 [B]	RN No 845 Sqn, Yeovilton	
ZE428	WS61 Sea King HC4 [VK]	RN No 846 Sqn, Yeovilton	
ZE432	BAC 1-11/479FU (DQ-FBV)	MoD(PE)/ETPS, DTEO Boscombe Down	
ZE433	BAC 1-11/479FU (DQ-FBQ)	MoD(PE)/GEC-Ferranti, Edinburgh	
ZE438	BAe Jetstream T3 [576]	RN, stored Shawbury	
ZE439	BAe Jetstream T3 [577]	RN FONA/Heron Flight, Yeovilton	
ZE440	BAe Jetstream T3 [578]	RN FONA/Heron Flight, Yeovilton	
ZE441	BAe Jetstream T3 [579]	RN FONA/Heron Flight, Yeovilton	
ZE449	SA330L Puma HC1 (9017M/PA-12)	MoD(PE)/Westland, Weston-super-Mare (under rebuild)	
ZE477	WS Lynx 3	IHM, Weston-super-Mare	
ZE495	Grob G103 Viking T1 (BGA3000) [VA]	RAF No 622 VGS, Upavon	
ZE496	Grob G103 Viking T1 (BGA3001) [VB]	RAF No 634 VGS, St Athan	
ZE497	Grob G103 Viking T1 (BGA3002)	*Crashed*	
ZE498	Grob G103 Viking T1 (BGA3003) [VC]	RAF No 614 VGS, Wethersfield	
ZE499	Grob G103 Viking T1 (BGA3004) [VD]	RAF ACCGS, Syerston	
ZE501	Grob G103 Viking T1 (BGA3006) [VE]	RAF ACCGS, Syerston	
ZE502	Grob G103 Viking T1 (BGA3007)	RAF No 645 VGS, Catterick	
ZE503	Grob G103 Viking T1 (BGA3008) [VG]	RAF No 645 VGS, Catterick	
ZE504	Grob G103 Viking T1 (BGA3009) [VH]	RAF No 634 VGS, St Athan	
ZE520	Grob G103 Viking T1 (BGA3010) [VJ]	RAF No 614 VGS, Wethersfield	
ZE521	Grob G103 Viking T1 (BGA3011)	RAF No 626 VGS, Predannack	
ZE522	Grob G103 Viking T1 (BGA3012) [VL]	RAF No 634 VGS, St Athan	
ZE524	Grob G103 Viking T1 (BGA3014) [VM]	RAF CGMF, Syerston	
ZE526	Grob G103 Viking T1 (BGA3016) [VN]	RAF No 636 VGS, Aberporth	
ZE527	Grob G103 Viking T1 (BGA3017)	RAF CGMF, Syerston	
ZE528	Grob G103 Viking T1 (BGA3018) [VQ]	RAF No 645 VGS, Catterick	
ZE529	Grob G103 Viking T1 (BGA3019)	RAF CGMF, Syerston (damaged)	
ZE530	Grob G103 Viking T1 (BGA3020) [VS]	RAF No 611 VGS, Watton	
ZE531	Grob G103 Viking T1 (BGA3021) [VT]	RAF No 617 VGS, Manston	
ZE532	Grob G103 Viking T1 (BGA3022)	RAF No 614 VGS, Wethersfield	
ZE533	Grob G103 Viking T1 (BGA3023) [VV]	RAF No 622 VGS, Upavon	
ZE534	Grob G103 Viking T1 (BGA3024) [VW]	RAF No 614 VGS, Wethersfield	
ZE550	Grob G103 Viking T1 (BGA3025) [VX]	RAF CGMF, Syerston	
ZE551	Grob G103 Viking T1 (BGA3026) [VY]	RAF No 614 VGS, Wethersfield	
ZE552	Grob G103 Viking T1 (BGA3027) [VZ]	RAF No 611 VGS, Watton	

Notes	Serial	Type (other identity) [code]	Owner/operator, location or fate
	ZE553	Grob G103 Viking T1 (BGA3028) [WA]	RAF No 611 VGS, Watton
	ZE554	Grob G103 Viking T1 (BGA3029) [WB]	RAF CGMF, Syerston
	ZE555	Grob G103 Viking T1 (BGA3030) [WC]	RAF No 645 VGS, Catterick
	ZE556	Grob G103 Viking T1 (BGA3031) [WD]	RAF CGMF, Syerston
	ZE557	Grob G103 Viking T1 (BGA3032) [WE]	RAF No 622 VGS, Upavon
	ZE558	Grob G103 Viking T1 (BGA3033) [WF]	RAF No 615 VGS, Kenley
	ZE559	Grob G103 Viking T1 (BGA3034) [WG]	RAF No 631 VGS, Sealand
	ZE560	Grob G103 Viking T1 (BGA3035) [WH]	RAF No 631 VGS, Sealand
	ZE561	Grob G103 Viking T1 (BGA3036) [WJ]	RAF No 621 VGS, Hullavington
	ZE562	Grob G103 Viking T1 (BGA3037) [WK]	RAF No 631 VGS, Sealand
	ZE563	Grob G103 Viking T1 (BGA3038) [WL]	RAF No 661 VGS, Kirknewton
	ZE564	Grob G103 Viking T1 (BGA3039) [WN]	RAF CGMF, Syerston
	ZE584	Grob G103 Viking T1 (BGA3040) [WP]	RAF No 661 VGS, Kirknewton
	ZE585	Grob G103 Viking T1 (BGA3041) [WQ]	RAF No 622 VGS, Upavon
	ZE586	Grob G103 Viking T1 (BGA3042) [WR]	RAF No 661 VGS, Kirknewton
	ZE587	Grob G103 Viking T1 (BGA3043) [WS]	RAF No 611 VGS, Watton
	ZE589	Grob G103 Viking T1 (BGA3045)	*Crashed*
	ZE590	Grob G103 Viking T1 (BGA3046) [WT]	RAF No 615 VGS, Kenley
	ZE591	Grob G103 Viking T1 (BGA3047) [WU]	RAF No 661 VGS, Kirknewton
	ZE592	Grob G103 Viking T1 (BGA3048) [WV]	RAF No 626 VGS, Predannack
	ZE593	Grob G103 Viking T1 (BGA3049) [WW]	RAF No 631 VGS, Sealand
	ZE594	Grob G103 Viking T1 (BGA3050) [WX]	RAF No 615 VGS, Kenley
	ZE595	Grob G103 Viking T1 (BGA3051) [WY]	RAF No 622 VGS, Upavon
	ZE600	Grob G103 Viking T1 (BGA3052) [WZ]	RAF No 622 VGS, Upavon
	ZE601	Grob G103 Viking T1 (BGA3053) [XA]	RAF No 615 VGS, Kenley
	ZE602	Grob G103 Viking T1 (BGA3054) [XB]	RAF No 621 VGS, Hullavington
	ZE603	Grob G103 Viking T1 (BGA3055) [XC]	RAF No 625 VGS, Hullavington
	ZE604	Grob G103 Viking T1 (BGA3056) [XD]	RAF No 617 VGS, Manston
	ZE605	Grob G103 Viking T1 (BGA3057) [XE]	RAF No 662 VGS, Arbroath
	ZE606	Grob G103 Viking T1 (BGA3058) [XF]	RAF No 625 VGS, Hullavington
	ZE607	Grob G103 Viking T1 (BGA3059) [XG]	RAF No 625 VGS, Hullavington
	ZE608	Grob G103 Viking T1 (BGA3060) [XH]	RAF No 621 VGS, Hullavington
	ZE609	Grob G103 Viking T1 (BGA3061) [XJ]	RAF CGMF, Syerston
	ZE610	Grob G103 Viking T1 (BGA3062) [XK]	RAF No 625 VGS, Hullavington
	ZE611	Grob G103 Viking T1 (BGA3063) [XL]	RAF No 636 VGS, Aberporth
	ZE613	Grob G103 Viking T1 (BGA3065) [XM]	RAF No 625 VGS, Hullavington
	ZE614	Grob G103 Viking T1 (BGA3066) [XN]	RAF No 661 VGS, Kirknewton

Serial	Type (other identity) [code]	Owner/operator, location or fate	Notes
ZE625	Grob G103 Viking T1 (BGA3067) [XP]	RAF No 625 VGS, Hullavington	
ZE626	Grob G103 Viking T1 (BGA3068)	RAF No 626 VGS, Predannack	
ZE627	Grob G103 Viking T1 (BGA3069) [XR]	RAF ACCGS, Syerston	
ZE628	Grob G103 Viking T1 (BGA3070) [XS]	RAF No 615 VGS, Kenley	
ZE629	Grob G103 Viking T1 (BGA3071) [XT]	RAF No 662 VGS, Arbroath	
ZE630	Grob G103 Viking T1 (BGA3072) [XU]	RAF No 662 VGS, Arbroath	
ZE631	Grob G103 Viking T1 (BGA3073) [XV]	RAF No 662 VGS, Arbroath	
ZE632	Grob G103 Viking T1 (BGA3074) [XW]	RAF No 617 VGS, Manston	
ZE633	Grob G103 Viking T1 (BGA3075) [XX]	RAF No 614 VGS, Wethersfield	
ZE635	Grob G103 Viking T1 (BGA3077) [XY]	RAF No 631 VGS, Sealand	
ZE636	Grob G103 Viking T1 (BGA3078) [XZ]	RAF No 636 VGS, Aberporth	
ZE637	Grob G103 Viking T1 (BGA3079) [YA]	RAF No 622 VGS, Upavon	
ZE650	Grob G103 Viking T1 (BGA3080) [YB]	RAF ACCGS, Syerston	
ZE651	Grob G103 Viking T1 (BGA3081) [YC]	RAF No 615 VGS, Kenley	
ZE652	Grob G103 Viking T1 (BGA3082)	RAF CGMF, Syerston	
ZE653	Grob G103 Viking T1 (BGA3083) [YE]	RAF No 631 VGS, Sealand	
ZE655	Grob G103 Viking T1 (BGA3085) (wreck)	RAF CGMF, Syerston	
ZE656	Grob G103 Viking T1 (BGA3086) [YH]	RAF No 617 VGS, Manston	
ZE657	Grob G103 Viking T1 (BGA3087) [YJ]	RAF No 617 VGS, Manston	
ZE658	Grob G103 Viking T1 (BGA3088) [YK]	RAF No 621 VGS, Hullavington	
ZE659	Grob G103 Viking T1 (BGA3089) [YL]	RAF No 611 VGS, Watton	
ZE677	Grob G103 Viking T1 (BGA3090)	RAF CGMF, Syerston (damaged)	
ZE678	Grob G103 Viking T1 (BGA3091) [YN]	RAF No 631 VGS, Sealand	
ZE679	Grob G103 Viking T1 (BGA3092) [YP]	RAF No 662 VGS, Arbroath	
ZE680	Grob G103 Viking T1 (BGA3093) [YQ]	RAF ACCGS, Syerston	
ZE681	Grob G103 Viking T1 (BGA3094) [YR]	RAF No 615 VGS, Kenley	
ZE682	Grob G103 Viking T1 (BGA3095) [YS]	RAF No 611 VGS, Watton	
ZE683	Grob G103 Viking T1 (BGA3096) [YT]	RAF No 645 VGS, Catterick	
ZE684	Grob G103 Viking T1 (BGA3097) [YU]	RAF No 621 VGS, Hullavington	
ZE685	Grob G103 Viking T1 (BGA3098) [YV]	RAF No 661 VGS, Kirknewton	
ZE686	Grob G103 Viking T1 (BGA3099)	MoD(PE)/Slingsby Kirkbymoorside	
ZE690	BAe Sea Harrier FA2 [003/L]	RN, St Athan	
ZE691	BAe Sea Harrier FA2 [710]	RN No 899 Sqn, Yeovilton	
ZE692	BAe Sea Harrier FA2 [711]	RN No 899 Sqn, Yeovilton	
ZE693	BAe Sea Harrier FA2 [001]	RN No 801 Sqn, Yeovilton	
ZE694	BAe Sea Harrier FA2 [123, 125]	RN, St Athan	
ZE695	BAe Sea Harrier FA2 [124]	RN, St Athan	
ZE696	BAe Sea Harrier FA2 [126]	RN No 800 Sqn, Yeovilton	
ZE697	BAe Sea Harrier FA2 [003]	RN No 801 Sqn, Yeovilton	
ZE698	BAe Sea Harrier FA2	MoD(PE)/BAe Dunsfold (conversion)	
ZE700	BAe 146 CC2	RAF No 32(The Royal) Sqn, Northolt	
ZE701	BAe 146 CC2	RAF No 32(The Royal) Sqn, Northolt	
ZE702	BAe 146 CC2	RAF No 32(The Royal) Sqn, Northolt	
ZE704	Lockheed TriStar C2 (N508PA)	RAF No 216 Sqn, Brize Norton	
ZE705	Lockheed TriStar C2 (N509PA)	RAF No 216 Sqn, Brize Norton	
ZE706	Lockheed TriStar C2A (N503PA)	RAF No 216 Sqn, Brize Norton	

Notes	Serial	Type (other identity) [code]	Owner/operator, location or fate
	ZE728	Panavia Tornado F3 (comp ZD903) [AL]	RAF, stored St Athan (for rebuild at BAe Warton)
	ZE729	Panavia Tornado F3 (comp ZD933)	RAF No 29 Sqn, Coningsby
	ZE731	Panavia Tornado F3 [GF]	RAF No 43 Sqn, Leuchars
	ZE732	Panavia Tornado F3 [BB]	RAF No 29 Sqn, Coningsby
	ZE734	Panavia Tornado F3 [GB]	RAF No 43 Sqn, Leuchars
	ZE735	Panavia Tornado F3 [AL]	RAF F3 OCU/No 56(R) Sqn, Coningsby
	ZE736	Panavia Tornado F3 (comp ZD937) [AX]	RAF F3 OCU/No 56(R) Sqn, Coningsby
	ZE737	Panavia Tornado F3 [FF]	RAF No 25 Sqn, Leeming
	ZE755	Panavia Tornado F3 [GJ]	RAF No 43 Sqn, Leuchars
	ZE756	Panavia Tornado F3	RAF AWC/F3 OEU, Coningsby
	ZE757	Panavia Tornado F3 [GK]	RAF No 43 Sqn, Leuchars
	ZE758	Panavia Tornado F3 [AU]	RAF F3 OCU/No 56(R) Sqn, Coningsby
	ZE759	Panavia Tornado F3 (comp ZD904)	*Crashed 28 September 1996, off Blackpool*
	ZE763	Panavia Tornado F3 [DG]	RAF No 11 Sqn, Leeming
	ZE764	Panavia Tornado F3 [DH]	RAF No 11 Sqn, Leeming
	ZE785	Panavia Tornado F3 [AT]	RAF F3 OCU/No 56(R) Sqn, Coningsby
	ZE786	Panavia Tornado F3 (comp ZD934) [AG]	RAF F3 OCU/No 56(R) Sqn, Coningsby
	ZE788	Panavia Tornado F3	RAF AWC/F3 OEU, Coningsby
	ZE790	Panavia Tornado F3 [GD]	RAF No 43 Sqn, Leuchars
	ZE791	Panavia Tornado F3 [HY]	RAF No 111 Sqn, Leuchars
	ZE793	Panavia Tornado F3 (comp ZD935)	RAF, stored St Athan (for rebuild at BAe Warton)
	ZE794	Panavia Tornado F3 [HQ]	RAF No 111 Sqn, Leuchars
	ZE808	Panavia Tornado F3 [FA]	RAF No 25 Sqn, Leeming
	ZE810	Panavia Tornado F3 [HP]	RAF No 111 Sqn, Leuchars
	ZE812	Panavia Tornado F3 [CW]	RAF No 5 Sqn, Coningsby
	ZE830	Panavia Tornado F3 [HU]	RAF No 111 Sqn, Leuchars
	ZE831	Panavia Tornado F3 [GG]	RAF No 43 Sqn, Leuchars
	ZE834	Panavia Tornado F3 [GM]	RAF No 43 Sqn, Leuchars
	ZE838	Panavia Tornado F3 [GH]	RAF No 43 Sqn, Leuchars
	ZE839	Panavia Tornado F3 [AR]	RAF F3 OCU/No 56(R) Sqn, Coningsby
	ZE862	Panavia Tornado F3 [AB]	*Collided with ZE166 near Sleaford, 10 January 1996*
	ZE887	Panavia Tornado F3 [DJ]	RAF No 11 Sqn, Leeming
	ZE888	Panavia Tornado F3 [FV]	RAF No 25 Sqn, Leeming
	ZE889	Panavia Tornado F3	RAF No 25 Sqn, Leeming
	ZE907	Panavia Tornado F3 [FM]	RAF No 25 Sqn, Leeming
	ZE908	Panavia Tornado F3 [HV]	RAF No 111 Sqn, Leuchars
	ZE911	Panavia Tornado F3 [GA]	*To Italy as MM7226, February 1997*
	ZE934	Panavia Tornado F3 [DX]	RAF No 11 Sqn, Leeming
	ZE936	Panavia Tornado F3 [DL]	RAF No 11 Sqn, Leeming
	ZE941	Panavia Tornado F3	RAF No 43 Sqn, Leuchars
	ZE942	Panavia Tornado F3 [DK]	RAF No 11 Sqn, Leeming
	ZE961	Panavia Tornado F3 [FD]	RAF No 25 Sqn, Leeming
	ZE962	Panavia Tornado F3 [FJ]	RAF No 25 Sqn, Leeming
	ZE963	Panavia Tornado F3 [GE]	RAF No 43 Sqn, Leuchars
	ZE964	Panavia Tornado F3 [DY]	RAF No 11 Sqn, Leeming
	ZE965	Panavia Tornado F3 [DW]	RAF No 11 Sqn, Leeming
	ZE966	Panavia Tornado F3 [DZ]	RAF No 11 Sqn, Leeming
	ZE967	Panavia Tornado F3 [FU]	RAF No 25 Sqn, Leeming
	ZE968	Panavia Tornado F3 [DM]	RAF No 11 Sqn, Leeming
	ZE969	Panavia Tornado F3 [DI]	RAF No 11 Sqn, Leeming
	ZE982	Panavia Tornado F3	RAF AWC/F3 OEU, Coningsby
	ZE983	Panavia Tornado F3 [DN]	RAF No 11 Sqn, Leeming
	ZF115	WS61 Sea King HC4	MoD(PE)/RWTS, DTEO Boscombe Down
	ZF116	WS61 Sea King HC4 [ZP]	RN No 848 Sqn, Yeovilton
	ZF117	WS61 Sea King HC4 [VQ]	RN No 846 Sqn, Yeovilton
	ZF118	WS61 Sea King HC4 [VP]	RN No 846 Sqn, Yeovilton
	ZF119	WS61 Sea King HC4 [VH]	RN AMG, Yeovilton
	ZF120	WS61 Sea King HC4 [K]	RN No 845 Sqn, Yeovilton
	ZF121	WS61 Sea King HC4 [VJ]	RN No 846 Sqn, Yeovilton
	ZF122	WS61 Sea King HC4 [VI]	RN No 846 Sqn, Yeovilton
	ZF123	WS61 Sea King HC4 [ZQ]	RN No 848 Sqn, Yeovilton
	ZF124	WS61 Sea King HC4 [L]	RN No 845 Sqn, Yeovilton
	ZF130	BAe 125-600B (G-BLUW)	MoD(PE)/BAe Dunsfold
	ZF135	Shorts Tucano T1	RAF No 1 FTS, Linton-on-Ouse
	ZF136	Shorts Tucano T1	RAF No 1 FTS, Linton-on-Ouse
	ZF137	Shorts Tucano T1	RAF No 1 FTS, Linton-on-Ouse

Serial	Type (other identity) [code]	Owner/operator, location or fate	Notes
ZF138	Shorts Tucano T1	RAF No 1 FTS, Linton-on-Ouse	
ZF139	Shorts Tucano T1	RAF No 1 FTS, Linton-on-Ouse	
ZF140	Shorts Tucano T1	RAF No 1 FTS, Linton-on-Ouse	
ZF141	Shorts Tucano T1	RAF, stored Shawbury	
ZF142	Shorts Tucano T1	RAF, stored Shawbury	
ZF143	Shorts Tucano T1	RAF No 1 FTS, Linton-on-Ouse	
ZF144	Shorts Tucano T1	RAF No 1 FTS, Linton-on-Ouse	
ZF145	Shorts Tucano T1	RAF, stored Shawbury	
ZF160	Shorts Tucano T1	RAF No 1 FTS, Linton-on-Ouse	
ZF161	Shorts Tucano T1	RAF CFS, Topcliffe	
ZF162	Shorts Tucano T1	RAF No 1 FTS, Linton-on-Ouse	
ZF163	Shorts Tucano T1	RAF No 1 FTS, Linton-on-Ouse	
ZF164	Shorts Tucano T1	RAF No 1 FTS, Linton-on-Ouse	
ZF165	Shorts Tucano T1	RAF, stored Shawbury	
ZF166	Shorts Tucano T1	RAF No 1 FTS, Linton-on-Ouse	
ZF167	Shorts Tucano T1	RAF, stored Shawbury	
ZF168	Shorts Tucano T1	RAF No 1 FTS, Linton-on-Ouse	
ZF169	Shorts Tucano T1	RAF No 1 FTS, Linton-on-Ouse	
ZF170	Shorts Tucano T1	RAF, stored Shawbury	
ZF171	Shorts Tucano T1	RAF, stored Shawbury	
ZF172	Shorts Tucano T1	RAF, stored Shawbury	
ZF200	Shorts Tucano T1	RAF No 1 FTS, Linton-on-Ouse	
ZF201	Shorts Tucano T1	RAF CFS, Topcliffe	
ZF202	Shorts Tucano T1	RAF, stored Shawbury	
ZF203	Shorts Tucano T1	RAF No 1 FTS, Linton-on-Ouse	
ZF204	Shorts Tucano T1	RAF, stored Shawbury	
ZF205	Shorts Tucano T1	RAF, stored Shawbury	
ZF206	Shorts Tucano T1	RAF No 1 FTS, Linton-on-Ouse	
ZF207	Shorts Tucano T1	RAF, stored Shawbury	
ZF208	Shorts Tucano T1	RAF, stored Shawbury	
ZF209	Shorts Tucano T1	RAF, stored Shawbury	
ZF210	Shorts Tucano T1	RAF, stored Shawbury	
ZF211	Shorts Tucano T1	RAF CFS, Topcliffe	
ZF212	Shorts Tucano T1	RAF No 1 FTS, Linton-on-Ouse	
ZF238	Shorts Tucano T1	RAF CFS, Topcliffe	
ZF239	Shorts Tucano T1	RAF, stored Shawbury	
ZF240	Shorts Tucano T1	RAF, stored Shawbury	
ZF241	Shorts Tucano T1	RAF No 1 FTS, Linton-on-Ouse	
ZF242	Shorts Tucano T1	RAF CFS, Topcliffe	
ZF243	Shorts Tucano T1	RAF, stored Shawbury	
ZF244	Shorts Tucano T1	RAF, stored Shawbury	
ZF245	Shorts Tucano T1	RAF, stored Shawbury	
ZF263	Shorts Tucano T1	RAF No 1 FTS, Linton-on-Ouse	
ZF264	Shorts Tucano T1	RAF No 1 FTS, Linton-on-Ouse	
ZF265	Shorts Tucano T1	RAF, stored Shawbury	
ZF266	Shorts Tucano T1	RAF No 1 FTS, Linton-on-Ouse	
ZF267	Shorts Tucano T1	RAF, stored Shawbury	
ZF268	Shorts Tucano T1	RAF No 1 FTS, Linton-on-Ouse	
ZF269	Shorts Tucano T1	RAF, stored Shawbury	
ZF270	Shorts Tucano T1	Crashed 13 May 1996, Wetwang, East Yorkshire	
ZF284	Shorts Tucano T1	RAF, stored Shawbury	
ZF285	Shorts Tucano T1	RAF, stored Shawbury	
ZF286	Shorts Tucano T1	RAF CFS, Topcliffe	
ZF287	Shorts Tucano T1	RAF, stored Shawbury	
ZF288	Shorts Tucano T1	RAF No 1 FTS, Linton-on-Ouse	
ZF289	Shorts Tucano T1	RAF, stored Shawbury	
ZF290	Shorts Tucano T1	RAF No 1 FTS, Linton-on-Ouse	
ZF291	Shorts Tucano T1	RAF, stored Shawbury	
ZF292	Shorts Tucano T1	RAF No 1 FTS, Linton-on-Ouse	
ZF293	Shorts Tucano T1	RAF, stored Shawbury	
ZF294	Shorts Tucano T1	RAF No 1 FTS, Linton-on-Ouse	
ZF295	Shorts Tucano T1	RAF No 1 FTS, Linton-on-Ouse	
ZF315	Shorts Tucano T1	RAF No 1 FTS, Linton-on-Ouse	
ZF317	Shorts Tucano T1	RAF, stored Shawbury	
ZF318	Shorts Tucano T1	RAF No 1 FTS, Linton-on-Ouse	
ZF319	Shorts Tucano T1	RAF No 1 FTS, Linton-on-Ouse	
ZF320	Shorts Tucano T1	RAF No 1 FTS, Linton-on-Ouse	
ZF338	Shorts Tucano T1	RAF, stored Shawbury	
ZF339	Shorts Tucano T1	RAF, stored Shawbury	
ZF340	Shorts Tucano T1	RAF, stored Shawbury	
ZF341	Shorts Tucano T1	RAF, stored Shawbury	
ZF342	Shorts Tucano T1	RAF, stored Shawbury	

Notes	Serial	Type (other identity) [code]	Owner/operator, location or fate
	ZF343	Shorts Tucano T1	RAF No 1 FTS, Linton-on-Ouse
	ZF344	Shorts Tucano T1	RAF, stored Shawbury
	ZF345	Shorts Tucano T1	RAF No 1 FTS, Linton-on-Ouse
	ZF346	Shorts Tucano T1	RAF No 1 FTS, Linton-on-Ouse
	ZF347	Shorts Tucano T1	RAF, stored Shawbury
	ZF348	Shorts Tucano T1	RAF No 1 FTS, Linton-on-Ouse
	ZF349	Shorts Tucano T1	RAF, stored Shawbury
	ZF350	Shorts Tucano T1	RAF No 1 FTS, Linton-on-Ouse
	ZF372	Shorts Tucano T1	RAF No 1 FTS, Linton-on-Ouse
	ZF373	Shorts Tucano T1	RAF, stored Shawbury
	ZF374	Shorts Tucano T1	RAF, stored Shawbury
	ZF375	Shorts Tucano T1	RAF CFS, Topcliffe
	ZF376	Shorts Tucano T1	RAF No 1 FTS, Linton-on-Ouse
	ZF377	Shorts Tucano T1	RAF, stored Shawbury
	ZF378	Shorts Tucano T1	RAF, stored Shawbury
	ZF379	Shorts Tucano T1	RAF CFS, Topcliffe
	ZF380	Shorts Tucano T1	RAF No 1 FTS, Linton-on-Ouse
	ZF405	Shorts Tucano T1	RAF No 1 FTS, Linton-on-Ouse
	ZF406	Shorts Tucano T1	RAF No 1 FTS, Linton-on-Ouse
	ZF407	Shorts Tucano T1	RAF, stored Shawbury
	ZF408	Shorts Tucano T1	RAF No 1 FTS, Linton-on-Ouse
	ZF409	Shorts Tucano T1	RAF, stored Shawbury
	ZF410	Shorts Tucano T1	RAF CFS, Topcliffe
	ZF411	Shorts Tucano T1	RAF No 1 FTS, Linton-on-Ouse
	ZF412	Shorts Tucano T1	RAF No 1 FTS, Linton-on-Ouse
	ZF413	Shorts Tucano T1	RAF No 1 FTS, Linton-on-Ouse
	ZF414	Shorts Tucano T1	RAF CFS, Topcliffe
	ZF415	Shorts Tucano T1	RAF, stored Shawbury
	ZF416	Shorts Tucano T1	RAF CFS, Topcliffe
	ZF417	Shorts Tucano T1	RAF No 1 FTS, Linton-on-Ouse
	ZF418	Shorts Tucano T1	RAF No 1 FTS, Linton-on-Ouse
	ZF445	Shorts Tucano T1	RAF No 1 FTS, Linton-on-Ouse
	ZF446	Shorts Tucano T1	RAF No 1 FTS, Linton-on-Ouse
	ZF447	Shorts Tucano T1	RAF CFS, Topcliffe
	ZF448	Shorts Tucano T1	RAF No 1 FTS, Linton-on-Ouse
	ZF449	Shorts Tucano T1	RAF CFS, Topcliffe
	ZF450	Shorts Tucano T1	RAF No 1 FTS, Linton-on-Ouse
	ZF483	Shorts Tucano T1	RAF CFS, Topcliffe
	ZF484	Shorts Tucano T1	RAF No 1 FTS, Linton-on-Ouse
	ZF485	Shorts Tucano T1 (G-BULU)	RAF No 1 FTS, Linton-on-Ouse
	ZF486	Shorts Tucano T1	RAF No 1 FTS, Linton-on-Ouse
	ZF487	Shorts Tucano T1	RAF No 1 FTS, Linton-on-Ouse
	ZF488	Shorts Tucano T1	RAF No 1 FTS, Linton-on-Ouse
	ZF489	Shorts Tucano T1	RAF No 1 FTS, Linton-on-Ouse
	ZF490	Shorts Tucano T1	RAF No 1 FTS, Linton-on-Ouse
	ZF491	Shorts Tucano T1	RAF, stored Shawbury
	ZF492	Shorts Tucano T1	RAF No 1 FTS, Linton-on-Ouse
	ZF510	Shorts Tucano T1	MoD(PE)/ETPS, DTEO Boscombe Down
	ZF511	Shorts Tucano T1	MoD(PE)/ETPS, DTEO Boscombe Down
	ZF512	Shorts Tucano T1	RAF No 1 FTS, Linton-on-Ouse
	ZF513	Shorts Tucano T1	RAF CFS, Topcliffe
	ZF514	Shorts Tucano T1	RAF No 1 FTS, Linton-on-Ouse
	ZF515	Shorts Tucano T1	RAF CFS, Topcliffe
	ZF516	Shorts Tucano T1	RAF No 1 FTS, Linton-on-Ouse
	ZF520	Piper PA-31 Navajo Chieftain 350	*Sold to the USA as N741T, May 1996*
	ZF521	Piper PA-31 Navajo Chieftain 350	MoD(PE), DTEO Llanbedr
	ZF522	Piper PA-31 Navajo Chieftain 350	*Sold to the USA as N174E, May 1996*
	ZF534	BAe EAP	Loughborough University
	ZF537	WS Lynx AH9	AAC, stored NARO, RNAY Fleetlands
	ZF538	WS Lynx AH9	AAC No 653 Sqn/3 Regiment, Wattisham
	ZF539	WS Lynx AH9 [5]	AAC No 659 Sqn/4 Regiment, Wattisham
	ZF540	WS Lynx AH9 [6]	AAC No 659 Sqn/4 Regiment, Wattisham
	ZF557	WS Lynx HMA8 [444/MR]	RN No 815 Sqn OEU, Portland
	ZF558	WS Lynx HMA8 [673]	RN No 815 Sqn OEU, Portland
	ZF560	WS Lynx HMA8 [404/IR]	RN No 815 Sqn, Portland
	ZF562	WS Lynx HMA8 [457/LA]	RN No 815 Sqn, Portland
	ZF563	WS Lynx HMA8 [671]	RN No 815 Sqn OEU, Portland
	ZF573	PBN 2T Islander CC2A (G-SRAY)	RAF Northolt Station Flight
	ZF577	BAC Lightning F53	Privately owned, stored Warrington
	ZF578	BAC Lightning F53	Privately owned, Cardiff
	ZF579	BAC Lightning F53	Privately owned, stored Warrington
	ZF580	BAC Lightning F53	BAe Samlesbury, at main gate
	ZF581	BAC Lightning F53	Privately owned, stored Warrington

Serial	Type (other identity) [code]	Owner/operator, location or fate	Notes
ZF582	BAC Lightning F53	Privately owned, stored Warrington	
ZF583	BAC Lightning F53	Solway Aviation Society, Carlisle	
ZF584	BAC Lightning F53	Ferranti Ltd, South Gyle, Edinburgh	
ZF585	BAC Lightning F53	Privately owned, stored Warrington	
ZF586	BAC Lightning F53	Privately owned, stored Warrington	
ZF587	BAC Lightning F53	Privately owned, stored Warrington	
ZF588	BAC Lightning F53	East Midlands Airport Aero Park	
ZF589	BAC Lightning F53	Privately owned, stored Warrington	
ZF590	BAC Lightning F53	Privately owned, stored Warrington	
ZF591	BAC Lightning F53	Privately owned, stored Warrington	
ZF592	BAC Lightning F53	Privately owned, stored Warrington	
ZF594	BAC Lightning F53	North-East Aircraft Museum, Usworth	
ZF595	BAC Lightning T55	Privately owned, stored Warrington	
ZF596	BAC Lightning T55	Privately owned, stored Warrington	
ZF597	BAC Lightning T55	Privately owned, stored Warrington	
ZF598	BAC Lightning T55	Midland Air Museum, Coventry	
ZF622	Piper PA-31 Navajo Chieftain 350	MoD(PE)/HATS, DTEO Boscombe Down	
ZF641	WS/Agusta EH-101 [PP1]	MoD(PE)/Westland, Yeovil	
ZF649	WS/Agusta EH-101 Merlin [PP5]	MoD(PE)/Westland, Yeovil	
ZG101	WS/Agusta EH-101 (mock-up) [GB]	Westland/Agusta, Yeovil	
ZG468	WS70 Blackhawk	Westland, Yeovil	
ZG471	BAe Harrier GR7 [61]	RAF No 1 Sqn, Wittering	
ZG472	BAe Harrier GR7 [O]	RAF AWC/SAOEU, DTEO Boscombe Down	
ZG474	BAe Harrier GR7 [64]	RAF No 1 Sqn, Wittering	
ZG476	BAe Harrier GR7 [WT]	Crashed 19 February 1996, Wittering	
ZG477	BAe Harrier GR7 [67]	RAF No 3 Sqn, Laarbruch	
ZG478	BAe Harrier GR7 [68]	RAF No 1 Sqn, Wittering	
ZG479	BAe Harrier GR7 [69]	RAF No 4 Sqn, Laarbruch	
ZG480	BAe Harrier GR7 [70]	RAF No 4 Sqn, Laarbruch	
ZG500	BAe Harrier GR7 [71]	RAF No 3 Sqn, Laarbruch	
ZG501	BAe Harrier GR7 [E]	RAF AWC/SAOEU, DTEO Boscombe Down	
ZG502	BAe Harrier GR7 [73]	RAF No 4 Sqn, Laarbruch	
ZG503	BAe Harrier GR7 [74]	RAF No 3 Sqn, Laarbruch	
ZG504	BAe Harrier GR7	RAF St Athan	
ZG505	BAe Harrier GR7 [76]	RAF No 1 Sqn, Wittering	
ZG506	BAe Harrier GR7 [77]	RAF No 3 Sqn, Laarbruch	
ZG507	BAe Harrier GR7 [78]	RAF No 3 Sqn/No 4 Sqn, Laarbruch	
ZG508	BAe Harrier GR7 [79]	RAF No 4 Sqn, Laarbruch	
ZG509	BAe Harrier GR7 [80]	MoD(PE)/BAe, Dunsfold	
ZG510	BAe Harrier GR7 [81]	RAF No 3 Sqn, Laarbruch	
ZG511	BAe Harrier GR7 [82]	MoD(PE)/BAe, Dunsfold	
ZG512	BAe Harrier GR7 [83]	RAF No 4 Sqn, Laarbruch	
ZG530	BAe Harrier GR7 [84]	RAF No 3 Sqn, Laarbruch	
ZG531	BAe Harrier GR7 [85]	RAF No 3 Sqn, Laarbruch	
ZG532	BAe Harrier GR7 [86]	RAF No 1 Sqn, Wittering	
ZG533	BAe Harrier GR7 [87]	RAF No 3 Sqn, Laarbruch	
ZG705	Panavia Tornado GR1A [J]	RAF No 13 Sqn, Marham	
ZG706	Panavia Tornado GR1A [E]	RAF AWC/SAOEU, DTEO Boscombe Down	
ZG707	Panavia Tornado GR1A [B]	RAF No 13 Sqn, Marham	
ZG709	Panavia Tornado GR1A [V]	RAF No 13 Sqn, Marham	
ZG710	Panavia Tornado GR4A [D]	MoD(PE)/BAe, Warton (conversion)	
ZG711	Panavia Tornado GR1A [P]	RAF No 13 Sqn, Marham	
ZG712	Panavia Tornado GR1A [F]	RAF No 13 Sqn, Marham	
ZG713	Panavia Tornado GR1A	RAF No 13 Sqn, Marham	
ZG714	Panavia Tornado GR1A [Q]	RAF St Athan (damaged)	
ZG726	Panavia Tornado GR1A [K[	RAF No 13 Sqn, Marham	
ZG727	Panavia Tornado GR1A [L]	RAF No 13 Sqn, Marham	
ZG728	Panavia Tornado F3 [CI]	For Italian AF as MM7229	
ZG729	Panavia Tornado GR1A [M]	RAF No 13 Sqn, Marham	
ZG730	Panavia Tornado F3 [CC]	For Italian AF as MM7230	
ZG731	Panavia Tornado F3 [BL]	RAF No 29 Sqn, Coningsby	
ZG732	Panavia Tornado F3 [BC]	For Italian AF as MM7227	
ZG733	Panavia Tornado F3 [AO]	For Italian AF as MM7228	
ZG734	Panavia Tornado F3 [BA]	For Italian AF as MM7231	
ZG735	Panavia Tornado F3 [AZ]	For Italian AF as MM7232	
ZG750	Panavia Tornado GR4 [III]	MoD(PE)/BAe, Warton (conversion)	
ZG751	Panavia Tornado F3 [C]	RAF No 1435 Flt, Mount Pleasant, FI	
ZG752	Panavia Tornado GR1 [XIII]	RAF No 13 Sqn, Marham	

Notes	Serial	Type (other identity) [code]	Owner/operator, location or fate
	ZG753	Panavia Tornado F3 [F]	RAF No 1435 Flt, Mount Pleasant, FI
	ZG754	Panavia Tornado GR1	RAF St Athan (rebuild)
	ZG755	Panavia Tornado F3 [BJ]	RAF No 29 Sqn, Coningsby
	ZG756	Panavia Tornado GR1 [AX]	RAF No 9 Sqn, Brüggen
	ZG757	Pilatus Tornado F3 [CA]	RAF No 5 Sqn, Coningsby
	ZG768	Panavia Tornado F3 [AX]	*For Italian AF as MM7233*
	ZG769	Panavia Tornado GR1 [AY]	RAF No 9 Sqn, Brüggen
	ZG770	Panavia Tornado F3 [BD]	RAF No 29 Sqn, Coningsby
	ZG771	Panavia Tornado GR1 [DW]	RAF No 31 Sqn, Brüggen
	ZG772	Panavia Tornado F3 [CO]	RAF No 5 Sqn, Coningsby
	ZG773	Panavia Tornado GR4	MoD(PE)/BAe Warton
	ZG774	Panavia Tornado F3	RAF No 5 Sqn, Coningsby
	ZG775	Panavia Tornado GR1 [DN]	RAF No 31 Sqn, Brüggen
	ZG776	Panavia Tornado F3	RAF F3 OCU/No 56(R) Sqn, Coningsby
	ZG777	Panavia Tornado GR1 [BS]	RAF No 14 Sqn, Brüggen
	ZG778	Panavia Tornado F3 [BG]	RAF No 29 Sqn, Coningsby
	ZG779	Panavia Tornado GR1 [DK]	RAF No 31 Sqn, Brüggen
	ZG780	Panavia Tornado F3 [H]	RAF No 1435 Flt, Mount Pleasant, FI
	ZG791	Panavia Tornado GR1 [DC]	RAF No 31 Sqn, Brüggen
	ZG792	Panavia Tornado GR1 [DD]	RAF No 31 Sqn, Brüggen
	ZG793	Panavia Tornado F3 [CY]	RAF No 5 Sqn, Coningsby
	ZG794	Panavia Tornado GR1 [BP]	RAF No 14 Sqn, Brüggen
	ZG795	Panavia Tornado F3 [CB]	RAF No 5 Sqn, Coningsby
	ZG796	Panavia Tornado F3 [CE]	RAF No 5 Sqn, Coningsby
	ZG797	Panavia Tornado F3 [BF]	RAF No 29 Sqn, Coningsby
	ZG798	Panavia Tornado F3 [CD]	RAF No 5 Sqn, Coningsby
	ZG799	Panavia Tornado F3 [D]	RAF No 1435 Flt, Mount Pleasant, FI
	ZG816	WS61 Sea King HAS6 [701/PW]	RN No 819 Sqn, Prestwick
	ZG817	WS61 Sea King HAS6 [504]	RN No 810 Sqn, Culdrose
	ZG818	WS61 Sea King HAS6 [707]	RN No 819 Sqn, Prestwick
	ZG819	WS61 Sea King HAS6 [270]	RN No 814 Sqn, Culdrose
	ZG820	WS61 Sea King HC4 [A]	RN No 845 Sqn, Yeovilton
	ZG821	WS61 Sea King HC4 [ZD]	RN No 848 Sqn, Yeovilton
	ZG822	WS61 Sea King HC4 [VN]	RN No 846 Sqn, Yeovilton
	ZG844	PBN 2T Islander AL1 (G-BLNE)	AAC No 1 Flt, Aldergrove
	ZG845	PBN 2T Islander AL1 (G-BLNT)	AAC AFWF, Middle Wallop
	ZG846	PBN 2T Islander AL1 (G-BLNU)	AAC No 1 Flt, Aldergrove
	ZG847	PBN 2T Islander AL1 (G-BLNV)	AAC No 1 Flt, Aldergrove
	ZG848	PBN 2T Islander AL1 (G-BLNY)	AAC No 1 Flt, Aldergrove
	ZG856	BAe Harrier GR7 [88]	RAF No 4 Sqn, Laarbruch
	ZG857	BAe Harrier GR7 [89]	RAF No 4 Sqn, Laarbruch
	ZG858	BAe Harrier GR7 [90]	RAF No 4 Sqn, Laarbruch
	ZG859	BAe Harrier GR7 [91]	MoD(PE)/BAe, Dunsfold
	ZG860	BAe Harrier GR7 [92]	RAF No 1 Sqn, Wittering
	ZG861	BAe Harrier GR7 [93]	RAF No 3 Sqn, Laarbruch
	ZG862	BAe Harrier GR7 [94]	RAF No 3 Sqn, Laarbruch
	ZG875	WS61 Sea King HAS6 [702/PW]	RN No 819 Sqn, Prestwick
	ZG879	Powerchute Raider Mk 1	MoD(PE)/Powerchute, Hereford
	ZG884	WS Lynx AH9	MoD(PE)/Westland, Yeovil
	ZG885	WS Lynx AH9 [7]	AAC No 659 Sqn/4 Regiment, Wattisham
	ZG886	WS Lynx AH9	AAC No 653 Sqn/3 Regiment, Wattisham
	ZG887	WS Lynx AH9	AAC No 653 Sqn/3 Regiment, Wattisham
	ZG888	WS Lynx AH9	AAC No 653 Sqn/3 Regiment, Wattisham
	ZG889	WS Lynx AH9	AAC No 653 Sqn/3 Regiment, Wattisham
	ZG914	WS Lynx AH9	AAC No 653 Sqn/3 Regiment, Wattisham
	ZG915	WS Lynx AH9	AAC No 653 Sqn/3 Regiment, Wattisham
	ZG916	WS Lynx AH9 [8]	AAC No 659 Sqn/4 Regiment, Wattisham
	ZG917	WS Lynx AH9 [9]	AAC No 659 Sqn/4 Regiment, Wattisham
	ZG918	WS Lynx AH9 [10]	AAC No 659 Sqn/4 Regiment, Wattisham
	ZG919	TWS Lynx AH9	AAC No 653 Sqn/3 Regiment, Wattisham
	ZG920	WS Lynx AH9	AAC No 653 Sqn/3 Regiment, Wattisham
	ZG921	WS Lynx AH9 [11]	AAC No 659 Sqn/4 Regiment, Wattisham
	ZG922	WS Lynx AH9	AAC No 653 Sqn/3 Regiment, Wattisham
	ZG923	WS Lynx AH9	AAC No 653 Sqn/3 Regiment, Wattisham
	ZG969	Pilatus PC-9 (HB-HQE)	BAe Warton
	ZG989	PBN 2T Islander Astor (G-DLRA)	MoD(PE)/PBN, Bembridge
	ZG993	PBN 2T Islander AL1 (G-BOMD)	AAC No Regiment, Gütersloh
	ZG994	PBN 2T Islander AL1 (G-BPLN)	AAC No 1 Flight, Aldergrove
	ZH101	Boeing E-3D Sentry AEW1	RAF No 8 Sqn/No 23 Sqn, Waddington
	ZH102	Boeing E-3D Sentry AEW1	RAF No 8 Sqn/No 23 Sqn, Waddington
	ZH103	Boeing E-3D Sentry AEW1	RAF No 8 Sqn/No 23 Sqn, Waddington
	ZH104	Boeing E-3D Sentry AEW1	RAF No 8 Sqn/No 23 Sqn, Waddington

Serial	Type (other identity) [code]	Owner/operator, location or fate	Notes
ZH105	Boeing E-3D Sentry AEW1	RAF No 8 Sqn/No 23 Sqn, Waddington	
ZH106	Boeing E-3D Sentry AEW1	RAF No 8 Sqn/No 23 Sqn, Waddington	
ZH107	Boeing E-3D Sentry AEW1	RAF No 8 Sqn/No 23 Sqn, Waddington	
ZH115	Grob G109B Vigilant T1 [TA]	RAF ACCGS, Syerston	
ZH116	Grob G109B Vigilant T1 [TB]	RAF No 664 VGS, Belfast City Airport	
ZH117	Grob G109B Vigilant T1 [TC]	RAF No 632 VGS, Ternhill	
ZH118	Grob G109B Vigilant T1	RAF No 612 VGS, Abingdon	
ZH119	Grob G109B Vigilant T1 [TE]	RAF No 635 VGS, Samlesbury	
ZH120	Grob G109B Vigilant T1 [TF]	RAF ACCGS, Syerston	
ZH121	Grob G109B Vigilant T1	RAF No 633 VGS, Cosford	
ZH122	Grob G109B Vigilant T1 [TH]	RAF No 616 VGS, Henlow	
ZH123	Grob G109B Vigilant T1 [TJ]	RAF ACCGS, Syerston	
ZH124	Grob G109B Vigilant T1 [TK]	RAF No 642 VGS, Linton-on-Ouse	
ZH125	Grob G109B Vigilant T1 [TL]	RAF No 633 VGS, Cosford	
ZH126	Grob G109B Vigilant T1 [TM]	RAF No 637 VGS, Little Rissington	
ZH127	Grob G109B Vigilant T1	RAF No 642 VGS, Linton-on-Ouse	
ZH128	Grob G109B Vigilant T1 [TP]	RAF No 624 VGS, Chivenor	
ZH129	Grob G109B Vigilant T1 [TQ]	RAF No 616 VGS, Henlow	
ZH144	Grob G109B Vigilant T1 [TR]	RAF No 616 VGS, Henlow	
ZH145	Grob G109B Vigilant T1 [TS]	RAF No 624 VGS, Chivenor	
ZH146	Grob G109B Vigilant T1 [TT]	RAF No 637 VGS, Little Rissington	
ZH147	Grob G109B Vigilant T1 [TU]	RAF No 613 VGS, Halton	
ZH148	Grob G109B Vigilant T1 [TV]	RAF No 637 VGS, Little Rissington	
ZH184	Grob G109B Vigilant T1 [TW]	RAF No 624 VGS, Chivenor	
ZH185	Grob G109B Vigilant T1 [TX]	RAF ACCGS, Syerston	
ZH186	Grob G109B Vigilant T1	RAF No 635 VGS, Samlesbury	
ZH187	Grob G109B Vigilant T1 [TZ]	RAF No 635 VGS, Samlesbury	
ZH188	Grob G109B Vigilant T1 [UA]	RAF No 635 VGS, Samlesbury	
ZH189	Grob G109B Vigilant T1 [UB]	RAF No 612 VGS, Abingdon	
ZH190	Grob G109B Vigilant T1 [UC]	RAF No 632 VGS, Ternhill	
ZH191	Grob G109B Vigilant T1	RAF No 612 VGS, Abingdon	
ZH192	Grob G109B Vigilant T1 [UE]	RAF ACCGS, Syerston	
ZH193	Grob G109B Vigilant T1 [UF]	RAF ACCGS, Syerston	
ZH194	Grob G109B Vigilant T1 [UG]	RAF No 613 VGS, Halton	
ZH195	Grob G109B Vigilant T1 [UH]	RAF No 663 VGS, Kinloss	
ZH196	Grob G109B Vigilant T1 [UJ]	RAF No 633 VGS, Cosford	
ZH197	Grob G109B Vigilant T1	RAF No 642 VGS, Linton-on-Ouse	
ZH200	BAe Hawk 200	MoD(PE), stored BAe Warton	
ZH205	Grob G109B Vigilant T1 [UL]	RAF ACCGS, Syerston	
ZH206	Grob G109B Vigilant T1	RAF CCMF, Syerston	
ZH207	Grob G109B Vigilant T1 [UN]	RAF No 632 VGS, Ternhill	
ZH208	Grob G109B Vigilant T1 [UP]	RAF No 612 VGS, Abingdon	
ZH209	Grob G109B Vigilant T1 [UQ]	RAF No 664 VGS, Belfast City Airport	
ZH211	Grob G109B Vigilant T1 [UR]	RAF No 663 VGS, Kinloss	
ZH247	Grob G109B Vigilant T1 [US]	RAF No 613 VGS, Halton	
ZH248	Grob G109B Vigilant T1	RAF No 642 VGS, Linton-on-Ouse	
ZH249	Grob G109B Vigilant T1 [UU]	RAF No 616 VGS, Henlow	
ZH257	B-V CH-47C Chinook (AE-520/ 9217M)	AAC Wattisham, instructional use	
ZH263	Grob G109B Vigilant T1 [UV]	RAF No 635 VGS, Samlesbury	
ZH264	Grob G109B Vigilant T1	RAF No 642 VGS, Linton-on-Ouse	
ZH265	Grob G109B Vigilant T1 [UX]	RAF No 633 VGS, Cosford	
ZH266	Grob G109B Vigilant T1 [UY]	RAF No 633 VGS, Cosford	
ZH267	Grob G109B Vigilant T1 [UZ]	RAF ACCGS, Syerston	
ZH268	Grob G109B Vigilant T1 [SA]	RAF No 616 VGS, Henlow	
ZH269	Grob G109B Vigilant T1 [SB]	RAF No 613 VGS, Halton	
ZH270	Grob G109B Vigilant T1 [SC]	RAF No 632 VGS, Ternhill	
ZH271	Grob G109B Vigilant T1 [SD]	RAF CGMF, Syerston	
ZH536	PBN 2T Islander CC2 (G-BSAH)	RAF Northolt Station Flight	
ZH540	WS61 Sea King HAR3A	RAF No 203(R) Sqn, St Mawgan	
ZH541	WS61 Sea King HAR3A	MoD(PE)/RWTS, DTEO Boscombe Down	
ZH542	WS61 Sea King HAR3A	RAF No 203(R) Sqn, St Mawgan	
ZH543	WS61 Sea King HAR3A	RAF No 203(R) Sqn, St Mawgan	
ZH544	WS61 Sea King HAR3A	RAF No 203(R) Sqn, St Mawgan	
ZH545	WS61 Sea King HAR3A	MoD(PE)/Westland, stored Yeovil	
ZH552	Panavia Tornado F3	RAF AWC/F3 OEU, Coningsby	
ZH553	Panavia Tornado F3 [AB]	RAF F3 OCU/No 56(R) Sqn, Coningsby	
ZH554	Panavia Tornado F3	RAF F3 OCU/No 56(R) Sqn, Coningsby	
ZH555	Panavia Tornado F3 [CV]	RAF No 5 Sqn, Coningsby	
ZH556	Panavia Tornado F3 [AK]	RAF F3 OCU/No 56(R) Sqn, Coningsby	
ZH557	Panavia Tornado F3 [CT]	RAF No 5 Sqn, Coningsby	
ZH559	Panavia Tornado F3 [AJ]	RAF F3 OCU/No 56(R) Sqn, Coningsby	
ZH588	Eurofighter 2000 (DA2)	MoD(PE)/BAe Warton	

Notes	Serial	Type (other identity) [code]	Owner/operator, location or fate
	ZH590	Eurofighter 2000(T) (DA4)	MoD(PE)/BAe Warton
	ZH629	BAe Hawk 102	*To Abu Dhabi AF as 1059*
	ZH634	BAe Hawk 102	*To Abu Dhabi AF as 1060*
	ZH635	BAe Hawk 102	*To Abu Dhabi AF as 1061*
	ZH636	BAe Hawk 102	*To Abu Dhabi AF as 1062*
	ZH637	BAe Hawk 102	*To Abu Dhabi AF as 1063*
	ZH638	BAe Hawk 102	*To Abu Dhabi AF as 1064*
	ZH639	BAe Hawk 102	*To Abu Dhabi AF as 1065*
	ZH640	BAe Hawk 102	*To Abu Dhabi AF as 1066*
	ZH641	BAe Hawk 102	*To Abu Dhabi AF as 1067*
	ZH642	BAe Hawk 102	*To Abu Dhabi AF as 1068*
	ZH647	WS/Agusta EH-101 (G-EHIL)	MoD(PE)/Westland, Yeovil
	ZH653	BAe Harrier T10	MoD(PE)/BAe Dunsfold
	ZH654	BAe Harrier T10	MoD(PE)/BAe Dunsfold
	ZH655	BAe Harrier T10	RAF, stored St Athan (damaged)
	ZH656	BAe Harrier T10 [104]	RAF No 3 Sqn, Laarbruch
	ZH657	BAe Harrier T10 [XX]	RAF HOCU/No 20(R) Sqn, Wittering
	ZH658	BAe Harrier T10 [N]	RAF HOCU/No 20(R) Sqn, Wittering
	ZH659	BAe Harrier T10 [O]	RAF No 1 Sqn, Wittering
	ZH660	BAe Harrier T10 [P]	RAF HOCU/No 20(R) Sqn, Wittering
	ZH661	BAe Harrier T10 [109]	RAF No 1 Sqn, Wittering
	ZH662	BAe Harrier T10 [R]	RAF HOCU/No 20(R) Sqn, Wittering
	ZH663	BAe Harrier T10 [Q]	RAF HOCU/No 20(R) Sqn, Wittering
	ZH664	BAe Harrier T10 [112]	RAF No 4 Sqn, Laarbruch
	ZH665	BAe Harrier T10 [S]	RAF HOCU/No 20(R) Sqn, Wittering
	ZH762	Westinghouse Skyship 500 (G-SKSC)	MoD(PE), DTEO Boscombe Down (on repair)
	ZH763	BAC 1-11/539GL (G-BGKE)	MoD(PE)/DRA, DTEO Boscombe Down
	ZH775	B-V Chinook HC2 (N7424J) [NS]	RAF No 27(R) Sqn, Odiham
	ZH776	B-V Chinook HC2 (N7424L) [NU]	RAF No 27(R) Sqn, Odiham
	ZH777	B-V Chinook HC2 (N7424M) [NY]	RAF No 27(R) Sqn, Odiham
	ZH796	BAe Sea Harrier FA2 [715]	RN No 899 Sqn, Yeovilton
	ZH797	BAe Sea Harrier FA2 [716]	RN No 899 Sqn, Yeovilton
	ZH798	BAe Sea Harrier FA2 [122]	RN No 800 Sqn, Yeovilton
	ZH799	BAe Sea Harrier FA2 [004]	RN No 801 Sqn, Yeovilton
	ZH800	BAe Sea Harrier FA2 [124]	RN No 800 Sqn, Yeovilton
	ZH801	BAe Sea Harrier FA2	RN, stored St Athan
	ZH802	BAe Sea Harrier FA2 [002]	RN No 801 Sqn, Yeovilton
	ZH803	BAe Sea Harrier FA2	RN, stored St Athan
	ZH804	BAe Sea Harrier FA2	BAe Dunsfold, for RN
	ZH805	BAe Sea Harrier FA2	BAe Dunsfold, for RN
	ZH806	BAe Sea Harrier FA2	BAe Dunsfold, for RN
	ZH807	BAe Sea Harrier FA2	BAe Dunsfold, for RN
	ZH808	BAe Sea Harrier FA2	BAe Dunsfold, for RN
	ZH809	BAe Sea Harrier FA2	BAe Dunsfold, for RN
	ZH810	BAe Sea Harrier FA2	BAe Dunsfold, for RN
	ZH811	BAe Sea Harrier FA2	BAe Dunsfold, for RN
	ZH812	BAe Sea Harrier FA2	BAe Dunsfold, for RN
	ZH813	BAe Sea Harrier FA2	BAe Dunsfold, for RN
	ZH814	Bell 212 (G-BGMH)	AAC No 7 Flt, Brunei
	ZH815	Bell 212 (G-BGCZ)	AAC No 7 Flt, Brunei
	ZH816	Bell 212 (G-BGMG)	AAC No 7 Flt, Brunei
	ZH821	WS/Agusta EH-101 Merlin HM1	MoD(PE)/Westland, Yeovil
	ZH822	WS/Agusta EH-101 Merlin HM1	Westland, Yeovil, for RN
	ZH823	WS/Agusta EH-101 Merlin HM1	Westland, Yeovil, for RN
	ZH824	WS/Agusta EH-101 Merlin HM1	Westland, Yeovil, for RN
	ZH825	WS/Agusta EH-101 Merlin HM1	Westland, Yeovil, for RN
	ZH826	WS/Agusta EH-101 Merlin HM1	Westland, Yeovil, for RN
	ZH827	WS/Agusta EH-101 Merlin HM1	Westland, Yeovil, for RN
	ZH828	WS/Agusta EH-101 Merlin HM1	Westland, Yeovil, for RN
	ZH829	WS/Agusta EH-101 Merlin HM1	Westland, Yeovil, for RN
	ZH830	WS/Agusta EH-101 Merlin HM1	Westland, Yeovil, for RN
	ZH831	WS/Agusta EH-101 Merlin HM1	Westland, Yeovil, for RN
	ZH832	WS/Agusta EH-101 Merlin HM1	Westland, Yeovil, for RN
	ZH833	WS/Agusta EH-101 Merlin HM1	Westland, Yeovil, for RN
	ZH834	WS/Agusta EH-101 Merlin HM1	Westland, Yeovil, for RN
	ZH835	WS/Agusta EH-101 Merlin HM1	Westland, Yeovil, for RN
	ZH836	WS/Agusta EH-101 Merlin HM1	Westland, Yeovil, for RN
	ZH837	WS/Agusta EH-101 Merlin HM1	Westland, Yeovil, for RN
	ZH838	WS/Agusta EH-101 Merlin HM1	Westland, Yeovil, for RN
	ZH839	WS/Agusta EH-101 Merlin HM1	Westland, Yeovil, for RN
	ZH840	WS/Agusta EH-101 Merlin HM1	Westland, Yeovil, for RN
	ZH841	WS/Agusta EH-101 Merlin HM1	Westland, Yeovil, for RN

Serial	Type (other identity) [code]	Owner/operator, location or fate	Notes
ZH842	WS/Agusta EH-101 Merlin HM1	Westland, Yeovil, for RN	
ZH843	WS/Agusta EH-101 Merlin HM1	Westland, Yeovil, for RN	
ZH844	WS/Agusta EH-101 Merlin HM1	Westland, Yeovil, for RN	
ZH845	WS/Agusta EH-101 Merlin HM1	Westland, Yeovil, for RN	
ZH846	WS/Agusta EH-101 Merlin HM1	Westland, Yeovil, for RN	
ZH847	WS/Agusta EH-101 Merlin HM1	Westland, Yeovil, for RN	
ZH848	WS/Agusta EH-101 Merlin HM1	Westland, Yeovil, for RN	
ZH849	WS/Agusta EH-101 Merlin HM1	Westland, Yeovil, for RN	
ZH850	WS/Agusta EH-101 Merlin HM1	Westland, Yeovil, for RN	
ZH851	WS/Agusta EH-101 Merlin HM1	Westland, Yeovil, for RN	
ZH852	WS/Agusta EH-101 Merlin HM1	Westland, Yeovil, for RN	
ZH853	WS/Agusta EH-101 Merlin HM1	Westland, Yeovil, for RN	
ZH854	WS/Agusta EH-101 Merlin HM1	Westland, Yeovil, for RN	
ZH855	WS/Agusta EH-101 Merlin HM1	Westland, Yeovil, for RN	
ZH856	WS/Agusta EH-101 Merlin HM1	Westland, Yeovil, for RN	
ZH857	WS/Agusta EH-101 Merlin HM1	Westland, Yeovil, for RN	
ZH858	WS/Agusta EH-101 Merlin HM1	Westland, Yeovil, for RN	
ZH859	WS/Agusta EH-101 Merlin HM1	Westland, Yeovil, for RN	
ZH860	WS/Agusta EH-101 Merlin HM1	Westland, Yeovil, for RN	
ZH861	WS/Agusta EH-101 Merlin HM1	Westland, Yeovil, for RN	
ZH862	WS/Agusta EH-101 Merlin HM1	Westland, Yeovil, for RN	
ZH863	WS/Agusta EH-101 Merlin HM1	Westland, Yeovil, for RN	
ZH864	WS/Agusta EH-101 Merlin HM1	Westland, Yeovil, for RN	
ZH865	Lockheed C-130J-30 Hercules C4 (N130JA)	Lockheed-Martin, Marietta	
ZH866	Lockheed C-130J-30 Hercules C4 (N130JE)	Lockheed-Martin, for RAF	
ZH867	Lockheed C-130J-30 Hercules C4 (N130JJ)	Lockheed-Martin, for RAF	
ZH868	Lockheed C-130J-30 Hercules C4 (N130JN)	Lockheed-Martin, for RAF	
ZH869	Lockheed C-130J-30 Hercules C4 (N130JV)	Lockheed-Martin, for RAF	
ZH870	Lockheed C-130J-30 Hercules C4	Lockheed-Martin, for RAF	
ZH871	Lockheed C-130J-30 Hercules C4	Lockheed-Martin, for RAF	
ZH872	Lockheed C-130J-30 Hercules C4	Lockheed-Martin, for RAF	
ZH873	Lockheed C-130J-30 Hercules C4	Lockheed-Martin, for RAF	
ZH874	Lockheed C-130J-30 Hercules C4	Lockheed-Martin, for RAF	
ZH875	Lockheed C-130J-30 Hercules C4	Lockheed-Martin, for RAF	
ZH876	Lockheed C-130J-30 Hercules C4	Lockheed-Martin, for RAF	
ZH877	Lockheed C-130J-30 Hercules C4	Lockheed-Martin, for RAF	
ZH878	Lockheed C-130J-30 Hercules C4	Lockheed-Martin, for RAF	
ZH879	Lockheed C-130J-30 Hercules C4	Lockheed-Martin, for RAF	
ZH880	Lockheed C-130J Hercules C5	Lockheed-Martin, for RAF	
ZH881	Lockheed C-130J Hercules C5	Lockheed-Martin, for RAF	
ZH882	Lockheed C-130J Hercules C5	Lockheed-Martin, for RAF	
ZH883	Lockheed C-130J Hercules C5	Lockheed-Martin, for RAF	
ZH884	Lockheed C-130J Hercules C5	Lockheed-Martin, for RAF	
ZH885	Lockheed C-130J Hercules C5	Lockheed-Martin, for RAF	
ZH886	Lockheed C-130J Hercules C5	Lockheed-Martin, for RAF	
ZH887	Lockheed C-130J Hercules C5	Lockheed-Martin, for RAF	
ZH888	Lockheed C-130J Hercules C5	Lockheed-Martin, for RAF	
ZH889	Lockheed C-130J Hercules C5	Lockheed-Martin, for RAF	
ZH890	Grob G109B Vigilant T1	RAF No 663 VGS, Kinloss	
ZH891	B-V Chinook HC2	Boeing, Philadelphia, for RAF	
ZH892	B-V Chinook HC2	Boeing, Philadelphia, for RAF	
ZH893	B-V Chinook HC2	Boeing, Philadelphia, for RAF	
ZH894	B-V Chinook HC2	Boeing, Philadelphia, for RAF	
ZH895	B-V Chinook HC2	Boeing, Philadelphia, for RAF	
ZH896	B-V Chinook HC2	Boeing, Philadelphia, for RAF	
ZH897	B-V Chinook HC3	Boeing, Philadelphia, for RAF	
ZH898	B-V Chinook HC3	Boeing, Philadelphia, for RAF	
ZH899	B-V Chinook HC3	Boeing, Philadelphia, for RAF	
ZH900	B-V Chinook HC3	Boeing, Philadelphia, for RAF	
ZH901	B-V Chinook HC3	Boeing, Philadelphia, for RAF	
ZH902	B-V Chinook HC3	Boeing, Philadelphia, for RAF	
ZH903	B-V Chinook HC3	Boeing, Philadelphia, for RAF	
ZH904	B-V Chinook HC3	Boeing, Philadelphia, for RAF	
ZH905	Panavia Tornado IDS	*To R Saudi AF as 7501, 3 October 1996*	
ZH906	Panavia Tornado IDS	*To R Saudi AF as 7502, 3 October 1996*	
ZH907	Panavia Tornado IDS	*To R Saudi AF as 7503, 7 November 1996*	
ZH908	Panavia Tornado IDS	*To R Saudi AF as 8301, 7 November 1996*	
ZH909	Panavia Tornado IDS	*To R Saudi AF as 8302, 9 January 1997*	

Notes	Serial	Type (other identity) [code]	Owner/operator, location or fate
	ZH910	Panavia Tornado IDS	*To R Saudi AF as 8303, 12 December 1996*
	ZH911	Panavia Tornado IDS	*To R Saudi AF as 6625, 12 December 1996*
	ZH912	Panavia Tornado IDS	*To R Saudi AF as 6626, 9 January 1997*
	ZH913	Panavia Tornado IDS	BAe Warton, for R Saudi AF
	ZH914	Panavia Tornado IDS	BAe Warton, for R Saudi AF
	ZH915	Panavia Tornado IDS	BAe Warton, for R Saudi AF
	ZH916	Panavia Tornado IDS	BAe Warton, for R Saudi AF
	ZH917	Panavia Tornado IDS	BAe Warton, for R Saudi AF
	ZH918	Panavia Tornado IDS	BAe Warton, for R Saudi AF
	ZH919	Panavia Tornado IDS	BAe Warton, for R Saudi AF
	ZH920	Panavia Tornado IDS	BAe Warton, for R Saudi AF
	ZH921	Panavia Tornado IDS	BAe Warton, for R Saudi AF
	ZH922	Panavia Tornado IDS	BAe Warton, for R Saudi AF
	ZH923	Panavia Tornado IDS	BAe Warton, for R Saudi AF
	ZH924	Panavia Tornado IDS	BAe Warton, for R Saudi AF
	ZH925	Panavia Tornado IDS	BAe Warton, for R Saudi AF
	ZH926	Panavia Tornado IDS	BAe Warton, for R Saudi AF
	ZH927	Panavia Tornado IDS	BAe Warton, for R Saudi AF
	ZH928	Panavia Tornado IDS	BAe Warton, for R Saudi AF
	ZH929	Panavia Tornado IDS	BAe Warton, for R Saudi AF
	ZH930	Panavia Tornado IDS	BAe Warton, for R Saudi AF
	ZH931	Panavia Tornado IDS	BAe Warton, for R Saudi AF
	ZH932	Panavia Tornado IDS	BAe Warton, for R Saudi AF
	ZH933	Panavia Tornado IDS	BAe Warton, for R Saudi AF
	ZH934	Panavia Tornado IDS	BAe Warton, for R Saudi AF
	ZH935	Panavia Tornado IDS	BAe Warton, for R Saudi AF
	ZH936	Panavia Tornado IDS	BAe Warton, for R Saudi AF
	ZH937	Panavia Tornado IDS	BAe Warton, for R Saudi AF
	ZH938	Panavia Tornado IDS	BAe Warton, for R Saudi AF
	ZH939	Panavia Tornado IDS	BAe Warton, for R Saudi AF
	ZH940	Panavia Tornado IDS	BAe Warton, for R Saudi AF
	ZH941	Panavia Tornado IDS	BAe Warton, for R Saudi AF
	ZH942	Panavia Tornado IDS	BAe Warton, for R Saudi AF
	ZH943	Panavia Tornado IDS	BAe Warton, for R Saudi AF
	ZH944	Panavia Tornado IDS	BAe Warton, for R Saudi AF
	ZH945	Panavia Tornado IDS	BAe Warton, for R Saudi AF
	ZH946	Panavia Tornado IDS	BAe Warton, for R Saudi AF
	ZH947	Panavia Tornado IDS	BAe Warton, for R Saudi AF
	ZH948	Panavia Tornado IDS	BAe Warton, for R Saudi AF
	ZH949	Panavia Tornado IDS	BAe Warton, for R Saudi AF
	ZH950	Panavia Tornado IDS	BAe Warton, for R Saudi AF
	ZH951	Panavia Tornado IDS	BAe Warton, for R Saudi AF
	ZH952	Panavia Tornado IDS	BAe Warton, for R Saudi AF
	ZH953	BAe Hawk 109	*To Indonesian Air Force as TT-1201, 8 May 1996*
	ZH954	BAe Hawk 109	*To Indonesian Air Force as TT-1202, 8 May 1996*
	ZH955	BAe Hawk 109	BAe Warton, for Indonesian Air Force as TT-103
	ZH956	BAe Hawk 109	*To Indonesian Air Force as TT-1204, 8 May 1996*
	ZH957	BAe Hawk 109	*To Indonesian Air Force as TT-101, 21 May 1996*
	ZH958	BAe Hawk 109	*To Indonesian Air Force as TT-102, 21 May 1996*
	ZH959	BAe Hawk 109	*To Indonesian Air Force as TT-1203, 17 July 1996*
	ZH960	BAe Hawk 109	*To Indonesian Air Force as TT-104, 21 May 1996*
	ZH961	WS Super Lynx Mk 21A	Westland, Yeovil, for Brazilian Navy as N-4000
	ZH962	WS Super Lynx Mk 21A	*To Brazilian Navy as N-4001, 9 September 1996*
	ZH963	WS Super Lynx Mk 21A	Westland, Yeovil, for Brazilian Navy as N-4002
	ZH964	WS Super Lynx Mk 21A	Westland, Yeovil, for Brazilian Navy as N-4003
	ZH965	WS Super Lynx Mk 21A	Westland, Yeovil, for Brazilian Navy as N-4004
	ZH966	WS Super Lynx Mk 21A	Westland, Yeovil, for Brazilian Navy as N-4005
	ZH967	WS Super Lynx Mk 21A	Westland, Yeovil, for Brazilian Navy as N-4006

Serial	Type (other identity) [code]	Owner/operator, location or fate	Notes
ZH968	WS Super Lynx Mk 21A	Westland, Yeovil, for Brazilian Navy as N-4007	
ZH969	WS Super Lynx Mk 21A	Westland, Yeovil, for Brazilian Navy as N-4008	
ZH970	WS Super Lynx Mk 21A	Westland, Yeovil, for Brazilian Navy as N-4009	
ZH971	WS Super Lynx Mk 21A	Westland, Yeovil, for Brazilian Navy	
ZH972	WS Super Lynx Mk 21A	Westland, Yeovil, for Brazilian Navy	
ZH973	WS Super Lynx Mk 21A	Westland, Yeovil, for Brazilian Navy	
ZH974	WS Super Lynx Mk 21A	Westland, Yeovil, for Brazilian Navy	
ZH979	Pilatus PC-9 (HB-HQX)	*To R Saudi AF as 905, 31 January 1996*	
ZH980	Pilatus PC-9 (HB-HRM)	*To R Saudi AF as 906, 31 January 1996*	
ZH981	Pilatus PC-9 (HB-HRN)	*To R Saudi AF as 907, 28 February 1996*	
ZH982	Pilatus PC-9 (HB-HRO)	*To R Saudi AF as 908, 28 February 1996*	
ZH983	Pilatus PC-9 (HB-HRP)	*To R Saudi AF as 909, 3 April 1996*	
ZH984	Pilatus PC-9 (HB-HRQ)	*To R Saudi AF as 910, 3 April 1996*	
ZH985	Pilatus PC-9 (HB-HRR)	*To R Saudi AF as 911, 29 April 1996*	
ZH986	Pilatus PC-9 (HB-HRS)	*To R Saudi AF as 912, 29 April 1996*	
ZH987	Pilatus PC-9 (HB-HRT)	*To R Saudi AF as 913, 5 June 1996*	
ZH988	Pilatus PC-9 (HB-HRU)	*To R Saudi AF as 914, 5 June 1996*	
ZH989	Pilatus PC-9 (HB-HRV)	*To R Saudi AF as 915, 21 June 1996*	
ZH990	Pilatus PC-9 (HB-HRW)	*To R Saudi AF as 916, 21 June 1996*	
ZH991	Pilatus PC-9 (HB-HRX)	*To R Saudi AF as 917, 31 July 1996*	
ZH992	Pilatus PC-9 (HB-HRY)	*To R Saudi AF as 918, 31 July 1996*	
ZH993	Pilatus PC-9 (HB-HRZ)	*To R Saudi AF as 919, 26 August 1996*	
ZH994	Pilatus PC-9 (HB-HRA)	*To R Saudi AF as 920, 26 August 1996*	
ZH995	BAe Hawk T65A	BAe Warton, for R Saudi AF as 7901	
ZH996	BAe Hawk T65A	BAe Warton, for R Saudi AF as 7902	
ZH997	BAe Hawk T65A	BAe Warton, for R Saudi AF	
ZH998	BAe Hawk T65A	BAe Warton, for R Saudi AF	
ZH999	BAe Hawk T65A	BAe Warton, for R Saudi AF	
ZJ100	BAe Hawk 102D	BAe Warton	
ZJ101	BAe Hawk T65A	BAe Warton, for R Saudi AF	
ZJ102	BAe Hawk T65A	BAe Warton, for R Saudi AF	
ZJ103	BAe Hawk T65A	BAe Warton, for R Saudi AF	
ZJ104	BAe Hawk T65A	BAe Warton, for R Saudi AF	
ZJ105	BAe Hawk T65A	BAe Warton, for R Saudi AF	
ZJ106	BAe Hawk T65A	BAe Warton, for R Saudi AF	
ZJ107	BAe Hawk T65A	BAe Warton, for R Saudi AF	
ZJ108	BAe Hawk T65A	BAe Warton, for R Saudi AF	
ZJ109	BAe Hawk T65A	BAe Warton, for R Saudi AF	
ZJ110	BAe Hawk T65A	BAe Warton, for R Saudi AF	
ZJ111	BAe Hawk T65A	BAe Warton, for R Saudi AF	
ZJ112	BAe Hawk T65A	BAe Warton, for R Saudi AF	
ZJ113	BAe Hawk T65A	BAe Warton, for R Saudi AF	
ZJ114	BAe Hawk T65A	BAe Warton, for R Saudi AF	
ZJ115	BAe Hawk T65A	BAe Warton, for R Saudi AF	
ZJ116	WS/Agusta EH-101 (G-OIOI) (PP8)	MoD(PE)/Westland, Yeovil	
ZJ117	WS/Agusta EH-101 Merlin HC3	Westland, Yeovil, for RAF	
ZJ118	WS/Agusta EH-101 Merlin HC3	Westland, Yeovil, for RAF	
ZJ119	WS/Agusta EH-101 Merlin HC3	Westland, Yeovil, for RAF	
ZJ120	WS/Agusta EH-101 Merlin HC3	Westland, Yeovil, for RAF	
ZJ121	WS/Agusta EH-101 Merlin HC3	Westland, Yeovil, for RAF	
ZJ122	WS/Agusta EH-101 Merlin HC3	Westland, Yeovil, for RAF	
ZJ123	WS/Agusta EH-101 Merlin HC3	Westland, Yeovil, for RAF	
ZJ124	WS/Agusta EH-101 Merlin HC3	Westland, Yeovil, for RAF	
ZJ125	WS/Agusta EH-101 Merlin HC3	Westland, Yeovil, for RAF	
ZJ126	WS/Agusta EH-101 Merlin HC3	Westland, Yeovil, for RAF	
ZJ127	WS/Agusta EH-101 Merlin HC3	Westland, Yeovil, for RAF	
ZJ128	WS/Agusta EH-101 Merlin HC3	Westland, Yeovil, for RAF	
ZJ129	WS/Agusta EH-101 Merlin HC3	Westland, Yeovil, for RAF	
ZJ130	WS/Agusta EH-101 Merlin HC3	Westland, Yeovil, for RAF	
ZJ131	WS/Agusta EH-101 Merlin HC3	Westland, Yeovil, for RAF	
ZJ132	WS/Agusta EH-101 Merlin HC3	Westland, Yeovil, for RAF	
ZJ133	WS/Agusta EH-101 Merlin HC3	Westland, Yeovil, for RAF	
ZJ134	WS/Agusta EH-101 Merlin HC3	Westland, Yeovil, for RAF	
ZJ135	WS/Agusta EH-101 Merlin HC3	Westland, Yeovil, for RAF	
ZJ136	WS/Agusta EH-101 Merlin HC3	Westland, Yeovil, for RAF	
ZJ137	WS/Agusta EH-101 Merlin HC3	Westland, Yeovil, for RAF	
ZJ138	WS/Agusta EH-101 Merlin HC3	Westland, Yeovil, for RAF	
ZJ139	Aérospatiale AS355F-1 Twin Squirrel HCC1 (G-NUTZ)	RAF No 32(The Royal) Sqn, Northolt	

Notes	Serial	Type (other identity) [code]	Owner/operator, location or fate
	ZJ140	Aérospatiale AS355F-1 Twin Squirrel HCC1 (G-FFHI)	RAF No 32(The Royal) Sqn, Northolt
	ZJ141	BAe Hawk 209	*To Indonesian AF as TT-1205, 2 July 1996*
	ZJ142	BAe Hawk 209	*To Indonesian AF as TT-1206, 2 July 1996*
	ZJ143	BAe Hawk 209	*To Indonesian AF as TT-1207, 17 July 1996*
	ZJ144	BAe Hawk 209	*To Indonesian AF as TT-1208, 16 August 1996*
	ZJ145	BAe Hawk 209	*To Indonesian AF as TT-1209, 16 August 1996*
	ZJ146	BAe Hawk 209	*To Indonesian AF as TT-1210, 3 September 1996*
	ZJ147	BAe Hawk 209	*To Indonesian AF as TT-1211, 3 September 1996*
	ZJ148	BAe Hawk 209	*To Indonesian AF as TT-1212, 1 October 1996*
	ZJ149	BAe Hawk 209	*To Indonesian AF as TT-1213, 1 October 1996*
	ZJ150	BAe Hawk 209	*To Indonesian AF as TT-1214, 5 November 1996*
	ZJ151	BAe Hawk 209	*To Indonesian AF as TT-1215, 5 November 1996*
	ZJ152	BAe Hawk 209	*To Indonesian AF as TT-1216, 3 December 1996*
	ZJ153	BAe Hawk 209	*To Indonesian AF as TT-1217, 3 December 1996*
	ZJ154	BAe Hawk 209	BAe Warton, for Indonesian AF as TT-1218
	ZJ155	BAe Hawk 209	BAe Warton, for Indonesian AF
	ZJ156	BAe Hawk 209	BAe Warton, for Indonesian AF
	ZJ157		
	ZJ158		
	ZJ159		
	ZJ160		
	ZJ161		
	ZJ162	WS61 Sea King Mk43B	*To Norwegian AF as 329, May 1996*
	ZJ163	WS61 Sea King Mk43B	*To Norwegian AF as 330, 1996*
	ZJ164	AS365N-2 Dauphin 2 (G-BTLC)	RN/Bond Helicopters, Plymouth
	ZJ165	AS365N-2 Dauphin 2 (G-NTOO)	RN/Bond Helicopters, Plymouth
	ZJ166	WS/McD AH-64D Apache AH1	Westland, for AAC
	ZJ167	WS/McD AH-64D Apache AH1	Westland, for AAC
	ZJ168	WS/McD AH-64D Apache AH1	Westland, for AAC
	ZJ169	WS/McD AH-64D Apache AH1	Westland, for AAC
	ZJ170	WS/McD AH-64D Apache AH1	Westland, for AAC
	ZJ171	WS/McD AH-64D Apache AH1	Westland, for AAC
	ZJ172	WS/McD AH-64D Apache AH1	Westland, for AAC
	ZJ173	WS/McD AH-64D Apache AH1	Westland, for AAC
	ZJ174	WS/McD AH-64D Apache AH1	Westland, for AAC
	ZJ175	WS/McD AH-64D Apache AH1	Westland, for AAC
	ZJ176	WS/McD AH-64D Apache AH1	Westland, for AAC
	ZJ177	WS/McD AH-64D Apache AH1	Westland, for AAC
	ZJ178	WS/McD AH-64D Apache AH1	Westland, for AAC
	ZJ179	WS/McD AH-64D Apache AH1	Westland, for AAC
	ZJ180	WS/McD AH-64D Apache AH1	Westland, for AAC
	ZJ181	WS/McD AH-64D Apache AH1	Westland, for AAC
	ZJ182	WS/McD AH-64D Apache AH1	Westland, for AAC
	ZJ183	WS/McD AH-64D Apache AH1	Westland, for AAC
	ZJ184	WS/McD AH-64D Apache AH1	Westland, for AAC
	ZJ185	WS/McD AH-64D Apache AH1	Westland, for AAC
	ZJ186	WS/McD AH-64D Apache AH1	Westland, for AAC
	ZJ187	TWS/McD AH-64D Apache AH1	Owestland, for AAC
	ZJ188	WS/McD AH-64D Apache AH1	Westland, for AAC
	ZJ189	WS/McD AH-64D Apache AH1	Westland, for AAC
	ZJ190	WS/McD AH-64D Apache AH1	Westland, for AAC
	ZJ191	WS/McD AH-64D Apache AH1	Westland, for AAC
	ZJ192	WS/McD AH-64D Apache AH1	Westland, for AAC
	ZJ193	WS/McD AH-64D Apache AH1	Westland, for AAC
	ZJ194	WS/McD AH-64D Apache AH1	Westland, for AAC
	ZJ195	WS/McD AH-64D Apache AH1	Westland, for AAC
	ZJ196	WS/McD AH-64D Apache AH1	Westland, for AAC
	ZJ197	WS/McD AH-64D Apache AH1	Westland, for AAC
	ZJ198	WS/McD AH-64D Apache AH1	Westland, for AAC
	ZJ199	WS/McD AH-64D Apache AH1	Westland, for AAC
	ZJ200	WS/McD AH-64D Apache AH1	Westland, for AAC

Serial	Type (other identity) [code]	Owner/operator, location or fate	Notes
ZJ201	BAe Hawk 200RDA	BAe Warton	
ZJ202	WS/McD AH-64D Apache AH1	Westland, for AAC	
ZJ203	WS/McD AH-64D Apache AH1	Westland, for AAC	
ZJ204	WS/McD AH-64D Apache AH1	Westland, for AAC	
ZJ205	WS/McD AH-64D Apache AH1	Westland, for AAC	
ZJ206	WS/McD AH-64D Apache AH1	Westland, for AAC	
ZJ207	WS/McD AH-64D Apache AH1	Westland, for AAC	
ZJ208	WS/McD AH-64D Apache AH1	Westland, for AAC	
ZJ209	WS/McD AH-64D Apache AH1	Westland, for AAC	
ZJ210	WS/McD AH-64D Apache AH1	Westland, for AAC	
ZJ211	WS/McD AH-64D Apache AH1	Westland, for AAC	
ZJ212	WS/McD AH-64D Apache AH1	Westland, for AAC	
ZJ213	WS/McD AH-64D Apache AH1	Westland, for AAC	
ZJ214	WS/McD AH-64D Apache AH1	Westland, for AAC	
ZJ215	WS/McD AH-64D Apache AH1	Westland, for AAC	
ZJ216	WS/McD AH-64D Apache AH1	Westland, for AAC	
ZJ217	WS/McD AH-64D Apache AH1	Westland, for AAC	
ZJ218	WS/McD AH-64D Apache AH1	Westland, for AAC	
ZJ219	WS/McD AH-64D Apache AH1	Westland, for AAC	
ZJ220	WS/McD AH-64D Apache AH1	Westland, for AAC	
ZJ221	WS/McD AH-64D Apache AH1	Westland, for AAC	
ZJ222	WS/McD AH-64D Apache AH1	Westland, for AAC	
ZJ223	WS/McD AH-64D Apache AH1	Westland, for AAC	
ZJ224	WS/McD AH-64D Apache AH1	Westland, for AAC	
ZJ225	WS/McD AH-64D Apache AH1	Westland, for AAC	
ZJ226	WS/McD AH-64D Apache AH1	Westland, for AAC	
ZJ227	WS/McD AH-64D Apache AH1	Westland, for AAC	
ZJ228	WS/McD AH-64D Apache AH1	Westland, for AAC	
ZJ229	WS/McD AH-64D Apache AH1	Westland, for AAC	
ZJ230	WS/McD AH-64D Apache AH1	Westland, for AAC	
ZJ231	WS/McD AH-64D Apache AH1	Westland, for AAC	
ZJ232	WS/McD AH-64D Apache AH1	Westland, for AAC	
ZJ233	WS/McD AH-64D Apache AH1	Westland, for AAC	
ZJ234	Bell 412EP Griffin HT1 (C-FZLM/G-BWZR)	MoD (PE)/RWTS, DTEO Boscombe Down	
ZJ235	Bell 412EP Griffin HT1 (N2291Q)	DHFS, RAF Valley	
ZJ236	Bell 412EP Griffin HT1 (C-FZLN)	DHFS, RAF Valley	
ZJ237	Bell 412EP Griffin HT1 (C-FZNF)	DHFS, RAF Valley	
ZJ238	Bell 412EP Griffin HT1	Bell, for RAF	
ZJ239	Bell 412EP Griffin HT1	Bell, for RAF	
ZJ240	Bell 412EP Griffin HT1	Bell, for RAF	
ZJ241	Bell 412EP Griffin HT1	Bell, for RAF	
ZJ242	Bell 412EP Griffin HT1	Bell, for RAF	
ZJ243	Eurocopter AS350BB Squirrel HT2 (G-BWZS)	MoD(PE)/RWTS, DTEO Boscombe Down	
ZJ244	Eurocopter AS350BB Squirrel HT1/HT2	Eurocopter, for DHFS	
ZJ245	Eurocopter AS350BB Squirrel HT1/HT2	Eurocopter, for DHFS	
ZJ246	Eurocopter AS350BB Squirrel HT1/HT2	Eurocopter, for DHFS	
ZJ247	Eurocopter AS350BB Squirrel HT1/HT2	Eurocopter, for DHFS	
ZJ248	Eurocopter AS350BB Squirrel HT1/HT2	Eurocopter, for DHFS	
ZJ249	Eurocopter AS350BB Squirrel HT1/HT2	Eurocopter, for DHFS	
ZJ250	Eurocopter AS350BB Squirrel HT1/HT2	Eurocopter, for DHFS	
ZJ251	Eurocopter AS350BB Squirrel HT1/HT2	Eurocopter, for DHFS	
ZJ252	Eurocopter AS350BB Squirrel HT1/HT2	Eurocopter, for DHFS	
ZJ253	Eurocopter AS350BB Squirrel HT1/HT2	Eurocopter, for DHFS	
ZJ254	Eurocopter AS350BB Squirrel HT1/HT2	Eurocopter, for DHFS	
ZJ255	Eurocopter AS350BB Squirrel HT1/HT2	Eurocopter, for DHFS	
ZJ256	Eurocopter AS350BB Squirrel HT1/HT2	Eurocopter, for DHFS	
ZJ257	Eurocopter AS350BB Squirrel HT1/HT2	Eurocopter, for DHFS	

Notes	Serial	Type (other identity) [code]	Owner/operator, location or fate
	ZJ258	Eurocopter AS350BB Squirrel HT1/HT2	Eurocopter, for DHFS
	ZJ259	Eurocopter AS350BB Squirrel HT1/HT2	Eurocopter, for DHFS
	ZJ260	Eurocopter AS350BB Squirrel HT1/HT2	Eurocopter, for DHFS
	ZJ261	Eurocopter AS350BB Squirrel HT1/HT2	Eurocopter, for DHFS
	ZJ262	Eurocopter AS350BB Squirrel HT1/HT2	Eurocopter, for DHFS
	ZJ263	Eurocopter AS350BB Squirrel HT1/HT2	Eurocopter, for DHFS
	ZJ264	Eurocopter AS350BB Squirrel HT1/HT2	Eurocopter, for DHFS
	ZJ265	Eurocopter AS350BB Squirrel HT1/HT2	Eurocopter, for DHFS
	ZJ266	Eurocopter AS350BB Squirrel HT1/HT2	Eurocopter, for DHFS
	ZJ267	Eurocopter AS350BB Squirrel HT1/HT2	Eurocopter, for DHFS
	ZJ268	Eurocopter AS350BB Squirrel HT1/HT2	Eurocopter, for DHFS
	ZJ269	Eurocopter AS350BB Squirrel HT1/HT2	Eurocopter, for DHFS
	ZJ270	Eurocopter AS350BB Squirrel HT1/HT2	Eurocopter, for DHFS
	ZJ271	Eurocopter AS350BB Squirrel HT1/HT2	Eurocopter, for DHFS
	ZJ272	Eurocopter AS350BB Squirrel HT1/HT2	Eurocopter, for DHFS
	ZJ273	Eurocopter AS350BB Squirrel HT1/HT2	Eurocopter, for DHFS
	ZJ274	Eurocopter AS350BB Squirrel HT1/HT2	Eurocopter, for DHFS
	ZJ275	Eurocopter AS350BB Squirrel HT1/HT2	Eurocopter, for DHFS
	ZJ276	Eurocopter AS350BB Squirrel HT1/HT2	Eurocopter, for DHFS
	ZJ277	Eurocopter AS350BB Squirrel HT1/HT2	Eurocopter, for DHFS
	ZJ278	Eurocopter AS350BB Squirrel HT1/HT2	Eurocopter, for DHFS
	ZJ279	Eurocopter AS350BB Squirrel HT1/HT2	Eurocopter, for DHFS
	ZJ280	Eurocopter AS350BB Squirrel HT1/HT2	Eurocopter, for DHFS
	ZJ281		
	ZJ282		
	ZJ283		
	ZJ284		
	ZJ285		
	ZJ286		
	ZJ287		
	ZJ288		
	ZJ289		
	ZJ290		
	ZJ291		
	ZJ292		
	ZJ293		
	ZJ294		
	ZJ295		
	ZJ296		
	ZJ297		
	ZJ298		
	ZJ299		
	ZJ300		
	ZJ301		
	ZJ302		
	ZJ303		
	ZJ304		
	ZJ305		
	ZJ306		
	ZJ307		

WS58 Wessex HC2 XR522 [A] in its last year with No 28 Squadron in Sek Kong. *PRM*

HS Nimrod MR2 XV240 of No 120 Sqn visiting its former base at RAF St Mawgan. *A. J. March*

SA Jetstream T1 XX492/A based with No 3 FTS/45(R) Sqn at RAF Cranwell. *D. J. March*

Grey-painted display Jaguar GR1A XZ108/A of No 16 (R) Sqn. *PRM*

WS Gazelle AH1 ZA777 with the Army Air Corps No 670 (*Blue Eagles*) Sqn at Middle Wallop. *PRM*

Lockheed Tristar ZD952 based at Brize Norton with No 216 Sqn. *D. J. March*

RAF Maintenance Command/ Support Command/Logistics Command 'M' number cross-reference

1764M/K4972	7548M/PS915	7859M/XP283	8021M/XL824
2015M/K5600	7554M/FS890	7860M/XL738	8022M/XN341
2292M/K8203	7555M/AR614	7862M/XR246	8023M/XD463
2361M/K6035	7556M/WK584	7863M/*XP248*	8027M/XM555
3118M/H5199/BK892	7564M/XE982	7864M/XP244	8032M/XH837
3858M/X7688	7570M/XD674	7865M/TX226	8033M/XD382
4354M/BL614	7582M/WP190	7866M/XH278	8034M/XL703
4552M/T5298	7583M/WP185	7868M/WZ736	8041M/XF690
5377M/EP120	7602M/WE600	7869M/WK935	8043M/XF836
5378M/AR614	7605M/WS692	7872M/*WZ826*/(XD826)	8046M/XL770
5405M/LF738	7606M/WV562	7881M/WD413	8049M/WE168
5466M/*BN230*/(LF751)	7607M/TJ138	7882M/XD525	8050M/XG329
5690M/MK356	7615M/WV679	7883M/*XT123*/(XT150)	8051M/XN929
5718M/BM597	7616M/WW388	7886M/XR985	8052M/WH166
5758M/DG202	7618M/WW442	7887M/XD375	8054AM/XM410
6457M/ML427	7622M/WV606	7890M/XD453	8054BM/XM417
6490M/LA255	7625M/WD356	7891M/XM693	8055AM/XM402
6850M/TE184	7631M/VX185	7894M/XD818	8055BM/XM404
6946M/RW388	7641M/XA634	7895M/WF784	8056M/XG337
6948M/DE673	7645M/WD293	7898M/XP854	8057M/XR243
6960M/MT847	7646M/VX461	7899M/XG540	8063M/WT536
7008M/EE549	7648M/XF785	7900M/WA576	8070M/EP120
7014M/N6720	7673M/WV332	7906M/WH132	8072M/PK624
7015M/NL985	7688M/WW421	7917M/WA591	8073M/TB252
7035M/*K2567*/(DE306)	7693M/WV483	7920M/WL360	8077M/XN594
7060M/VF301	7696M/WV493	7923M/XT133	8078M/XM351
7090M/EE531	7698M/WV499	7925M/WV666	8079M/XN492
7118M/LA198	7703M/WG725	7928M/XE849	8080M/XM480
7119M/LA226	7704M/TW536	7930M/WH301	8081M/XM468
7150M/PK683	7705M/WL505	7931M/RD253	8082M/XM409
7154M/WB188	7706M/WB584	7932M/WZ744	8086M/TB752
7174M/VX272	7709M/WT933	7933M/XR220	8088M/XN602
7175M/VV106	7711M/PS915	7937M/WS843	8092M/WK654
7200M/VT812	7712M/WK281	7938M/XH903	8094M/WT520
7243M/TE462	7715M/XK724	7939M/XD596	8101M/WH984
7244M/*MK673*/(TB382)	7716M/WS776	7940M/XL764	8102M/WT486
7256M/TB752	7718M/WA577	7955M/XH767	8103M/WR985
7257M/TB252	7719M/WK277	7957M/XF545	8106M/WR982
7279M/TB752	7729M/WB758	7959M/WS774	8108M/WV703
7281M/TB252	7734M/XD536	7960M/WS726	8114M/WL798
7288M/PK724	7737M/XD602	7961M/WS739	8117M/WR974
7293M/RW393	7741M/VZ477	7964M/WS760	8118M/WZ549
7323M/VV217	7750M/*WK864*/(WL168)	7965M/WS792	8119M/WR971
7325M/R5868	7751M/WL131	7967M/WS788	8121M/XM474
7326M/VN485	7755M/WG760	7970M/WP907	8124M/XD614
7362M/475081/(VP546)	7758M/PM651	7971M/XK699	8128M/WH775
7416M/WN907	7759M/PK664	7973M/WS807	8131M/WT507
7421M/WT660	7761M/XH318	7976M/XK418	8140M/XJ571
7422M/WT684	7762M/XE670	7979M/XM529	8141M/XN688
7428M/WK198	7770M/WT746	7980M/XM561	8142M/XJ560
7432M/WZ724	7793M/XG523	7982M/XH892	8143M/XN691
7438M/*18671*/(WP905)	7796M/WJ676	7983M/XD506	8147M/XR526
7443M/WX853	7798M/XH783	7984M/XN597	8151M/WV795
7458M/WX905	7806M/TA639	7986M/WG777	8153M/WV903
7464M/XA564	7809M/XA699	7988M/XL149	8154M/WV908
7467M/WP978	7816M/WG763	7990M/XD452	8155M/WV797
7470M/XA553	7817M/TX214	7997M/XG452	8156M/XE339
7473M/XE946	7825M/WK991	7998M/*XM515*/(XD515)	8158M/XE369
7491M/WT569	7827M/XA917	8001M/WV395	8159M/XD528
7496M/WT612	7829M/XH992	8005M/WG768	8160M/XD622
7499M/WT555	7839M/WV781	8009M/XG518	8161M/XE993
7510M/WT694	7840M/XK482	8010M/XG547	8162M/WM913
7525M/WT619	7841M/WV783	8012M/VS562	8163M/XP919
7530M/WT648	7851M/WZ706	8016M/XT677	8164M/*WN105*/(WF299)
7532M/WT651	7852M/XG506	8017M/XL762	8165M/WH791
7533M/WT680	7854M/XM191	8018M/XN344	8169M/WH364
7544M/WN904	7855M/XK416	8019M/WZ869	8171M/XJ607

8173M/XN685	8395M/WF408	8561M/XS100	8709M/XG209
8176M/*WH791*	8396M/XK740	8565M/*WT720*/(E-408)	8710M/XG274
8177M/*WM311*/(WM224)	8399M/WR539	8566M/XV279	8711M/XG290
8179M/XN928	8401M/XP686	8568M/XP503	8713M/XG225
8182M/XN953	8402M/XN769	8569M/XR535	8714M/XK149
8183M/*XN972*/(XN962)	8406M/XP831	8570M/XR954	8718M/XX396
8184M/WT520	8407M/XP585	8573M/XM708	8719M/XT257
8185M/WH946	8408M/XS186	8575M/XP542	8720M/XP353
8186M/WR977	8409M/XS209	8576M/XP502	8721M/XP354
8187M/WH791	8413M/XM192	8578M/XR534	8722M/WJ640
8189M/WD646	8414M/XM173	8581M/WJ775	8723M/XL567
8190M/XJ918	8417M/XM144	8582M/XE874	8724M/XW923
8192M/XR658	8422M/XM169	8583M/BAPC 94	8726M/XP299
8196M/XE920	8427M/XM172	8584M/WH903	8727M/XR486
8198M/WT339	8429M/XH592	8585M/XE670	8728M/WT532
8203M/XD377	8431M/XR651	8586M/XE643	8729M/WJ815
8205M/XN819	8435M/XN512	8587M/XP677	8730M/XD186
8206M/WG419	8436M/XN554	8588M/XR681	8731M/XP361
8207M/WD318	8437M/*WX643*/(WG362)	8589M/XR700	8732M/XJ729
8208M/WG303	8439M/WZ846	8590M/XM191	8733M/XL318
8209M/WG418	8440M/WD935	8591M/XA813	8736M/XF375
8210M/WG471	8442M/XP411	8595M/XH278	8738M/*XF519*/(XJ695)
8211M/WK570	8445M/XK968	8598M/WP270	8739M/XH170
8213M/WK626	8453M/XP745	8600M/XX761	8740M/WE173
8214M/WP864	8457M/XS871	8602M/*PF179*/(XR541)	8741M/XW329
8215M/WP869	8458M/XP672	8606M/XP530	8743M/WD790
8216M/WP927	8459M/XR650	8608M/XP540	8746M/XH171
8217M/WZ866	8460M/XP680	8610M/XL502	8749M/XH537
8218M/WB645	8462M/XX477	8611M/WF128	8751M/XT255
8229M/XM355	8463M/XP355	8617M/XM709	8753M/WL795
8230M/XM362	8464M/XJ758	8618M/*XM693*/(XP504)	8762M/WH740
8231M/XM375	8465M/W1048	8620M/XP534	8763M/WH665
8234M/XN458	8466M/L-866	8621M/XR538	8767M/XX635
8235M/XN549	8467M/WP912	8624M/*XR991*/(XS102)	8768M/A-522
8236M/XP573	8468M/MM5701/(BT474)	8627M/XP558	8769M/A-528
8237M/XS179	8470M/584219	8628M/XJ380	8770M/XL623
8238M/XS180	8471M/701152	8630M/*WX643*/(WG362)	8771M/XM602
8344M/WH960	8472M/120227/(VN679)	8631M/XR574	8772M/WR960
8345M/XG540	8473M/WP190	8634M/WP314	8777M/XX914
8350M/WH840	8474M/494083	8638M/XS101	8778M/XM598
8352M/XN632	8475M/360043/(PJ876)	8640M/XR977	8779M/XM607
8355M/*KG374*/(KN645)	8476M/24	8642M/XR537	8780M/WK102
8357M/WK576	8477M/4101/(DG200)	8645M/XD163	8781M/WE982
8359M/WF825	8478M/10639	8648M/XK526	8782M/XH136
8360M/WP863	8479M/730301	8653M/XS120	8783M/XW272
8361M/WB670	8481M/191614	8655M/XN126	8785M/XS642
8362M/WG477	8482M/112372/(VK893)	8656M/XP405	8786M/XN495
8364M/WG464	8483M/420430	8657M/VZ634	8791M/XP329
8365M/XK421	8484M/5439	8661M/XJ727	8792M/XP345
8366M/XG454	8485M/997	8662M/XR458	8793M/XP346
8367M/XG474	8486M/BAPC 99	8664M/WJ603	8794M/XP398
8368M/XF926	8487M/J-1172	8666M/XE793	8796M/XK943
8369M/WE139	8488M/WL627	8667M/WP972	8797M/XX947
8370M/N1671	8491M/WJ880	8668M/WJ821	8799M/WV787
8371M/XA847	8492M/WJ872	8671M/XJ435	8800M/XG226
8372M/K8042	8493M/XR571	8672M/XP351	8805M/XT772
8373M/P2617	8494M/XP557	8673M/XD165	8807M/XL587
8375M/NX611	8495M/XR672	8674M/XP395	8810M/XJ825
8376M/RF398	8501M/XP640	8676M/XL577	8814M/XM927
8377M/R9125	8502M/XP686	8677M/*XF519*/(XJ695)	8818M/XK527
8378M/*T9707*	8503M/XS451	8678M/XE656	8819M/XS479
8379M/DG590	8507M/XS215	8679M/XF526	8820M/VP952
8380M/Z7197	8508M/XS218	8680M/XF527	8821M/XX115
8382M/VR930	8509M/XT141	8681M/XG164	8822M/VP957
8383M/K9942	8513M/XN724	8682M/XP404	8824M/VP971
8384M/X4590	8514M/XS176	8684M/XJ634	8828M/XS587
8385M/N5912	8535M/XN776	8687M/XJ639	8830M/XF515
8386M/NV778	8538M/XN781	8693M/WH863	8831M/XG160
8387M/T6296	8545M/XN726	8696M/WH773	8832M/XG172
8388M/XL993	8546M/XN728	8700M/ZD234	8833M/XL569
8389M/VX573	8548M/WT507	8702M/XG196	8834M/XL572
8392M/SL674	8549M/WT534	8703M/VW453	8836M/XL592
8393M/XK987	8554M/TG511	8706M/XF383	8838M/*34037*/(429356)
8394M/WG422	8560M/XR569	8708M/XF509	8839M/XG194

8840M/XG252	8948M/XX757	9049M/XW404	9149M/XW375
8844M/XJ676	8949M/XX743	9050M/XG577	9150M/*FX760*
8845M/XS572	8950M/XX956	9052M/WJ717	9151M/XT907
8847M/XX344	8951M/XX727	9054M/XT766	9152M/XV424
8848M/XZ135	8952M/XX730	9055M/XT770	9153M/XW360
8851M/XT595	8953M/XX959	9056M/XS488	9154M/XW321
8852M/XV337	8954M/XZ384	9057M/ZE361	9155M/WL679
8853M/XT277	8955M/XX110	9059M/ZE360	9157M/XV422
8855M/XT284	8956M/XN577	9060M/ZE356	9158M/XV467
8857M/XW544	8957M/XN582	9061M/XW335	9159M/XV468
8860M/XW549	8958M/XN501	9062M/XW351	9162M/XZ991
8861M/XW528	8960M/XM455	9064M/XT867	9163M/XV415
8862M/XN473	8961M/XS925	9065M/XV577	9165M/XV408
8863M/XG154	8967M/XV263	9066M/XV582	9166M/XW323
8867M/XK532	8968M/XM471	9067M/XV586	9167M/XV744
8868M/WH775	8969M/XR753	9070M/XV581	9168M/XZ132
8869M/WH957	8972M/XR754	9072M/XW768	9169M/XW547
8870M/WH964	8973M/XS922	9073M/XW924	9170M/XZ994
8871M/WJ565	8974M/XM473	9074M/XV738	9171M/XT895
8873M/XR453	8978M/XX837	9075M/XV753	9172M/XW304
8874M/XE597	8979M/XV747	9076M/XV808	9173M/XW418
8875M/XE624	8983M/XM478	9077M/XZ967	9174M/XZ131
8876M/*VM791*/(XA312)	8984M/XN551	9078M/XV752	9175M/P1344
8877M/XP159	8985M/WK127	9079M/XZ130	9176M/XW430
8879M/XX948	8986M/XV261	9083M/ZE353	9177M/XW328
8880M/XF435	8987M/XM358	9084M/ZE354	9178M/XS793
8881M/XG254	8988M/XN593	9085M/ZE364	9179M/XW309
8883M/XX946	8990M/XM419	9087M/XX753	9180M/XW311
8884M/VX275	8992M/XP547	9090M/XW353	9181M/XW358
8885M/XW922	8995M/XM425	9091M/XW434	9183M/*XF519*/(XJ695)
8886M/XA243	8996M/XM414	9092M/XH669	9185M/XZ987
8888M/XA231	8997M/XX669	9093M/WK124	9186M/XF967
8889M/XN239	8998M/XT864	9095M/XW547	9187M/XW405
8890M/WT532	9002M/XW763	9096M/WV322	9188M/XW364
8892M/XL618	9003M/XZ390	9097M/XW366	9189M/ZD350
8895M/XX746	9004M/XZ370	9098M/XV406	9190M/XW318
8896M/XX821	9005M/XZ374	9100M/XL188	9191M/XW416
8897M/XX969	9006M/XX967	9101M/WL756	9192M/XW361
8898M/XX119	9007M/XX968	9103M/XV411	9193M/XW367
8899M/XX756	9008M/XX140	9108M/XT475	9194M/XW420
8900M/XZ368	9009M/XX763	9109M/XW312	9195M/XW330
8901M/XZ383	9010M/XX764	9110M/XX736	9196M/XW370
8902M/XX739	9011M/XM412	9111M/XW421	9197M/XX637
8903M/XX747	9012M/XN494	9112M/XM475	9198M/XS641
8904M/XX966	9014M/XN584	9113M/XV500	9199M/XW290
8905M/XX975	9015M/XW320	9115M/XV863	9200M/XW425
8906M/XX976	9017M/ZE449	9117M/XV161	9201M/ZD667
8907M/XZ371	9018M/XW365	9118M/XV253	9202M/*433*
8908M/XZ382	9019M/XX824	9119M/XW303	9203M/*3066*
8909M/XV784	9020M/XX825	9120M/XW419	9205M/*E449*
8910M/XL160	9021M/XX826	9122M/XZ997	9206M/F6314
8911M/XH673	9022M/XX958	9123M/XT773	9207M/8417/18
8915M/XH132	9023M/XX844	9124M/XW427	9208M/F938
8917M/XM372	9026M/XP629	9125M/XW410	9209M/164
8918M/XX109	9027M/XP556	9126M/XW413	9210M/MF628
8919M/XT486	9028M/XP563	9127M/XW432	9211M/733682
8920M/XT469	9029M/XS217	9128M/XW292	9212M/*KL216* (45-49295)
8921M/XT466	9030M/XR674	9129M/XW294	9213M/N5182
8922M/XT467	9031M/XP688	9130M/XW327	9215M/XL164
8923M/XX819	9032M/XR673	9131M/*DD931*	9216M/XL190
8924M/XP701	9033M/XS181	9132M/XX977	9217M/ZH257
8925M/XP706	9034M/XP638	9133M/*413573*	9218M/XL563
8931M/XV779	9036M/XM350	9134M/XT288	9219M/FXZ971
8932M/XR718	9037M/XN302	9136M/XT891	9220M/XZ995
8934M/XR749	9038M/XV810	9137M/XN579	9221M/XZ966
8935M/XR713	9039M/XN586	9139M/XV863	9222M/XZ968
8937M/XX751	9040M/XZ138	9140M/XZ287	9223M/XL616
8938M/WV746	9041M/XW763	9141M/XV118	9224M/XL568
8941M/XT456	9042M/XL954	9143M/XN589	9225M/XX885
8943M/XE799	9044M/XS177	9144M/XV353	9226M/XV865
8944M/WZ791	9045M/XN636	9145M/XV863	9227M/XB812
8945M/XX818	9046M/XM349	9146M/XW299	9228M/ZD991
8946M/XZ389	9047M/XW409	9147M/XW301	9229M/ZA678
8947M/XX726	9048M/XM403	9148M/XW436	9230M/ZA676

RAF Maintenance cross-reference

9231M	9239M	9247M/XV420	9254M
9232M/XV332	9241M	9248M/WB627	9255M
9233M/XZ431	9242M	9249M	9256M
9234M/XV864	9243M/XX163	9250M/162068	9257M
9236M	9244M	9251M	9258M
9237M/XF995	9245M	9252M	9259M
9238M/ZA717	9246M/XS714	9253M	9260M

Agusta A109A ZE411 of 8 Flt Army Air Corps at Netheravon.

Panavia Tornado F3 ZE830/HU of No 111 Sqn at RAF Leuchars. *PRM*

RN Landing Platform and Shore Station Code-letters

Code	Deck Letters	Vessel Name & Pennant No	Vessel Type & Unit
—	AS	RFA *Argus* (A135)	Aviation Training ship
365/6	AY	HMS *Argyll* (F232)	Type 23 (815 Sqn)
328/9	BA	HMS *Brave* (F94)	Type 22 (815 Sqn)
514	BD	A&AEE Boscombe Down	(810 Sqn)
—	BE	RFA *Blue Rover* (A270)	Fleet tanker
333	BM	HMS *Birmingham* (D86)	Type 42 (815 Sqn)
342/3	BT	HMS *Brilliant* (F90)	Type 22 (815 Sqn)
—	BV	HMS *Black Rover* (A273)	Fleet tanker
402/3	BX	HMS *Battleaxe* (F89)	Type 22 (815 Sqn)
335	CF	HMS *Cardiff* (D108)	Type 42 (815 Sqn)
350/1	CL	HMS *Cumberland* (F85)	Type 22 (815 Sqn)
515	CM	HMS *Chatham* (F87)	Type 22 (810 Sqn)
338/9	CT	HMS *Campbeltown* (F86)	Type 22 (815 Sqn)
—	CU	RNAS Culdrose (HMS *Seahawk*)	
336/7	CV	HMS *Coventry* (F98)	Type 22 (815 Sqn)
412/3	CW	HMS *Cornwall* (F99)	Type 22 (815 Sqn)
—	DC	HMS *Dumbarton Castle* (P268)	Fishery protection
—	DG	RFA *Diligence* (A132)	Maintenance
411	EB	HMS *Edinburgh* (D97)	Type 42 (815 Sqn)
434/5	ED	HMS *Endurance* (A176)	Ice Patrol (815 Sqn)
420	EX	HMS *Exeter* (D89)	Type 42 (815 Sqn)
—	FA	RFA *Fort Austin* (A386)	Support ship
—	FG	RFA *Fort Grange* (A385)	Support ship
—	FL	RNAY Fleetlands	
—	FS	HMS *Fearless* (L10)	Assault
410	GC	HMS *Gloucester* (D96)	Type 42 (815 Sqn)
—	GD	RFA *Sir Galahad* (L3005)	Landing ship
—	GN	RFA *Green Rover* (A268)	Fleet tanker
—	GR	RFA *Sir Geraint* (L3027)	Landing ship
437	GT	HMS *Grafton* (F241)	Type 23 (815 Sqn)
—	GV	RFA *Gold Rover* (A271)	Fleet tanker
344	GW	HMS *Glasgow* (D88)	Type 42 (815 Sqn)
—	GY	RFA *Grey Rover* (A269)	Fleet tanker
—	HC	HMS *Hecla* (A133)	Survey ship
—	HR	HMS *Herald*	Survey ship
—	ID	HMS *Intrepid* (L11)	Assault
404	IR	HMS *Iron Duke* (F234)	Type 23 (815 Sqn)
—	L	HMS *Illustrious* (R06)	Carrier
457	LA	HMS *Lancaster* (F229)	Type 23 (815 Sqn)
—	LC	HMS *Leeds Castle* (P258)	Fishery protection
405/6	LO	HMS *London* (F95)	Type 22 (815 Sqn)
332	LP	HMS *Liverpool* (D92)	Type 42 (815 Sqn)
363/4	MA	HMS *Marlborough* (F233)	Type 23 (815 Sqn)
360	MC	HMS *Manchester* (D95)	Type 42 (815 Sqn)
415	MM	HMS *Monmouth* (F235)	Type 23 (815 Sqn)
444	MR	HMS *Montrose* (F236)	Type 23 (815 Sqn)
—	N	HMS *Invincible* (R05)	Carrier
345	NC	HMS *Newcastle* (D87)	Type 42 (815 Sqn)
361/2	NF	HMS *Norfolk* (F230)	Type 23 (815 Sqn)
372	NL	HMS *Northumberland* (F238)	Type 23 (815 Sqn)
417	NM	HMS *Nottingham* (D91)	Type 42 (815 Sqn)
—	OD	RFA *Olmeda* (A124)	Fleet tanker
—	ON	RFA *Olna* (A123)	Fleet tanker
—	OW	RFA *Olwen* (A122)	Fleet tanker
—	PO	RNAS Portland (HMS *Osprey*)	
—	PV	RFA *Sir Percival* (L3036)	Landing ship
—	PW	Prestwick Airport (HMS *Gannet*)	
—	R	HMS *Ark Royal* (R09)	Carrier
—	RG	RFA *Regent* (A486)	Support ship
474	RM	HMS *Richmond* (F239)	Type 23 (815 Sqn)
—	RS	RFA *Resource* (A480)	Support ship
352/3	SD	HMS *Sheffield* (F96)	Type 23 (815 Sqn)
355	SM	HMS *Somerset* (F240)	Type 23 (815 Sqn)
334	SN	HMS *Southampton* (D90)	Type 42 (815 Sqn)
422	SU	HMS *Sutherland* (F242)	Type 23 (815 Sqn)
—	TM	RFA *Sir Tristram* (L3505)	Landing ship
374/5	VB	HMS *Beaver* (F93)	Type 22 (815 Sqn)

RN Landing Platforms

Code	Deck Letters	Vessel Name & Pennant No	Vessel Type & Unit
—	VL	RNAS Yeovilton (HMS *Heron*)	
462	WM	HMS *Westminster* (F237)	Type 23 (815 Sqn)
376	XB	HMS *Boxer* (F92)	Type 22 (815 Sqn)
407	YK	HMS *York* (D98)	Type 42 (815 Sqn)
—	—	RFA *Fort Victoria* (A387)	Auxiliary Oiler
—	—	RFA *Fort George* (A388)	Auxiliary Oiler

Shorts Tucano T1 ZF417 of No 1 FTS touching down at Biggin Hill following an airshow display. *PRM*

WS Lynx AH9 ZG921 of AAC No 659 Sqn based at Wattisham. *D. J. March*

	0	1	2	3	4	5	6	7	8	9
32									BA	BA
33			LP	BM	SN	CF	CV	CV	CT	CT
34			BT	BT	GW	NC				
35	CL	CL	SD	SD		SM				
36	MC	NF	NF	MA	MA	AY	AY			
37			NL		VB	VB	XB			
40			BX	BX	IR	LO	LO	YK		
41	GC	EB	CW	CW		MM		NM		
42	EX		SU							
43					ED	ED		GT		
44					MR					
45								LA		
46			WM							
47					RM					

RN Code – Squadron – Base – Aircraft Cross-Check

Deck/Base Code Numbers	Letters	Unit	Location	Aircraft Type(s)
000 — 005	R	801 Sqn	Yeovilton	Sea Harrier FA2
010 — 020	L/R	820 Sqn	Culdrose	Sea King HAS6
122 — 129	N	800 Sqn	Yeovilton	Sea Harrier FA2
180 — 188	L/R	849 Sqn	Culdrose	Sea King AEW2A/HU5
264 — 274	N	814 Sqn	Culdrose	Sea King HAS6
300 — 308	PO	815 Sqn	Portland	Lynx HAS3
320 — 479	*	815 Sqn	Portland	Lynx HAS3/HMA8
500 — 515	CU	810 Sqn	Culdrose	Sea King HAS6
538 — 559	CU	705 Sqn	Culdrose	Gazelle HT2
560 — 575	CU	750 Sqn	Culdrose	Jetstream T2
576 — 579	—	FONA	Yeovilton	Jetstream T3
580 — 599	—	706 Sqn	Culdrose	Sea King HU5/HAS6
630 — 638	PO	702 Sqn	Portland	Lynx HAS3
640 — 648	PO	702 Sqn	Portland	Lynx HAS3
670 — 672	PO	815 Sqn OEU	Portland	Lynx HMA8
699 — 709	PW	819 Sqn	Prestwick	Sea King HAS6
710 — 717	VL	899 Sqn	Yeovilton	Sea Harrier FA2
718 — 722	VL	899 Sqn	Yeovilton	Harrier T4/T4N/T8
820 — 826	CU	771 Sqn	Culdrose	Sea King HU5

*See foregoing separate ships' Deck Letter Analysis
Note that only the 'last two' digits of the Code are worn by some aircraft types, especially helicopters.

Some *historic, classic and warbird* aircraft carry the markings of overseas air arms and can be seen in the UK, mainly preserved in museums and collections or taking part in air shows.

Notes	Serial	Type (other identity)	Owner/operator, location
	Argentina		
	0729	Beech T-34C Turbo Mentor	FAA Museum, stored Wroughton
	0767	Aermacchi MB339AA	Rolls-Royce Heritage Trust, Filton
	A-515	FMA IA58 Pucara (ZD485)	RAF Cosford Aerospace Museum
	A-517	FMA IA58 Pucara (G-BLRP)	Privately owned, Channel Islands
	A-522	FMA IA58 Pucara (8768M)	FAA Museum, at NE Aircraft Museum, Usworth
	A-528	FMA IA58 Pucara (8769M)	Norfolk & Suffolk Avn Museum, Flixton
	A-533	FMA IA58 Pucara (ZD486)	Museum of Army Flying, Middle Wallop
	A-549	FMA IA58 Pucara (ZD487)	Imperial War Museum, Duxford
	AE-406	Bell UH-1H Iroquois	Museum of Army Flying, Middle Wallop
	AE-409	Bell UH-1H Iroquois [656]	Museum of Army Flying, Middle Wallop
	AE-422	Bell UH-1H Iroquois	FAA Museum, RNAS Yeovilton
	Australia		
	A2-4	Supermarine Seagull V (VH-ALB)	RAF Museum, Hendon
	A8-324	Bristol 156 Beaufighter X	The Fighter Collection, Duxford
	A16-199	Lockheed Hudson IIIA (G-BEOX) [SF-R]	RAF Museum, Hendon
	A17-48	DH82A Tiger Moth (G-BPHR)	Privately owned, Swindon
	A19-144	Bristol 156 Beaufighter XIC (JM135)	The Fighter Collection, Duxford
	A92-480	GAF Jindivik 4A	DTEO Llanbedr, on display
	A92-664	GAF Jindivik 4A	Maes Artro Craft Village, Llanbedr
	Belgium		
	FT-36	Lockheed T-33A	Dumfries & Galloway Avn Mus, Dumfries
	HD-75	Hanriot HD1 (G-AFDX)	RAF Museum, Hendon
SG-3	VS379 Spitfire FR XIV (RN201/ SG-31/G-BSKP)	Privately owned, Duxford
	Brazil		
	1317	Embraer T-27 Tucano	Shorts, Belfast (engine test bed)
	Canada		
	622	Piasecki HUP-3 Retriever (51-16622/N6699D)	IHM, Weston-super-Mare
	920	VS Stranraer (CF-BXO) [Q-N]	RAF Museum, Hendon
	5450	Hawker Hurricane XII (G-TDTW)	Hawker Restorations Ltd, Milden
	9059	Bristol 149 Bolingbroke IVT	Privately owned, Portsmouth
9754	Consolidated PBY-5A Catalina (VR-BPS) [P]	Plane Sailing Ltd, Duxford
	9893	Bristol 149 Bolingbroke IVT	Imperial War Museum store, Duxford
	9940	Bristol 149 Bolingbroke IVT	Royal Scottish Mus'm of Flight, E Fortune
16693	Auster J/1N Alpha (G-BLPG) [693]	Privately owned, Headcorn
18013	DHC1 Chipmunk 22 (G-TRIC) [013]	Privately owned, North Weald
	18393	Avro Canada CF-100 (G-BCYK)	Imperial War Museum, Duxford
18671	DHC1 Chipmunk 22 (WP905/ 7438M/G-BNZC) [671]	Privately owned, Wombleton
20310	CCF T-6J Harvard IV (G-BSBG)	Privately owned, Liverpool
20385	CCF T-6J Harvard IV (G-BGPB)	The Aircraft Restoration Co, Duxford
	21417	Canadair CT-133 Silver Star	Yorkshire Air Museum, Elvington
	23140	Canadair CL-13 Sabre [AX] (fuselage)	Midland Air Museum, Coventry
	23380	Canadair CL-13 Sabre <rf>	RAF Millom Museum, Haverigg
	China		
	1532008	Nanchang CJ-6A Chujiao (G-BVFX) [08]	Privately owned, Slinfold
	2232028	Nanchang CJ-6A Chujiao (G-BVVF) [69]	Privately owned, Bishop Auckland

Serial	Type (other identity)	Owner/operator, location	Notes
Czech Republic			
3677	Letov S-102 (MiG-15) (613677)	Royal Scottish Museum of Flight, E Fortune	
3794	Letov S-102 (MiG-15) (623794)	Imperial War Museum, Duxford	
9147	Mil Mi-4	IHM, Weston-super-Mare	
Denmark			
A-011	SAAB A-35XD Draken	NATO Aircraft Museum, New Waltham, Humberside	
AR-107	SAAB S-35XD Draken	Newark Air Museum, Winthorpe	
E-402	Hawker Hunter F51	Privately owned, Staverton	
E-409	Hawker Hunter F51 (*XF383*)	City of Norwich Aviation Museum	
E-419	Hawker Hunter F51	North-East Aircraft Museum, Usworth	
E-420	Hawker Hunter F51 (G-9-442)	Privately owned, Walton-on-Thames	
E-421	Hawker Hunter F51	Brooklands Museum, Weybridge	
E-423	Hawker Hunter F51 (G-9-444)	SWWAPS, Lasham	
E-424	Hawker Hunter F51 (G-9-445)	South Yorkshire Avn Museum, Firbeck	
E-425	Hawker Hunter F51	Midland Air Museum, Coventry	
E-430	Hawker Hunter F51	Vallance By-Ways, Charlwood, Surrey	
ET-272	Hawker Hunter T7 <ff>	Phoenix Aviation, Bruntingthorpe	
ET-273	Hawker Hunter T7 <ff>	South Yorkshire Avn Museum, Firbeck	
L-866	Consolidated PBY-6A Catalina (8466M)	RAF Cosford Aerospace Museum	
R-756	Lockheed F-104G Starfighter	Midland Air Museum, Coventry	
S-881	Sikorsky S-55C	IHM, Weston-super-Mare	
S-882	Sikorsky S-55C	IHM, Weston-super-Mare	
S-885	Sikorsky S-55C	Privately owned,	
S-886	Sikorsky S-55C	IHM, Weston-super-Mare	
S-887	Sikorsky S-55C	IHM, Weston-super-Mare	
Egypt			
0446	Mikoyan MiG-21UM <ff>	Thameside Aviation Museum, Tilbury	
2684	Mikoyan MiG-19 <ff>		
7907	Sukhoi Su-7 <ff>	Robertsbridge Aviation Society, Mayfield	
France			
37	Nord 3400 (G-ZARA) [MAB]	Privately owned, Boston	
57	Dassault Mystäre IVA [8-MT]	Imperial War Museum, Duxford	
59	Dassault Mystäre IVA [2-SF]	Privately owned, Cardiff	
68	Nord 3400 [MHA]	Privately owned, Coventry	
70	Dassault Mystäre IVA	Midland Air Museum, Coventry	
73	Morane-Saulnier MS505 (G-BWRF)	Island Aeroplane Company, Sandown	
79	Dassault Mystäre IVA [8-NB]	Norfolk & Suffolk Avn Museum, Flixton	
83	Dassault Mystäre IVA [8-MS]	Newark Air Museum, Winthorpe	
84	Dassault Mystäre IVA [8-NF]	Lashenden Air Warfare Museum, Headcorn	
85	Dassault Mystäre IVA [8-MV]	British Aviation Heritage, Bruntingthorpe	
101	Dassault Mystäre IVA [8-MN]	Bomber County Aviation Museum, Hemswell	
FR108	SO1221 Djinn [CDL]	IHM, Weston-super-Mare	
120	SNCAN Stampe SV4C (G-AZGC)	Privately owned, Reading	
121	Dassault Mystäre IVA	City of Norwich Aviation Museum	
143	Morane-Saulnier MS733 Alcyon (G-MSAL)	Privately owned, Booker	
FR145	SO1221 Djinn [CDL]	Privately owned,	
146	Dassault Mystäre IVA [8-MC]	North-East Aircraft Museum, Usworth	
192	MH1521M Broussard (G-BKPT) [44-GI]	Privately owned, Rednal	
290	Dewoitine D27 (F-AZJD)	The Old Flying Machine Company, Duxford	
318	Dassault Mystäre IVA [8-NY]	Dumfries & Galloway Avn Mus, Dumfries	
319	Dassault Mystäre IVA [8-ND]	Rebel Air Museum, Andrewsfield	
396	Stampe SV4A (G-BWRE)	Island Aeroplane Company, Sandown	
538	Dassault Mirage IIIE	Yorkshire Air Museum, Elvington	
1197	Bleriot XI <R> (G-BPVE)	Bianchi Avn Film Services, Booker	
S3398	Spad XIII <R> (G-BFYO) [2]	American Air Museum, Duxford	
42157	NA F-100D Super Sabre [11-ML]	North-East Aviation Museum, Usworth	
42204	NA F-100D Super Sabre [11-MQ]		
63938	NA F-100F Super Sabre [11-MU]	Lashenden Air Warfare Museum, Headcorn	
18-1528	PA-18 Cub 95 (F-MBCH)	Privately owned, stored Southampton	
MS824	Morane-Saulnier Type N <R> (G-AWBU)	Privately owned, Booker	

Historic Aircraft

Notes	Serial	Type (other identity)	Owner/operator, location
	Germany		
—		Fieseler Fi103 (V-1) (BAPC 36)	Kent Battle of Britain Mus'm, Hawkinge
—		Fieseler Fi103R-IV (V-1) (BAPC 91)	Lashenden Air Warfare Museum, Headcorn
—		Fieseler Fi103 (V-1) (BAPC 92)	RAF Museum, Hendon
—		Fieseler Fi103 (V-1) (BAPC 93)	Imperial War Museum, Duxford
—		Fieseler Fi103 (V-1) (8583M/ BAPC 94)	RAF Cosford Aerospace Museum
—		Fieseler Fi103 (V-1) (BAPC 158)	Defence School, Chattenden
—		Fieseler Fi103 (V-1) (BAPC 237)	RAF Museum Restoration Centre, Cardington
—		Focke-Achgelis Fa330A-1 (8469M)	RAF Cosford Aerospace Museum
	3	SNCAN 1101 Noralpha (G-BAYV)	Macclesfield Historical Av Soc, Barton
	4	Focke Wulf Fw190 <R> (G-BSLX)	Privately owned, Carlisle
	7	Klemm Kl35D (G-BWRD)	Island Aeroplane Company, Sandown
	8	Focke Wulf Fw190 <R> (G-WULF)	The Real Aeroplane Company, Breighton
	14	Fiat G46-3B (G-BBII)	Privately owned, stored Staverton
	14	Messerschmitt Bf109 <R> (BAPC 67)	Kent Battle of Britain Museum, Hawkinge
	14	Pilatus P-2 (G-BJAX)	Privately owned, stored Duxford
	102/17	Fokker Dr1 Dreidekker <R> (BAPC 88)	FAA Museum, RNAS Yeovilton
	114	SNCAN 1101 Noralpha (G-BSMD)	The Old Flying Machine Company, Duxford
	152/17	Fokker Dr1 Dreidekker <R> (G-ATJM)	
	210/16	Fokker EIII (BAPC 56)	Science Museum, South Kensington
	422/15	Fokker EIII <R> (G-AVJO)	Privately owned, Booker
	425/17	Fokker Dr1 Dreidekker <R> (BAPC 133)	Kent Battle of Britain Museum, Hawkinge
	425/17	Fokker Dr1 Dreidekker <R> (G-BWRJ)	Island Aeroplane Company, Sandown
	450/17	Fokker Dr1 Dreidekker <R> (G-BVGZ)	Museum of Army Flying, Middle Wallop
	626/18	Fokker DVII <R> (N6268)	Blue Max Movie Aircraft Museum, Booker
	959	Mikoyan MiG-21SPS	Old Flying Machine Company, Duxford
	1190	Messerschmitt Bf109E-3	Privately owned, Bournemouth
	1227	Focke-Wulf Fw190A-5 (G-FOKW) [OG+HO]	Flying A Services
	1480	Messerschmitt Bf109 <R> (BAPC 66) [6]	Kent Battle of Britain Museum, Hawkinge
	3235	Messerschmitt Bf110C-4 [LN+ER]	Sussex Spraying Services, Lancing
	3579	Messerschmitt Bf109E-1	Charleston Aviation Services, Colchester
	4101	Messerschmitt Bf109E-3 (DG200/8477M) [12]	RAF Museum, Hendon
	4502	Messerschmitt Bf110E-2 [M8+ZE]	Sussex Spraying Services, Lancing
	5052	Messerschmitt Bf110F-2	Sussex Spraying Services, Lancing
	5858	Junkers Ju87R-4 [L1+BL]	Privately owned, Milden
	6357	Messerschmitt Bf109 <R> (BAPC 74) [6]	Kent Battle of Britain Museum, Hawkinge
	7198/18	LVG CVI (G-AANJ)	The Shuttleworth Collection, Old Warden
	8147	Messerschmitt Bf109F-4	Charleston Aviation Services, Colchester
	8417/18	Fokker DVII (9207M)	RAF Museum Restoration Centre, Cardington
	10132	Messerschmitt Bf109F-4	Privately owned, Milden
	10639	Messerschmitt Bf109G-2/Trop (RN228/8478M/G-USTV) [6]	Imperial War Museum, Duxford
	12802	Antonov An-2T (D-FOFM)	Island Aeroplane Company, Sandown
	28368	Flettner Fl282/B-V20 Kolibri (frame only)	Midland Air Museum, Coventry
	100143	Focke-Achgelis Fa330A-1	Imperial War Museum, Duxford
	100502	Focke-Achgelis Fa330A-1	The Real Aeroplane Company, Breighton
	100509	Focke-Achgelis Fa330A-1	Science Museum, stored South Kensington
	100545	Focke-Achgelis Fa330A-1	Fleet Air Arm Museum stored, Wroughton
	100549	Focke-Achgelis Fa330A-1	Lashenden Air Warfare Museum, Headcorn
	112372	Messerschmitt Me262A-2a (AM.51/VK893/8482M) [9K-XK]	RAF Cosford Aerospace Museum
	120227	Heinkel He162A-2 Salamander (VH513/8472M) [2]	RAF Museum, Hendon
	120235	Heinkel He162A-1 Salamander (AM.68)	Imperial War Museum, Lambeth

Serial	Type (other identity)	Owner/operator, location	Notes
151591	Messerschmitt Bf109G-10 (D-HDME) [2]	Privately owned, Duxford	
166238	Hispano HA1.112MIL Buchon (G-BOML) [3]	The Old Flying Machine Company, Duxford	
191316	Messerschmitt Me163B Komet	Science Museum, South Kensington	
191614	Messerschmitt Me163B Komet (8481M)	RAF Cosford Aerospace Museum	
191659	Messerschmitt Me163B Komet (8480M) [15]	Royal Scottish Mus'm of Flight, E Fortune	
191660	Messerschmitt Me163B Komet [3]	Imperial War Museum, Duxford	
360043	Junkers Ju88R-1 (PJ876/8475M) [D5+EV]	RAF Museum, Hendon	
420430	Messerschmitt Me410A-1/U2 (AM.72/8483M) [3U+CC]	RAF Cosford Aerospace Museum	
477663	Fieseler Fi103 (V-1) (BAPC 198)	Imperial War Museum, Lambeth	
442795	Fieseler Fi103 (V-1) (BAPC 199)	Science Museum, South Kensington	
475081	Fieseler Fi156C-7 Storch (VP546/ AM.101/7362M)[GM+AK]	RAF Cosford Aerospace Museum	
494083	Junkers Ju87D-3 (8474M) [RI+JK]	RAF Museum, Hendon	
584219	Focke Wulf Fw190F-8/U1 (AM.29/8470M) [38]	RAF Museum, Hendon	
701152	Heinkel He111H-23 (8471M) [NT+SL]	RAF Museum, Hendon	
730301	Messerschmitt Bf110G-4 (AM.34/8479M) [D5+RL]	RAF Museum, Hendon	
733682	Focke Wulf Fw190A-8/R7 (AM.75/9211M)	Imperial War Museum, Lambeth	
1Z+NK	Amiot AAC1/Ju52 (Port.AF 6316)	Imperial War Museum, Duxford	
2+1	Focke Wulf Fw190 <R> (G-SYFW) [7334]	Privately owned, Guernsey, CI	
20+48	Mikoyan MiG-23BN [702]	DTEO Boscombe Down	
22+35	Lockheed F-104G Starfighter	SWWAPS, Lasham	
22+57	Lockheed F-104G Starfighter	NATO Aircraft Museum, New Waltham, Humberside	
28+02	Aero L-39ZO Albatros (140/G-BWTS)	Aces High Ltd, North Weald	
28+10	Aero L-39ZO Albatros (150/G-BWTT)	Aces High Ltd, North Weald	
96+21	Mil Mi-24D	Imperial War Museum, Duxford	
96+26	Mil Mi-24D	IHM, Weston-super-Mare	
97+04	Putzer Elster B (G-APVF)	Privately owned, Tadlow	
6J+PR	CASA 2.111D (G-AWHB)	Aces High Ltd, North Weald	
AM+YA	Zlin Z381 Bestmann (G-AMYA)	Privately owned, Wombleton, N Yorks	
BU+CC	CASA 1.131E Jungmann (G-BUCC)	Privately owned, Goodwood	
BU+CK	CASA 1.131E Jungmann (G-BUCK)	Privately owned, White Waltham	
C850	Albatros DV <R>	Macclesfield Hist Avn Society	
CC+43	Pilatus P-2 (G-CJCI)	Privately owned, Norwich	
CF+HF	Morane-Saulnier MS502 (EI-AUY)	Imperial War Museum, Duxford	
D5397/17	Albatros DVA <R> (G-BFXL)	FAA Museum, RNAS Yeovilton	
FI+S	Morane-Saulnier MS505 (G-BIRW)	Royal Scottish Mus'm of Flight, E Fortune	
JA+120	Canadair CL-13 Sabre 4 (MM19607)	Privately owned	
LG+01	Bücker Bü133C Jungmeister (G-AYSJ)	The Fighter Collection, Duxford	
LG+03	Bücker Bü133C Jungmeister (G-AEZX)	Privately owned, Milden	
NJ+C11	Nord 1002 (G-ATBG)	Privately owned, Duxford	
S5+B06	CASA 1.131E Jungmann 2000 (G-BSFB)	Privately owned, Stretton	
TA+RC	Morane-Saulnier MS505 (G-BPHZ)	The Aircraft Restoration Co, Duxford	
TQ+BJ	Focke-Wulf Fw44 Stieglitz (LV-ZAU)	Privately owned, Booker	

Ghana

Serial	Type (other identity)	Owner/operator, location	Notes
G-102	SA122 Bulldog	Privately owned, Henstridge	
G-103	SA122 Bulldog (G-BWIB)	Privately owned, Henstridge	
G-105	SA122 Bulldog	Privately owned, Henstridge	
G-107	SA122 Bulldog (G-BCUO)	Privately owned, Henstridge	
G-108	SA122 Bulldog (G-BCUP)	Privately owned, Henstridge	
G-112	SA122 Bulldog (G-BCUV)	Privately owned, Henstridge	

Notes	Serial	Type (other identity)	Owner/operator, location
	Greece		
	51-6171	NA F-86D Sabre	North-East Aircraft Museum, Usworth
	52-6541	Republic F-84F Thunderflash [541]	North-East Aircraft Museum, Usworth
	Hong Kong		
	HKG-5	SA128 Bulldog (G-BULL)	Privately owned, Slinfold
	Hungary		
	501	Mikoyan MiG-21PF	Imperial War Museum, Duxford
	503	Mikoyan MiG-21SMT (G-BRAM)	Aces High Ltd, North Weald
	India		
	Q497	EE Canberra T4 (fuselage)	BAe Warton Fire Service
	Iraq		
	243	Hawker Fury FB10 (G-BTTA)	The Old Flying Machine Co, Duxford
	333	DH115 Vampire T55	Military Aircraft Pres'n Grp, Barton
	26186	Bell 214ST (tail only)	Museum of Army Flying, Middle Wallop
	Israel		
	41	NA P-51D Mustang (G-LYNE)	Privately owned, Teesside
	Italy		
	MM5701	Fiat CR42 (BT474/8468M) [13-95]	RAF Museum, Hendon
	MM53432	NA T-6D Texan [RM-11]	Privately owned, South Wales
	MM53692	CCF T-6G Texan	RAeS Medway Branch, Rochester
	MM54099	NA T-6G Texan (G-BRBC) [RR-56]	Privately owned, Chigwell
	MM54-2372	PA-18 Super Cub 95	Privately owned,
	W7	Avia FL3 (G-AGFT)	Privately owned, Leicester
	Japan		
	—	Yokosuka MXY 7 Ohka II (BAPC 159)	Defence School, Chattenden
	24	Kawasaki Ki100-1B (8476M/ BAPC 83)	RAF Cosford Aerospace Museum
	5439	Mitsubishi Ki46-III (8484M/ BAPC 84)	RAF Cosford Aerospace Museum
	15-1585	Yokosuka MXY 7 Ohka II (BAPC 58)	Science Museum, at FAA Museum, RNAS Yeovilton
	997	Yokosuka MXY 7 Ohka II (8485M/ BAPC 98)	Gr Manchester Mus of Science & Industry
	I-13	Yokosuka MXY 7 Ohka II (8486M/ BAPC 99)	RAF Cosford Aerospace Museum
	Jordan		
	109	DH100 Vampire FB6 (J-1106/ G-BVPO)	RJAF Historic Flight, Bournemouth
	209	DH115 Vampire T55 (U-1216/ G-BVLM/ZH563)	RJAF Historic Flight, Bournemouth
	712	Hawker Hunter F58 (J-4025/ G-BWKC) [E]	RJAF Historic Flight, Bournemouth
	800	Hawker Hunter T7 (G-BOOM) [F]	RJAF Historic Flight, Bournemouth
	843	Hawker Hunter F58 (J-4075/ G-BWKA) [H]	RJAF Historic Flight, Bournemouth
	Netherlands		
	204	Lockheed SP-2H Neptune [V]	RAF Cosford Aerospace Museum
	361	Hawker Fury FB10 (N36SF)	Privately owned, Bournemouth
	B-168	Noorduyn AT-16 Harvard IIB (FE984)	British Aerial Museum, Duxford (spares use)
	E-15	Fokker S-11 Instructor (G-BIYU)	Privately owned, White Waltham
	E-31	Fokker S-11 Instructor (G-BEPV)	Privately owned, Elstree
	N-202	Hawker Hunter F6 [10] <ff>	Privately owned, Eaglescott
	N-250	Hawker Hunter F6 (G-9-185) <ff>	Science Museum, Wroughton
	N-268	Hawker Hunter FGA78 (Qatar QA-10)	Yorkshire Air Museum, Elvington
	N-315	Hawker Hunter T7	Jet Avn Preservation Grp, Long Marston
	R-163	Piper L-21B Super Cub (54-2453/ G-BIRH)	Privately owned, Lee-on-Solent
	R-167	Piper L-21B Super Cub (54-2457/ G-LION)	Privately owned, Turweston, Bucks

Serial	Type (other identity)	Owner/operator, location	Notes
New Zealand			
NZ5648	Goodyear FG-1D Corsair (NX55JP) [648]	Old Flying Machine Co, Duxford	
North Korea			
1211	WSK Lim-5 (MiG-17F) (G-BWUF)	The Old Flying Machine Company, Duxford	
Norway			
56321	SAAB S91B Safir (G-BKPY) [U-AB]	Newark Air Museum, Winthorpe	
Poland			
05	WSK SM-2 (Mi-2) (1005)	IHM, Weston-super-Mare	
07	WSK SM-1 (Mi-1) (2007)	IHM, Weston-super-Mare	
309	WSK SBLim-2A (MiG-15UTI) <ff>	Royal Scottish Museum of Flight, E Fortune	
1018	WSK TS-11 Iskra (1H-1018)	British Aviation Heritage, Bruntingthorpe	
1120	WSK Lim-2 (MiG-15bis)	RAF Museum, Hendon	
1408	WSK TS-11 Iskra (3H-1408)	The Old Flying Machine Company, Duxford	
09008	WSK SBLim-2A (MiG-15UTI)	Privately owned, Bruntingthorpe	
Portugal			
1345	OGMA/DHC1 Chipmunk T20 (CS-DAQ/G-OACP)	Privately owned, Spanhoe Lodge	
1360	OGMA/DHC1 Chipmunk T20 (CS-DAP)	Privately owned, Spanhoe Lodge	
1366	OGMA/DHC1 Chipmunk T20 (CS-DAO)	Privately owned, Spanhoe Lodge	
1367	OGMA/DHC1 Chipmunk T20	Privately owned, Spanhoe Lodge	
1377	DHC1 Chipmunk 22 (G-BARS)	Privately owned, Wombleton	
1741	CCF Harvard IV (G-HRVD)	Air Atlantique Historic Flight, Coventry	
Qatar			
QA12	Hawker Hunter FGA78 <ff>	The Planets Leisure Centre, Woking	
QP30	WS Lynx Mk 28 (G-BFDV/TD013)	AAC SEAE, Arborfield	
QP31	WS Lynx Mk 28	RNAY Fleetlands Apprentice School	
QP32	WS Lynx Mk 28	RN, stored RNAY Fleetlands	
Russia (& former Soviet Union)			
2	Yakovlev Yak-52 (9311708/ G-YAKS)	Privately owned, North Weald	
03	Mil Mi-24D (3532461715415)	Privately owned, Hawarden	
04	Mikoyan MiG-23ML (024003607)	Privately owned, Hawarden	
04	Yakovlev Yak-52 (9211612/ RA-22521)	Privately owned, Wellesbourne Mountford	
05	Yakovlev Yak-50 (832507/ YL-CBH)	Privately owned, Hawarden	
06	Let L-29 Delfin (591636/YL-PAE)	Privately owned, Cumbernauld	
06	Mil Mi-24D (3532464505029)	Privately owned, Hawarden	
07	Yakovlev Yak-18M (G-BMJY)	Privately owned, North Weald	
09	Let L-29 Delfin (591378/YL-PAD)	Privately owned, Cumbernauld	
12	Let L-29 Delfin (194555/ES-YLM)	Privately owned, Manston	
15	Yakovlev Yak-52 (844605/ G-BVVW)	Privately owned, Sudbury, Suffolk	
18	Let L-29 Delfin (591771/YL-PAF)	Privately owned, Hawarden	
19	Yakovlev Yak-52 (811202/YL-CBI)	Privately owned, Hawarden	
20	Lavochkin La-11	The Fighter Collection, Duxford	
20	Yakovlev Yak-52 (790404/YL-CBJ)	Privately owned, Hawarden	
23	Mikoyan MiG-27D (83712515040)	Privately owned, Hawarden	
26	Yakovlev Yak-52 (9111306/ G-BVXK)	Privately owned, White Waltham	
27	SPP Yak C-11 (G-OYAK)	Privately owned, North Weald	
31	Yakovlev Yak-52 (9111311)	Privately owned, Rendcomb	
35	Sukhoi Su-17M-3 (25102)	Privately owned, Hawarden	
37	Let L-29 Delfin (491119/YL-PAA)	Privately owned, Cumbernauld	
40	Let L-29 Delfin (491165/YL-PAB)	Privately owned, Cumbernauld	
40	Yakovlev Yak-55M (RA-01333)	Privately owned,	
42	Yakovlev Yak-52 (LY-AMU)	Privately owned, North Weald	
43	Yakovlev Yak-52 (877601/ G-BWSV)	Privately owned, Sudbury, Suffolk	
46	Yakovlev Yak-52 (9111413/) RA-44413	Privately owned, White Waltham	

Historic Aircraft

Notes	Serial	Type (other identity)	Owner/operator, location
	50	Mikoyan MiG-23MF (023003508)	Privately owned, Hawarden
	51	Let L-29 Delfin (491273/YL-PAG)	Privately owned, Hawarden
	51	Yakovlev Yak-50 (812004/ G-BWYK)	Privately owned, Little Gransden
	52	Yakovlev Yak-52 (877610/ G-BVVA)	Privately owned, Fowlmere, Herts
	52	Yakovlev Yak-52 (878202/ G-BWVR)	Privately owned, Sowerby Bridge, West Yorkshire
	53	Curtiss P-40C Warhawk (41-13390)	The Fighter Collection, Duxford
	54	Sukhoi Su-17M (69004)	Privately owned, Hawarden
	55	Yakovlev Yak-52 (9111505/ G-BVOK)	Intrepid Aviation, North Weald
	56	Yakovlev Yak-52 (811504/LY-AKW)	Privately owned, Strathallan
	56	Yakovlev Yak-52 (9111506/ RA-44516)	Privately owned, White Waltham
	69	Yakovlev Yak-50 (G-BTZB)	The Fighter Collection, Duxford
	69	Yakovlev Yak-52 (855509/LY-ALS)	Privately owned, North Weald
	71	Mikoyan MiG-27K (61912507006)	Privately owned, Hawarden
	72	Yakovlev Yak-52 (9111608/ RA-01325)	Privately owned, Newcastle
	88	Yakovlev Yak-52 (866807/ G-BWSW)	Privately owned, Sudbury, Suffolk
	100	Yakovlev Yak-52 (866904/G-YAKI)	Privately owned, Popham
	112	Yakovlev Yak-52 (822610/LY-AFB)	Privately owned, Little Gransden
	1342	Yakovlev Yak-1 (G-BTZD)	Privately owned, Audley End
	6247	WSK SBLim-2A (MiG-15UTI) (622047/G-OMIG)	The Old Flying Machine Company, Duxford
	165221	WSK-Mielec An-2T (G-BTCU) [77]	Privately owned, Henstridge
	899404	Yakovlev Yak-52 (G-CCCP)	Privately owned, Little Gransden
	1-12	Yakovlev Yak-52 (9011013/ RA-02293)	Privately owned, Halfpenny Green
	(RK858)	VS361 Spitfire LF IX	The Fighter Collection, Duxford
	(SM639)	VS361 Spitfire LF IX	Privately owned, Norwich

Singapore

Notes	Serial	Type (other identity)	Owner/operator, location
	311	BAC Strikemaster 84 (N2146S/ G-SARK)	Classic Jets Flying Museum, Biggin Hill

Slovakia

Notes	Serial	Type (other identity)	Owner/operator, location
	7708	Mikoyan MiG-21MF	RAF Benevolent Fund, DTEO Boscombe Down

South Africa

Notes	Serial	Type (other identity)	Owner/operator, location
	6130	Lockheed Ventura II (AJ469)	RAF Cosford Aerospace Museum, stored

Spain

Notes	Serial	Type (other identity)	Owner/operator, location
	B.21-103	CASA 2.111B (He111H-16)	Old Flying Machine Company, Spain
	C.4E-88	Messerschmitt Bf109E	Privately owned, Hungerford
	E.1-9	CASA 1.133L Jungmeister (G-BVXJ)	The Real Aeroplane Company, Breighton
	E.3B-153	CASA 1.131E Jungmann (G-BPTS) [781-75]	Old Flying Machine Company, Duxford
	(E.3B-369)	CASA 1.131E Jungmann (G-BPDM) [781-32]	Privately owned, Chilbolton
	(E.3B-540)	CASA 1.131E Jungmann (G-BRSH) [781-25]	The Real Aeroplane Company, Breighton
	ES.1-16	CASA 1.133L Jungmeister	Privately owned, Stretton, Cheshire
	T.9-16	DHC4 Caribou (N52NC)	Privately owned, Coventry
	T.9-19	DHC4 Caribou (N55NC)	Privately owned, Coventry
	T.9-20	DHC4 Caribou (N56NC)	Privately owned, Coventry
	T.9-22	DHC4 Caribou (N57NC)	Privately owned, Coventry

Sweden

Notes	Serial	Type (other identity)	Owner/operator, location
	05108	DH60 Moth	Privately owned, Langham
	29640	SAAB J-29F [20-08]	Midland Air Museum, Coventry
	32028	SAAB 32A Lansen (G-BMSG)	Privately owned, Cranfield
	35075	SAAB J-35J Draken [40]	Imperial War Museum, Duxford

Switzerland

Notes	Serial	Type (other identity)	Owner/operator, location
	A-10	CASA 1.131E Jungmann (G-BECW)	Privately owned, Headcorn
	A-57	CASA 1.131E Jungmann (G-BECT)	Privately owned, Shoreham
	A-806	Pilatus P3-03 (G-BTLL)	Privately owned, stored Headcorn

Serial	Type (other identity)	Owner/operator, location	Notes
C-558	EKW C-3605	Aerobuild Ltd, stored Gransden	
J-1008	DH100 Vampire FB6	Mosquito Aircraft Museum, London Colney	
J-1149	DH100 Vampire FB6 (G-SWIS)	Jet Heritage, Bournemouth	
J-1172	DH100 Vampire FB6 (8487M)	RAF Museum Restoration Centre, Cardington	
J-1573	DH112 Venom FB50 (G-VICI)	Source Classic Jet Flight, Bournemouth	
J-1605	DH112 Venom FB50 (G-BLID)	Vallance By-Ways, Charlwood, Surrey	
J-1611	DH112 Venom FB50 (G-DHTT)	Source Classic Jet Flight, Bournemouth	
J-1614	DH112 Venom FB50 (G-BLIE)	Privately owned, E Dereham, Norfolk	
J-1632	DH112 Venom FB50 (G-VNOM)	De Havilland Aviation, Swansea	
J-1704	DH112 Venom FB54	RAF Cosford Aerospace Museum, stored	
J-1712	DH112 Venom FB54	Jet Heritage, Bournemouth (dismantled)	
J-1758	DH112 Venom FB54 (N203DM)	Privately owned, North Weald	
J-4021	Hawker Hunter F58 (G-BWIU)	Historic Flying Ltd, North Weald	
J-4031	Hawker Hunter F58 (G-BWFR)	The Old Flying Machine Company, Duxford	
J-4058	Hawker Hunter F58 (G-BWFS)	The Old Flying Machine Company, Duxford	
J-4081	Hawker Hunter F58 (G-BWKB)	RJAF Historic Flight, Bournemouth	
J-4083	Hawker Hunter F58 (G-EGHH)	Jet Heritage, Bournemouth	
J-4090	Hawker Hunter F58 (G-SIAL)	Privately owned, Exeter	
J-4091	Hawker Hunter F58	British Aviation Heritage, Bruntingthorpe	
J-4105	Hawker Hunter F58A (G-BWOU)	The Old Flying Machine Company, Duxford	
U-80	Bücker Bü133D Jungmeister (G-BUKK)	Privately owned, White Waltham	
U-95	Bücker Bü133C Jungmeister (G-BVGP)	Privately owned, Rednal, Shropshire	
U-110	Pilatus P-2 (G-PTWO)	Privately owned, Earls Colne	
U-142	Pilatus P-2 (G-BONE)	Privately owned, Goudhurst	
U-1234	DH115 Vampire T55 (G-DHAV)	De Havilland Aviation, Swansea	
V-54	SE3130 Alouette II (G-BVSD)	Privately owned, Shoreham	

USA

Serial	Type (other identity)	Owner/operator, location	Notes
2	Boeing-Stearman N2S-5 Kaydet (G-AZLE)	Privately owned, Denham	
5	Boeing P-26A Peashooter <R> (G-BEEW)	Privately owned, Barton	
23	Fairchild PT-23 (N49272)	Privately owned, Halfpenny Green	
26	Boeing-Stearman A75N-1 Kaydet (G-BAVO)	Privately owned, Streethay, Lichfield	
27	NA SNJ-7 Texan (G-BRVG)	Intrepid Aviation Co, North Weald	
28	Boeing-Stearman PT-13D Kaydet (N8162G)	Privately owned, Swanton Morley	
33	Boeing-Stearman N2S-5 Kaydet (G-THEA)	Privately owned, Sutton Bridge	
41	NA T-6G Texan (G-DDMV) [BA]	Privately owned, Sywell	
44	PA-18 Super Cub 95 (G-BJLH) [33-K]	Privately owned, Felthorpe	
44	Piper L-21B Super Cub (54-2405/ G-BWHH)	Privately owned, Popham	
57	WS55 Whirlwind HAS7 (XG592)	*Task Force* Adventure Park, Cowbridge, S Glam	
85	WAR P-47 Thunderbolt <R> (N47DL/G-BTBI)	Privately owned, Carlisle	
88	NA P-51D Mustang <R>	The Old Flying Machine Company, stored Duxford	
106	Grumman F8F-2 Bearcat (N800H) [A]	The Fighter Collection, Duxford	
112	Boeing-Stearman PT-13D Kaydet (G-BSWC)	Privately owned, Old Sarum	
118	Boeing-Stearman PT-13A Kaydet (G-BSWC)	Privately owned, Swanton Morley	
208	Boeing-Stearman N2S-5 Kaydet	Privately owned, Spanhoe Lodge, Northants	
243	Boeing-Stearman A75N-1 Kaydet (G-BUKE)	Privately owned, Goodwood	
295	Ryan PT-22 Recruit (N56028)	Privately owned, Oaksey Park, Wilts	
379	Boeing-Stearman PT-13D Kaydet (G-ILLE)	Privately owned, Compton Abbas	
441	Boeing-Stearman N2S-4 Kaydet (G-BTFG)	Privately owned, Bryngwyn Bach, Clwyd	
540	Piper L-4H Grasshopper (43-29877/G-BCNX)	Privately owned, Monewden	

Historic Aircraft

Notes	Serial	Type (other identity)	Owner/operator, location
	628	Beech D17S (N18V)	Privately owned, stored North Weald
	796	Boeing-Stearman PT-13D Kaydet (N43SV)	Privately owned, Rendcomb
	854	Ryan PT-22 Recruit (G-BTBH)	Privately owned, Wellesbourne Mountford
	855	Ryan PT-22 Recruit (N56421)	Privately owned, Halfpenny Green
	897	Aeronca 11AC Chief (G-BJEV) [E]	Privately owned, English Bicknor, Glos
	1164	Beech D18S (G-BKGL)	Classic Wings, Duxford
	1180	Boeing-Stearman N2S-3 Kaydet (G-BRSK)	Privately owned, Tibenham
	1411	Grumman G44A Widgeon (N444M)	Privately owned, Biggin Hill
	2807	NA T-6G Texan (G-BHTH) [V-103]	Privately owned, Thruxton
	5547	Lockheed T-33A (19036)	Newark Air Museum, Winthorpe
	6771	Republic F-84F Thunderstreak (BAF FU-6)	RAF Cosford Aerospace Museum, stored
	7797	Aeronca L-16A (G-BFAF)	Privately owned, Finmere
	8178	NA F-86A Sabre (48-0178/ G-SABR) [FU-178]	Golden Apple Operations/OFMC, Duxford
	8242	NA F-86A Sabre (48-0242) [FU-242]	American Air Museum, Duxford
	01532	Northrop F-5E Tiger II <R>	RAF Alconbury on display
	14286	Lockheed T-33A	American Air Museum, Duxford
	O-14419	Lockheed T-33A	Midland Air Museum, Coventry
	14863	NA AT-6D Harvard III (G-BGOR)	Privately owned, Goudhurst, Kent
	15154	Bell OH-58A Kiowa (FY70)	R. Military College of Science, Shrivenham
	15195	Fairchild PT-19A Cornell	RAF Museum, stored Cardington
	16136	Boeing-Stearman A75N-1 Kaydet (G-BRUJ) [205]	Privately owned, Liverpool
	16445	Bell AH-1F Hueycobra (FY69)	R. Military College of Science, Shrivenham
	16579	Bell UH-1H Iroquois (FY66)	IHM, Weston-super-Mare
	16718	Lockheed T-33A	City of Norwich Aviation Museum
	17473	Lockheed T-33A	Midland Air Museum, Coventry
	O-17899	Convair VT-29B	Imperial War Museum, Duxford
	18169	Boeing-Stearman PT-17 Kaydet (CF-EQS)	American Air Museum, Duxford
	18263	Boeing-Stearman PT-17 Kaydet (N38940) [822]	Privately owned, Tibenham
	19252	Lockheed T-33A	Tangmere Military Aviation Museum
	24518	Kaman HH-43F Huskie (24535)	Midland Air Museum, Coventry
	28521	CCF Harvard IV (G-TVIJ) [TA-521]	The Old Flying Machine Company, Duxford
	29963	Lockheed T-33A	Privately owned, Cardiff
	30861	NA TB-25J Mitchell (N9089Z)	Privately owned, North Weald
	31145	Piper L-4B Grasshopper (G-BBLH) [G-26]	Privately owned, Biggin Hill
	31952	Aeronca O-58B Defender (G-BRPR)	Privately owned, Earls Colne
	34037	NA TB-25N Mitchell (N9115Z/ 8838M)	RAF Museum, Hendon
	37414	McD F-4C Phantom (FY63)	Midland Air Museum, Coventry
	37699	McD F-4C Phantom (FY63)	Midland Air Museum, Coventry
	38674	Thomas-Morse S4 Scout <R> (G-MTKM)	Privately owned, Rugby
	39624	Wag Aero Sport Trainer (G-BVMH) [39-D]	Privately owned, Lincoln
	40467	Grumman F6F-5K Hellcat (G-BTCC) [19]	The Fighter Collection, Duxford
	41386	Thomas-Morse S4 Scout <R> (G-MJTD)	Privately owned, Hitchin
	42163	NA F-100D Super Sabre [HE]	Dumfries & Galloway Avn Mus, Dumfries
	42165	NA F-100D Super Sabre [VM]	American Air Museum, Duxford
	42174	NA F-100D Super Sabre [UH]	Midland Air Museum, Coventry
	42196	NA F-100D Super Sabre [LT]	Norfolk & Suffolk Avn Museum, Flixton
	42223	NA F-100D Super Sabre	Newark Air Museum, Winthorpe
	46867	Grumman FM-2 Wildcat (N909WJ)	Flying A Services, Earls Colne
	53319	Grumman TBM-3R Avenger (G-BTDP) [319-RB]	Privately owned, North Weald
	54137	CCF Harvard IV (G-CTKL) [69]	Privately owned, North Weald
	54433	Lockheed T-33A	Norfolk & Suffolk Avn Museum, Flixton
	54439	Lockheed T-33A	North-East Aircraft Museum, Usworth
	60312	McDonnell F-101F Voodoo [AR]	Midland Air Museum, Coventry
	60689	Boeing B-52D Stratofortress	American Air Museum, Duxford
	63000	NA F-100D Super Sabre (42160) [FW-000]	Privately owned, Cardiff

Serial	Type (other identity)	Owner/operator, location	Notes
63000	NA F-100D Super Sabre (42212) [FW-000]	USAF Croughton, Oxon, at gate	
63319	NA F-100D Super Sabre (42269) [FW-319]	RAF Lakenheath, on display	
63428	Republic F-105G Thunderchief (24428)	USAF Croughton, Oxon, at gate	
66692	Lockheed U-2CT	American Air Museum, Duxford	
69327	Grumman TBM-3E Avenger (CF-KCG)	American Air Museum, Duxford	
70270	McDonnell F-101B Voodoo (fuselage)	Midland Air Museum, Coventry	
80425	Grumman F7F-3P Tigercat (N7235C) [WT]	The Fighter Collection, Duxford	
82062	DHC U-6A Beaver	Midland Air Museum, Coventry	
91007	Lockheed T-33A (G-NASA) [TR-007]	De Havilland Aviation, Swansea	
93542	CCF Harvard IV (G-BRLV) [LTA-542]	Privately owned, White Waltham	
111836	NA AT-6C Harvard IIA (G-TSIX) [JZ-6]	The Real Aeroplane Company, Breighton	
111989	Cessna L-19A Bird Dog (N33600)	Museum of Army Flying, Middle Wallop	
115042	NA T-6G Texan (G-BGHU) [TA-042]	Privately owned, Headcorn	
115302	Piper L-18C Super Cub (G-BJTP) [TP]	Privately owned, Winterbourne, Bristol	
115684	Piper L-21A Super Cub (G-BKVM) [DC]	Privately owned, Woodhall Spa	
121714	Grumman F8F-2P Bearcat (NX700HL) [100-S]	The Fighter Collection, Duxford	
121752	Grumman F8F-2P Bearcat (NX800H) [106-A]	The Fighter Collection, Duxford	
122179	CV F4U-5NL Corsair (N179PT)	Flying A Services, Earls Colne	
122351	Beech C-45G (51-11665/G-BKRG)	Aces High Ltd, North Weald	
124485	Boeing B-17G Fortress (G-BEDF) [DF-A]	B-17 Preservation Ltd, Duxford	
126922	Douglas AD-4NA Skyraider (G-RAID) [402-AK]	The Fighter Collection, Duxford	
140547	NA T-28C Trojan (N2800Q)	Privately owned	
146289	NA T-28C Trojan (N99153) [2W]	Norfolk & Suffolk Aviation Museum, Flixton	
150225	WS58 Wessex 60 (G-AWOX) [123]	IHM, Weston-super-Mare	
151632	NA TB-25N Mitchell (G-BWGR)	Aces High Ltd, North Weald	
153008	McD F-4N Phantom	RAF Alconbury, BDRT	
155529	McD F-4S Phantom (ZE359) [AJ-114]	American Air Museum, Duxford	
155848	McD F-4S Phantom [WT-11]	FAA Museum stored, RNAS Yeovilton	
159233	HS AV-8A Harrier [CG-33]	FAA Museum, RNAS Yeovilton	
160810	Bell AH-1T Sea Cobra <ff>	GEC, Rochester	
162068	McD AV-8B Harrier II (9250M) (fuselage)	RAF Wittering, BDRT	
162071	McD AV-8B Harrier II (fuselage)	Rolls-Royce, Filton	
211072	Boeing-Stearman PT-17 Kaydet (N50755)	Privately owned, Swanton Morley	
217786	Boeing-Stearman PT-13D Kaydet (G-BRTK) [177]	Privately owned, Old Buckenham	
219993	Bell P-39Q Airacobra (N319DP)	The Fighter Collection	
226671	Republic P-47M Thunderbolt (NX47DD)[MX-X]	The Fighter Collection, Duxford	
231983	Boeing B-17G Fortress (F-BDRS) [IY-G]	American Air Museum, Duxford	
233752	Fairchild PT-19A Cornell (G-BVCV) [52]	Privately owned, White Waltham	
236800	Piper L-4A Grasshopper (42-38410/G-BHPK) [44-A]	Privately owned, Tibenham	
237123	Waco CG-4A Hadrian (BAPC 157) (fuselage)	Yorkshire Air Museum, Elvington	
243809	Waco CG-4A Hadrian (BAPC 185)	Museum of Army Flying, Middle Wallop	
252983	Schweizer TG-3A	American Air Museum, Duxford	
269097	Bell P-63A Kingcobra (G-BTWR)	The Fighter Collection, Duxford	
314887	Fairchild Argus III (G-AJPI)	Privately owned, Swanton Morley	
315509	Douglas C-47A (G-BHUB) [W7-S]	American Air Museum, Duxford	
329405	Piper L-4H Grasshopper (G-BCOB) [23-A]	Privately owned, South Walsham	
329417	Piper L-4A Grasshopper (42-38400/G-BDHK)	Privately owned, Coleford	

Historic Aircraft

Notes	Serial	Type (other identity)	Owner/operator, location
	329471	Piper L-4H Grasshopper (G-BGXA) [44-F]	Privately owned, Martley, Worcs
	329601	Piper L-4H Grasshopper (G-AXHR) [44-D]	Privately owned, Nayland
	329854	Piper L-4H Grasshopper (G-BMKC) [44-R]	Privately owned, St Just
	329934	Piper L-4H Grasshopper (G-BCPH) [72-B]	Privately owned, White Waltham
	330238	Piper L-4H Grasshopper (G-LIVH) [24-A]	Privately owned, Barton
	330485	Piper L-4H Grasshopper (G-AJES) [44-C]	Privately owned, Saltash
	343251	Boeing-Stearman N2S-5 Kaydet (G-NZSS) [27]	Privately owned, Cumbernauld
	413573	NA P-51D Mustang (9133M/ N6526D) [B6-V]	RAF Museum, Hendon
	431171	NA B-25J Mitchell (N7614C)	American Air Museum, Duxford
	436021	Piper J-3C Cub 65 (G-BWEZ)	Privately owned, Cumbernauld
	454467	Piper L-4J Grasshopper (G-BILI) [44-J]	Privately owned, White Waltham
	454537	Piper L-4J Grasshopper (G-BFDL) [04-J]	Privately owned, Pontefract
	461748	Boeing B-29A Superfortress (G-BHDK) [Y]	American Air Museum, Duxford
	463221	NA P-51D Mustang (G-BTCD) [G4-S]	The Fighter Collection, Duxford
	472216	NA P-51D Mustang (G-BIXL) [AJ-L]	Privately owned, North Weald
	472218	CAC-18 Mustang 22 (A68-192/ G-HAEC) [WZ-I]	The Old Flying Machine Company, Duxford
	472258	NA P-51D Mustang (473979) [WZ-I]	Imperial War Museum, Lambeth
	472773	NA P-51D Mustang (G-SUSY) [AJ-C]	Privately owned, Sywell
	474008	NA P-51D Mustang (473339/ N51RR) [VF-R]	Intrepid Aviation Co, North Weald
	479744	Piper L-4H Grasshopper (G-BGPD) [49-M]	Privately owned, Enstone
	479766	Piper L-4H Grasshopper (G-BKHG) [63-D]	Privately owned, Goldcliff, Gwent
	480015	Piper L-4H Grasshopper (G-AKIB)	Privately owned, Bodmin
	480133	Piper L-4J Grasshopper (G-BDCD) [44-B]	Privately owned, Slinfold
	480321	Piper L-4J Grasshopper (G-FRAN) [44-H]	Privately owned, Rayne, Essex
	480480	Piper L-4J Grasshopper (G-BECN) [44-E]	Privately owned, Kersey, Suffolk
	480636	Piper L-4J Grasshopper (G-AXHP) [58-A]	Privately owned, Southend
	480752	Piper L-4J Grasshopper (G-BCXJ) [39-E]	Privately owned, Old Sarum
	483868	Boeing B-17G Fortress (N5237V) [A-N]	RAF Museum, Hendon
	511701A	Beech C-45H (G-BSZC) [AF258]	Privately owned, Bryngwyn Bach
	607327	PA-18 Super Cub 95 (G-ARAO) [09-L]	Privately owned, Lambley
	2-134	NA T-6G Texan (114700)	Aces High Ltd, North Weald
	3-1923	Aeronca O-58B Defender (G-BRHP)	Privately owned, Chiseldon
	18-2001	Piper L-18C Super Cub (52-2401/ G-BIZV)	Privately owned, Oxenhope
	40-1766	Boeing-Stearman PT-17 Kaydet	Privately owned, Swanton Morley
	41-33275	NA AT-6C Texan (G-BICE) [CE]	Privately owned, Ipswich
	42-12417	NA AT-16 Harvard IIB	Thameside Aviation Museum, East Tilbury
	42-58678	Taylorcraft DF-65 (G-BRIY) [IY]	Privately owned, North Weald
	42-78044	Aeronca 11AC Chief (G-BRXL)	Privately owned, High Cross, Herts
	42-84555	NA AT-6D Harvard III (FAP.1662/ G-ELMH) [EP-H]	Privately owned, Crowfield
	42-93510	Douglas C-47A Skytrain [CM] <ff>	Privately owned, Kew
	42-100611	Douglas C-47A Skytrain [4U] <ff>	Museum of Berkshire Aviation, Woodley
	43-9628	Douglas A-20G Havoc <ff>	Privately owned, Hinckley, Leics
	44-14574	NA P-51D Mustang (fuselage)	East Essex Aviation Museum, Clacton

Serial	Type (other identity)	Owner/operator, location	Notes
44-79609	Piper L-4H Grasshopper (G-BHXY) [PR]	Privately owned, Bodmin	
44-80594	Piper L-4J Grasshopper (G-BEDJ)	Privately owned, White Waltham	
45-49192	Republic P-47D Thunderbolt (N47DD)	American Air Museum, Duxford	
51-14526	NA T-6G Texan (G-BRWB)	Privately owned, Duxford	
51-15227	NA T-6G Texan (G-BKRA) [10]	Privately owned, Shoreham	
51-15673	Piper L-18C Super Cub (53-4781/ G-CUBI)	Privately owned, Felixkirk	
52-8543	CCF T-6J Harvard IV (G-BUKY) [16]	Privately owned, North Weald	
52-8578	CCF T-6J Harvard IV (D-FABE) [78]	Island Aeroplane Company, Sandown	
54-2447	Piper L-21B Super Cub (G-SCUB)	Privately owned, Anwick	
54-2474	Piper L-21B Super Cub (G-PCUB)	Privately owned, Headcorn	
54-21261	Lockheed T-33A (N33VC)	Old Flying Machine Company, Duxford	
64-17657	Douglas A-26A Invader (N99218) <ff>	Tower Museum, Ludham, Norfolk	
65-777	McD F-4C Phantom (37419) [LN]	RAF Lakenheath, on display	
67-120	GD F-111E Aardvark (70120) [UH]	American Air Museum, Duxford	
68-060	GD F-111E Aardvark (80060) <ff>	Dumfries & Galloway Avn Mus, Dumfries	
72-448	GD F-111E Aardvark (80011) [LN]	RAF Lakenheath, on display	
76-029	McD F-15A Eagle (60029)	RAF Lakenheath, BDRT	
76-124	McD F-15B Eagle (60124) [LN, 48 LSS]	RAF Lakenheath	
77-259	Fairchild A-10A Thunderbolt (70259) [AR]	American Air Museum, Duxford	
80-219	Fairchild GA-10A Thunderbolt (00219) [AR]	RAF Alconbury, on display	
92-048	McD F-15A Eagle (40131) [LN]	RAF Lakenheath, on display	
146-11042	Wolf WII <R> (G-BMZX) [7]	Privately owned, Haverfordwest	
146-11083	Wolf WII <R> (G-BNAI) [5]	Privately owned, Haverfordwest	
H-57	Piper L-4A Grasshopper (42-36375/G-AKAZ)	Privately owned, Duxford	
I-492	Ryan PT-22 Recruit (G-BPUD)	Privately owned, Swanton Morley	

Yugoslavia

Serial	Type (other identity)	Owner/operator, location	Notes
30140	Soko P-2 Kraguj (G-RADA) [140]	Privately owned,	
30146	Soko P-2 Kraguj (G-BSXD) [146]	Privately owned, Durrington, W Sussex	
30149	Soko P-2 Kraguj (G-SOKO) [149]	Privately owned, Liverpool	

North American F-86A Sabre 48-0178 owned by Golden Mile Operations and displayed by OFMC at Duxford. *D. J. March*

Notes	Serial	Type (other identity)	Owner/operator, location
	34	Miles M14A Magister (N5392)	Engineering Wing stored, Baldonnel
	141	Avro 652A Anson C19	Engineering Wing stored, Baldonnel
	164	DHC1 Chipmunk T20	Engineering Wing stored, Baldonnel
	168	DHC1 Chipmunk T20	No 2 Support Wing, Gormanston
	172	DHC1 Chipmunk T20	Training Wing stored, Gormanston
	173	DHC1 Chipmunk T20	South East Aviation Enthusiasts, Waterford
	176	DH104 Dove 4 (VP-YKF)	South East Aviation Enthusiasts, Waterford
	177	Percival P56 Provost T51 (G-BLIW)	Privately owned, Shoreham
	181	Percival P56 Provost T51	Privately owned, Thatcham
	183	Percival P56 Provost T51	Irish Aviation Museum Store, Dublin
	184	Percival P56 Provost T51	South East Aviation Enthusiasts, Waterford
	187	DH115 Vampire T55	Av'n Society of Ireland, stored, Waterford
	189	Percival P56 Provost T51	Baldonnel Fire Section
	191	DH115 Vampire T55	Irish Aviation Museum Store, Dublin
	192	DH115 Vampire T55	South East Aviation Enthusiasts, Waterford
	193	DH115 Vampire T55 <ff>	Baldonnel Fire Section
	195	Sud SA316 Alouette III	No 3 Support Wing, Baldonnel
	196	Sud SA316 Alouette III	No 3 Support Wing, Baldonnel
	197	Sud SA316 Alouette III	No 3 Support Wing, Baldonnel
	198	DH115 Vampire T11 (XE977)	Engineering Wing, Baldonnel
	199	DHC1 Chipmunk T22	Training Wing stored, Gormanston (spares)
	202	Sud SA316 Alouette III	No 3 Support Wing, Baldonnel (under repair)
	203	Reims-Cessna FR172H	No 2 Support Wing, Gormanston
	205	Reims-Cessna FR172H	No 2 Support Wing, Gormanston
	206	Reims-Cessna FR172H	No 2 Support Wing, Gormanston
	207	Reims-Cessna FR172H	No 2 Support Wing, Gormanston
	208	Reims-Cessna FR172H	No 2 Support Wing, Gormanston
	209	Reims-Cessna FR172H	No 2 Support Wing, Gormanston
	210	Reims-Cessna FR172H	No 2 Support Wing, Gormanston
	211	Sud SA316 Alouette III	No 3 Support Wing, Baldonnel
	212	Sud SA316 Alouette III	No 3 Support Wing, Baldonnel
	213	Sud SA316 Alouette III	No 3 Support Wing, Baldonnel
	214	Sud SA316 Alouette III	No 3 Support Wing, Baldonnel
	215	Fouga CM170 Super Magister	No 1 Support Wing, Baldonnel
	216	Fouga CM170 Super Magister	No 1 Support Wing, Baldonnel
	217	Fouga CM170 Super Magister	No 1 Support Wing, Baldonnel
	218	Fouga CM170 Super Magister	No 1 Support Wing, Baldonnel
	219	Fouga CM170 Super Magister	No 1 Support Wing, Baldonnel
	220	Fouga CM170 Super Magister	No 1 Support Wing, Baldonnel
	221	Fouga CM170 Super Magister [79/3-KE]	Engineering Wing, Baldonnel
	222	SIAI SF-260WE Warrior	Training Wing, Baldonnel
	225	SIAI SF-260WE Warrior	Training Wing, Baldonnel
	226	SIAI SF-260WE Warrior	Training Wing, Baldonnel
	227	SIAI SF-260WE Warrior	Training Wing, Baldonnel
	229	SIAI SF-260WE Warrior	Training Wing, Baldonnel
	230	SIAI SF-260WE Warrior	Training Wing, Baldonnel
	231	SIAI SF-260WE Warrior	Training Wing, Baldonnel
	233	SIAI SF-260MC (I-SYAS)	Engineering Wing stored, Baldonnel
	237	Aérospatiale SA341F Gazelle	Advanced FTS, Baldonnel
	240	Beech Super King Air 200	Transport & Training Squadron, Baldonnel
	241	Aérospatiale SA341F Gazelle	Advanced FTS, Baldonnel
	243	Reims-Cessna FR172K	No 2 Support Wing, Gormanston
	244	Aérospatiale SA365F Dauphin II	No 3 Support Wing, Baldonnel
	245	Aérospatiale SA365F Dauphin II	No 3 Support Wing, Baldonnel
	246	Aérospatiale SA365F Dauphin II	No 3 Support Wing, Baldonnel
	247	Aérospatiale SA365F Dauphin II	No 3 Support Wing, Baldonnel
	248	Aérospatiale SA365F Dauphin II	No 3 Support Wing, Baldonnel
	251	Grumman G1159C Gulfstream IV	Transport & Training Squadron, Baldonnel
	252	Airtech CN.235 MPA Persuader	Transport & Training Squadron, Baldonnel
	253	Airtech CN.235 MPA Persuader	Transport & Training Squadron, Baldonnel

Aircraft included in this section are a selection of those likely to be seen visiting UK civil and military airfields on transport flights, exchange visits, exercises and for air shows. It is not a comprehensive list of *all* aircraft operated by the air arms concerned.

ALGERIA
Force Aérienne Algérienne/
Al Quwwat al Jawwiya al
Jaza'eriya
    Lockheed C-130H Hercules
    4911 (7T-WHT)
    4912 (7T-WHS)
    4913 (7T-WHY)
    4914 (7T-WHZ)
    4924 (7T-WHR)
    4926 (7T-WHQ)
    4928 (7T-WHJ)
    4930 (7T-WHI)
    4934 (7T-WHF)
    4935 (7T-WHE)

    Lockheed C-130H-30
    Hercules
    4984 (7T-WHN)
    4987 (7T-WHO)
    4989 (7T-WHL)
    4997 (7T-WHA)
    5224 (7T-WHB)

AUSTRALIA
Royal Australian Air Force
    Boeing 707-338C/368C*
    33 Sqn, Amberley
    A20-261*
    A20-623
    A20-624
    A20-627
    A20-629

    Lockheed C-130H Hercules
    36 Sqn, Richmond, NSW
    A97-001
    A97-002
    A97-003
    A97-004
    A97-005
    A97-006
    A97-007
    A97-008
    A97-009
    A97-010
    A97-011
    A97-012

    Lockheed C-130E Hercules
    37 Sqn, Richmond, NSW
    A97-159
    A97-160
    A97-167
    A97-168
    A97-171
    A97-172
    A97-177
    A97-178
    A97-180
    A97-181
    A97-189
    A97-190

Lockheed P-3C/P-3W*
Orion
10/11 Sqns, Edinburgh, NSW
A9-656	11 Sqn
A9-657*	11 Sqn
A9-658	11 Sqn
A9-659	11 Sqn
A9-660*	11 Sqn
A9-661	11 Sqn
A9-662	11 Sqn
A9-663	11 Sqn
A9-664	11 Sqn
A9-665*	11 Sqn
A9-751	10 Sqn
A9-752	10 Sqn
A9-753	10 Sqn
A9-755	10 Sqn
A9-756	10 Sqn
A9-757	10 Sqn
A9-758	10 Sqn
A9-759	10 Sqn
A9-760*	10 Sqn

AUSTRIA
Öesterreichische
Luftstreitkräfte
    SAAB 105ÖE
    Fliegerregiment III
      1 Staffel/JbG, Linz
    (yellow)
    1102/B
    1104/D
    1105/E
    1106/F
    1107/G
    1108/H
    1109/I
    1110/J
    (green)
    1111/A
    1112/B
    1114/D
    1116/F
    1117/G
    1120/J
    (red)
    1122/B
    1123/C
    1124/D
    1125/E
    1126/F
    1127/G
    1128/H
    1129/I
    1130/J
    (blue)
    1131/A
    1132/B
    1133/C
    1134/D
    1135/E
    1136/F
    1137/G
    1139/I
    1140/J

    Short SC7 Skyvan 3M
    Fliegerregiment I
      Flachenstaffel, Tulln
    5S-TA
    5S-TB

BELGIUM
Force Aérienne Belge/
    Belgische Luchtmacht
    D-BD Alpha Jet E
    7/11 Smaldeel (1 Wg),
      Bevekom
    AT-01
    AT-02
    AT-03
    AT-05
    AT-06
    AT-08
    AT-09
    AT-10
    AT-11
    AT-12
    AT-13
    AT-14
    AT-15
    AT-16
    AT-17
    AT-18
    AT-19
    AT-20
    AT-21
    AT-22
    AT-23
    AT-24
    AT-25
    AT-26
    AT-27
    AT-28
    AT-29
    AT-30
    AT-31
    AT-32
    AT-33

    Boeing 727-29C
    21 Smaldeel, Melsbroek
    CB-01
    CB-02

    Dassault Falcon 900B
    21 Smaldeel, Melsbroek
    CD-01

    Swearingen Merlin IIIA
    21 Smaldeel, Melsbroek
    CF-01
    CF-02

CF-04	
CF-05	
CF-06	

Lockheed C-130H Hercules
20 Smaldeel, Melsbroek

CH-01	
CH-02	
CH-03	
CH-04	
CH-05	
CH-07	
CH-08	
CH-09	
CH-10	
CH-11	
CH-12	

Dassault Falcon 20E
21 Smaldeel, Melsbroek

CM-01	
CM-02	

Hawker-Siddeley HS748 Srs 2A
21 Smaldeel, Melsbroek

CS-01	
CS-02	
CS-03	

General Dynamics F-16A/F-16B*
1,2,350 Smaldeel, Florennes (2 Wg);
23,31,349 Smaldeel, OCU, Kleine-Brogel (10 Wg);
SABCA, Gosselies

FA-27	SABCA
FA-39	23 Sm
FA-47	349 Sm
FA-48	350 Sm
FA-49	349 Sm
FA-50	350 Sm
FA-53	349 Sm
FA-55	349 Sm
FA-56	23 Sm
FA-57	23 Sm
FA-58	23 Sm
FA-60	31 Sm
FA-61	349 Sm
FA-65	23 Sm
FA-66	31 Sm
FA-67	23 Sm
FA-68	2 Sm
FA-69	1 Sm
FA-70	2 Sm
FA-71	23 Sm
FA-72	31 Sm
FA-73	23 Sm
FA-74	31 Sm
FA-75	349 Sm
FA-76	349 Sm
FA-77	1 Sm
FA-78	31 Sm
FA-80	349 Sm
FA-81	1 Sm
FA-82	1 Sm
FA-83	349 Sm
FA-84	31 Sm
FA-86	31 Sm
FA-87	23 Sm
FA-88	350 Sm
FA-89	1 Sm
FA-90	31 Sm

FA-91	349 Sm
FA-92	31 Sm
FA-93	23 Sm
FA-94	1 Sm
FA-95	349 Sm
FA-96	1 Sm
FA-97	349 Sm
FA-98	2 Sm
FA-99	349 Sm
FA-100	349 Sm
FA-101	1 Sm
FA-102	2 Sm
FA-103	349 Sm
FA-104	23 Sm
FA-106	2 Sm
FA-107	1 Sm
FA-108	2 Sm
FA-109	1 Sm
FA-110	350 Sm
FA-111	1 Sm
FA-112	2 Sm
FA-114	349 Sm
FA-115	2 Wg
FA-116	350 Sm
FA-117	349 Sm
FA-118	2 Sm
FA-119	1 Sm
FA-120	31 Sm
FA-121	1 Sm
FA-122	2 Sm
FA-123	349 Sm
FA-124	23 Sm
FA-125	1 Sm
FA-126	349 Sm
FA-127	1 Sm
FA-128	2 Sm
FA-129	1 Sm
FA-130	2 Sm
FA-131	1 Sm
FA-132	2 Sm
FA-133	349 Sm
FA-134	2 Sm
FA-135	1 Sm
FA-136	23 Sm
FB-01*	OCU
FB-02*	OCU
FB-04*	OCU
FB-05*	OCU
FB-07*	OCU
FB-08*	OCU
FB-09*	OCU
FB-10*	OCU
FB-12*	2 Sm
FB-14*	1 Sm
FB-15*	1 Sm
FB-17*	OCU
FB-18*	OCU
FB-19*	350 Sm
FB-20*	2 Wg
FB-21*	1 Sm
FB-22*	10 Wg
FB-23*	1 Sm
FB-24*	2 Sm

Fouga CM170R Magister
33 Smaldeel (1 Wg), Bevekom

MT-04	
MT-13	
MT-14	
MT-26	
MT-30	
MT-34	
MT-35	

MT-36	
MT-37	*wfu*
MT-40	
MT-44	
MT-48	

Westland Sea King Mk48/48A*
40 Smaldeel, Koksijde

RS-01	
RS-02	
RS-03*	
RS-04	
RS-05	

SIAI Marchetti SF.260MB/SF.260D*
Ecole de Pilotage Elementaire (5 Sm/1 Wg), Bevekom

ST-02	
ST-03	
ST-04	
ST-06	
ST-09	
ST-12	
ST-15	
ST-17	
ST-18	
ST-19	
ST-20	
ST-21	
ST-22	
ST-23	
ST-24	
ST-25	
ST-26	
ST-27	
ST-30	
ST-31	
ST-32	
ST-34	
ST-35	
ST-36	
ST-40*	
ST-41*	
ST-42*	
ST-43*	
ST-44*	
ST-45*	
ST-46*	
ST-47*	
ST-48*	

Aviation Légère de la Force Terrestre/ Belgische Landmacht Sud Alouette II
16 BnHLn, Bierset; SLV, Brasschaat

A-22	16 BnHLn
A-37	16 BnHLn
A-38	*wfu*
A-40	SLV
A-41	SLV
A-42	16 BnHLn
A-43	16 BnHLn
A-44	16 BnHLn
A-45	16 BnHLn
A-46	16 BnHLn
A-47	16 BnHLn
A-49	SLV
A-50	16 BnHLn
A-53	16 BnHLn

A-54 SLV
A-55 SLV
A-57 SLV
A-59 16 BnHLn
A-61 SLV
A-62 16 BnHLn
A-64 SLV
A-65 SLV
A-66 SLV
A-68 16 BnHLn
A-70 SLV
A-72 SLV
A-73 16 BnHLn
A-74 SLV
A-75 16 BnHLn
A-77 16 BnHLn
A-78 16 BnHLn
A-79 SLV
A-80 16 BnHLn
A-81 16 BnHLn

**Britten-Norman BN-2A/
BN-2B-21* Islander**
16 BnHLn, Bierset;
SLV, Brasschaat
B-01/LA 16 BnHLn
B-02/LB SLV
B-03/LC SLV
B-04/LD SLV
B-07/LG 16 BnHLn
B-08/LH 16 BnHLn
B-09/LI* 16 BnHLn
B-10/LJ 16 BnHLn
B-11/LK SLV
B-12/LL SLV

Agusta A109HA/HO*
17 BnHATk, Bierset;
18 BnHATk, Bierset;
SLV, Brasschaat
H-01* SLV
H-02* SLV
H-03* SLV
H-04* 17 BnHATk
H-05* 17 BnHATk
H-06* 17 BnHATk
H-07* 17 BnHATk
H-08* 18 BnHATk
H-09* 18 BnHATk
H-10* 18 BnHATk
H-11* SLV
H-12* SLV
H-13* SLV
H-14* SLV
H-15* SLV
H-16* 18 BnHATk
H-17* 17 BnHATk
H-18* 18 BnHATk
H-19 17 BnHATk
H-20 18 BnHATk
H-21 18 BnHATk
H-22 17 BnHATk
H-23 18 BnHATk
H-24 17 BnHATk
H-25 18 BnHATk
H-26 18 BnHATk
H-27 18 BnHATk
H-28 18 BnHATk
H-29 18 BnHATk
H-30 18 BnHATk
H-31 18 BnHATk
H-32 18 BnHATk
H-33 18 BnHATk

H-34 17 BnHATk
H-35 17 BnHATk
H-36 17 BnHATk
H-37 17 BnHATk
H-38 17 BnHATk
H-39 18 BnHATk
H-40 18 BnHATk
H-41 17 BnHATk
H-42 17 BnHATk
H-43 17 BnHATk
H-44 17 BnHATk
H-45 17 BnHATk
H-46 17 BnHATk

Force Navale Belge/Belgische Zeemacht
SA316B Alouette III
Koksijde Heli Flight
M-1 (OT-ZPA)
M-2 (OT-ZPB)
M-3 (OT-ZPC)

Gendarmerie/Rijkswacht
Britten-Norman PBN-2T Islander
Base: Melsbroek
G-05 (OT-GLA)

Cessna 182 Skylane
Base: Melsbroek
G-01 C.182Q
G-04 C.182R

MDH MD.900 Explorer
Base: Melsbroek
G-10
G-11
G-12

Sud Alouette II
Base: Melsbroek
G-90
G-92
G-93
G-94
G-95

BRAZIL
Força Aérea Brasileira
Boeing KC-137
2º GT 2º Esq, Galeão
2401
2402
2403
2404

Lockheed C-130E Hercules
1º GT, 1º Esq, Galeão;
1º GTT, 1º Esq, Afonsos
2451 C-130E 1º GTT
2453 C-130E 1º GTT
2454 C-130E 1º GTT
2455 C-130E 1º GTT
2456 C-130E 1º GTT
2458 SC-130E 1º GT
2459 SC-130E 1º GT
2461 KC-130H 1º GT
2462 KC-130H 1º GT
2463 C-130H 1º GT
2464 C-130H 1º GT
2465 C-130H 1º GT
2466 C-130H 1º GT
2467 C-130H 1º GT

CANADA
Canadian Forces
**Lockheed CC-130E/
CC-130E(SAR)*
Hercules**
413 Sqn, Greenwood (SAR)
(14 Wing);
418 Sqn, Edmonton (SAR)
(18 Wing)
424 Sqn, Trenton (SAR)
(8 Wing);
426 Sqn, Trenton (8 Wing);
429 Sqn, Trenton (8 Wing);
435 Sqn, Edmonton
(18 Wing);
436 Sqn, Trenton (8 Wing)
130305* 8 Wing
130306* 14 Wing
130307 8 Wing
130308* 14 Wing
130310* 8 Wing
130311* 14 Wing
130313 18 Wing
130314* 8 Wing
130315 8 Wing
130316 8 Wing
130317 8 Wing
130319 18 Wing
130320 8 Wing
130323 8 Wing
130324 8 Wing
130325 8 Wing
130326 8 Wing
130327 18 Wing
130328 8 Wing

**Lockheed CC-130H/
CC-130H(T)* Hercules**
130332 8 Wing
130333 8 Wing
130334 8 Wing
130335 8 Wing
130336 8 Wing
130337 8 Wing
130338* 18 Wing
130339* 18 Wing
130340* 18 Wing
130341* 18 Wing
130342* 18 Wing

**Lockheed CC-130H-30
Hercules**
130343
130344

**Boeing CC-137
(B.707-347C)**
437 Sqn, Trenton (8 Wing)
13703
13704

Lockheed CP-140 Aurora
404/405/415 Sqns,
Greenwood (14 Wing);
407 Sqn, Comox (19 Wing)
140101 14 Wing
140102 14 Wing
140103 407 Sqn
140104 407 Sqn
140105 407 Sqn
140106 14 Wing
140107 14 Wing
140108 14 Wing
140109 14 Wing

140110	14 Wing
140111	14 Wing
140112	407 Sqn
140113	14 Wing
140114	14 Wing
140115	14 Wing
140116	407 Sqn
140117	407 Sqn
140118	14 Wing

Lockheed CP-140A Arcturus

140119	14 Wing
140120	14 Wing
140121	14 Wing

Canadair CC-144A/B/ CE-144A Challenger
412 Sqn, Ottawa-Uplands
  (7 Wing);
434 Sqn, Shearwater
  (12 Wing)

144601	CC-144A	434 Sqn
144602	CC-144A	434 Sqn
144603	CE-144A	434 Sqn
144604	CC-144A	434 Sqn
144605	CC-144A	434 Sqn
144606	CE-144A	434 Sqn
144607	CE-144A	434 Sqn
144608	CE-144A	434 Sqn
144609	CE-144A	434 Sqn
144610	CC-144A	434 Sqn
144611	CE-144A	434 Sqn
144614	CC-144B	412 Sqn
144615	CC-144B	412 Sqn
144616	CC-144B	412 Sqn

Airbus CC-150 Polaris (A310-304)
437 Sqn, Trenton (8 Wing)

15001	216
15002	212
15003	
15004	
15005	204

CHILE
Fuerza Aérea de Chile
  Boeing 707

901	321B
902	351C
903	330B
905	385C

Extra EA-300
Los Halcones

021	[1]
022	[2]
023	[3]
024	[6]
025	[5]
027	[4]
...	[7]

Lockheed C-130B/H Hercules
Grupo 10, Santiago

993	C-130B
994	C-130H
995	C-130H
996	C-130H
997	C-130B
998	C-130B
999	C-130B

CZECH REPUBLIC
Ceske Vojenske Letectvo
  Aero L-39/L-59 Albatros
  LZS 1, Lině;
  41, 42 & 43 slt/4 zSL, Cáslav;
  322 tlt/32 zTL, Náměšt;
  341 vlt/34 zSL, Pardubice;
  LZú, Praha/Kbely

0001	L-39MS	LZú
0004	L-39MS	341 vlt/34 zSL
0005	L-39MS	341 vlt/34 zSL
0006	L-39MS	341 vlt/34 zSL
0103	L-39C	341 vlt/34 zSL
0105	L-39C	341 vlt/34 zSL
0106	L-39C	341 vlt/34 zSL
0107	L-39C	341 vlt/34 zSL
0108	L-39C	341 vlt/34 zSL
0113	L-39C	341 vlt/34 ZSL
0115	L-39C	341 vlt/34 ZSL
0440	L-39C	341 vlt/34 zSL
0441	L-39C	341 vlt/34 zSL
0444	L-39C	341 vlt/34 zSL
0445	L-39C	341 vlt/34 zSL
0448	L-39C	341 vlt/34 zSL
2341	L-39ZA	4 zSL
2344	L-39ZA	4 zSL
2347	L-39ZA	4 zSL
2350	L-39ZA	4 zSL
2415	L-39ZA	4 zSL
2418	L-39ZA	4 zSL
2421	L-39ZA	4 zSL
2424	L-39ZA	322 tlt/32 zTL
2427	L-39ZA	4 zSL
2430	L-39ZA	4 zSL
2433	L-39ZA	4 zSL
2436	L-39ZA	4 zSL
3903	L-39ZA	4 zSL
4605	L-39C	341 vlt/34 ZSL [5]
4606	L-39C	341 vlt/34 ZSL
4607	L-39C	341 vlt/34 ZSL
5013	L-39ZA	LZS 1
5015	L-39ZA	322 tlt/32 zTL
5017	L-39ZA	322 tlt/32 zTL
5019	L-39ZA	322 tlt/32 zTL

Antonov An-24V
61 dlt/6 zDL, Praha/Kbely

2904
5803
7109
7110

Antonov An-26/ AN-26Z-1M*
344 pzdlt/34 zSL, Pardubice;
61 dlt/6 zDL, Praha/Kbely;
LZú, Praha/Kbely

2408	61 dlt/6 zDL
2409	61 dlt/6 zDL
2507	61 dlt/6 zDL
3209*	344 pzdlt/34 zSL

Antonov An-30
344 pzdlt/34 zSL, Pardubice

1107

Let 410 Turbolet
61 dlt/6 zDL, Praha/Kbely;
344 pzdlt/34 zSL, Pardubice

0402	L-410MA 344 pzdlt/34 zSL
0403	L-410MA 344 pzdlt/34 zSL
0501	L-410MA 61 dlt/6 zDL
0503	L-410MA 344 pzdlt/34 zSL
0712	L-410UVP-S 344 pzdlt/34 zSL
0731	L-410UVP 61 dlt/6 zDL
0926	L-410UVP-T 61 dlt/6 zDL [4]
0928	L-410UVP-T 344 pzdlt/34 zSL
0929	L-410UVP-T 61 dlt/6 zDL [2]
1132	L-410UVP-T 61 dlt/6 zDL [3]
1134	L-410UVP 344 pzdlt/34 zSL
1504	L-410UVP 344 pzdlt/34 zSL
1523	L-410FG 344 pzdlt/34 zSL
1525	L-410FG 344 pzdlt/34 zSL
1526	L-410FG
2312	L-410UVP 61 dlt/6 zDL
2601	L-410UVP 61 dlt/6 zDL
2602	L-410UVP 61 dlt/6 zDL

Let 610M
61 dlt/6 zDL, Praha/Kbely;
LZú Praha/Kbely

0003	61 dlt/6 zDL
0005	LZú

Mil Mi-24
331 vrlt/33 zVrL, Přerov

0102	Mi-24D
0103	Mi-24D
0140	Mi-24D
0142	Mi-24D
0146	Mi-24D
0147	Mi-24D
0151	Mi-24D
0214	Mi-24D
0216	Mi-24D
0217	Mi-24D
0218	Mi-24D
0219	Mi-24D
0220	Mi-24D
0221	Mi-24D
0701	Mi-24V1
0702	Mi-24V1
0703	Mi-24V1
0705	Mi-24V1
0709	Mi-24V1
0710	Mi-24V1
0788	Mi-24V1
0789	Mi-24V1
0790	Mi-24V1
0812	Mi-24V1
0815	Mi-24V1
0816	Mi-24V1
0834	Mi-24V2
0835	Mi-24V2
0836	Mi-24V2
0837	Mi-24V2
0838	Mi-24V2
0839	Mi-24V2
0928	Mi-24V2
4010	Mi-24D
4011	Mi-24D
6050	Mi-24DU

**Sukhoi Su-22M-4K/
Su-22UM-3K***
321 tlt/32 zTL, Náměšt

2217		
2218		
2619	34	NA-2D
2620	35	NA-2D
2701	36	
3313	24	NA-2A
3314	23	
3315	39	NA-2B
3402	05	
3403	08	NA-1B
3404	09	
3405		
3406		
3407	10	
3701	02	NA-1A
3703	43	NA-1D
3704	44	NA-1D
3705	51	
3706	52	NA-1E
3802	26	NA-2B
3803	27	NA-2B
4005	30	NA-2C
4006	31	NA-2C
4007	32	NA-2C
4008	29	NA-2B
4010	28	NA-2B
4011	22	NA-2A
4208	53	NA-1E
4209	54	NA-1E
6602	*	
7103	03	NA-1A*
7104	40	NA-2C*
7309	41	NA-2D*
7310	25	NA-2A*

Sukhoi Su-25K/Su-25UBK*
322 tlt/32 zTL, Náměšt

1002
1004
1005
3348*
5003
5006
5007
5008
5039
5040
6019
6020
8076
8077
8078
8079
8080
8081
9013
9014
9093
9094
9098
9099

Tupolev Tu-134A
61 dlt/6 zDL, Praha/Kbely
1407

Tupolev Tu-154B-2
61 dlt/6 zDL, Praha/Kbely
0601

**DENMARK
Kongelige Danske Flyvevåbnet
Lockheed C-130H Hercules**
Eskadrille 721, Vaerløse
B-678
B-679
B-680

**General Dynamics
F-16A/F-16B***
Eskadrille 723, Aalborg;
Eskadrille 726, Aalborg;
Eskadrille 727, Skrydstrup;
Eskadrille 730, Skrydstrup

E-004	Esk 726
E-005	Esk 726
E-006	Esk 726
E-007	Esk 726
E-008	Esk 726
E-011	
E-016	Esk 726
E-017	Esk 726
E-018	Esk 726
E-024	Esk 723
E-069	
E-070	
E-074	
E-075	
E-107	
E-174	Esk 727
E-176	Esk 726
E-177	Esk 723
E-178	Esk 730
E-180	Esk 726
E-181	Esk 723
E-182	Esk 730
E-183	Esk 723
E-184	Esk 723
E-187	Esk 727
E-188	Esk 723
E-189	Esk 723
E-190	Esk 723
E-191	Esk 730
E-192	Esk 730
E-193	Esk 727
E-194	Esk 730
E-195	Esk 723
E-196	Esk 723
E-197	Esk 723
E-198	Esk 730
E-199	Esk 723
E-200	Esk 723
E-202	Esk 730
E-203	Esk 723
E-596	Esk 723
E-597	Esk 730
E-598	Esk 730
E-599	Esk 730
E-600	Esk 727
E-601	Esk 727
E-602	Esk 730
E-603	Dansk 727
E-604	Esk 726
E-605	Esk 727
E-606	Esk 730
E-607	Esk 723
E-608	Esk 723
E-609	Esk 727
E-610	Esk 727
E-611	Esk 727
ET-022*	Esk 730
ET-197*	Esk 726
ET-198*	Esk 726
ET-199*	Esk 726
ET-204*	Esk 727
ET-206*	Esk 730
ET-207*	Esk 727
ET-208*	Esk 730
ET-210*	Esk 727
ET-612*	Esk 727
ET-613*	Esk 727
ET-614*	Esk 723
ET-615*	Esk 727

**Grumman G.1159A
Gulfstream III**
Eskadrille 721, Vaerløse
F-249
F-313
F-401

SAAB T-17 Supporter
Flyveskolen, Karup (FLSK);
Haerens Flyvetjaeneste
    (Danish Army), Vandel;
Eskadrille 721, Vaerløse

T-401	Karup Stn Flt
T-402	FLSK
T-403	Karup Stn Flt
T-404	FLSK
T-405	Karup Stn Flt
T-407	FLSK
T-408	Esk 721
T-409	FLSK
T-410	Karup Stn Flt
T-411	FLSK
T-412	Karup Stn Flt
T-413	FLSK
T-414	FLSK
T-415	FLSK
T-417	Army
T-418	FLSK
T-419	FLSK
T-420	FLSK
T-421	FLSK
T-423	FLSK
T-425	Aalborg Stn Flt
T-426	FLSK
T-427	FLSK
T-428	FLSK
T-429	FLSK
T-430	FLSK
T-431	FLSK
T-432	FLSK

Sikorsky S-61A Sea King
Eskadrille 722, Vaerløse
*Detachments at:
Aalborg, Ronne, Skrydstrup*
U-240
U-275
U-276
U-277
U-278
U-279
U-280
U-481

**Søvaernets Flyvetjaeneste
(Navy)
Westland Lynx Mk 80/90***
Eskadrille 722, Vaerløse
S-035
S-134
S-142
S-170
S-175
S-181

S-191		**FRANCE**		64	315-WG	
S-249*		**Armée de l'Air**		65	315-WH	
S-256*		**Aérospatiale SN601**		66	315-WI	
		Corvette		67	315-WJ	
Haerens Flyvetjaeneste		CEV, Bretigny		68	315-WK	
(Army)		1	MV	69	315-WL	
Hughes 500M		2	MW	70	315-WM	
Base: Vandel		10	MX	71	315-WN	
H-201				72	315-WO	
H-202		**Aérospatiale TB-30**		73	315-WP	
H-203		**Epsilon**		74	315-WQ	
H-205		*Cartouche Dorée*,		75	315-WR	
H-206		(EPAA 315) Cognac;		76	315-WS	
H-207		DV 05.312, Salon de		77	315-WT	
H-209		Provence;		78	315-WU	
H-210		EPAA 315, Cognac		79	315-WV	
H-211		1	315-UA	80	315-WW	
H-213		2	315-UB	81	315-WX	
H-244		3	FZ	82	315-WY	
H-245		4	315-UC	83	315-WZ	
H-246		5	315-UD	84	315-XA	
		6	315-UE	85	315-XB	
Aérospatiale AS.550C-2		7	315-UF	86	315-XC	
Fennec		8	315-UG	87	315-XD	
Base: Vandel		9	315-UH	88	315-XE	
P-090		10	315-UI	89	315-XF	
P-234		12	315-UK	90	315-XG	
P-254		13	315-UL	91	315-XH	
P-275		14	315-UM	92	F-SEXI	[1]*
P-276		15	315-UN	93	315-XJ	
P-287		16	315-UO	94	315-XK	
P-288		17	315-UP	95	315-XL	
P-319		18	315-UQ	96	315-XM	
P-320		19	315-UR	97	315-XN	
P-352		20	315-US	98	315-XO	
P-369		21	315-UT	99	315-XP	
		23	315-UV	100	F-SEXQ	[2]*
		24	315-UW	101	315-XR	
ECUADOR		25	315-UX	102	315-XS	
Fuerza Aérea Ecuatoriana		26	315-UY	103	315-XT	
Lockheed C-130H Hercules		27	315-UZ	104	315-XU	
FAE-812		28	315-VA	105	F-SEXV	[4]*
FAE-893		29	315-VB	106	315-XW	
		30	315-VC	107	315-XX	
EGYPT		31	315-VD	108	315-XY	
Al Quwwat al-Jawwiya		32	315-VE	109	315-XZ	
Ilmisriya		33	315-VF	110	315-YA	
Lockheed C-130H/		34	315-VG	111	315-YB	
C-130H-30* Hercules		35	315-VH	112	315-YC	
16 Sqn, Cairo West		36	315-VI	113	315-YD	
1271/SU-BAB		37	315-VJ	114	315-YE	
1272/SU-BAC		38	315-VK	115	315-YF	
1273/SU-BAD		39	315-VL	116	315-YG	
1274/SU-BAE		40	315-VM	117	F-SEYH	[3]*
1275/SU-BAF		41	315-VN	118	315-YI	
1277/SU-BAI		42	315-VO	119	315-YJ	
1278/SU-BAJ		43	315-VP	120	315-YK	
1279/SU-BAK		44	315-VQ	121	315-YL	
1280/SU-BAL		45	315-VR	122	315-YM	
1281/SU-BAM		46	315-VS	123	315-YN	
1282/SU-BAN		47	315-VT	124	315-YO	
1283/SU-BAP		48	315-VU	125	315-YP	
1284/SU-BAQ		49	315-VV	126	315-YQ	
1285/SU-BAR		50	315-VW	127	315-YR	
1286/SU-BAS		51	2-BD	128	315-YS	
1287/SU-BAT		52	315-VX	129	315-YT	
1288/SU-BAU		53	315-VY	130	315-YU	
1289/SU-BAV		54	315-VZ	131	315-YV	
1290/SU-BEW		56	315-WA	132	315-YW	
1291/SU-BEX		57	F-ZVLB	133	315-YX	
1292/SU-BEY		60	315-WC	134	315-YY	
1293/SU-BKS*		61	315-WD	135	315-YZ	
1294/SU-BKT*		62	315-WE	136	315-ZA	
1295/SU-BKU*		63	315-WF	137	315-ZB	

138	312-VX	
139	315-ZD	
140	315-ZE	
141	315-ZF	
142	315-ZG	
143	315-ZH	
144	315-ZI	
145	315-ZJ	
146	315-ZK	
148	315-ZL	
149	315-ZM	
150	315-ZN	
152	315-ZO	
153	315-ZP	
154	315-ZQ	
155	315-ZR	
158	315-ZS	
159	315-ZT	

Airbus A.300B2-103
CEV, Bretigny
03

Airbus A.310-304
ET 03.060 'Esterel', Paris/Charles de Gaulle

421	F-RADA
422	F-RADB

Airtech CN-235M-100
ETL 01.062 'Vercours', Creil;
ETOM 00.082 'Maine', Faaa-Tahiti

043	62-IA	01.062
045	62-IB	01.062
065	62-IC	00.082
066	62-ID	01.062
071	62-IE	01.062
072	62-IF	00.082
105	62-IG	01.062
107	62-IH	01.062

Boeing C-135 Stratotanker
ERV 00.093 'Bretagne', Istres

470	C-135FR	93-CA
471	C-135FR	93-CB
475	C-135FR	93-CF
735	C-135FR	93-CG
736	C-135FR	93-CH
737	C-135FR	93-CI
738	C-135FR	93-CJ
740	C-135FR	93-CL
12739	C-135FR	93-CK
23497	KC-135R	93-CM
23516	KC-135R	
23525	KC-135R	93-CN
38033	KC-135R	
38472	C-135FR	93-CC
38474	C-135FR	93-CE

Boeing E-3F Sentry
EDCA 00.036, Avord

201	36-CA
202	36-CB
203	36-CC
204	36-CD

CASA 212-300 Aviocar
CEV, Bretigny

377	MO
378	MP
386	MQ
387	MR
388	MS

Cessna 310
CEV, Bretigny & Melun

046	310L	AV
185	310N	AU
187	310N	BJ
188	310N	BK
190	310N	BL
192	310N	BM
193	310N	BG
194	310N	BH
242	310K	AW
244	310K	AX
513	310N	BE
693	310N	BI
820	310Q	CL
981	310	BF

D-BD Alpha Jet
Patrouille de France (PDF), Salon de Provence;
EC 02.007 'Argonne', St Dizier;
ETO 01.008 'Saintonge' & ETO 02.008 'Nice' Cazaux;
ERS 01.091 'Gascogne', Mont-de-Marsan
EAC 314, Tours;
CEAM (330), Mont-de-Marsan;
AMD-BA, Istres;
CEV, Bretigny;
EPNER, Istres

01	F-ZJTS	CEV
02	F-ZWRU	AMD-BA
E1		CEV
E3	8-NC	02.008
E4		CEV
E5	8-NS	02.008
E7		
E8		CEV
E9		
E10	8-NM	02.008
E11	8-MW	01.008
E12		CEV
E13	314-TK	
E14	314-LE	
E15		
E17	8-NK	02.008
E18	8-MD	01.008
E19	314-TS	
E20		
E21	314-UO	
E22	314-TG	
E23	F-TERO	*PDF* [0]
E24		
E25	314-LL	
E26	314-LC	
E27		
E28	8-M	01.008
E29	314-TM	
E30	8-NR	02.008
E31		
E32	8-NQ	02.008
E33	8-NN	02.008
E34	314-TC	
E35	314-UF	
E36	314-LT	
E37	F-TERI	*PDF* [8]
E38		
E40		
E41	314-LC	
E42	7-PX	02.007
E43	314-TZ	
E44		CEV
E45	330-AK	CEAM
E46		CEV
E47	314-LO	
E48	8-MO	01.008
E49		
E51	314-UB	
E52		
E53	314-LV	
E55	314-UN	
E58	7-PY	02.007
E59	314-LY	
E60		EPNER
E61	7-PP	02.007
E63	314-TA	
E64	314-TL	
E65	8-MU	01.008
E66	8-ME	01.008
E67	314-TB	
E68		
E69	8-NX	02.008
E70		
E72	314-LA	
E73	314-TV	
E74		
E75	314-TU	
E76	7-PW	02.007
E79	314-LN	
E80		CEV
E81	314-LR	
E82	8-MM	01.008
E83	8-NG	02.008
E84	8-MH	01.008
E85	330-AL	CEAM
E86		
E87	314-LU	
E88	314-TF	
E89	F-TERE	*PDF* [2]
E90	314-LF	
E91	8-NL	02.008
E92	314-UE	
E93	314-LD	
E94		
E95		
E96	8-MT	01.008
E97	F-TERL	*PDF* [7]
E98		
E99	314-LW	
E100		EPNER
E101	314-LX	
E102	8-MC	01.008
E103	314-LM	
E104	F-TERB	*PDF* [4]
E105	F-TERF	*PDF* [6]
E106	F-TERJ	*PDF* [9]
E107	314-LS	
E108	8-NJ	02.008
E109	8-NI	02.008
E110	8-MG	01.008
E112		
E113	314-LK	
E114	314-UC	
E115	8-MS	01.008
E116		
E117	314-UH	
E118	314-TX	
E119	7-PZ	02.007
E120		
E121		
E122	8-NF	02.008
E123	8-ML	01.008
E124	8-NB	02.008
E125	F-TERH	*PDF*
E126	314-LI	

Serial	Code	Unit
E127		
E128		
E129	314-TO	
E130	314-TI	
E131		
E132	314-UJ	
E133	8-NE	02.008
E134	8-MA	01.008
E135	314-LP	
E136	314-TN	
E137	314-LB	
E138		
E139	330-AH	CEAM
E140	F-TERD	PDF [3]
E141	F-TERA	PDF [1]
E142	MB	CEAM
E143	8-MJ	01.008
E144	8-NU	02.008
E145		
E146	MG	01.091
E147	8-NH	02.008
E148		
E149	314-UG	
E150	314-TY	
E151	314-TR	
E152	8-MP	01.008
E153	8-NA	02.008
E154	8-MA	01.008
E155		
E156		
E157	314-LG	
E158	8-NT	02.008
E159	8-ND	02.008
E160		
E161		
E162	314-LH	
E163	314-TQ	
E164	8-NO	02.008
E165	314-TP	
E166	8-MR	01.008
E167		
E168	314-TN	
E169		
E170	314-UI	
E171	314-TD	
E173	F-TERP	PDF [5]
E174		
E175	314-UK	
E176	8-MT	01.008

Dassault Falcon 20

CEV, Bretigny[1], Cazaux[2], Istres[3] & Melun[4];
ETEC 02.065, Villacoublay;
SIET 98.120, Cazaux;
CITac 00.339, Luxeuil

Serial	Code	Unit
22	CS	CEV[3]
49	120-FA	
79	CT	CEV[1]
86	CG	CEV[2]
93	F-RAED	02.065
96	CB	CEV[1]
104	CW	CEV[1]
115	339-JG	
124	CC	CEV[1]
131	CD	CEV[1]
138	CR	CEV[2]
145	CU	CEV[1]
167	F-RAEB	02.065
182	339-JA	
186	339-JE	
188	CX	CEV[4]
238	F-RAEE	02.065
252	CA	CEV[1]
260	A	02.065
263	CY	CEV[1]
268	(F-RAEF)	02.065
288	CV	CEV[1]
291	(F-RAEG)	02.065
342	C	02.065
375	CZ	CEV[1]
422	65-EH	02.065
451	339-JC	
483	339-JI	

Dassault Falcon 50

ET 01.060, Villacoublay

Serial	Code	Unit
5	(F-RAFI)	
27	(F-RAFK)	
34	(F-RAFL)	
78	(F-RAFJ)	

Dassault Falcon 900

ET 01.060, Villacoublay

Serial	Code	Unit
2	(F-RAFP)	
4	F-RAFQ	

Dassault Mirage IVP

ERS 01.091 'Gascogne', Mont-de-Marsan

Serial	Code
8/01	AG
11	AJ
13	AL
23	AV
25	AX
31	BD
48	BU
52	BY
56	CC
59	CF
61	CH
62	CI

Dassault Mirage F.1B

EC 03.033 'Lorraine', Reims;
CEAM (330), Mont-de-Marsan

Serial	Code	Unit
501		
502	33-FE	03.033
503		
504	330-AD	CEAM
505		
507	33-FP	03.033
509	33-FG	03.033
510		
511	33-FF	03.033
512		
513		
514	33-FU	03.033
516	33-FH	03.033
517		
518	33-FI	03.033
519	33-FB	03.033
520	33-FL	03.033

Dassault Mirage F.1C/F.1CT*

GC 02.030 'Normandie Niemen' & GC 03.030 'Alsace', Colmar;
EC 03.033 'Lorraine', Reims;
EC 04.033 'Vexin', Djibouti;
CEAM (330), Mont-de-Marsan;
CEV, Bretigny & Istres

Serial	Code	Unit
2		
4	12-YE	CEV
5	33-FA	03.033
9	wfu	
10		
15		
20		
24	33-FS	03.033
30		
31	330-AC	CEAM
32		
36		
38		
47		
52	33-FK	03.033
62	33-FD	03.033
64	33-FC	03.033
70		
72	330-AG	CEAM
74		
76	33-FQ	03.033
80	33-LJ	04.033
81	33-FT	03.033
82	33-LK	04.033
83	33-FO	03.033
84		
85	33-FV	03.033
87	33-FR	03.033
90		
100	33-LA	04.033
103	33-FX	03.033
201		
202	33-LG	04.033
203		
205		
206		
207*	330-AO	CEAM
210	33-FJ	03.033
211	33-FW	03.033
213	33-FN	03.033
214	33-LH	04.033
218	33-LD	04.033
219*		
220*	30-ST	03.030
221*	30-QR	02.030
223*	30-QT	02.030
224	33-LE	04.033
225*	30-QC	02.030
226*	30-QO	02.030
227*	330-AP	CEAM
228*	30-SN	03.030
229*	30-QF	02.030
230*	30-QM	02.030
231*		
232*	30-SP	03.030
233*	30-QG	02.030
234*	30-QL	02.030
235*	30-QS	02.030
236*	30-SW	03.030
237*	30-SE	03.030
238*	30-SB	03.030
239*	30-QD	02.030
241*	30-SI	03.030
242*	30-SG	03.030
243*	30-QN	02.030
244*		
245*	30-SA	03.030
246*	30-QJ	02.030
247*	30-QP	02.030
248*	30-QQ	02.030
249*		
251*	330-AY	CEAM
252*	30-SK	03.030
253*		
254*	330-AJ	CEAM
255*	30-QK	02.030
256*	30-SL	03.030

257*	30-SD	03.030
258*	30-SM	03.030
259*	30-QU	02.030
260*	30-SO	03.030
261*	30-SV	03.030
262*	30-SP	03.030
264*	30-QH	02.030
265*	30-SR	03.030
267*	30-QB	02.030
268*	30-SF	03.030
271*	30-SM	03.030
272*	30-SQ	03.030
273*	30-SJ	03.030
274*		
275*	30-SX	03.030
278*	30-QA	02.030
279*	30-SC	03.030
280*	30-QE	02.030
281*	30-QI	02.030
283*	30-SV	03.030

Dassault Mirage F.1CR

ER 01.033 'Belfort' &
ER 02.033 'Savoie', Reims;
CEAM (330), Mont-de-
Marsan;
CEV, Istres

601		CEV
602		CEV
603	33-CB	01.033
604	33-CE	01.033
605	33-NF	02.033
606	33-NP	02.033
607	330-AB	CEAM
608	33-NG	02.033
610	33-NQ	02.033
611	33-CO	01.033
612	33-NJ	02.033
613	33-NK	02.033
614	33-CN	01.033
615	33-CU	01.033
616	330-AB	CEAM
617	33-CI	01.033
620	33-CT	01.033
622	33-CR	01.033
623	33-CM	01.033
624	33-NY	02.033
627	33-NI	02.033
628	33-NN	02.033
629	33-CG	01.033
630	33-NL	02.033
631	33-CD	01.033
632	33-NE	02.033
634	33-CK	01.033
635	33-NS	02.033
636	33-CS	01.033
637	33-CP	01.033
638	33-NU	02.033
640	33-NV	02.033
641	33-NT	02.033
642	33-NC	02.033
643	330-AF	CEAM
645	33-NO	02.033
646	33-NW	02.033
647	33-NX	02.033
648	33-CF	01.033
649	33-CZ	01.033
650	33-CJ	01.033
651	33-NB	02.033
653	33-CQ	01.033
654	33-CL	01.033
655	33-NR	02.033
656	33-NH	02.033
657	33-CV	01.033
658	33-CW	01.033
659		
660	33-ND	02.033
661	33-CX	01.033
662	33-NA	02.033

**Dassault Mirage 2000B/
2000B-5***

AMD-BA, Istres;
CEV, Bretigny;
EC 02.002 'Côte d'Or', Dijon;
EC 01.005 'Vendée',
EC 02.005 'Ile de France'
& EC 03.005
'Comtat-Venaissin',
Orange;
EC 01.012 'Cambrésis' &
EC 02.012 'Picardie',
Cambrai

BX1*	(501)	CEV
BY1*		AMD-BA
502	2-FA	02.002
504*	BOB	CEV
505	2-FB	02.002
506	2-FC	02.002
507	2-FD	02.002
508	2-FE	02.002
509	2-FF	02.002
510	2-FG	02.002
511	2-FH	02.002
512	2-FQ	02.002
513	2-FR	02.002
514	2-FK	02.002
515		
516	2-EO	01.002
518	2-FU	02.002
519	2-FV	02.002
520	2-FW	02.002
521	2-FX	02.002
522	2-FY	02.002
523	5-OJ	02.005
524	330-AZ	CEAM
525	12-KN	02.012
526	12-KM	02.012
527	5-NO	01.005
528	330-AN	CEAM
529	5-AA	03.005
530	12-YA	01.012
531		
532		

**Dassault Mirage 2000C/
2000C-5***

CEAM (330), Mont-de-
Marsan;
CEV, Istres;
EC 01.002 'Cicogne' &
EC 02.002 'Côte
d'Or', Dijon;
EC 01.005 'Vendée',
EC 02.005 'Ile de France'
& EC 03.005
'Comtat-Venaissin',
Orange;
EC 01.012 'Cambrésis' &
EC 02.012 'Picardie',
Cambrai

1	2-EP	CEV
2		CEV
3	2-ER	01.002
4	2-FP	02.002
5	2-FM	02.002
8	2-FI	02.002
9	2-EB	01.002
11	2-EF	01.002
12		
13	2-ES	01.002
14		
15	2-EK	01.002
16	2-EL	01.002
17	2-EM	01.002
18	2-FL	02.002
19	2-EA	01.002
20	2-EQ	01.002
21	2-EG	01.002
22	2-EH	01.002
25	2-EJ	01.002
27	2-FJ	02.002
28	2-FZ	02.002
29	2-ED	01.002
30	2-FN	02.002
32	2-EP	01.002
34	2-ET	01.002
35	2-EE	01.002
36	2-EN	01.002
37	2-EU	01.002
38	5-ND	01.005
39	5-OF	02.005
40	5-NJ	01.005
41	5-NL	01.005
42	5-AB	03.005
43	5-AE	03.005
44	5-AQ	03.005
45	5-OM	02.005
46	5-NB	01.005
47	5-ON	02.005
48	5-AF	03.005
49	5-AL	03.005
51*		
52	5-OC	02.005
53	5-AJ	03.005
54	5-AR	03.005
55	5-OH	02.005
56	5-OA	02.005
57	5-OL	02.005
58	5-AM	03.005
59	5-OB	02.005
61	5-OD	02.005
62	5-AC	03.005
63	5-OK	02.005
64	330-AQ	CEAM
65	5-OO	02.005
66	5-AN	03.005
67	5-OQ	02.005
68	5-AI	03.005
69	5-OR	02.005
70	5-AO	03.005
71	5-AD	03.005
72	5-OE	02.005
73	5-NN	01.005
74	5-OP	02.005
76	5-NP	01.005
77*		CEV
78	5-NE	01.005
79	5-NF	01.005
80	330-AS	CEAM
81		
82	5-NM	01.005
83		
84	5-NH	01.005
85		
86	5-AG	03.005
87	5-NK	01.005
88	5-NG	01.005
89	12-YB	01.012
90	12-KO	02.012
91	12-YO	01.012
92	330-AW	CEAM

93	330-AR	CEAM
94	12-KA	02.012
95		
96	12-KK	02.012
97	12-KP	02.012
98	12-YJ	01.012
99	12-YP	01.012
100	5-NQ	01.005
101	12-KJ	02.012
102	12-YE	01.012
103	12-YN	01.012
104	12-YK	01.012
105	12-YL	01.012
106	12-KL	02.012
107	12-YR	01.012
108	5-NC	01.005
109	12-YI	01.012
111	12-KI	02.012
112		
113		
114	12-YG	01.012
115	12-KC	02.012
116	12-KG	02.012
117	12-YD	01.012
118	12-KH	02.012
119	12-KD	02.012
120	12-YM	01.012
121	12-KF	02.012
122	12-YC	01.012
123	12-KR	02.012
124	12-KB	02.012

Dassault Mirage 2000D

EC 01.003 'Navarre',
EC 02.003 'Champagne' &
EC 03.003 'Ardennes',
Nancy;
CEAM (330), Mont-de-Marsan;
AMD-BA, Istres

D01		AMD-BA
601	3-IA	01.003
602	3-XG	03.003
603	3-IC	01.003
604	3-XK	03.003
605	3-IE	01.003
606	3-XM	03.003
607		CEV
608	3-XB	03.003
609	3-XD	03.003
610	3-II	01.003
611	3-XS	03.003
612	330-AX	CEAM
613	330-AE	CEAM
614	3-IJ	01.003
615	330-AM	CEAM
616	3-IL	01.003
617	3-XA	03.003
618	3-IG	01.003
619	3-XO	03.003
620	3-IM	01.003
621	3-XC	03.003
622	3-IH	01.003
623	3-IB	01.003
624	3-XF	03.003
625	3-IK	01.003
626		
627	3-IN	01.003
628	3-XI	03.003
629	3-XJ	03.003
630	3-IO	01.003
631	3-IF	01.003
632	3-XL	03.003
633	3-XN	03.003
634	3-ID	01.003
635	3-XP	03.003
636	3-XR	03.003
637	3-IP	01.003
638	3-IQ	01.003
639	3-XQ	03.003
640	3-IR	01.003
641	3-JA	02.003
642		
643		
644		
645		

Dassault Mirage 2000N

EC 02.003 'Champagne', Nancy;
EC 01.004 'Dauphiné' &
EC 02.004 'Lafayette', Luxeuil;
EC 03.004 'Limousin', Istres
CEAM (330), Mont-de-Marsan;

301		
302	4-CA	03.004
303		CEV
304	3-CB	03.004
305	4-BF	02.004
306	4-CQ	03.004
307	4-CC	03.004
308	4-CD	03.004
309	4-BA	02.004
310	4-CE	03.004
311	4-BD	02.004
312	4-CF	03.004
313	4-BE	02.004
314	4-CG	03.004
315	4-BZ	02.004
316	4-CH	03.004
317		
318	4-CI	03.004
319	4-BI	02.004
320		
322	4-BK	02.004
323	4-CJ	03.004
325	4-BL	02.004
326	4-CM	03.004
327	4-BM	02.004
329	4-CN	03.004
330	4-CO	03.004
331	4-CP	03.004
332	4-BN	02.004
333	4-AB	01.004
334	330-AV	CEAM
335	4-BJ	02.004
336	4-BP	02.004
337	4-BU	02.004
338	4-AC	01.004
339	4-AD	01.004
340	4-AA	01.004
341	4-AF	01.004
342	4-AG	01.004
343	4-AH	01.004
344	4-AJ	01.004
345	4-AK	01.004
347	4-BT	02.004
348	3-AL	01.004
349	4-AO	01.004
350	3-JR	02.003
351	4-AQ	01.004
353	3-JS	02.003
354	3-JC	02.003
355	4-AL	01.004
356	3-JE	02.003
357	3-JF	02.003
358	3-JG	02.003
359	3-JH	02.003
360	3-JI	02.003
361	3-JJ	02.003
362	3-JK	02.003
363	3-JL	02.003
364	3-JM	02.003
365	3-JN	02.003
366	4-BO	02.004
367	4-AS	01.004
368	4-AR	01.004
369	4-BQ	02.004
370	4-AT	01.004
371	4-AV	01.004
372	4-BR	02.004
373	4-BH	02.004
374	4-BS	02.004
375	3-JB	02.003

Dassault Rafale-B

AMD-BA, Istres

B01		AMD-BA

DHC-6 Twin Otter 200/300*

GAM 00.056 'Vaucluse', Evreux;
EdC 00.070, Chateaudun;
ETL 01.062 'Vercours', Creil;
CEAM (330), Mont-de-Marsan;

292	CC	00.056
298	CD	00.056
300	CE	00.056
603*	MB	00.070
730*	CA	01.062
742*	IA	CEAM
743*	MA	00.070
745*	IB	CEAM
786*	CT	01.062
790*	CW	01.062

Douglas DC-8-53[1]/55F[2]/72CF[3]

EE 00.051 'Aubrac', Evreux;
ET 03.060 'Esterel',
Paris/Charles de Gaulle

45570[1]	F-RAFE	00.051
45819[2]	F-RAFC	03.060
46013[3]	F-RAFG	03.060
46043[3]	F-RAFD	03.060
46130[3]	F-RAFF	03.060

Embraer EMB.121AA Xingu

ETE 00.043 'Médoc', Bordeaux;
ETE 00.044 'Mistral', Aix-en-Provence;
EAT 319, Avord;
CEAM (330), Mont-de-Marsan;
CITac 00.339, Luxeuil

054	YX	EAT 319
064	YY	EAT 319
072	YA	EAT 319
073	YB	EAT 319
075	YC	EAT 319
076	YD	EAT 319
078	YE	EAT 319
080	YF	EAT 319
082	YG	EAT 319
084	YH	EAT 319
086	YI	EAT 319
089	YJ	EAT 319
091	YK	EAT 319

092	YL	EAT 319
095	YM	EAT 319
096	YN	EAT 319
098	YO	EAT 319
099	YP	EAT 319
101	YR	EAT 319
102	YS	EAT 319
103	YT	EAT 319
105	YU	EAT 319
107	YV	EAT 319
108	YW	EAT 319
111	YQ	EAT 319

Embraer EMB.312F Tucano
GI 312, Salon de Provence

438	312-UW
439	312-UX
456	312-JA
457	312-JB
458	312-JC
459	312-JD
460	312-JE
461	312-JF
462	312-JG
463	312-JH
464	312-JI
465	312-JJ
466	312-JK
467	312-JL
468	312-JM
469	312-JN
470	312-JO
471	312-JP
472	312-JQ
473	312-JR
474	312-JS
475	312-JT
477	312-JU
478	312-JV
479	312-JX
480	312-JY
481	312-JZ
482	312-UA
483	312-UB
484	312-UC
485	312-UD
486	312-UE
487	312-UF
488	312-UG
489	312-UH
490	312-UI
491	312-UJ
492	312-UK
493	312-UL
494	312-UM
495	312-UN
496	312-UO
497	312-UP
498	312-UQ
499	312-UR
500	312-US
501	312-UT
502	312-UU
503	312-UV

Lockheed C-130H/ C-130H-30* Hercules
ET 02.061 'Franche-Comté', Orléans

5114	61-PA
5116	61-PB
5119	61-PC
5140	61-PD
5142*	61-PE
5144*	61-PF
5150*	61-PG
5151*	61-PH
5152*	61-PI
5153*	61-PJ
5226*	61-PK
5227*	61-PL

Morane Saulnier 760 Paris
CEAM (330), Mont-de-Marsan;
CEV, Bretigny & Istres;
EAC 314, Tours;
EAM 09.112, Reims;
EAM 09.115, Orange;
EAM 09.116, Luxeuil;
EAM 09.121, Nancy;
EAM 09.126, Solenzara;
EAM 09.132, Colmar;
EAM 09.133, Nancy;
ENOSA 316, Toulouse;
ETE 00.041 'Verdun', Metz;
ETEC 01.065, Villacoublay;
GI 312, Salon de Provence

1	330-DA	CEAM
19		
23	3-KA	09.121
25	*wfu*	
26	330-DR	CEAM
27	41-AR	00.041
30	4-WA	09.116
34	133-CG	09.133
35	115-QG	09.115
36	316-DH	ENOSA
38	115-MF	09.115
44	314-DD	EAC 314
45	316-DI	ENOSA
54	330-DQ	CEAM
56	DJ	ENOSA
57	4-WD	09.116
58	312-DG	GI 312
59	133-CF	09.133
61	312-DF	GI 312
62		
65	330-DP	CEAM
68	NB	CEV
70	65-LF	01.065
71	41-AC	00.041
73	330-DF	CEAM
75	116-CB	09.116
82	126-HH	09.126
83	NC	CEV
91	316-DM	ENOSA
92	316-DL	ENOSA
93	330-IC	CEAM
94	115-MF	09.115
100	NG	CEV
113	NI	CEV
114	NJ	CEV
115	OV	CEV
116	ON	CEV
118	NQ	CEV
119	NL	CEV

Nord 262/262A[A]/262D[D]/ 262D-AEN[N] Frégate
CEV, Istres;
EPNER, Istres;
ETE 00.041 'Verdun', Metz;
ETE 00.043 'Médoc', Bordeaux;
ETE 00.044 'Mistral', Aix-en-Provence;
ETEC 01.065, Villacoublay;
EdC 00.070, Chateaudun;
ENOSA 316, Toulouse;
CIEH 341, Toulouse;
CEAM (330), Mont-de-Marsan

1		CEV
3	OH	CEV
55[A]	MH	EPNER
58[A]	MJ	EPNER
64[D]	AA	CIEH 341
66[D]	AB	01.065
67[A]	MI	CEV
68[D]	AC	01.065
76[N]	DA	ENOSA
77[D]	AK	01.065
78[D]	AF	01.065
80[D]	AW	00.041
81[D]	AH	CEV
83[N]	DB	ENOSA
86[N]	DD	ENOSA
87[N]	DC	ENOSA
88[D]	AL	00.044
89[D]	AZ	01.065
91[D]	AT	00.043
92[N]	DE	ENOSA
93[D]	AP	CIEH 341
94[D]	AU	00.044
95[D]	AR	00.041
105[D]	AE	00.041
106[D]	AY	01.065
107[D]	AX	00.043
108[D]	AG	CIEH 341
109[D]	AM	00.043
110[D]	AS	00.041

SEPECAT Jaguar A
CEV, Bretigny & Istres;
EC 01.007 'Provence',
EC 02.007 'Argonne' &
EC 03.007 'Languedoc', St Dizier;
EC 03.011 'Corse', Toul;
CEAM (330), Mont-de-Marsan;
CITac 00.339, Luxeuil

A1		
A2	11-RA	03.011
A3		CEV
A7	*wfu*	
A13		
A14	7-PO	02.007
A15	7-HG	01.007
A17		
A23	7-HH	01.007
A25	7-PU	02.007
A26	11-MH	
A28	7-HB	01.007
A29	7-PE	02.007
A34	7-ID	03.007
A35	7-IH	02.007
A37	11-RB	03.011
A38	7-PV	02.007
A39	7-HI	01.007
A40	7-HO	01.007
A41		
A43	7-HF	01.007
A46	7-HP	01.007
A47	7-HJ	01.007
A48		
A49	11-RD	03.011
A50	7-IE	03.007
A53	7-HD	01.007
A54	11-MN	

France

A55	7-PA	02.007
A58	7-HL	01.007
A61	11-RG	03.011
A64	7-IS	03.007
A66	7-IB	03.007
A70		
A75	7-IJ	03.007
A79		
A80		
A82	7-HM	01.007
A84	7-HA	01.007
A86	7-IO	03.007
A87	7-HN	01.007
A88	7-II	03.007
A89	11-RE	03.011
A90	11-MI	
A92	7-HC	01.007
A93		
A94		
A96	7-ID	03.007
A97	11-RH	03.011
A98		
A99	11-RJ	03.011
A100	7-HK	01.007
A101		
A103	11-RI	03.011
A104	7-IT	03.007
A107	7-IG	03.007
A108	11-RF	03.011
A112	11-MA	
A113	7-IR	03.007
A115		
A117		
A120	11-MR	
A122	11-RL	03.011
A123	11-RQ	03.011
A124	7-IM	03.007
A127	7-PC	02.007
A128	7-IU	03.007
A129	11-RP	03.011
A130		
A131	7-IC	03.007
A133	11-MT	
A135	11-RU	03.011
A137	7-IA	03.007
A138		
A139	11-RC	03.011
A140		
A141	11-RT	03.011
A144	7-IF	03.007
A145	7-IQ	03.007
A148	7-IL	03.007
A149	11-RK	03.011
A150		
A151	11-RS	03.011
A153	11-RO	03.011
A154	7-IN	03.007
A157	11-MW	
A158	11-RM	03.011
A159	11-RV	03.011
A160	7-IV	03.007

SEPECAT Jaguar E

E1		CEV
E2	7-PG	02.007
E3	339-WF	00.339
E4		
E5	11-RY	03.011
E6	7-PD	02.007
E7		
E8	339-WG	00.339
E9	7-PL	02.007
E10	7-IC	03.007
E11	339-WH	00.339
E12	7-PI	02.007
E13	7-PF	02.007
E15		
E18	11-RN	03.011
E19	7-PN	02.007
E20	7-PR	02.007
E21	7-PB	02.007
E22	339-WK	00.339
E23		
E24	7-PH	02.007
E25		
E27		
E28	7-PS	02.007
E29	339-WJ	00.339
E30	7-PK	02.007
E32		
E33		
E35	7-PJ	02.007
E36	339-WI	00.339
E37	7-PQ	02.007
E39		
E40		

SOCATA TBM 700

ETE 00.041 'Verdun', Metz;
ETE 00.043 'Médoc', Bordeaux;
ETE 00.044 'Mistral', Aix-en-Provence;
ETEC 02.065, Villacoublay;
CEAM (330), Mont-de-Marsan;

33	65-XA	02.065
35	43-XB	00.043
70	43-XC	00.043
77	65-XD	02.065
78	65-XE	02.065
80	65-XF	02.065
93	330-IC	CEAM
94	44-XG	00.044
95	65-XH	02.065
103	41-XI	00.041
104	41-XJ	00.041
105	65-XK	02.065
106	MN	CEV

Transall C-160/C-160H[1]/C-160NG[2]/C-160NG GABRIEL[3]/C-160R[4]

CEV, Bretigny;
EET 01.054 'Dunkerque', Metz;
ETOM 00.055 'Ouessant', Dakar;
EA 01.059 'Bigorre', Evreux (C160H);
ET 01.061 'Touraine' & ET 03.061 'Poitou', Orléans (C160A/F);
ET 01.064 'Bearn' & ET 02.064 'Anjou', Evreux (C160NG);
CEAM (330), Mont-de-Marsan

R02[4]	61-MI	01.061
A04	BI	CEV
R06[4]	61-ZB	03.061
R1[4]	61-MA	01.061
F2	61-MB	01.061
R3[4]	61-MC	01.061
R4[4]	61-MD	01.061
R5[4]	61-ME	01.061
R11[4]	61-MF	01.061
R12	61-MG	01.061
R13[4]		01.061
R15[4]	61-MJ	01.061
F16	61-MK	01.061
R17[4]		01.061
R18[4]	61-MM	01.061
R42[4]		01.061
F43	61-MO	01.061
R44		01.061
F45	61-MQ	01.061
F46	61-MR	01.061
F48	61-MT	01.061
F49	61-MU	01.061
F51	61-MW	01.061
F52	61-MX	01.061
F53	61-MY	01.061
F54	61-MZ	01.061
F55	61-ZC	03.061
F86	61-ZD	03.061
F87	61-ZE	03.061
F88	61-ZF	03.061
F89	61-ZG	03.061
F90	61-ZH	03.061
F91	61-ZI	03.061
R92[4]	61-ZJ	03.061
R93[4]	61-ZK	03.061
F94	61-ZL	03.061
F95	61-ZM	03.061
F96	61-ZN	03.061
R97[4]	61-ZA	03.061
F98	61-ZP	03.061
R99[4]	61-ZQ	03.061
F100	61-ZR	03.061
R153[4]		03.061
F154	61-ZT	03.061
F155	61-ZU	03.061
F157	61-ZW	03.061
F158	61-ZX	03.061
F159	61-ZY	03.061
F160	61-ZZ	03.061
F201[2]	64-GA	01.064
F202[2]	64-GB	02.064
R203[4]	330-IS	CEAM
F204[2]	64-GD	02.064
F205[2]	64-GE	01.064
F206[2]	64-GF	02.064
F207[2]	64-GG	01.064
F208[2]	64-GH	02.064
F210[2]	64-GJ	02.064
F211[2]	64-GK	01.064
F212[2]	64-GL	02.064
F213[2]	64-GM	01.064
F214[2]	64-GN	02.064
F215[2]	64-GO	01.064
F216[3]	54-GT	01.054
F217[2]	64-GQ	01.064
F218[2]	64-GR	02.064
F221[3]	54-GS	01.054
F224[2]	64-GX	02.064
F225[2]	64-GY	01.064
F226[2]	64-GZ	02.064
H01[1]	59-BA	01.059
H02[1]	59-BB	01.059
H03[1]	59-BC	01.059
H04[1]	59-BD	01.059

Aéronavale/Marine
Aérospatiale SA.321G Super Frelon

32 Flotille, Lanvéoc;
33 Flotille, San Mandrier

101	32F
102	33F
106	32F

118	32F
120	32F
134	33F
137	33F
141	32F
144	32F
148	33F
149	32F
160	33F
162	32F
163	33F
164	32F
165	33F

Breguet Br.1050M Alizé
4 Flotille, Lann Bihoué;
6 Flotille, Nimes-Garons;
ES 59, Hyères

11	6F
12	4F
17	4F
22	4F
24	6F
25	4F
26	4F
30	6F
31	4F
33	4F
41	4F
43	4F
47	4F
48	6F
49	6F
50	4F
51	6F
52	4F
53	6F
55	4F
56	4F
59	6F
60	6F
64	6F
65	4F
67	59S
73	6F
76	6F

Breguet Br.1150 Atlantique 2
21 Flotille, Nimes-Garons;
23 Flotille/24 Flotille, Lann Bihoué;
CEV, Bretigny

02	21F
03	CEV
04	21F
1	23F/24F
2	23F/24F
3	23F/24F
4	23F/24F
5	23F/24F
6	23F/24F
7	23F/24F
8	21F
9	23F/24F
10	23F/24F
11	23F/24F
12	23F/24F
13	23F/24F
14	21F
15	21F
16	21F
17	23F/24F

18	21F
19	23F/24F
20	23F/24F
21	23F/24F
22	23F/24F
23	
24	
25	23F/24F
26	
27	
28	
29	
30	

Dassault Etendard IVP/IVMP*
16 Flotille, Landivisiau

101	
107*	
109*	
114*	
115*	
118*	
120*	
153*	
162*	
163*	

Dassault Super Etendard
11 Flotille, Landivisiau;
17 Flotille, Landivisiau;
CEV, Bretigny & Istres;
ES 59, Landivisiau

1	11F
2	17F
3	11F
4	11F
6	59S
8	11F
10	17F
11	59S
12	11F
13	11F
14	11F
15	59S
16	11F
17	17F
18	59S
19	11F
23	17F
24	11F
25	17F
26	11F
28	11F
29	
30	11F
31	17F
32	11F
33	11F
34	11F
35	17F
37	59S
38	11F
39	
41	11F
42	
43	11F
44	17F
45	17F
46	11F
47	17F
48	11F
49	11F
50	17F

51	11F
52	11F
53	
55	17F
57	11F
59	17F
60	11F
61	11F
62	11F
64	11F
65	11F
66	17F
68	CEV
69	17F
71	11F

Dassault Falcon 10(MER)
ES 3, Hyères;
ES 57, Landivisiau

32	3S
101	57S
129	57S
133	57S
143	57S
185	57S

Dassault Falcon Guardian
ES 9 Noumea;
ES 12 Papeete;
CEPA, Istres

48	12S
65	9S
72	12S
77	9S
80	CEPA

Dassault Rafale-M

M01	AMD-BA
M02	AMD-BA

Embraer EMB.121AN Xingu
ERCS, Cuers;
ES 2, Lann Bihoué;
ES 3, Hyères;
ES 11, Le Bourget;
ES 52, Lann Bihoué;
ES 57, Landivisiau

30	11S
47	11S
55	52S
65	11S
66	2S
67	52S
68	52S
69	2S
70	11S
71	52S
74	52S
77	52S
79	52S
81	2S
83	52S
85	52S
87	52S
90	52S

LTV F-8P Crusader
12 Flotille, Landivisiau

3	
4	
5	
7	
8	
10	

11
17
19
22
23
29
32
34
35
37
39

**Morane Saulnier 760
Paris**
ES 57, Landivisiau
32
33
40
41
42
46
85
87
88

Nord 262 Frégate
ERCS, Cuers;
ES 2, Lann Bihoué;
ES 3, Hyères;
ES 11, Le Bourget;
ES 56, Nimes-Garons;
ES 57, Landivisiau

1	262C	ERCS
16	262A	2S
28	262A	2S
43	262A	ERCS
45	262E	2S
46	262A	11S
51	262E	56S
52	262A	56S
53	262E	56S
59	262A	3S
60	262A	2S
61	262A	2S
62	262A	11S
63	262A	3S
65	262A	2S
69	262A	56S
70	262A	2S
71	262A	2S
72	262E	56S
73	262A	2S
75	262A	56S
79	262A	56S
100	262E	56S
104	262C	11S

Piper Navajo
ES 3, Hyères
227
925

**Westland Lynx HAS2 (FN);
HAS4 (FN)***
31 Flotille, San Mandrier;
34 Flotille, Lanvéoc;
ES 20, St Raphael

260	20S
262	35F
263	31F
264	31F
265	34F
266	31F
267	31F
268	
269	31F
270	31F
271	34F
272	31F
273	34F
274	34F
275	31F
276	34F
278	34F
620	34F
621	34F
622	34F
623	34F
624	31F
625	34F
627	31F
801*	31F
802*	31F
803*	31F
804*	31F
806*	34F
807*	31F
808*	31F
810*	31F
811*	34F
812*	31F
813*	34F
814*	34F

**Aviation Legére de l'Armée
de Terre (ALAT)
Cessna F.406 Caravan II**
3GHL, Rennes

0008	ABM
0010	ABN

SOCATA TBM 700
3GHL, Rennes

99	ABO
100	ABP
115	ABQ

GERMANY
**Luftwaffe, Marineflieger
Boeing 707-307C**
1/FBS, Köln-Bonn
10+01
10+02
10+03
10+04

Airbus A310-304
1/FBS, Köln-Bonn
10+21
10+22
10+23
10+24
10+25

Tupolev Tu-154M
1/FBS, Köln-Bonn
11+01
11+02

**Canadair CL601-1A
Challenger**
1/FBS, Köln-Bonn
12+01
12+02
12+03
12+04
12+05
12+06
12+07

VFW-Fokker 614-100
1/FBS, Köln-Bonn
17+01
17+02
17+03

**Mikoyan MiG-29A/
MiG-29UB***
JG-73, Laage;
WTD-61, Ingolstadt

29+01	JG-73
29+02	JG-73
29+03	JG-73
29+04	JG-73
29+05	JG-73
29+07	JG-73
29+08	JG-73
29+10	JG-73
29+11	JG-73
29+12	JG-73
29+14	JG-73
29+15	JG-73
29+16	JG-73
29+17	JG-73
29+18	JG-73
29+19	JG-73
29+20	JG-73
29+22*	JG-73
29+23*	JG-73
29+24*	JG-73
29+25*	JG-73
98+06	WTD-61
98+08	WTD-61

McD F-4F Phantom
JG-71, Wittmundhaven;
JG-72, Hopsten;
JG-73, Pferdsfeld;
JG-74, Neuburg/Donau;
TsLw-1, Kaufbeuren;
WTD-61, Ingolstadt

37+01	JG-72
37+03	JG-71
37+04	TsLw-1
37+05	JG-72
37+06	JG-73
37+07	JG-72
37+08	JG-74
37+09	JG-73
37+10	JG-73
37+11	JG-72
37+12	JG-73
37+13	JG-74
37+14	TsLw-1
37+15	WTD-61
37+16	WTD-61
37+17	JG-74
37+18	JG-72
37+19	JG-72
37+20	JG-73
37+21	JG-73
37+22	JG-72
37+23	JG-72
37+24	JG-72
37+25	JG-73
37+26	JG-72
37+28	JG-71
37+29	JG-73
37+30	JG-73
37+31	JG-74
37+32	JG-74
37+33	JG-73
37+34	JG-73
37+35	JG-72

37+36	JG-73
37+37	JG-72
37+38	JG-73
37+39	JG-71
37+40	JG-73
37+41	JG-73
37+42	JG-73
37+43	JG-73
37+44	JG-73
37+45	JG-73
37+47	JG-73
37+48	JG-74
37+49	JG-74
37+50	JG-73
37+52	JG-73
37+53	JG-74
37+54	JG-74
37+55	JG-74
37+57	JG-73
37+58	JG-73
37+60	JG-74
37+61	JG-74
37+63	JG-74
37+64	JG-74
37+65	JG-71
37+66	JG-74
37+67	JG-74
37+69	JG-73
37+70	JG-74
37+71	JG-74
37+73	JG-74
37+75	JG-72
37+76	JG-74
37+77	JG-74
37+78	JG-71
37+79	JG-74
37+81	JG-74
37+82	JG-71
37+83	JG-74
37+84	JG-74
37+85	JG-71
37+86	JG-71
37+88	JG-72
37+89	JG-74
37+90	JG-71
37+92	JG-74
37+93	JG-72
37+94	JG-71
37+96	JG-74
37+97	JG-74
37+98	JG-71
38+00	JG-74
38+01	JG-72
38+02	JG-71
38+03	JG-72
38+04	JG-71
38+05	JG-72
38+06	JG-71
38+07	JG-71
38+08	JG-74
38+09	JG-71
38+10	JG-71
38+11	JG-71
38+12	JG-71
38+13	WTD-61
38+14	JG-71
38+16	JG-74
38+17	JG-71
38+18	JG-71
38+20	JG-72
38+21	JG-72
38+24	JG-74
38+25	JG-71
38+26	JG-71

38+27	JG-71
38+28	JG-71
38+29	JG-72
38+30	JG-71
38+31	JG-72
38+32	JG-71
38+33	JG-74
38+34	JG-73
38+36	JG-71
38+37	JG-72
38+38	JG-73
38+39	JG-72
38+40	JG-71
38+42	JG-72
38+43	JG-72
38+44	JG-72
38+45	JG-72
38+46	JG-74
38+47	JG-72
38+48	JG-71
38+49	JG-72
38+50	JG-72
38+51	JG-73
38+53	JG-74
38+54	JG-72
38+55	JG-72
38+56	JG-72
38+57	JG-72
38+58	JG-72
38+60	JG-72
38+61	JG-72
38+62	JG-72
38+63	JG-72
38+64	JG-72
38+66	JG-72
38+67	JG-72
38+68	JG-72
38+69	JG-72
38+70	JG-72
38+72	JG-73
38+73	JG-72
38+74	JG-72
38+75	JG-72
99+91	WTD-61

D-BD Alpha Jet A
FLG FFB, Fürstenfeldbruck;
WTD-61, Ingolstadt

40+01	WTD-61
40+02	WTD-61
40+03	FLG FFB
40+05	FLG FFB
40+09	FLG FFB
40+11	FLG FFB
40+12	FLG FFB
40+15	WTD-61
40+18	FLG FFB
40+22	FLG FFB
40+26	FLG FFB
40+27	FLG FFB
40+35	FLG FFB
40+40	FLG FFB
40+44	FLG FFB
40+49	FLG FFB
40+56	WTD-61
40+57	WTD-61
40+59	TsLw-3
40+65	WTD-61
40+76	FLG FFB
40+78	TsLw-3
40+85	FLG FFB
40+93	FLG FFB
40+94	FLG FFB
41+02	FLG FFB

41+04	FLG FFB
41+09	FLG FFB
41+14	FLG FFB
41+25	FLG FFB
41+26	FLG FFB
41+29	FLG FFB
41+30	WTD-61
41+34	FLG FFB
41+35	FLG FFB
41+36	FLG FFB
41+37	FLG FFB
41+38	FLG FFB
41+39	WTD-61
41+42	FLG FFB
41+45	FLG FFB
41+49	FLG FFB
41+53	FLG FFB
41+55	FLG FFB
41+56	FLG FFB
41+57	WTD-61
41+58	FLG FFB
41+59	FLG FFB
41+61	FLG FFB
41+62	FLG FFB
41+63	FLG FFB
41+64	FLG FFB
41+66	FLG FFB
41+67	FLG FFB
41+68	FLG FFB
41+71	FLG FFB
41+72	FLG FFB
41+73	FLG FFB
41+74	FLG FFB
41+75	FLG FFB

**Panavia Tornado
Strike/Trainer[1]/ECR[2]**
Tactical Training Center,
 Holloman AFB, New
 Mexico, USA (49 FW);
TTTE, RAF Cottesmore;
AkG-51, Schleswig/Jagel;
JbG-31, Nörvenich;
JbG-32, Lechfeld;
JbG-33, Böchel;
JbG-34, Memmingen;
JbG-38, Jever;
MFG-2, Eggebek;
TsLw-1, Kaufbeuren;
WTD-61, Ingolstadt

43+01[1]	[G-20]	TTTE
43+02[1]	[G-21]	TTTE
43+03[1]	[G-22]	TTTE
43+04[1]	JbG-31	
43+05[1]	[G-24]	TTTE
43+06[1]	[G-25]	TTTE
43+07[1]	[G-26]	TTTE
43+08[1]	JbG-34	
43+09[1]	[G-28]	TTTE
43+10[1]	[G-29]	TTTE
43+11[1]	[G-30]	TTTE
43+13	[G-71]	TTTE
43+14	[G-72]	TTTE
43+15[1]	[G-31]	TTTE
43+16[1]	[G-32]	TTTE
43+17[1]	[G-33]	TTTE
43+18	JbG-34	
43+19	49 FW	
43+20	AkG-51	
43+22[1]	JbG-38	
43+23[1]	JbG-38	
43+25	[G-75]	TTTE
43+26	JbG-38	
43+27	JbG-34	

Serial	Unit	Note	Serial	Unit	Serial	Unit	Note
43+28	49 FW		44+13	TsLw-1	44+95	JbG-38	
43+29[1]	JbG-31		44+14	JbG-31	44+96	JbG-31	
43+30	JbG-38		44+15[1]	JbG-38	44+97	JbG-33	
43+31[1]	JbG-31		44+16	JbG-31	44+98	JbG-38	
43+32	[G-73]	TTTE	44+17	AkG-51	45+00	JbG-33	
43+33[1]	JbG-38		44+19	JbG-31	45+01	JbG-38	
43+34	TsLw-1		44+20[1]	49 FW	45+02	JbG-33	
43+35[1]	JbG-38		44+21	JbG-31	45+03	JbG-33	
43+36	49 FW		44+22	JbG-33	45+04	JbG-38	
43+37[1]	JbG-38		44+23	JbG-33	45+05	JbG-33	
43+38	AkG-51		44+24	AkG-51	45+06	JbG-33	
43+40	JbG-38		44+25[1]	JbG-38	45+07	JbG-33	
43+41	JbG-31		44+26	JbG-31	45+08	JbG-33	
43+42[1]	[G-39]	TTTE	44+27	JbG-33	45+09	JbG-33	
43+43[1]	JbG-38		44+28	JbG-31	45+10	JbG-31	
43+44[1]	AkG-51		44+29	JbG-31	45+11	JbG-33	
43+45[1]	AkG-51		44+30	JbG-31	45+12[1]	MFG-2	
43+46	AkG-51		44+31	JbG-31	45+13[1]	MFG-2	
43+47	AkG-51		44+32	JbG-38	45+14[1]	MFG-2	
43+48	AkG-51		44+33	JbG-33	45+15[1]	MFG-2	
43+50	AkG-51		44+34	AkG-51	45+16[1]	MFG-2	
43+52	JbG-38		44+36[1]	JbG-38	45+17	JbG-33	
43+53	JbG-38		44+37[1]	JbG-38	45+18	AkG-51	
43+54	JbG-34		44+38[1]	AkG-51	45+19	JbG-33	
43+55	MFG-2		44+39[1]	JbG-33	45+20	AkG-51	
43+57	AkG-51		44+40	JbG-33	45+21	JbG-33	
43+58	JbG-34		44+41	JbG-31	45+22	JbG-33	
43+59	JbG-38		44+42	AkG-51	45+23	JbG-31	
43+60	JbG-34		44+43	JbG-34	45+24	JbG-33	
43+61	TsLw-1		44+44	JbG-31	45+25	AkG-51	
43+62	JbG-34		44+46	JbG-34	45+26	MFG-2	
43+63	JbG-34		44+48	JbG-33	45+27	MFG-2	
43+64	JbG-38		44+50	AkG-51	45+28	MFG-2	
43+65	JbG-38		44+51	JbG-38	45+29	JbG-33	
43+67	JbG-34		44+52	JbG-31	45+30	MFG-2	
43+68	JbG-34		44+53	AkG-51	45+31	MFG-2	
43+69	JbG-38		44+54	JbG-33	45+32	*Cr 24 Aug 96*	
43+70	JbG-38		44+55	JbG-38	45+33	MFG-2	
43+71	JbG-38		44+56	JbG-34	45+34	MFG-2	
43+72	JbG-38		44+57	JbG-31	45+35	MFG-2	
43+73	AkG-51		44+58	JbG-34	45+36	AkG-51	
43+75	[G-77]	TTTE	44+59	JbG-31	45+37	MFG-2	
43+76	JbG-38		44+60	JbG-31	45+38	MFG-2	
43+77	JbG-33		44+61	AkG-51	45+39	MFG-2	
43+78	JbG-34		44+62	JbG-33	45+40	MFG-2	
43+79	[G-76]	TTTE	44+63	JbG-33	45+41	MFG-2	
43+80	AkG-51		44+64	JbG-38	45+42	MFG-2	
43+81	AkG-51		44+65	AkG-51	45+43	JbG-38	
43+82	AkG-51		44+66	JbG-31	45+44	MFG-2	
43+85	JbG-38		44+68	AkG-51	45+45	MFG-2	
43+86	JbG-38		44+69	AkG-51	45+46	MFG-2	
43+87	MFG-2		44+70	49 FW	45+47	MFG-2	
43+88	AkG-51		44+71	JbG-31	45+48	MFG-2	
43+90[1]	JbG-38		44+72[1]	JbG-33	45+49	MFG-2	
43+91[1]	JbG-32		44+73[1]	JbG-32	45+50	MFG-2	
43+92[1]	JbG-31		44+75[1]	JbG-33	45+51	JbG-31	
43+94[1]	JbG-38		44+76	JbG-34	45+52	MFG-2	
43+96	AkG-51		44+77	JbG-31	45+53	MFG-2	
43+97[1]	JbG-32		44+78	JbG-31	45+54	MFG-2	
43+98	AkG-51		44+79	JbG-33	45+55	JbG-32	
43+99	JbG-34		44+80	JbG-33	45+56	MFG-2	
44+00	JbG-31		44+81	JbG-34	45+57	JbG-34	
44+01[1]	49 FW		44+82	JbG-31	45+59	MFG-2	
44+02	JbG-31		44+83	JbG-33	45+60[1]	JbG-38	
44+03	JbG-34		44+84	JbG-33	45+61[1]	JbG-34	
44+04	JbG-33		44+85	JbG-33	45+62[1]	JbG-38	
44+05[1]	AkG-51		44+86	JbG-38	45+64	TsLw-1	
44+06	JbG-34		44+87	AkG-51	45+65	49FW	
44+07	JbG-38		44+88	AkG-51	45+66	MFG-2	
44+08	JbG-38		44+89	JbG-33	45+67	MFG-2	
44+09	JbG-33		44+90	JbG-33	45+68	MFG-2	
44+10[1]	JbG-38		44+91	JbG-33	45+69	MFG-2	
44+11	JbG-34		44+92	JbG-38	45+70[1]	JbG-33	
44+12	JbG-38		44+94	JbG-33	45+71	MFG-2	

Serial	Unit
45+72	MFG-2
45+73[1]	JbG-31
45+74	MFG-2
45+76	JbG-38
45+77[1]	JbG-33
45+78	JbG-34
45+79	JbG-31
45+81	JbG-34
45+82	AkG-51
45+83	49 FW
45+84	AkG-51
45+85	AkG-51
45+86	JbG-33
45+87	JbG-34
45+88	JbG-33
45+89	JbG-34
45+90	JbG-31
45+91	AkG-51
45+92	AkG-51
45+93	AkG-51
45+94	JbG-33
45+95	JbG-34
45+96	49 FW
45+98	AkG-51
45+99[1]	AkG-51
46+00	JbG-38
46+01	JbG-34
46+02	JbG-33
46+03	JbG-34
46+04[1]	JbG-38
46+05[1]	MFG-2
46+06[1]	JbG-32
46+07	JbG-34
46+08	JbG-34
46+09	JbG-34
46+10	WTD-61
46+11	MFG-2
46+12	MFG-2
46+13	JbG-34
46+14	JbG-34
46+15	MFG-2
46+18	MFG-2
46+19	MFG-2
46+20	MFG-2
46+21	MFG-2
46+22	MFG-2
46+23[2]	JbG-32
46+24[2]	JbG-32
46+25[2]	JbG-32
46+26[2]	JbG-32
46+27[2]	JbG-32
46+28[2]	JbG-32
46+29[2]	JbG-32
46+30[2]	JbG-32
46+31[2]	JbG-32
46+32[2]	JbG-32
46+33[2]	JbG-32
46+34[2]	JbG-32
46+35[2]	JbG-32
46+36[2]	JbG-32
46+37[2]	JbG-32
46+38[2]	JbG-32
46+39[2]	JbG-32
46+40[2]	JbG-32
46+41[2]	JbG-32
46+42[2]	JbG-32
46+43[2]	JbG-32
46+44[2]	JbG-32
46+45[2]	JbG-32
46+46[2]	JbG-32
46+47[2]	JbG-32
46+48[2]	JbG-32
46+49[2]	JbG-32
46+50[2]	JbG-32
46+51[2]	JbG-32
46+52[2]	JbG-32
46+53[2]	JbG-32
46+54[2]	JbG-32
46+55[2]	JbG-32
46+56[2]	JbG-32
46+57[2]	JbG-32
98+02	WTD-61
98+03[2]	WTD-61
98+59	WTD-61
98+60	WTD-61
98+79[2]	WTD-61
98+97[2]	WTD-61

Transall C-160D
LTG-61, Landsberg;
LTG-62, Wunstorf;
LTG-63, Hohn;
WTD-61, Ingolstadt

Serial	Unit
50+06	LTG-63
50+07	LTG-61
50+08	LTG-61
50+09	LTG-62
50+10	LTG-62
50+17	LTG-62
50+29	LTG-62
50+33	LTG-62
50+34	LTG-63
50+35	LTG-62
50+36	LTG-63
50+37	LTG-62
50+38	LTG-62
50+40	LTG-61
50+41	LTG-63
50+42	LTG-63
50+44	LTG-61
50+45	LTG-61
50+46	LTG-62
50+47	LTG-61
50+48	LTG-62
50+49	LTG-61
50+50	LTG-62
50+51	LTG-62
50+52	LTG-62
50+53	LTG-62
50+54	LTG-63
50+55	LTG-62
50+56	LTG-61
50+57	LTG-61
50+58	LTG-62
50+59	LTG-63
50+60	LTG-62
50+61	LTG-63
50+62	LTG-62
50+64	LTG-61
50+65	LTG-61
50+66	LTG-61
50+67	LTG-63
50+68[2]	LTG-61
50+69[2]	LTG-61
50+70	LTG-63
50+71	LTG-63
50+72	LTG-61
50+73	LTG-62
50+74	LTG-61
50+75	WTD-61
50+76	LTG-63
50+77	LTG-63
50+78	LTG-62
50+79	LTG-63
50+81	LTG-63
50+82	LTG-62
50+83	LTG-62
50+84	LTG-61
50+85	LTG-63
50+86	LTG-62
50+87	LTG-63
50+88	LTG-61
50+89	LTG-62
50+90	LTG-61
50+91	LTG-62
50+92	LTG-61
50+93	LTG-63
50+94	LTG-63
50+95	LTG-62
50+96	LTG-61
50+97	LTG-62
50+98	LTG-61
50+99	LTG-61
51+00	LTG-62
51+01	LTG-62
51+02	LTG-63
51+03	LTG-63
51+04	LTG-61
51+05	LTG-62
51+06	LTG-63
51+07	LTG-62
51+08	LTG-63
51+09	LTG-63
51+10	LTG-61
51+11	LTG-62
51+12	LTG-63
51+13	LTG-61
51+14	LTG-63
51+15	LTG-61

LET L-410UVP-T/UVP-S*
3/FBS, Berlin-Tegel

Serial
53+08
53+09*
53+10*
53+11*
53+12*

Dornier Do.228
WTD-61, Ingolstadt;
MFG-3, Nordholz

Serial	Unit
57+01	MFG-3
57+02	MFG-3
57+03	MFG-3
98+78	WTD-61

Breguet Br.1151 Atlantic
*Elint
MFG-3, Nordholz

Serial
61+01
61+02*
61+03*
61+04
61+05
61+06*
61+08
61+09
61+10
61+11
61+12
61+13
61+14
61+15
61+16
61+17
61+18
61+19*
61+20*

Westland Lynx Mk88
MFG-3, Nordholz

Serial		
83+02		
83+03		
83+04		
83+05		
83+06		
83+07		
83+08		
83+09		
83+10		
83+11		
83+12		
83+13		
83+14		
83+15		
83+17		
83+18		
83+19		

Westland Sea King HAS41
MFG-5, Kiel-Holtenau

Serial		
89+50		
89+51		
89+52		
89+53		
89+54		
89+55		
89+56		
89+57		
89+58		
89+59		
89+60		
89+61		
89+62		
89+63		
89+64		
89+65		
89+66		
89+67		
89+68		
89+69		
89+70		
89+71		

Eurofighter EF2000

98+29	WTD-61 (ZH586)	

Heeresfliegertruppe
MBB Bo.105
HFlgRgt-15, Rheine-Bentlage;
HFlgRgt-16, Celle;
HFlgRgt-25, Laupheim;
HFlgRgt-26, Roth;
HFlgRgt-35, Mendig;
HFlgRgt-36, Fritzlar;
HFVS-910, Bückeburg;
HFWS, Bückeburg;
TsLw-3, Fassberg;
WTD-61, Ingolstadt

Serial	Type	Unit
80+01	Bo.105M	HFR-35
80+02	Bo.105M	TsLw-3
80+03	Bo.105M	HFWS
80+04	Bo.105M	HFWS
80+05	Bo.105M	HFR-35
80+06	Bo.105M	TsLw-3
80+07	Bo.105M	HFWS
80+08	Bo.105M	HFR-25
80+09	Bo.105M	HFWS
80+10	Bo.105M	HFR-25
80+11	Bo.105M	HFWS
80+12	Bo.105M	HFWS
80+13	Bo.105M	HFR-15
80+14	Bo.105M	HFWS
80+15	Bo.105M	HFR-15
80+16	Bo.105M	HFR-15
80+17	Bo.105M	HFWS
80+18	Bo.105M	HFR-15
80+19	Bo.105M	HFR-15
80+20	Bo.105M	HFR-15
80+21	Bo.105M	HFR-26
80+22	Bo.105M	
80+23	Bo.105M	HFR-15
80+24	Bo.105M	HFR-15
80+25	Bo.105M	HFR-15
80+26	Bo.105M	HFR-35
80+27	Bo.105M	HFR-35
80+28	Bo.105M	TsLw-3
80+29	Bo.105M	HFR-35
80+30	Bo.105M	HFR-35
80+31	Bo.105M	HFR-35
80+32	Bo.105M	HFR-35
80+33	Bo.105M	HFR-35
80+34	Bo.105M	HFR-25
80+35	Bo.105M	
80+36	Bo.105M	HFR-25
80+37	Bo.105M	HFR-25
80+38	Bo.105M	HFR-25
80+39	Bo.105M	HFR-25
80+40	Bo.105M	HFR-26
80+41	Bo.105M	HFR-25
80+42	Bo.105M	HFR-25
80+43	Bo.105M	HFR-25
80+44	Bo.105M	HFR-25
80+46	Bo.105M	TsLw-3
80+47	Bo.105M	HFR-25
80+48	Bo.105M	HFR-25
80+49	Bo.105M	
80+50	Bo.105M	
80+51	Bo.105M	HFR-15
80+52	Bo.105M	HFR-15
80+53	Bo.105M	
80+54	Bo.105M	HFR-15
80+55	Bo.105M	
80+56	Bo.105M	
80+57	Bo.105M	HFR-35
80+58	Bo.105M	HFR-35
80+59	Bo.105M	HFR-35
80+60	Bo.105M	HFR-35
80+62	Bo.105M	HFR-35
80+64	Bo.105M	HFR-35
80+65	Bo.105M	HFR-15
80+66	Bo.105M	HFR-15
80+67	Bo.105M	HFR-15
80+68	Bo.105M	HFR-15
80+69	Bo.105M	HFR-15
80+70	Bo.105M	HFR-15
80+71	Bo.105M	HFR-15
80+72	Bo.105M	HFR-15
80+73	Bo.105M	HFR-15
80+74	Bo.105M	HFR-15
80+75	Bo.105M	
80+76	Bo.105M	HFR-15
80+77	Bo.105M	HFR-35
80+78	Bo.105M	HFR-35
80+79	Bo.105M	HFR-35
80+80	Bo.105M	HFR-35
80+81	Bo.105M	HFR-25
80+82	Bo.105M	HFR-25
80+83	Bo.105M	HFR-25
80+84	Bo.105M	HFR-25
80+85	Bo.105M	HFR-25
80+86	Bo.105M	
80+87	Bo.105M	HFR-25
80+88	Bo.105M	
80+89	Bo.105M	HFR-36
80+90	Bo.105M	
80+91	Bo.105M	HFR-35
80+92	Bo.105M	
80+93	Bo.105M	
80+94	Bo.105M	HFR-25
80+95	Bo.105M	
80+96	Bo.105M	HFR-25
80+97	Bo.105M	HFR-35
80+98	Bo.105M	HFR-25
80+99	Bo.105M	HFR-26
81+00	Bo.105M	HFR-25
86+01	Bo.105P	HFR-16
86+02	Bo.105P	HFWS
86+03	Bo.105P	HFWS
86+04	Bo.105P	HFR-36
86+05	Bo.105P	HFWS
86+06	Bo.105P	HFWS
86+07	Bo.105P	HFWS
86+08	Bo.105P	TsLw-3
86+09	Bo.105P	HFWS
86+10	Bo.105P	HFVS-910
86+11	Bo.105P	HFWS
86+12	Bo.105P	HFWS
86+13	Bo.105P	HFWS
86+14	Bo.105P	HFR-16
86+15	Bo.105P	TsLw-3
86+16	Bo.105P	HFWS
86+17	Bo.105P	HFVS-910
86+18	Bo.105P	HFR-26
86+19	Bo.105P	HFR-26
86+20	Bo.105P	HFWS
86+21	Bo.105P	HFR-36
86+22	Bo.105P	HFWS
86+23	Bo.105P	HFWS
86+24	Bo.105P	HFVS-910
86+25	Bo.105P	HFR-16
86+26	Bo.105P	HFR-16
86+27	Bo.105P	HFR-26
86+28	Bo.105P	TsLw-3
86+29	Bo.105P	HFR-16
86+30	Bo.105P	HFR-26
86+31	Bo.105P	HFR-16
86+32	Bo.105P	HFR-26
86+33	Bo.105P	HFR-26
86+34	Bo.105P	HFR-26
86+35	Bo.105P	HFR-26
86+36	Bo.105P	HFR-36
86+37	Bo.105P	HFR-16
86+38	Bo.105P	HFR-36
86+39	Bo.105P	HFR-16
86+40	Bo.105P	
86+41	Bo.105P	HFR-16
86+42	Bo.105P	HFR-26
86+43	Bo.105P	HFR-16
86+44	Bo.105P	HFR-26
86+45	Bo.105P	HFR-26
86+46	Bo.105P	HFR-26
86+47	Bo.105P	HFR-16
86+48	Bo.105P	HFR-16
86+49	Bo.105P	
86+50	Bo.105P	HFR-16
86+51	Bo.105P	HFR-36
86+52	Bo.105P	HFR-16
86+53	Bo.105P	HFR-36
86+54	Bo.105P	HFR-16
86+55	Bo.105P	HFR-16
86+56	Bo.105P	HFR-36
86+57	Bo.105P	HFR-16
86+58	Bo.105P	HFR-36
86+59	Bo.105P	HFR-16
86+60	Bo.105P	HFR-16
86+61	Bo.105P	HFR-26
86+62	Bo.105P	HFVS-910
86+63	Bo.105P	HFR-26
86+64	Bo.105P	HFR-26

Serial	Type	Unit
86+65	Bo.105P	HFR-26
86+66	Bo.105P	HFVS-910
86+67	Bo.105P	HFR-26
86+68	Bo.105P	HFR-16
86+69	Bo.105P	HFR-26
86+70	Bo.105P	HFR-16
86+71	Bo.105P	HFR-36
86+72	Bo.105P	HFR-36
86+73	Bo.105P	HFR-36
86+74	Bo.105P	HFR-16
86+75	Bo.105P	HFR-16
86+76	Bo.105P	HFR-26
86+77	Bo.105P	HFR-16
86+78	Bo.105P	HFR-26
86+79	Bo.105P	
86+80	Bo.105P	HFR-16
86+81	Bo.105P	HFR-16
86+83	Bo.105P	HFR-16
86+84	Bo.105P	HFR-26
86+85	Bo.105P	HFR-16
86+86	Bo.105P	HFR-16
86+87	Bo.105P	HFR-16
86+88	Bo.105P	HFR-16
86+89	Bo.105P	HFR-16
86+90	Bo.105P	HFR-26
86+91	Bo.105P	HFR-26
86+92	Bo.105P	HFR-36
86+93	Bo.105P	HFVS-910
86+94	Bo.105P	HFR-26
86+95	Bo.105P	HFR-16
86+96	Bo.105P	HFR-26
86+97	Bo.105P	HFR-36
86+98	Bo.105P	HFR-26
86+99	Bo.105P	HFR-26
87+00	Bo.105P	HFR-26
87+01	Bo.105P	HFR-26
87+02	Bo.105P	HFR-26
87+03	Bo.105P	HFR-26
87+04	Bo.105P	HFR-26
87+06	Bo.105P	HFR-36
87+07	Bo.105P	HFR-26
87+08	Bo.105P	HFR-16
87+09	Bo.105P	HFR-36
87+10	Bo.105P	HFR-26
87+11	Bo.105P	HFR-36
87+12	Bo.105P	HFR-36
87+13	Bo.105P	HFR-36
87+14	Bo.105P	HFR-36
87+15	Bo.105P	HFR-36
87+16	Bo.105P	HFR-36
87+17	Bo.105P	HFR-36
87+18	Bo.105P	HFR-36
87+19	Bo.105P	HFR-36
87+20	Bo.105P	HFR-26
87+21	Bo.105P	HFWS
87+22	Bo.105P	HFR-16
87+23	Bo.105P	
87+24	Bo.105P	HFR-16
87+25	Bo.105P	HFR-26
87+26	Bo.105P	HFR-16
87+27	Bo.105P	HFR-16
87+28	Bo.105P	HFR-16
87+29	Bo.105P	HFR-26
87+30	Bo.105P	HFR-16
87+31	Bo.105P	HFR-16
87+32	Bo.105P	HFR-16
87+33	Bo.105P	HFR-26
87+34	Bo.105P	HFR-26
87+35	Bo.105P	HFR-26
87+36	Bo.105P	HFR-26
87+37	Bo.105P	HFR-26
87+38	Bo.105P	HFR-36
87+39	Bo.105P	HFR-36
87+40	Bo.105P	
87+41	Bo.105P	HFR-16
87+42	Bo.105P	HFR-36
87+43	Bo.105P	HFR-36
87+44	Bo.105P	HFR-36
87+45	Bo.105P	HFR-16
87+46	Bo.105P	HFR-16
87+47	Bo.105P	HFR-16
87+48	Bo.105P	HFR-16
87+49	Bo.105P	HFR-16
87+50	Bo.105P	HFR-26
87+51	Bo.105P	HFR-16
87+52	Bo.105P	HFR-16
87+53	Bo.105P	HFR-26
87+54	Bo.105P	HFR-26
87+55	Bo.105P	HFR-26
87+56	Bo.105P	HFR-26
87+57	Bo.105P	HFR-26
87+58	Bo.105P	HFR-26
87+59	Bo.105P	HFR-36
87+60	Bo.105P	HFR-36
87+61	Bo.105P	HFR-36
87+62	Bo.105P	HFR-36
87+63	Bo.105P	HFWS
87+64	Bo.105P	HFR-36
87+65	Bo.105P	HFR-36
87+66	Bo.105P	HFR-36
87+67	Bo.105P	HFWS
87+68	Bo.105P	HFR-16
87+69	Bo.105P	HFR-26
87+70	Bo.105P	HFR-16
87+71	Bo.105P	HFR-26
87+72	Bo.105P	HFR-16
87+73	Bo.105P	HFR-16
87+74	Bo.105P	HFVS-910
87+75	Bo.105P	HFR-16
87+76	Bo.105P	HFR-16
87+77	Bo.105P	HFR-16
87+78	Bo.105P	HFR-16
87+79	Bo.105P	HFR-16
87+80	Bo.105P	HFR-26
87+81	Bo.105P	HFR-16
87+82	Bo.105P	HFR-16
87+83	Bo.105P	HFR-16
87+84	Bo.105P	HFVS-910
87+85	Bo.105P	HFR-26
87+86	Bo.105P	HFR-26
87+87	Bo.105P	HFR-16
87+88	Bo.105P	HFR-26
87+89	Bo.105P	HFR-26
87+90	Bo.105P	HFWS
87+91	Bo.105P	HFR-26
87+92	Bo.105P	HFR-26
87+93	Bo.105P	HFR-26
87+94	Bo.105P	HFR-26
87+95	Bo.105P	HFR-26
87+96	Bo.105P	HFR-26
87+97	Bo.105P	HFR-26
87+98	Bo.105P	HFR-26
87+99	Bo.105P	HFR-36
88+01	Bo.105P	HFR-26
88+02	Bo.105P	HFR-36
88+03	Bo.105P	HFR-36
88+04	Bo.105P	HFR-16
88+05	Bo.105P	HFVS-910
88+06	Bo.105P	HFR-36
88+07	Bo.105P	HFR-36
88+08	Bo.105P	HFR-36
88+09	Bo.105P	HFR-36
88+10	Bo.105P	HFVS-910
88+11	Bo.105P	HFR-36
88+12	Bo.105P	HFR-36
98+20	Bo.105C	WTD-61
98+21	Bo.105C	WTD-61
98+27	Bo.105C	HFWS
98+28	Bo.105C	WTD-61

Sikorsky/VFW CH-53G

HFlgRgt-15, Rheine-Bentlage;
HFlgRgt-25, Laupheim;
HFlgRgt-35, Mendig;
HFWS, Bückeburg;
TsLw-3, Fassberg;
WTD-61, Ingolstadt

Serial	Unit
84+01	WTD-61
84+02	WTD-61
84+03	HFR-15
84+04	TsLw-3
84+05	HFR-35
84+06	HFR-35
84+07	HFWS
84+08	HFR-35
84+09	HFR-25
84+10	HFWS
84+11	HFWS
84+12	HFR-15
84+13	TsLw-3
84+14	HFWS
84+15	HFR-25
84+16	HFWS
84+17	HFR-25
84+18	HFWS
84+19	HFWS
84+20	HFR-35
84+21	HFWS
84+22	HFR-35
84+23	HFR-25
84+24	HFR-35
84+25	HFR-35
84+26	HFR-35
84+27	HFR-35
84+28	HFR-35
84+29	HFR-35
84+30	HFR-35
84+31	HFR-35
84+32	HFR-35
84+33	HFR-35
84+34	HFR-35
84+35	HFR-35
84+36	HFR-35
84+37	HFR-35
84+38	HFR-35
84+39	HFR-35
84+40	HFR-25
84+41	HFWS
84+42	HFR-25
84+43	HFR-25
84+44	HFR-25
84+45	HFR-25
84+46	HFR-35
84+47	HFR-25
84+48	HFR-25
84+49	HFWS
84+50	HFR-25
84+51	HFR-25
84+52	HFR-25
84+53	HFR-25
84+54	HFR-25
84+55	HFR-25
84+56	HFR-25
84+57	HFR-25
84+58	HFR-25
84+59	HFR-25
84+60	HFR-25
84+62	HFR-25
84+63	HFR-25
84+64	HFR-35
84+65	HFR-35
84+66	HFR-35
84+67	HFR-35

84+68	HFR-15
84+69	HFR-15
84+70	HFR-15
84+71	HFR-15
84+72	HFR-15
84+73	HFR-15
84+74	HFR-15
84+75	HFR-15
84+76	HFR-15
84+77	HFR-15
84+78	HFR-15
84+79	HFR-15
84+80	HFR-15
84+82	HFR-15
84+83	HFR-15
84+84	HFR-15
84+85	HFR-15
84+86	HFR-15
84+87	HFR-15
84+88	HFR-15
84+89	HFR-15
84+90	HFR-15
84+91	HFR-15
84+92	HFR-35
84+93	HFR-35
84+94	HFR-35
84+95	HFR-25
84+96	HFR-25
84+97	HFR-25
84+98	HFR-15
84+99	HFR-15
85+00	HFR-15
85+01	HFR-35
85+02	HFR-35
85+03	HFR-35
85+04	HFR-25
85+05	HFR-25
85+06	HFR-25
85+07	HFR-15
85+08	HFR-15
85+09	HFR-15
85+10	HFR-35
85+11	HFR-25
85+12	HFR-15

Eurocopter AS.665 Tiger
WTD-61, Ingolstadt
98+23
98+25

GREECE
Hellinikí Aeroporía
Lockheed C-130H Hercules
356 MTM, Elefsis
*ECM
741*
742
743
744
745
746
747
749
750
751
752

HUNGARY
**Magyar Honvédseg Repülö
Csapatai**
Antonov An-26
Szolnok Mixed Air Carrier
Regiment

202	(02202)
203	(02203)
204	(02204)
208	(02208)
209	(02209)
405	(03405)
406	(03406)
407	(03407)
603	(03603)

ISRAEL
Heyl ha Avir
Boeing 707
122 Sqn, 134 Sqn, Tel Aviv

115/4X-JYV	EC-707	
120/4X-JYP	RC-707	
128/4X-JYL	RC-707	
137/4X-JYM	RC-707	
140/4X-JYT	KC-707	
242/4X-JYQ	VC-707	
246/4X-JYS	EC-707	
248/4X-JYU	KC-707	
250/4X-JYY	KC-707	
255/4X-JYB	EC-707	
258/4X-JYC	EC-707	
260	KC-707	
264/4X-JYH	VC-707	

Lockheed C-130 Hercules
103 Sqn, 131 Sqn, Tel Aviv

102/4X-FBA	C-130H
106/4X-FBB	C-130H
208/4X-FBP	C-130E
301	C-130E
304	C-130E
305	C-130E
307	C-130E
309	C-130H
310/4X-FBG	C-130E
311/4X-FBD	C-130E
312	C-130E
313	C-130E
314	C-130E
316	C-130E
318	C-130E
420	C-130H
427	C-130H
428	C-130H
435/4X-FBT	C-130H
436	C-130H
448	C-130H
522	KC-130H
545	KC-130H

ITALY
Aeronautica Militare Italiana
Aeritalia G222
46ª Brigata Aerea, Pisa;
14º Stormo, Pratica di Mare;
RSV, Pratica di Mare

MM62101	RS-45	TCM
MM62102	46-20	TCM
MM62103	46-37	TCM
MM62104	46-91	TCM
MM62105	46-82	TCM
MM62107	(14)	VS
MM62109	46-96	TCM
MM62110	46-81	TCM
MM62111	46-83	TCM
MM62112	46-85	TCM
MM62114	46-80	TCM
MM62115	46-22	TCM
MM62117	46-25	TCM
MM62118	46-24	TCM
MM62119	46-21	TCM
MM62120	46-90	TCM
MM62121	46-86	TCM
MM62122	46-23	TCM
MM62123	46-28	TCM
MM62124	46-88	TCM
MM62125	46-87	TCM
MM62126	46-26	TCM
MM62127	46-27	TCM
MM62130	RS-51	TCM
MM62132	46-32	TCM
MM62133	46-93	TCM
MM62134	46-33	TCM
MM62135	46-94	TCM
MM62136	46-97	TCM
MM62137	46-95	TCM
MM62138	(14)	RM
MM62139	14-20	RM
MM62140	14-21	RM
MM62141	14-22	RM
MM62142	(14)	RM
MM62143	46-36	TCM
MM62144	46-98	TCM
MM62145	46-50	TCM
MM62146	46-51	TCM
MM62147	46-52	TCM
MM62152	46-38	TCM
MM62153	46-99	TCM
MM62154		TCM
MM62155		TCM

Aeritalia-EMB AMX/AMX-T*
2º Stormo, Rivolto;
3º Stormo, Villafranca;
32º Stormo, Amendola;
51º Stormo, Istrana;
RSV, Pratica di Mare

MMX595	Aeritalia
MMX596	Alenia
MMX597	Alenia
MMX599	Alenia
MM7089	
MM7090	RS-12
MM7091	32-64
MM7092	RS-14
MM7093	3-11
MM7094	3-37
MM7095	(51)
MM7096	32-03
MM7097	3-36
MM7098	3-35
MM7099	
MM7100	3-44
MM7101	(51)
MM7102	2-03
MM7103	
MM7104	51-44
MM7105	32-13
MM7106	51-37
MM7107	
MM7110	2-14
MM7111	3-16
MM7112	32-01
MM7114	
MM7115	2-12
MM7116	32-11
MM7117	3-34
MM7118	2-11
MM7119	
MM7120	3-33
MM7122	3-32
MM7123	3-13
MM7124	3-40
MM7125	3-30
MM7126	
MM7127	3-12

MM7128	
MM7129	3-30
MM7130	32-02
MM7131	RS-13
MM7132	(51)
MM7133	(51)
MM7134	51-30
MM7135	51-32
MM7138	2-25
MM7139	(51)
MM7140	(51)
MM7141	51-55
MM7142	51-37
MM7143	51-41
MM7144	3-42
MM7145	3-22
MM7146	(51)
MM7147	32-04
MM7148	2-21
MM7149	
MM7150	32-65
MM7151	(51)
MM7152	3-43
MM7153	3-45
MM7154	51-54
MM7155	32-05
MM7156	32-10
MM7157	32-06
MM7158	
MM7159	
MM7160	51-30
MM7161	2-21
MM7162	51-45
MM7163	3-02
MM716	51-34
MM7165	3-51
MM7166	3-24
MM7167	2-01
MM7168	2-04
MM7169	2-06
MM7170	2-23
MM7171	2-15
MM7172	2-07
MM7173	2-16
MM7174	3-05
MM7175	3-01
MM7176	2-20
MM7177	2-22
MM7178	24
MM7179	2-02
MM7180	3-03
MM7181	3-07
MM7182	3-52
MM7183	3-53
MM7184	3-06
MM7185	3-54
MM7186	
MM7187	
MM7188	
MM7189	
MM7190	
MM7191	
MM7192	
MM7193	
MM55024*	Aeritalia
MM55025*	(RSV)
MM55026*	32-43
MM55027*	32-42
MM55028*	3-56
MM55029*	3-55
MM55030*	32-41
MM55031*	32-40
MM55032*	
MM55033*	

MM55034*	18
MM55035*	32-50
MM55036*	32-51
MM55037*	3-27
MM55038*	
MM55039*	
MM55040*	32-52
MM55041*	
MM55042*	
MM55043*	51-61
MM55044*	
MM55045*	

Aermacchi MB339A/ MB339CD[1]
Frecce Tricolori
(MB339PAN)
(313 Gruppo), Rivolto;
61° Stormo, Lecce;
14° Stormo, Pratica di Mare;
Aermacchi, Venegono;
RSV, Pratica di Mare

MM54438	61-93
MM54439	6*
MM54440	61-00
MM54442	61-95
MM54443	61-50
MM54445	8*
MM54446	61-01
MM54447	61-02
MM54448	61-03
MM54449	61-04
MM54450	61-94
MM54451	61-86
MM54452	61-41
MM54453	61-05
MM54454	61-06
MM54455	61-07
MM54456	RS-10
MM54457	61-11
MM54458	61-12
MM54459	61-13
MM54460	61-14
MM54461	(RSV)
MM54462	61-16
MM54463	61-17
MM54467	61-23
MM54468	61-24
MM54471	61-27
MM54472	61-30
MM54473	*
MM54475	1*
MM54476	
MM54477	9*
MM54478	*
MM54479	10*
MM54480	0*
MM54482	*
MM54483	7*
MM54484	3*
MM54485	11*
MM54486	*
MM54487	61-31
MM54488	61-32
MM54489	61-33
MM54490	61-34
MM54491	61-35
MM54492	61-36
MM54493	61-37
MM54494	61-40
MM54496	61-42
MM54497	61-43
MM54498	61-44

MM54499	61-45
MM54500	4*
MM54503	61-51
MM54504	61-52
MM54505	61-53
MM54506	61-54
MM54507	61-55
MM54508	61-56
MM54509	61-57
MM54510	61-60
MM54511	(RSV)
MM54512	61-62
MM54513	61-63
MM54514	61-64
MM54515	61-65
MM54516	61-66
MM54517	12*
MM54518	61-70
MM54532	61-71
MM54533	61-72
MM54534	61-73
MM54535	61-74
MM54536	5*
MM54537	
MM54538	61-75
MM54539	61-76
MM54540	61-77
MM54541	61-80
MM54542	61-81
MM54543	61-82
MM54544[1]	Aermacchi
MM54545	61-84
MM54546	61-85
MM54547	61-87
MM54548	61-90
MM54549	61-91
MM54550	61-92
MM54551	2*
MM55052	61-96
MM55053	61-97
MM55054	61-15
MM55055	61-20
MM55058	61-41
MM55059	61-26

Boeing 707-328B/-3F5C*
14° Stormo, Pratica di Mare;
31° Stormo, Roma-Ciampino

MM62148	14-01
MM62149	14-02
MM62150*	(31)
MM62151*	14-04

Breguet Br 1150 Atlantic
30° Stormo, Cagliari;
41° Stormo, Catania

MM40108	41-70
MM40109	30-71
MM40110	41-72
MM40111	41-73
MM40112	30-74
MM40113	30-75
MM40114	41-76
MM40115	41-77
MM40116	30-01
MM40117	41-02
MM40118	30-03
MM40119	30-04
MM40120	41-05
MM40121	41-06
MM40122	30-07
MM40123	30-10
MM40124	41-11
MM40125	30-12

Dassault Falcon 50
31° Stormo, Roma-Ciampino
MM62020
MM62021
MM62026
MM62029

Eurofighter EF2000
Aeritalia, Torino/Caselle
MMX602

Grumman G.1159A Gulfstream III
31° Stormo, Roma-Ciampino
MM62022
MM62025

Lockheed F-104 Starfighter
4° Stormo, Grosseto;
5° Stormo, Rimini;
9° Stormo, Grazzanise;
37° Stormo, Trapani;
51° Stormo, Istrana;
53° Stormo, Cameri;
RSV, Pratica di Mare

F-104S

Serial	Code
MM6701	
MM6703	51-01
MM6704	5-44
MM6705	
MM6710	
MM6713	
MM6714	9-50
MM6716	*wfu*
MM6717	9-32
MM6719	
MM6720	9-40
MM6721	51-06
MM6722	5-45
MM6726	4-6
MM6727	9-45
MM6730	9-33
MM6731	
MM6732	4-5
MM6733	4-7
MM6734	9-43
MM6735	51-22
MM6736	
MM6737	5-43
MM6739	
MM6740	*wfu*
MM6741	37-21
MM6742	4-53
MM6744	5-07
MM6747	37-24
MM6748	
MM6749	9-41
MM6750	37-04
MM6756	37-10
MM6759	37-26
MM6760	4-50
MM6761	4-3
MM6762	
MM6763	
MM6764	
MM6767	
MM6768	
MM6769	
MM6770	5-30
MM6771	5-31
MM6772	
MM6773	
MM6774	4-1
MM6775	9-50
MM6776	51-15
MM6778	4-4
MM6780	
MM6781	51-14
MM6782	37-15
MM6784	37-27
MM6785	5-25
MM6786	5-32
MM6787	
MM6788	5-01
MM6789	37-02
MM6791	
MM6792	5-21
MM6794	37-20
MM6795	5-40
MM6796	5-37
MM6797	
MM6798	37-01
MM6800	
MM6802	
MM6804	51-07
MM6805	4-10
MM6807	
MM6808	9-30
MM6809	
MM6810	5-41
MM6812	5-33
MM6814	53-16
MM6815	37-07
MM6816	
MM6817	51-02
MM6818	
MM6819	
MM6821	5-16
MM6822	*wfu*
MM6823	
MM6824	51-04
MM6825	
MM6826	4-51
MM6827	53-20
MM6828	4-55
MM6830	5-27
MM6831	4-22
MM6833	5-22
MM6835	
MM6836	5-10
MM6838	9-46
MM6839	
MM6840	4-2
MM6841	
MM6842	
MM6844	37-23
MM6845	5-11
MM6847	37-11
MM6848	
MM6849	
MM6850	51-12
MM6870	51-04
MM6872	53-15
MM6873	9-31
MM6875	
MM6876	
MM6879	
MM6880	*wfu*
MM6881	5-42
MM6886	5-02
MM6887	
MM6890	4-11
MM6908	4-52
MM6909	
MM6910	37-12
MM6912	4-20
MM6913	51-10
MM6914	9-42
MM6915	5-15
MM6916	*wfu*
MM6918	37-22
MM6920	5-35
MM6921	9-52
MM6922	5-04
MM6923	4-21
MM6924	
MM6925	37-05
MM6926	
MM6929	51-11
MM6930	
MM6932	51-05
MM6934	9-51
MM6935	
MM6936	5-36
MM6937	9-42
MM6938	9-46
MM6939	
MM6940	
MM6941	51-20
MM6942	4-16
MM6943	
MM6944	
MM6946	37-06

TF-104G

Serial	Code
MM54226	4-23
MM54228	4-26
MM54232	4-29
MM54233	4-30
MM54237	4-32
MM54250	4-33
MM54251	4-34
MM54253	4-35
MM54254	4-36
MM54255	4-37
MM54256	4-38
MM54257	4-39
MM54258	4-40
MM54260	4-41
MM54261	4-42
MM54552	
MM54553	4-44
MM54554	4-48
MM54555	4-45
MM54556	4-47
MM54557	
MM54558	4-46

Lockheed C-130H Hercules
46ª Brigata Aerea, Pisa

Serial	Code
MM61988	46-02
MM61989	46-03
MM61990	46-04
MM61991	46-05
MM61992	46-06
MM61993	46-07
MM61994	46-08
MM61995	46-09
MM61997	46-11
MM61998	46-12
MM61999	46-13
MM62001	46-15

McDonnell Douglas DC-9-32
31° Stormo, Roma-Ciampino
MM62012
MM62013

Panavia Tornado ADV/Trainer[1]
36° Stormo, Gioia del Colle;
53° Stormo, Cameri

Serial	Code	
MM7202	36-12	(ZE832)
MM7203	36-02	(ZE761)
MM7204	36-05	(ZE730)

MM7205 36-06 (ZE787)
MM7206 36-07 (ZE760)
MM7207 36-10 (ZE762)
MM7208 36-11 (ZE811)
MM7209 36-13 (ZE835)
MM7210 36-14 (ZE836)
MM7211 36-16 (ZE792)
MM7225 53-02 (ZE252)
MM7226 53-21 (ZE911)
MM7227 53-05 (ZG732)
MM7228 53-03 (ZG733)
MM7229 53-06 (ZG728)
MM7230 53-07 (ZG730)
MM7231 53-11 (ZG734)
MM7232 53-10 (ZG735)
MM7233 53-04 (ZG768)
MM7234 53-14 (ZE167)
MM55056[1] 36-01 (ZE202)
MM55057[1] 36-03 (ZE837)
MM55060[1] 53-01 (ZE208)
MM55061[1] 53-12 (ZE205)

Panavia Tornado Strike/Trainer[1]/ECR[2]
TTTE, RAF Cottesmore;
6° Stormo, Ghedi;
36° Stormo, Gioia del Colle;
50° Stormo, Piacenza;
RSV, Pratica di Mare
MM586
MM7002 36-35
MM7003 I-93 TTTE
MM7004 36-37
MM7005 6-31
MM7006
MM7007 50-07
MM7008
MM7009 50-45
MM7010 6-33
MM7011
MM7013 6-03
MM7014
MM7015 50-05
MM7016 6-16
MM7017 6-37
MM7018 6-18
MM7019 19
MM7020 50-43
MM7021 6-21
MM7022
MM7023 36-31
MM7025
MM7026 50-06
MM7027
MM7028
MM7029 50-41
MM7030 6-35
MM7031 50-01
MM7033 6-11
MM7034 6-30
MM7035 35
MM7036 6-43
MM7037 6-07
MM7038 36-33
MM7039 50-03
MM7040 36-35
MM7041 50-42
MM7042 6-22
MM7043 6-13
MM7044
MM7046 50-46
MM7047 6-12
MM7048 36-54 (Alenia)
MM7049 50-44

MM7050 36-44
MM7051 6-01
MM7052 6-32
MM7053 53
MM7054 6-54
MM7055 6-55
MM7056 6-46
MM7057 6-47
MM7058 36-36
MM7059 6-31
MM7060
MM7061 36-41
MM7062 36-53
MM7063 36-43
MM7064 50-04
MM7065 6-14
MM7066 66
MM7067 36-45
MM7068
MM7070
MM7071 6-42
MM7072 6-36
MM7073 6-27
MM7075
MM7078 50-02
MM7079[2] (Alenia)
MM7080 6-41
MM7081 6-02
MM7082 RS-02
MM7083 36-30
MM7084 6-34
MM7085 36-50 (Alenia)
MM7086 86
MM7087 50-40
MM7088 6-04
MM55000[1] I-42 TTTE
MM55001[1] I-40 TTTE
MM55002[1] I-41 TTTE
MM55003[1] I-43 TTTE
MM55004[1] 6-15
MM55005[1] 6-40
MM55006[1] 6-03
MM55007[1] 50-51
MM55008[1]
MM55009[1] 36-56
MM55010[1] 50-50
MM55011[1] 36-55

Piaggio RP-180 Avanti
31° Stormo, Roma-Ciampino;
53° Stormo, Cameri;
RSV, Pratica di Mare
MM62159 RSV
MM62160 54 RSV
MM62161 (53)
MM62162 (31)
MM62163 RSV
MM62164 RSV

Piaggio-Douglas PD-808/[1]PD-808-GE/[2]PD-808-RM/[3]PD-808-TA
14° Stormo, Pratica di Mare;
31° Stormo, Roma-Ciampino;
RSV, Pratica di Mare
MM577[3] RS-48
MM578[3] RS-49
MM61948 (14)
MM61949 (14)
MM61950 (14)
MM61951 (31)
MM61952[1] (14)
MM61953[3] (14)
MM61954[3] (31)
MM61955[1] (14)

MM61956[2] (14)
MM61957[3] (14)
MM61958[1] (14)
MM61959[1] (14)
MM61960[1] (14)
MM61961[1] (14)
MM61962[1] (14)
MM62014[2] (14)
MM62015[2] (14)
MM62017[2] (14)

Marina Militare Italiana
McDonnell AV-8B/TAV-8B Harrier II+
Gruppo Aerei Imbarcati, Taranto/Grottaglie
AV-8B
MM7199 1-03
MM7200 1-04
MM7201 1-05
MM7212 1-06
MM7213 1-07
MM7214 1-08
MM7215 1-09
MM7216 1-10
MM7217 1-11
MM7218 1-12
MM7219 1-13
MM7220 1-14
MM7221 1-15
MM7222 1-16
MM7223 1-17
MM7224 1-18
TAV-8B
MM55032 1-01
MM55033 1-02

JAPAN
Japan Air Self Defence Force
Boeing 747-47C
701 Hikotai, Chitose
20-1101
20-1102

JORDAN
Al Quwwat al Jawwiya al Malakiya al Urduniya
Lockheed C-130H Hercules
3 Sqn, Amman
344
345
346
347

KUWAIT
Al Quwwat al Jawwiya al Kuwaitiya
McDonnell Douglas DC9-32
42 Sqn, Ali Al Salem
KAF 321

McDonnell Douglas MD-83
42 Sqn, Ali Al Salem
KAF 26

Lockheed L100-30 Hercules
41 Sqn, Kuwait International
KAF 323
KAF 324
KAF 325

LUXEMBOURG
NATO
Boeing E-3A
NAEWF, Geilenkirchen
LX-N90442
LX-N90443
LX-N90444
LX-N90445
LX-N90446
LX-N90447
LX-N90448
LX-N90449
LX-N90450
LX-N90451
LX-N90452
LX-N90453
LX-N90454
LX-N90455
LX-N90456
LX-N90458
LX-N90459

Boeing 707-329C
NAEWF, Geilenkirchen
LX-N19996
LX-N20198
LX-N20199

MALAYSIA
**Royal Malaysian Air Force/
Tentera Udara Diraja Malaysia**
Lockheed C-130 Hercules
4 Sqn, Simpang;
14 Sqn, Simpang;
20 Sqn, Butterworth

Serial	Type	Sqn
M30-01	C-130H	14 Sqn
M30-02	C-130H	14 Sqn
M30-03	C-130H	14 Sqn
M30-04	C-130H	14 Sqn
M30-05	C-130H	14 Sqn
M30-06	C-130H	14 Sqn
M30-07	C-130H(MP)	4 Sqn
M30-08	C-130H(MP)	4 Sqn
M30-09	C-130H(MP)	4 Sqn
M30-10	C-130H	14 Sqn
M30-11	C-130H-30	20 Sqn
M30-12	C-130H-30	20 Sqn
M30-13	C-130H-30	20 Sqn
M30-14	C-130H-30	14 Sqn
M30-15	C-130H-30	14 Sqn
M30-16	C-130H-30	14 Sqn

MOROCCO
**Force Aérienne Royaume
Marocaine/Al Quwwat al
Jawwiya al Malakiya
Marakishiya**
Airtech CN.235M-100
Escadrille de Transport,
Rabat

023	CNA-MA
024	CNA-MB
025	CNA-MC
026	CNA-MD
027	CNA-ME
028	CNA-MF
031	CNA-MG

CAP-230
Marche Verte

04	CN-ABD
05	CN-ABF
06	CN-ABI
07	CN-ABJ
08	CN-ABK
09	CN-ABL
22	CN-ABM
23	CN-ABN
24	CN-ABO

**Lockheed C-130H
Hercules**
Escadrille de Transport,
Rabat

4535	CN-AOA
4551	CN-AOC
4575	CN-AOD
4581	CN-AOE
4583	CN-AOF
4713	CN-AOG
4717	CN-AOH
4733	CN-AOI
4738	CN-AOJ
4739	CN-AOK
4742	CN-AOL
4875	CN-AOM
4876	CN-AON
4877	CN-AOO
4888	CN-AOP
4892	CN-AOQ
4907	CN-AOR
4909	CN-AOS
4940	CN-AOT

NETHERLANDS
Koninklijke Luchtmacht
**Aérospatiale AS.532U2
Cougar**
300 Sqn, Gilze-Rijen
S-400
S-419
S-433
S-438
S-440
S-441
S-444
S-445
S-447
S-450
S-453
S-454

Agusta-Bell AB.412SP
SAR Flight, Leeuwarden
R-01
R-02
R-03

**Boeing-Vertol CH-47D
Chinook**
298 Sqn, Soesterberg
D-101
D-102
D-103
D-104
D-105
D-106
D-661
D-662
D-663
D-664
D-665
D-666
D-667

Fokker F-27-200MPA
336 Sqn, Hato, Antilles
M-1
M-2

Fokker 50
334 Sqn, Eindhoven
U-05
U-06

Fokker 60UTA-N
334 Sqn, Eindhoven
U-01
U-02
U-03
U-04

**General Dynamics
F-16A/F-16B***
TGp/306/311/312 Sqns,
Volkel;
313/315 Sqns, Twenthe;
322/323 Sqns, Leeuwarden

J-001	312 Sqn
J-002	315 Sqn
J-003	312 Sqn
J-004	311 Sqn
J-005	315 Sqn
J-006	315 Sqn
J-008	315 Sqn
J-009	315 Sqn
J-010	312 Sqn
J-011	315 Sqn
J-013	312 Sqn
J-014	315 Sqn
J-015	312 Sqn
J-016	311 Sqn
J-017	315 Sqn
J-018	311 Sqn
J-019	311 Sqn
J-020	315 Sqn
J-021	312 Sqn
J-055	315 Sqn
J-057	315 Sqn
J-058	311 Sqn
J-059	315 Sqn
J-060	306 Sqn
J-061	311 Sqn
J-062	312 Sqn
J-063	312 Sqn
J-064*	312 Sqn
J-065*	311 Sqn
J-066*	311 Sqn
J-067*	312 Sqn
J-068*	312 Sqn
J-135	315 Sqn
J-136	322 Sqn
J-137	322 Sqn
J-138	323 Sqn
J-139	323 Sqn
J-140	322 Sqn
J-141	323 Sqn
J-142	323 Sqn
J-143	306 Sqn
J-144	322 Sqn
J-145	315 Sqn
J-146	315 Sqn
J-192	322 Sqn
J-193	312 Sqn
J-194	322 Sqn
J-196	323 Sqn
J-197	322 Sqn
J-198	311 Sqn
J-199	322 Sqn
J-201	312 Sqn
J-202	322 Sqn
J-203	322 Sqn
J-204	322 Sqn
J-205	322 Sqn

J-206	312 Sqn	J-637	306 Sqn	B-77	
J-207	322 Sqn	J-638	306 Sqn	B-78*	
J-208*	322 Sqn	J-640	306 Sqn	B-79	
J-209*	322 Sqn	J-641	306 Sqn	B-80	
J-210*	313 Sqn	J-642	306 Sqn	B-83	
J-211*	322 Sqn	J-643	306 Sqn		
J-213	312 Sqn	J-644	306 Sqn	**McD AH-64A Apache**	
J-215	312 Sqn	J-646	306 Sqn	301 Sqn, Gilze-Rijen	
J-218	313 Sqn	J-647	306 Sqn	25430	
J-220	311 Sqn	J-648	306 Sqn	25465	
J-223	*wfu*	J-649*	306 Sqn	25471	
J-226	312 Sqn	J-650*	323 Sqn	25472	
J-228	315 Sqn	J-651*	306 Sqn	25474	
J-230	313 Sqn	J-652*	306 Sqn	25480	
J-231	312 Sqn	J-653*	TGp	25482	
J-232	313 Sqn	J-654*	323 Sqn	25485	
J-235	311 Sqn	J-655*	323 Sqn	68970	
J-236	312 Sqn	J-656*	323 Sqn	68983	
J-239	313 Sqn	J-657*	323 Sqn	69029	
J-241	311 Sqn	J-864	306 Sqn	69033	
J-243	306 Sqn	J-866	306 Sqn		
J-246	315 Sqn	J-867	306 Sqn	**McDonnell Douglas**	
J-248	312 Sqn	J-868	323 Sqn	**KDC-10**	
J-249	306 Sqn	J-869	323 Sqn	334 Sqn, Eindhoven	
J-250	311 Sqn	J-870	323 Sqn	T-235	
J-251	323 Sqn	J-871	323 Sqn	T-264	
J-253	315 Sqn	J-872	323 Sqn		
J-254	312 Sqn	J-873	323 Sqn	**Pilatus PC-7**	
J-255	315 Sqn	J-874	322 Sqn		
J-256	311 Sqn	J-875	323 Sqn		
J-257	315 Sqn	J-876	323 Sqn	**Sud Alouette III**	
J-259*	315 Sqn	J-877	322 Sqn	299 Sqn, Gilze-Rijen	
J-261*	313 Sqn	J-878	323 Sqn	A-177	
J-262*	313 Sqn	J-879	312 Sqn	A-246	
J-264*	322 Sqn	J-881	323 Sqn	A-253	
J-265*	313 Sqn	J-882*	323 Sqn	A-260	
J-266*	313 Sqn	J-884*	315 Sqn	A-261	
J-267*	315 Sqn	J-885*	311 Sqn	A-275	
J-268*	315 Sqn			A-292	
J-269*	313 Sqn	**Grumman G-1159C**		A-301	
J-270*	313 Sqn	**Gulfstream IV**		A-350	*wfu*
J-360	322 Sqn	334 Sqn, Eindoven		A-451	
J-361	322 Sqn	V-11		A-471	
J-362	322 Sqn			A-494	
J-363	322 Sqn	**Lockheed C-130H-30**		A-515	
J-364	322 Sqn	**Hercules**		A-521	
J-365	322 Sqn	334 Sqn, Eindhoven		A-522	
J-366	322 Sqn	G-273		A-542	
J-367	322 Sqn	G-275			
J-368*	315 Sqn			**Marine Luchtvaart Dienst**	
J-369*	323 Sqn	**MBB Bo.105CB/**		**Lockheed P-3C Orion**	
J-508	312 Sqn	**Bo.105CB-4***		MARPAT (320 Sqn & 321	
J-509	315 Sqn	299 Sqn, Gilze-Rijen		Sqn), Valkenburg,	
J-510	315 Sqn	B-37*		Sigonella and Keflavik	
J-511	312 Sqn	B-38		300	
J-512	311 Sqn	B-39*		301	
J-513	312 Sqn	B-40*		302	
J-514	315 Sqn	B-41*		303	
J-515	315 Sqn	B-42		304	
J-516	315 Sqn	B-43		305	
J-616	322 Sqn	B-44		306	
J-617	323 Sqn	B-47		307	
J-619	311 Sqn	B-48		308	
J-620	322 Sqn	B-63		309	
J-622	311 Sqn	B-64		310	
J-623	322 Sqn	B-66		311	
J-624	322 Sqn	B-67		312	
J-627	306 Sqn	B-68			
J-628	306 Sqn	B-69		**Westland SH-14D Lynx**	
J-630	306 Sqn	B-70		HELIGRP (7 Sqn & 860 Sqn),	
J-631	306 Sqn	B-71		De Kooij (7 Sqn operates	
J-632	306 Sqn	B-72		860 Sqn aircraft on loan)	
J-633	306 Sqn	B-74		260	
J-635	306 Sqn	B-75		261	
J-636	306 Sqn	B-76		262	

264	
265	
266	
267	
268	
269	
270	
271	
272	
273	
274	
276	
277	
278	
279	
280	
281	
282	
283	

NEW ZEALAND
Royal New Zealand Air Force
  Boeing 727-22C
  40 Sqn, Whenuapai
  NZ7271
  NZ7272

  Lockheed C-130H Hercules
  40 Sqn, Whenuapai
  NZ7001
  NZ7002
  NZ7003
  NZ7004
  NZ7005

  Lockheed P-3K Orion
  5 Sqn, Whenuapai
  NZ4201
  NZ4202
  NZ4203
  NZ4204
  NZ4205
  NZ4206

NIGERIA
Federal Nigerian Air Force
  Lockheed C-130H Hercules
  Lagos
  NAF-910
  NAF-912
  NAF-913
  NAF-914
  NAF-915
  NAF-916
  NAF-917
  NAF-918
  NAF-918 (NAF 916)

NORWAY
Kongelige Norske
  Luftforsvaret
  Bell 412SP
  339 Skv, Bardufoss;
  720 Skv, Rygge

139	339 Skv
140	720 Skv
141	720 Skv
142	339 Skv
143	339 Skv
144	339 Skv
145	339 Skv
146	339 Skv
147	339 Skv

148	339 Skv
149	339 Skv
161	339 Skv
162	339 Skv
163	720 Skv
164	720 Skv
165	720 Skv
166	720 Skv
167	720 Skv

Dassault Falcon 20 ECM
717 Skv, Gardermoen
041
053
0125

DHC-6 Twin Otter
719 Skv, Bodø
057
062
184

**General Dynamics
F-16A/F-16B***
331   Skv, Bodø   (r/w/bl);
332   Skv, Rygge *(y/bk)*;
334   Skv, Bodø   (r/w);
338   Skv, Ørland

272	332 Skv
273	332 Skv
274	332 Skv
275	332 Skv
276	332 Skv
277	332 Skv
279	332 Skv
281	332 Skv
282	332 Skv
284	332 Skv
285	332 Skv
288	338 Skv
289	338 Skv
291	338 Skv
292	338 Skv
293	338 Skv
295	338 Skv
297	338 Skv
298	338 Skv
299	338 Skv
302*	332 Skv
304*	332 Skv
305*	332 Skv
306*	332 Skv
658	334 Skv
659	334 Skv
660	334 Skv
661	334 Skv
662	334 Skv
663	334 Skv
664	334 Skv
665	334 Skv
666	334 Skv
667	334 Skv
668	334 Skv
669	334 Skv
670	334 Skv
671	338 Skv
672	331 Skv
673	331 Skv
674	331 Skv
675	331 Skv
677	331 Skv
678	331 Skv
680	331 Skv

681	331 Skv
682	331 Skv
683	331 Skv
686	331 Skv
687	331 Skv
688	331 Skv
689*	338 Skv
690*	338 Skv
691*	334 Skv
692*	334 Skv
693*	338 Skv
711*	331 Skv
712*	331 Skv

Lockheed C-130H Hercules
335 Skv, Gardermoen
952
953
954
955
956
957

Lockheed P-3C Orion
333 Skv, Andøya
3296
3297
3298
3299

Lockheed P-3N Orion
333 Skv, Andøya
4576
6603

Northrop F-5A
336 Skv, Rygge
128
130
131
133
134
896
902

Northrop F-5B
336 Skv, Rygge
136
243
244
387
906
907
908
909

**Westland Sea King Mk43/
Mk43A[A]/Mk43B[B]**
330 Skv, Bodø
060[A]
062
066[A]
069[A]
070[A]
071[B]
072[A]
073[A]
074[A]
189
322[B]
329[B]
330[B]

Kystvakt (Coast Guard)
  Westland Lynx Mk86
  337 Skv, Bardufoss
  207
  216
  228
  232
  237
  350

OMAN
Royal Air Force of Oman
  BAC 1-11/485GD
  4 Sqn, Seeb
  551
  552
  553

  Lockheed C-130H Hercules
  4 Sqn, Seeb
  501
  502
  503

  Short Skyvan 3M
  2 Sqn, Seeb
  901
  902
  903
  904
  905
  906
  907
  908
  910
  911
  912
  913
  914
  915
  916

PAKISTAN
Pakistan Fiza'ya
  Boeing 707-340C
  68-19866   12 Sqn
  69-19635   12 Sqn

PERU
Fuerza Aérea Peruana
  Douglas DC-8-62AF
  370 (OB-1372)
  371 (OB-1373)

POLAND
Polskie Wojska Lotnicze
  Antonov An-26
  13 PLT, Belice
  1307
  1308
  1309
  1310
  1402
  1403
  1406
  1407
  1508
  1509
  1602
  1603
  1604

Yakovlev Yak-40
36 SPLT, Warszawa
036
037
038
039
040
041
042
043
044
045
047
048

PORTUGAL
Força Aérea Portuguesa
  Aérospatiale SA.330C Puma
  711 Esq, Lajes;
  751 Esq, Montijo
  19502   751 Esq
  19503   751 Esq
  19504   751 Esq
  19505   751 Esq
  19506   751 Esq
  19508   711 Esq
  19509   711 Esq
  19511   711 Esq
  19512   751 Esq
  19513   751 Esq

CASA 212A/212ECM* Aviocar
401 Esq, Sintra;
502 Esq, Sintra;
503 Esq, Lajes
16501*   502 Esq
16502*   401 Esq
16503   502 Esq
16504   502 Esq
16505   502 Esq
16506   502 Esq
16507   502 Esq
16508   502 Esq
16509   502 Esq
16510   401 Esq
16511   502 Esq
16512   401 Esq
16513   503 Esq
16514   503 Esq
16515   503 Esq
16517   503 Esq
16519   401 Esq
16520   503 Esq
16521*   401 Esq
16522*   401 Esq
16523*   401 Esq
16524*   401 Esq

CASA 212-300 Aviocar
401 Esq, Sintra
17201
17202

D-BD Alpha Jet
103 Esq, Beja;
301 Esq, Beja
15201
15205
15208
15209
15210
15211

15214
15215
15217
15218
15221
15223
15224
15225
15226
15227
15228
15229
15230
15231
15232
15233
15234
15235
15236
15237
15238
15241
15242
15243
15244
15246
15247
15248
15249
15250

Dassault Falcon 20DC
504 Esq, Lisbon/Montijo
17103

Dassault Falcon 50
504 Esq, Lisbon/Montijo
17401
17402
17403

Lockheed C-130H/ C-130H-30* Hercules
501 Esq, Lisbon/Montijo
16801*
16802*
16803
16804
16805
16806*

Lockheed (GD) F-16A/F-16B*
201 Esq, Monte Real
15101
15102
15103
15104
15105
15106
15107
15108
15109
15110
15111
15112
15113
15114
15115
15116
15117
15118*
15119*
15120*

Lockheed P-3P Orion
601 Esq, Lisbon/Montijo
14801
14802
14803
14804
14805
14806

LTV A-7P/TA-7P* Corsair II
302 Esq, Monte Real;
304 Esq, Monte Real
15502
15503
15504
15506
15507
15508
15509
15511
15512
15513
15514
15515
15516
15519
15521
15522
15524
15528
15531
15532
15536
15537
15538
·15539
15544
15545*
15546*
15547*
15549*
15550*

RUSSIA
Voenno-Vozdushniye Sily
Rossioki Federatsii
(Russia Air Force)
Sukhoi Su-27
TsAGI, Gromov Flight
Institute Zhukhovsky

595	(27595)	Su-27P
597	(27597)	Su-30
598	(27598)	Su-27P

SAUDI ARABIA
Al Quwwat al Jawwiya
as Sa udiya
Boeing E-3A/KE-3A*
Sentry
18 Sqn, Riyadh
1801
1802
1803
1804
1805
1811*
1812*
1813*
1814*
1815*
1816*
1817*
1818*

Lockheed C-130 Hercules
1 Sqn, Riyadh;
4 Sqn, Jeddah;
16 Sqn, Jeddah;
32 Sqn, Jeddah

112	VC-130H	1 Sqn
451	C-130E	4 Sqn
452	C-130H	4 Sqn
455	C-130E	4 Sqn
461	C-130H	4 Sqn
462	C-130H	4 Sqn
463	C-130H	4 Sqn
464	C-130H	4 Sqn
465	C-130H	4 Sqn
466	C-130H	4 Sqn
467	C-130H	4 Sqn
468	C-130H	4 Sqn
470	C-130H	4 Sqn
471	C-130H-30	4 Sqn
472	C-130H	4 Sqn
473	C-130H	4 Sqn
474	C-130H	4 Sqn
475	C-130H	4 Sqn
476	C-130H	4 Sqn
477	C-130H	4 Sqn
478	C-130H	4 Sqn
479	C-130H	4 Sqn
1601	C-130H	16 Sqn
1602	C-130H	16 Sqn
1603	C-130H	16 Sqn
1604	C-130H	16 Sqn
1605	C-130H	16 Sqn
1606	C-130E	16 Sqn
1607	C-130E	16 Sqn
1608	C-130E	16 Sqn
1609	C-130E	16 Sqn
1610	C-130E	16 Sqn
1611	C-130E	16 Sqn
1612	C-130H	16 Sqn
1613	C-130H	16 Sqn
1614	C-130H	16 Sqn
1615	C-130H	16 Sqn
1618	C-130H	16 Sqn
1619	C-130H	16 Sqn
1622	C-130H-30	16 Sqn
1623	C-130H-30	16 Sqn
1624	C-130H	16 Sqn
1625	C-130H	16 Sqn
1626	C-130H	16 Sqn
1627	C-130H	16 Sqn
1628	C-130H	16 Sqn
3201	KC-130H	2 Sqn
3202	KC-130H	32 Sqn
3203	KC-130H	32 Sqn
3204	KC-130H	32 Sqn
3205	KC-130H	32 Sqn
3206	KC-130H	32 Sqn
3207	KC-130H	32 Sqn
3208	KC-130H	32 Sqn

SINGAPORE
Republic of Singapore Air Force
Lockheed C-130 Hercules
122 Sqn, Paya Labar

720	KC-130B
721	KC-130B
724	KC-130B
725	KC-130B
730	C-130H
731	C-130H
732	C-130H
733	C-130H
734	KC-130H
735	KC-130H

SLOVAKIA
Slovenské Vojenske Letectvo
Aero L.39/L.59 (L.39MS)
Albatros
31 SLK/3 Letka, Sliač;
33 SBoLK/2 Letka, Malacky;
VSL, Košice;
White Albatroses, Košice
  (*WA*)

0002	L-39MS	VSL
0003	L-39MS	VSL
0101	L-39C	*WA* [4]
0102	L-39C	*WA* [6]
0103	L-39C	VSL
0111	L-39C	*WA* [5]
0112	L-39C	*WA* [1]
0442	L-39C	*WA* [0]
0443	L-39C	*WA* [7]
0730	L-39V	VSL
0745	L-39V	VSL
1725	L-39ZA	33 SBoLK
1730	L-39ZA	33 SBoLK
3905	L-39ZA	33 SBoLK
4355	L-39C	*WA* [3]
4357	L-39C	*WA* [2]
4701	L-39ZA	31 SLK
4703	L-39ZA	31 SLK
4705	L-39ZA	31 SLK
4707	L-39ZA	31 SLK
4711	L-39ZA	31 SLK

Antonov An-12BP
32 ZmDK/1 Letka, Pieštany
2209

Antonov An-24V
32 ZmDK/1 Letka, Pieštany
2903
5605

Antonov An-26
32 ZmDK/1 Letka, Pieštany
2506
3208

Let 410
VSL, Košice;
32 ZmDK/1 Letka, Pieštany

0404	L-410M	32 ZmDK
0405	L-410M	32 ZmDK
0730	L-410UVP	32 ZmDK
0927	L-410T	VSL
0930	L-410T	VSL
1133	L-410T	VSL
1203	L-410FG	32 ZmDK
1504	L-410UVP	
1521	L-410FG	32 ZmDK
1810	L-410UVP-E	32 ZmDK
2006	L-410UVP-E	32 ZmDK
2311	L-410UVP	32 ZmDK

Mikoyan MiG-29A/UB*
31 SLK/1 Letka, Sliač;
0619
0820
0921
1303*
2022
2123
3709
3911
4401*
5113
5304*
5515

5817
6526
6627
6728
6829
6930
7501
8003
8605
9207
9308

Sukhoi Su-25K/BK*
33 SBoLK/2 Letka, Malacky
1006
1007
1008
1027
3237*
5033
5036
6017
6018
8073
8074
8075

Tupolev Tu-154B-2
32 ZmDK/1 Letka, Bratislava
0420

SOUTH AFRICA
South African Air Force/
Suid Afrikaanse Lugmag
Boeing 707
60 Sqn, Waterkloof

AF-615(1415)	328C	
AF-617(1417)	328C	
AF-619(1419)	328C	
AF-621(1421)	344C	
AF-623(1423)	344C	

SPAIN
Ejército del Aire
Airtech CN.235M-10 (T.19A)/
CN.235M-100 (T.19B)
Ala 35, Getafe

T.19A-01	35-60
T.19A-02	35-61
T.19B-03	35-21
T.19B-04	35-22
T.19B-05	35-23
T.19B-06	35-24
T.19B-07	35-25
T.19B-08	35-26
T.19B-09	35-27
T.19B-10	35-28
T.19B-11	35-29
T.19B-12	35-30
T.19B-13	35-31
T.19B-14	35-32
T.19B-15	35-33
T.19B-16	35-34
T.19B-17	35-35
T.19B-18	35-36
T.19B-19	35-37
T.19B-20	35-38

Boeing 707
408 Esc, Torrejón;
Grupo 45, Torrejón

T.17-1	331B	45-10
T.17-2	331B	45-11
T.17-3	368C	45-12
TM.17-4	351C	408-21

CASA 101 Aviojet
Grupo 54, Torrejón;
Grupo de Escuelas de
Matacán (74);
AGA, San Javier (79);
Patrulla Aguila, San Javier*

E.25-01	79-01	
E.25-02	793-02	
E.25-04		
E.25-05	79-05	
E.25-06	79-06	
E.25-07	79-07	[8]*
E.25-08	79-08	
E.25-09	79-09	
E.25-10	79-10	
E.25-11	79-11	
E.25-12	79-12	
E.25-13	79-13	[3]*
E.25-14	79-14	[4]*
E.25-15	79-15	
E.25-16	79-16	
E.25-17	79-17	
E.25-18	79-18	
E.25-19	79-19	
E.25-20	79-20	
E.25-21	79-21	[2]*
E.25-22	79-22	
E.25-23	74-02	[5]*
E.25-24	79-24	
E.25-25	79-25	[6]*
E.25-26	79-26	
E.25-27	79-27	
E.25-28	79-28	[1]*
E.25-29	79-29	
E.25-30	79-30	
E.25-31	79-31	
E.25-33		
E.25-34	79-34	
E.25-35	79-35	
E.25-36	79-36	
E.25-37	79-37	
E.25-38	79-38	
E.25-40	79-40	
E.25-41	79-41	
E.25-42	793-32	
E.25-43	79-43	
E.25-44	79-44	
E.25-45	79-45	
E.25-46	79-46	
E.25-47	79-47	
E.25-48	79-48	
E.25-49	79-49	
E.25-50	79-33	
E.25-51	74-07	
E.25-52	74-08	
E.25-53	411-07	
E.25-54	79-35	
E.25-55	44-05	
E.25-56	79-56	
E.25-57	74-12	
E.25-59		
E.25-61		
E.25-62	74-16	
E.25-63	74-17	
E.25-64	74-13	
E.25-65	79-95	
E.25-66		
E.25-67		
E.25-68	74-22	
E.25-69	79-97	
E.25-71		
E.25-72	74-26	
E.25-73	79-98	
E.25-74	74-28	

E.25-75	
E.25-76	
E.25-78	79-02
E.25-79	74-32
E.25-80	74-33
E.25-81	74-34
E.25-83	74-35
E.25-84	79-04
E.25-86	74-37
E.25-87	74-38
E.25-88	74-39

CASA 212 Aviocar
212 (XT.12)/212A (T.12B)/
212B (TR.12A)/
212D (TE.12B)/
212DE (TM.12D)/
212E (T.12C)/
212S (D.3A)/
212S1 (D.3B)
Ala 22, Morón;
Ala 37, Villanubla;
Ala 46, Gando, Las Palmas;
CLAEX, Torrejón (54);
Grupo 72, Alcantarilla;
Grupo Esc, Matacán (74);
AGA (Ala 79), San Javier;
403 Esc, Getafe;
408 Esc, Torrejón;
721 Esc, Alcantarilla;
801 Esc, Palma/Son San
Juan;
803 Esc, Cuatro Vientos

D.3A-1	801 Esc
D.3A-2	803-11
D.3B-3	803 Esc
D.3B-4	801 Esc
D.3B-5	801 Esc
D.3B-6	803-12
D.3B-7	803 Esc
D.3B-8	22-92
D.3B-9	803-14
XT.12A-1	54-10
XT.12A-2	54-12
TR.12A-3	403-01
TR.12A-4	403-02
TR.12A-5	403-03
TR.12A-6	403-04
TR.12A-7	403-05
TR.12A-8	403-06
TE.12B-9	74-83
TE.12B-10	79-92
T.12B-12	74-82
T.12B-13	74-70
T.12B-14	37-01
T.12B-15	37-02
T.12B-16	74-71
T.12B-17	37-03
T.12B-18	46-31
T.12B-19	46-32
T.12B-20	37-04
T.12B-21	37-05
T.12B-22	37-06
T.12B-23	72-01
T.12B-24	37-07
T.12B-25	74-72
T.12B-26	72-02
T.12B-27	46-33
T.12B-28	72-03
T.12B-29	37-08
T.12B-30	74-73
T.12B-31	46-34
T.12B-33	72-04
T.12B-34	74-74

T.12B-35	37-09	**Lockheed P-3A/P-3B***		C.15-40	15-27		
T.12B-36	37-10	**Orion**		C.15-41	15-28		
T.12B-37	72-05	Grupo 22, Morón		C.15-42	15-29		
T.12B-38	35-10	P.3-01	22-21	C.15-43	15-30		
T.12B-39	74-75	P.3-03	22-22	C.15-44	12-02		
TE.12B-40	79-93	P.3-08	22-31*	C.15-45	12-03		
TE.12B-41	79-94	P.3-09	22-32*	C.15-46	12-04		
TE.12B-42	744-42	P.3-10	22-33*	C.15-47	15-31		
T.12C-43	46-50	P.3-11	22-34*	C.15-48	12-06		
T.12C-44	37-50	P.3-12	22-35*	C.15-49	12-07		
T.12B-46	74-76			C.15-50	12-08		
T.12B-47	72-06	**Lockheed Hercules**		C.15-51	12-09		
T.12B-48	37-11	**C-130H/C-130H-30**[1]		C.15-52	12-10		
T.12B-49	46-36	311 Esc/312 Esc (Ala 31),		C.15-53	12-11		
T.12B-50	74-77	Zaragoza		C.15-54	12-12		
T.12B-51	74-78	TL.10-1	31-01[1]	C.15-55	12-13		
T.12B-52		T.10-2	31-02	C.15-56	12-14		
T.12B-53	46-37	T.10-3	31-03	C.15-57	12-15		
T.12B-54	37-54	T.10-4	31-04	C.15-58	12-16		
T.12B-55	46-38	T.10-8	31-05	C.15-59	12-17		
T.12B-56	74-79	T.10-9	31-06	C.15-60	12-18		
T.12B-57	72-08	T.10-10	31-07	C.15-61	12-19		
T.12B-58	74-78			C.15-62	12-20		
T.12C-59	37-51	**Lockheed KC-130H**		C.15-63	15-32		
T.12C-60	37-52	**Hercules**		C.15-64	12-22		
T.12C-61	37-53	312 Esc (Ala 31), Zaragosa		C.15-65	12-23		
T.12B-63	37-14	TK.10-5	31-50	C.15-66	12-24		
T.12B-64	46-40	TK.10-6	31-51	C.15-67	15-33		
T.12B-65	74-80	TK.10-7	31-52	C.15-68	12-26		
T.12B-66	72-09	TK.10-11	31-53	C.15-69	12-27		
T.12B-67	74-81	TK.10-12	31-54	C.15-70	12-28		
T.12B-68	37-15			C.15-72	12-30		
T.12B-69	37-16	**McDonnell Douglas**		C.15-73	21-02		
T.12B-70	37-17	**EF-18A/EF-18B* Hornet**		C.15-74			
T.12B-71	37-18	Ala 12, Torrejón;		C.15-75	21-05		
TM.12D-72	408-01	Grupo 15, Zaragoza;		C.15-76	21-07		
TM.12D-73	408-02	Grupo 21, Morón		C.15-77	21-08		
TM.12D-74	408-03	CE.15-1	15-70*	C.15-78	21-15		
		CE.15-2	15-71*	C.15-79	21-		
Cessna 560 Citation VI		CE.15-3	15-72*	C.15-80	21-		
403 Esc, Getafe		CE.15-4	15-73*	C.15-81	21-		
TR.20-01	403-11	CE.15-5	15-74*	C.15-82	21-		
TR.20-02	403-12	CE.15-6	15-75*	C.15-83	21-		
		CE.15-7	15-76*	C.15-84	21-		
Dassault Falcon 20		CE.15-8	12-71*	C.15-85			
Grupo 45, Torrejón;		CE.15-9	15-77*	C.15-86			
408 Esc, Torrejón		CE.15-10	12-73*	C.15-87			
T.11-1	45-02	CE.15-11	12-74*	C.15-88			
TM.11-2	45-03	CE.15-12	12-75*	C.15-89			
TM.11-3	408-11	C.15-13	12-01	C.15-90			
TM.11-4	408-12	C.15-14	15-01	C.15-91			
T.11-5	45-05	C.15-15	15-02	C.15-92			
		C.15-16	15-03	C.15-93			
Dassault Falcon 50		C.15-18	15-05	C.15-94			
Grupo 45, Torrejón		C.15-20	15-07	C.15-95			
T.16-1	45-20	C.15-21	15-08	C.15-96			
		C.15-22	15-09				
		C.15-23	15-10	**Arma Aérea de l'Armada**			
		C.15-24	15-11	**Española**			
Dassault Falcon 900		C.15-25	15-12	**BAe/McDonnell Douglas**			
Grupo 45, Torrejón		C.15-26	15-13	**EAV-8B/EAV-8B+/**			
T.18-1	45-40	C.15-27	15-14	**TAV-8B+ Harrier II**			
T.18-2	45-41	C.15-28	15-15	**EAV-8B**			
		C.15-29	15-16	Esc 009, Rota			
Eurofighter EF2000		C.15-30	15-17	VA.2-2	01-902		
CASA, Getafe		C.15-31	15-18	VA.2-3	01-903		
XCE.16-01		C.15-32	15-19	VA.2-4	01-904		
		C.15-33	15-20	VA.2-5	01-905		
		C.15-34	15-21	VA.2-6	01-906		
Fokker F.27M		C.15-35	15-22	VA.2-7	01-907		
Friendship 400MPA		C.15-36	15-23	VA.2-9	01-909		
802 Esc, Gando, Las Palmas		C.15-37	15-24	VA.2-10	01-910		
D.2-01	802-10	C.15-38	15-25	VA.2-11	01-911		
D.2-02	802-11	C.15-39	15-26	VA.2-12	01-912		
D.2-03	802-12						

EAV-8B+

VA.2-14	01-914
VA.2-15	01-915
VA.2-16	01-916
VA.2-17	01-917
VA.2-18	01-918
VA.2-19	01-919
VA.2-20	01-920
VA.2-21	01-921
VA.2-22	01-922

TAV-8B+

VA.2-23	01-923

Cessna 550 Citation II
Esc 004, Rota

U.20-1	01-405
U.20-2	01-406
U.20-3	01-407

SUDAN
Silakh al Jawwiya as'Sudaniya
Lockheed C-130H Hercules
1100
1101
1102
1103
1104
1105

SWEDEN
Kungliga Svenska Flygvapnet
Aerospatiale AS.332M-1 Super Puma (Hkp.10)
Flottiljer 7, Såtenäs;
Flottiljer 15, Söderhamn;
Flottiljer 17, Ronneby/ Kallinge;
Flottiljer 21, Luleå/Kallax

10401	91	F7
10402	92	F7
10403	93	F21
10404	94	F15
10405	95	F15
10406	96	F15
10407	97	F17
10408	98	F15
10409	99	F17
10410	90	F17
10411	88	F21
10412	89	F15

Beechcraft Super King Air (Tp.101)
Flottiljer 7, Satenäs;
Flottiljer 17, Ronneby/ Kallinge;
Flottiljer 21, Lulea/Kallax

101002	012	F21
101003	013	F17
101004	014	F7

Grumman G.1159C Gulfstream IV (Tp.102/S.102B*)
Flottiljer 7, Såtenäs;
Flottiljer 16, Uppsala

102001	021	F7
102002*	022	F16
102003*	023	F16

Lockheed C-130 Hercules (Tp.84)
Flottiljer 7, Satenäs

84001	841	C-130E
84002	842	C-130E
84003	843	C-130H
84004	844	C-130H
84005	845	C-130H
84006	846	C-130H
84007	847	C-130H
84008	848	C-130H

Rockwell Sabreliner-40 (Tp.86)
FMV, Malmslätt

86001	861
86002	862

SAAB JAS 39 Gripen
Flottiljer 7, Satenäs;
FMV, Malmslätt

39-2	JAS 39	[52]	FMV
39-3	JAS 39	[53]	FMV
39-4	JAS 39	[54]	FMV
39-5	JAS 39	[55]	SAAB
39101	JAS 39	[51]	FMV
39103	JAS 39	[03]	F7
39104	JAS 39	[04]	F7
39105	JAS 39	[05]	F7
39106	JAS 39	[06]	F7
39107	JAS 39	[07]	F7
39108	JAS 39	[08]	F7
39109	JAS 39	[09]	F7
39110	JAS 39	[10]	F7
39111	JAS 39	[11]	F7
39112	JAS 39	[12]	F7
39113	JAS 39	[13]	F7
39114	JAS 39	[14]	F7
39115	JAS 39	[15]	F7
39116	JAS 39	[16]	F7
39117	JAS 39	[17]	F7
39118	JAS 39	[18]	F7
39119	JAS 39	[19]	F7
39120	JAS 39	[20]	F7
39121	JAS 39	[21]	F7
39122	JAS 39	[22]	F7
39123	JAS 39	[23]	F7
39124	JAS 39	[24]	F7
39125	JAS 39	[25]	F7
39126	JAS 39	[26]	F7
39127	JAS 39	[27]	F7
39128	JAS 39	[28]	F7
39129	JAS 39	[29]	F7
39130	JAS 39	[30]	F7
39131	JAS 39	[31]	F7
39800	JAS 39B	[58]	FMV
39801	JAS 39B	{70]	F7

SAAB SF.340B (Tp.100)/ SF.340AEW&C (S.100B)*
Flottiljer 16, Uppsala;
FMV, Malmslätt

100001	001	F16
100002*	002	FMV
100003*	003	FMV
100004*	004	FMV

Swearingen Metro III (Tp.88)
FC, Malmslätt

88003	883

Marine Flygtjänst
Vertol 107-II-5 (Hkp.4C)
1 Hkp Div, Berga

04061	61
04063	63
04064	64

Kawasaki-Vertol KV.107-II (Hkp.4C)
1 Hkp Div, Berga;
2 Hkp Div, Säve;
3 Hkp Div, Ronneby/Kallinge;
FC, Malmslätt (Air Force)

04065	65	2 Hkp Div
04067	67	2 Hkp Div
04068	68	2 Hkp Div
04069	69	1 Hkp Div
04070	70	1 Hkp Div
04071	71	2 Hkp Div
04072	72	FC
04073	73	1 Hkp Div
04074	74	3 Hkp Div
04075	75	3 Hkp Div

Armen
MBB Bo.105CB (Hkp.9B)
Armeflyget 1 (AF1), Boden;
Armeflyget 2 (AF2), Malmslätt;
FC, Malmslätt (Air Force)

09201	01	AF2
09202	02	AF1
09203	03	AF2
09204	04	AF2
09205	05	AF1
09206	06	AF1
09207	07	AF1
09208	08	AF1
09209	09	AF2
09210	10	AF1
09211	11	AF1
09212	12	AF1
09213	13	AF2
09214	14	AF2
09215	15	AF2
09216	16	AF2
09217	17	AF2
09218	18	AF1
09219	19	AF1
09220	20	AF2
09221	90	FC

SWITZERLAND
Schweizerische Flugwaffe
Aérospatiale AS.532 Super Puma
Leichte Fliegerstaffeln 5 (LtSt 5), Interlaken;
Leichte Fliegerstaffeln 6 (LtSt 6), Alpnach;
Leichte Fliegerstaffeln 8 (LtSt 8), Ulrichen
Detachments at Alpnach, Emmen, Meiringen, Payerne & Sion

T-311
T-312
T-313
T-314
T-315
T-316
T-317
T-318
T-319
T-320
T-321
T-322
T-323
T-324
T-325

Dassault Falcon 50
Swiss Air Force, Dübendorf
T-783

Dassault Mirage III
Flieger Staffel 3 (FlSt 3),
  Sion;
Flieger Staffel 4 (FlSt 4),
  Payerne;
Flieger Staffel 10 (FlSt 10),
  Buochs;
Flieger Staffel 16 (FlSt 16),
  Buochs;
Flieger Staffel 17 (FlSt 17),
  Payerne;
Gruppe fur Rustunggdienste
  (GRD), Emmen;
Instrumentation Flieger
  Staffel 14 (InstruFlSt 14),
  Payerne

Mirage IIIDS

J-2001	InstruFlSt 14

Mirage IIIUDS

J-2011	InstruFlSt 14
J-2012	InstruFlSt 14

Mirage IIIS

J-2301	
J-2302	GRD
J-2303	GRD
J-2304	FlSt 10
J-2305	FlSt 10
J-2306	FlSt 16/17
J-2308	FlSt 16/17
J-2309	FlSt 16
J-2311	FlSt 10
J-2312	
J-2313	FlSt 10
J-2314	FlSt 16
J-2315	
J-2317	
J-2318	FlSt 16
J-2319	FlSt 16/17
J-2321	FlSt 16/17
J-2322	
J-2324	FlSt 10
J-2325	
J-2326	FlSt 16
J-2327	FlSt 16
J-2329	FlSt 16
J-2330	FlSt 16/17
J-2331	FlSt 16/17
J-2332	FlSt 10
J-2333	FlSt 16/17
J-2334	FlSt 16
J-2335	FlSt 16/17

Mirage IIIRS

R-2101	FlSt 10
R-2102	FlSt 10
R-2103	FlSt 10
R-2104	FlSt 10
R-2105	FlSt 10
R-2106	FlSt 10
R-2108	FlSt 10
R-2109	FlSt 10
R-2110	FlSt 10
R-2111	FlSt 10
R-2112	FlSt 10
R-2113	FlSt 10
R-2114	FlSt 10
R-2115	FlSt 10
R-2116	FlSt 10
R-2117	FlSt 10
R-2118	FlSt 10

Mirage IIIBS

U-2004	InstruFlSt 14

Gates Learjet 35A
Swiss Air Force, Dübendorf
T-781

McDonnell Douglas F/A-18
Hornet F/A-18C

J-5001
J-5002
J-5003
J-5004
J-5005
J-5006
J-5007
J-5008
J-5009
J-5010
J-5011
J-5012
J-5013
J-5014
J-5015
J-5016
J-5017
J-5018
J-5019
J-5020
J-5021
J-5022
J-5023
J-5024
J-5025
J-5026

F/A-18D

J-5231
J-5232
J-5233
J-5234
J-5235
J-5236
J-5237
J-5238

Northrop F-5 Tiger II
Flieger Staffel 1 (FlSt 1),
  Turtman;
Flieger Staffel 6 (FlSt 6),
  Sion;
Flieger Staffel 8 (FlSt 8),
  Meiringen;
Flieger Staffel 11 (FlSt 11),
  Meiringen;
Flieger Staffel 13 (FlSt 13),
  Meiringen;
Flieger Staffel 18 (FlSt 18),
  Payerne;
Flieger Staffel 19 (FlSt 19),
  Mollis;
Gruppe fur Rustunggdienste
  (GRD), Emmen;
Instrumentation Flieger
Staffel 14 (InstruFlSt 14),
  Dübendorf;
Patrouille Suisse, Emmen
  (P. Suisse)

F-5E

J-3001	GRD
J-3002	FlSt 11
J-3003	FlSt 11
J-3004	FlSt 11
J-3005	FlSt 18
J-3006	FlSt 11
J-3007	FlSt 11
J-3008	InstruFlSt 14
J-3009	FlSt 11
J-3010	FlSt 18
J-3011	FlSt 13
J-3012	FlSt 11
J-3014	FlSt 11
J-3015	FlSt 11
J-3016	FlSt 11
J-3019	FlSt 11
J-3020	FlSt 18
J-3021	FlSt 18
J-3022	FlSt 19
J-3023	FlSt 11
J-3023	FlSt 13
J-3025	FlSt 11
J-3026	FlSt 18
J-3027	FlSt 18
J-3029	FlSt 19
J-3030	FlSt 6
J-3031	FlSt 13
J-3032	FlSt 13
J-3033	FlSt 19
J-3034	FlSt 13
J-3035	FlSt 19
J-3036	FlSt 13
J-3037	FlSt 13
J-3038	FlSt 18
J-3039	FlSt 13
J-3040	
J-3041	FlSt 19
J-3043	FlSt 13
J-3044	FlSt 1
J-3045	FlSt 19
J-3046	FlSt 18
J-3047	FlSt 13
J-3049	FlSt 1
J-3050	FlSt 19
J-3051	FlSt 1
J-3052	FlSt 13
J-3053	FlSt 13
J-3054	FlSt 18
J-3055	FlSt 18
J-3056	FlSt 1
J-3057	
J-3058	FlSt 13
J-3060	FlSt 1
J-3061	FlSt 13
J-3062	FlSt 18
J-3063	FlSt 1
J-3064	FlSt 13
J-3065	FlSt 13
J-3066	
J-3067	FlSt 1
J-3068	FlSt 13
J-3069	FlSt 13
J-3070	FlSt 8
J-3072	FlSt 13
J-3073	FlSt 13
J-3074	FlSt 13
J-3075	FlSt 13
J-3076	FlSt 13
J-3077	FlSt 8
J-3079	FlSt 1
J-3080	P. Suisse
J-3081	P. Suisse [1]
J-3082	FlSt 11
J-3083	P. Suisse [3]
J-3084	P. Suisse [4]
J-3085	P. Suisse [5]
J-3086	P. Suisse
J-3087	P. Suisse [6]
J-3088	P. Suisse
J-3089	P. Suisse
J-3090	P. Suisse [2]
J-3091	P. Suisse
J-3092	FlSt 13

J-3093	FISt 18
J-3094	FISt 1
J-3095	
J-3096	FISt 18
J-3097	GRD
J-3098	FISt 19

F-5F

J-3201	FISt 1
J-3202	FISt 1
J-3203	FISt 18
J-3204	GRD
J-3205	FISt 13
J-3206	
J-3207	FISt 13
J-3208	FISt 11
J-3209	FISt 13
J-3210	FISt 11
J-3211	
J-3212	

TURKEY
Türk Hava Kuvvetleri
Boeing KC-135R Stratotanker
Tanker Aircraft Sqn, Incirlik

23512
23563
23568
72591
72592
80110

Cessna 650 Citation VII
224 Filo, Ankara/Etimes gut

93-7024	ETI-024
93-7026	ETI-026

Grumman G.1159C Gulfstream IV
224 Filo, Ankara/Etimes gut

003

Lockheed C-130B Hercules
222 Filo, Erkilet

10960
10963
23496
70527
80736
91527

Lockheed C-130E Hercules
222 Filo, Erkilet

00991	12-991
01468	12-468
01947	12-947
13186	12-186
13187	12-187
13188	12-188
13189	12-189
17949	12-949

Transall C-160D
221 Filo, Erkilet

019	
020	12-020
021	
022	12-022
023	12-023
024	12-024
025	12-025
026	12-026
027	12-027
028	12-028
029	
030	12-030
031	12-031
032	12-032
033	12-033
034	12-034
035	12-035
036	12-036
037	12-037
038	12-038
039	12-039
040	12-040

UNITED ARAB EMIRATES
United Arab Emirates Air Force
Abu Dhabi
Lockheed C-130H Hercules

1211
1212
1213
1214

Dubai
Lockheed L.100-30 Hercules

311
312

Swearingen Merlin IIIA CF01 based at 21 Smaldeel, Melsboek, with the Belgian Air Force. *A. P. March*

Fouga CM 170 Super Magister 219, one of seven based with No 1 Support Wing, Irish Air Corps, at Baldonnel. *PRM*

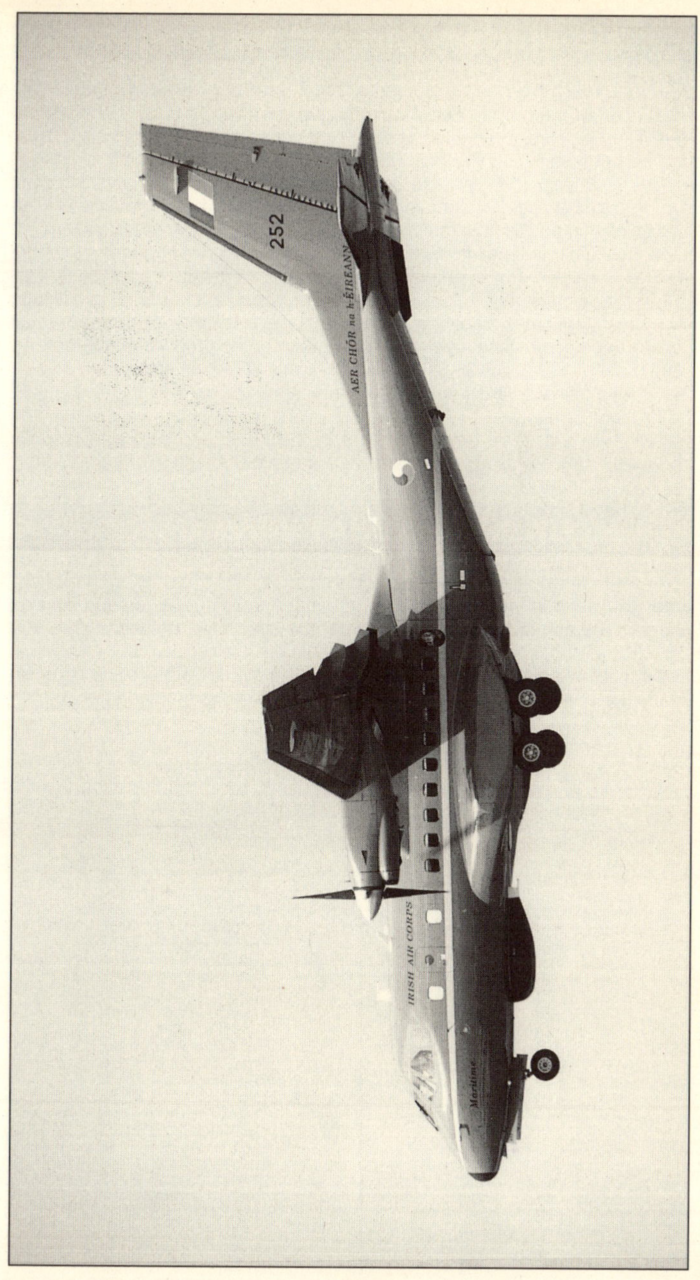

Airtech CN.235 MPA Persuader 252/7 of the Irish Air Corps Maritime Squadron based at Baldonnel. *PRM*

US Military Aircraft Markings

All USAF aircraft have been allocated a fiscal year (FY) number since 1921. Individual aircraft are given a serial according to the fiscal year in which they are ordered. The numbers commence at 0001 and are prefixed with the year of allocation. For example F-15C Eagle 40001 (84-001) was the first aircraft ordered in 1984. The fiscal year (FY) serial is carried on the technical data block which is usually stencilled on the left-hand side of the aircraft just below the cockpit. The number displayed on the fin is a corruption of the FY serial. Most tactical aircraft carry the fiscal year in small figures followed by the last three or four digits of the serial in large figures. For example Lakenheath-based F-15E Eagle 10311 carries 91-0311/LN on its tail. Large transport and tanker aircraft such as C-130s and KC-135s sometimes display a five-figure number commencing with the last digit of the appropriate fiscal year and four figures of the production number. An example of this is KC-135R 58-0128 which displays 80128 on its fin.

USN serials follow a straightforward numerical sequence which commenced, for the present series, with the allocation of 00001 to an SB2C Helldiver by the Bureau of Aeronautics in 1940. Numbers in the 165000 series are presently being issued. They are usually carried in full on the rear fuselage of the aircraft.

UK based USAF Aircraft

The following aircraft are normally based in the UK. They are listed in numerical order of type with individual aircraft in serial number order, as depicted on the aircraft. The number in brackets is either the alternative presentation of the five-figure number commencing with the last digit of the fiscal year, or the fiscal year where a five-figure serial is presented on the aircraft. Where it is possible to identify the allocation of aircraft to individual squadrons by means of colours carried on fin or cockpit edge, this is also provided.

Notes	Type	Notes	Type
	McDonnell Douglas		90-0256 (00256) F-15E *bl*
	F-15C Eagle/F-15D Eagle/		90-0257 (00257) F-15E *bl*
	F-15E Strike Eagle		90-0258 (00258) F-15E *bl*
	48 FW, RAF Lakenheath [LN]		90-0259 (00259) F-15E *bl*
	492 FS *blue*/white		90-0260 (00260) F-15E *bl*
	493 FS black/*yellow*		90-0261 (00261) F-15E *bl*
	494 FS *red*/white		90-0262 (00262) F-15E *bl* [48 OG]
	86-0147 (60147) F-15C *y*		91-0300 (10300) F-15E *bl*
	86-0154 (60154) F-15C *y*		91-0301 (10301) F-15E *bl*
	86-0156 (60156) F-15C *y*		91-0302 (10302) F-15E *bl*
	86-0159 (60159) F-15C *y*		91-0303 (10303) F-15E *bl*
	86-0160 (60160) F-15C *y*		91-0304 (10304) F-15E *bl*
	86-0163 (60163) F-15C *y*		91-0305 (10305) F-15E *bl*
	86-0164 (60164) F-15C *y* [493 FS]		91-0306 (10306) F-15E *r*
	86-0165 (60165) F-15C *y*		91-0307 (10307) F-15E *bl*
	86-0166 (60166) F-15C *y* [48 OG]		91-0308 (10308) F-15E *bl*
	86-0167 (60167) F-15C *y*		91-0309 (10309) F-15E *bl*
	86-0169 (60169) F-15C *y*		91-0310 (10310) F-15E *bl*
	86-0171 (60171) F-15C *y*		91-0311 (10311) F-15E *bl*
	86-0172 (60172) F-15C *y*		91-0312 (10312) F-15E *bl*
	86-0173 (60173) F-15C *y*		91-0313 (10313) F-15E *r* [3rd AF]
	86-0174 (60174) F-15C *y*		91-0314 (10314) F-15E *r* [494 FS]
	86-0175 (60175) F-15C *y*		91-0315 (10315) F-15E *r*
	86-0176 (60176) F-15C *y*		91-0316 (10316) F-15E *r*
	86-0178 (60178) F-15C *y*		91-0317 (10317) F-15E *r*
	86-0180 (60180) F-15C *y*		91-0318 (10318) F-15E *r*
	86-0182 (60182) F-15D *y*		91-0319 (10319) F-15E *r*
	90-0248 (00248) F-15E *m* [48 FW]		91-0320 (10320) F-15E *r*
	90-0251 (00251) F-15E *bl* [492 FS]		91-0321 (10321) F-15E *r*
	90-0255 (00255) F-15E *bl*		91-0322 (10322) F-15E *r*

Type			Notes
91-0323	(10323)	F-15E	r
91-0324	(10324)	F-15E	r
91-0325	(10325)	F-15E	bl
91-0326	(10326)	F-15E	bl
91-0327	(10327)	F-15E	r
91-0328	(10328)	F-15E	r
91-0329	(10329)	F-15E	bl
91-0330	(10330)	F-15E	r
91-0331	(10331)	F-15E	r
91-0332	(10332)	F-15E	bl
91-0333	(10333)	F-15E	r
91-0334	(10334)	F-15E	r
91-0335	(10335)	F-15E	r
91-0601	(10601)	F-15E	r
91-0602	(10602)	F-15E	r
91-0603	(10603)	F-15E	r
91-0604	(10604)	F-15E	r
91-0605	(10605)	F-15E	r
92-0364	(20364)	F-15E	r

Sikorsky MH-53J
21 SOS, 352 SOG
RAF Mildenhall

01625	(FY70)
01626	(FY70)
10930	(FY68)
14993	(FY67)
31648	(FY73)
95784	(FY69)
95790	(FY69)

Lockheed C-130 Hercules
7 SOS* & 67 SOS, 352 SOG
RAF Mildenhall

37814	(FY63)	C-130E
40476	(FY84)	MC-130H*
60213	(FY66)	MC-130P
61699	(FY86)	MC-130H*
70023	(FY87)	MC-130H*
80193	(FY88)	MC-130H*
80194	(FY88)	MC-130H*
95819	(FY69)	MC-130P
95820	(FY69)	MC-130P
95823	(FY69)	MC-130P
95831	(FY69)	MC-130P

Boeing KC-135R Stratotanker
351 ARS, 100 ARW [D]
RAF Mildenhall (r/w/bl)

23541	(FY62)
38023	(FY63)
38877	(FY63)
71439	(FY57)
71456	(FY57)
71474	(FY57)
71499	(FY57)
71506	(FY57)
91482	(FY59)

UK based US Navy Aircraft

Beech UC-12M Super King Air
Naval Air Facility, Mildenhall [8G]
3837 (163837)
3840 (163840)
3843 (163843)

Fairchild A-10A Thunderbolt II 81-988 (10988) of 52 FW at Spangdahlem AB, Germany. *A. P. March*

These aircraft are normally based in Western Europe with the USAFE. They are shown in numerical order of type designation, with individual aircraft in serial number order as carried on the aircraft. An alternative five-figure presentation of the serial is shown in brackets where appropriate. Fiscal year (FY) details are also provided if necessary. The unit allocation and operating bases are given for most aircraft.

Notes	Type		
	Lockheed U-2R		
	OL-FR, 9 RW, Istres, France [BB]		
	01066	(FY80)	
	01068	(FY80)	
	01092	(FY80)	
	McDonnell Douglas		
	C-9A Nightingale		
	75 AAS, 86 AW Ramstein, Germany		
	SHAPE, Chievres, Belgium[1]		
	FY71		
	10876[1] (VIP)		
	10879		
	10880		
	10881		
	10882		
	FY67		
	22585		
	Fairchild A-10A/OA-10A*		
	Thunderbolt II		
	SP: 52 FW Spangdahlem, Germany		
	81 FS *black*		
	81-951	(10951)	*bk*
	81-952	(10952)* *m*	[52 FW]
	81-954	(10954)* *bk*	
	81-956	(10956)* *bk*	
	81-962	(10962) *bk*	
	81-963	(10963) *bk*	
	81-966	(10966) *bk*	
	81-976	(10976) *bk*	
	81-978	(10978)* *bk*	
	81-980	(10980) *bk*	[81 FS]
	81-983	(10983 *bk*	
	81-984	(10984) *bk*	
	81-985	(10985)* *bk*	
	81-988	(10988) *bk*	
	81-991	(10991)* *bk*	
	81-992	(10992) *bk*	
	82-649	(20649)* *bk*	
	82-650	(20650) *bk*	
	82-654	(20654) *bk*	
	82-655	(20655) *bk*	
	82-656	(20656) *bk*	
	Beech C-12C/C-12D/C-12F		
	[1]JUSMG, Ankara, Turkey		
	[2]US Embassy Flight, Athens		
	[3]US Embassy Flight, Budapest		
	FY83		
	30495	C-12D[3]	
	FY73		
	31206	C-12C[1]	
	31216	C-12C[1]	
	31218	C-12C[2]	
	FY84		
	40180	C-12F[3]	
	FY76		
	60173	C-12C[1]	

Notes	Type		
	McDonnell Douglas		
	F-15C/F-15D* Eagle		
	SP: 52 FW Spangdahlem, Germany		
	53 FS *yellow/black*		
	78-514	(80514) *y*	
	79-012	(90012)* *y*	
	79-025	(90025) *y*	
	79-057	(90057) *y*	
	79-064	(90064) *y*	
	80-004	(00004) *y*	
	80-012	(00012) *y*	
	80-052	(00052) *m*	[52 FW]
	84-001	(40001) *y*	[53 FS]
	84-003	(40003) *y*	
	84-005	(40005) *y*	
	84-008	(40008) *y*	
	84-009	(40009) *y*	[52 FW]
	84-010	(40010) *y*	
	84-014	(40014) *y*	
	84-015	(40015) *y*	
	84-019	(40019) *y*	
	84-023	(40023) *y*	
	84-024	(40024) *y*	
	84-025	(40025) *y*	
	84-027	(40027) *y*	
	84-044	(40044)* *y*	
	Lockheed (GD) F-16C/F-16D*		
	AV: 31 FW Aviano, Italy		
	510 FS *purple/white*		
	555 FS *blue/yellow*		
	SP: 52 FW Spangdahlem, Germany		
	22 FS *red/white*		
	23 FS *blue/white*		
	87-350	(70350) AV *pr*	
	87-351	(70351) AV *bl*	
	87-355	(70355) AV *pr*	
	87-359	(70359) AV *bl*	
	88-413	(80413) AV *pr*	[510 FS]
	88-425	(80425) AV *bl*	
	88-435	(80435) AV *bl*	
	88-443	(80443) AV *pr*	
	88-444	(80444) AV *pr*	
	88-446	(80446) AV *pr*	
	88-491	(80491) AV *pr*	
	88-525	(80525) AV *pr*	[31 OSS]
	88-526	(80526) AV *bl*	
	88-529	(80529) AV *pr*	
	88-532	(80532) AV *bl*	[31 OG]
	88-535	(80535) AV *bl*	
	88-541	(80541) AV *pr*	
	88-550	(80550) AV *bl*	[555 FS]
	89-001	(92001) AV *m*	[31 FW]
	89-009	(92009) AV *bl*	
	89-011	(92011) AV *pr*	
	89-016	(92016) AV *bl*	
	89-023	(92023) AV *bl*	
	89-024	(92024) AV *bl*	
	89-026	(92026) AV *pr*	

Type	Notes	Type	Notes
89-029 (92029) AV *bl*		**Grumman C-20A**	
89-030 (92030) AV *pr*		**Gulfstream III**	
89-035 (92035) AV *bl*		76 AS, 86 AW Ramstein, Germany	
89-038 (92038) AV *bl*		*FY83*	
89-039 (92039) AV *bl*		30500	
89-044 (92044) AV *pr*		30501	
89-046 (92046) AV *pr*		30502	
89-047 (92047) AV *pr*			
89-049 (92049) AV *pr*		**Gates C-21A Learjet**	
89-050 (92050) AV *pr*		76 AS, 86 AW Ramstein, Germany	
89-057 (92057) AV *bl*		*7005 ABS/HQ USEUCOM, Stuttgart, Germany	
89-137 (92137) AV *bl*		*FY84*	
89-178 (92178)* AV *pr*		40068*	
90-709 (00709) AV *pr*		40081*	
90-795 (00795)* AV *bl*		40082*	
90-796 (00796)* AV *pr*		40083*	
90-800 (00800)* AV *bl*		40084	
90-813 (00813) SP *r*		40085	
90-818 (00818) SP *r*		40086	
90-827 (00827) SP *r*		40087	
90-828 (00828) SP *r*		40108	
90-829 (00829) SP *r* [22 FS]		40109	
90-831 (00831) SP *r*		40110	
90-833 (00833) SP *r*		40111	
90-843 (00843)* SP *r*		40112	
90-846 (00846)* SP *r*			
91-336 (10336) SP *r* [22 FS]		**Sikorsky HH-60G Blackhawk**	
91-337 (10337) SP *r*		56 RQS, 85 Wg Keflavik, Iceland [IS]	
91-338 (10338) SP *r*		26117 (FY88)	
91-339 (10339) SP *r*		26205 (FY89)	
91-340 (10340) SP *r*		26206 (FY89)	
91-341 (10341) SP *r*		26208 (FY89)	
91-342 (10342) SP *r*		26212 (FY89)	
91-343 (10343) SP *r*			
91-344 (10344) SP *r*		**Lockheed C-130E Hercules**	
91-351 (10351) SP *r*		37 AS, 86 AW Ramstein, Germany	
91-352 (10352) SP *m* [52 FW]		[RS] (*bl/w*)	
91-402 (10402) SP *bl*		01260 (FY70)	
91-403 (10403) SP *bl* [23 FS]		01264 (FY70)	
91-405 (10405) SP *bl*		01271 (FY70)	
91-406 (10406) SP *bl* [23 FS]		01274 (FY70)	
91-407 (10407) SP *bl*		10935 (FY68)	
91-408 (10408) SP *bl*		10938 (FY68)	
91-409 (10409) SP *bl*		10943 (FY68)	
91-410 (10410) SP *bl*		10947 (FY68)	
91-412 (10412) SP *m* [52 FW]		17681 (FY64)	
91-414 (10414) SP *bl*		18240 (FY64)	
91-415 (10415) SP *bl*		37885 (FY63)	
91-416 (10416) SP *bl*		37887 (FY63)	
91-417 (10417) SP *bl*		40502 (FY64)	
91-418 (10418) SP *bl*		40527 (FY64)	
91-419 (10419) SP *bl*		40533 (FY64)	
91-420 (10420) SP *bl*		40550 (FY64)	
91-421 (10421) SP *bl*		96566 (FY69)	
91-464 (10464)* SP *r*		96582 (FY69)	
91-472 (10472)* SP *bl*		96583 (FY69)	
91-474 (10474)* SP *bl*			
92-915 (23915) SP *bl*			
92-918 (23918) SP *bl*			

Notes	Type		Notes	Type
	Lockheed P-3 Orion			**Sikorsky CH-53E/MH-53E***
	CinCAFSE, NAF Sigonella, Italy			**Sea Stallion**
	NAF Keflavik, Iceland;			HC-4, NAF Sigonella, Italy
	VQ-2, NAF Rota, Spain			162505 HC-47*
	150495 UP-3A	NAF Keflavik		162506 HC-48*
	150515 VP-3A	CinCAFSE		162509 HC-49*
	156520 P-3C [10]	VQ-2		162516 HC-46*
	156525 P-3C [11]	VQ-2		163053 HC-44*
	157320 EP-3E	VQ-2		163057 HC-41*
	157326 EP-3E [22]	VQ-2		163065 HC-43*
				163068 HC-42*

Beech UC-12M Super King Air
[1] NAF Sigonella, Italy
[2] NAF Rota, Spain
3838 (163838)[1]
3839 (163839)[2]
3841 (163841)[1]
3842 (163842)[2]
3844 (163844)[1]

Canadian Armed Forces CC-150 Polaris 15005/204 of 437 Sqn/8 Wg bearing UN markings. *D. J. March*

Type	Notes
Beech C-12 Super King Air	
7th ATC, Grafenwöhr;	
207 Avn Co, Heidelberg;	
LANDSOUTHEAST, Izmir, Turkey;	
HQ/USEUCOM, Stuttgart;	
6th Avn Det, Vicenza, Italy;	
'A' Co, 5 Batt, 158 Avn Reg't,	
Wiesbaden;	
1 MIB, Wiesbaden	
FY80	
23373 RC-12D 1 MIB	
FY84	
40144 C-12F 7th ATC	
40150 C-12F 207 Avn Co	
40151 C-12F 207 Avn Co	
40152 C-12F 207 Avn Co	
40153 C-12F 207 Avn Co	
40154 C-12F 207 Avn Co	
40155 C-12F 6 Avn Det	
40156 C-12F 207 Avn Co	
40157 C-12F 5/158 ACo	
40158 C-12F HQ/USEUCOM	
40159 C-12F HQ/USEUCOM	
40160 C-12F HQ/USEUCOM	
40161 C-12F 6 Avn Det	
40162 C-12F 6 Avn Det	
40163 C-12F *to USA*	
40164 C-12F LANDSOUTHEAST	
40165 C-12F 7th ATC	
40181 C-12F *to USA*	
FY94	
40315 C-12R 207 Avn Co	
40316 C-12R 206 Avn Co	
40317 C-12R 207 Avn Co	
40318 C-12R 207 Avn Co	
40319 C-12R 207 Avn Co	
FY95	
50088 C-12R 207 Avn Co	
FY85	
50147 RC-12K 1 MIB	
50148 RC-12K 1 MIB	
50150 RC-12K 1 MIB	
50151 RC-12K 1 MIB	
50152 RC-12K 1 MIB	
50153 RC-12K 1 MIB	
50154 RC-12K 1 MIB	
50155 RC-12K 1 MIB	
Boeing-Vertol CH-47D Chinook	
'A' Co, 5 Batt, 159 Avn Reg't	
Giebelstadt;	
'E' Co, 502 Avn Reg't, Aviano	
FY87	
70072 5/159 ACo	
70073 5/159 ACo	
70079 5/159 ACo	
70081 5/159 ACo	
70082 5/159 ACo	
70083 5/159 ACo	
70085 5/159 ACo	
70086 5/159 ACo	
70088 5/159 ACo	
70089 5/159 ACo	
70091 5/159 ACo	
70092 5/159 ACo	
70094 5/159 ACo	
70096 5/159 ACo	
70112 5/159 ACo	

Type	Notes
FY88	
80098 502 ECo	
80099 502 ECo	
80100 502 ECo	
80101 502 ECo	
80102 502 ECo	
80103 502 ECo	
80104 502 ECo	
80106 502 ECo	
FY89	
90138 502 ECo	
90139 502 ECo	
90140 502 ECo	
90141 502 ECo	
92142 502 ECo	
90143 502 ECo	
90144 502 ECo	
90145 502 ECo	
Sikorsky UH-60 Black Hawk	
7-1 Avn, Ansbach;	
45 Med Co, Ansbach;	
1-1 Cav, Budingen;	
357th Avn Det/SHAPE, Chievres;	
'C' Co, 7th Btn, 158 Avn Reg't,	
Giebelstadt;	
8-158 Avn, Giebelstadt;	
'C' Co, 6th Btn, 159 Avn Reg't,	
Giebelstadt;	
2-227 Avn, Hanau;	
3-227 Avn, Hanau;	
'A' Co, 7th Btn, 227 Avn Reg't, Hanau;	
207th Aviation Co, Heidelberg;	
2-6 Cavalry, Illesheim;	
6-6 Cavalry, Illesheim;	
236th Med Co (HA), Landstuhl;	
'A' Co, 5th Btn, 158 Avn Reg't,	
Wiesbaden;	
159th Med Co, Wiesbaden	
UH-60A	
FY81	
23578 B/70 TRANS	
23584 *to USA*	
23590 236 Med Co	
23594 7-1 Avn	
23609 7/227 ACo	
23613 B/70 TRANS	
23617	
23623 7/158 CCo	
23626 236 Med Co	
FY82	
23647 1 HCo	
23660 7/158 CCo	
23661 *to USA*	
23663 7-1 Avn	
23664 *to USA*	
23665 7/227 ACo	
23667 7/158 CCo	
23668 7/158 CCo	
23669 5/158 ACo	
23672 236 Med Co	
23675 45 Med Co	
23676 *to USA*	
23682 7/227 ACo	
23684 5/158 ACo	
23685 236 Med Co	
23686 236 Med Co	
23691 5/158 ACo	
23692 7/158 CCo	

Notes	Type		Notes	Type	
	23693	45 Med Co		26023	7/158 CCo
	23695	*to USA*		26024	7/158 CCo
	23699	6/159 CCo		26025	7/158 CCo
	23702	7-1 Avn		26026	5/159 ACo
	23722			26027	7/158 CCo
	23723	159 Med Co		26028	7/158 CCo
	23726	45 Med Co		26031	7-1 Avn
	23727	236 Med Co		26034	7/227 ACo
	23729	45 Med Co		26037	
	23730	236 Med Co		26038	5/158 ACo
	23731	*to USA*		26039	
	23733	*to USA*		26040	7-1 Avn
	23735	236 Med Co		26041	6/159 CCo
	23736	236 Med Co		26042	5/158 ACo
	23737	159 Med Co		26045	
	23738	159 Med Co		26050	7-227 Avn
	23739	*to USA*		26051	5/158 ACo
	23743	*to USA*		26052	7/227 ACo
	23744			26053	7-227 Avn
	23745	45 Med Co		26054	236 Med Co
	23746			26055	159 Med Co
	23748	7-1 Avn		26056	5/158 ACo
	23750	159 Med Co		26058	159 Med Co
	23751	159 Med Co		26063	
	23753	159 Med Co		26067	7/227 ACo
	23754	45 Med Co		26068	7/227 ACo
	23755	45 Med Co		26070	
	23756	159 Med Co		26071	7/227 ACo
	23757	207 Avn Co		26072	7/227 ACo
	23761	7/227 ACo		26073	
	FY83			26075	45 Med Co
	23854	5/158 ACo		26077	3-227 Avn
	23855	207 Avn Co		26080	159 Med Co
	23869			26083	5/159 ACo
	FY84			26085	2-227 Avn
	23951	45 Med Co		26086	3-227 Avn
	FY85			*FY89*	
	24391	45 Med Co		26138	2-6 Cav
	FY86			26142	2-227 Avn
	24498	7/227 ACo		26145	3-227 Avn
	24530	7-1 Avn		26146	45 Med Co
	24531			26151	159 Med Co
	24532	45 Med Co		26153	7-1 Avn
	24538	207 Avn Co		26155	7/227 ACo
	24550	236 Med Co		26164	7-1 Avn
	24551	236 Med Co		26165	207 Avn Co
	24552	159 Med Co		**UH-60L**	
	24554	7/227 ACo		*FY95*	
	24555	6/159 CCo		26621	7-1 Avn
	FY87			26628	7-1 Avn
	24579	5/158 ACo		26629	7-1 Avn
	24581	159 Med Co		26630	7/158 CCo
	24583	357 Avn Det		26631	7-1 Avn
	24584	357 Avn Det		26632	7-1 Avn
	24589	207 Avn Co		26633	7/158 CCo
	24621	207 Avn Co		26635	7-1 Avn
	24628	7-1 Avn		26636	7-1 Avn
	24634	6/159 CCo		26637	7-1 Avn
	24642	7-1 Avn		26638	7-1 Avn
	24643	7-1 Avn		26639	7-1 Avn
	24644			26640	7-1 Avn
	24645	45 Med Co		26641	6/159 CCo
	24647	7-1 Avn		26642	7-1 Avn
	24650	159 Med Co		26643	6/159 CCo
	24656			26644	7-1 Avn
	26001	45 Med Co		26646	
	26002	45 Med Co		26649	6/159 CCo
	26003	7/227 ACo		26650	6/159 CCo
	26004	7/1 ACo		26651	7/158 CCo
	FY88			26652	6/159 CCo
	26019	7/227 ACo		26653	6/159 CCo
	26020			26674	6/159 CCo
	26021	5/158 ACo		26676	6/159 CCo

Type	Notes	Type	Notes
McD AH-64A Apache		70415	1-1 Avn
1-1 Avn, Ansbach;		70417	1-1 Avn
2-227 Avn, 3-227 Avn, Hanau;		70418	1-1 Avn
2-6 Cav, 6-6 Cav, Illesheim;		70419	1-1 Avn
7/159 ACo, Illesheim		70420	1-1 Avn
FY84		70423	1-1 Avn
24218	2-6 Cav	70428	2-6 Cav
24244	6-6 Cav	70432	
24247		70434	3-227 Avn
24250	3-227 Avn	70435	2-227 Avn
24262	2-6 Cav	70436	1-1 Avn
24266	2-6 Cav	70437	
24277	2-6 Cav	70438	3-227 Avn
24290	2-6 Cav	70439	1-1 Avn
24293	2-6 Cav	70440	3-227 Avn
24296	2-6 Cav	70441	6-6 Cav
24297	2-6 Cav	70442	1-1 Avn
24299		70443	2-6 Cav
24303	2-6 Cav	70444	2-227 Avn
24304	2-6 Cav	70445	3-227 Avn
FY85		70446	3-227 Avn
25357	2-6 Cav	70447	3-227 Avn
25397		70449	3-227 Avn
25424		70451	2-227 Avn
25460	1-1 Avn	70455	2-227 Avn
25469	7/159 ACo	70459	
25473	1-1 Avn	70465	1-1 Avn
25474	*to KLu*	70470	1-1 Avn
25475	2-6 Cav	70471	1-1 Avn
25476		70473	
25478	1-1 Avn	70474	1-1 Avn
25479	1-1 Avn	70475	3-227 Avn
25485	*to KLu*	70477	1-1 Avn
FY86		70478	1-1 Avn
68940	2-6 Cav	70479	*to USA*
68941	6-6 Cav	70481	
68942	2-6 Cav	70482	
68943	2-6 Cav	70487	2-227 Avn
68946	2-6 Cav	70496	3-227 Avn
68947	6-6 Cav	70498	*to USA*
68948	2-6 Cav	70503	2-227 Avn
68949	2-6 Cav	70504	2-227 Avn
68950	6-6 Cav	70505	3-227 Avn
68951	2-6 Cav	70506	2-227 Avn
68952	2-6 Cav	*FY88*	
68955	6-6 Cav	80197	2-227 Avn
68956	2-6 Cav	80198	2-227 Avn
68957	2-6 Cav	80199	2-227 Avn
68959	2-6 Cav	80203	6-6 Cav
68960	2-6 Cav	80204	6-6 Cav
68961	2-6 Cav	80212	6-6 Cav
68981	2-6 Cav	80213	6-6 Cav
69010	2-6 Cav	80214	6-6 Cav
69011	2-6 Cav	80215	6-6 Cav
69019	2-6 Cav	80216	6-6 Cav
69026	2-6 Cav	80217	6-6 Cav
69030	2-6 Cav	80219	6-6 Cav
69032	2-6 Cav	80222	6-6 Cav
69037	2-6 Cav	80225	6-6 Cav
69039		80228	6-6 Cav
69048	2-6 Cav	80229	6-6 Cav
FY87		80232	6-6 Cav
70408	1-1 Avn	80233	6-6 Cav
70409	1-1 Avn	80234	6-6 Cav
70410	3-227 Avn	80236	6-6 Cav
70411	6-6 Cav	80243	6-6 Cav
70412	1-1 Avn	80246	6-6 Cav
70413	1-1 Avn	80250	6-6 Cav

The following aircraft are normally based in the USA but are likely to be seen visiting the UK from time to time. The presentation is in numerical order of the type, commencing with the B-**1B** and concluding with the C-**141**. The aircraft are listed in numerical progression by the serial actually carried externally. Fiscal year information is provided, together with details of mark variations and in some cases operating units. Where base-code letter information is carried on the aircrafts' tails, this is detailed with the squadron/base data; for example the 7th Wing's B-1B 30069 carries the letters DY on its tail, thus identifying the Wing's home base as Dyess AFB, Texas.

Notes	Type		
	Rockwell B-1B Lancer		
	7 Wg Dyess AFB, Texas [DY]:		
	9 BS (*bk*) & 28 BS (*bl/w*);		
	28 BW Ellsworth AFB, South Dakota		
	[EL]: 37 BS (*bk/y*);		
	127 BS/184 BW, Kansas ANG,		
	McConnell AFB, Kansas;		
	128 BS/116 BW, Georgia ANG,		
	Robins AFB, Georgia [GA];		
	366 Wg Mountain Home AFB, Idaho		
	[MO]: 34 BS (*r/bk*);		
	410 TS Edwards AFB, California		
	FY83		
	30065	7 Wg	*bk*
	30066	7 Wg	*bl/w*
	30067	7 Wg	*bk*
	30068	7 Wg	*bl/w*
	30069	7 Wg	*bl/w*
	30070	7 Wg	*bl/w*
	30071	7 Wg	*bk*
	FY84		
	40049	410 TS	
	40050	7 Wg	*bl/w*
	40051	7 Wg	*bk*
	40053	7 Wg	*bl/w*
	40054	7 Wg	*bl/w*
	40055	7 Wg	*bl/w*
	40056	7 Wg	*bl/w*
	40057	7 Wg	*bk*
	40058	7 Wg	*bk*
	FY85		
	50059	128 BS	
	50060	127 BS	
	50061	28 BW	*bk/y*
	50062	7 Wg	*bk*
	50064	28 BW	*bk/y*
	50065	7 Wg	*bl/w*
	50066	28 BW	*bk/y*
	50067	7 Wg	*bl/w*
	50068	410 TS	
	50069	127 BS	
	50070	127 BS	
	50071	7 Wg	*bl/w*
	50072	7 Wg	*bk*
	50073	7 Wg	*bl/w*
	50074	7 Wg	*bl/w*
	50075	28 BW	*bk/y*
	50077	28 BW	*bk/y*
	50078	28 BW	*bk/y*
	50079	28 BW	*bk/y*
	50080	127 BS	
	50081	127 BS	
	50082	7 Wg	*bk*
	50083	28 BW	*bk/y*
	50084	28 BW	*bk/y*
	50085	28 BW	*bk/y*

Notes	Type		
	50086	28 BW	*bk/y*
	50087	28 BW	*bk/y*
	50088	127 BS	
	50089	28 BW	*bk/y*
	50090	28 BW	*bk/y*
	50091	366 Wg	*r/bk*
	50092	28 BW	*bk/y*
	FY86		
	60093	28 BW	*bk/y*
	60094	28 BW	*bk/y*
	60095	127 BS	
	60096	28 BW	*bk/y*
	60097	366 Wg	*r/bk*
	60098	28 BW	*bk/y*
	60099	28 BW	*bk/y*
	60100	7 Wg	*bl/w*
	60101	7 Wg	*bl/w*
	60102	28 BW	*bk/y*
	60103	7 Wg	*bk*
	60104	366 Wg	*r/bk*
	60105	7 Wg	*bl/w*
	60107	7 Wg	*bk*
	60108	7 Wg	*bl/w*
	60109	7 Wg	*bl/w*
	60110	7 Wg	*bl/w*
	60111	28 BW	*bk/y*
	60112	7 Wg	*bk*
	60113	28 BW	*bk/y*
	60114	28 BW	*bk/y*
	60115	127 BS	
	60116	366 Wg	*r/bk*
	60117	7 Wg	*bl/w*
	60118	366 Wg	*r/bk*
	60119	7 Wg	*bl/w*
	60120	7 Wg	*bk*
	60121	366 Wg	*r/bk*
	60122	7 Wg	*bl/w*
	60123	7 Wg	*bk*
	60124	128 BS	
	60125	366 Wg	*r/bk*
	60126	7 Wg	*bl/w*
	60127	127 BS	
	60128	28 BW	*bk/y*
	60129	127 BS	
	60130	7 Wg	*bl/w*
	60131	366 Wg	*r/bk*
	60132	7 Wg	*bl/w*
	60133	28 BW	*bk/y*
	60134	366 Wg	*r/bk*
	60135	7 Wg	*bk*
	60136	127 BS	
	60137	7 Wg	*bl/w*
	60138	366 Wg	*r/bk*
	60139	366 Wg	*r/bk*
	60140	7 Wg	*bl/w*

Type			Notes
Northrop B-2 Spirit			
420 TS/412 TW Edwards AFB,			
California [ED];			
509 BW Whiteman AFB,			
Missouri [WM]: 393 BS & 715 BS			
FY90			
00040	509 BW		
00041	509 BW		
FY92			
20700	509 BW		
FY82			
21066	Northrop		
21067	412 TW		
21068	412 TW		
21069	412 TW		
21070	412 TW		
21071	412 TW		
FY93			
31085	509 BW		
31086	509 BW		
31087			
FY88			
80328	509 BW		
80329	509 BW		
80330	509 BW		
80331	509 BW		
80332	509 BW		
FY89			
90127	509 BW		
90128	509 BW		
90129	509 BW		

Type			Notes
Boeing E-3 Sentry			
552 ACW			
961 AACS/18 Wg (*or*)			
Kadena AB, Japan [ZZ];			
962 AACS/3 Wg (*gn*) Elmendorf AFB,			
Alaska [AK];			
963 AACS (*bk*)			
964 AACS (*r*)			
965 AACS (*y*)			
966 AACTS (*bl*) Tinker AFB,			
Oklahoma [OK]			
FY80			
00137	E-3C	*bk*	
00138	E-3C	*y*	
00139	E-3C	*bk*	
FY81			
10004	E-3C	*bk*	
10005	E-3C	*m*	
FY71			
11407	E-3B	*m*	
11408	E-3B	*y*	
FY82			
20006	E-3C	*y*	
20007	E-3C	*y*	
FY83			
30008	E-3C	*or*	
30009	E-3C	*bk*	
FY73			
31674	E-3C	Boeing	
31675	E-3B	*r*	
FY75			
50556	E-3B	*bk*	
50557	E-3B	*r*	
50558	E-3B	*y*	
50559	E-3B	*gn*	
50560	E-3B	*bk*	
FY76			
61604	E-3B	*y*	
61605	E-3B	*m*	
61606	E-3B	*or*	
61607	E-3B	*bl*	

Type			Notes
FY77			
70351	E-3B	*gn*	
70352	E-3B	*r*	
70353	E-3B	*bl*	
70355	E-3B	*r*	
70356	E-3B	*y*	
FY78			
80576	E-3B	*bk*	
80577	E-3B	*or*	
80578	E-3B	*y*	
FY79			
90001	E-3B	*bk*	
90002	E-3B	*r*	
90003	E-3B	*or*	

Type			Notes
Boeing E-4B			
1ACCS/55 Wg Offutt AFB,			
Nebraska [OF]			
31676	(FY73)		
31677	(FY73)		
40787	(FY74)		
50125	(FY75)		

Type			Notes
Lockheed C-5 Galaxy			
60 AMW Travis AFB, California:			
21 AS & 22 AS (*bk/bl* & *bk/gd*);			
68 AS/433 AW AFRES, Kelly AFB,			
Texas;			
97 AMW Altus AFB, Oklahoma:			
56 AS (*r/y*);			
137 AS/105 AW Stewart AFB,			
New York (*bl*);			
337 AS/439 AW AFRES,			
Westover ARB,			
Massachusetts (*bl* & *r*);			
436 AW Dover AFB, Delaware:			
3 AS & 9 AS (*y/r* & *y/bl*)			
FY70			
00445	C-5A	68 AS	
00446	C-5A	68 AS	
00447	C-5A	436 AW	*y/r*
00448	C-5A	337 AS	*bl/r*
00449	C-5A	60 AMW	
00450	C-5A	97 AMW	*r/y*
00451	C-5A	436 AW	*y/bl*
00452	C-5A	436 AW	*y/r*
00453	C-5A	97 AMW	*r/y*
00454	C-5A	60 AMW	
00455	C-5A	436 AW	
00456	C-5A	97 AMW	*r/y*
00457	C-5A	60 AMW	*bk/gd*
00458	C-5A	97 AMW	*r/y*
00459	C-5A	60 AMW	*bk/gd*
00460	C-5A	137 AS	*bl*
00461	C-5A	68 AS	
00462	C-5A	97 AMW	*r/y*
00463	C-5A	436 AW	*y/bl*
00464	C-5A	97 AMW	*r/y*
00465	C-5A	436 AW	*y/r*
00466	C-5A	97 AMW	*r/y*
00467	C-5A	436 AW	*y/r*
FY83			
31285	C-5B	436 AW	*y/r*
FY84			
40059	C-5B	436 AW	*y/r*
40060	C-5B	60 AMW	*bk/bl*
40061	C-5B	436 AW	*y/r*
40062	C-5B	60 AMW	*bk/gd*
FY85			
50001	C-5B	436 AW	*m*
50002	C-5B	60 AMW	*bk/bl*
50003	C-5B	436 AW	*y/bl*
50004	C-5B	60 AMW	*bk/bl*
50005	C-5B	436 AW	*y/bl*

Notes	Type			
	50006	C-5B	60 AMW	*bk/gd*
	50007	C-5B	436 AW	*y/bl*
	50008	C-5B	60 AMW	*bk/gd*
	50009	C-5B	436 AW	
	50010	C-5B	60 AMW	*bk/gd*
	FY86			
	60011	C-5B	436 AW	*y/bl*
	60012	C-5B	60 AMW	*bk/bl*
	60013	C-5B	436 AW	*y/bl*
	60014	C-5B	60 AMW	*bk/bl*
	60015	C-5B	436 AW	*y/r*
	60016	C-5B	60 AMW	*bk/bl*
	60017	C-5B	436 AW	*y/bl*
	60018	C-5B	60 AMW	*bk/gd*
	60019	C-5B	436 AW	*y/r*
	60020	C-5B	436 AW	*y/bl*
	60021	C-5B	60 AMW	*bk/gd*
	60022	C-5B	60 AMW	*bk/bl*
	60023	C-5B	436 AW	*y/bl*
	60024	C-5B	60 AMW	*bk/bl*
	60025	C-5B	436 AW	*y/r*
	60026	C-5B	60 AMW	*bk/gd*
	FY66			
	68304	C-5A	337 AS	*bl/r*
	68305	C-5A	68 AS	
	68306	C-5A	68 AS	
	68307	C-5A	68 AS	
	FY87			
	70027	C-5B	436 AW	*y/bl*
	70028	C-5B	60 AMW	*bk/bl*
	70029	C-5B	436 AW	*y/r*
	70030	C-5B	60 AMW	*bk/bl*
	70031	C-5B	436 AW	*y/r*
	70032	C-5B	60 AMW	*bl*
	70033	C-5B	436 AW	*y/r*
	70034	C-5B	60 AMW	*bk/gd*
	70035	C-5B	436 AW	*y/bl*
	70036	C-5B	60 AMW	*bk/gd*
	70037	C-5B	436 AW	*y/r*
	70038	C-5B	60 AMW	*bk/bl*
	70039	C-5B	436 AW	*y/r*
	70040	C-5B	60 AMW	*bk/gd*
	70041	C-5B	436 AW	*y/bl*
	70042	C-5B	60 AMW	*bk/gd*
	70043	C-5B	436 AW	*y/bl*
	7004	C-5B	60 AMW	*bk/gd*
	70045	C-5B	436 AW	*y/r*
	FY67			
	70167	C-5A	337 AS	*bl*
	70168	C-5A	68 AS	
	70169	C-5A	137 AS	*bl*
	70170	C-5A	137 AS	*bl*
	70171	C-5A	68 AS	
	70173	C-5A	137 AS	*bl*
	70174	C-5A	137 AS	*bl*
	FY68			
	80211	C-5A	337 AS	*bl/r*
	80212	C-5A	137 AS	*bl*
	80213	C-5C	60 AMW	*bl*
	80214	C-5A	436 AW	*y/r*
	80215	C-5A	337 AS	*bl*
	80216	C-5C	60 AMW	*bk/bl*
	80217	C-5A	436 AW	*y/bl*
	80219	C-5A	337 AS	*r*
	80220	C-5A	68 AS	
	80221	C-5A	68 AS	
	80222	C-5A	337 AS	*r*
	80223	C-5A	68 AS	
	80224	C-5A	137 AS	*bl*
	80225	C-5A	337 AS	*bl/r*
	80226	C-5A	137 AS	*bl*
	FY69			
	90001	C-5A	97 AMW	*r/y*
	90002	C-5A	68 AS	
	90003	C-5A	337 AS	*bl/r*

Notes	Type			
	90004	C-5A	68 AS	
	90005	C-5A	337 AS	*bl/r*
	90006	C-5A	68 AS	
	90007	C-5A	68 AS	
	90008	C-5A	137 AS	*bl*
	90009	C-5A	137 AS	*bl*
	90010	C-5A	60 AMW	*bk/gd*
	90011	C-5A	337 AS	*r*
	90012	C-5A	137 AS	*bl*
	90013	C-5A	337 AS	*bl/r*
	90014	C-5A	60 AMW	*bk/gd*
	90015	C-5A	137 AS	*bl*
	90016	C-5A	68 AS	
	90017	C-5A	337 AS	*bl/r*
	90018	C-5A	60 AMW	*bk/bl*
	90019	C-5A	337 AS	*bl*
	90020	C-5A	337 AS	*bl/r*
	90021	C-5A	137 AS	*bl*
	90022	C-5A	337 AS	*r*
	90023	C-5A	60 AMW	*bk/bl*
	90024	C-5A	436 AW	*y/r*
	90025	C-5A	60 AMW	*bk/gd*
	90026	C-5A	60 AMW	*bk/bl*
	90027	C-5A	436 AW	

Boeing E-8 J-STARS
Grumman, Melbourne, Florida;
12 ACCS/93 ACW, Robins AFB,
  Georgia [WR] (*gn*)

Notes	Type		
	FY90		
	00175	E-8C	
	FY92		
	23289	E-8C	93 ACW
	23290	E-8C	
	FY93		
	30011	E-8C	93 ACW
	FY93		
	31097	E-8C	
	FY94		
	40284	E-8C	
	40285	E-8C	
	FY95		
	50121	E-8C	
	FY86		
	60416	E-8A	93 ACW
	60417	E-8A	

McDonnell-Douglas KC-10A
  Extender
60 AMW, Travis AFB, California:
  6 ARS (*bk/r*) & 9 ARS (*bk/bl*);
305 AMW McGuire AFB, New Jersey:
  2 ARS (*bl/r*) & 32 ARS (*bl*)

Notes	Type		
	FY82		
	20191	60 AMW	*bk/bl*
	20192	60 AMW	*bk/r*
	20193	60 AMW	
	FY83		
	30075	305 AMW	*bl*
	30076	60 AMW	*bk/bl*
	30077	60 AMW	*bk/r*
	30078	60 AMW	*bk/bl*
	30079	305 AMW	*bl/r*
	30080	60 AMW	*bk/bl*
	30081	305 AMW	*bl*
	30082	305 AMW	*bl*
	FY84		
	40185	60 AMW	*bk/bl*
	40186	305 AMW	*bl/r*
	40187	60 AMW	*bk/bl*
	40188	305 AMW	*bl*
	40189	60 AMW	*bk/bl*
	40190	305 AMW	*bl/r*
	40191	60 AMW	*bk/bl*
	40192	305 AMW	*bl/r*

Type			
FY85			
50027	305 AMW	*bl/r*	
50028	305 AMW	*bl/r*	
50029	60 AMW	*bk/r*	
50030	305 AMW	*bl*	
50031	305 AMW	*bl*	
50032	305 AMW	*bl*	
50033	305 AMW	*bl*	
50034	305 AMW	*bl/r*	
FY86			
60027	305 AMW	*bl*	
60028	305 AMW	*bl/r*	
60029	60 AMW	*bk/r*	
60030	305 AMW	*bl/r*	
60031	60 AMW	*bk/r*	
60032	60 AMW	*bk/bl*	
60033	60 AMW	*bk/r*	
60034	305 AMW	*bl*	
60035	305 AMW	*bl*	
60036	60 AMW	*bk/r*	
60037	60 AMW	*bk/r*	
60038	60 AMW	*bk/r*	
FY87			
70117	60 AMW	*bk/r*	
70118	60 AMW	*bk/bl*	
70119	60 AMW	*bk/r*	
70120	305 AMW	*bl*	
70121	305 AMW	*bl/r*	
70122	305 AMW	*bl/r*	
70123	305 AMW	*bl*	
70124	305 AMW	*bl/r*	
FY79			
90433	305 AMW	*bl*	
90434	305 AMW	*bl/r*	
91710	305 AMW	*bl/r*	
91711	305 AMW	*bl*	
91712	305 AMW	*bl/r*	
91713	305 AMW	*bl*	
91946	60 AMW	*bk/r*	
91947	60 AMW	*bk/r*	
91948	60 AMW	*bk/bl*	
91949	305 AMW	*bl/r*	
91950	60 AMW	*bk/bl*	
91951	60 AMW	*bk/r*	

McDonnell-Douglas C-17 Globemaster III

97 AMW Altus AFB, Oklahoma:
   57 AS (*r/y*);
417 TS Edwards AFB, California [ED]
437 AW Charleston AFB,
   South Carolina:
    14 AS & 17 AS (*y/bl*)

Type			
FY90			
00532	C-17A	437 AW	*y/bl*
00533	C-17A	437 AW	*y/bl*
00534	C-17A	437 AW	*y/bl*
00535	C-17A	437 AW	*y/bl*
FY92			
23291	C-17A	437 AW	*y/bl*
23292	C-17A	437 AW	*y/bl*
23293	C-17A	437 AW	*y/bl*
23294	C-17A	437 AW	
FY93			
30599	C-17A	437 AW	*y/bl*
30600	C-17A	437 AW	*y/bl*
30601	C-17A	437 AW	*y/bl*
30602	C-17A	97 AMW	*r/y*
30603	C-17A	97 AMW	*r/y*
30604	C-17A	437 AW	*y/bl*
FY94			
40065	C-17A	437 AW	*y/bl*
40066	C-17A	437 AW	*y/bl*
40067	C-17A	437 AW	*y/bl*
40068	C-17A	437 AW	*y/bl*

Type			
40069	C-17A	437 AW	*y/bl*
40070	C-17A	437 AW	*y/bl*
FY95			
50102	C-17A	437 AW	*y/bl*
50103	C-17A		
50104	C-17A		
50105	C-17A		
50106	C-17A		
50107	C-17A		
FY96			
60001	C-17A		
60002	C-17A		
60003	C-17A		
60004	C-17A		
60005	C-17A		
60006	C-17A		
60007	C-17A		
60008	C-17A		
FY87			
70025	YC-17A	417 TS	
FY88			
80265	C-17A	437 AW	*y/bl*
80266	C-17A	437 AW	*y/bl*
FY89			
91189	C-17A	437 AW	*y/bl*
91190	C-17A	437 AW	*y/bl*
91191	C-17A	437 AW	*y/bl*
91192	C-17A	437 AW	*y/bl*

Boeing C-18

452 TS/452 TS Edwards AFB,
   California;
966 AACTS /552 ACW (*bl*)
   Tinker AFB, Oklahoma [OK]

Type			
FY81			
10891	EC-18B	452 TS	
10892	EC-18B	452 TS	
10893	EC-18D	452 TS	
10894	EC-18B	452 TS	
10895	EC-18D	452 TS	
10896	EC-18B	452 TS	
10898	C-18A	452 TS	
FY84			
41398	TC-18E	966 AACTS	
41399	TC-18E	966 AACTS	

Grumman C-20 Gulfstream II/III/IV

89 AW/99 AS Andrews AFB, Maryland;
US Army Andrews AFB, Maryland

C-20B Gulfstream III

Type		
FY86		
60201	89 AW	
60202	89 AW	
60203	89 AW	
60204	89 AW	
60206	89 AW	
60403	89 AW	

C-20C Gulfstream III

Type		
FY85		
50049	89 AW	
50050	89 AW	

C-20E Gulfstream III

Type		
FY87		
70139	US Army	
70140	US Army	

C-20F Gulfstream IV

Type		
FY91		
10108	OSAC/US Army	

C-20H Gulfstream IV

Type		
FY90		
00300	89 AW	
FY92		
20375	89 AW	

Notes	Type		
	C-20J Gulfstream II		
	FY89		
	90266	US Army	
	Boeing C-22B/C-22C[1]		
	201 AS/113 FW DC ANG,		
	Andrews AFB, Maryland		
	FY83		
	34610		
	34615		
	34616		
	34618[1]		
	Boeing VC-25A		
	89 AW Andrews AFB, Maryland		
	FY82		
	28000		
	FY92		
	29000		
	Boeing CT-43A		
	12 FTW Randolph AFB, Texas [RA]:		
	558 FTS (*bk/y*);		
	76 AS/86 AW Ramstein, Germany;		
	200 AS/140 FW Colorado ANG,		
	Buckley ANGB, Colorado;		
	310 AS/24 Wg Howard AFB,		
	Panama, Canal Zone [HW]		
	FY71		
	11403	12 FTW	*bk/y*
	11404	12 FTW	*bk/y*
	11405	12 FTW	*bk/y*
	11406	12 FTW	*bk/y*
	FY72		
	20283	310 AS	
	20288	200 AS	
	FY73		
	31150	12 FTW	*bk/y*
	31151	12 FTW	*bk/y*
	31152	12 FTW	*bk/y*
	31153	12 FTW	*bk/y*
	31154	200 AS	
	31155	12 FTW	*bk/y*
	31156	12 FTW	*bk/y*
	Boeing B-52H Stratofortress		
	2 BW Barksdale AFB, Louisiana [LA]:		
	11 BS (*gd*), 20 BS (*bl*) & 96 BS (*r*);		
	5 BW Minot AFB, North Dakota [MT]:		
	23 BS (*r/w*);		
	93 BS/917 Wg AFRES, Barksdale		
	AFB, Louisiana [BD] (*y/bl*);		
	419 TS/412 TW Edwards AFB,		
	California [ED]		
	FY60		
	00001	2 BW	*bl*
	00002	2 BW	*r*
	00003	93 BS	*y/bl*
	00004	5 BW	*r/w*
	00005	5 BW	*r/w*
	00007	5 BW	*r/w*
	00008	2 BW	*r*
	00009	2 BW	*r*
	00010	2 BW	*r*
	00011	2 BW	*bl*
	00012	2 BW	*gd*
	00013	2 BW	*r*
	00014	2 BW	*bl*
	00015	5 BW	*r/w*
	00016	2 BW	*r*
	00017	2 BW	*gd*
	00018	5 BW	*r/w*
	00019	2 BW	*gd*
	00020	2 BW	*bl*

Notes	Type		
	00021	5 BW	*r/w*
	00022	2 BW	*r*
	00023	5 BW	*r/w*
	00024	5 BW	*r/w*
	00025	2 BW	*bl*
	00026	5 BW	*r/w*
	00028	2 BW	*r*
	00029	5 BW	*r/w*
	00030	2 BW	*r*
	00031	2 BW	*bl*
	00032	2 BW	*bl*
	00033	5 BW	*r/w*
	00034	5 BW	*r/w*
	00035	2 BW	*gd*
	00036		
	00037	2 BW	*r*
	00038	2 BW	*gd*
	00041	93 BS	*y/bl*
	00042	2 BW	*gd*
	00043	2 BW	*bl*
	00044		
	00045	93 BS	*y/bl*
	00046	2 BW	
	00047	5 BW	*r/w*
	00048	2 BW	*gd*
	00049	2 BW	*bl*
	00050	419 TS	
	00051	5 BW	*r/w*
	00052	5 BW	*r/w*
	00053	2 BW	*r*
	00054	2 BW	*r*
	00055	5 BW	*r/w*
	00056		
	00057	2 BW	*bl*
	00058	2 BW	*gd*
	00059	2 BW	*r*
	00060	5 BW	*r/w*
	00061	2 BW	
	00062	2 BW	*bl*
	FY61		
	10001	5 BW	*r/w*
	10002	2 BW	*bl*
	10003	2 BW	*gd*
	10004	2 BW	*bl*
	10005	5 BW	*r/w*
	10006	2 BW	
	10007	5 BW	*r/w*
	10008	93 BS	*y/bl*
	10009	2 BW	*r*
	10010	2 BW	*bl*
	10011	2 BW	*gd*
	10012	2 BW	*gd*
	10013	2 BW	*r*
	10014	2 BW	*gd*
	10015	2 BW	*gd*
	10016	2 BW	*gd*
	10017	93 BS	*y/bl*
	10018	5 BW	*r/w*
	10019	5 BW	*r/w*
	10020	2 BW	*r*
	10021	93 BS	*y/bl*
	10022	93 BS	*y/bl*
	10023	2 BW	*bl*
	10024	2 BW	*r*
	10025	2 BW	*r*
	10027	5 BW	*r/w*
	10028	2 BW	*r*
	10029	93 BS	*y/bl*
	10031	2 BW	*gd*
	10032	93 BS	*y/bl*
	10034	5 BW	*r/w*
	10035	2 BW	*gd*
	10036	5 BW	*r/w*
	10038	2 BW	*gd*
	10039	5 BW	*r/w*

Type	Notes

Lockheed C-130 Hercules
1 SOS/353 SOG Kadena AB, Japan;
3 Wg Elmendorf AFB, Alaska [AK]:
  517 AS (*w*);
4 SOS/16 SOW Hurlburt Field,
  Florida;
5 SOS/919 SOW AFRES, Duke Field,
  Florida;
7 SOS/352 SOG, RAF Mildenhall, UK;
7 Wg Dyess AFB, Texas [DY]:
  39 AS (*r*) & 40 AS (*bl*);
8 SOS/16 SOW Hurlburt Field,
  Florida;
9 SOS/16 SOW Eglin AFB, Florida;
15 SOS/16 SOW Hurlburt Field,
  Florida;
16 SOS/16 SOW Hurlburt Field,
  Florida;
17 SOS/353 SOG Kadena AB,
Japan;
23 Wg Pope AFB,
  North Carolina [FT]:
  2 AS (*r/y*) & 41 AS (*gn/or*);
37 AS/86 AW Ramstein AB,
  Germany [RS] (*bl/w*);
41 ECS/355 Wg Davis-Monthan
  AFB, Arizona [DM] (*bl*);
42 ACCS/355 Wg Davis-Monthan
  AFB, Arizona [DM] (*w*);
43 ECS/355 Wg Davis-Monthan
  AFB, Arizona [DM] (*r*);
46 TW Eglin AFB, Florida [ET];
52 AS/347 Wg Moody AFB,
  Georgia [MY] (*gn*);
53 WRS/403 Wg AFRES,
  Keesler AFB, Missouri [KT];
58 SOW/550 SOS Kirtland AFB,
  New Mexico;
67 SOS/352 SOG RAF Mildenhall,
  UK;
71 RQS/1 FW Patrick AFB,
  Florida [FF] (*bl*);
95 AS/440 AW AFRES,
  General Mitchell ARS,
  Wisconsin [MK] (*y/w*);
96 AS/934 AW AFRES,
  Minneapolis/St Paul,
  Minnesota [MS] (*pr*);
102 RQS/106 RQW Suffolk Field,
  New York ANG [LI];
105 AS/118 AW Nashville,
  Tennessee ANG;
109 AS/133 AW
  Minneapolis/St Paul,
  Minnesota ANG [MN] (*y*);
115 AS/146 AW NAS Point Mugu,
  California ANG [CI] (*gn*);
122 FS/159 FW NAS New Orleans,
  Louisiana ANG [JZ];
129 RQS/129 RQW Moffet Field,
  California ANG [CA] (*bl*);
130 AS/130 AW Charleston
  West Virginia ANG [WV] (*bl*);
135 AS/135 AW Martin Field,
  Maryland ANG [MD];
139 AS/109 AW Schenectady,
  New York ANG [NY];
142 AS/166 AW Greater Wilmington,
  Delaware ANG [DE] (*bl*);
143 AS/143 AW Quonset,
  Rhode Island ANG [RI] (*r*);
144 AS/176 CW Kulis ANGB,
  Alaska ANG;
154 TS/189 AW Little Rock,
  Arkansas ANG (*r*);

156 AS/145 AW Charlotte,
  North Carolina ANG [NC] (*bl*);
157 FS/169 FW McEntire ANGB,
  South Carolina ANG;
158 AS/165 AW Savannah,
  Georgia ANG [GA] (*r*);
164 AS/179 AW Mansfield,
  Ohio ANG [OH];
165 AS/123 AW Standiford Field,
  Kentucky ANG [KY];
167 AS/167 AW Martinsburg,
  West Virginia ANG [WV] (*r*);
169 AS/182 AW Peoria,
  Illinois ANG [IL];
171 AS/191 AW Selfridge ANGB,
  Michigan ANG (*y/bk*);
180 AS/139 AW St Joseph,
  Missouri ANG [XP];
181 AS/136 AW NAS Dallas,
  Texas ANG [TX];
185 AS/137 AW Oklahoma,
  Oklahoma ANG [OK] (*bl*);
187 AS/153 AW Cheyenne,
  Wyoming ANG [WY];
189 AS/124 AW Boise, Idaho ANG;
192 AS/152 AW Reno,
  Nevada ANG [NV] (*w*);
193 SOS/193 SOW Harrisburg,
  Pennsylvania ANG [PA];
204 AS/154 CW Hickam AFB,
  Hawaii ANG;
210 RQS/176 CW Kulis ANGB,
  Alaska ANG [AK];
301 RQS/939 RQW AFRES,
  Patrick AFB, Florida [FL];
304 RQS/939 RQW AFRES,
  Portland, Oregon [PD] (*y*);
314 AW Little Rock AFB,
  Arkansas [LK]:
  50 AS (*r*), 53 AS (*bk*),
61 AS (*gn*) & 62 AS (*bl*);
327 AS/913 AW AFRES,
  NAS Willow Grove,
  Pennsylvania [WG] (*bk*);
328 AS/914 AW AFRES, Niagara Falls,
  New York [NF] (*gn*);
357 AS/908 AW AFRES,
  Maxwell AFB, Alabama [MX] (*bl*);
374 AW Yokota AB, Japan [YJ]:
  36 AS (*r*);
418 TS/412 TW Edwards AFB,
  California [ED];
514 TS/412 TW Hill AFB, Utah;
700 AS/94 AW AFRES,
  Dobbins ARB, Georgia [DB] (*bk/w*);
711 SOS/919 SOW AFRES,
  Duke Field, Florida;
731 AS/302 AW AFRES,
  Peterson AFB, Colorado [CR] (*gn*);
757 AS/910 AW AFRES, Youngstown
  ARS, Ohio [YO] (*bl*);
758 AS/911 AW AFRES, Pittsburgh
  ARS, Pennsylvania [PI] (*bk/y*);
773 AS/910 AW AFRES,
  Youngstown ARS, Ohio [YO] (*r*);
815 AS/403 Wg AFRES, Keesler
  AFB, Missouri [KT] (*r*)

FY90

00161	MC-130H	15 SOS	
00162	MC-130H	15 SOS	
00163	AC-130U	4 SOS	
00164	AC-130U	4 SOS	
00165	AC-130U	4 SOS	
00166	AC-130U	4 SOS	
00167	AC-130U	4 SOS	

Notes	Type			
	FY80			
	00320	C-130H	158 AS	*r*
	00321	C-130H	158 AS	*r*
	00322	C-130H	158 AS	*r*
	00323	C-130H	158 AS	*r*
	00324	C-130H	158 AS	*r*
	00325	C-130H	158 AS	*r*
	00326	C-130H	158 AS	*r*
	00332	C-130H	158 AS	*r*
	FY90			
	01057	C-130H	181 AS	
	01058	C-130H	130 AS	*bl*
	FY70			
	01259	C-130E	23 Wg	*gn/or*
	01260	C-130E	37 AS	*bl/w*
	01261	C-130E	23 Wg	*gn/or*
	01262	C-130E	23 Wg	*gn/or*
	01263	C-130E	23 Wg	*gn/or*
	01264	C-130E	37 AS	*bl/w*
	01265	C-130E	23 Wg	
	01266	C-130E	23 Wg	*gn/or*
	01267	C-130E	23 Wg	*gn/or*
	01268	C-130E	23 Wg	*r/y*
	01269	C-130E	23 Wg	*gn/or*
	01270	C-130E	23 Wg	*r/y*
	01271	C-130E	37 AS	*bl/w*
	01272	C-130E	23 Wg	
	01273	C-130E	23 Wg	
	01274	C-130E	37 AS	*bl/w*
	01275	C-130E	23 Wg	*r/y*
	01276	C-130E	23 Wg	*gn/or*
	FY90			
	01791	C-130H	164 AS	
	01792	C-130H	164 AS	
	01793	C-130H	164 AS	
	01794	C-130H	164 AS	
	01795	C-130H	164 AS	
	01796	C-130H	164 AS	
	01797	C-130H	164 AS	
	01798	C-130H	164 AS	
	02103	HC-130N	210 RQS	
	09107	C-130H	757 AS	*bl*
	09108	C-130H	757 AS	*bl*
	FY81			
	10626	C-130H	700 AS	*bk/w*
	10627	C-130H	700 AS	*bk/w*
	10628	C-130H	700 AS	*bk/w*
	10629	C-130H	700 AS	*bk/w*
	10630	C-130H	700 AS	*bk/w*
	10631	C-130H	700 AS	*bk/w*
	FY68			
	10934	C-130E	23 Wg	*r/y*
	10935	C-130E	37 AS	*bl/w*
	10937	C-130E	23 Wg	*gn/or*
	10938	C-130E	37 AS	*bl/w*
	10939	C-130E	23 Wg	*gn/or*
	10940	C-130E	23 Wg	*gn/or*
	10941	C-130E	23 Wg	*r/y*
	10942	C-130E	23 Wg	*r/y*
	10943	C-130E	37 AS	*bl/w*
	10947	C-130E	37 AS	*bl/w*
	10948	C-130E	314 AW	*gn*
	10949	C-130E	*wfu*	
	FY91			
	11231	C-130H	165 AS	
	11232	C-130H	165 AS	
	11233	C-130H	165 AS	
	11234	C-130H	165 AS	
	11235	C-130H	165 AS	
	11236	C-130H	165 AS	
	11237	C-130H	165 AS	
	11238	C-130H	165 AS	
	11239	C-130H	165 AS	
	11651	C-130H	165 AS	
	11652	C-130H	165 AS	
	11653	C-130H	165 AS	

Notes	Type			
	FY61			
	12358	C-130E	171 AS	*y/bk*
	12359	C-130E	115 AS	*gn*
	12361	C-130E	192 AS	*w*
	12363	C-130E	314 AW	*bk*
	12367	C-130E	115 AS	*gn*
	12369	C-130E	109 AS	*y*
	12370	C-130E	171 AS	*y/bk*
	12371	C-130E	171 AS	*y/bk*
	12372	C-130E	115 AS	*gn*
	FY64			
	14852	HC-130P	71 RQS	*bl*
	14853	HC-130P	71 RQS	*bl*
	14854	MC-130P	9 SOS	
	14855	HC-130P	304 RQS	*y*
	14856	HC-130P	W/O	
	14858	MC-130P	58 SOW	
	14859	C-130H	711 SOS	
	14860	HC-130P	304 RQS	*y*
	14861	WC-130H	53 WRS	
	14862	EC-130H	645 MS	
	14863	HC-130P	71 RQS	*bl*
	14864	HC-130P	301 RQS	
	14865	HC-130P	304 RQS	*y*
	14866	WC-130H	53 WRS	
	17680	C-130E	314 AW	*bk*
	17681	C-130E	37 AS	*bl/w*
	18240	C-130E	37 AS	*bl/w*
	FY91			
	19141	C-130H	773 AS	*r*
	19142	C-130H	757 AS	*bl*
	19143	C-130H	773 AS	*r*
	19144	C-130H	773 AS	*r*
	FY82			
	20054	C-130H	144 AS	
	20055	C-130H	144 AS	
	20056	C-130H	144 AS	
	20057	C-130H	144 AS	
	20058	C-130H	144 AS	
	20059	C-130H	144 AS	
	20060	C-130H	144 AS	
	20061	C-130H	144 AS	
	FY92			
	20253	AC-130U	4 SOS	
	20547	C-130H	314 AW	*r*
	20548	C-130H	314 AW	*r*
	20549	C-130H	314 AW	*r*
	20550	C-130H	314 AW	*r*
	20551	C-130H	314 AW	*r*
	20552	C-130H	314 AW	*r*
	20553	C-130H	314 AW	*r*
	20554	C-130H	314 AW	*r*
	21094	LC-130H	139 AS	
	21095	LC-130H	139 AS	
	FY72			
	21288	C-130E	374 AW	*r*
	21289	C-130E	374 AW	*r*
	21290	C-130E	374 AW	*r*
	21291	C-130E	314 AW	*bk*
	21292	C-130E	314 AW	*gn*
	21293	C-130E	314 AW	*gn*
	21294	C-130E	314 AW	*gn*
	21295	C-130E	314 AW	*bl*
	21296	C-130E	314 AW	*bk*
	21298	C-130E	314 AW	*bl*
	21299	C-130E	374 AW	*r*
	FY92			
	21451	C-130H	156 AS	*bl*
	21452	C-130H	156 AS	*bl*
	21453	C-130H	156 AS	*bl*
	21454	C-130H	156 AS	*bl*
	21531	C-130H	187 AS	
	21532	C-130H	187 AS	
	21533	C-130H	187 AS	

Type			Notes
21534	C-130H	187 AS	
21535	C-130H	187 AS	
21536	C-130H	187 AS	
21537	C-130H	187 AS	
21538	C-130H	187 AS	
FY62			
21784	C-130E	154 TS	*r*
21786	C-130E	109 AS	*y*
21787	C-130E	154 TS	*r*
21788	C-130E	154 TS	*r*
21789	C-130E	314 AW	*bk*
21790	C-130E	154 TS	*r*
21791	EC-130E	42 ACCS	*w*
21792	C-130E	115 AS	*gn*
21793	C-130E	115 AS	*gn*
21795	C-130E	154 TS	*r*
21798	C-130E	154 TS	*r*
21799	C-130E	115 AS	*gn*
21801	C-130E	115 AS	*gn*
21804	C-130E	154 TS	*r*
21806	C-130E	96 AS	*pr*
21807	C-130E	327 AS	*bk*
21808	C-130E	314 AW	*bk*
21810	C-130E	314 AW	*bl*
21811	C-130E	115 AS	*gn*
21812	C-130E	109 AS	*y*
21816	C-130E	314 AW	*bl*
21817	C-130E	109 AS	*y*
21818	EC-130E	42 ACCS	*w*
21819	C-130E	192 AS	*w*
21820	C-130E	171 AS	*y/bk*
21821	C-130E	314 AW	*bl*
21822	C-130E	192 AS	*w*
21823	C-130E	96 AS	*pr*
21824	C-130E	154 TS	*r*
21825	EC-130E	42 ACCS	*gy*
21826	C-130E	115 AS	*gn*
21827	C-130E	314 AW	*bl*
21828	C-130E	192 AS	*w*
21829	C-130E	109 AS	*y*
21832	EC-130E	42 ACCS	*w*
21833	C-130E	115 AS	*gn*
21834	C-130E	96 AS	*pr*
21835	C-130E	96 AS	*pr*
21836	EC-130E	42 ACCS	*w*
21837	C-130E	109 AS	*y*
21839	C-130E	96 AS	*pr*
21842	C-130E	171 AS	*y/bk*
21843	MC-130E	711 SOS	
21844	C-130E	96 AS	*pr*
21846	C-130E	109 AS	*y*
21847	C-130E	96 AS	*pr*
21848	C-130E	96 AS	*pr*
21849	C-130E	815 AS	*r*
21850	C-130E	314 AW	*bk*
21851	C-130E	115 AS	*gn*
21852	C-130E	96 AS	*pr*
21855	MC-130E	16 SOS	
21856	C-130E	143 AS	*r*
21857	EC-130E	42 ACCS	*w*
21858	C-130E	192 AS	*w*
21859	C-130E	192 AS	*w*
21862	C-130E	115 AS	*gn*
21863	EC-130E	42 ACCS	*gy*
21864	C-130E	109 AS	*y*
21866	C-130E	314 AW	
FY92			
23021	C-130H	773 AS	*r*
23022	C-130H	773 AS	*r*
23023	C-130H	773 AS	*r*
23024	C-130H	773 AS	*r*
23281	C-130H	328 AS	*gn*
23282	C-130H	328 AS	*gn*
23283	C-130H	328 AS	*gn*
23284	C-130H	328 AS	*gn*

Type			Notes
23285	C-130H	328 AS	*gn*
23286	C-130H	328 AS	*gn*
23287	C-130H	328 AS	*gn*
23288	C-130H	328 AS	*gn*
FY83			
30486	C-130H	139 AS	
30487	C-130H	139 AS	
30488	C-130H	139 AS	
30489	C-130H	139 AS	
30490	LC-130H	139 AS	
30491	LC-130H	139 AS	
30492	LC-130H	139 AS	
30493	LC-130H	139 AS	
FY93			
31036	C-130H	314 AW	*r*
31037	C-130H	314 AW	*r*
31038	C-130H	314 AW	*r*
31039	C-130H	314 AW	*r*
31040	C-130H	314 AW	*r*
31041	C-130H	314 AW	*r*
31096	LC-130H	139 AS	
FY83			
31212	MC-130H	15 SOS	
FY93			
31455	C-130H	156 AS	*bl*
31456	C-130H	156 AS	*bl*
31457	C-130H	156 AS	*bl*
31458	C-130H	156 AS	*bl*
31459	C-130H	156 AS	*bl*
31461	C-130H	156 AS	*bl*
31462	C-130H	156 AS	*bl*
31463	C-130H	156 AS	*bl*
FY73			
31580	EC-130H	43 ECS	*r*
31581	EC-130H	43 ECS	*r*
31582	C-130H	374 AW	*r*
31583	EC-130H	43 ECS	*r*
31584	EC-130H	43 ECS	*r*
31585	EC-130H	41 ECS	*bl*
31586	EC-130H	41 ECS	*bl*
31587	EC-130H	41 ECS	*bl*
31588	EC-130H	41 ECS	*bl*
31590	EC-130H	43 ECS	*r*
31592	EC-130H	43 ECS	*r*
31594	EC-130H	41 ECS	*bl*
31595	EC-130H	43 ECS	*r*
31597	C-130H	374 AW	*r*
31598	C-130H	374 AW	*r*
FY93			
32041	C-130H	204 AS	
32042	C-130H	204 AS	
32104	HC-130N	210 RQS	
32105	HC-130N	210 RQS	
32106	HC-130N	210 RQS	
37311	C-130H	731 AS	*gn*
37312	C-130H	731 AS	*gn*
37313	C-130H	731 AS	*gn*
37314	C-130H	731 AS	*gn*
FY63			
37764	C-130E	815 AS	*r*
37765	C-130E	314 AW	*bl*
37767	C-130E	314 AW	*bl*
37768	C-130E	314 AW	*bl*
37769	C-130E	327 AS	*bk*
37770	C-130E	815 AS	*r*
37773	EC-130E	193 SOS	
37776	C-130E	327 AS	*bk*
37777	C-130E	135 AS	
37778	C-130E	314 AW	*bk*
37781	C-130E	314 AW	*gn*
37782	C-130E	143 AS	*r*
37783	EC-130E	193 SOS	
37784	C-130E	52 AS	*gn*
37785	MC-130E	711 SOS	
37786	C-130E	192 AS	*w*

Notes	Type			
	37788	C-130E	143 AS	r
	37790	C-130E	52 AS	gn
	37791	C-130E	314 AW	bl
	37792	C-130E	169 AS	
	37794	C-130E	71 RQS	bl
	37796	C-130E	314 AW	bk
	37799	C-130E	314 AW	bl
	37800	C-130E	169 AS	
	37804	C-130E	314 AW	bl
	37805	C-130E	815 AS	r
	37808	C-130E	314 AW	gn
	37809	C-130E	52 AS	gn
	37811	C-130E	143 AS	r
	37812	C-130E	169 AS	
	37813	C-130E	52 AS	gn
	37814	C-130E	67 SOS	
	37815	C-130E	193 SOS	
	37816	C-130E	193 SOS	
	37817	C-130E	815 AS	r
	37818	C-130E	169 AS	
	37819	C-130E	374 AW	r
	37821	C-130E	52 AS	gn
	37822	C-130E	815 AS	r
	37823	C-130E	327 AS	bk
	37824	C-130E	143 AS	r
	37825	C-130E	135 AS	
	37826	C-130E	327 AS	bk
	37828	EC-130E	193 SOS	
	37829	C-130E	314 AW	gn
	37830	C-130E	314 AW	bk
	37831	C-130E	135 AS	
	37832	C-130E	327 AS	bk
	37833	C-130E	327 AS	bk
	37834	C-130E	327 AS	bk
	37835	C-130E	314 AW	bk
	37837	C-130E	374 AW	r
	37838	C-130E	314 AW	bl
	37839	C-130E	314 AW	gn
	37840	C-130E	143 AS	r
	37841	C-130E	314 AW	gn
	37842	C-130E	17 SOS	
	37845	C-130E	314 AW	bk
	37846	C-130E	52 AS	gn
	37847	C-130E	154 TS	r
	37848	C-130E	327 AS	bk
	37849	C-130E	189 AS	
	37850	C-130E	52 AS	gn
	37851	C-130E	192 AS	w
	37852	C-130E	328 AS	gn
	37853	C-130E	327 AS	bk
	37854	C-130E	314 AW	gn
	37856	C-130E	815 AS	r
	37857	C-130E	314 AW	gn
	37858	C-130E	169 AS	
	37859	C-130E	143 AS	r
	37860	C-130E	314 AW	bl
	37861	C-130E	314 AW	gn
	37864	C-130E	314 AW	bl
	37865	C-130E	374 AW	r
	37866	C-130E	314 AW	bk
	37867	C-130E	327 AS	bk
	37868	C-130E	143 AS	r
	37869	EC-130E	193 SOS	
	37871	C-130E	52 AS	gn
	37872	C-130E	169 AS	
	37874	C-130E	314 AW	bk
	37876	C-130E	314 AW	gn
	37877	C-130E	169 AS	
	37879	C-130E	374 AW	r
	37880	C-130E	314 AW	bl
	37882	C-130E	314 AW	bk
	37883	C-130E	327 AS	bk
	37884	C-130E	52 AS	gn
	37885	C-130E	37 AS	bl/w
	37887	C-130E	37 AS	bl/w

Notes	Type			
	37888	C-130E	314 AW	gn
	37889	C-130E	143 AS	r
	37890	C-130E	314 AW	bl
	37892	C-130E	327 AS	bk
	37893	C-130E	314 AW	bk
	37894	C-130E	314 AW	gn
	37895	C-130E	171 AS	y/bk
	37896	C-130E	314 AW	gn
	37897	C-130E	169 AS	
	37898	C-130E	8 SOS	
	37899	C-130E	314 AW	bl
	39810	C-130E	52 AS	gn
	39812	C-130E	314 AW	bk
	39813	C-130E	171 AS	y/bk
	39814	C-130E	314 AW	bl
	39815	C-130E	171 AS	y/bk
	39816	EC-130E	193 SOS	
	39817	EC-130E	193 SOS	
FY84				
	40204	C-130H	700 AS	bk/w
	40205	C-130H	700 AS	bk/w
	40206	C-130H	142 AS	bl
	40207	C-130H	142 AS	bl
	40208	C-130H	142 AS	bl
	40209	C-130H	142 AS	bl
	40210	C-130H	142 AS	bl
	40211	C-130H	142 AS	bl
	40212	C-130H	142 AS	bl
	40213	C-130H	142 AC	bl
	40475	MC-130H	15 SOS	
	40476	MC-130H	7 SOS	
FY64				
	40495	C-130E	23 Wg	gn/or
	40496	C-130E	23 Wg	r/y
	40498	C-130E	23 Wg	r/y
	40499	C-130E	23 Wg	r/y
	40500	NC-130E	645 MS	
	40502	C-130E	37 AS	bl/w
	40504	C-130E	23 Wg	r/y
	40510	C-130E	135 AS	
	40512	C-130E	154 TS	r
	40514	C-130E	135 AS	
	40515	C-130E	135 AS	
	40517	C-130E	23 Wg	gn/or
	40518	C-130E	314 AW	gn
	40519	C-130E	314 AW	bl
	40520	C-130E	135 AS	
	40521	C-130E	135 AS	
	40523	MC-130E	8 SOS	
	40525	C-130E	23 Wg	gn/or
	40526	C-130E	135 AS	
	40527	C-130E	37 AS	bl/w
	40529	C-130E	23 Wg	gn/or
	40531	C-130E	23 Wg	
	40533	C-130E	37 AS	bl/w
	40535	C-130E	314 AW	bl
	40537	C-130E	23 Wg	gn/or
	40538	C-130E	314 AW	bk
	40539	C-130E	23 Wg	gn/or
	40540	C-130E	23 Wg	m
	40541	C-130E	314 AW	bk
	40542	C-130E	314 AW	bk
	40544	C-130E	135 AS	
	40550	C-130E	37 AS	bl/w
	40551	MC-130E	8 SOS	
	40555	MC-130E	8 SOS	
	40557	C-130E	314 AW	bl
	40559	MC-130E	8 SOS	
	40561	MC-130E	5 SOS	
	40562	MC-130E	8 SOS	
	40565	MC-130E	711 SOS	
	40566	MC-130E	8 SOS	
	40567	MC-130E	8 SOS	
	40568	MC-130E	8 SOS	

Type			Notes
40569	C-130E	314 AW	bl
40570	C-130E	23 Wg	gn/or
40571	MC-130E	711 SOS	
40572	MC-130E	711 SOS	
FY74			
41658	C-130H	3 Wg	w
41659	C-130H	3 Wg	w
41660	C-130H	374 AW	r
41661	C-130H	374 AW	r
41663	C-130H	7 Wg	bl
41664	C-130H	374 AW	r
41665	C-130H	7 Wg	bl
41666	C-130H	7 Wg	bl
41667	C-130H	7 Wg	r
41668	C-130H	3 Wg	w
41669	C-130H	7 Wg	r
41670	C-130H	7 Wg	r
41671	C-130H	7 Wg	bl
41673	C-130H	7 Wg	bl
41674	C-130H	7 Wg	r
41675	C-130H	7 Wg	r
41676	C-130H	3 Wg	w
41677	C-130H	7 Wg	bl
41679	C-130H	7 Wg	bl
41680	C-130H	7 Wg	r
41682	C-130H	374 AW	r
41684	C-130H	374 AW	r
41685	C-130H	374 AW	r
41687	C-130H	7 Wg	r
41688	C-130H	7 Wg	bl
41689	C-130H	7 Wg	bl
41690	C-130H	3 Wg	w
41691	C-130H	7 Wg	r
41692	C-130H	3 Wg	w
42061	C-130H	7 Wg	r
42062	C-130H	3 Wg	w
42063	C-130H	7 Wg	bl
42065	C-130H	7 Wg	bl
42066	C-130H	3 Wg	w
42067	C-130H	7 Wg	r
42069	C-130H	7 Wg	r
42070	C-130H	3 Wg	w
42071	C-130H	3 Wg	w
42072	C-130H	7 Wg	bl
42130	C-130H	7 Wg	r
42131	C-130H	3 Wg	w
42132	C-130H	7 Wg	r
42133	C-130H	374 AW	r
42134	C-130H	7 Wg	r
FY94			
43026	C-130J	Lockheed	
43027	C-130J	Lockheed	
46701	C-130H	167 AS	r
46702	C-130H	167 AS	r
46703	C-130H	167 AS	r
46704	C-130H	167 AS	r
46705	C-130H	167 AS	r
46706	C-130H	167 AS	r
46707	C-130H	167 AS	r
46708	C-130H	167 AS	r
47310	C-130H	731 AS	gn
47315	C-130H	731 AS	gn
47316	C-130H	731 AS	gn
47317	C-130H	731 AS	gn
47318	MC-130H	731 AS	gn
47319	C-130H	731 AS	gn
47320	C-130H	731 AS	gn
47321	C-130H	731 AS	gn
FY85			
50011	MC-130H	15 SOS	
50012	MC-130H	15 SOS	
FY55			
50022	NC-130A	46 TW	
FY85			
50035	C-130H	357 AS	bl

Type			Notes
50036	C-130H	357 AS	bl
50037	C-130H	357 AS	bl
50038	C-130H	357 AS	bl
50039	C-130H	357 AS	bl
50040	C-130H	357 AS	bl
50041	C-130H	357 AS	bl
50042	C-130H	357 AS	bl
FY65			
50962	EC-130H	42 ACCS	w
50963	WC-130H	53 WRS	
50964	C-130E	301 RQS	
50966	WC-130H	53 WRS	
50967	WC-130H	53 WRS	
50968	WC-130H	53 WRS	
50969	C-130E	711 SOS	
50970	HC-130P	304 RQS	y
50971	MC-130P	5 SOS	
50972	C-130E	711 SOS	
50973	HC-130P	71 RQS	bl
50974	HC-130P	71 RQS	bl
50975	MC-130P	58 SOW	
50976	HC-130P	304 RQS	y
50977	WC-130H	53 WRS	
50978	HC-130P	102 RQS	
50979	NC-130H	514 TS	
50980	WC-130H	53 WRS	
50981	HC-130P	129 RQS	bl
50982	HC-130P	71 RQS	bl
50983	HC-130H	129 RQS	bl
50984	WC-130H	53 WRS	
50985	WC-130H	53 WRS	
50986	HC-130P	71 RQS	bl
50987	HC-130P	71 RQS	bl
50988	HC-130P	71 RQS	bl
50989	EC-130H	41 ECS	bl
50991	MC-130P	9 SOS	
50992	MC-130P	17 SOS	
50993	MC-130P	17 SOS	
50994	MC-130P	17 SOS	
FY95			
51001	C-130H	109 AS	y
51002	C-130H	109 AS	y
FY85			
51361	C-130H	181 AS	
51362	C-130H	181 AS	
51363	C-130H	181 AS	
51364	C-130H	181 AS	
51365	C-130H	181 AS	
51366	C-130H	181 AS	
51367	C-130H	181 AS	
51368	C-130H	181 AS	
FY95			
56709	C-130H	167 AS	r
56710	C-130H	167 AS	r
56711	C-130H	167 AS	r
56712	C-130H	167 AS	r
FY66			
60212	MC-130P	58 SOW	
60213	MC-130P	67 SOS	
60215	MC-130P	17 SOS	
60216	MC-130P	5 SOS	
60217	MC-130P	9 SOS	
60219	MC-130P	5 SOS	
60220	MC-130P	9 SOS	
60221	HC-130P	129 RQS	bl
60222	HC-130P	102 RQS	
60223	MC-130P		
60224	HC-130P	129 RQS	bl
60225	MC-130P	9 SOS	
FY86			
60410	C-130H	758 AS	bk/y
60411	C-130H	758 AS	bk/y
60412	C-130H	758 AS	bk/y
60413	C-130H	758 AS	bk/y
60414	C-130H	758 AS	bk/y

Notes	Type			
	60415	C-130H	758 AS	*bk/y*
	60418	C-130H	758 AS	*bk/y*
	60419	C-130H	758 AS	*bk/y*
	FY96			
	61003	C-130H	109 AS	*y*
	61004	C-130H	109 AS	*y*
	61005	C-130H	109 AS	*y*
	61006	C-130H	109 AS	*y*
	61007	C-130H	109 AS	*y*
	61008	C-130H	109 AS	*y*
	FY86			
	61391	C-130H	180 AS	
	61392	C-130H	180 AS	
	61393	C-130H	180 AS	
	61394	C-130H	180 AS	
	61395	C-130H	180 AS	
	61396	C-130H	180 AS	
	61397	C-130H	180 AS	
	61398	C-130H	180 AS	
	61699	MC-130H	7 SOS	
	FY96			
	67322	C-130H	731 AS	*gn*
	67323	C-130H	731 AS	*gn*
	67324	C-130H	731 AS	*gn*
	67325	C-130H	731 AS	*gn*
	FY87			
	70023	MC-130H	7 SOS	
	70024	MC-130H	15 SOS	
	70125	MC-130H	58 SOW	
	70126	MC-130H	58 SOW	
	70127	MC-130H	58 SOW	
	70128	AC-130U	418 TS	
	79281	C-130H		
	79282	C-130H		
	79283	C-130H		
	79284	C-130H	357 AS	*bl*
	79285	C-130H		
	79286	C-130H	357 AS	*bl*
	79287	C-130H		
	79288	C-130H		
	FY88			
	80191	MC-130H	1 SOS	
	80192	MC-130H	1 SOS	
	80193	MC-130H	7 SOS	
	80194	MC-130H	7 SOS	
	80195	MC-130H	1 SOS	
	80264	MC-130H	1 SOS	
	FY78			
	80806	C-130H	185 AS	*bl*
	80807	C-130H	185 AS	*bl*
	80808	C-130H	185 AS	*bl*
	80809	C-130H	185 AS	*bl*
	80810	C-130H	185 AS	*bl*
	80811	C-130H	185 AS	*bl*
	80812	C-130H	185 AS	*bl*
	80813	C-130H	185 AS	*bl*
	FY88			
	81301	C-130H	130 AS	*bl*
	81302	C-130H	130 AS	*bl*
	81303	C-130H	130 AS	*bl*
	81304	C-130H	130 AS	*bl*
	81305	C-130H	130 AS	*bl*
	81306	C-130H	130 AS	*bl*
	81307	C-130H	130 AS	*bl*
	81308	C-130H	130 AS	*bl*
	81803	MC-130H	1 SOS	
	82101	HC-130N	102 RQS	
	82102	HC-130N	102 RQS	
	84401	C-130H	95 AS	*y/w*
	84402	C-130H	95 AS	*y/w*
	84403	C-130H	95 AS	*y/w*
	84404	C-130H	95 AS	*y/w*
	84405	C-130H	95 AS	*y/w*
	84406	C-130H	95 AS	*y/w*

Notes	Type			
	84407	C-130H	95 AS	*y/w*
	84408	C-130H	95 AS	*y/w*
	FY89			
	90280	MC-130H	15 SOS	
	90281	MC-130H	15 SOS	
	90282	MC-130H	15 SOS	
	90283	MC-130H	15 SOS	
	FY79			
	90473	C-130H	144 AS	
	90474	C-130H	185 AS	*bl*
	90475	C-130H	204 AS	
	90476	C-130H	157 FS	
	90477	C-130H	158 AS	*r*
	90478	C-130H	204 AS	
	90479	C-130H	204 AS	
	90480	C-130H	122 FS	
	FY89			
	90509	AC-130U	4 SOS	
	90510	AC-130U	4 SOS	
	90511	AC-130U	4 SOS	
	90512	AC-130U	4 SOS	
	90513	AC-130U	4 SOS	
	90514	AC-130U	4 SOS	
	91051	C-130H	105 AS	
	91052	C-130H	105 AS	
	91053	C-130H	105 AS	
	91054	C-130H	105 AS	
	91055	C-130H	142 AS	*bl*
	91056	C-130H	180 AS	
	91181	C-130H	105 AS	
	91182	C-130H	105 AS	
	91183	C-130H	105 AS	
	91184	C-130H	105 AS	
	91185	C-130H	105 AS	
	91186	C-130H	105 AS	
	91187	C-130H	105 AS	
	91188	C-130H	105 AS	
	FY69			
	95819	MC-130P	67 SOS	
	95820	MC-130P	67 SOS	
	95821	MC-130P	58 SOW	
	95822	MC-130P	17 SOS	
	95823	MC-130P	67 SOS	
	95824	HC-130N	301 RQS	
	95825	MC-130P	5 SOS	
	95826	MC-130P		
	95827	MC-130P	5 SOS	
	95828	MC-130P	9 SOS	
	95829	HC-130N	301 RQS	
	95830	HC-130N	301 RQS	
	95831	MC-130P	67 SOS	
	95832	MC-130P	9 SOS	
	95833	HC-130N	301 RQS	
	96566	C-130E	37 AS	*bl/w*
	96568	AC-130H	6 SOS	
	96569	AC-130H	16 SOS	
	96570	AC-130H	16 SOS	
	96572	AC-130H	16 SOS	
	96573	AC-130H	16 SOS	
	96574	AC-130H	16 SOS	
	96575	AC-130H	16 SOS	
	96577	AC-130H	16 SOS	
	96579	C-130E	314 AW	*gn*
	96580	C-130E	23 Wg	*gn/or*
	96582	C-130E	37 AS	*bl/w*
	96583	C-130E	37 AS	*bl/w*
	FY89			
	99101	C-130H	757 AS	*bl*
	99102	C-130H	757 AS	*bl*
	99103	C-130H	757 AS	*bl*
	99104	C-130H	757 AS	*bl*
	99105	C-130H	757 AS	*bl*
	99106	C-130H	757 AS	*bl*

Type	Notes
Boeing C-135/C-137	
6 ARW MacDill AFB, Florida:	
91 ARS (*y/bk*);	
18 Wg Kadena AB, Japan [ZZ]:	
909 ARS (*w*);	
19 ARW Robins AFB, Georgia:	
99 ARS (*y/bl*) & 712 ARS (*y/w*);	
22 ARW McConnell AFB, Kansas:	
344 ARS (*y/bk*), 349 ARS (*y/bl*)	
350 ARS (*y/r*) & 384 ARS (*y/pr*);	
55 Wg Offutt AFB, Nebraska [OF]:	
7 ACCS (*bl*), 38 RS, 45 RS	
& 343 RS (*gn*);	
63 ARS/927 ARW AFRES,	
Selfridge ANGB, Michigan (*pr/w*);	
65 AS/15 ABW, Hickam AFB,	
Hawaii;	
72 ARS/434 ARW AFRES,	
Grissom AFB, Indiana (*bl*);	
74 ARS/434 ARW AFRES,	
Grissom AFB, Indiana (*r/w*);	
77 ARS/916 ARW AFRES, Seymour	
Johnson AFB, North Carolina (*gn*);	
89 AW Andrews AFB, Maryland	
(1 AS);	
92 ARW Fairchild AFB,Washington:	
43 ARS (*bl*), 92 ARS (*bk*),	
96 ARS (*gn*), 97 ARS (*y*) &	
98 ARS (*r*);	
97 AMW Altus AFB, Oklahoma:	
55 ARS (*y/r*);	
100 ARW RAF Mildenhall, UK [D]:	
351 ARS (*r/w/bl*);	
106 ARS/117 ARW Birmingham,	
Alabama ANG (*w/r*);	
108 ARS/126 ARW, Greater Peoria	
Airport, Illinois ANG (*w/bl*);	
108 ARW McGuire AFB, New Jersey	
ANG: 141 ARS (*bk/y*) &	
150 ARS (*bl*);	
116 ARS/141 ARW Fairchild AFB,	
Washington ANG (*gn/w*);	
117 ARS/190 ARW Forbes Field,	
Kansas ANG (*bl/y*);	
121 ARW Rickenbacker ANGB, Ohio	
ANG: 145 ARS & 166 ARS (*bl*);	
126 ARS/128 ARW Mitchell Field,	
Wisconsin ANG (*w/bl*);	
132 ARS/101 ARW Bangor,	
Maine ANG (*w/gn*);	
133 ARS/157 ARW Pease ANGB,	
New Hampshire ANG (*bl*);	
136 ARS/107 ARW Niagara Falls,	
New York ANG (*bl*);	
151 ARS/134 ARW Knoxville,	
Tennessee ANG (*w/or*);	
153 ARS/186 ARW Meridian,	
Mississippi ANG (*bk/gd*);	
168 ARS/168 ARW Eielson AFB,	
Alaska ANG (*bl/y*);	
171 ARW Greater Pittsburgh,	
Pennsylvania ANG:	
146 ARS (*y/bk*) & 147 ARS (*bk/y*);	
173 ARS/155 ARW Lincoln,	
Nebraska ANG (*r/w*);	
191 ARS/151 ARW, Salt Lake City,	
Utah ANG (*bl/bk*);	
196 ARS/163 ARW March ARB,	
California ANG (*bl/w*);	
197 ARS/161 ARW Phoenix,	
Arizona ANG;	
203 ARS/154 CW Hickam AFB,	
Hawaii ANG (*y/bk*);	
314 ARS/940 ARW AFRES,	
McClellan AFB,California (*or/bk*);	

Type			Notes
319 ARW Grand Forks AFB,			
North Dakota:			
905 ARS (*bl*), 906 ARS (*y*),			
911 ARS (*r*) & 912 ARS (*w*);			
366 Wg Mountain Home AFB,			
Idaho [MO]: 22 ARS (*y/gn*);			
452 AMW/336 ARS AFRES,			
March ARB, California (*y*);			
452 TS/412 TW, Edwards AFB,			
California (*bl*);			
465 ARS/507 ARW AFRES,			
Tinker AFB, Oklahoma (*bl/y*);			
645 Materiel Sqn, Greenville, Texas			
FY60			
00313	KC-135R	22 ARW	
00314	KC-135R	74 ARS	*r/w*
00315	KC-135R	126 ARS	*w/bl*
00316	KC-135E	116 ARS	*gn/w*
00318	KC-135R	203 ARS	*y/bk*
00319	KC-135R	22 ARW	
00320	KC-135R	319 ARW	*w*
00321	KC-135R	319 ARW	*y*
00322	KC-135R	72 ARS	*bl*
00323	KC-135R	203 ARS	*y/bk*
00324	KC-135R	319 ARW	*bl*
00327	KC-135E	191 ARS	*bl/bk*
00328	KC-135R	92 ARW	*bk*
00329	KC-135R	203 ARS	*y/bk*
00331	KC-135R	97 AMW	*y/r*
00332	KC-135R	319 ARW	*w*
00333	KC-135R	97 AMW	*y/r*
00334	KC-135R	168 ARS	*bl/y*
00335	KC-135T	22 ARW	*y/bk*
00336	KC-135T	92 ARW	*gn*
00337	KC-135T	92 ARW	*bl*
00339	KC-135T	92 ARW	*bk*
00341	KC-135R	121 ARW	*bl*
00342	KC-135T	319 ARW	*y*
00343	KC-135T	319 ARW	*w*
00344	KC-135T	22 ARW	*y/bk*
00345	KC-135T	92 ARW	*bl*
00346	KC-135T	92 ARW	*gn*
00347	KC-135R	121 ARW	*bl*
00348	KC-135R	6 ARW	*y/bk*
00349	KC-135R	77 ARS	*gn*
00350	KC-135R	6 ARW	*y/bk*
00351	KC-135R	6 ARW	*y/bk*
00353	KC-135R	319 ARW	*y*
00355	KC-135R	6 ARW	*y/bk*
00356	KC-135R	22 ARW	*y/bl*
00357	KC-135R	22 ARW	*y/bk*
00358	KC-135R	136 ARS	*bl*
00359	KC-135R	74 ARS	*r/w*
00360	KC-135R	319 ARW	*r*
00362	KC-135R	22 ARW	*y/r*
00363	KC-135R	72 ARS	*bl*
00364	KC-135R	74 ARS	*r/w*
00365	KC-135R	366 Wg	*y/gn*
00366	KC-135R	366 Wg	*y/gn*
00367	KC-135R	121 ARW	*bl*
00372	C-135E	452 TS	*bl*
00374	EC-135E	452 TS	*bl*
00375	C-135E	452 TS	*bl*
00376	C-135E	89 AW	
FY61			
10264	KC-135R	121 ARW	*bl*
10266	KC-135R	173 ARS	*r/w*
10267	KC-135R	19 ARW	
10268	KC-135E	314 ARS	*or/bk*
10270	KC-135E	63 ARS	*pr/w*
10271	KC-135E	63 ARS	*pr/w*
10272	KC-135R	74 ARS	*r/w*
10275	KC-135R	22 ARW	
10276	KC-135R	173 ARS	*r/w*
10277	KC-135R	366 Wg	*y/gn*

Notes		Type			
	10280	KC-135E	452 AMW	y
	10281	KC-135E	197 ARS	
	10284	KC-135R	92 ARW	bk
	10288	KC-135R	18 Wg	w
	10290	KC-135R	203 ARS	y/bk
	10292	KC-135R	22 ARW	y/pr
	10293	KC-135R	22 ARW	y/r
	10294	KC-135R	92 ARW	y
	10295	KC-135R	319 ARW	
	10298	KC-135R	126 ARS	w/bl
	10299	KC-135R	92 ARW	y
	10300	KC-135R	19 ARW	y/w
	10302	KC-135R	18 Wg	w
	10303	KC-135E	452 AMW	y
	10304	KC-135R	319 ARW	
	10305	KC-135R	22 ARW	y/bk
	10306	KC-135R	6 ARW	y/bk
	10307	KC-135R	74 ARS	r/w
	10308	KC-135R	97 AMW	y/r
	10309	KC-135R	126 ARS	w/bl
	10310	KC-135R	33 ARS	bl
	10311	KC-135R	22 ARW	y/r
	10312	KC-135R	92 ARW	y
	10313	KC-135R	77 ARS	gn
	10314	KC-135R	319 ARW	
	10315	KC-135R	18 Wg	w
	10317	KC-135R	319 ARW	bl
	10318	KC-135R	319 ARW	w
	10320	KC-135R	92 ARW	y
	10321	KC-135R	92 ARW	y
	10323	KC-135R	92 ARW	y
	10324	KC-135R	465 ARS	bl/y
	10326	EC-135E	452 TS	bl
	10327	EC-135N	CinC CC	
	10329	EC-135E	452 TS	bl
	10330	EC-135E	452 TS	bl
	12662	RC-135S	55 Wg	bk
	12663	RC-135S	55 Wg	
	12665	WC-135W	wfu	
	12666	WC-135W	645 MS	
	12667	WC-135W	55 Wg	bk
	12668	C-135C	65 AS	
	12669	C-135C	452 TS	bl
	12670	OC-135B	55 Wg	bl
	12672	OC-135B	55 Wg	bl
	12674	OC-135B	55 Wg	
FY64				
	14828	KC-135R	22 ARW	y/r
	14829	KC-135R	97 AMW	y/r
	14830	KC-135R	319 ARW	r
	14831	KC-135R	92 ARW	y
	14832	KC-135R	203 ARS	y/bk
	14833	KC-135R	22 ARW	y/pr
	14834	KC-135R	74 ARS	r/w
	14835	KC-135R	18 Wg	w
	14836	KC-135R	319 ARW	r
	14837	KC-135R	319 ARW	w
	14838	KC-135R	22 ARW	y/pr
	14839	KC-135R	136 ARS	bl
	14840	KC-135R	121 ARW	bl
	14841	RC-135V	55 Wg	gn
	14842	RC-135V	55 Wg	gn
	14843	RC-135V	55 Wg	gn
	14844	RC-135V	55 Wg	gn
	14845	RC-135V	55 Wg	gn
	14846	RC-135V	55 Wg	gn
	14847	RC-135U	55 Wg	gn
	14848	RC-135V	55 Wg	gn
	14849	RC-135U	55 Wg	gn
FY67				
	19417	EC-137D	19 ARW	
FY62				
	23498	KC-135R	92 ARW	bk
	23499	KC-135R	22 ARW	y/r
	23500	KC-135R	126 ARS	w/bl

Notes		Type			
	23502	KC-135R	97 AMW	y/r
	23503	KC-135R	92 ARW	r
	23504	KC-135R	319 ARW	bl
	23505	KC-135R	319 ARW	w
	23506	KC-135R	133 ARS	bl
	23507	KC-135R	319 ARW	
	23508	KC-135R	19 ARW	y/bk
	23509	KC-135R	77 ARS	gn
	23510	KC-135R	74 ARS	r/w
	23511	KC-135R	121 ARW	bl
	23513	KC-135R	366 Wg	y/gn
	23514	KC-135R	203 ARS	y/bk
	23515	KC-135R	133 ARS	bl
	23517	KC-135R	18 Wg	w
	23518	KC-135R	72 ARS	bl
	23519	KC-135R	319 ARW	r
	23520	KC-135R	319 ARW	
	23521	KC-135R	72 ARS	bl
	23523	KC-135R	19 ARW	y/w
	23524	KC-135R	106 ARS	w/r
	23526	KC-135R	173 ARS	r/w
	23527	KC-135E	108 ARW	bk/y
	23528	KC-135R	97 AMW	y/r
	23529	KC-135R	97 AMW	y/r
	23530	KC-135R	72 ARS	bl
	23531	KC-135R	121 ARW	bl
	23533	KC-135R	6 ARW	y/bk
	23534	KC-135R	22 ARW	
	23537	KC-135R	319 ARW	r
	23538	KC-135R	92 ARW	y
	23540	KC-135R	92 ARW	y
	23541	KC-135R	100 ARW	r/w/bl
	23542	KC-135R	77 ARS	gn
	23543	KC-135R	72 ARS	bl
	23544	KC-135R	19 ARW	y/w
	23545	KC-135R	19 ARW	w
	23546	KC-135R	92 ARW	y
	23547	KC-135R	133 ARS	bl
	23548	KC-135R	22 ARW	y/r
	23549	KC-135R	6 ARW	y/bk
	23550	KC-135R	97 AMW	y/r
	23551	KC-135R	97 AMW	y/r
	23552	KC-135R	319 ARW	w
	23553	KC-135R	22 ARW	y/r
	23554	KC-135R	19 ARW	
	23556	KC-135R	77 ARS	gn
	23557	KC-135R	319 ARW	bl
	23558	KC-135R	92 ARW	bk
	23559	KC-135R	22 ARW	y/pr
	23561	KC-135R	319 ARW	w
	23562	KC-135R	319 ARW	w
	23564	KC-135R	97 AMW	y/r
	23565	KC-135R	97 AMW	y/r
	23566	KC-135E	132 ARS	w/gn
	23569	KC-135R	19 ARW	y/bl
	23571	KC-135R	168 ARS	bl/y
	23572	KC-135R	366 Wg	y/gn
	23573	KC-135R	97 AMW	y/r
	23575	KC-135R	6 ARW	y/bk
	23576	KC-135R	133 ARS	bl
	23577	KC-135R	77 ARS	gn
	23578	KC-135R	92 ARW	r
	23580	KC-135R	97 AMW	y/r
	23581	EC-135C	55 Wg	bl
	23582	EC-135C	55 Wg	bl
	23585	EC-135C	55 Wg	bl
	24125	RC-135W	55 Wg	
	24126	C-135B	108 ARW	bk/y
	24127	C-135B	65 AS	
	24129	TC-135W	55 Wg	gn
	24130	RC-135W	55 Wg	
	24131	RC-135W	55 Wg	gn
	24132	RC-135W	55 Wg	gn
	24133	TC-135S	55 Wg	bk

Type			Notes	Type			Notes
24134	RC-135W	55 Wg	*gn*	38871	KC-135R	319 ARW	*r*
24135	RC-135W	55 Wg	*gn*	38872	KC-135R	136 ARS	*bl*
24138	RC-135W	55 Wg	*gn*	38873	KC-135R	319 ARW	*r*
24139	RC-135W	55 Wg	*gn*	38874	KC-135R	319 ARW	*w*
26000	C-137C	89 AW		38875	KC-135R	366 Wg	*y/gn*
FY72				38876	KC-135R	168 ARS	*bl/y*
27000	C-137C	89 AW		38877	KC-135R	100 ARW	*r/w/bl*
FY63				38878	KC-135R	97 AMW	*y/r*
37976	KC-135R	319 ARW	*bl*	38879	KC-135R	18 Wg	*w*
37977	KC-135R	319 ARW	*bl*	38880	KC-135R	465 ARS	*bl/y*
37978	KC-135R	97 AMW	*y/r*	38881	KC-135R	319 ARW	*y*
37979	KC-135R	97 AMW	*y/r*	38883	KC-135R	319 ARW	*w*
37980	KC-135R	22 ARW	*y/r*	38884	KC-135R	22 ARW	
37981	KC-135R	136 ARS	*bl*	38885	KC-135R	18 Wg	*w*
37982	KC-135R	6 ARW	*y/bk*	38886	KC-135R	319 ARW	*bl*
37984	KC-135R	106 ARS	*w/r*	38887	KC-135R	22 ARW	*y/r*
37985	KC-135R	465 ARS	*bl/y*	38888	KC-135R	97 AMW	*y/r*
37987	KC-135R	18 Wg	*w*	39792	RC-135V	55 Wg	*gn*
37988	KC-135R	173 ARS	*r/w*	*FY55*			
37991	KC-135R	173 ARS	*r/w*	53118	EC-135K	*wfu*	
37992	KC-135R	121 ARW	*bl*	53125	EC-135Y	CinC CC	
37993	KC-135R	121 ARW	*m*	53132	NKC-135E	452 TS	*bl*
37995	KC-135R	19 ARW	*y/bl*	53135	NKC-135E	452 TS	*bl*
37996	KC-135R	72 ARS	*bl*	53141	KC-135E	116 ARS	*gn/w*
37997	KC-135R	19 ARW	*y/w*	53143	KC-135E	197 ARS	
37999	KC-135R	18 Wg	*w*	53145	KC-135E	314 ARS	*or/bk*
38000	KC-135R	22 ARW		53146	KC-135E	108 ARW	*bk/y*
38002	KC-135R	19 ARW	*y/bl*	*FY85*			
38003	KC-135R	22 ARW	*y/r*	56973	C-137C	89 AW	
38004	KC-135R	366 Wg	*y/gn*	56974	C-137C	89 AW	
38006	KC-135R	19 ARW	*y/w*	*FY56*			
38007	KC-135R	106 ARS	*w/r*	63593	KC-135E	108 ARW	*bk/y*
38008	KC-135R	22 ARW	*y/r*	63604	KC-135E	117 ARS	*bl/y*
38011	KC-135R	18 Wg	*w*	63606	KC-135E	132 ARS	*w/gn*
38012	KC-135R	18 Wg	*w*	63607	KC-135E	151 ARS	*w/or*
38013	KC-135R	121 ARW	*bl*	63609	KC-135E	151 ARS	*w/or*
38014	KC-135R	18 Wg	*w*	63611	KC-135E	171 ARW	*y/bk*
38015	KC-135R	168 ARS	*bl/y*	63612	KC-135E	171 ARW	*y/bk*
38017	KC-135R	92 ARW	*bk*	63622	KC-135E	132 ARS	*w/gn*
38018	KC-135R	173 ARS	*r/w*	63623	KC-135E	452 AMW	*y*
38019	KC-135R	22 ARW	*y/pr*	63626	KC-135E	171 ARW	*y/bk*
38020	KC-135R	97 AMW	*y/r*	63630	KC-135E	171 ARW	*y/bk*
38021	KC-135R	319 ARW	*bl*	63631	KC-135E	191 ARS	*bl/bk*
38022	KC-135R	22 ARW	*y/r*	63638	KC-135E	197 ARS	
38023	KC-135R	100 ARW	*r/w/bl*	63640	KC-135E	132 ARS	*w/gn*
38024	KC-135R	465 ARS	*bl/y*	63641	KC-135E	117 ARS	*bl/y*
38025	KC-135R	18 Wg	*w*	63643	KC-135E	151 ARS	*w/or*
38026	KC-135R	319 ARW	*y*	63645	KC-135E	314 ARS	*or/bk*
38027	KC-135R	92 ARW	*gn*	63648	KC-135E	171 ARW	*y/bk*
38028	KC-135R	168 ARS	*bl/y*	63650	KC-135E	116 ARS	*gn/w*
38029	KC-135R	126 ARS	*w/bl*	63654	KC-135E	132 ARS	*w/gn*
38030	KC-135R	203 ARS	*y/bk*	63658	KC-135E	117 ARS	*bl/y*
38031	KC-135R	22 ARW	*y/bk*	*FY57*			
38032	KC-135R	72 ARS	*bl*	71418	KC-135R	153 ARS	*bk/gd*
38034	KC-135R	319 ARW	*w*	71419	KC-135R	319 ARW	*w*
38035	KC-135R	106 ARS	*w/r*	71421	KC-135E	116 ARS	*gn/w*
38036	KC-135R	136 ARS	*bl*	71422	KC-135E	63 ARS	*pr/w*
38037	KC-135R	92 ARW	*bl*	71423	KC-135E	171 ARW	*bk/y*
38038	KC-135R	133 ARS	*bl*	71425	KC-135E	151 ARS	*w/or*
38039	KC-135R	465 ARS	*bl/y*	71426	KC-135E	197 ARS	
38040	KC-135R	319 ARW	*y*	71427	KC-135R	121 ARW	*bl*
38041	KC-135R	72 ARS	*bl*	71428	KC-135R	196 ARS	*bl/w*
38043	KC-135R	168 ARS	*bl/y*	71429	KC-135E	117 ARS	*bl/y*
38044	KC-135R	319 ARW	*y*	71430	KC-135R	133 ARS	*bl*
38045	KC-135R	319 ARW	*r*	71431	KC-135E	108 ARW	*bk/y*
38046	EC-135C	55 Wg	*bl*	71432	KC-135R	106 ARS	*w/r*
38048	EC-135C	55 Wg	*bl*	71433	KC-135E	197 ARS	
38050	EC-135C	452 TS	*bl*	71434	KC-135E	116 ARS	*gn/w*
38052	EC-135C	55 Wg	*bl*	71435	KC-135R	22 ARW	*y/r*
38053	EC-135C	55 Wg	*bl*	71436	KC-135E	196 ARS	*bl/w*
38054	EC-135C	55 Wg	*bl*	71437	KC-135R	77 ARS	*gn/w*
38058	KC-135D	117 ARS	*bl/y*	71438	KC-135E	63 ARS	*pr/w*
38059	KC-135D	117 ARS	*bl/y*	71439	KC-135R	100 ARW	*r/w/bl*
38060	KC-135D	117 ARS	*bl/y*	71440	KC-135R	319 ARW	*bl*
38061	KC-135D	117 ARS	*bl/y*	71441	KC-135E	108 ARS	*w/bl*

Notes	Type			
	71443	KC-135E	132 ARS	*w/gn*
	71445	KC-135E	108 ARW	*bk/y*
	71447	KC-135E	171 ARW	*y/bk*
	71448	KC-135E	132 ARS	*w/gn*
	71450	KC-135E	132 ARS	*w/gn*
	71451	KC-135E	116 ARS	*gn/w*
	71452	KC-135E	197 ARS	
	71453	KC-135R	106 ARS	*w/r*
	71454	KC-135R	6 ARW	*y/bk*
	71455	KC-135E	151 ARS	*w/or*
	71456	KC-135R	100 ARW	*r/w/bl*
	71458	KC-135E	108 ARS	*w/bl*
	71459	KC-135E	196 ARS	*bl/w*
	71460	KC-135E	117 ARS	*bl/y*
	71461	KC-135R	173 ARS	*r/w*
	71462	KC-135R	121 ARW	*bl*
	71463	KC-135E	117 ARS	*bl/y*
	71464	KC-135E	108 ARW	*bk/y*
	71465	KC-135E	151 ARS	*w/or*
	71468	KC-135E	452 AMW	*y*
	71469	KC-135R	121 ARW	*bl*
	71471	KC-135E	132 ARS	*w/gn*
	71472	KC-135R	72 ARS	*bl*
	71473	KC-135R	319 ARW	
	71474	KC-135R	100 ARW	*r/w/bl*
	71475	KC-135E	197 ARS	
	71478	KC-135E	151 ARS	*w/or*
	71479	KC-135E	452 AMW	*y*
	71480	KC-135E	108 ARS	*w/bl*
	71482	KC-135E	117 ARS	*bl/y*
	71483	KC-135R	18 Wg	*w*
	71484	KC-135E	197 ARS	
	71485	KC-135E	151 ARS	*w/or*
	71486	KC-135R	92 ARW	
	71487	KC-135R	72 ARS	*bl*
	71488	KC-135R	97 AMW	*y/r*
	71491	KC-135E	132 ARS	*w/gn*
	71492	KC-135E	151 ARS	*w/or*
	71493	KC-135R	6 ARW	*y/bk*
	71494	KC-135E	108 ARS	*w/bl*
	71495	KC-135E	197 ARS	
	71496	KC-135E	197 ARS	
	71497	KC-135E	191 ARS	*bl/bk*
	71499	KC-135R	100 ARW	*r/w/bl*
	71501	KC-135E	116 ARS	*gn/w*
	71502	KC-135R	319 ARW	*y*
	71503	KC-135E	151 ARS	*w/or*
	71504	KC-135E	63 ARS	*pr/w*
	71505	KC-135E	132 ARS	*w/gn*
	71506	KC-135R	100 ARW	*r/w/bl*
	71507	KC-135E	108 ARW	*bk/y*
	71508	KC-135R	203 ARS	*y/bk*
	71509	KC-135E	171 ARW	*bk/y*
	71510	KC-135E	191 ARS	*bl/bk*
	71511	KC-135E	314 ARS	*or/bk*
	71512	KC-135E	452 AMW	*y*
	71514	KC-135R	126 ARS	*w/bl*
	72589	KC-135E	55 Wg	*bl*
	72593	KC-135R	121 ARW	*bl*
	72594	KC-135E	108 ARS	*w/bl*
	72595	KC-135E	171 ARW	*bk/y*
	72597	KC-135R	153 ARS	*bk/gd*
	72598	KC-135E	452 AMW	*y*
	72599	KC-135R	77 ARS	*gn*
	72600	KC-135E	116 ARS	*gn/w*
	72601	KC-135E	151 ARS	*w/or*
	72602	KC-135E	108 ARW	*bl*
	72603	KC-135E	452 AMW	*y*
	72604	KC-135E	171 ARW	*y/bk*
	72605	KC-135R	22 ARW	*y/bl*
	72606	KC-135E	108 ARW	*bl*
	72607	KC-135E	171 ARW	*bk/y*
	72608	KC-135E	171 ARW	*bk/y*
	FY58			
	80001	KC-135R	97 AMW	*y/r*

Notes	Type			
	80003	KC-135E	108 ARS	*w/bl*
	80004	KC-135R	153 ARS	*bk/gd*
	80005	KC-135E	117 ARS	*bl/y*
	80006	KC-135E	191 ARS	*bl/bk*
	80008	KC-135R	196 ARS	*bl/w*
	80009	KC-135R	126 ARS	*w/bl*
	80010	KC-135R	153 ARS	*bk/gd*
	80011	KC-135R	22 ARW	*y/bl*
	80012	KC-135E	191 ARS	*bl/bk*
	80013	KC-135E	63 ARS	*pr/w*
	80014	KC-135E	108 ARS	*w/bl*
	80015	KC-135R	74 ARS	*r/w*
	80016	KC-135R	22 ARW	*y/bk*
	80017	KC-135E	171 ARW	*y/bk*
	80018	KC-135R	22 ARW	*y/pr*
	80020	KC-135E	116 ARS	*gn/w*
	80021	KC-135R	126 ARS	*w/bl*
	80023	KC-135R	136 ARS	*bl*
	80024	KC-135E	171 ARW	*y/bk*
	80027	KC-135R	18 Wg	*w*
	80030	KC-135R	106 ARS	*w/r*
	80032	KC-135E	108 ARW	*bl*
	80034	KC-135R	97 AMW	*y/r*
	80035	KC-135R	22 ARW	*y/bl*
	80036	KC-135R	22 ARW	*y/bl*
	80037	KC-135E	171 ARW	*bk/y*
	80038	KC-135R	77 ARS	*gn*
	80040	KC-135E	108 ARW	*bl*
	80041	KC-135E	63 ARS	*pr/w*
	80042	KC-135T	319 ARW	*y*
	80043	KC-135E	191 ARS	*bl/bk*
	80044	KC-135E	108 ARW	*bk/y*
	80045	KC-135T	92 ARW	*gn*
	80046	KC-135T	92 ARW	*r*
	80047	KC-135T	319 ARW	*w*
	80049	KC-135T	92 ARW	*bl*
	80050	KC-135T	92 ARW	*r*
	80051	KC-135R	465 ARS	*bl/y*
	80052	KC-135E	452 AMW	*y*
	80053	KC-135E	314 ARS	*or/bk*
	80054	KC-135T	92 ARW	*gn*
	80055	KC-135T	92 ARW	*r*
	80056	KC-135R	153 ARS	*bk/gd*
	80057	KC-135E	108 ARS	*w/bl*
	80058	KC-135E	314 ARS	*or/bk*
	80059	KC-135R	153 ARS	*bk/gd*
	80060	KC-135T	92 ARW	*gn*
	80061	KC-135T	319 ARW	
	80062	KC-135T	92 ARW	*gn*
	80063	KC-135R	465 ARS	*bl/y*
	80064	KC-135E	314 ARS	*or/bk*
	80065	KC-135T	319 ARW	*bl*
	80066	KC-135R	465 ARS	*bl/y*
	80067	KC-135E	108 ARS	*w/bl*
	80068	KC-135E	108 ARS	*w/bl*
	80069	KC-135T	92 ARW	*bl*
	80071	KC-135T	22 ARW	*y/bk*
	80072	KC-135T	92 ARW	*gn*
	80073	KC-135R	106 ARS	*w/r*
	80074	KC-135T	92 ARW	*r*
	80075	KC-135R	72 ARS	*bl*
	80076	KC-135R	74 ARS	*r/w*
	80077	KC-135T	92 ARW	*gn*
	80078	KC-135E	108 ARW	*bl*
	80079	KC-135R	465 ARS	*bl/y*
	80080	KC-135E	191 ARS	*bl/bk*
	80082	KC-135E	116 ARS	*gn/w*
	80083	KC-135R	121 ARW	*bl*
	80084	KC-135T	92 ARW	*r*
	80085	KC-135E	452 AMW	*y*
	80086	KC-135T	92 ARW	*bk*
	80087	KC-135E	108 ARW	*bl*
	80088	KC-135T	22 ARW	*y/bk*
	80089	KC-135T	22 ARW	*y/bk*

Type			Notes
80090	KC-135E	314 ARS	or/bk
80092	KC-135R	133 ARS	bl
80093	KC-135R	319 ARW	r
80094	KC-135T	92 ARW	bl
80095	KC-135T	22 ARW	y/r
80096	KC-135E	314 ARS	or/bk
80098	KC-135R	133 ARS	bl
80099	KC-135T	22 ARW	bk
80100	KC-135R	6 ARW	y/bk
80102	KC-135R	74 ARS	r/w
80103	KC-135T	92 ARW	
80104	KC-135R	136 ARS	bl
80106	KC-135R	106 ARS	w/r
80107	KC-135E	191 ARS	bl/bk
80108	KC-135E	314 ARS	or/bk
80109	KC-135R	153 ARS	bk/gd
80111	KC-135E	108 ARW	bk/y
80112	KC-135T	92 ARW	bl
80113	KC-135R	319 ARW	bl
80114	KC-135R	319 ARW	r
80115	KC-135E	108 ARW	bl
80116	KC-135E	197 ARS	
80117	KC-135T	92 ARW	r
80118	KC-135R	22 ARW	y/bl
80119	KC-135R	319 ARW	r
80120	KC-135R	97 AMW	/r
80121	KC-135R	465 ARS	bl/y
80122	KC-135R	168 ARS	bl/y
80123	KC-135R	19 ARW	y/w
80124	KC-135R	22 ARW	y/bl
80125	KC-135T	92 ARW	y
80126	KC-135R	22 ARW	y/bl
80128	KC-135R	22 ARW	y/bk
80129	KC-135T	92 ARW	y
80130	KC-135R	126 ARS	w/bl
86971	C-137B	89 AW	

FY59

Type			Notes
91444	KC-135R	121 ARW	bl
91445	KC-135E	116 ARS	gn/w
91446	KC-135R	153 ARS	bk/gd
91447	KC-135E	63 ARS	pr/w
91448	KC-135R	196 ARS	bl/w
91450	KC-135R	196 ARS	bl/w
91451	KC-135E	63 ARS	pr/w
91452	KC-135E	116 ARS	gn/w
91453	KC-135R	121 ARW	bl
91455	KC-135R	153 ARS	bk/gd
91456	KC-135E	108 ARW	bk/y
91457	KC-135E	171 ARW	bk/y
91458	KC-135R	121 ARW	bl
91459	KC-135R	97 AMW	y/r
91460	KC-135T	92 ARW	bl
91461	KC-135R	168 ARS	bl/y
91462	KC-135T	22 ARW	y/bk
91463	KC-135R	173 ARS	r/w
91464	KC-135T	92 ARW	r
91466	KC-135R	136 ARS	bl
91467	KC-135T	92 ARW	y
91468	KC-135T	92 ARW	gn
91469	KC-135R	77 ARS	gn
91470	KC-135T	92 ARW	bl
91471	KC-135T	92 ARW	r
91472	KC-135R	203 ARS	y/bk
91473	KC-135E	191 ARS	bl/bk
91474	KC-135T	92 ARW	bl
91475	KC-135R	6 ARW	y/bk
91476	KC-135R	97 AMW	y/r
91477	KC-135E	63 ARS	pr/w
91478	KC-135R	153 ARS	bk/gd
91479	KC-135E	171 ARW	y/bk
91480	KC-135T	92 ARW	y
91482	KC-135R	100 ARW	r/w/bl
91483	KC-135R	121 ARW	bl
91484	KC-135E	171 ARW	bk/y
91485	KC-135E	108 ARW	bl
91486	KC-135R	22 ARW	
91487	KC-135E	108 ARS	w/bl
91488	KC-135R	18 Wg	w
91489	KC-135E	191 ARS	bl/bk
91490	KC-135T	92 ARW	bk
91492	KC-135R	92 ARW	bk
91493	KC-135E	132 ARS	w/gn
91495	KC-135R	173 ARS	r/w
91496	KC-135E	171 ARW	y/bk
91497	KC-135E	108 ARW	bl
91498	KC-135R	366 Wg	y/gn
91499	KC-135R	196 ARS	bl/w
91500	KC-135R	19 ARW	y/bl
91501	KC-135R	22 ARW	
91502	KC-135R	22 ARW	y/r
91503	KC-135E	108 ARW	bk/y
91504	KC-135T	92 ARW	bl
91505	KC-135R	196 ARS	bl/w
91506	KC-135E	171 ARW	bk/y
91507	KC-135R	22 ARW	y/bl
91508	KC-135R	319 ARW	r
91509	KC-135R	196 ARS	bl/w
91510	KC-135T	22 ARW	y/bk
91511	KC-135R	319 ARW	
91512	KC-135T	92 ARW	gn
91513	KC-135T	22 ARW	y/pr
91514	KC-135E	55 Wg	bl
91515	KC-135R	22 ARW	y/r
91516	KC-135R	196 ARS	bl/w
91517	KC-135R	18 Wg	w
91518	EC-135K	89 AW	
91519	KC-135E	171 ARW	y/bk
91520	KC-135T	92 ARW	y
91521	KC-135R	168 ARS	bl/y
91522	KC-135R	136 ARS	bl
91523	KC-135T	92 ARW	gn

Lockheed C-141B Starlifter

60 AMW Travis AFB, California:
19 AS & 20 AS (*bk/r* & *bk/si*);
62 AW McChord AFB, Washington:
4 AS, 7 AS & 8 AS (*gn/bl*) (*gn*)
(*gn/r*);
97 AMW Altus AFB, Oklahoma:
57 AS (*r/y*);
155 AS/164 AW Memphis,
Tennessee ANG (*r*);
183 AS/172 AW Jackson Field AFB,
Mississippi ANG (*bl*);
305 AMW McGuire AFB, New Jersey:
6 AS & 13 AS (*bl*);
437 AW Charleston AFB, South
Carolina: 15 AS & 16 AS (*y/bl*);
445 AW AFRES, Wright-Patterson
AFB, Ohio: 89 AS & 356 AS (*w/r*);
452 AMW AFRES, March ARB,
California: 729 AS & 730 AS (*r/y*);
756 AS/459 AW AFRES,
Andrews AFB, Maryland (y/*bk*)

FY61

Type		Notes
12778	155 AS	r

FY63

Type		Notes
38076	62 AW	gn/r
38080	155 AS	r
38081	62 AW	gn/bl
38082	62 AW	n/r
38083	*wfu*	
38084	452 AMW	r/y
38085	452 AMW	r/y
38086	62 AW	
38087	62 AW	gn/r
38088	60 AMW	
38089	62 AW	gn/r

FY64

Type		Notes
40609	97 AMW	r/y
40610	437 AW	y/bl

C-141B

Notes	Type			Notes	Type		
	40611	437 AW	y/bl		50266	437 AW	y/bl
	40612	437 AW	y/bl		50267	62 AW	gn/r
	40613	305 AMW	bl		50268	60 AMW	bk/si
	40614	183 AS	bl		50269	437 AW	y/bl
	40615	437 AW	y/bl		50270	437 AW	y/bl
	40616	305 AMW	bl		50271	756 AS	y/bk
	40618	437 AW	y/bl		50272	305 AMW	bl
	40619	437 AW	y/bl		50273	437 AW	y/bl
	40620	756 AS	y/bk		50275	437 AW	y/bl
	40621	305 AMW	bl		50276	305 AMW	bl
	40622	183 AS	bl		50277	62 AW	gn/r
	40623	305 AMW	bl		50279	437 AW	y/bl
	40625	305 AMW	bl		50280	60 AMW	bk/r
	40627	155 AS	r		59401	437 AW	y/bl
	40628	305 AMW	bl		59403	60 AMW	bk/si
	40629	305 AMW	bl		59404	62 AW	gn/si
	40630	305 AMW	bl		59405	305 AMW	bl
	40631	437 AW	y/bl		59408	305 AMW	bl
	40632	183 AS	bl		59409	445 AW	w/r
	40633	62 AW	gn/r		59411	305 AMW	bl
	40635	62 AW	gn/si		59412	445 AW	w/r
	40637	756 AS	y/bk		59413	305 AMW	bl
	40638	305 AMW	bl		59414	452 AMW	r/y
	40639	97 AMW	r/y		*FY66*		
	40640	183 AS	bl		60128	62 AW	gn/bl
	40643	60 AMW	bk/r		60130	183 AS	bl
	40644	97 AMW	r/y		60131	437 AW	y/bl
	40645	756 AS	y/bk		60132	445 AW	w/r
	40646	305 AMW	bl		60133	305 AMW	bl
	40649	437 AW	y/bl		60134	445 AW	w/r
	40651	97 AMW	r/y		60135	437 AW	y/bl
	40653	62 AW	gn/bl		60136	452 AMW	r/y
	FY65				60137	62 AW	gn
	50216	756 AS	y/bk		60139	155 AS	r
	50217	305 AMW			60140	62 AW	gn/r
	50218	62 AW	gn/r		60141	62 AW	gn/r
	50219	60 AMW			60144	305 AMW	bl
	50220	305 AMW	bl		60145	62 AW	gn/r
	50221	305 AMW	bl		60146	97 AMW	r/y
	50222	155 AS	r		60147	60 AMW	bk/r
	50223	305 AMW	bl		60148	60 AMW	bk/r
	50224	305 AMW	bl		60149	437 AW	y/bl
	50225	452 AMW	r/y		60151	452 AMW	r/y
	50226	756 AS	y/bk		60152	452 AMW	r/y
	50227	445 AW	w/r		60153	756 AS	y/bk
	50229	452 AMW	r/y		60155	305 AMW	bl
	50230	60 AMW	bk/r		60156	62 AW	gn/bl
	50231	60 AMW	bk/si		60157	155 AS	r
	50232	445 AW	w/r		60158	62 AW	gn/bl
	50234	60 AMW	bk/r		60159	62 AW	gn/si
	50235	62 AW	gn/si		60160	60 AMW	bk/r
	50237	445 AW	w/r		60161	62 AW	gn/r
	50238	60 AMW	bk/r		60162	305 AMW	bl
	50239	60 AMW	bk/si		60163	305 AMW	bl
	50240	62 AW	gn/bl		60164	183 AS	bl
	50241	62 AW	gn/r		60165	62 AW	
	50242	60 AMW	bk/si		60166	60 AMW	
	50243	97 AMW	r/y		60167	437 AW	y/bl
	50244	62 AW	gn/si		60168	437 AW	y/bl
	50245	452 AMW	r/y		60169	305 AMW	bl
	50248	452 AMW	r/y		60171	62 AW	gn/r
	50249	445 AW	w/r		60172	97 AMW	r/y
	50250	445 AW	w/r		60174	756 AS	y/bk
	50251	60 AMW	bk/r		60175	62 AW	gn/si
	50252	60 AMW			60177	445 AW	w/r
	50254	60 AMW	bk/si		60178	305 AMW	bl
	50256	445 AW	w/r		60179	62 AW	gn/r
	50257	452 AMW	r/y		60181	452 AMW	r/y
	50258	445 AW	w/r		60182	452 AMW	r/y
	50259	60 AMW	bk/r		60183	60 AMW	bk/r
	50260	60 AMW	bk/si		60184	62 AW	gn/bl
	50261	445 AW	gy/r		60185	183 AS	bl
	50263	62 AW	gn/bl		60187	437 AW	y/bl

Type			Notes	Type			Notes
60190	183 AS	bl		67958	62 AW	gn/bl	
60191	183 AS	bl		67959	445 AW	w/r	
60192	62 AW	gn/bl		FY67			
60193	452 AMW	r/y		70001	62 AW	gn/r	
60194	437 AW	y/bl		70002	437 AW	y/bl	
60195	62 AW	gn/r		70003	62 AW	gn/bl	
60196	437 AW	y/bl		70004	437 AW	y/bl	
60197	62 AW	gn/r		70005	62 AW	gn/r	
60198	62 AW	gn/si		70007	60 AMW	bk/si	
60199	756 AS	y/bk		70009	62 AW	gn/r	
60200	97 AMW	r/y		70010	437 AW	y/bl	
60201	452 AMW	r/y		70011	437 AW	y/bl	
60202	437 AW	y/bl		70012	437 AW	y/bl	
60203	97 AMW	r/y		70013	437 AW	y/bl	
60204	97 AMW	r/y		70014	437 AW	y/bl	
60205	97 AMW	r/y		70015	452 AMW	r/y	
60206	62 AW	gn/bl		70016	437 AW	y/bl	
60207	305 AMW	bl		70018	62 AW	gn/bl	
60208	62 AW	gn/bl		70019	305 AMW	bl	
60209	437 AW	y/bl		70020	305 AMW	bl	
67944	60 AMW	bk/si		70021	155 AS	r	
67946	62 AW	gn/bl		70022	60 AMW	bk/r	
67947	437 AW	y/bl		70024	155 AS	r	
67948	305 AMW	bl		70025	305 AMW	bl	
67949	62 AW	gn/r		70026	437 AW	y/bl	
67950	445 AW	w/r		70027	60 AMW	bk/r	
67951	62 AW	gn/r		70028	62 AW	gn/si	
67952	452 AMW	r/y		70029	155 AS	r	
67953	445 AW	w/r		70031	445 AW	gy/r	
67954	445 AW	w/r		70164	97 AMW	r/y	
67955	437 AW	y/bl		70165	305 AMW	bl/r	
67956	62 AW			70166	305 AMW	(VIP)	
67957	452 AMW	r/y					

Colourful D-BD Alpha Jet E134/8-MA of the French *Armée de l'Air* during an operational visit to RAF St Mawgan. *PRM*

Boeing E-6 Mercury
Boeing, McConnell AFB, Kansas;
VQ-3 & VQ-4, Sea Control Wing 1 (SCW-1),
  Tinker AFB, Oklahoma

162782	E-6A	VQ-4
162783	E-6A	VQ-3
162784	E-6A	VQ-3
163918	E-6A	Boeing
163919	E-6A	VQ-3
163920	E-6A	VQ-3
164386	E-6A	VQ-3
164387	E-6A	VQ-3
164388	E-6A	VQ-3
164404	E-6A	VQ-4
164405	E-6A	VQ-4
164406	E-6B	Boeing
164407	E-6A	VQ-4
164408	E-6A	VQ-4
164409	E-6A	VQ-4
164410	E-6A	VQ-4

McDonnell Douglas C-9B Skytrain II/DC-9-32*
SOES Cherry Point MCAS, North Carolina;
VR-46 Atlanta, Georgia [JS];
VR-51 Glenview NAS, Illinois [RV];
VR-52 Willow Grove NAS, Pennsylvania [JT];
VR-56 Norfolk NAS, Virginia [JU];
VR-57 North Island NAS, California [RX];
VR-58 Jacksonville NAS, Florida [JV];
VR-59 Dallas, Texas [RY];
VR-60 Memphis NAS, Tennessee [RT];
VR-61 Whidbey Island NAS, Washington [RS];
VR-62 South Weymouth NAS, Massachusetts [JW]

159113	[RX]	VR-57
159114	[RX]	VR-57
159115	[RX]	VR-57
159116	[RX]	VR-57
159117	[JU]	VR-56
159118	[JU]	VR-56
159119	[JU]	VR-56
159120	[JU]	VR-56
160046		SOES
160047		SOES
160048	[JV]	VR-58
160049	[JV]	VR-58
160050	[JV]	VR-58
160051	[JV]	VR-58
161266	[JS]	VR-46
161529	[RY]	VR-59
161530	[RY]	VR-59
162753	[JT]	VR-52
162754	[JT]	VR-52
163036*	[JT]	VR-52
163037*	[JT]	VR-52
163208*	[RY]	VR-59
163511*	[JS]	VR-46
163512*	[JS]	VR-46
163513*	[JS]	VR-46
164605*	[RS]	VR-61
164606*	[RS]	VR-61
164607*	[RS]	VR-61
164608*	[RS]	VR-61

Boeing TC-18F
Sea Control Wing 1 (SCW-1), Tinker AFB,
  Oklahoma

165342	
165343	

**Grumman C-20D Gulfstream III/
C-20G Gulfstream IV***
CFLSW, NAF Washington;
HQ US Marine Corps, NAF Washington;
VR-48, NAF Washington [JR];
CFLSW Detachment, NAS Barbers Point, Hawaii
  [RG]

163691		CFLSW
163692		CFLSW
165093*	[JR]	VR-48
165094*	[JR]	VR-48
165151*	[RG	CFLSW
165152*	[RG]	CFLSW
165153*		HQ USMC

Lockheed C-130 Hercules
NAWC, Patuxent River, Maryland;
VR-53 Martinsburg, West Virginia [WV];
VR-54 New Orleans NAS, Louisiana [CW];
VR-55 Moffett Field NAS, California [RU];
VR-62 Brunswick NAS, Maine [JW];
VMGR-152 Futenma MCAS, Japan [QD];
VMGR-234 NAS Fort Worth, Texas [QH];
VMGR-252 Cherry Point MCAS, North Carolina [BH];
VMGRT-253 Cherry Point MCAS, North Carolina
  [GR];
VMGR-352 El Toro MCAS, California [QB];
VMGR-452 Stewart Field, New York [NY]

147572	[QB]	KC-130F	VMGR-352
147573	[QD]	KC-130F	VMGR-152
148246	[GR]	KC-130F	VMGRT-253
148247	[QD]	KC-130F	VMGR-152
148248	[QD]	KC-130F	VMGR-152
148249	[GR]	KC-130F	VMGRT-253
148890	[GR]	KC-130F	VMGRT-253
148891	[BH]	KC-130F	VMGR-252
148892	[GR]	KC-130F	VMGRT-253
148893	[QH]	KC-130F	VMGR-234
148894	[GR]	KC-130F	VMGRT-253
148895	[BH]	KC-130F	VMGR-252
148896	[BH]	KC-130F	VMGR-252
148897	[BH]	KC-130F	VMGR-252
148898	[BH]	KC-130F	VMGR-252
148899	[BH]	KC-130F	VMGR-252
149788	[BH]	KC-130F	VMGR-252
149789	[BH]	KC-130F	VMGR-252
149791	[QB]	KC-130F	VMGR-352
149792	[QB]	KC-130F	VMGR-352
149795	[QB]	KC-130F	VMGR-352
149796	[QB]	KC-130F	VMGR-352
149798	[QB]	KC-130F	VMGR-352
149799	[QD]	KC-130F	VMGR-152
149800	[QB]	KC-130F	VMGR-352
149803	[GR]	KC-130F	VMGRT-253
149804	[GR]	KC-130F	VMGRT-253
149806		KC-130F	NAWC
149807	[QD]	KC-130F	VMGR-152
149808	[BH]	KC-130F	VMGR-252
149811	[GR]	KC-130F	VMGRT-253
149812	[QD]	KC-130F	VMGR-152
149815	[QB]	KC-130F	VMGR-352
149816	[QD]	KC-130F	VMGR-152
150684	[GR]	KC-130F	VMGRT-253
150686	[BH]	KC-130F	VMGR-252
150687	[GR]	KC-130F	VMGRT-253
150688	[GR]	KC-130F	VMGRT-253
150689	[QB]	KC-130F	VMGR-352
150690	[QD]	KC-130F	VMGR-152
151891		TC-130G	Blue Angels
160013	[QD]	KC-130R	VMGR-152

160014	[QB]	KC-130R	VMGR-352	164759	[NY]	KC-130T	VMGR-452
160015	[QB]	KC-130R	VMGR-352	164760	[QH]	KC-130T	VMGR-234
160016	[QB]	KC-130R	VMGR-352	164762		C-130T	NAWC
160017	[QB]	KC-130R	VMGR-352	164763	[CW]	C-130T	VR-54
160018	[QD]	KC-130R	VMGR-152	164993	[CW]	C-130T	VR-54
160019	[QD]	KC-130R	VMGR-152	164994	[WV]	C-130T	VR-53
160020	[QD]	KC-130R	VMGR-152	164995	[CW]	C-130T	VR-54
160021	[QB]	KC-130R	VMGR-352	164996	[WV]	C-130T	VR-53
160022	[QB]	KC-130R	VMGR-352	164997	[WV]	C-130T	VR-53
160240	[QB]	KC-130R	VMGR-352	164998	[WV]	C-130T	VR-53
160625	[BH]	KC-130R	VMGR-252	164999	[NY]	KC-130T	VMGR-452
160626	[BH]	KC-130R	VMGR-252	165000	[NY]	KC-130T	VMGR-452
160627	[BH]	KC-130R	VMGR-252	165158	[CW]	C-130T	VR-54
160628	[BH]	KC-130R	VMGR-252	165159	[RU]	C-130T	VR-55
162308	[QH]	KC-130T	VMGR-234	165160	[RU]	C-130T	VR-55
162309	[QH]	KC-130T	VMGR-234	165161	[RU]	C-130T	VR-55
162310	[QH]	KC-130T	VMGR-234	165162	[NY]	KC-130T	VMGR-452
162311	[QH]	KC-130T	VMGR-234	165163	[NY]	KC-130T	VMGR-452
162785	[QH]	KC-130T	VMGR-234	165313	[JW]	C-130T	VR-62
162786	[QH]	KC-130T	VMGR-234	165314	[JW]	C-130T	VR-62
163022	[QH]	KC-130T	VMGR-234	165315	[NY]	KC-130T	VMGR-452
163023	[QH]	KC-130T	VMGR-234	165316	[NY]	KC-130T	VMGR-452
163310	[QH]	KC-130T	VMGR-234	165348	[JW]	C-130T	VR-62
163311	[QH]	KC-130T	VMGR-234	165349	[JW]	C-130T	VR-62
163591	[NY]	KC-130T	VMGR-452	165350	[RU]	C-130T	VR-55
163592	[NY]	KC-130T	VMGR-452	165351	[RU]	C-130T	VR-55
164105	[NY]	KC-130T	VMGR-452	165352	[NY]	KC-130T	VMGR-452
164106	[NY]	KC-130T	VMGR-452	165353	[NY]	KC-130T	VMGR-452
164180	[NY]	KC-130T	VMGR-452	165378	[RU]	C-130T	VR-55
164181	[NY]	KC-130T	VMGR-452	165379	[RU]	C-130T	VR-55
164441	[QH]	KC-130T	VMGR-234	165 . . .		KC-130J	VMGR- . .
164442	[QH]	KC-130T	VMGR-234	165 . . .		KC-130J	VMGR- . .
164597	[NY]	KC-130T-30	VMGR-452	165 . . .		KC-130J	VMGR- . .
164598	[QH]	KC-130T-30	VMGR-234	165 . . .		KC-130J	VMGR- . .

Lockheed C-130H Hercules 347 *Guts Airline* of No 3 Sqn, Royal Jordanian Airforce, landing at RAF Fairford. *D. J. March*

Notes	Serial	Type (other identity)	Owner/operator, location
	United Kingdom		
	G-AZXA	Beech C55 Baron	FR Aviation, Bournemouth
	G-BNSO	Slingsby T.67M Firefly 2	Hunting Aircraft Ltd/JEFTS, Barkston Heath
	G-BNSR	Slingsby T.67M Firefly 2	Hunting Aircraft Ltd/JEFTS, Barkston Heath
	G-BUUA	Slingsby T.67M Firefly 2	Hunting Aircraft Ltd/JEFTS, Barkston Heath
	G-BUUB	Slingsby T.67M Firefly 2	Hunting Aircraft Ltd/JEFTS, Barkston Heath
	G-BUUD	Slingsby T.67M Firefly 2	Hunting Aircraft Ltd/JEFTS, Barkston Heath
	G-BUUE	Slingsby T.67M Firefly 2	Hunting Aircraft Ltd/JEFTS, Barkston Heath
	G-BUUF	Slingsby T.67M Firefly 2	Hunting Aircraft Ltd/JEFTS, Barkston Heath
	G-BUUG	Slingsby T.67M Firefly 2	Hunting Aircraft Ltd/JEFTS, Barkston Heath
	G-BUUH	Slingsby T.67M Firefly 2	Hunting Aircraft Ltd/JEFTS, Barkston Heath
	G-BUUI	Slingsby T.67M Firefly 2	Hunting Aircraft Ltd/JEFTS, Barkston Heath
	G-BUUJ	Slingsby T.67M Firefly 2	Hunting Aircraft Ltd/JEFTS, Barkston Heath
	G-BUUK	Slingsby T.67M Firefly 2	Hunting Aircraft Ltd/JEFTS, Barkston Heath
	G-BUUL	Slingsby T.67M Firefly 2	Hunting Aircraft Ltd/JEFTS, Barkston Heath
	G-BVHC	Grob G.115D-2 Heron	Shorts Bros/NFGF, Plymouth
	G-BVHD	Grob G.115D-2 Heron	Shorts Bros/NFGF, Plymouth
	G-BVHE	Grob G.115D-2 Heron	Shorts Bros/NFGF, Plymouth
	G-BVHF	Grob G.115D-2 Heron	Shorts Bros/NFGF, Plymouth
	G-BVHG	Grob G.115D-2 Heron	Shorts Bros/NFGF, Plymouth
	G-BWXA	Slingsby T.67M Firefly 260	Hunting Aircraft Ltd/JEFTS, Barkston Heath
	G-BWXB	Slingsby T.67M Firefly 260	Hunting Aircraft Ltd/JEFTS, Barkston Heath
	G-BWXC	Slingsby T.67M Firefly 260	Hunting Aircraft Ltd/JEFTS, Barkston Heath
	G-BWXD	Slingsby T.67M Firefly 260	Hunting Aircraft Ltd/JEFTS, Barkston Heath
	G-BWXE	Slingsby T.67M Firefly 260	Hunting Aircraft Ltd/JEFTS, Barkston Heath
	G-BWXF	Slingsby T.67M Firefly 260	Hunting Aircraft Ltd/JEFTS, Barkston Heath
	G-BWXG	Slingsby T.67M Firefly 260	Hunting Aircraft Ltd/JEFTS, Barkston Heath
	G-BWXH	Slingsby T.67M Firefly 260	Hunting Aircraft Ltd/JEFTS, Barkston Heath
	G-BWXI	Slingsby T.67M Firefly 260	Hunting Aircraft Ltd/JEFTS, Barkston Heath
	G-BWXJ	Slingsby T.67M Firefly 260	Hunting Aircraft Ltd/JEFTS, Barkston Heath
	G-BWXK	Slingsby T.67M Firefly 260	Hunting Aircraft Ltd/JEFTS, Barkston Heath
	G-BWXL	Slingsby T.67M Firefly 260	Hunting Aircraft Ltd/MJEFTS, Barkston Heath
	G-BWXM	Slingsby T.67M Firefly 260	Hunting Aircraft Ltd/JEFTS, Barkston Heath
	G-BWXN	Slingsby T.67M Firefly 260	Hunting Aircraft Ltd/JEFTS, Barkston Heath
	G-BWXO	Slingsby T.67M Firefly 260	Hunting Aircraft Ltd/JEFTS, Barkston Heath
	G-BWXP	Slingsby T.67M Firefly 260	Hunting Aircraft Ltd/JEFTS, Barkston Heath
	G-BWXR	Slingsby T.67M Firefly 260	Hunting Aircraft Ltd/JEFTS, Barkston Heath
	G-BWXS	Slingsby T.67M Firefly 260	Hunting Aircraft Ltd/JEFTS, Barkston Heath
	G-BWXT	Slingsby T.67M Firefly 260	Hunting Aircraft Ltd/JEFTS, Barkston Heath
	G-BWXU	Slingsby T.67M Firefly 260	Hunting Aircraft Ltd/JEFTS, Barkston Heath
	G-BWXV	Slingsby T.67M Firefly 260	Hunting Aircraft Ltd/JEFTS, Barkston Heath
	G-BWXW	Slingsby T.67M Firefly 260	Hunting Aircraft Ltd/JEFTS, Barkston Heath
	G-BWXX	Slingsby T.67M Firefly 260	Hunting Aircraft Ltd/JEFTS, Barkston Heath
	G-BWXY	Slingsby T.67M Firefly 260	Hunting Aircraft Ltd/JEFTS, Barkston Heath
	G-BWXZ	Slingsby T.67M Firefly 260	Hunting Aircraft Ltd/JEFTS, Barkston Heath
	G-BWZR	Bell 412EP	FBS Ltd/DHFS, Shawbury
	G-BWZS	Eurocopter AS350BA Ecureuil	FBS Ltd/DHFS, Shawbury
	G-FCAL	Cessna 441 Conquest	FR Aviation, Bournemouth
	G-FFRA	Dassault Falcon 20DC (N902FR)	FR Aviation, Bournemouth
	G-FRAD	Dassault Falcon 20E (G-BCYF)	FR Aviation, Bournemouth
	G-FRAE	Dassault Falcon 20E (N910FR)	FR Aviation, Bournemouth
	G-FRAF	Dassault Falcon 20E (N911FR)	FR Aviation, Bournemouth
	G-FRAH	Dassault Falcon 20DC (N900FR)	FR Aviation, Bournemouth
	G-FRAI	Dassault Falcon 20E (N901FR)	FR Aviation, Bournemouth
	G-FRAJ	Dassault Falcon 20E (N903FR)	FR Aviation, Bournemouth
	G-FRAK	Dassault Falcon 20DC (N905FR)	FR Aviation, Bournemouth
	G-FRAL	Dassault Falcon 20DC (N904FR)	FR Aviation, Bournemouth
	G-FRAM	Dassault Falcon 20DC (N907FR)	FR Aviation, Bournemouth

Serial	Type (other identity)	Owner/operator, location	Notes
G-FRAO	Dassault Falcon 20DC (N906FR)	FR Aviation, Bournemouth	
G-FRAP	Dassault Falcon 20DC (N908FR)	FR Aviation, Bournemouth	
G-FRAR	Dassault Falcon 20DC (N909FR)	FR Aviation, Bournemouth	
G-FRAS	Dassault Falcon 20C (117501)	FR Aviation, Bournemouth	
G-FRAT	Dassault Falcon 20C (117502)	FR Aviation, Bournemouth	
G-FRAU	Dassault Falcon 20C (117504)	FR Aviation, Bournemouth	
G-FRAW	Dassault Falcon 20ECM (117507)	FR Aviation, Bournemouth	
G-FRAX	Cessna 441 Conquest	FR Aviation, Bournemouth	
G-FRAZ	Cessna 441 Conquest	FR Aviation, Bournemouth	
G-FRBA	Dassault Falcon 20C	FR Aviation, Bournemouth	
G-FRBY	Beech E55 Baron	FR Aviation, Bournemouth	
G-HONG	Slingsby T.67M Firefly 2 [6]	Hunting Aircraft Ltd/JEFTS, Barkston Heath	
G-KONG	Slingsby T.67M Firefly 2	Hunting Aircraft Ltd/JEFTS, Barkston Heath	
G-LEAR	Gates LearJet 35A	Northern Executive Aviation, Manchester	

Algeria

Serial	Type (other identity)	Owner/operator, location	Notes
7T-VPA	Dassault Falcon 900 (81)	Ministry of Defence, Boufarik	
7T-VPB	Dassault Falcon 900 (82)	Ministry of Defence, Boufarik	
7T-VPR	G.1159C Gulfstream IVSP (1288)	Ministry of Defence, Boufarik	
7T-VPS	G.1159C Gulfstream IVSP (1291)	Ministry of Defence, Boufarik	

Bahrain

Serial	Type (other identity)	Owner/operator, location	Notes
A9C-BA	Boeing 727-2M7	Govt of Bahrain	
A9C-BB	G.1159A Gulfstream III	Govt of Bahrain	
A9C-BG	G.1159 Gulfstream IITT	Govt of Bahrain	

Botswana

Serial	Type (other identity)	Owner/operator, location	Notes
OK1	G.1159C Gulfstream IV	Botswana Defence Force	

Brunei

Serial	Type (other identity)	Owner/operator, location	Notes
V8-007	G.1159C Gulfstream IV (V8-SR1)	Brunei Govt, Bandar Seri Bergawan	
V8-008	G.1159C Gulfstream IV	Brunei Govt, Bandar Seri Bergawan	
V8-009	G.1159C Gulfstream IVSP (V8-MSB)	Brunei Govt, Bandar Seri Bergawan	
V8-AC1	Boeing 747SP-21 (V8-JBB/V8-JP1)	Brunei Govt, Bandar Seri Bergawan	
V8-AL1	Boeing 747-430	Brunei Govt, Bandar Seri Bergawan	
V8-BKH	Airbus A.340-212 (V8-PJB)	Brunei Govt, Bandar Seri Bergawan	
V8-DPD	Airbus A.310-304 (V8-HM1)	Brunei Govt, Bandar Seri Bergawan	
V8-JBB	Airbus A.340-213	Brunei Govt, Bandar Seri Bergawan	
V8-JP1	Airbus A.340-211 (V8-BKH)	Brunei Govt, Bandar Seri Bergawan	
V8-MJB	Boeing 767-27G	Brunei Govt, Bandar Seri Bergawan	
V8-SR1	G.1159C Gulfstream IV (V8-AL1/V8-009)	Brunei Govt, Bandar Seri Bergawan	

Bulgaria

Serial	Type (other identity)	Owner/operator, location	Notes
LZ D 050	Tupolev Tu-134A (1303)	Bulgarian Air Force, 16 TAB, Sofia/Dobroslavtzi	

Czech Republic

Serial	Type (other identity)	Owner/operator, location	Notes
OK-BYA	Canadair CL.601-3A Challenger	Czech Govt, Praha/Kbely	
OK-BYF	Let L-410UVP-E	Czech Govt, Praha/Kbely	
OK-BYH	Yakovlev Yak-40	Czech Govt, Praha/Kbely	
OK-BYI	Yakovlev Yak-40	Czech Govt, Praha/Kbely	
OK-BYJ	Yakovlev Yak-40	Czech Govt, Praha/Kbely	
OK-BYK	Yakovlev Yak-40	Czech Govt, Praha/Kbely	
OK-BYZ	Tupolev Tu-154M	Czech Govt, Praha/Kbely	
OK-VCP	Tupolev Tu-154M	Czech Govt, Praha/Kbely	

Egypt

Serial	Type (other identity)	Owner/operator, location	Notes
SU-AXJ	Boeing 707-366C	Egyptian Govt, Cairo	
SU-BGM	G.1159C Gulfstream IV	Egyptian Air Force/Govt, Cairo	
SU-BGU	G.1159A Gulfstream III	Egyptian Air Force/Govt, Cairo	
SU-BGV	G.1159A Gulfstream III	Egyptian Air Force/Govt, Cairo	
SU-GGG	Airbus A.340-211	Egyptian Govt, Cairo	

Civil Registrations

Notes	Serial	Type (other identity)	Owner/operator, location
	France		
	F-GPAA	Dassault Falcon 20ECM (117505/G-FRAV)	AVDEF, Nimes-Garons
	F-GPAB	Dassault Falcon 20E (G-FRAC)	AVDEF, Nimes-Garons
	F-SEBI	Dassault Falcon 20E-5 (315)	CNET, Lannion
	F-SEBK	Aérospatiale ATR-42	CNET, Rennes
	Greece		
	SX-ECH	Dassault Falcon 900	Greek Govt/Olympic Airways, Athens
	Israel		
	4X-COV	Hawker 800XP	Israeli Govt, Tel Aviv
	Jordan		
	JY-HAH	G.1159A Gulfstream III	Govt of Jordan, Amman
	JY-HKJ	L.1011 TriStar 500	Govt of Jordan, Amman
	JY-HZH	G.1159A Gulfstream III	Govt of Jordan, Amman
	Kazakhstan		
	UN-001	Boeing 747SP-31	Govt of Kazakhstan, Almaty
	UN-002	Boeing 757-2M6	Govt of Kazakhstan, Almaty
	Kuwait		
	9K-AJA	G.1159C Gulfstream IV	Kuwaiti Govt/Kuwaiti Airways, Safat
	9K-AJB	G.1159C Gulfstream IV	Kuwaiti Govt/Kuwaiti Airways, Safat
	9K-AJC	G.1159C Gulfstream IV	Kuwaiti Govt/Kuwaiti Airways, Safat
	9K-ALD	Airbus A.310-308	Kuwaiti Govt, Safat
	Lithuania		
	LY-AMB	L.1329 Jetstar 731	Lithuanian Govt, Vilnius
	Morocco		
	CNA-NL	G.1159 Gulfstream IITT	Govt of Morocco, Rabat
	CNA-NR	Boeing 707-3W6C	Govt of Morocco, Rabat
	CNA-NS	Boeing 707-138B	Govt of Morocco, Rabat
	CNA-NU	G.1159A Gulfstream III	Govt of Morocco, Rabat
	Netherlands		
	PH-KBX	Fokker 70	Dutch Royal Flight, Schiphol
	PH-SBK	Beechcraft Super King Air 200	MLD 2 MOTU, Maastricht
	Oman		
	A4O-AB	G.1159C Gulfstream IV	Govt of Oman, Seeb
	A4O-AC	G.1159C Gulfstream IV	Govt of Oman, Seeb
	A4O-SO	Boeing 747SP-27	Govt of Oman, Seeb
	A4O-SP	Boeing 747SP-27	Govt of Oman, Seeb
	Qatar		
	A7-AAD	Dassault Falcon 900	Qatari Govt, Doha
	A7-AAE	Dassault Falcon 900	Qatari Govt, Doha
	A7-HHK	Airbus A.340-211	Qatari Govt, Doha
	Saudi Arabia		
	HZ-103	G.1159C Gulfstream IV	Royal Saudi AF, No 1 Sqn, Riyadh
	HZ-108	G.1159A Gulfstream III	Royal Saudi AF, No 1 Sqn, Riyadh
	HZ-111	Lockheed VC-130H Hercules	Royal Saudi AF, No 1 Sqn, Riyadh
	HZ-114	Lockheed VC-130H Hercules	Royal Saudi AF, No 1 Sqn, Riyadh
	HZ-115	Lockheed VC-130H Hercules	Royal Saudi AF, No 1 Sqn, Riyadh
	HZ-116	Lockheed VC-130H Hercules	Royal Saudi AF, No 1 Sqn, Riyadh
	HZ-117	Lockheed L.100-30 Hercules	Royal Saudi AF, No 1 Sqn, Riyadh
	HZ-128	Lockheed L.100-30 Hercules	Royal Saudi AF, No 1 Sqn, Riyadh
	HZ-129	Lockheed L.100-30 Hercules	Royal Saudi AF, No 1 Sqn, Riyadh
	HZ-AIJ	Boeing 747SP-68	Saudi Royal Flight, Jeddah
	HZ-HM1A	Boeing 747-3G1	Saudi Royal Flight, Jeddah
	HZ-HM1B	Boeing 747SP-68	Saudi Royal Flight, Jeddah
	HZ-HM4	Boeing 737-268	Saudi Royal Flight, Jeddah
	HZ-HM5	L.1011 TriStar 500	Saudi Royal Flight, Jeddah
	HZ-HM6	L.1011 TriStar 500	Saudi Royal Flight, Jeddah
	HZ-MS3	G.1159A Gulfstream III	Armed Forces Medical Services, Riyadh
	HZ-MS019	Lockheed C-130H Hercules	Armed Forces Medical Services, Riyadh

Serial	Type (other identity)	Owner/operator, location	Notes
Slovakia			
OM-BYE	Yakovlev Yak-40	Slovak Govt, Bratislava/Ivanka	
OM-BYL	Yakovlev Yak-40	Slovak Govt, Bratislava/Ivanka	
OM-BYO	Tupolev Tu.154M	Slovak Govt, Bratislava/Ivanka	
South Africa			
ZS-NAN	Dassault Falcon 900	South African Air Force, No 21 Sqn, Waterkloof	
Switzerland			
HB-GII	Beechcraft Super King Air 350C	Flugwaffe, Flugswaffenbrigade 31, Dübendorf	
Turkey			
TC-ATA	G.1159C Gulfstream IV	Govt of Turkey, Istanbul	
TC-GAP	G.1159C Gulfstream IV	Govt of Turkey, Istanbul	
United Arab Emirates			
A6-AUH	Dassault Falcon 900	Govt of Abu Dhabi	
A6-ESH	Boeing 737-2W8	Govt of Sharjah	
A6-HEH	G.1159A Gulfstream III	Dubai Air Wing	
A6-HHH	G.1159C Gulfstream IV	Dubai Air Wing	
A6-PFD	Airbus A.300C4-620	Govt of Abu Dhabi	
A6-SHZ	Airbus A.300B4-620	Govt of Abu Dhabi	
A6-SMM	Boeing 747SP-31	Govt of Dubai	
A6-SMR	Boeing 747SP-31	Govt of Dubai	
A6-UAE	Dassault Falcon 900	Govt of Abu Dhabi	
A6-ZKM	Dassault Falcon 900	Govt of Abu Dhabi	
A6-ZSN	Boeing 747SP-Z5	Govt of Dubai	
United States			
N88JA	Gates LearJet 35A	US Navy, Sigonella	
N94	BAe 125-800A (C-29A) (88-0269)	Federal Aviation Administration, Oklahoma	
N95	BAe 125-800A (C-29A) (88-0270)	Federal Aviation Administration, Oklahoma	
N96	BAe 125-800A (C-29A) (88-0271)	Federal Aviation Administration, Oklahoma	
N97	BAe 125-800A (C-29A) (88-0272)	Federal Aviation Administration, Oklahoma	
N98	BAe 125-800A (C-29A) (88-0273)	Federal Aviation Administration, Oklahoma	
N99	BAe 125-800A (C-29A) (88-0274)	Federal Aviation Administration, Oklahoma	
N350JF	Gates LearJet 35A	US Navy, Sigonella	

General Dynamics F-16A J-508 of No 306 Squadron Royal Netherlands Air Force, 1996 display aircraft based at Volkel. *PRM*